CW00337820

Richmond House: a temporary home for the House of Commons
image by Forbes Massey

ALLFORD
HALL
MONAGHAN
MORRIS

Proud to support The Bartlett School of Architecture

Elizabeth House, Waterloo
image by Forbes Massey

Morelands, 5-23 Old Street
London EC1V 9HL
0207 251 5261 info@ahmm.co.uk
www.ahmm.co.uk

Exploring The Bartlett Summer Show 2018

Contents

BARTLETT

SUMMER
2019

Introduction

Welcome to our 2019 Summer Show Book, offering a sumptuous glimpse into the vast array of extraordinary projects dreamt up, researched and made in a myriad of ways by over 600 of our 1300 students, including all those taking our ARB/RIBA accredited programmes, as well as those taking our Architectural & Interdisciplinary Studies BSc, and Engineering & Architectural Design MEng.

By definition, many of these students are declaring an explicit interest in having a future within the profession, either at its centre or its frontier. The question many of them ask about the decades ahead is, what kind of profession will that be? How might it relate to the talent, visions, passions, ethics, diversity, and values of this generation and their successors? For this school, now in its 178th year, these questions are not only embedded in our ethos, but crucially in our profile. Over 70% of our academic staff are part-time, the majority of whom are practitioners in many diverse forms from architecture to engineering, art to writing, enterprise to innovation. 30% of our staff are on research-based appointments, of whom a growing percentage are part-time and practice-based. These unique and invaluable strengths underpin our relevance and responsiveness. They offer proximity to a living and evolving discipline, and they channel critical and creative dialogue through our studios on a daily basis, project by project, tutorial by tutorial.

Our students, representing over 50 different nationalities, play the most vital part in all this. As this book demonstrates in abundance, they are keen, talented and ambitious, each with their own perspective on the brief they have taken on. Yet, perhaps the most important quality they possess is their immediate ability to challenge and influence our direction; from the ideas and contexts we explore, to the subjects we unravel, and the way we operate.

Being a student today is profoundly different to the relevant experiences of even our youngest members of staff, let alone our most senior. From the extraordinary opportunities afforded by the power of the digital age in information, communication, tooling and intelligence, to the challenges of managing the significant investment in studentship from year to year. Within this setting, we thank our students for their voice on all matters, particularly on the importance of wellbeing and social life, which has led to changes in staffing allocations and space usage. We salute the delivery of *Outlet*, a new entirely student-led publication and, recently, the inspiring 'Architecture Education Declares' campaign.

Six years ago we offered eight programmes of study. This year, in launching Landscape Architecture MA/MLA and Bio-Integrated Design MArch/MSc, that total is now 25, supported across two sites: our Bloomsbury HQ and our experimental laboratories at Here East. They are creating new and exciting connections to complementary and collaborative domains both beyond our department, and beyond the profession. These domains are witnessed by all our students through their everyday exchanges and experiences at open crits, project fairs and exhibitions. From studio to studio, and project to project, there's a palpable sense that the school is fulfilling the potential of architectural research and education like never before. New generations of graduates are emerging with big ideas on where they want the world to be, and as you can see here, they have accrued a precious momentum that we must all cherish and admire.

And finally, our sincere thanks to Professor Alan Penn, who stands down as Dean of our faculty this summer, after ten extraordinary years. His unwavering support and commitment to education, research and wellbeing are profoundly appreciated by us all.

Professor Frédéric Migayrou
Chair, Bartlett Professor of Architecture,
The Bartlett School of Architecture

Professor Bob Sheil
Director of The Bartlett School of Architecture

At work in the studio

Presenting at the Open Crits, 2019

Architecture BSc (ARB/RIBA Part 1)

Architecture BSc (ARB/RIBA Part 1)

Programme Directors: Luke Pearson, Sara Shafiei

The boundaries of the architectural profession are constantly shifting, confronted by technology, politics, culture and our environment. In this context, Architecture BSc develops primary knowledge and understanding about the core principles of the discipline, providing a platform from which experimental and challenging design work can emerge.

The programme teaches students the fundamentals of architecture, developing their critical ability to think about what it means to synthesise architectural designs and what methods they can utilise to do so. This involves drawing and making that operates between and across the analogue and digital. Our students carve spaces from the chiaroscuro of the drawn surface, fuse handmade ceramics with robotically-milled substrates and create architectures experienced through virtual reality. Underpinning this experimentation is a rigorous approach, not only to spatial planning but also to technology, where structural strategies, environmental design and sustainability principles, alongside computation, allow our students to produce complex and layered buildings.

Our Year 1 cohort is organised as a single group before a design unit system begins in Year 2. The first year is a 'contextual' year in which architectural expertise is developed through diverse experimentation and exploration. Several modules, including 'The History of Cities and their Architecture' and 'Making Cities', meld ideas from different programmes and areas of research within The Bartlett, bringing undergraduates into contact with students from different disciplines to develop an understanding of the historical and social role of the architect.

In Years 2 and 3, our units offer unique expertise and a broad range of approaches, allowing students to connect their studies to their developing interests. The 14 undergraduate units explore diverse themes and agendas, including the relationship between architecture and landscape, digital simulation and fabrication, the role of narrative in architecture and the political context of design in London and beyond. Each unit establishes a methodology that builds core skills and expands them in new directions. Following tailored research briefs, units undertake an in-depth field trip, forging links with other architectural schools and studios to help our students understand the complexities of producing architecture in radically different environments.

Throughout the course of the degree, students relate their design projects to all other taught modules. This culminates in Year 3, where design and technology are developed in synthesis, complemented by self-selected thematic interests in history and theory. By the end of their undergraduate studies, our students are equipped to engage with the design of architecture in a sophisticated manner, whilst also placing their own practice and research into wider socio-political, historical and environmental contexts.

This year, ambitious design projects from our undergraduate students vary, from architecture that tackles the post-Hurricane Katrina housing crisis of New Orleans, to reinventions of the traditional London pub as a new form of post-digital social space for an increasingly teetotal generation. Buildings exploring ceramic fabrication techniques combining handmade gestures with robotic procedures sit alongside museums using augmented and virtual reality to confront the memories of marginalised societies. Buildings that bind the fractured borderlands of Hong Kong and Shenzhen sit alongside suburban houses designed to be viewed through the digital eyes of self-driving cars. Architectures that celebrate the cinematic construction of space coexist with social housing schemes and kit-of-parts structures that explore playful, participatory forms of design. The diversity of approaches and the daring acts of design that emerge demonstrate that as our undergraduate students carefully study the fundamentals of architecture, they make sure to keep an eye on the ever-shifting boundaries of the profession.

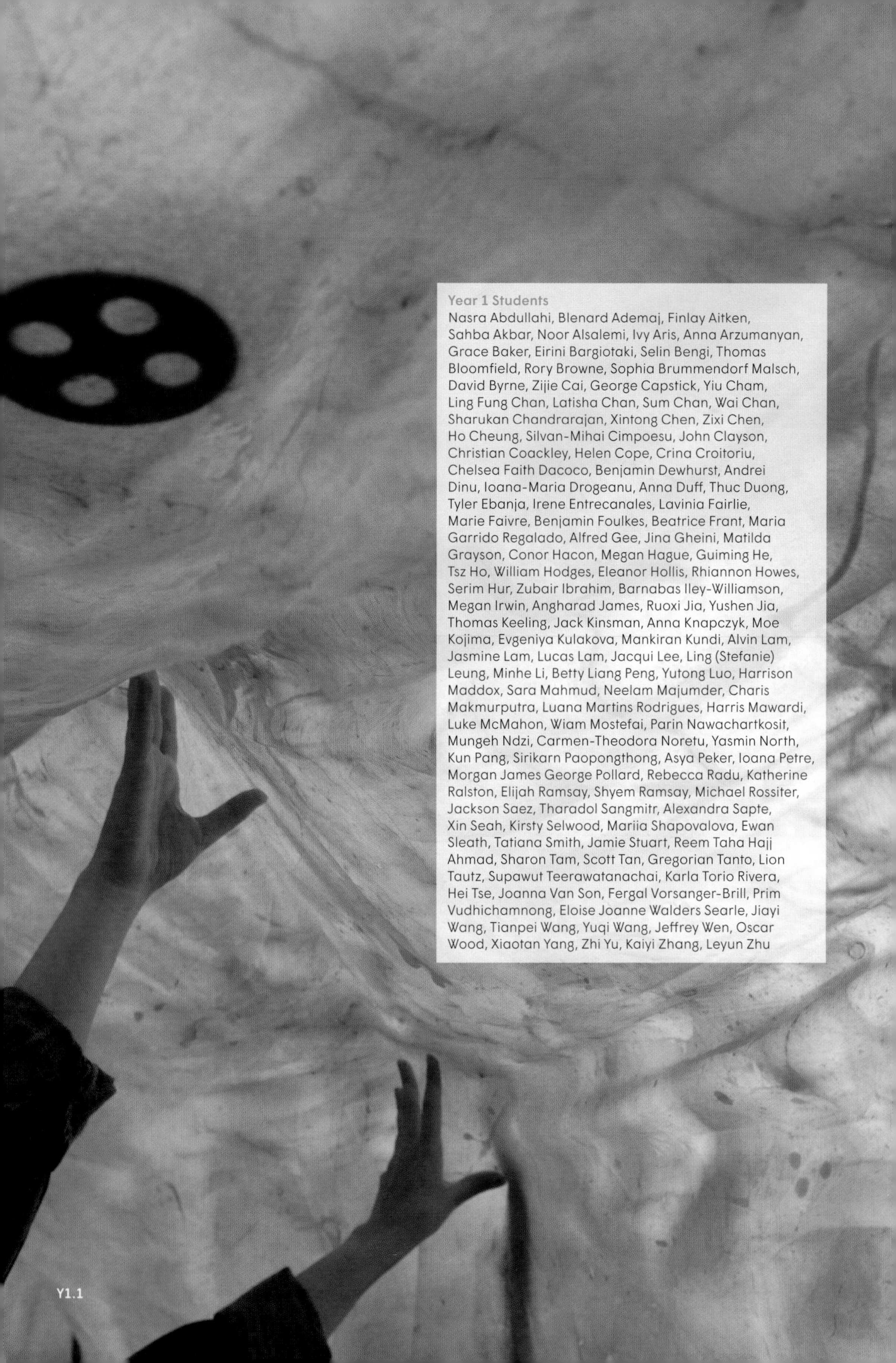

Year 1 Students

Nasra Abdullahi, Blenard Ademaj, Finlay Aitken, Sahba Akbar, Noor Alsalemi, Ivy Aris, Anna Arzumanyan, Grace Baker, Eirini Bargiotaki, Selin Bengi, Thomas Bloomfield, Rory Browne, Sophia Brummendorf Malsch, David Byrne, Zijie Cai, George Capstick, Yiu Cham, Ling Fung Chan, Latisha Chan, Sum Chan, Wai Chan, Sharukan Chandrarajan, Xintong Chen, Zixi Chen, Ho Cheung, Silvan-Mihai Cimpoesu, John Clayson, Christian Coackley, Helen Cope, Crina Croitoriu, Chelsea Faith Dacoco, Benjamin Dewhurst, Andrei Dinu, Ioana-Maria Drogeanu, Anna Duff, Thuc Duong, Tyler Ebanja, Irene Entrecanales, Lavinia Fairlie, Marie Faivre, Benjamin Foulkes, Beatrice Frant, Maria Garrido Regalado, Alfred Gee, Jina Gheini, Matilda Grayson, Conor Hacon, Megan Hague, Guiming He, Tsz Ho, William Hodges, Eleanor Hollis, Rhiannon Howes, Serim Hur, Zubair Ibrahim, Barnabas Iley-Williamson, Megan Irwin, Angharad James, Ruoxi Jia, Yushen Jia, Thomas Keeling, Jack Kinsman, Anna Knapczyk, Moe Kojima, Evgeniya Kulakova, Mankiran Kundi, Alvin Lam, Jasmine Lam, Lucas Lam, Jacqui Lee, Ling (Stefanie) Leung, Minhe Li, Betty Liang Peng, Yutong Luo, Harrison Maddox, Sara Mahmud, Neelam Majumder, Charis Makmurputra, Luana Martins Rodrigues, Harris Mawardi, Luke McMahon, Wiam Mostefai, Parin Nawachartkosit, Mungeh Ndzi, Carmen-Theodora Noretu, Yasmin North, Kun Pang, Sirikarn Paopongthong, Asya Peker, Ioana Petre, Morgan James George Pollard, Rebecca Radu, Katherine Ralston, Elijah Ramsay, Shyem Ramsay, Michael Rossiter, Jackson Saez, Tharadol Sangmitr, Alexandra Sapte, Xin Seah, Kirsty Selwood, Mariia Shapovalova, Ewan Sleath, Tatiana Smith, Jamie Stuart, Reem Taha Hajj Ahmad, Sharon Tam, Scott Tan, Gregorian Tanto, Lion Tautz, Supawut Teerawatanachai, Karla Torio Rivera, Hei Tse, Joanna Van Son, Fergal Vorsanger-Brill, Prim Vudhichamnong, Eloise Joanne Walders Searle, Jiayi Wang, Tianpei Wang, Yuqi Wang, Jeffrey Wen, Oscar Wood, Xiaotan Yang, Zhi Yu, Kaiyi Zhang, Leyun Zhu

Islands of Ground and Water

Year 1

Co-Directors: Max Dewdney, Frosso Pimenides

The first year at The Bartlett is a transformative process for students to look afresh at the world and develop a collective spirit that encourages an exchange of ideas, skills and cultures.

The theme for the year was 'Islands of Ground and Water', exploring the shifting relationship between natural, urban and rural contexts, and how the placement and inhabitation of buildings within a city can have an impact on the world beyond their site. Islands are natural formations whose form questions the condition of 'the edge', accessibility and the relationship between ground and water.

The sites of investigation were Venice and East London. Students examined and speculated on the relationship that both cities have to the water, and began the year with a project that introduced them to surveying a fragment of a building and re-examining the real, the possible and the imagined.

Our installation projects are always based on the juxtaposition of an existing context and a thematic intervention. They aim to temporarily 'adjust' a familiar place into something strange and extraordinary. This year, they took place on the Lea Navigation in East London, where students designed and built six temporary installations that adjusted the context of the canal, and culminated in an event at the local community centre.

We then travelled to Venice, where we explored six themes: light and water; placement; route, view and vista; negotiation of water; and ground and water. The project served as a bridge between the installation and the main building project.

Following the theme 'Islands of Ground and Water', the main building project explored the dual conditions of 'urban' and 'rural' on the Isle of Dogs. Through the design of a small building, students questioned: 'What is rural?' and 'What is urban?'. The selected sites sit on the edge of the Isle of Dogs on the River Thames in London, and students were invited to investigate the different ways in which the ground met the water. The design strategy followed principles of 'architectural acupuncture', whereby projects acted as urban incisions that bridged the isolation, privacy, lack of community and life on the site. Just like acupuncture on the body, micro-interventions in the city have a wider impact that addresses the context beyond the footprint of the sites.

During the nine-month lifespan of our first-year studio, students are encouraged to engage with design exploration and undertake a journey that treats failure and success as equally crucial. 'Dreaming the impossible and building the extraordinary' is the underpinning philosophy of the year. Students are encouraged to embrace and celebrate the struggles of the design process, to be optimistic, to be daring, and to have fun.

Associates: Lucy Leonard, Gavin Robotham, Jasmin Sohi, Emmanouil Stavrakakis

Tutors: Alastair Browning, Joel Cady, Zachary Fluker, Alicia Gonzalez Lafita Perez, Stefan Lengen, Samantha Lynch, Thomas Parker, Marcel Rahm, Colin Smith, Jasmin Sohi, Emmanouil Stavrakakis

Thanks to: Dimitris Argyros, Abigail Ashton, Julia Backhaus, Pascal Bronner, Andy Bryce, Barbara-Ann Campbell-Lange, Marcus Cole, Elizabeth Dow, Julika Gittner, Tamsin Hanke, Simon Herron, Thomas Hillier, Susanne Isa, Will Jefferies, Fergus Knox, Chee-Kit Lai, Laura Mark, Ana Monrabal-Cook, Chiara Montgomerie, Elliot Nash, Jack Newton, Brian O'Reilly, Ralph Parker, Luke Pearson, Theo Petrochilos, Jonathan Pile, Gill Scampton, Sara Shafiei, David Shanks, Neil Spiller, Matthew Springett, Jerry Tate, Nick Tyler, Afra Van't Land, Viktoria Viktorija, Patrick Weber, Simon Withers, Paolo Zaide

Special thanks to: Matt Bowles, Nat Chard, Peter Cook, Niamh Grace, Jordanna Greaves, Jonathan Hill, Owen Hopkins, Steve Johnson, Perry Kulper, CJ Lim, Níall McLaughlin, Jeremy Melvyn, John O'Driscoll, Alan Penn, Uilleac Pimenides, Indigo Rohrer, Joseph Rykwert, Bob Sheil, Gillian Smith, Harmit Soora, Phil Tabor, Elizabeth Thornhill, Paul Weston, James Willis

Y1.1 Group Installation Project 'Below Venice'. This ceiling made of latex includes aspects of Venice (the water) and London (the ground). A map of Venice is transferred onto the latex surface, with different scales to highlight land and water ratios. Parts of the map are composed using writing found on historic trading maps highlighting the city's trading pasts.
Y1.2 Finlay Aitken'Music Below Venice – The Landscape City'. This is a hybrid drawing of two projects: a topographic exploration of how cities can share a hillside with nature, uncovering different levels of natural occupied space, and an intimate pool of sounds below the Venetian skin.
Y1.3 Xiaotan (Alex) Yang 'Farmers' Market and Teahouse'. A multifunctional farmers' market sits on top of a viaduct in the Isle of Dogs. Through the changing components of the design, the space changes into a teahouse and a dining room.
Y1.4 Supawut Teerawatanachai 'Campo Santa Maria Formosa Reimagined'. The routes of a tourist, fish seller and birds are mapped towards the Campo Santa Maria Formosa square in Venice. This model interprets the interaction between each group of users and the city elements of Venice.
Y1.5 Anna Arzumanyan 'Jazz Club with Music Practice Rooms'. The language of the building is taken from jazz improvisation. The colour scheme follows the jazz club aesthetic. The journey to the club under the lightwells, which change colour throughout the day, creates a unique spatial effect.
Y1.6 Ivy Aris 'The Parrhesia Forum and Kitchen'. The building acts as a membrane between those who wish to donate food to the collective kitchen, fuelling the idea of community, whilst simultaneously offering those who feel marginalised the opportunity to cook for themselves and others, whilst engaging in the Ancient Greek concept of parrhesia (speaking candidly).
Y1.7 Kirsty Selwood 'Light through Water – An Element of Venice'. Inspired by the water and light conditions observed in Venice, the wax cube acts as a lightbox to create an atmosphere that can reflect off the model inside.
Y1.8 Barnabas Iley-Williamson 'The Pickling Island'. A trench extends into the River Thames, keeping jars of produce cool, whilst cooking and dining areas overhead provide a communal place to rest and share food.
Y1.9 Joanna Van Son 'Bathhouse Amidst Ruins'. The project takes the decaying conditions of the slipway and the Victorian concept of the terracotta bathhouse (and communal bathing) to reconnect the community to their bodies and each other. The bathhouse combats individual and communal alienation and disconnection.
Y1.10 Reem Taha Hajj Ahmad 'Marionette Theatre and Workshop'. This project presents a marionette theatre with a lemonade and lollipop kiosk, a workshop for primary school children and a puppet-maker. The building is formed through the inhabitation of suspended frames that respond to the tides and the wind onsite.
Y1.11 Ruoxi (Cici) Jia 'Gut-It House: Sheep's-Gut String Workshop'. The building emphasises the idea of 'stretchiness' and uses traditional sheep's-gut violin strings. It applies the idea of extendable stretchiness to the form of the building and allows elements to be stretched from the main spaces along the slipway. The building consists of both the making and living spaces for a string-maker.
Y1.12 Christian Coackley 'The Bike Hangout'. The building acts as a hub for isolated young cycling enthusiasts who want to meet others, work on their bikes, and find a sense of belonging on the Isle of Dogs. The users are looked after by Manny, the building's caretaker, who encourages them to source bike parts locally and bring them back to the Bike Hangout.
Y1.13 Benjamin Foulkes 'Optical Acupuncture: Home for a Photographer'. The building brings the outside world into the space through the use of pinhole light apertures, turning rooms into camera obscuras. Photographic paper lines the interior surfaces, capturing the images before they are developed in the photographer's darkroom. The building is occasionally open to the public as a place of observation.
Y1.14 Group Installation Project 'Lagoon'. Eight floating 'islands' and three towers are designed as a response to the urban landscape of the Venetian lagoon. This new landscape aims to respond to the movement of the water: it moves when the water moves. This movement is signified by a small bell attached to the structures. Each tower has a small container within it, which is filled with fog, as a commentary on the weather of Venice and London.
Y1.15 Group Installation Project 'Rusting Ruskin'. This installation explores an exchange between the exterior and interior spaces of a community centre. Inspired by the unique waterways of both Venice and London, an instrument amplifies and transfers the soundscape of the Lea Navigation – whose banks lie adjacent to the walls – into this particular corridor.
Y1.16 Group Installation Project 'Irrigational Tool'. In London and Venice the water merges with the inhabited land. This project refers to a pile structure, like the one Venice was built upon, which holds an unusual irrigation tool. Its form is inspired by traditional Venetian rowing boats. Its naked skeleton attracts the attention of the observer and is used to reveal what is hidden in the water landscape.
Y1.17 Group Installation Project 'Lollipop Shields'. Staking a claim upon the ground of Hackney Wick, this installation is a portal between modern-day London and 19th-century Venice; specifically the siege of 1848 and the victory of the Venetians over Habsburg imperial rule. Here, shields pierce the ground like billowing flags perforating the canalside.
Y1.18 Xiaotan (Alex) Yang 'Shifting Venice'. An exploration of the spatial relationship between the floating city of Venice and unpredictable water levels. Fragments of Venetian façades are recollected from memory to construct a journey.
Y1.19 Kaiyi (Kelvin) Zhang 'The Real, the Possible and the Imagined'. This drawing is composed from memories of inhabited rooms, unused doors and windows, which blend in with fragments from the present-day Hoxton Docks.
Y1.20 Xin (Sean) Seah 'Unearthing Thames Embankment'. The unearthed Thames Embankment and Thames Path have been integral in connecting communities; though the embankment itself creates a division, distancing people from the wildlife that resides there at low tide. This project connects these two vastly different worlds: a blacksmithing workshop forges bird baths from flotsam and jetsam deposited along the riverbank.

Y1.2

Y1.3

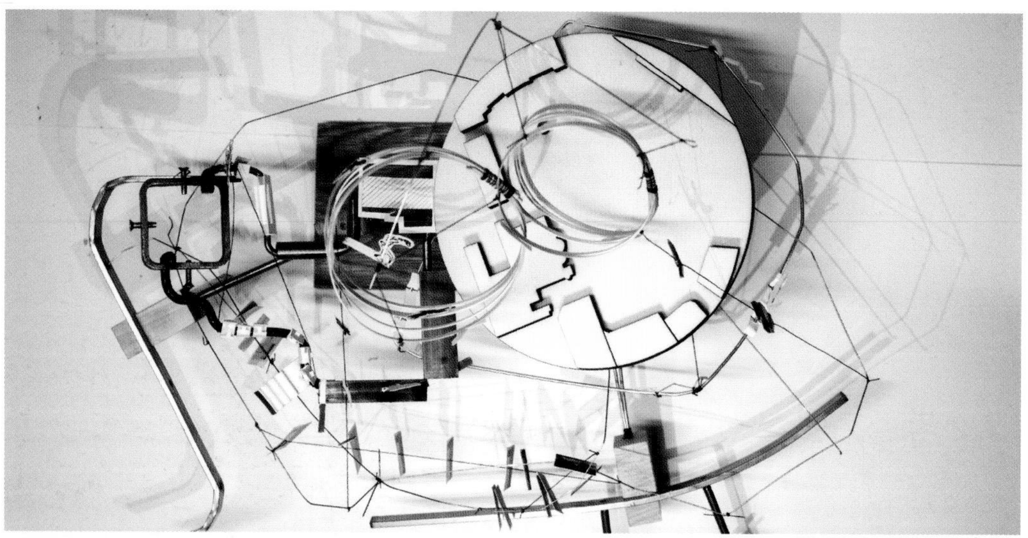
Y1.4

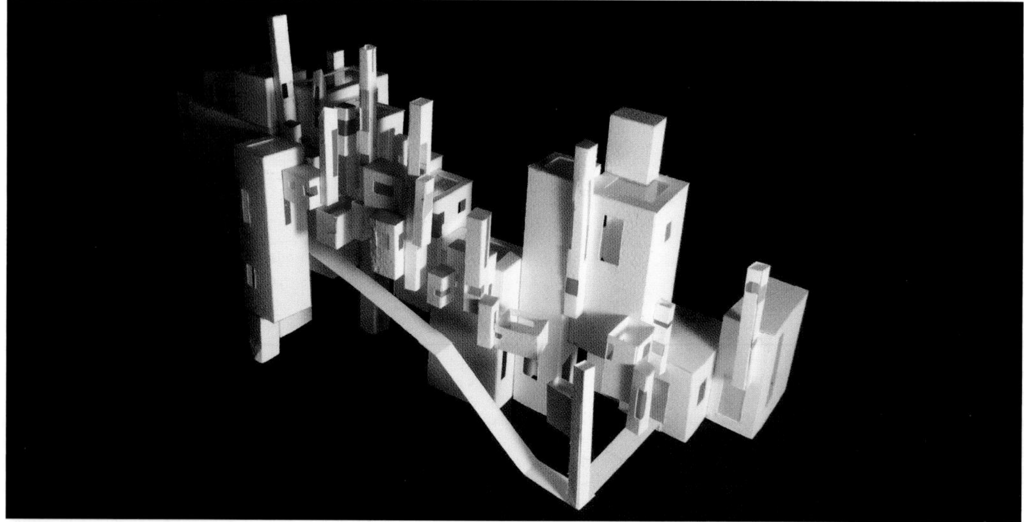
Y1.5

Y1.6

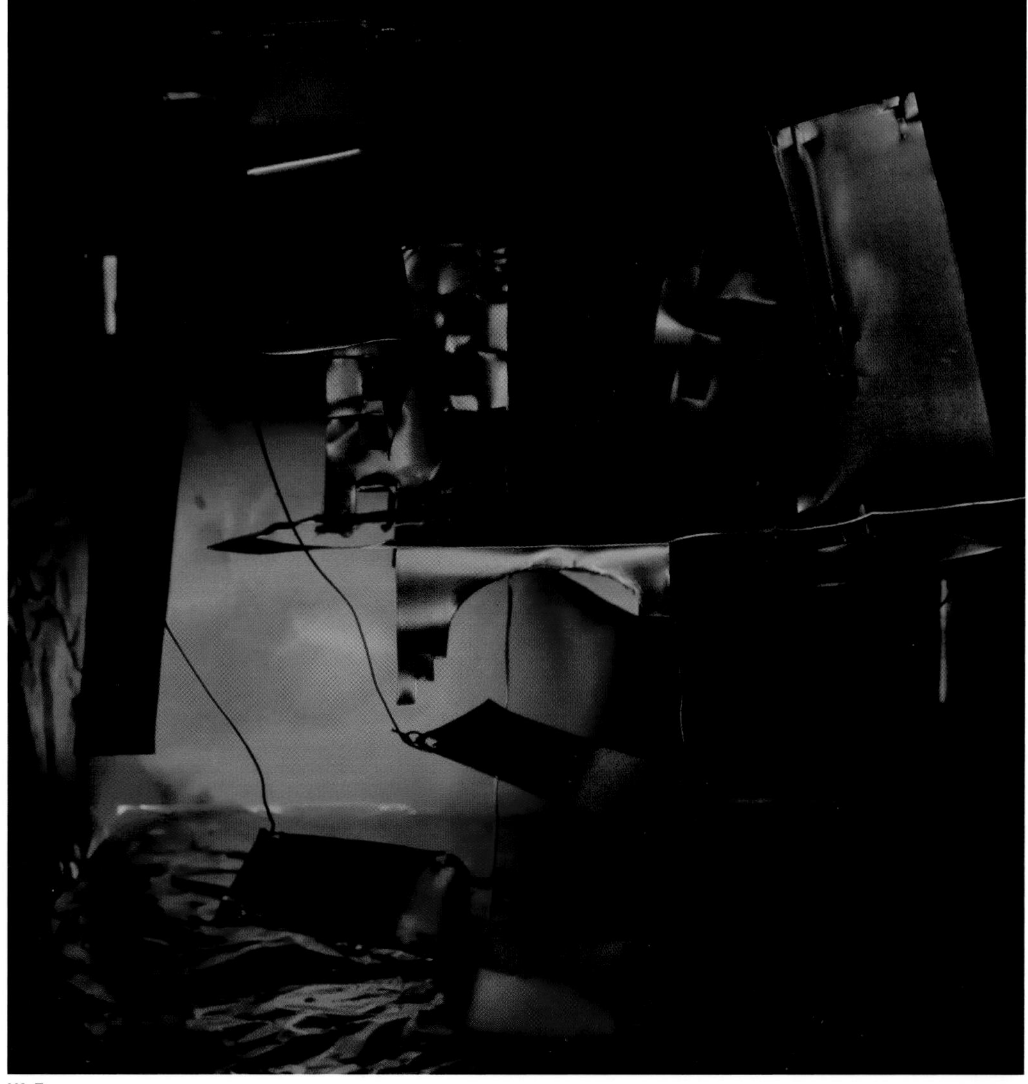

Y1.7

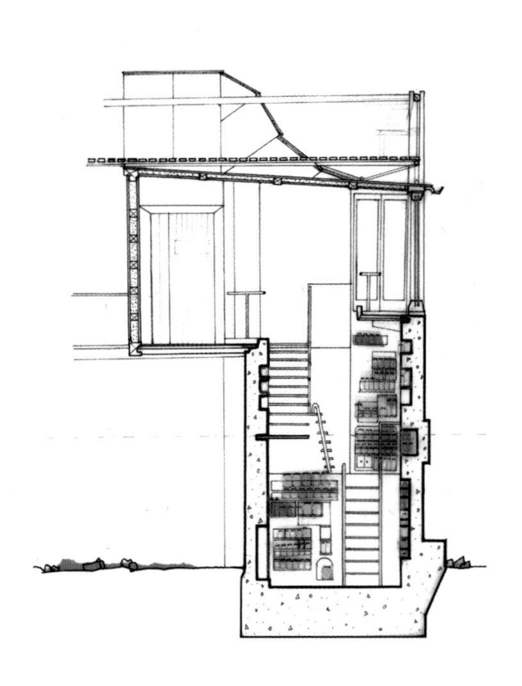

Y1.8

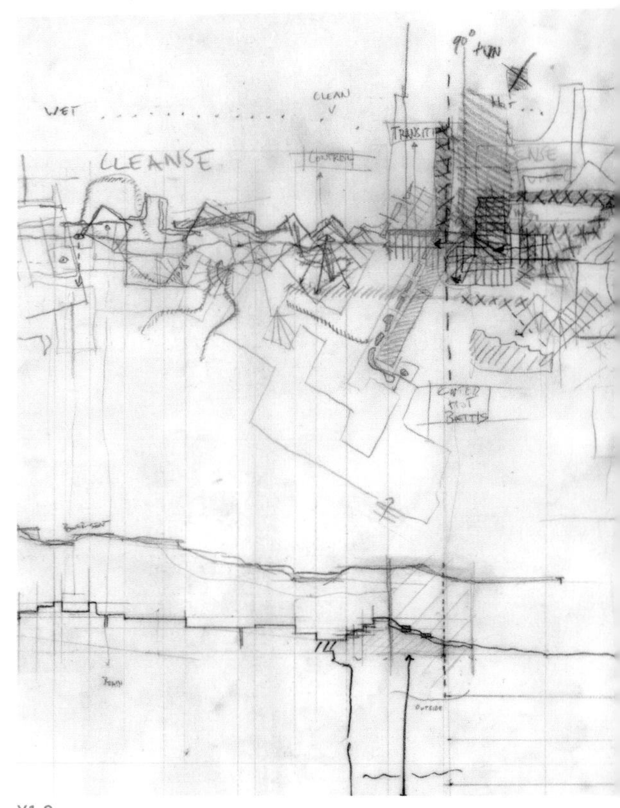

Y1.9

Y1.10

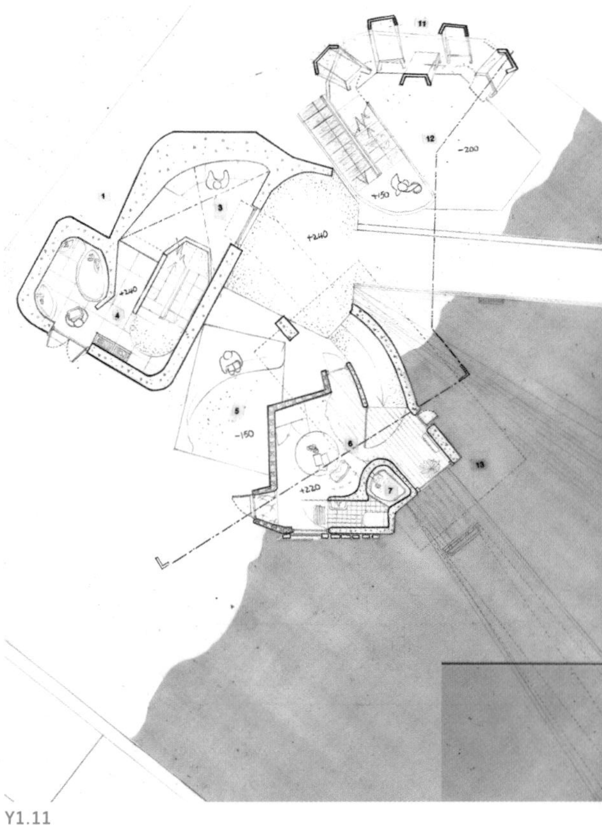

Y1.11

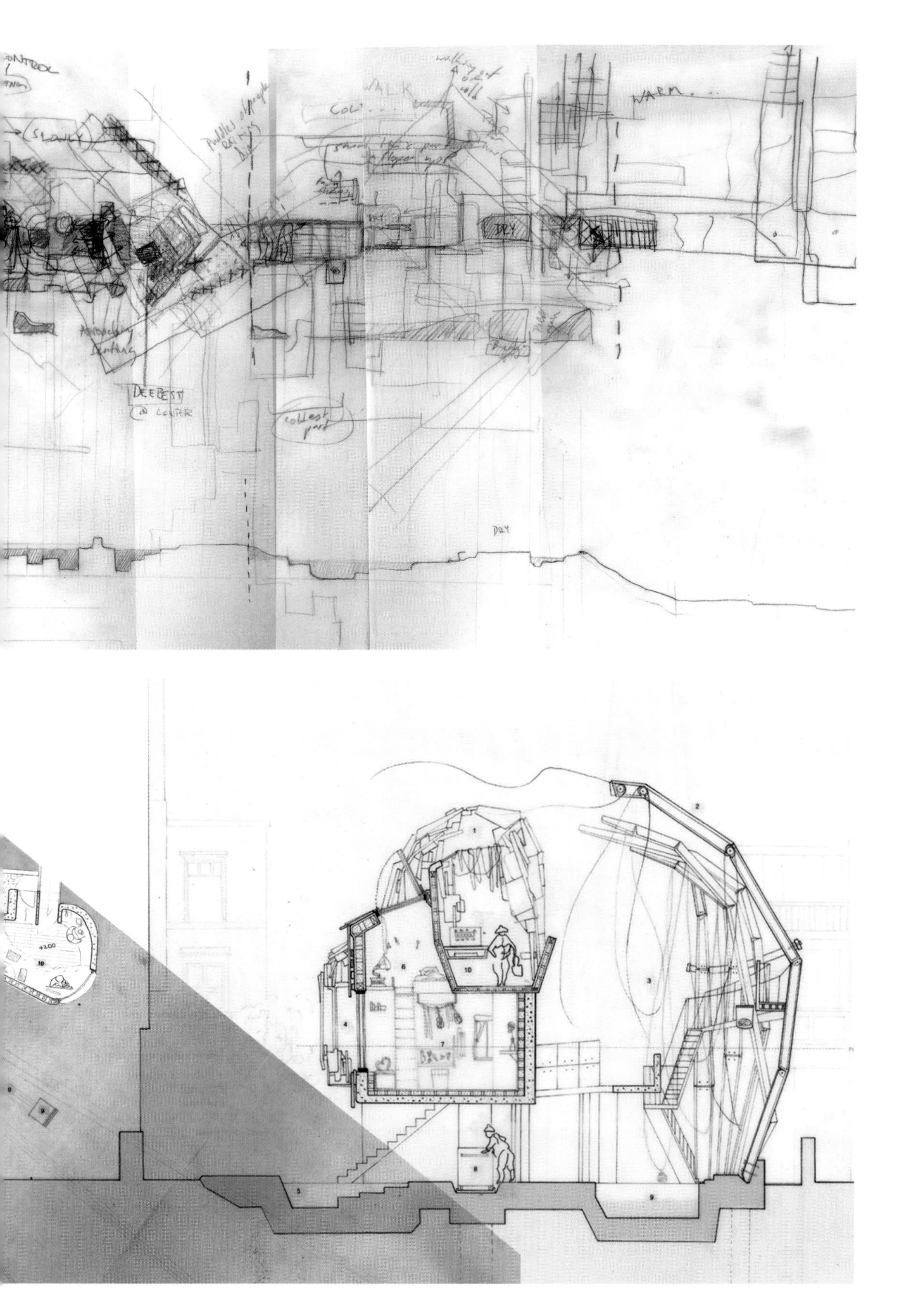

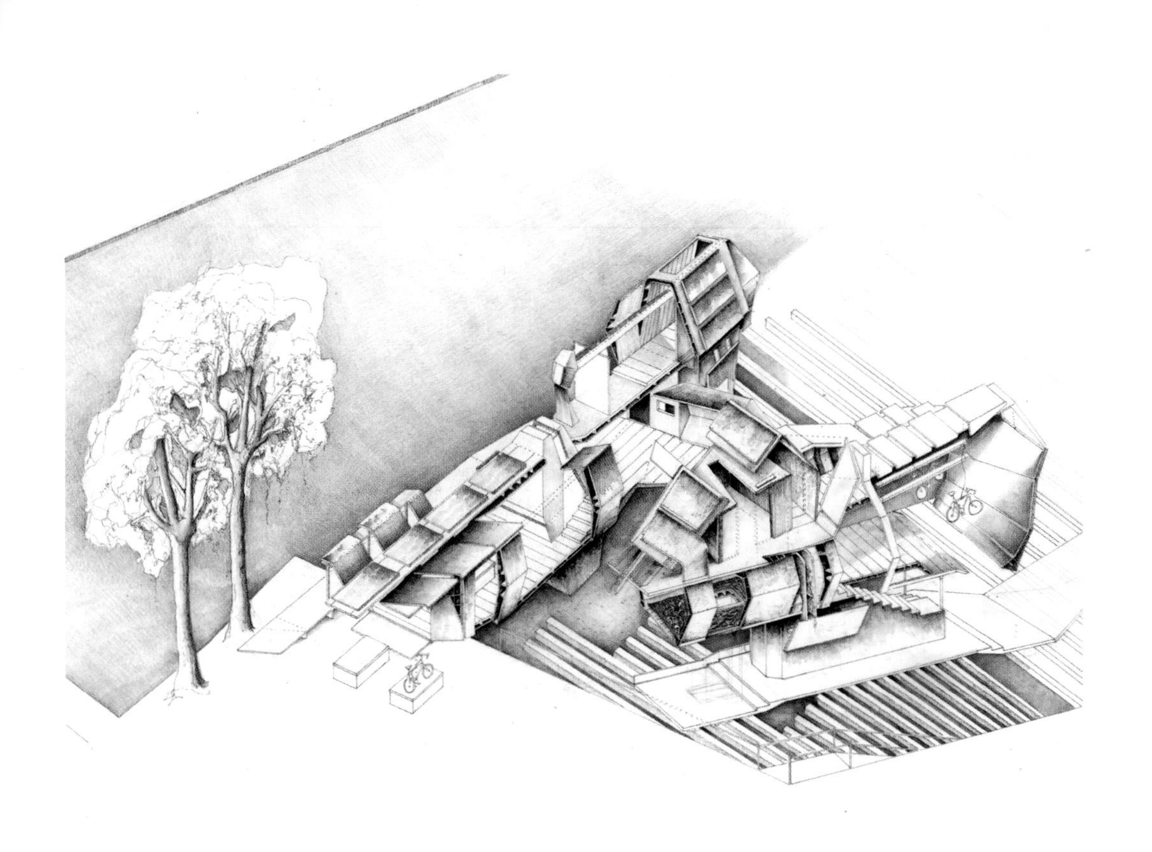

Y1.12

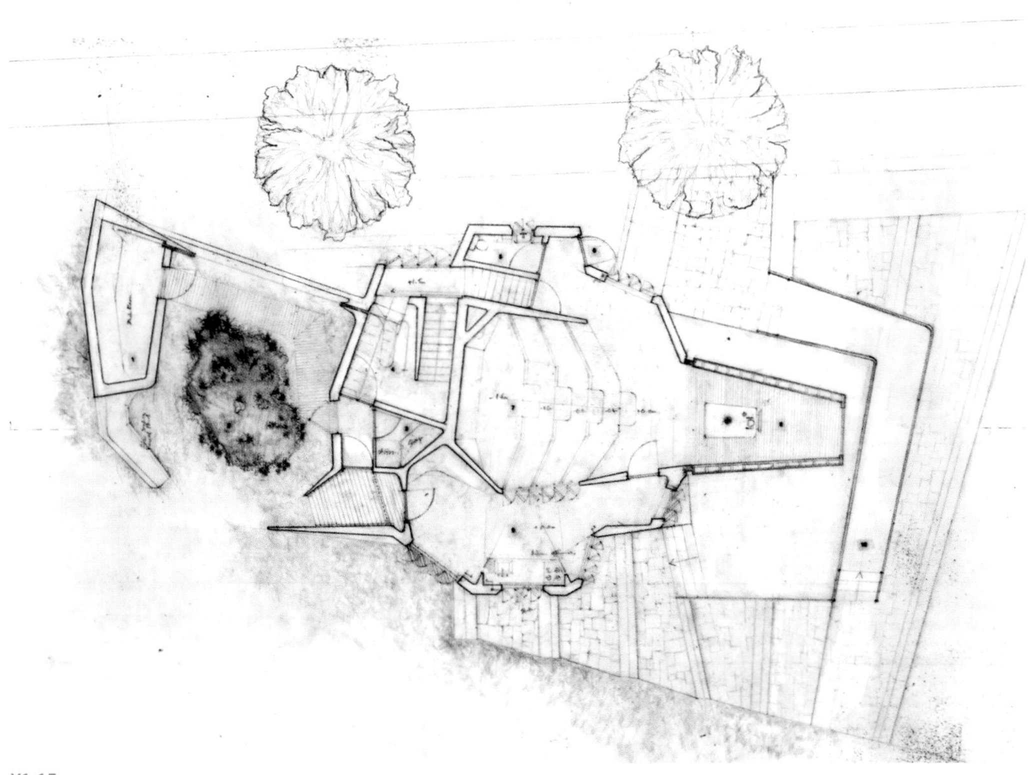

Y1.13

Y1.14

Y1.15

Y1.16

Y1.17

Y1.18

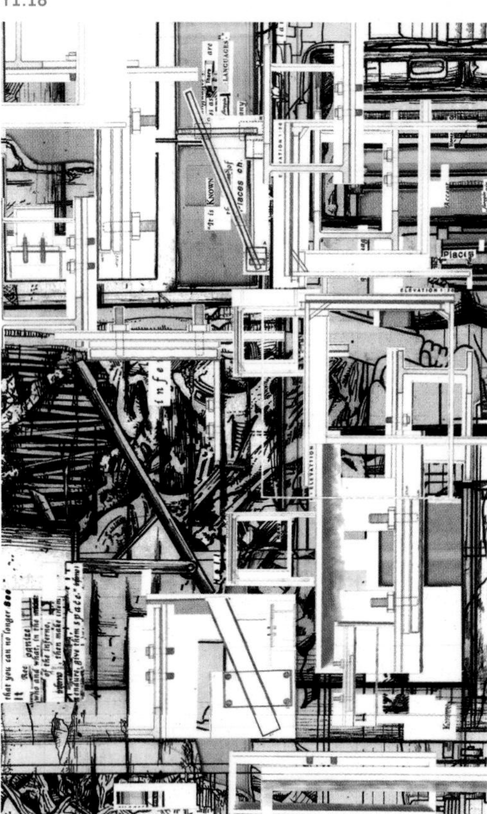

Y1.19

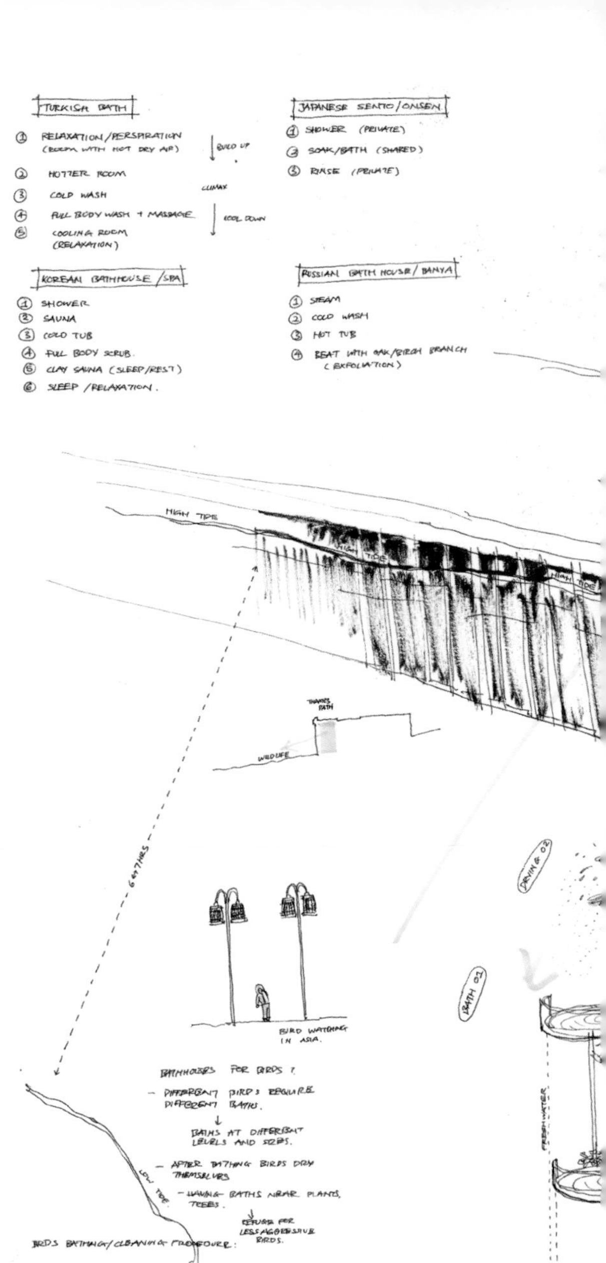

Y1.20

STUDIO SWINE
VIDEO REF
MOBILE FOUNDRY:
TURNING CANS
INTO STOOLS.
WASTE
VEGETABLE
OIL
LEAF BLOWER
FUNNEL FOR
OIL
BATTERY
CONTROL
VALVE
TROLLEY USED AS
FRAME.
CAN CITY
JOGGERS
CYCLIST
DOG WALKERS.
GUY THAT LIVES IN THE WALL?
SITE?
PIGEONS
BATH PODS
SEAGULL
SHELTER
BATH BASIN FOR BIRDS
ALONG RIVER BANK.
MIST
SECTION
SHELTER
FROM
WIND.
EXISTING WASTE / STRUCTURE
LOW TIDE
LOW TIDE
LOW TIDE
LOW TIDE
SEAGULLS

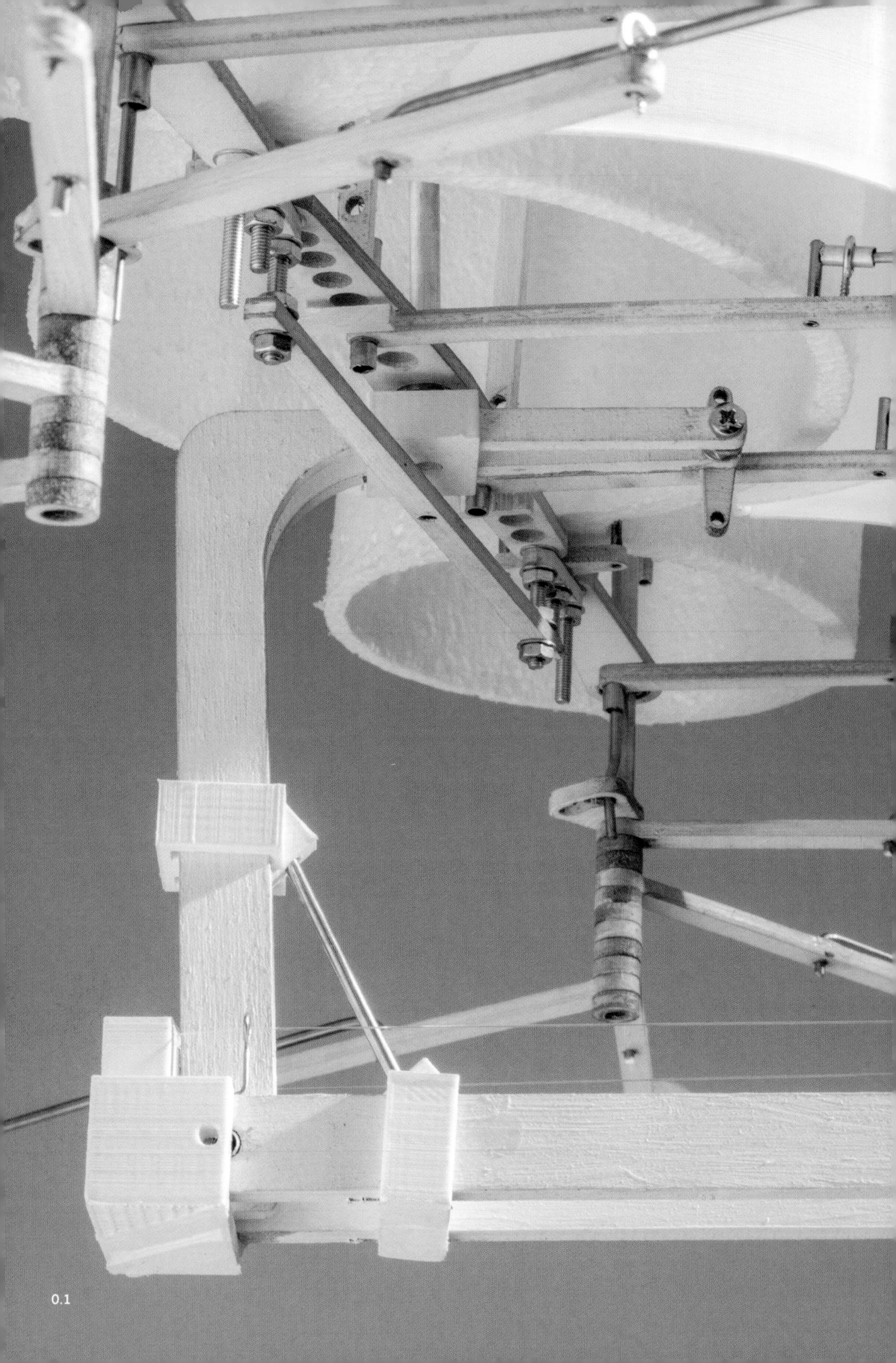

0.1

Continuum

UG0

Murray Fraser, Michiko Sumi

One doesn't need to study a building for too long to realise that it is a continuum, not an artifact. Buildings are not fixed entities or static objects but are, in fact, never finished. They change over time, in their spatial atmosphere and patterns of usage and programmes, and they get added to and subtracted from until their eventual decline. What does this mean for architects when designing a building? How should, or can, one allow for change and transformation over the lifespan of individual architectures? How does one draw a line between what is included within a building – ostensibly its interior – and what is not – its exterior? How do new modes of trans-spatial communication and lifestyle transform the idea of buildings as cultural continuums?

Equally crucial, buildings also need to negotiate with the surrounding city, with the latter formed of a myriad collection of buildings that, likewise, exist as continuums. To what extent, then, do the users of buildings become creative participants, even agents, in the process of becoming? To what extent do buildings exist within their own relatively autonomous state, changing only under their own defined conditions? As potential mediations between these two opposing poles, the spatial and material investigations carried out by architects consider the connections and disruptions that coexist within a building when treated as a continuum.

Following an initial project of their own devising, students were asked to develop their individual briefs for buildings, or other urban interventions, on sites they selected around London. This year's field trip was to Bangkok, where we visited floating markets, the ancient temples in the former capital of Ayutthaya, and a range of recently designed buildings, including the Kantana Film Institute designed by Boomserm Premthada (winner of this year's Royal Academy Dorfman Award).

As ever, the unit's underlying aim is for students to learn how to carry out a process of intensive research into contemporary architectural ideas, urban conditions, cultural relations and practices of everyday life, and then learn how to use these findings to create innovative and challenging forms of architecture for the contemporary city. Students are expected to use the unique speculative space offered by academic study and combine this with a commitment to social engagement and urban improvement. A clear understanding of the technological, environmental and developmental issues involved in design projects is vital. Furthermore, to develop their design proposals, students are expected to capitalise on the full range of methods of investigation and representation available to them: physical models, digital fabrication, photography, drawings, computer models, renderings, animations, films, and more.

Year 2
Charlotte Carr, Yuge (Julie) Chen, Sofya Daniltseva, Alice Guglielmi, Dongheon (Julian) Lee, Aaliyah McKoy, Hanlin (Finn) Shi, Tao Shi, Amy Zhou

Year 3
Daeyong Bae, Bryn Davies, Benedict Edwards, Millicent Green, Yiu (Anson) Lee, Yingying (Iris) Lou, Agnes Parker

Thanks to our critics and consultants: Tim Barwell, Anthony Boulanger, Eva Branscome, Matthew Butcher, Barbara-Ann Campbell-Lange, Jun Chan, Sam Coulton, Malina Dabrowska, Tamineh Hooshyar Emami, Guillermo Grauvoge, Ewa Hazla, Jonathan Hill, John I'Anson, Guan Lee, Yeoryia Manolopoulou, Luke Olsen, Achilleas Papakyriakou, Stuart Piercy, Jack Sardeson, Jack Sargent, Sara Shafiei, Ben Stringer, Mika Zacharias

Partners: Atelier One, Faber Architects

Thanks to our sponsors: Bean Buro, Forterra Building Products Ltd

0.1 **Daeyong Bae, Y3** 'The Dentist's Chair'. This close-up shot is of the underside of an abstracted process model that encapsulates the four classic pillars of dentistry: excavation, bracing, bridging and veneering. In conceiving the human mouth as a continuous construction site that requires work throughout one's life, the model sets the feel and tone for the proposed building project to follow.
0.2, 0.8–0.9, 0.15 **Daeyong Bae, Y3** 'Self-Excavating Building'. Convoy's Wharf in Deptford is a significant historic site, dating back to before a dockyard was established there in the early-16th century. A development plan recently threatened to swamp the site with luxury housing. This proposal adopts an alternative approach, envisaging a vast archaeological park for residents to enjoy and watch tall scratching devices slowly remove the soil. Shown first in its mechanical model form, in which scratchers sit on their pontoons, powered by tidal drop; then, its poetic expression; a sgraffito plan drawing made using erasure to suggest the gradual revealing of the sub-layers; and lastly, a site strategy plan, depicting viewing walkways and platforms. The overall scheme includes two crucial reused elements: the twin-vaulted Olympia Building with its 1850s cast wrought-iron frame, veneered with mottled whitewashed timber shingles. A sequence of new laboratories and community spaces are clipped onto the existing timber jetty that runs parallel to the shoreline.
0.3–0.5 **Millicent Green, Y3** 'The School for Dexterity'. Plan; collection of process models; hybrid clay-etched sectional drawing. Situated in Bow Locks in Limehouse, the proposed school explores the relationship between hand and machine through the tactility of clay – the quintessential, unpredictable London material – and our desire to touch. Acting as a teaching device in itself, the building is comprised of imperfect ergonomic spaces used for dexterous activities. Here, the clay is developed by machine and intervenedwith by hand, thereby allowing for human error within the mechanised process. The wider ambition of the project is to question where beauty can be found in construction today.
0.6 **Hanlin (Finn) Shi, Y2** 'Park Conveniences'. Material model. CAD-CAM digital fabrication techniques are used to simulate the pattern made by leaves dried out and stiffened with resin. The resultant form is used to shape the roof over a suite of semi-sunken public conveniences on the Outer Circle in Regent's Park in London, designed to provide a pit-stop for park goers.
0.7, 0.14 **Hanlin (Finn) Shi, Y2** 'Made in ~~China~~ Chelsea'. Keen to undercut the prices of the East India Company's porcelain imports from China, Britain's first chinaware factory opened in the mid-18th century, close to Cheyne Walk in Chelsea. On a site nearby (Upper Cheyne Row), this project seeks to revive the industry in acknowledgement of the longstanding cultural link between the two countries. The drawing shows the dominating presence of the large 'bottle kilns' used to fire porcelain goods, as well as the careful combination of the sweeping Chinese timber roof forms, traditionally found in temples, with local vernacular of London stock brickwork.
0.10–0.11 **Benedict Edwards, Y3** 'An Alternative Building Site'. Partial perspective section; rendered bird's-eye perspective. A prototype scheme located on Cleveland Street in London, as a response to the construction industry in post-Brexit Britain and foreign workers being replaced by drones and robots. By rethinking the construction site through a focus on the suppression of dangerous dusts and the facilitation of near-future robotics, a double-diagrid envelope system is proposed, to be reused at building sites around London, with almost every element modular and able to be rented. The 'flesh' envelope holds the site facilities, with a small technical college atop it, alongside larger event spaces for hire.
0.12–0.13 **Bryn Davies, Y3** 'Night and Day'. Partial section; rendered night-time perspective. This proposal for a ferry terminal at Westferry Circus in Canary Wharf, offers a transitional node for social interaction and increased physical/mental wellbeing for shift-workers. Set on the riverfront, it constructs a synergy between the River Thames's natural cycles and the regimented timetable of Canary Wharf. Through layered translucent materials and screens, the building offers a regulated progression of spatial and lighting conditions to prepare the circadian clocks of shift-workers.
0.16 **Charlotte Carr, Y2** 'Stage-Set Journey'. Using the exaggerated perspective effects of theatrical stages – like the Teatro Olimpico Vicenza in Italy – and the pastel colours of Wes Anderson's films, this distorted model represents the key moments on a bus journey from Camden to The Bartlett in Bloomsbury. The final upper balcony is a landing on the twisting steel staircase that snakes up inside The Bartlett's building.
0.17 **Tao Shi, Y2** 'Four Times of the Day'. Overlaid perspective. For this project, William Hogarth's 1736 series of paintings *Four Times of the Day* was dissected and used as a guide to review London at the time. A new pavilion next to St Paul's Church in Covent Garden – depicted by Hogarth – is proposed. The design connects the past to the present, thus equating architecture with historical commemoration. This idea of a continuum in time and space was taken further in the main project, for the old Foundling Hospital in Coram's Fields, of which Hogarth was a patron.
0.18 **Amy Zhou, Y2** 'Landscape of Buildings'. Cutaway axonometric. This project is sited on Brent Reservoir in an area of London with a large Chinese population. It proposes a natural garden influenced by ancient Chinese gardens, and includes inhabitable community spaces for socialising. The design explores the idea of a continuum of time and the four seasons, with the evolution of the nature-scape considered in relation to the seemingly consistent state of the built elements. Taking inspiration from Feng Shui, the elements of water and wood are dominant, and views over the adjacent reservoir enhance the naturalistic feel of the site.
0.19 **Aaliyah McKoy, Y2** 'Vertical Market'. This model is part of a concept for a high-density market building on Ridley Road in London that sits vertically in a thin tower rather than horizontally on the street. The sense of being on a rambling promenade is enhanced by the design's highly irregular form, complete with external staircases and lifts to take people and goods up and down.
0.20–0.23 **Agnes Parker, Y3** 'Towie: Toxic Overflow Waste in Essex'. Material model; concrete test pieces; plan; section. 1,264 landfill sites along the British coastline are eroding, leaking and spilling into the water; the majority of which are in the Thames flood zone. These landfills contain material from the Anthropocene age: whole items, broken fragments and toxic chemicals. Sited on a rubble-strewn beach in Tilbury in Essex, this project proposes laboratory residences for climate researchers and artists. The structures dot the terrain and have thick concrete cores to encase toxic elements beneath them. Slow erosion reshapes them gracefully as they crumble away into the sea.

0.2

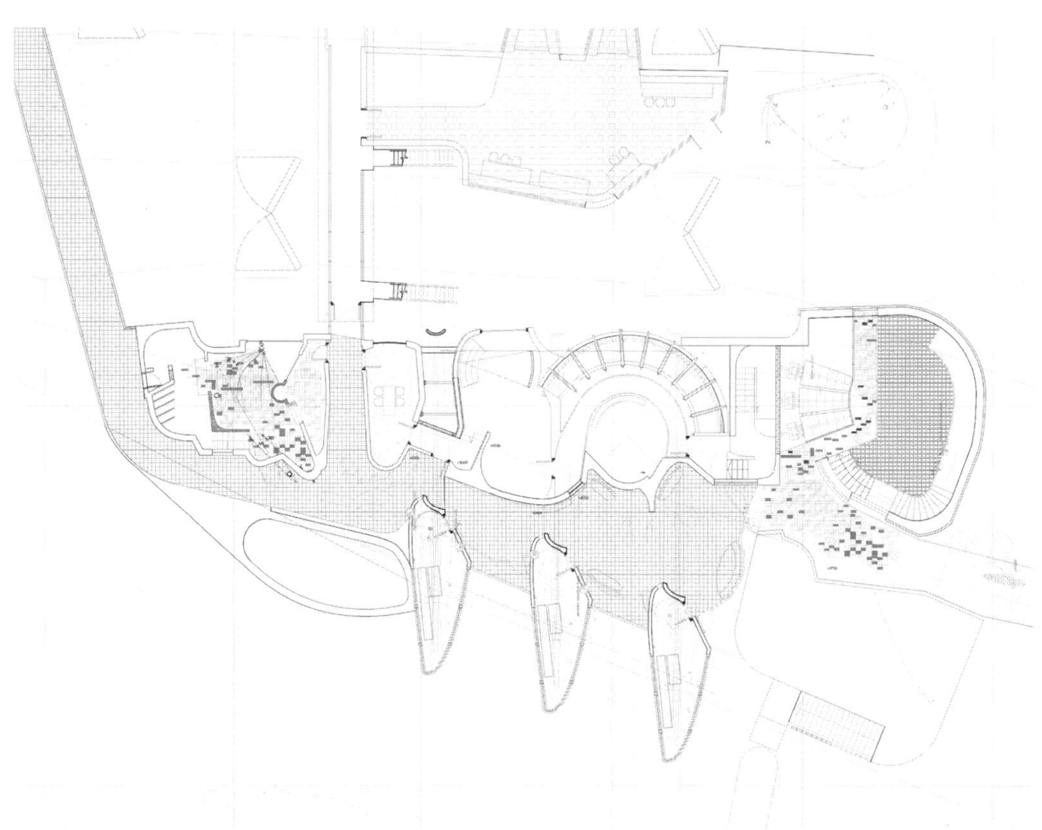

0.3

0.4

0.5

0.6

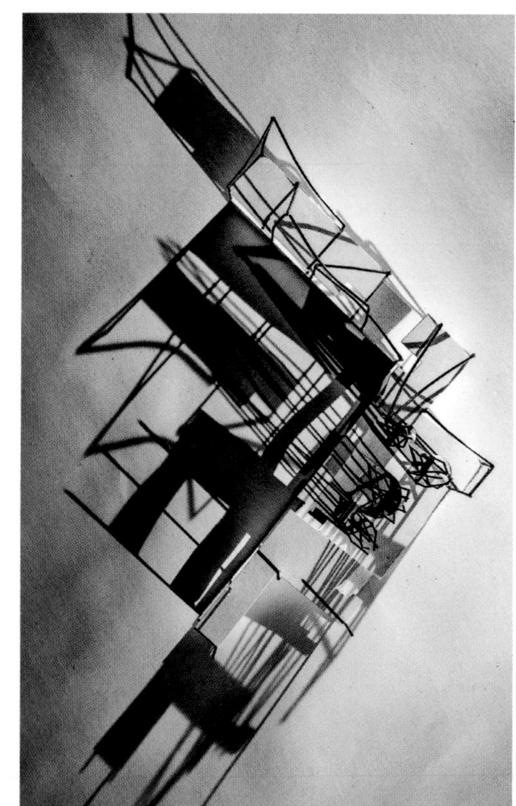

0.7

0.8

0.9

0.10

0.11

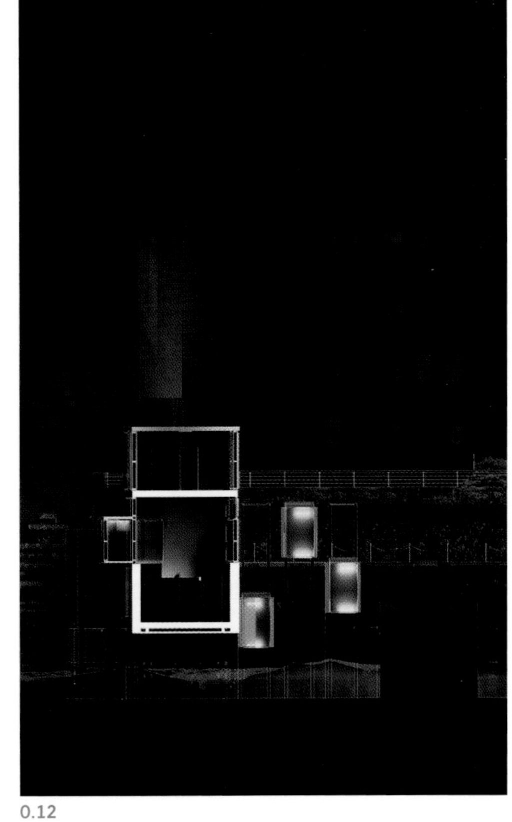

0.12

0.13

0.14

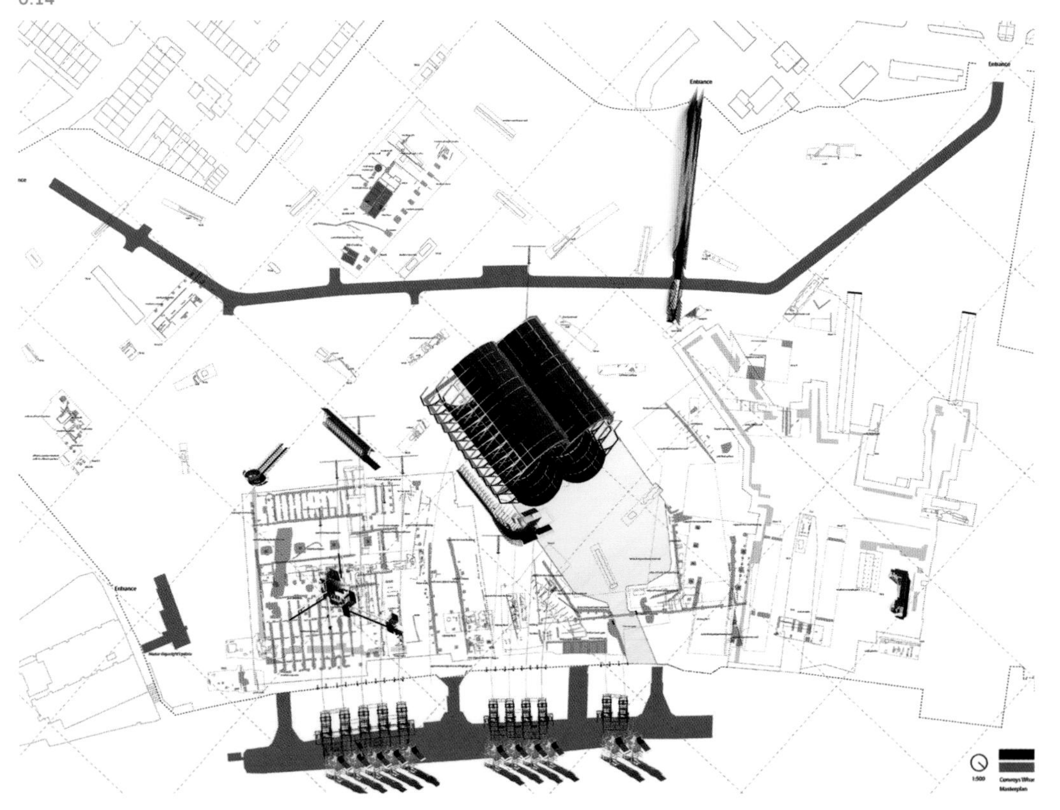
Entrance
Entrance
Entrance
1:500
Convoys Wharf
Masterplan

0.15

0.16

0.17

0.18

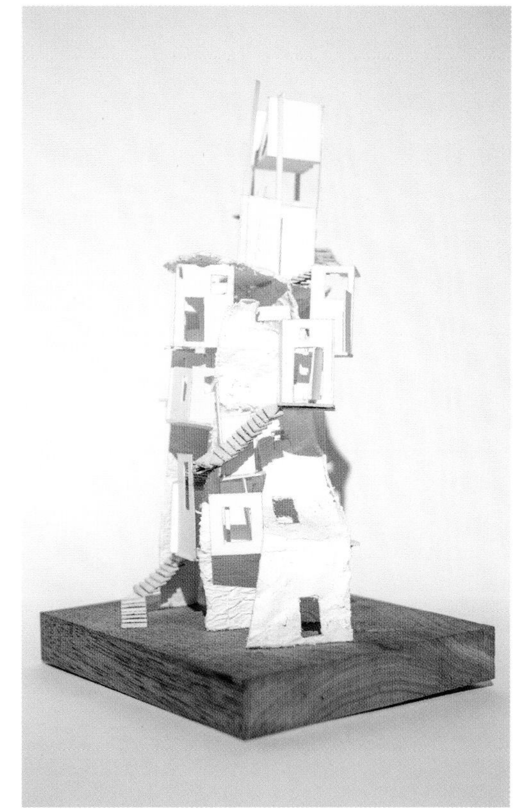
0.19

0.20

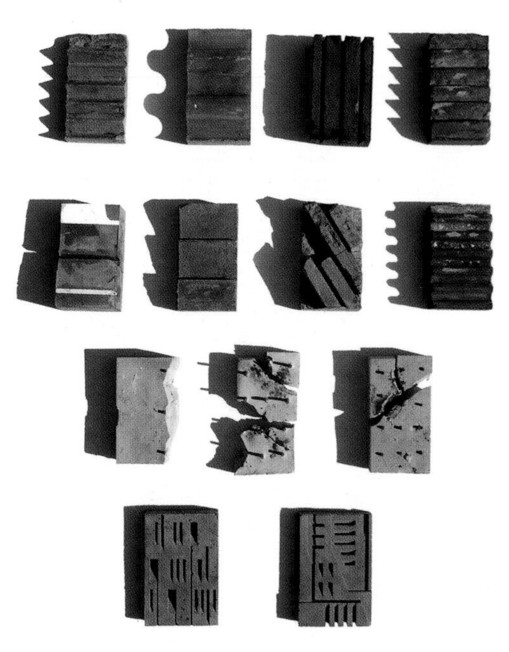

0.21

0.22

0.23

1.1

Binary

Mads Hulsroy-Peterson, Eleanor Lakin

This year, UG1 pursued an architectural agenda driven by the concept of 'binary' in the broadest sense of the word: an architecture that is generated by the tension between diametric extremes or two polar-opposite states.

On a micro scale, we are inspired by the innate and embodied behaviours of materials, pre-determined by molecular, cellular or even atomic compositions; whilst on a macro scale, site-specific extremes, such as environmental conditions, cultural relationships or human psychology trigger design responses. The collective behaviour of pixels in digital matrices or components in mechanical processes inspire a machine architecture, where binary inputs inform pre-defined outputs.

Our work inherently evolves and adapts, and is thus heavily contextualised within a certain place and time. The existing condition, construction, occupancy and even the post-occupancy phases of our proposals are all key considerations throughout our design development. We nurture a design process where the speculated is swiftly realised throughout the design process, and where the making, testing and prototyping of scaled or 1:1 components of our proposals are examined, both physically and digitally, to be re-imagined on site as part of the built whole.

We started the year by identifying moments of binary within a site on Canvey Island in Essex. We designed and made physical devices, installations and small building proposals that responded to our observations. Responses included a 'biomimetic sanctuary' that heals the polluted landscape beneath it; a smuggler's bothy, with a skin that responds to solar inputs, to camouflage or reveal the shelter at specific times of the day and year; and a dystopian fairground ride, where the track and vehicle work collectively to create an analogue, spatial and musical machine.

Following our site trip to Berlin, we applied the knowledge gained to develop highly resolved building proposals, which embodied the essence of the early binary investigations. Proposals included a 'Freedom of Speech Centre' that explores the city's relationship to freedom of expression, the building's façade becoming a physical embodiment of the manifesto spoken within; 'Landscape of Glimpses', a radical self-expression club inspired by Berlin's underground culture, incorporating a melting wax façade and fibreoptic arrays; and a 'Field Recording Museum', which draws on Berlin's historical and cultural relationship with monuments and their immortalising of the past, by recording and playing back intangible audio moments found within the city through the textures in the fabric of the building.

Year 2
Temilayo Ajayi, Bengisu Demir, Defne Kocamustafaogullari, Yue Yu

Year 3
Alp Amasya, Issariyaporn Chotitawan, Elizabeth Day, Jiana Lin, Faustyna Smolilo

Partners: AKT II, Bare Conductive, BlindPig, Jason Bruges Studio, Piercy & Company

Consultants and critics: Stefan Dzisiewski-Smith, Stephen Gage, Anam Afroze Hasan, Kirstine Jaeger, Daria Jelonek, Tetsuro Nagata, Christine Peters, Danae Polyviou, David Shanks, Guy Woodhouse

1.1–1.2, 1.16 **Alp Amasya, Y3** 'The Landscape of Glimpses'. Inspired by the hedonism of the Berlin underground, 'The Landscape of Glimpses' is a radical self-expression club, which challenges and erodes the boundaries of societal norms. Over time, the semi-subterranean building merges the public space above with the hidden depths of the club below, through its semi-translucent melting-wax façade and fibre optic arrays.
1.3 **Elizabeth Day, Y3** 'Climate Centre'. Located in one of the most polluted areas of Berlin, the 'Climate Centre' aims to both cleanse and purify the local environment, as well as inform and educate visitors in sustainable living. An array of self-grown, perforated mycelium fins filter prevailing air currents of pollutants, and also support a series of pod enclosures that accommodate both public and private laboratory and educational spaces. The biodegradable mycelium 'pixels' are grown on site and are, therefore, easily replaced once expired.
1.4 **Yue Yu, Y2** 'Disaster Follies'. This project proposes a series of emergency follies situated on the seawall at Canvey Island in Essex. By exploring the outcomes of an extreme condition – the detonation of 1,400 tonnes of explosives onboard the wrecked ship, SS Richard Montgommery, that ran aground in the Thames Estuary in 1944 – the follies collectively act as a warning and defence system to protect local residents.
1.5 **Defne Kocamustafaogullari, Y2** 'Techno Realm'. This project commemorates the euphoric era of 90s Berlin and the drive for escapism that the city, at the time, encapsulated. The building transforms from day to night, reconfiguring from a museum to a music venue, incorporating the layered and repetitive nature of electronic music in its mechanical character. The tunable acoustics in the dynamic ceiling, the energy harvested in the wall-mounted solar reflectors and the phosphorescent way-finding device, are key ways in which the building adapts itself to perform.
1.6 **Issariyaporn Chotitawan, Y3** 'Smuggler's Bothy'. This proposal imagines Canvey Island as an underground gateway to London. Tracking the journey of present-day smugglers, it proposes a series of shelters sited at key locations along the route. By exploring the concept of camouflage, each unique bothy is concealed within its distinct landscape and is only revealed to the smuggler at their angle of approach and at a particular time of the day.
1.7, 1.10 **Alp Amasya, Y3** 'Spydoscope'. This project diffuses the distinct boundary created by the flood wall on the beach-front on Canvey Island, connecting the two contrasting and extreme landscapes on either side. The covert viewing device is directed towards different views and ultimately creates paranoia and division amongst the communities on the island.
1.8 **Issariyaporn Chotitawan, Y3** 'Loneliness Recreational Creative Hub'. The 'Loneliness Recreational Creative Hub' has rated Berlin as one of Europe's most difficult cities to settle in, and looks to help integrate visitors and provide opportunities for interaction. The proposal's reflective 'limbs' extend out into the adjacent park, inviting people, light and images of the surrounding landscape into the social space within. Reflective satellites at various locations within the park rotate to ensure light paths are directed into the building at all times of the day.
1.9 **Defne Kocamustafaogullari, Y2** 'The Toxic Ride'. Located in the so-called 'oil-land', 'The Toxic Ride' is a dystopian fairground ride whose track and vehicle work collectively to create an analogue, spatial and musical machine. The unsettling experience amplifies the contradiction of the toxicity and joy that characterises Canvey Island.
1.11–1.13 **Jiana Lin, Y3** 'Field Recording Museum'. Drawing on Berlin's historical and cultural relationship with monuments and their immortalising of the past, the 'Field Recording Museum' aims to record and play back intangible audio moments found within the city. A network of textures integrated throughout the circulation and exhibition spaces of the internal fabric of the building create sound vibrations when played.
1.14 **Faustyna Smolilo, Y3** 'Crabbing Shack'. Located in the Thames Estuary off the shore of Canvey Island, the 'Crabbing Shack' uses the traditional activity of crabbing, local to Canvey, to integrate new communities. Its architecture takes inspiration from fishing apparatus, gently adjusting to the natural levels, tides and buoyancy of the water to accommodate various activities within the space.
1.15 **Faustyna Smolilo, Y3** 'The Freedom of Speech Centre'. Located close to the Luther Bridge in Berlin, 'The Freedom of Speech Centre' affirms the city's affinity with freedom of expression, providing a platform from which views can be shared and learnt. A matrix of copper-façade pixels transforms with patination so that the building becomes a physical embodiment of the manifesto spoken within. Copper pixel sizes vary, each size relating to a key view, thus ensuring that the message is discernible from the outside as well as within.

1.2

1.3

1.4

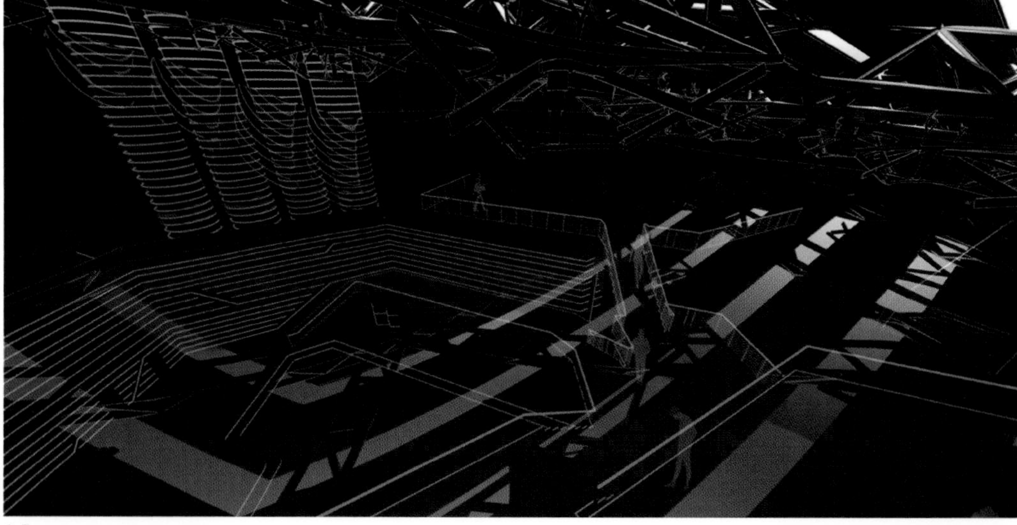

1.5

1.6

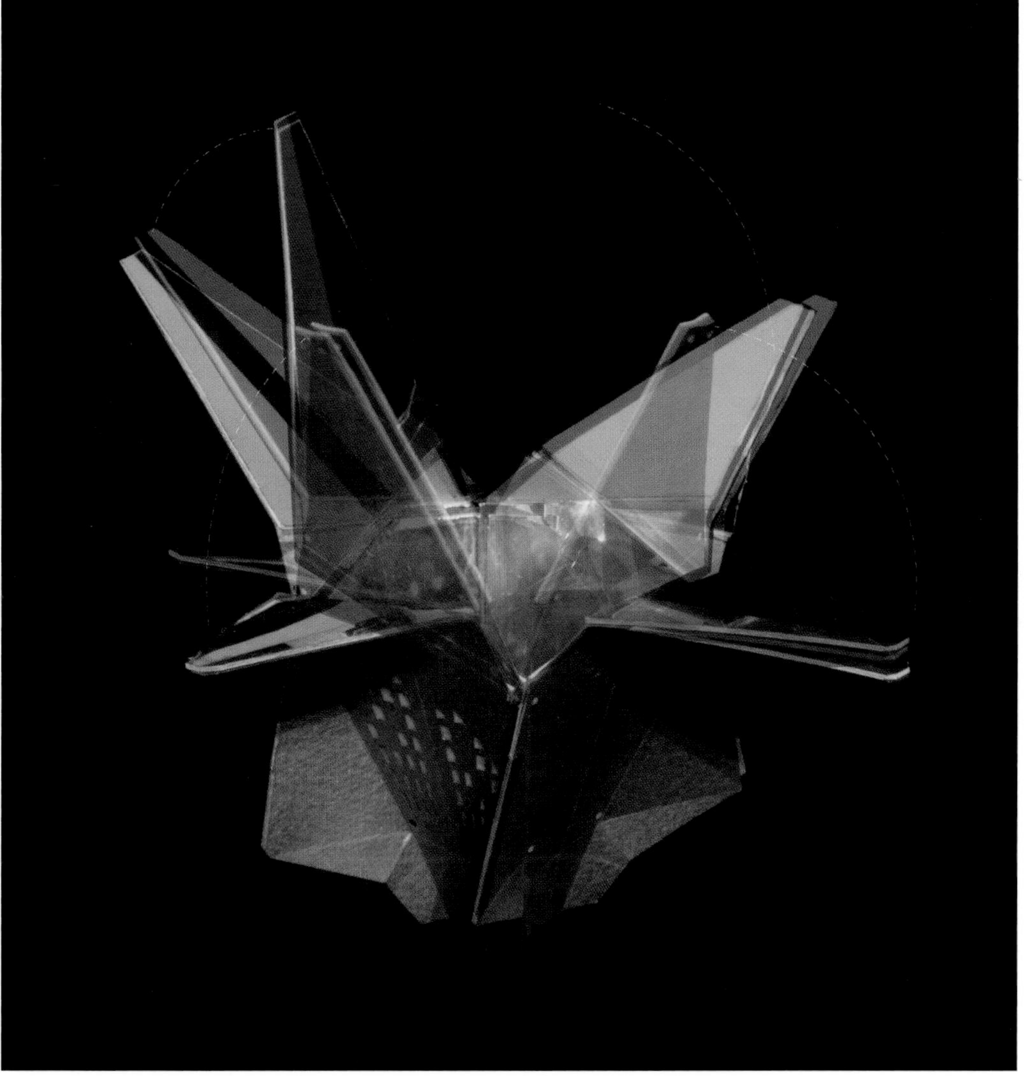

1.7

1.8

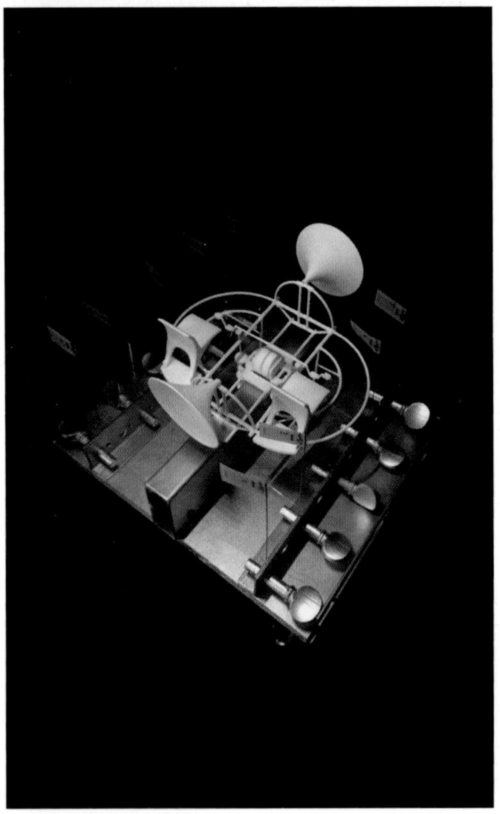

1.9

1.10

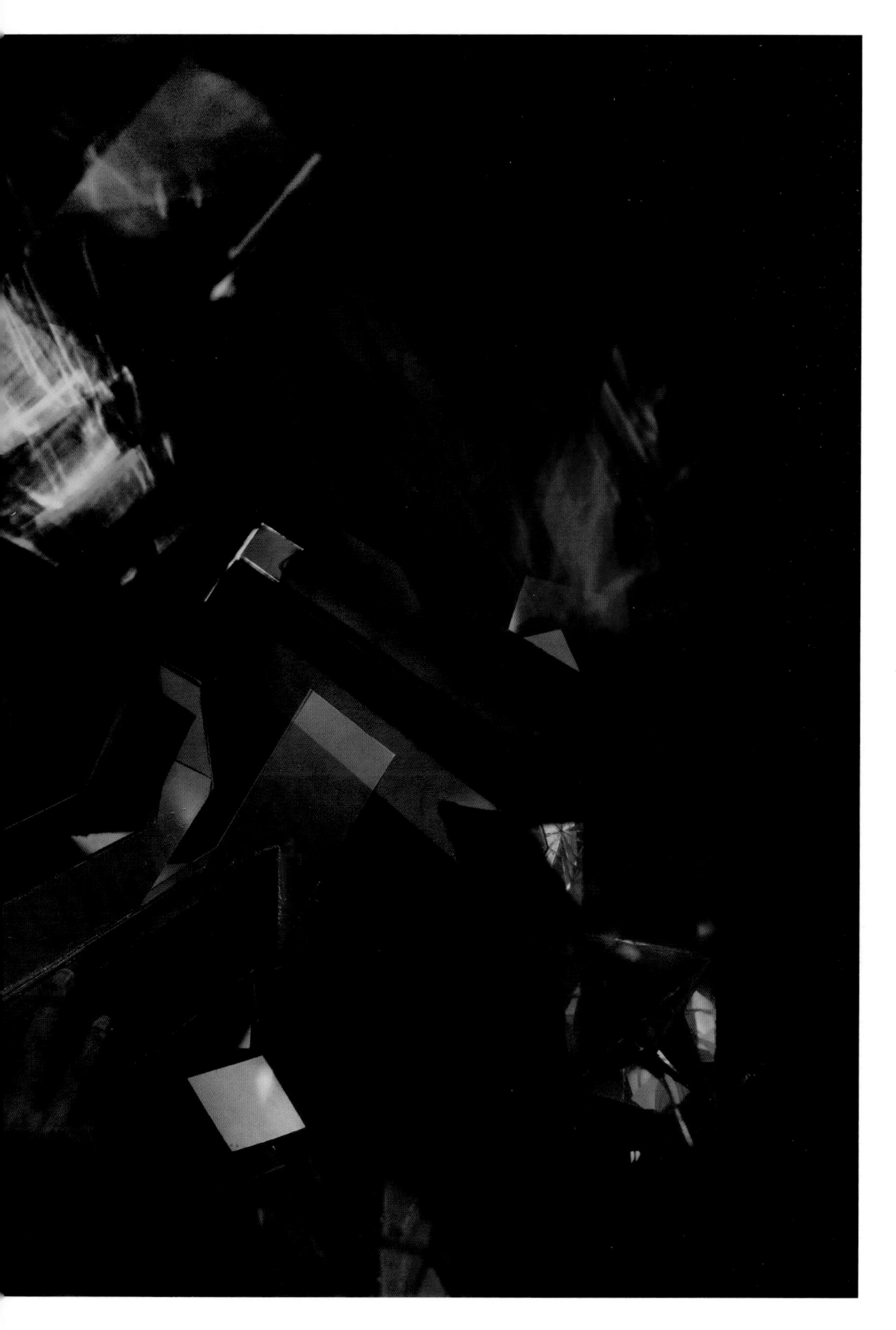

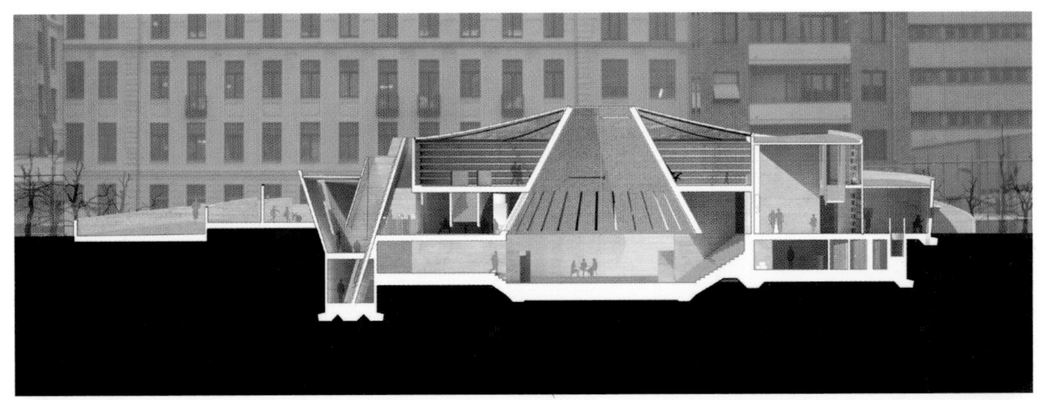
1.11

1.12

1.13

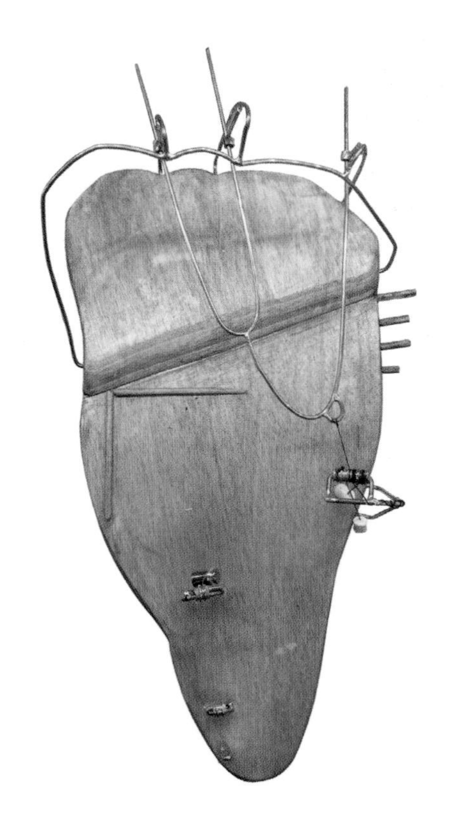

1.14

1.15

1.16

2.1

Urban Cliff

UG2

Maria Knutsson-Hall, Barry Wark

This year, we explored the 'urban cliff' hypothesis, which identifies that our cities are often akin to the habitat templates of cliffs. This is based upon the similarities in their physical composition, whereby both have a lack of soil and rooting space, with moisture ranging from dry to waterlogged due to their hard and impervious surfaces. These conditions are apparent in abandoned buildings, pavements and along railway lines where our built environment is less polished and forgotten. Rather than try to implement a superficial and manicured nature, the unit instead looked to exploit these qualities and viewed it as fertile ground for the exploration of moments of wilderness in architecture.

We travelled to Morocco's Eastern border with the Sahara Desert and the Atlas Mountain range, visiting Fes, Chefchaouen, Marrakesh and Ait Ben-Haddou. During our excursions, we cast a critical eye on traditional construction and vernacular architecture, observing and examining how these tight-knit cities form out of a necessity to escape the intense heat. The unit focused on civic architecture in Marrakesh, addressing projections on near future scenarios. The proposals explored issues such as mismanagement of natural resources, tourism, gentrification of the medina, education and other social services. Many projects also integrated new forms of public space into central Marrakesh to facilitate the varying lifestyles of the inhabitants of Ville Nouvelle and those of the old city.

In searching for urban cliff conditions, it was impossible not to take influence from Marrakesh's famous riads, or courtyard houses. The calm, vegetated interiors of the buildings, with their delicate ornament, formed a strong contrast to the more robust and austere external conditions of the medina. Many of the students' projects play on this internal/external duality found throughout the city, and employ the same passive cooling systems to regulate the thermal conditions in their proposals.

Inspired by the energy of the city, its deeply textured walls and its overgrown courtyards, the projects endeavoured to capture these qualities in an architecture that is at once progressive and, at the same time, inspired by its context. Balancing moments of high intensity with serenity, the work reimagines a variety of traditional materials through avant-garde design and fabrication tools. The proposals ultimately integrate water and vegetation in novel, considered and meaningful ways, to create alluring moments of atmospheric wilderness within the Marrakesh medina.

Year 2
Jean Bell, Nicholas Collee, James Della Valle, Ceren Erten, Paul Kohlhaussen, Ian Lim, Sut (Eunice) Lo, Natali Rayya, Josef Stoger, Kar (Tiffanie) Tseng

Year 3
Sheryl Beh, Katarzyna Dabrowska, Imogen Dhesi, Karishma Khajuria, Yue (Nicole) Ren, Benjamin Webster

Many thanks to our technical tutor James Palmer for his invaluable contribution to the unit and to Sonia Magdziarz for her passion and positivity in the teaching of the skills workshops

Thank you to our guest critics and those offering their comments and support throughout the year: Richard Beckett, Tom Budd, Barbara-Ann Campbell-Lange, Sir Peter Cook, Christina Grytten, Shireen Hamdan, Simon Herron, Andreas Koerner, Chee-Kit Lai, Justin Nicholls, Sara Shafiei, Sam Welham

We are grateful to our sponsor Populous for their continuing support of the unit

2.1 UG2, Y2 and Y3 'Model Display'. Collective output of the units model-centred, design methodology. These include spatial studies, material composites, tectonic assemblies and final building models.
2.2, 2.3, 2.7, 2.10 Imogen Dhesi, Y3 'Riad Al Nisa'. This project is a building for the women of Marrakesh who have become isolated or ostracised from their communities. Developed from the riad typology, it provides accommodation, vegetated courtyards and a new public space. This space functions as a mint tea garden and enables the building's residents to interact and foster relationships with their neighbours. It is characterised by an opulent water feature, adapted to the Marrakesh climate, that passively cools the building whilst also providing an acoustic and atmospheric experience.
2.4–2.5 Benjamin Webster, Y3 'Modular Tectonic Experiments'. Early experiments investigating the potential of extruded earth and ceramic components to be assembled into larger structures.
2.6 Sheryl Beh, Y3 'Chinese Tourism Centre'. Chinese tourists visiting Morocco have increased since a visa requirement was removed. This project creates a building that assists these tourists in orientating themselves within the medina and, also, in training local tour guides in basic Mandarin language skills.
2.8 Ceren Erten, Y2 'Visiting School'. This project creates a school where children from rural areas can come and stay for a period of time in Marrakesh and access facilities that might not be available to them in their villages. The aim is that it will allow the country to develop its literacy rate and further its digital skills. The building is composed of classrooms and accommodation and, simultaneously, creates a cool underbelly, forming much-needed public space.
2.9 Josef Stoger, Y2 'Fashion School'. Motivated by the rich heritage of fashion in Marrakesh, the project looks to foster a culture that rejects the global fashion industry in the creation of a style that is idiosyncratic to the city. The proposal is for a dedicated fashion school where the building is inspired by the Berber tents and loose-fit fabrics adorned by older generations.
2.11 Yue (Nicole) Ren, Y3 'Souvenir Auction House'. Many souvenirs in the Marrakesh medina are not the product of careful hand-craft but are mass produced and imported from China. This proposal is for an auction house where traders can bid on larger quantities of these goods. It draws upon the smoothed-out aesthetic of many of the city's buildings where, over time, they become bulbous as more layers of earth and clay are applied to their façades.
2.12 James Della Valle, Y2 'Light Entertainment'. This project builds on idea of the souk as a space for entertainment and performance. The proposal refurbishes a dilapidated collection of buildings to the north of Jemaa el-Fnaa Square, creating a series of urban incisions composed of lightweight walls, amphitheatres and rooftop canopies that act to frame and promote informal performance. The model is a 1:20 detail of how these incisions might meet the existing fabric.
2.13 Nicholas Collee, Y2 'House of Football'. This project creates a much-needed sports amenity in a poor part of the medina. It explores components and in-situ 'post-carving', after construction, to create visual complexity as a wayfinding strategy.
2.14 Ian Lim, Y2 'Souvenir Riad'. With Instagram tourism on the rise, what value is there in pictures as a souvenir? Questioning this phenomena, this project proposes that true value in travelling might be to obtain a unique experience or handmade souvenir. The result is a workshop building where visitors can create their own souvenirs guided by local craftspeople.
2.15 Katarzyna Dabrowska, Y3 'The Felt Garden'. This project explores notions of life and death in the creation of a garden, where felt urns are filled with seeds and the ashes of the deceased. Over time, the seeds germinate and become luscious plants. As generations pass, the felt bags disintegrate, allowing for new residents to bring life to the garden.
2.16 Jean Bell, Y2 'Rooftop Renewal-Casting Experiments'. This project embodies ideas about how one might capture the materiality and richness of the historic medina in which it is sited. It looks at casting with rubber moulds taken from existing wall conditions. The formwork of the new proposal is lined with the casts.
2.17 Karishma Khajuria, Y3 'Unfulfilled Aspirations'. This project endeavours to create a space where the women of Marrakesh are able to fulfil life ambitions. The building provides sanctuary, education and leisure. Conceived as a small neighbourhood with several riads and passageways, it is cooled and thermally regulated by screens and water channels.
2.18 Benjamin Webster, Y3 'Bab Doukala Riads'. As the medina of Marrakesh is becoming gentrified, many people are being displaced to the outskirts of the city. The proposal is for new affordable housing in the interstitial space between the old medina wall and the new city. The housing design, inspired by the riad typology, is arranged around central courtyards hosting vegetation and water. The structure is created out of modular elements which utilise the courtyards to passively cool the building.
2.19 Sut (Eunice) Lo, Y2 'Medina Market'. There are many places to buy food in the medina but few places to sit and enjoy it. This project explores a new kind of market space for the medina that is, at once, a series of food stalls and, at the same time, a shaded and vegetated public space.
2.20 Natali Rayya, Y2 'Equine Veterinary Clinic'. Donkeys are still widely used throughout the medina to transport goods. Working long hours under intense heat can often put a lot of strain on these animals. This project creates a clinic where the animals can have check-ups and treatment, and is supported by a visitor centre where they can interact with retired and recovering animals in a garden courtyard.
2.21 Kar (Tiffanie) Tseng, Y2 'Tannery Working Men's Club'. Morocco is known for its tanneries. The intense heat and smell during the production process can be too much for many visitors. The workers, however, endure these conditions daily with little respite or retreat. This project creates a humble working men's club for the tanners where they can shower, rest and converse, away from the harsh sun. The building is thermally regulated through a series of wind towers that can be seen poking up from the medina floor.
2.22–2.23 Paul Kohlhaussen, Y2 'Hammam Bab Doukala'. The hammam in Morocco forms one of the most democratic and inclusive public spaces. This project explores the idea that the hammam can bridge the widening gulf between those of the medina and the new city, as Marrakesh evolves with increased tourism. The building is formed of a series of spatial gradients ranging from gender specific to mixed, hammam to spa and inside to outside. The design is characterised by new ceramic ornaments inspired by the interiors of the city's architecture. These ceramics vary to either filter water or create ceiling conditions where condensation is collected and reused.

2.2

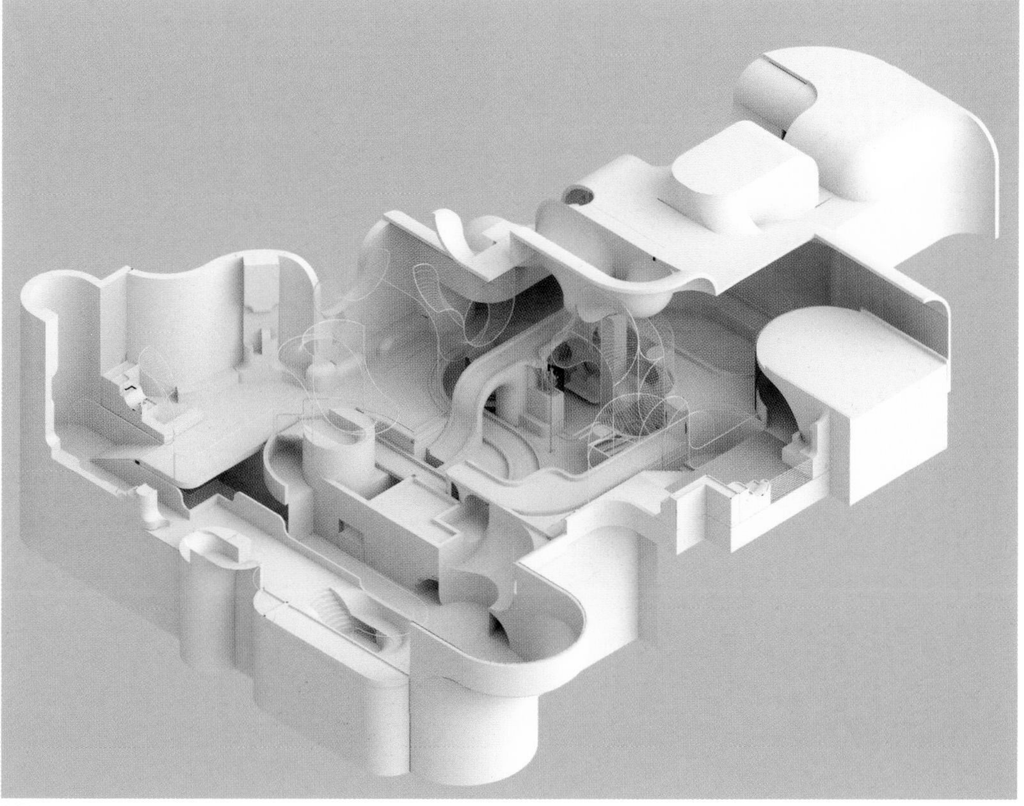

2.3

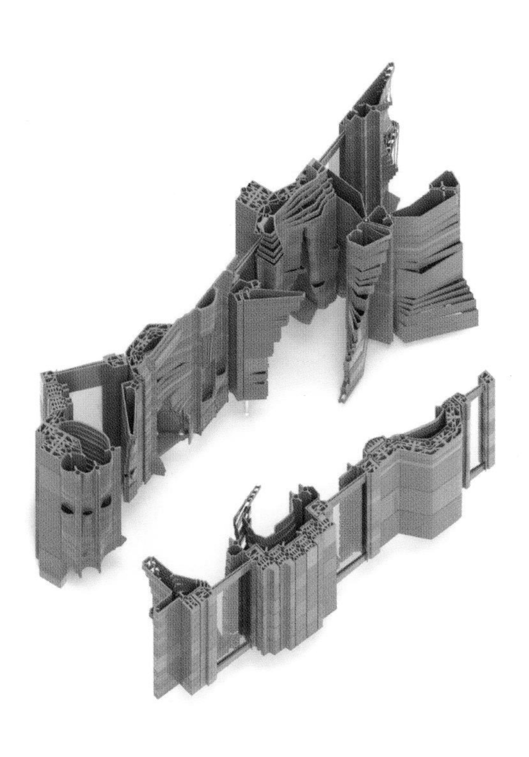

2.4

2.5

2.6

2.7

2.8

2.9

2.10

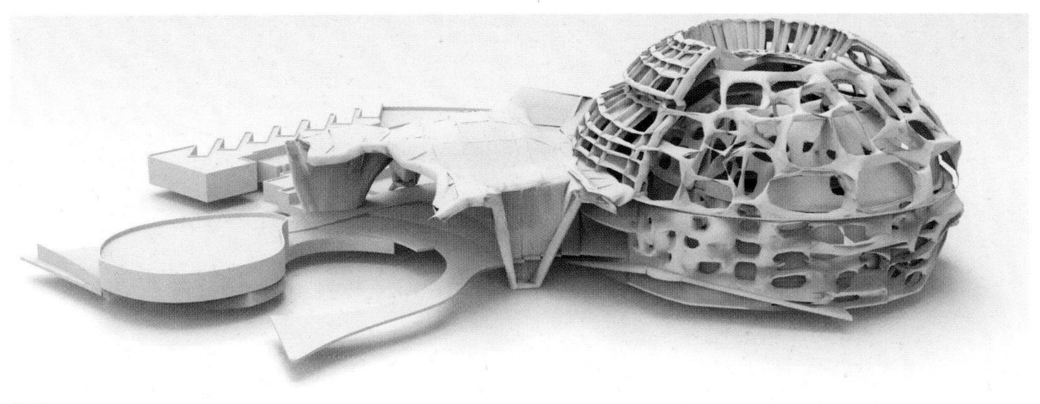

2.11

2.12

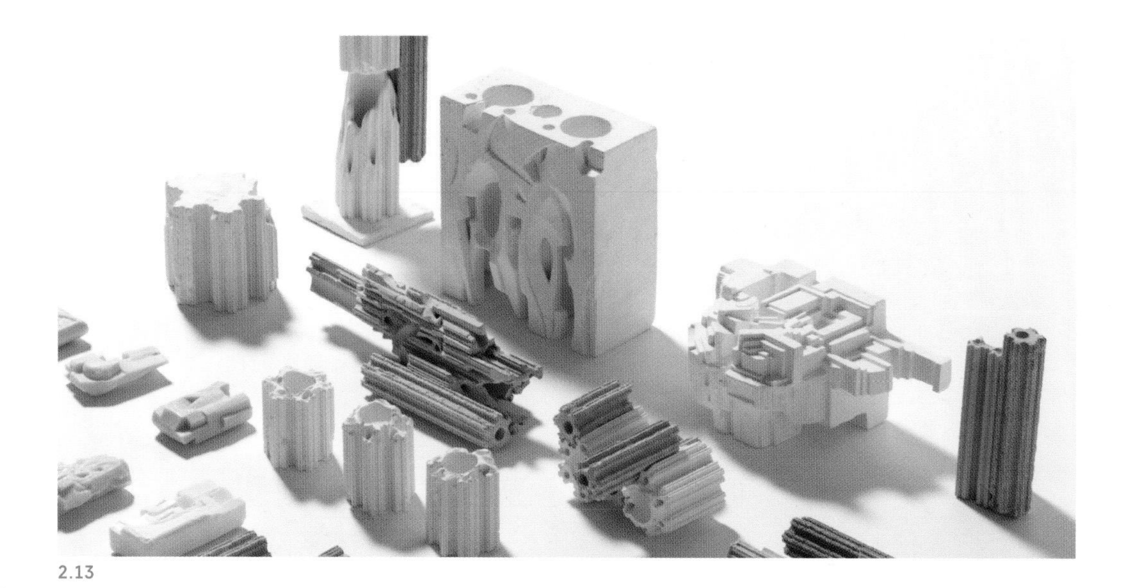

2.13

2.14

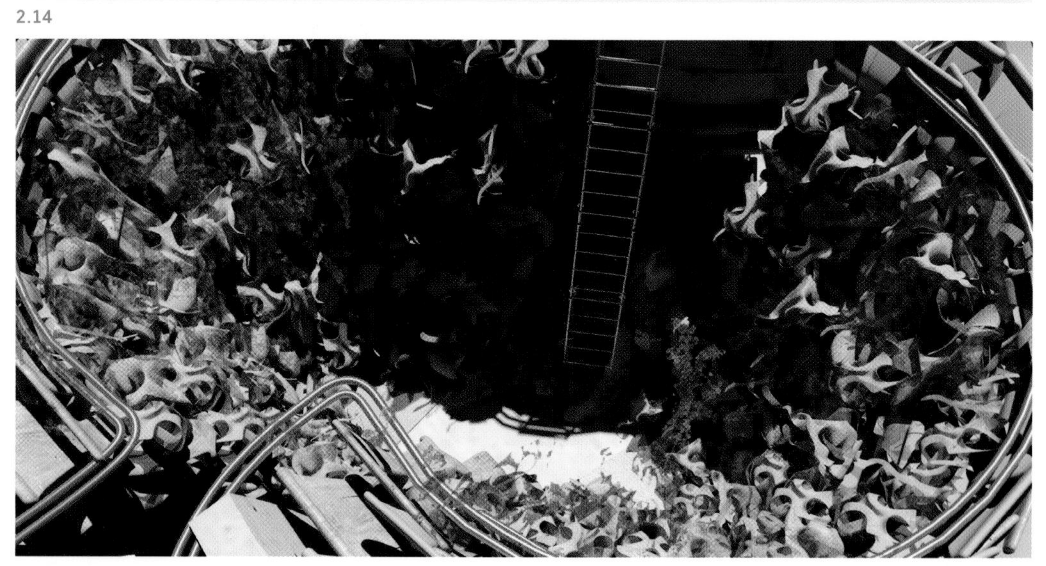

2.15

2.16

2.17

2.18

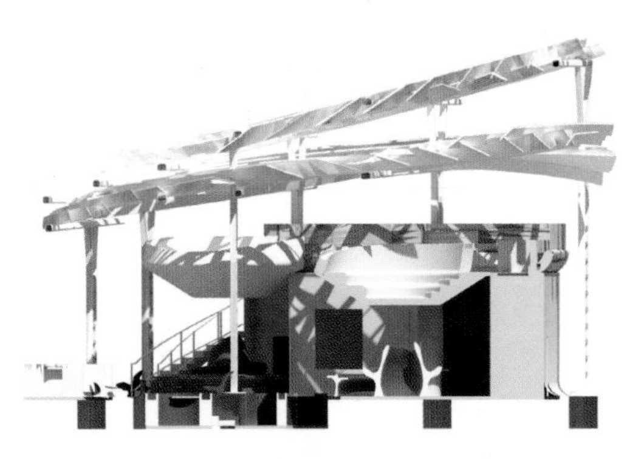

2.19

2.20

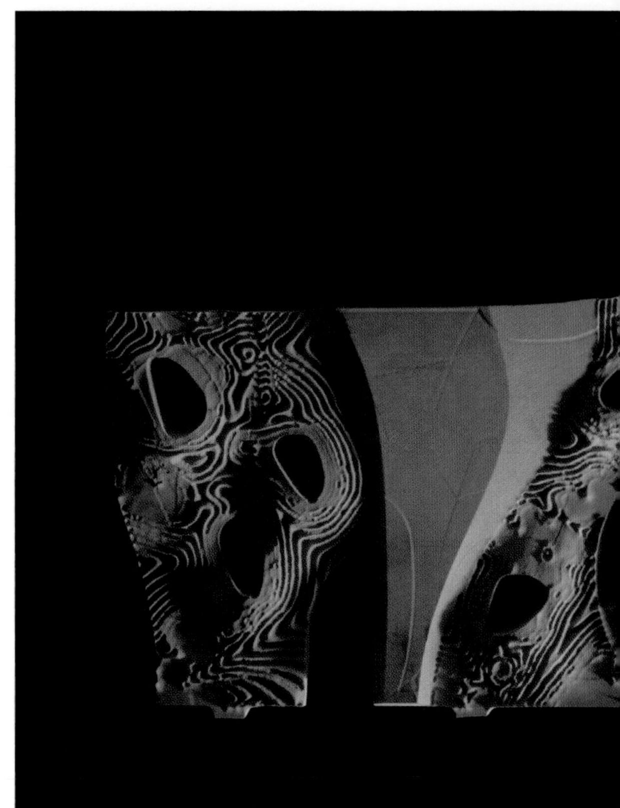

2.22

2.21

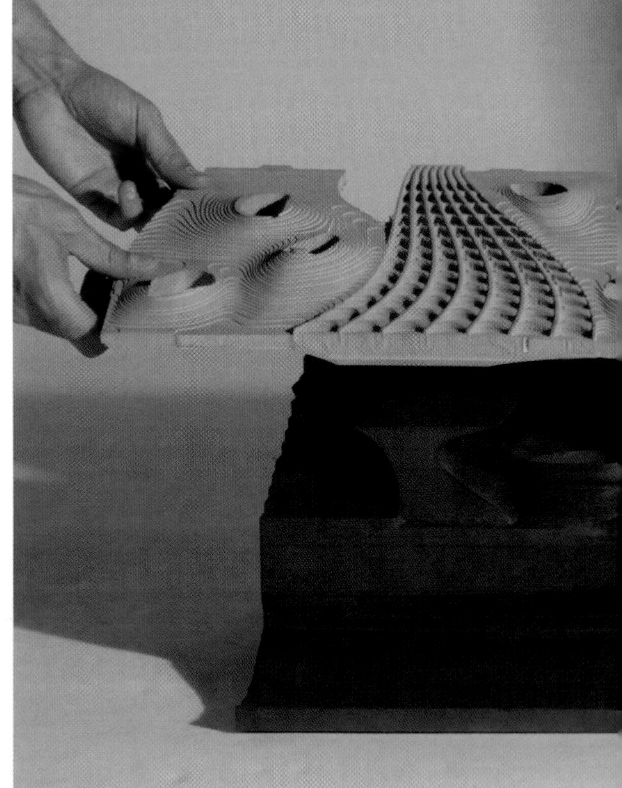

2.23

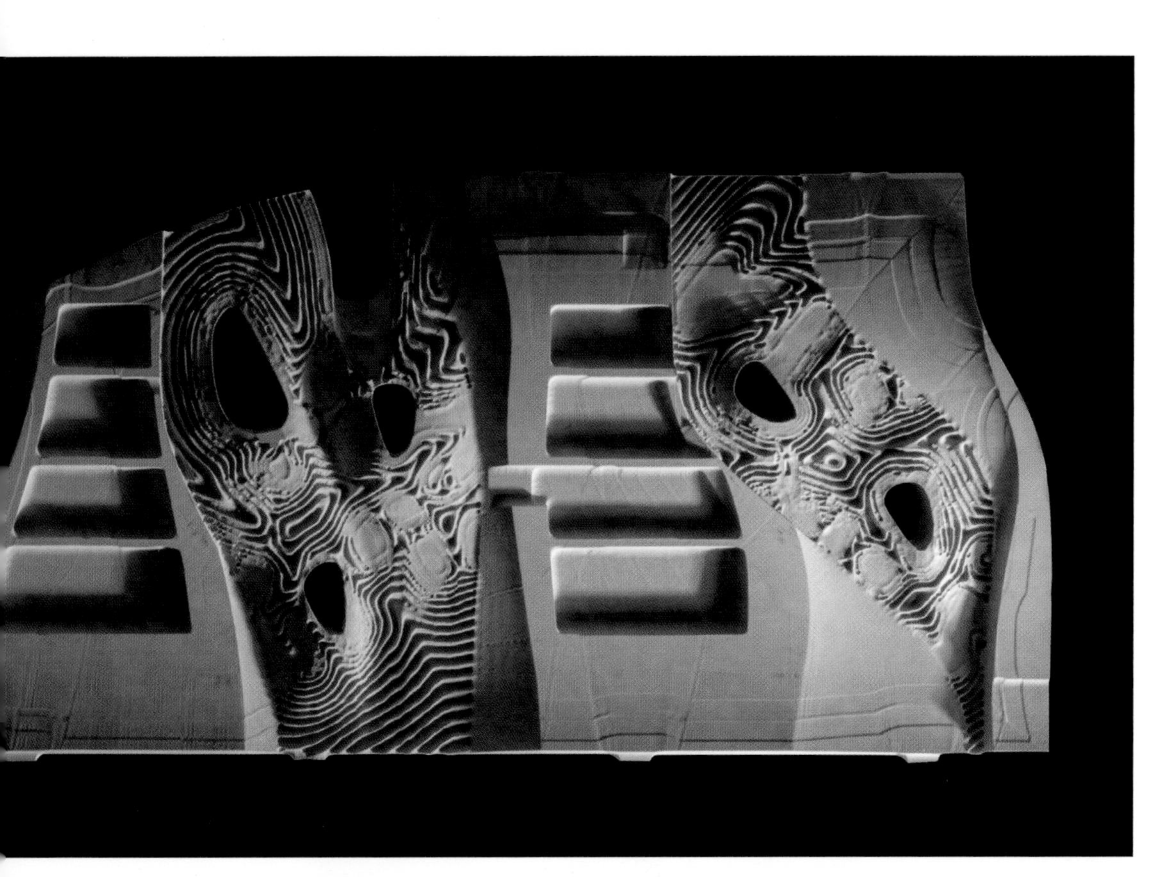

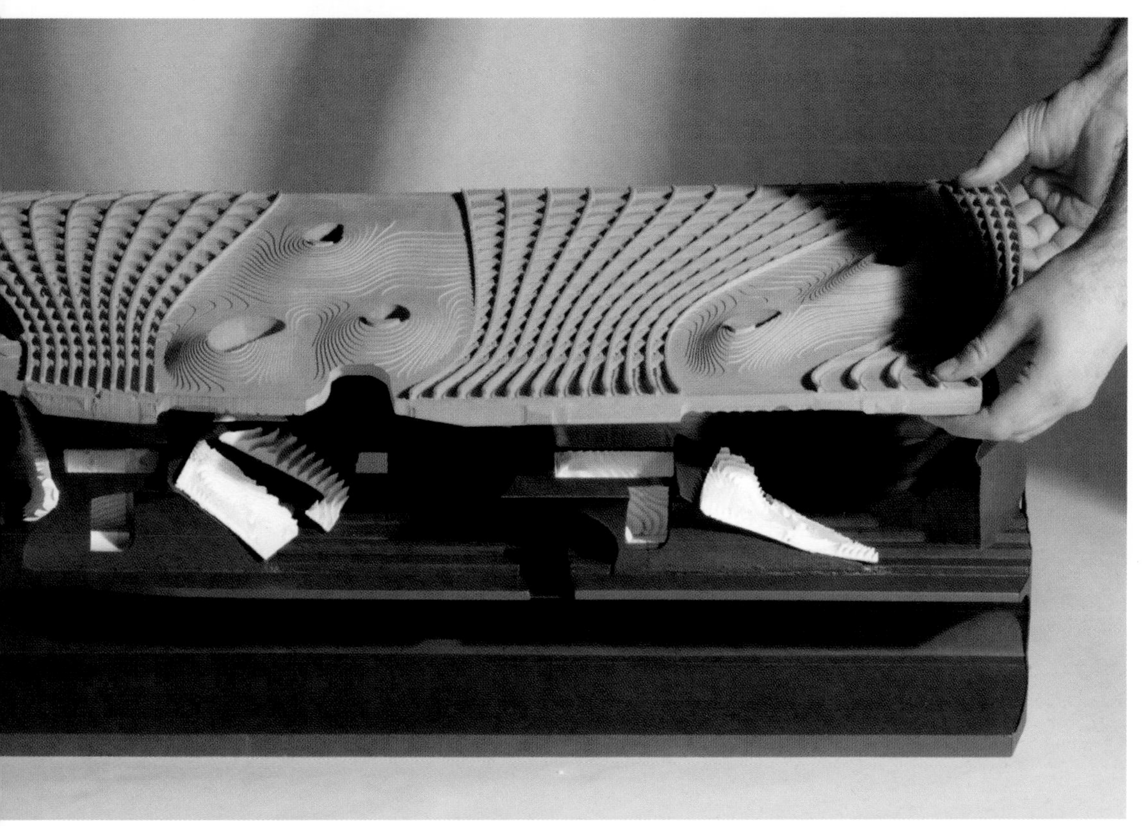

3.1

The Right Side of Paradise UG3

Ifigeneia Liangi, Daniel Wilkinson

This year, UG3 investigated the animalesque, animalistic and animal-ish through architectural figuration. Architecture, as we know it, is grounded in the anthropomorphic. To disrupt this, we used the intricacies of animality to challenge notions of space and design. We didn't design architecture for animals but, instead, acted as architectural animals ourselves, observing the protean design possibilities that resulted.

The Latin origin of the word 'figure' translates as 'something that gives form', whether as a number, symbol, depiction of a person or animal, or a trope. In architecture, a figure can be literal – a sculpture, painting or projection – or allegorical – in tropes that are both playful and meaningful.

The idea that as humans we are different to animals is a modern concept, as the complexities of animal behaviour continue to amaze us, whilst also outlining the limits of our intelligence. Aristotle thought that birds either hibernated under water, transformed into other birds or travelled to the moon for the winter. Meanwhile, Sigmund Freud only started writing about dreams after repeatedly failing to locate the genitals of eels, despite dissecting hundreds of them.

Animals have many strange histories within architecture, too: A secret sculpture of a bull's head peers down from the façade of the Duomo in Florence, thought to have been created by the stonemason as an act of revenge on a scorned lover; during the Middle Ages, people would seal live cats within the walls of a new house to give the building a 'soul'; the Tyrian purple on the ceiling of the Sistine Chapel is created mainly from crushed clams, and the Indian yellow is the powdered urine of cows; the drawings for the fortifications of Florence, often considered the most radical architectural plans of all time, were based on studies of crabs and, prior to the Industrial Revolution, the majority of workers on a construction site would have likely been animals.

As soon as humans began to draw, they started drawing animals; architectural drawings came later. Over the first term, UG3 developed an architect's zoomorphic fantasy, working in a variety of media, questioning ideas of the animalistic and figuration. We then travelled to Florence and Rome, where we encountered caged architectural critters, chubby Botticellian angels, Sorrentino's *The Great Beauty* and Fellini's *The Voice of the Moon*. We visited the ruins of Casa Sperimentale and the marble quarries of Carrara, and we met the magical figures and wild beasts of La Scarzuola and Bomarzo. The unit then made architectural propositions for either Florence or Rome, incorporating animalistic figurative ideas, of buildings as wild beasts and creatures of paradise.

Year 2
Giorgos Christofi, Charlotte Cole, Maria Gerzon, Rebecca Honey, Zicong (Charles) Liang, Heba Mohsen, Michela Morreale, Punnapa Pairojtanachai, Luke Topping, Siyuan (Amy) Yao, See (Phyllis) Yu

Year 3
Jahba Anan, Ting (Sharon) Lee, George Stewart, Yaqi Su, Venessa Yau

Thanks to our consultants and critics: Kyveli Anastasiadi, Barbara-Ann Campbell-Lange, Nat Chard, Jason Coe, Elizabeth Dow, Stylianos Giamarelos, Naomi Gibson, Stefana Gradinariu, Jonathan Hill, Joe Johnson, Alastair King, Vsevolod Kondratiev-Popov, Matthew Lenkiewicz, Oscar Maguire, Vasilis Marcou Ilchuk, Emma-Kate Matthews, Katherine Ramchand, David Shanks, Sayan Skandarajah, Amy Sullivan-Bodiam, Seamus Ward, Gabriel Warshafsky

3.1, 3.17 Giorgos Christofi, Y2 'The Lantern of the Holy Humbleness'. The 'Church of the Holy Humbleness' reimagines the practices and rituals of Christianity within Rome, using the donkey that carried Christ as a figure of worship. Within the church, donkeys are present literally, figuratively and allegorically. Donkeys and humans become inseparable from the architectural fabric during mass, the former braced within the altar for ceremonies, whilst the latter are braced within their sodden pews. The church is surrounded by a fresco workers' union who restore and replace the works devoted to labour and humility within the church.
3.2 Heba Mohsen, Y2 'Memento Mori'. Looking to close the distance between birth, sex and death through the ideas of Wilhelm Reich, this project blurs the line between tectonics and decoration. Death becomes a lady who occupies the spaces, surfaces and structures of the project.
3.3 Jahba Anan, Y3 'Jahba Becomes a Bird'. Jahba became a bird by investigating and beautifying the strains, ruptures and scarification of the Greek myth where Cygnus metamorphosised into a swan. By investigating the violence of human to animal transformations that litter mythology, contortion is used as a tool for considering ideas of beauty, posture and sexual practice within the animal kingdom.
3.4 Venessa Yau, Y3 'A Spatial Summoning'. Using descriptions from tales of the kraken – a legendary, giant squid-like creature – a summoning of form was created from the blending of slimes and their viscosities in this project. It considers an architecture that values mass over space and an experience of gliding through stuff.
3.5 Luke Topping, Y2 'Being in Mass'. Working next to the tomb of Marcus Vergilius Eurysaces in Rome, this project was designed as a chapel, a bakery and a bank, according to the needs and interests of a baker-architect. Through its occupation and maintenance, the project is marked by the simultaneous rising of the priest, the loaf and the thatch.
3.6 See (Phyllis) Yu, Y2 'Phyllos'. This project is a spatial, material and formal investigation into a ceramic trigger for an octopodean urbanism, informed by recent studies of the octopus cities of Octlantis and Octopolis.
3.7 Ting (Sharon) Lee, Y3 'Sharon's Garden of Earthly Delights'. Working on the site of Lorenzo de Medici's lost sculpture garden in Florence – the model for the first schools of design during the Renaissance – a sculpture school was imagined as a playground for ceramic investigations. By using the school's kiln as part of an environmental strategy for establishing different micro-climates for the growing of fruit, the results of raku firing techniques determined the aesthetic and environmental conditions of the project.
3.8 Charlotte Cole, Y2 'The Altar of The Dead'. Responding to the persistent presence of bees within accounts of purgatory – from the ancient Egyptians to the modern era – this project builds on Italy's animalistic history of purgatory chapels. Looking to incorporate this history within the contemporary religious climate of Rome and Pope Francis' attempts to bring the country's different Catholic sects together, the living, the dead and the hives are considered as equally valid in their differing modes of occupation in the chapel.
3.9 Maria Gerzon, Y2 'The Directors of Secrets – A Medieval Mystery Play for Contemporary Rome'. Following the procession of a number of animalistic architectures across Rome, a temporary theatre occupies Piazza della Pigna at specific moments in its cultural calendar. A contemporary reimagining of the travelling medieval mystery play, each component of the theatre plays both a practical and metaphorical role in the performances it enables.
3.10 Punnapa Pairojtanachai, Y3 'The Cutealist Cup Noodle Factory'. Beginning with a cute reimagining of brutalism, this project for a noodle factory is located in the back streets of Rome, close to the Trevi Fountain. Once a year, the building spills and inflates outside of itself as part of a festival that involves the production of the biggest noodle in the world.
3.11 Rebecca Honey, Y2 'A Skin for Dreaming'. Using the technical apparatus of the cuttlefish as an analogue for an architecture, this project engages with the materiality of the animal for the drawing forth of a design. Whilst the creature's ink and limbs provided the tools for the early stages of investigation, the increasing smell and slime were a restraint. The cuttlefish's ability to hypnotise its prey by pulsating its skin was recreated with a live crab.
3.12–3.13 Venessa Yau, Y3 'A Chocolate Tempering Playground'. Continuing an interest in pours and viscosity, this project looks at the possibility of making a chocolate factory entirely from chocolate. Reacting to the environmental variables of Rome and the site-specificity of an island in the Tiber, a concrete was developed which contained 30% cocoa beans – 'Choc-crete' – as a response to EU regulations on what can be legally considered 'chocolate'. The remaining dark, milk and white chocolate components of the project melt into storage pens in the river before being reconstructed following the heat of the summer.
3.14 Siyuan (Amy) Yao, Y2 'Where the Dolls are Born'. Working within the pit of an ancient ruin, this project is a puppeteer's theatre and residence, and is also a puppet itself. Mirroring the posture of our own bodies throughout the day, the house is at its most upright in the morning and gradually gets smaller, until the building goes to bed alongside its occupants in the evening.
3.15 Yaqi Su, Y3 'Rome Plays Itself'. Taking three key scenes from the films *The Belly of an Architect* (1987), *Obsession* (1976) and *The Great Beauty* (2013), this project looks to the history of Florence and Rome as cinematic characters inseparable from the tales they have been instrumental in telling. By manipulating the natural light conditions in Rome, the proposed film studios reveal and disguise themselves through sharkstooth scrim façades, whilst also being able to recreate, at the director's request, the varying light conditions of each city through an adjustable and filtering roof.
3.16 George Stewart, Y3 'School of Looking'. This project proposes a school where light becomes an occupant, alongside the staff and students. A visual curriculum was developed where the act of looking is exposed as being a cultural construct. A mother figure occupies the central chamber of the school, watching over the school's students as they learn by looking themselves.

3.2

3.3

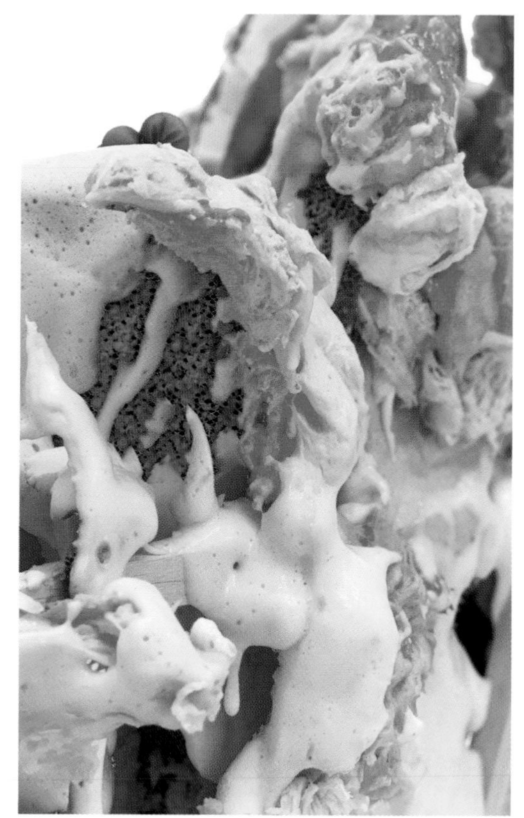

3.4

3.5

3.6

3.7

3.8

3.9

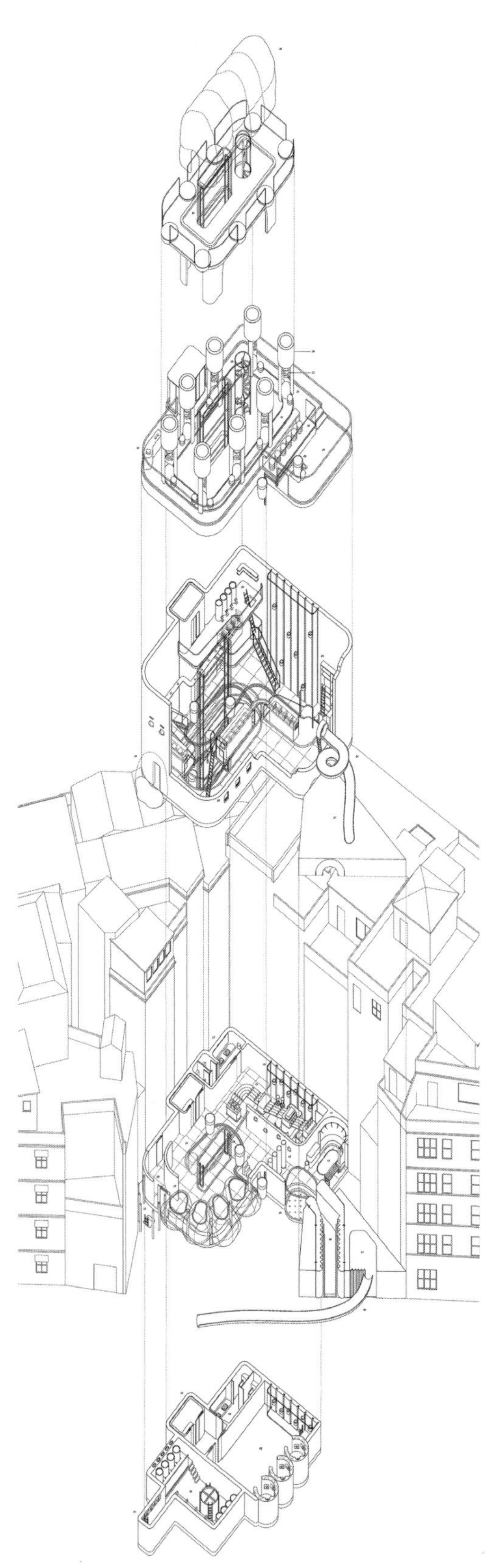

3.10

3.11

3.12

3.13

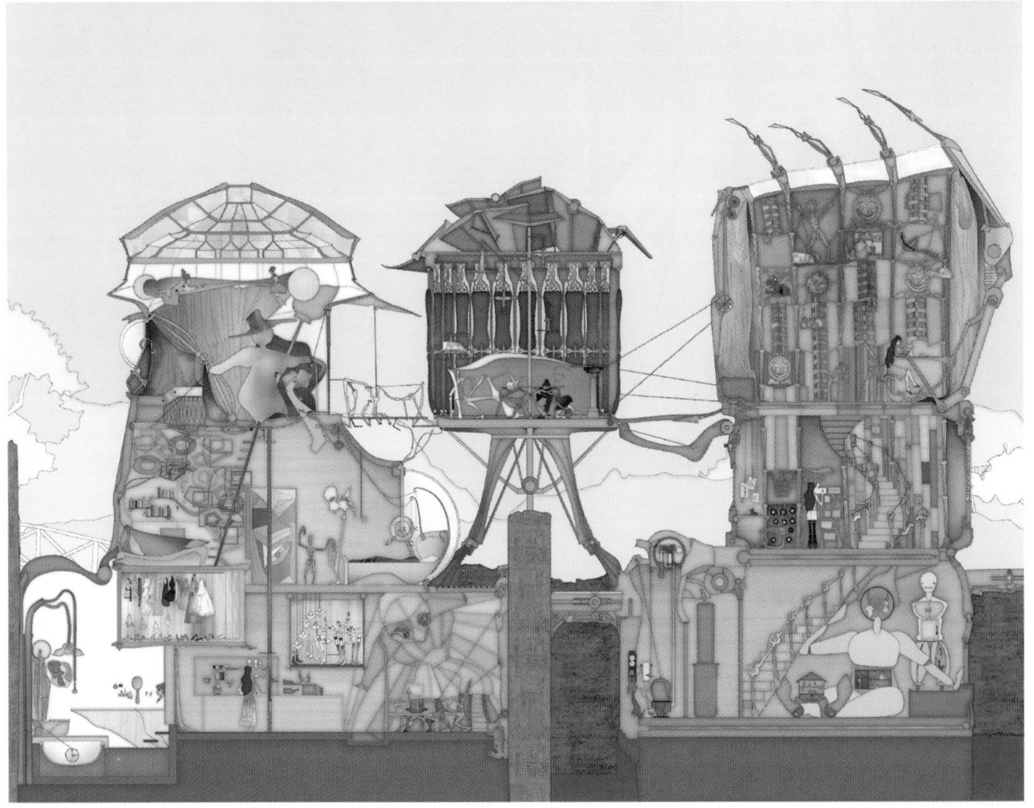

3.14

3.15

3.16

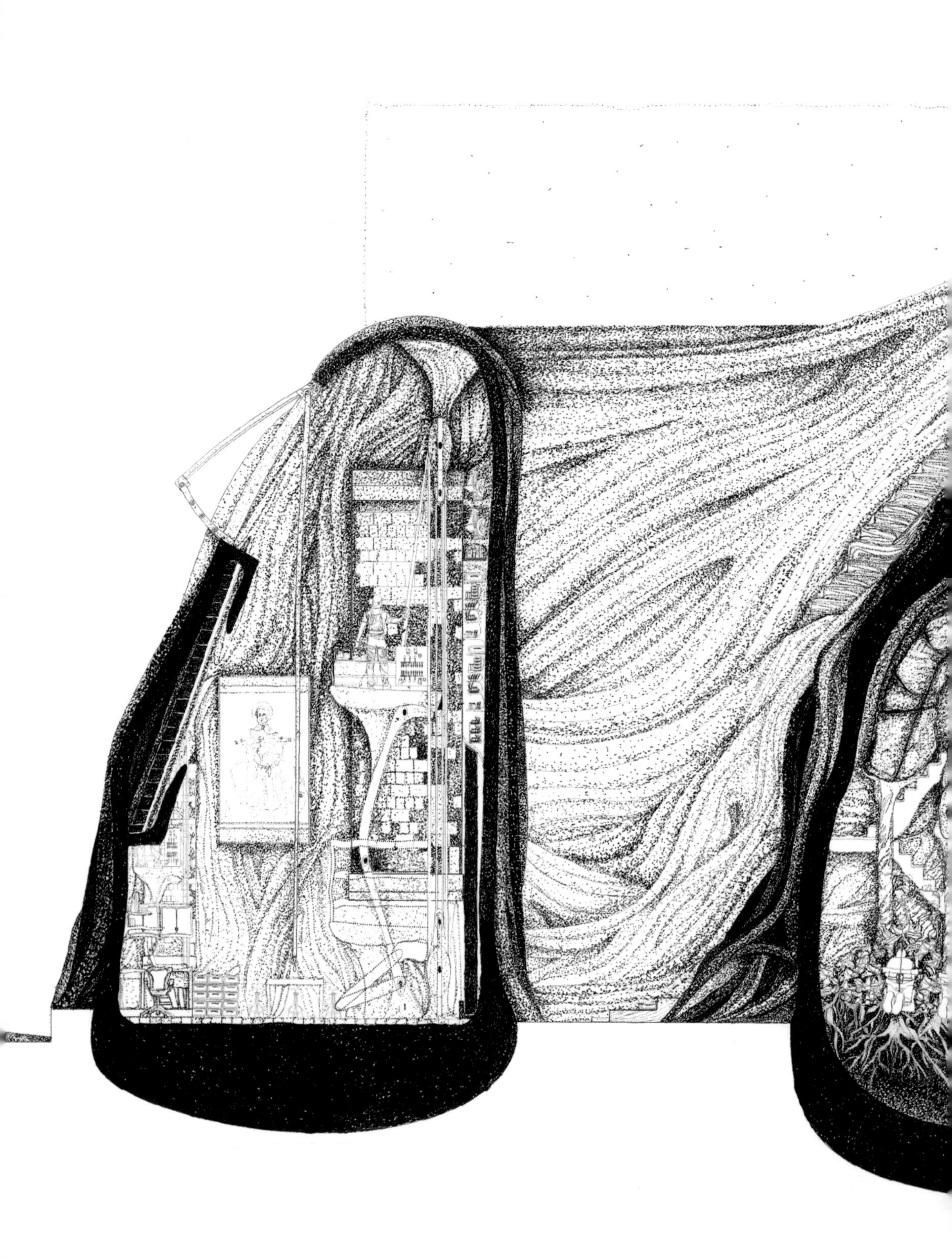

3.17

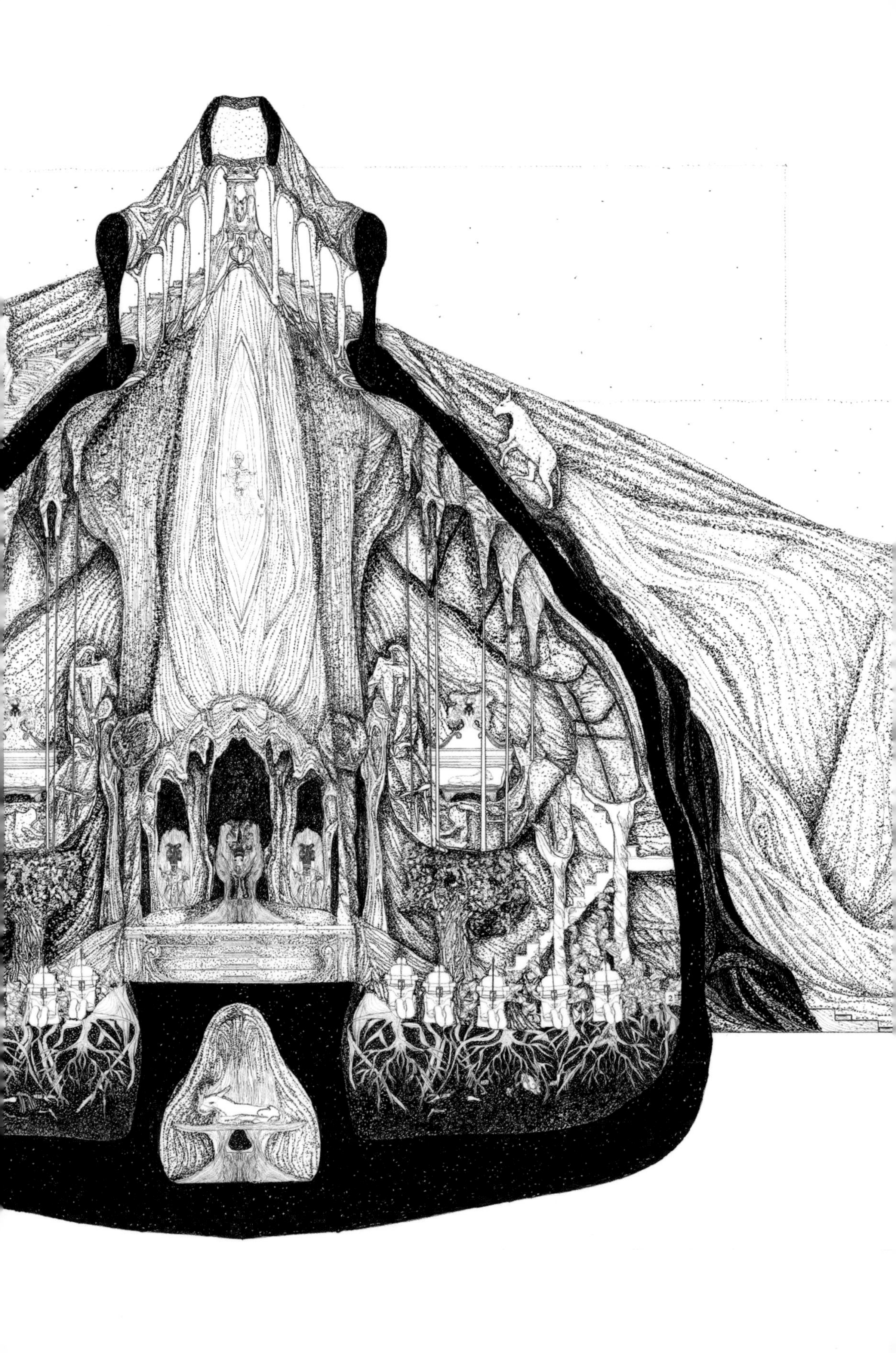

4.1

Great Expectations

UG4

Hugh McEwen, Greg Nordberg, Catrina Stewart

In UG4, we believe that you can change the world with architecture. The unit's approach is concerned primarily with the social, cultural and political conditions of today, explored through alternative environmental, material and programmatic strategies. Using thorough analysis, narratives and material investigations, our projects speculate and invent new building typologies.

This year, we have individually confronted the generic and meaningless forms of architecture that have resulted from austerity. Austerity has created a society that is risk-averse and architecture that is used as an anaesthetic for occupants, rather than a means for good. Using design as a critical tool, we have proposed projects that make possible futures real and, in doing so, become powerful polemic tools that enable us, and others, to question our values.

The site for these speculations is the stretch between the City of London and Canary Wharf. London is expanding at an unprecedented rate and this, together with increasing levels of pollution, waste and a housing crisis, means that we face challenging times ahead. Can the fabric of a capitalist city be disassembled and repurposed to propose an alternative economy? Can a pluralistic and ad-hoc architecture create more with less? We are designing for a future where millennials seek experiences over possessions, where co-habitees wear shared haute couture rather than squabbling over the remote, and workers inhabit buildings powered by their own waste rather than oil.

On our field trip to Northern India, we collected examples of radical individualism in Rajasthan: decorated trucks, paintings of cities and hand-carved astrological instruments. These were used to create a catalogue of architecture to reuse, containing a collection of materials, elements and narratives that showcased radical individualism as new models to investigate through the projects.

The architecture that the unit has proposed views reuse as essential and is a new architectural response to austerity that views waste as valuable in its discarded state. Using materials such as recycled plastics, glazed tiles, blitzcrete and recycled polystyrene, we have focused on longevity rather than assuming that we will always have more resources, framing discussions in terms of both resource and social sustainability.

Year 2
Tisha Aramkul, Christina Econimidou, Isabelle Gin, Gabriel Healy, Evan O'Sullivan, Chinwe Obi, Thomas Richardson, Zuzanna Rostocka, Yunzi Wang

Year 3
Christopher Collyer, Nanci Fairless Nicholson, Maria Petalidou, Muyun Qiu, Joshua Richardson, Justine Shirley, James Van Caloen

Thank you to Marcus Andren, Mat Barnes, Paul Bisbrown, Duncan Blackmore, Graham Burn, Phineas Harper, Joseph Henry, Alex Hill, Charles Holland, Theo Jones, Anna Mill, Joe Morris, Ellie Sampson, Elly Ward, Owain Williams

Thank you to our sponsors: U+I, Metropolitan Workshop

4.1, 4.4–4.6 **Joshua Richardson, Y3** 'The Microbial Medi-Clinic'. This health centre, located in Wapping, is designed to combat the exponential rise in superbugs. The clinic contains both naturally anti-microbial spaces, which discourage the use of antibiotics, as well as 'pro-biotic' spaces that strengthen natural immunity to infection. The clinic is modelled on a notion that health is a public luxury and proactively working on one's health can be an act of leisure and respite. Like Alvar Aalto's Paimio Sanitorium or the Peckham Health Centre, 'The Microbial Medi-Clinic' is a 'legacy project': a prototype in realising the future of health and architecture.
4.2–4.3 **Christopher Collyer, Y3** 'The Gig Economy Guild'. This project is an exploration of precarity in contemporary societal living and architecture. Focusing on the gig economy and the precariat – a group of people defined by labour instability, social insecurity and occupational identity – this project seeks to establish a discursive, allegorical architecture that is simultaneously precarious and secure. It celebrates the radical yet dangerous nature of precariousness whilst, also, facilitating community and resilience to a group who have become increasingly exploited and isolated.
4.7–4.9 **Maria Petalidou, Y3** 'The Service Exchange Bank'. Canary Wharf has been a site of trade and exchange throughout its history. Radical redevelopment in the 1980s, however, created a site of social and aesthetic division. 'The Service Exchange Bank' tries to bridge the gap between Canary Wharf and its surroundings by creating a centre where services are exchanged based on the supply and demand of the local population; from economic skills to plumbing. Its architecture combines elements from the site.
4.10 **Evan O'Sullivan, Y2** 'The Weather Sanatorium'. Holidays are socially and physically good for us but their financial, environmental and political impact is increasingly unaffordable. By controlling the weather through architecture in this project, the perfect holiday is created on the banks of the River Thames.
4.11 **Gabriel Healy, Y2** 'The Plastic Mint'. A discussion on luxury, this project looks at recycling plastic into a new monetary system. The ceremonial building re-frames waste as a valuable item, whilst questioning the value of souvenirs and fast fashion.
4.12 **Isabelle Gin, Y2** 'Ministry of Water'. London's cycle of flooding and drought has been exacerbated through poor management by water companies. By nationalising the water system, this project provides a space to educate the public on this crisis, and allows interaction between the minister for water and the public.
4.13–4.14 **Muyun Qiu, Y3** 'An International Haven for the Exiled'. By exploiting legally ambiguous opportunities in its architecture and programme, and complying with the legal framework of the UK, this project creates a dedicated 'international zone' beyond the UK border, sited in the south dock of Canary Wharf. Responding to the UK's current political climate, and the social issues that have arisen as a result, it provides shelter, amenities and support for those suffering from the UK's increasingly tight immigration policy.
4.15–4.17 **Nanci Fairless Nicholson, Y3** 'The Circadian Realignment Centre'. Exposure to the sun has synchronised our biological circadian rhythm to coincide with the 24-hour clock. There is, however, increasing disruption to this natural rhythm from shift work, long-haul flights and blue light from screens. This project creates spaces to realign the circadian rhythm, using careful studies on light temperature and colour perception. It enables overnight porters, early morning cleaners and late-night traders to experience the day as it should be, whilst improving health and increasing productivity.
4.18–4.20 **Thomas Richardson, Y2** 'Ageing Gracefully'. This project proposes a model for a new type of care home that tackles loneliness, using a domestic architecture for living, gardening and cooking, but proposing it at an urban scale.
4.21–4.22, 4.24 **James Van Caloen, Y3** 'The Data Guild'. Situated at the northern edge of Canary Wharf, 'The Data Guild' responds to the possibility of a 'Digital Dark Age', where information on obsolete formats becomes unreadable by future ages. In the monastery-like building, precious digital information is transcribed onto physical supports, whilst local inhabitants can delete sensitive aspects of their online identity. Information is, thus, both preserved and obliterated.
4.23 **Zuzanna Rostocka, Y2** 'Dance Macabre'. Dying is bad for our health. This project is a new form of garden cemetery that decreases the environmental impact of burial, and creates a landscape to come to terms with death through music and dance.
4.25–4.27 **Justine Shirley, Y3** 'The London Housing Commission'. Situated on Whitechapel Road, this project houses the fragmented government agencies and private sector bodies who are responsible for addressing London's housing crisis. It seeks to break down the compartmentalised nature of housing development and delivery. In turn, its continually self-built architecture serves as a pedagogic tool to encourage innovation and risk-taking in local authority housing, and provokes change amongst London's residents.

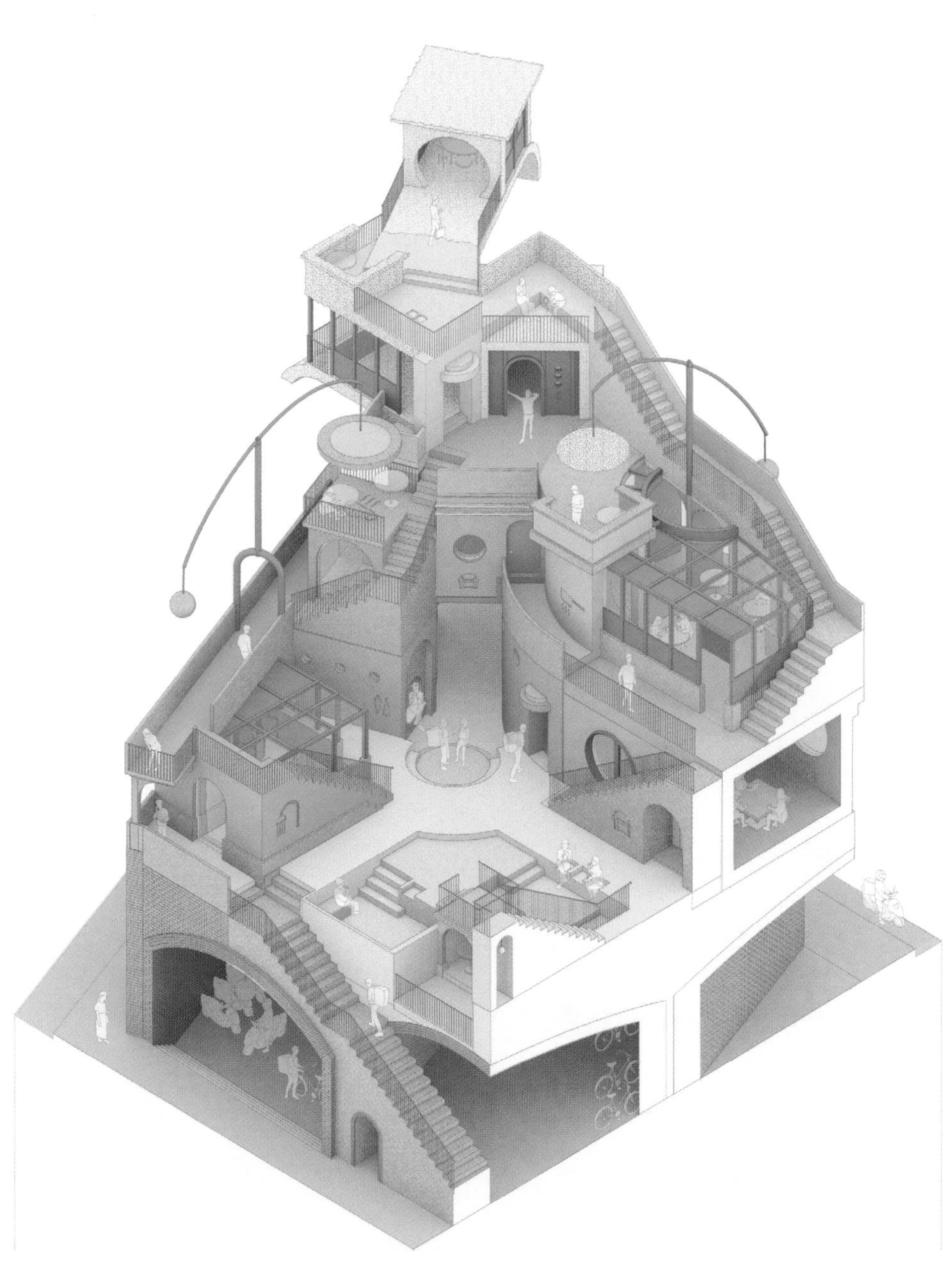

4.2

4.3

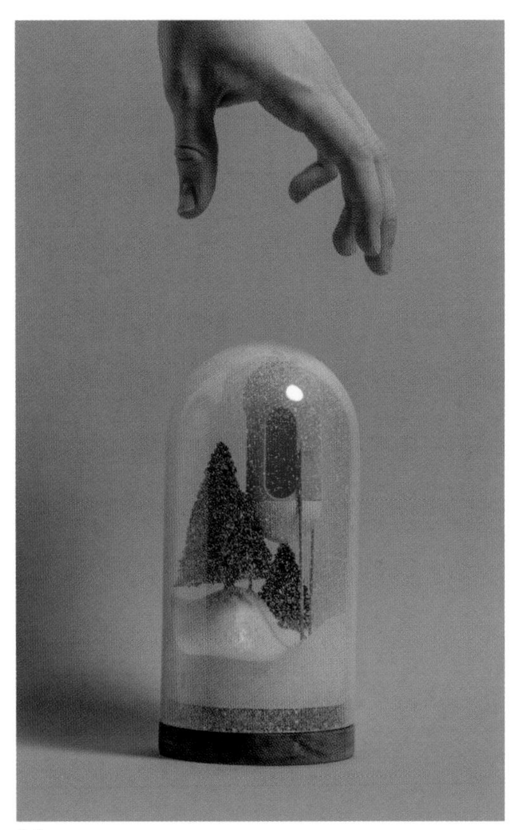

4.4

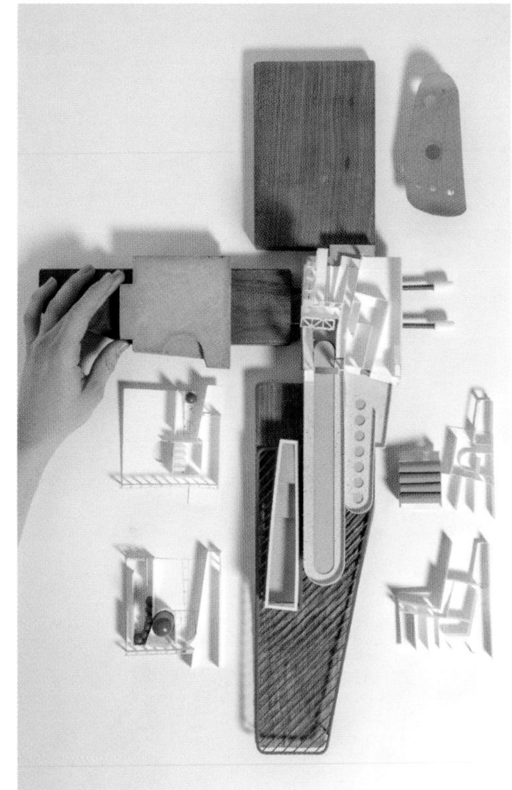

4.5

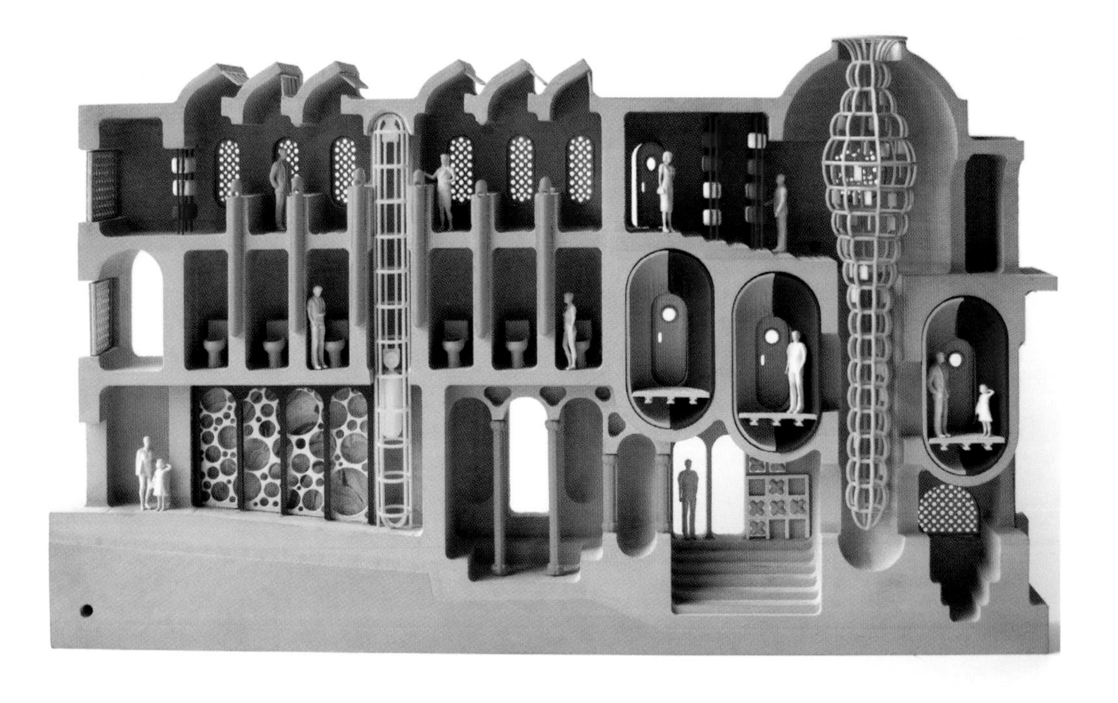

4.6

4.7

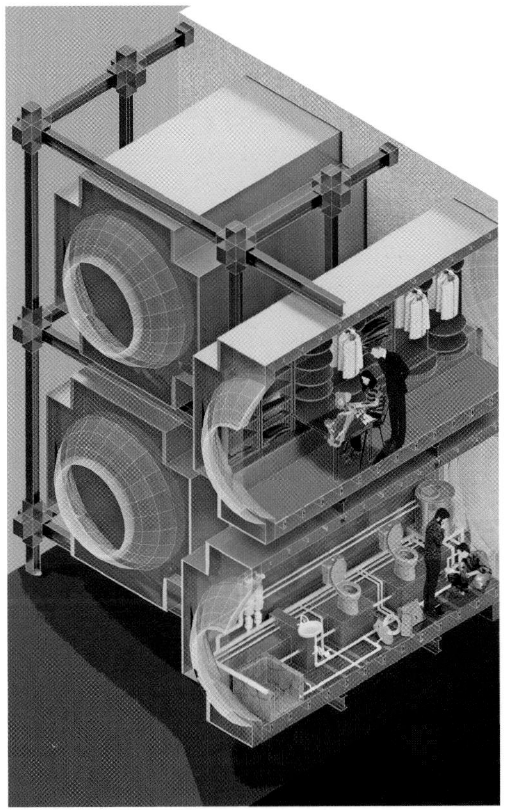
4.8

4.9

4.10

4.11

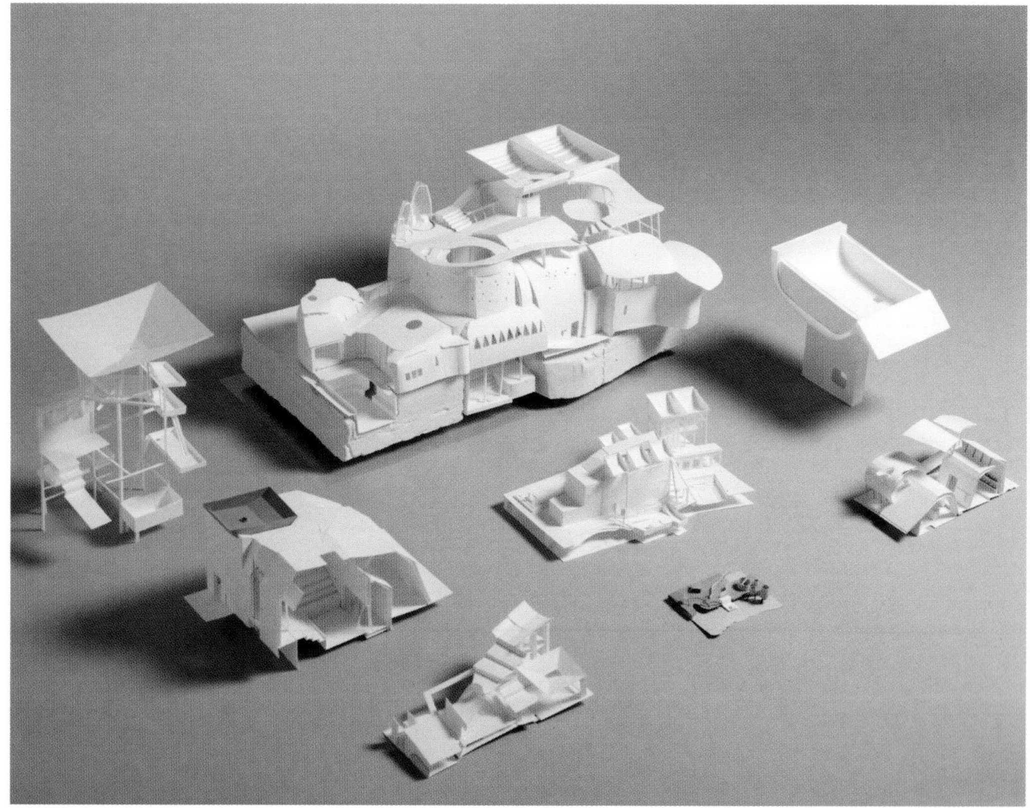

4.12

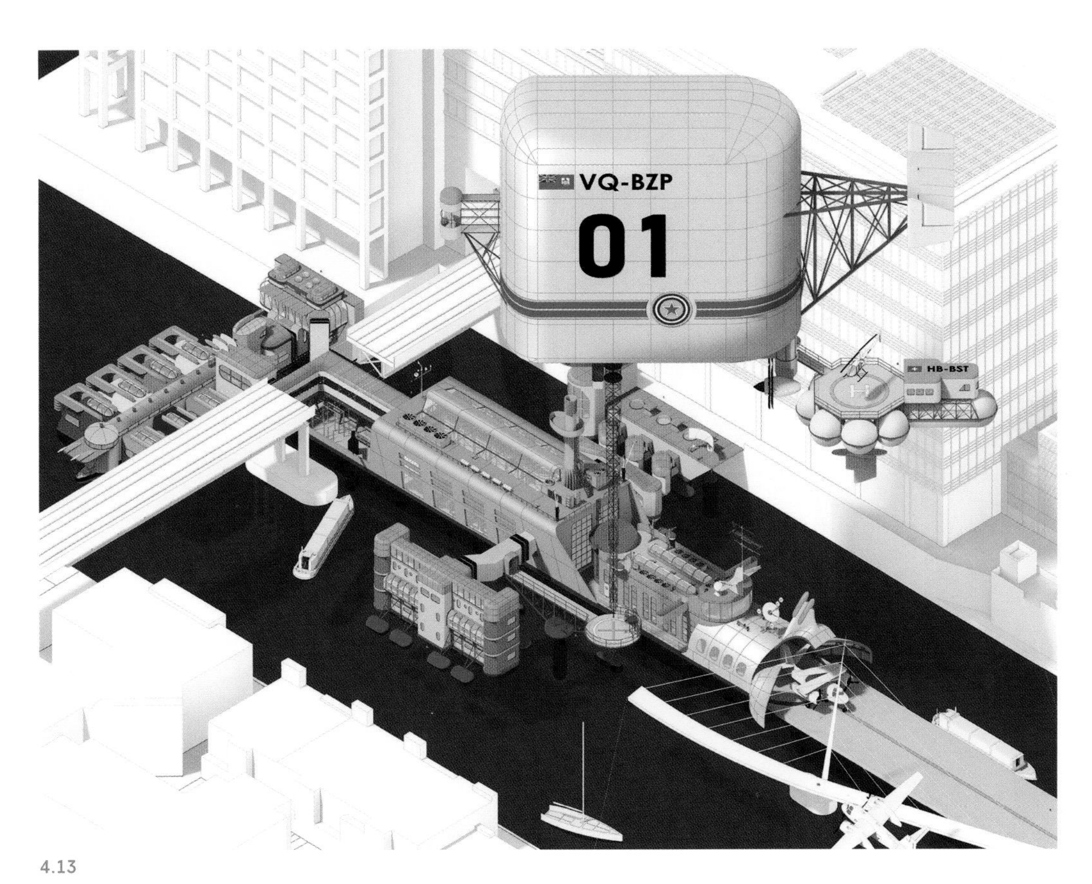

4.13

4.14

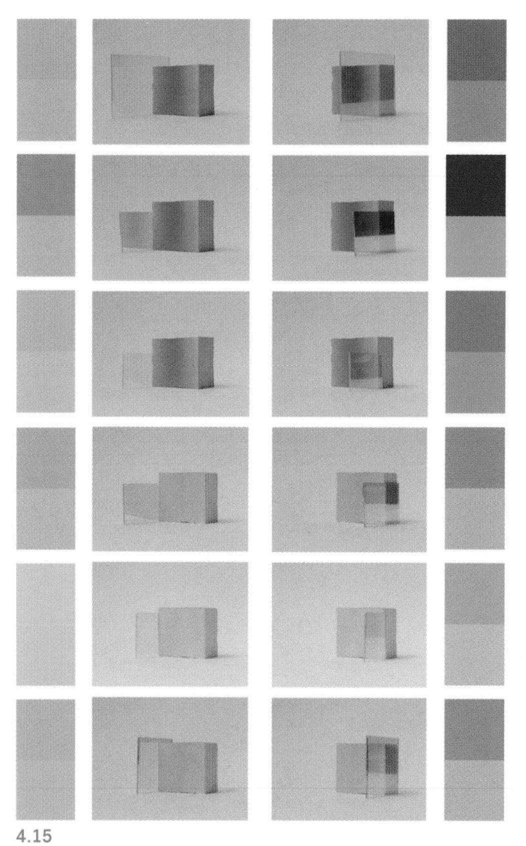
4.15

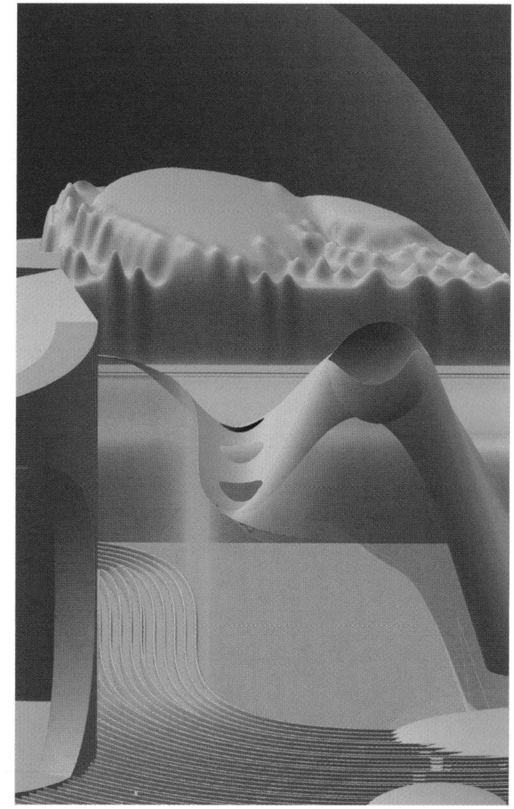
4.16

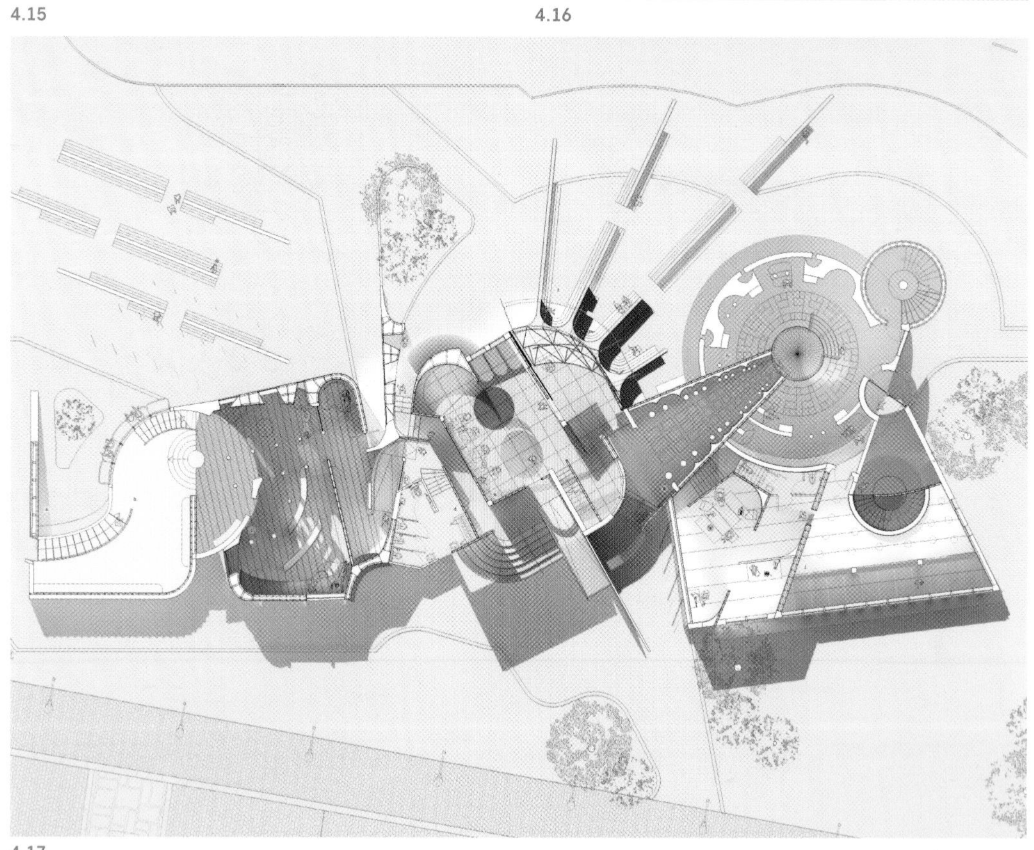
4.17

4.18

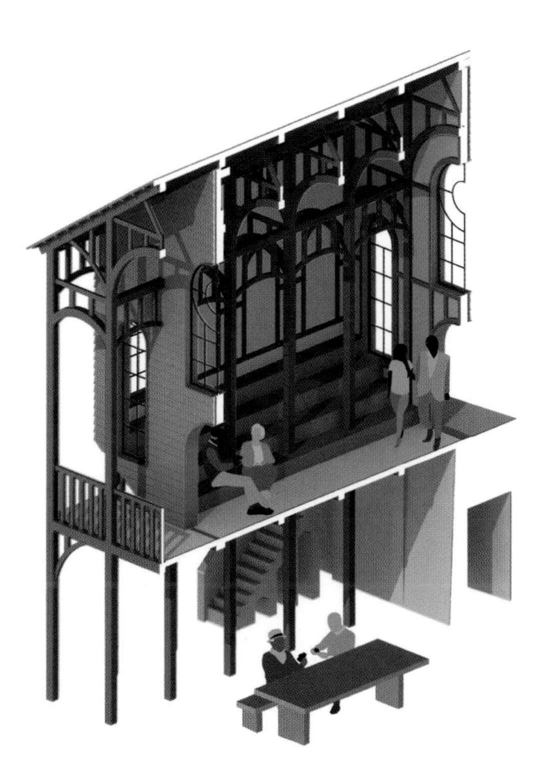

4.19

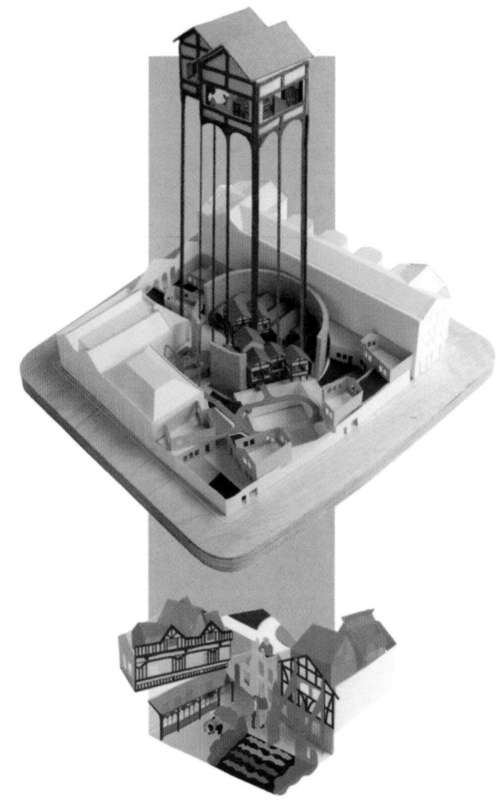

4.20

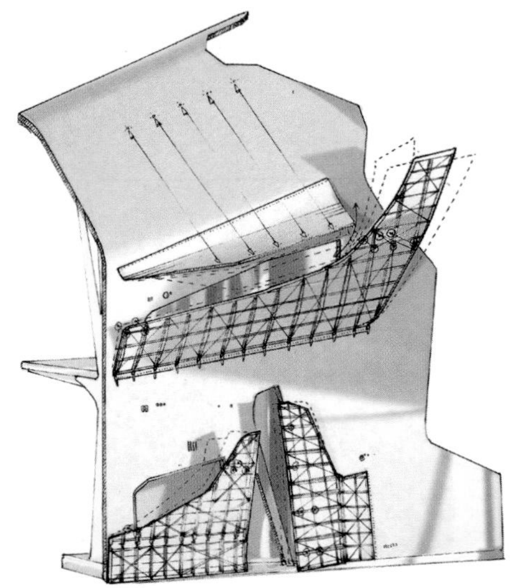
4.21

4.22

4.23

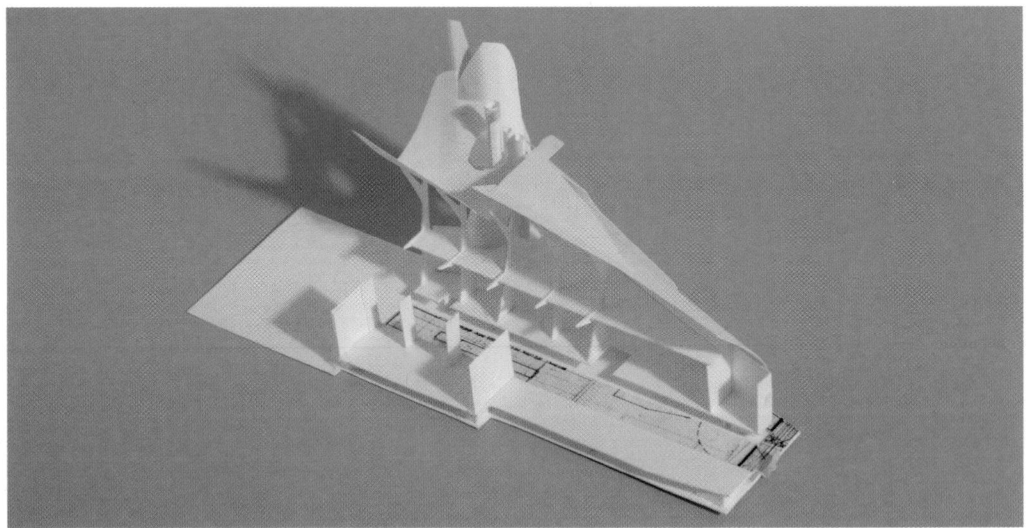
4.24

4.25

4.26

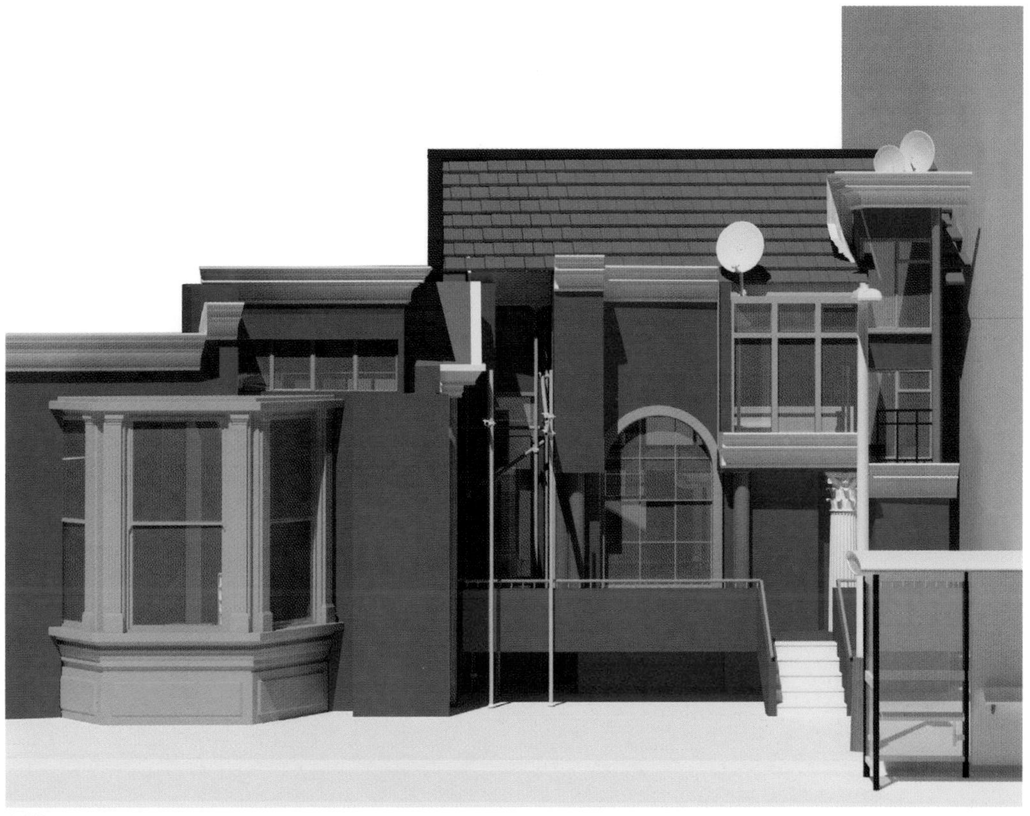
4.27

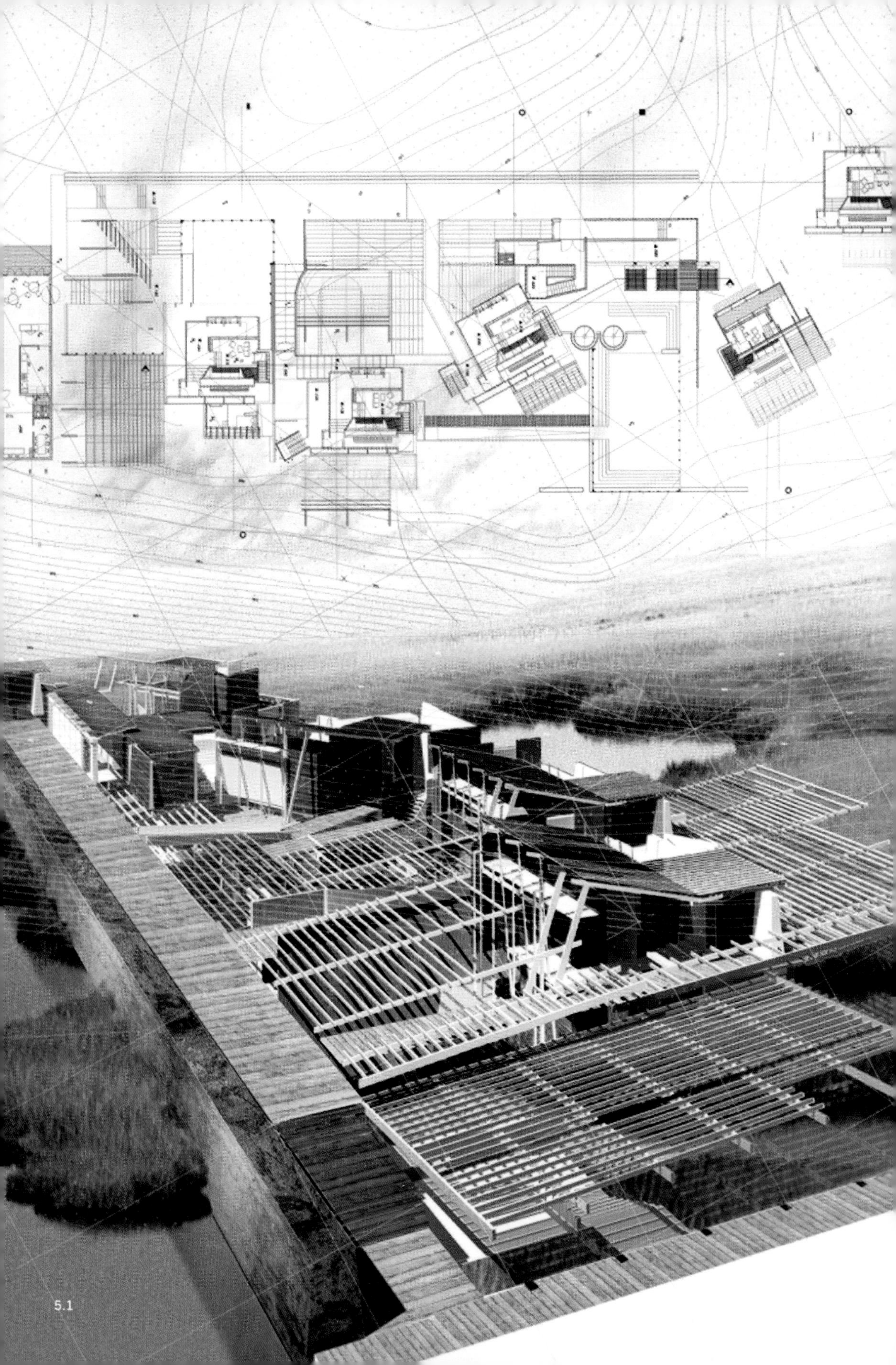

5.1

Hinterland: Beyond the Borders

Julia Backhaus, Ben Hayes

Cities get a lot of attention. Following decades of urban triumphalism much of architectural production has focused on metropolitan territories; yet, cities only account for approximately 2% of the Earth's surface. Rem Koolhaas's current research on the future of the countryside argues that by looking at the remaining 98%, we are looking at the future of the world.

This year, UG5 explored the hidden dimensions of the city's hinterland: a territory lying beyond the visible and the known. Historically, cities have functioned as the epicentres of political and economic power. They controlled and managed the agricultural and resource-rich rural countryside, and its hinterland, and this dual relationship was the breeding ground for local culture. Today, new technologies, infrastructure and open trade render this relationship as remarkably complex. As we travel deeper into the digital age, cities seem to rely less and less on their neighbouring countryside to feed, maintain and entertain them. They have been emancipated from the constraints of geography. Now, we have global cities with global hinterlands, where distances, dependencies and boundaries between sites of production and consumption are radically redefined and in constant flux.

The city of Shenzhen in Hong Kong, and its uncharted border zone, became the testbed for our explorations. In term 1, we speculated about this residual landscape as a new metropolitan playground. Could this hinterland become a new experimental foreground? For the main building project, our areas of interrogation reached from abandoned Hakka villages to trade, traditions and craftsmanship; from the small house policy to the aquatic maze of water flows; from ancient traditions to cutting-edge technology and from the dynamics of cross-border education to China's consumer electronics, games and robotics, where the virtual collides with the physical world.

Our field trip took us through multiple thresholds, from the super-urban to the super-rural. We started the trip in Hong Kong, an island of skyscrapers, mountains, tropical forests and beaches, and explored the city's outer limits, extreme topography, concrete-reinforced mountain slopes and reclaimed grounds. From here, we crossed the border zone, a residual landscape locked between two megacities: Shenzhen, a fast-moving city and a mecca for makers – with fabrication laboratories, robotics, electronic markets, drone factories and architecture by I.M.Pei, OMA, Coop Himmelb(l)au and Urbanus – and Guilin, with its majestic rural landscape, reminding us that days could also pass in slow motion.

Year 2
Niamh Cahill, Daniel Eytan Grubner, Anahita Hosseini Ardehali, Edmund King, Cheuk Yan (Felix) Lau, Mabel McCabe, Nandinzul Munkhbayar, Barbara Sawko, Alice Shanahan, Yujie Wu

Year 3
Maria Patricia Castelo, Eleanor Harding, Amy Kempa, Emily Mak, Marcus Yang Mohan, Szymon Padlewski,
Zifeng Ye

We would like to thank our technical tutors, Jack Newton and Anja Kempa, as well as Damian Eley and Kartikeya Rajput for their generous time and superb technical support. Special thanks to Thomas Parker, Joanne Chen and Theo Games for honing the students' computational skills

Thank you also to our critics: Laura Allen, Peter Cook, Pedro Font, Stephen Gage, Theo Games, Kaown Ho, Bruce Irwin, Anja Kempa, CJ Lim, Luke Olsen, Jack Newton, Thomas Parker, Luke Pearson, Sara Shafiei, Mark Smout, Sabine Storp

5.1 **Amy Kempa, Y3** 'Manufacturing Living'. In this project, rural Hong Kong – a landscape of abandonment – becomes a speculative model of countryside living, revitalising the rural through the implementation of industry. Embedded within a rapidly declining environment, it imagines a symbiotic exchange between the heavily polluting underbelly of TaoBao LED manufacturing and its parasitic camouflage of idyllic rural living above. Light forms the architectural driver, where the unique nature of production provides a landscape of constant illumination.
5.2 **Zifeng Ye, Y3** 'The Blue Frontier'. A proposal for an experimental community located on the Plover Cove Reservoir in Hong Kong. This project responds to the city's recurring proposals to reclaim land from the reservoir and proposes that Plover Cove be its first floating town. The project utilises water entering into the reservoir to create animated public and domestic spaces for the enjoyment of visitors and residents.
5.3 **Emily Mak, Y3** 'Dust Matter(s)'. Set in the context of the thriving industrial city of Shenzhen, this speculative project proposes an experiential facility that aims to educate the public on the dust in the air that is often unnoticed. The building itself functions as an air filter and makes visible the impact, weight and mass of dust. The immersive journey is a live cautionary tale on the effects of air pollution in the city.
5.4, 5.7 **Marcus Yang Mohan, Y3** 'Rooftop Escapades'. Informed by Hong Kong's history of informal rooftop classrooms, 'Rooftop Escapades' proposes a rooftop educational facility that drapes over the existing urban landscape, forming alcoves that serve as spaces for play and learning. Concrete – the ubiquitous material of the city – is re-examined as a soft tactile language that can protect, nurture and embrace.
5.5 **Barbara Sawko, Y2** 'Robotic Toy Workshop'. This project proposes a building that educates children from both sides of the border zone between mainland China and Hong Kong. They will learn programming and robotics, but also creative thinking and looking at things from different points of view. Taking inspiration from Chinese Yin Yang ideology, the centre will focus on balanced development of both the mind and the body.
5.6 **Szymon Padlewski, Y3** 'Hidden in Plain Sight'. Proposing a building that acts as an architectural decoy, confusing and tricking outside observers to create a surveillance-free space, this 'church of freedom' offers a democratic space where the people of Shenzhen can express their thoughts and opinions and share ideas. A prototype testing ambiguous architecture based on optical illusions and camouflage, the building obscures and confuses external and internal visual surveillance.
5.8 **Anahita Hosseini Ardehali, Y2** 'The First Frontier'. It is the near future and, with their expanding space programme, China are looking to colonise Mars and the Moon. The building proposes a space travel agency that aims to capture the cosmic sublime. It is a place for visitors to experience recreations of certain phenomena from these astronomical bodies in hope of promoting the excitement of space travel.
5.9 **Nandinzul Munkhbayar, Y2** 'Thinkers' Hotel-cum-Landscape'. Narrating traditional Chinese philosophies, this project raises awareness of stress levels at work and attempts to offer spatial opportunities to help nourish mental health. Adopting an interwoven spatial language, it intersperses live/work spaces with gardens and waterscapes where guests are met with social encounters and sensory experiences.
5.10 **Alice Shanahan, Y2** 'Small Farm Policy'. Responding to controversial governmental policies, this project proposes a new village typology that facilitates rural growth in the hinterlands post-2047. The building brings the visitor on a journey through the landscape before entering the housing system above, based on a modular system centring around a singularly designed column.
5.11 **Niamh Cahill, Y2** 'Casting Xingping'. In response to the need for more sustainable tourism along the Li River, this project proposes a theatre that provides a platform for the revival of Chinese shadow theatre. As night falls, the landscape becomes the backdrop for projections of light, creating an immersive experience amongst the dramatic karst landscape. A community centre by day, the building is designed as a shadow theatre with the roof filtering light into the various spaces.
5.12 **Yujie Wu, Y2** 'Celebration as Preservation'. A post-demolition urban village community centre becomes democratic place for both past and future residents. By respecting the spacial format of the demolished urban village, people are provided opportunities to experience the scale of the past living space. The community library and the market underneath keep the legacy of the demolished urban village, and give the original function back to its space.
5.13 **Cheuk Yan (Felix) Lau, Y2** 'The New Tourist Rafts Terminal'. The terminal strives to respond to the contrast in tourism in the area during different seasons, and to resolve the poor management of the tourist sightseeing rafts along the Li River in XingPingZhen, China. The flexible intervention adapts to and embraces the seasonal changes, expanding and contracting according to the demand for space in different seasons.
5.14–5.16 **Maria Patricia Castelo, Y3** 'Vertical Landscapes'. A proposal for a vertical urban park that focuses on bringing the sublime quality of nature to a dense city context, providing Hong Kong city dwellers with access to scenic natural landscapes. The park provides plants that filter air users may take a vertical, winding hike up the building.
5.17 **Mabel McCabe, Y2** 'Institute for Food Innovation'. This project explores sustainable future foods: fake meat and insects. With buildings on opposite sides of the water, circulation is key to making sure the visitor explores every area, from food kitchens to a lecture theatre. All senses are experienced in eating a wealth of new foods, whilst travelling on a journey to discover how it is made and ending at the sunset restaurant.
5.18 **Daniel Eytan Grubner, Y2** 'Rebranding and Reviving Chinese Oysters'. Located in a region with a rich history of aquaculture, this building proposal is comprised of an oyster supplement factory and experimental medicine clinic. The theatricality of the industry is accentuated by encouraging public entry to manufacturing spaces and offering wellness treatments within the factory's operation.
5.19 **Eleanor Harding, Y3** 'Embassy of the Unseen'. This alternative embassy uses a responsive architecture to communicate its occupation and needs to the overlooking luxury tower blocks, whilst shifting scales to maximise approachability on the ground. The 'unseen' (people with no visibility within the city) are exemplified as the 'live-in maids' and the 'working poor'. The embassy exploits legal loopholes around land ownership in favour of those with no space of their own.

5.2

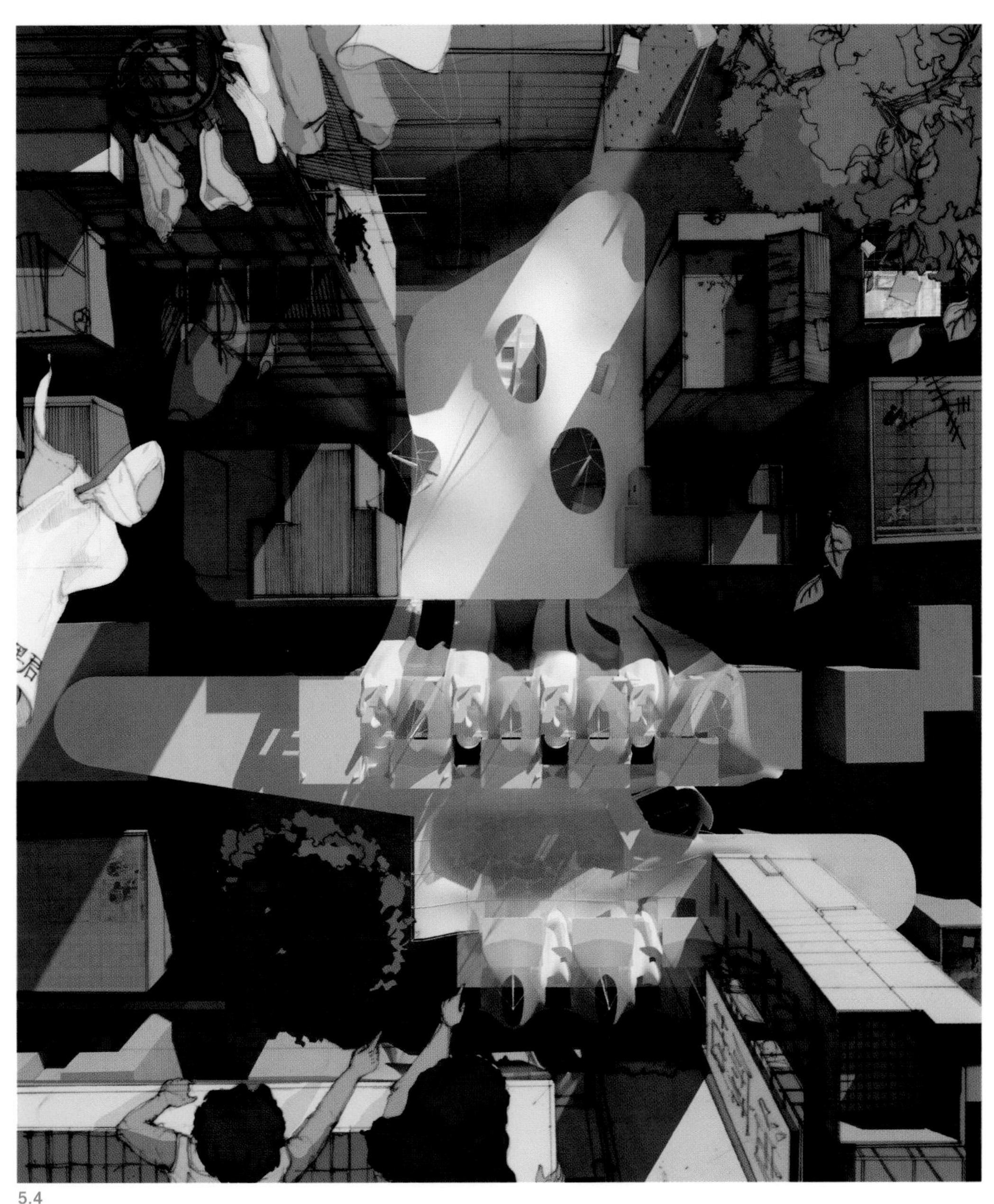

5.4

5.5

5.6

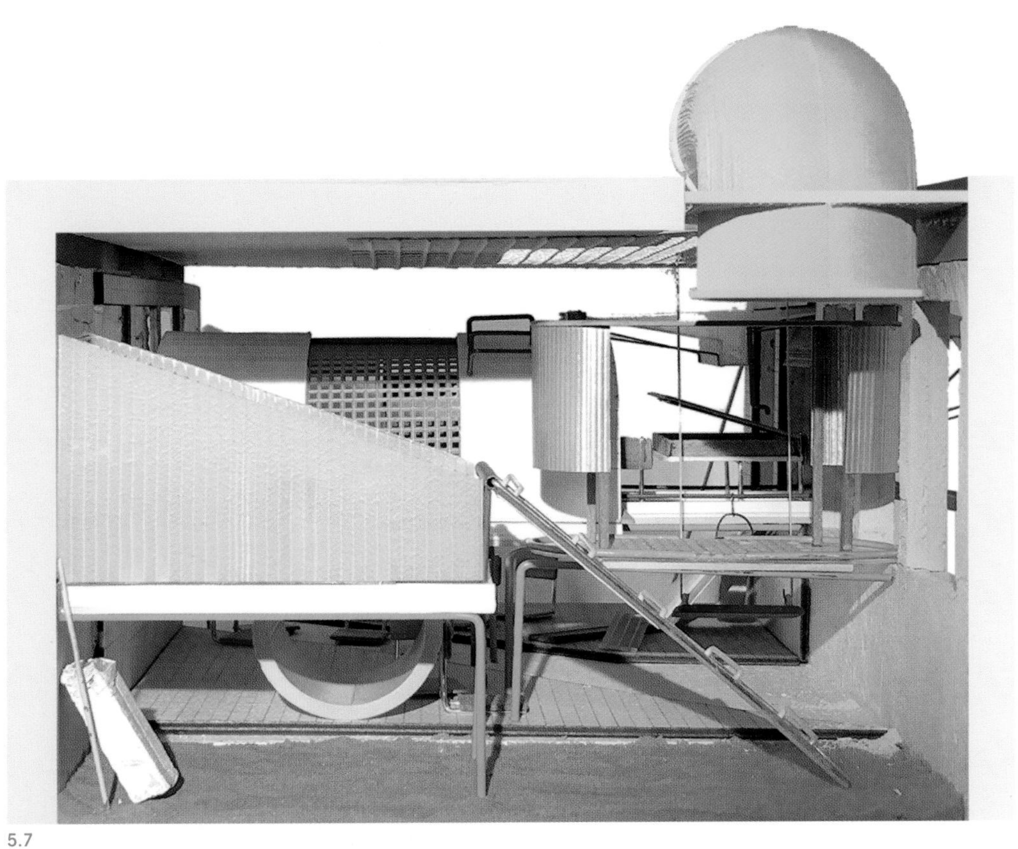

5.7

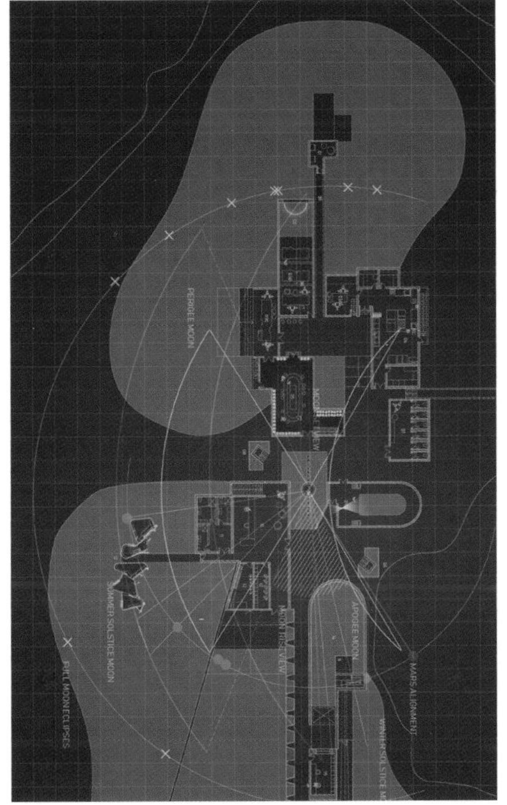
PERIGEE MOON
SUMMER SOLSTICE MOON
FULL MOON ECLIPSES
MOON RISE VIEW
APOGEE MOON
MARS ALIGNMENT

5.8

5.9

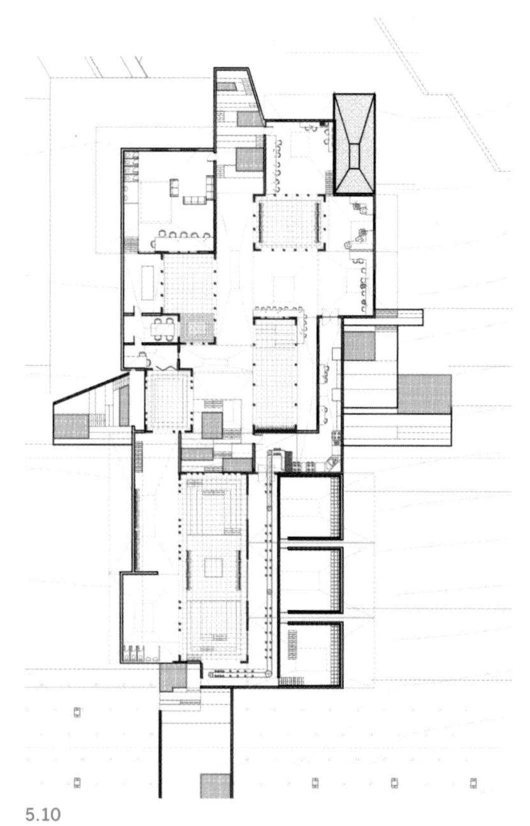

5.10

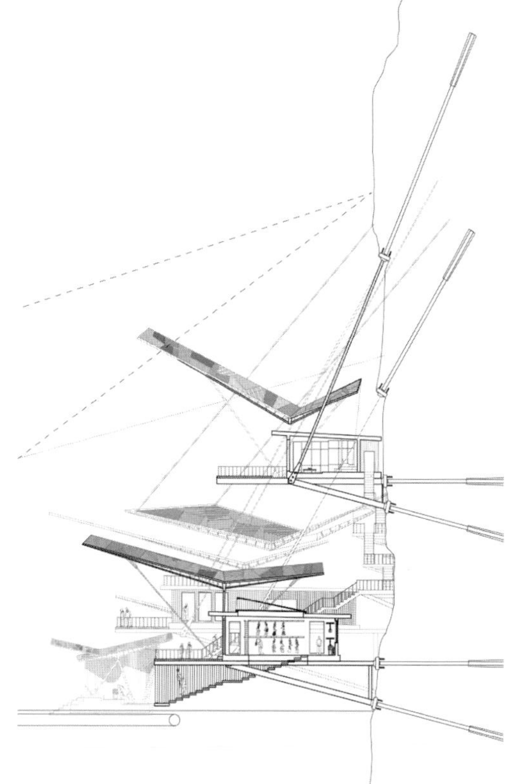

5.11

5.12

5.13

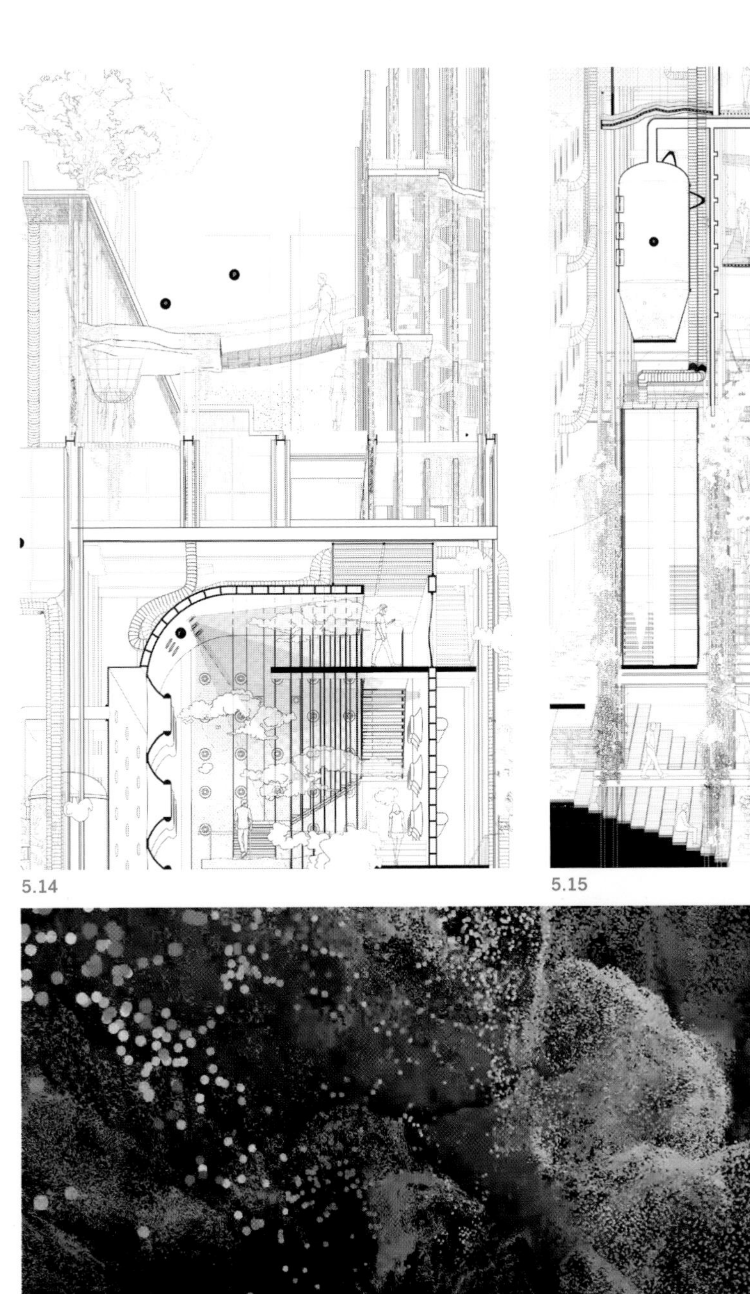

5.14

5.15

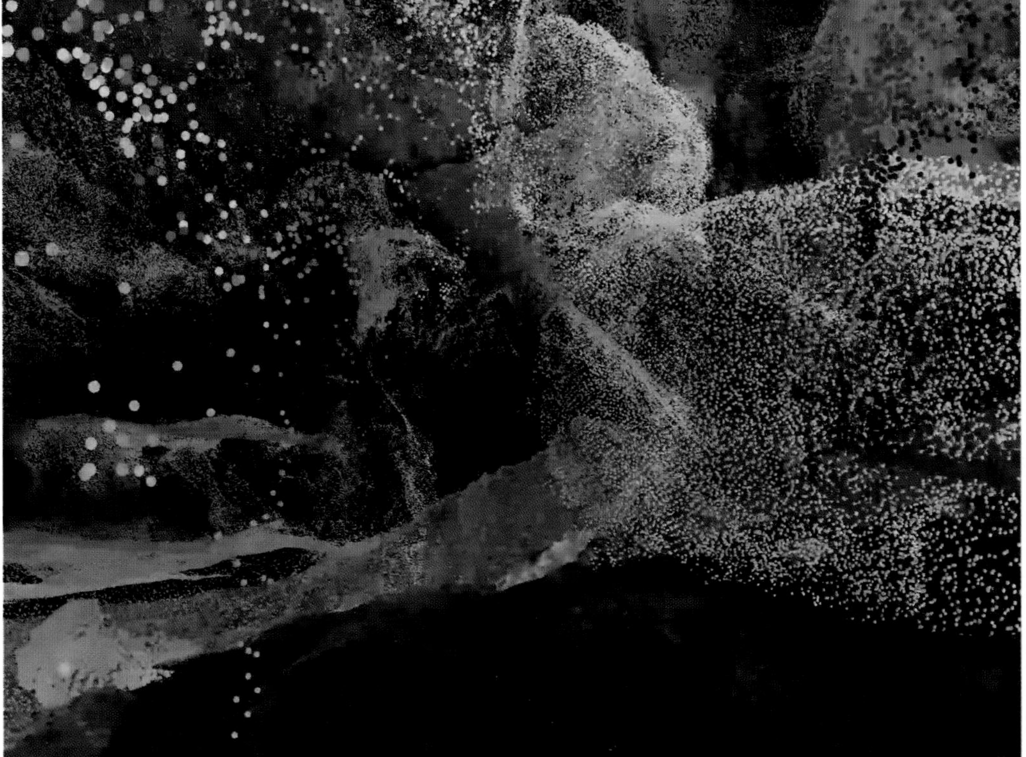

5.16

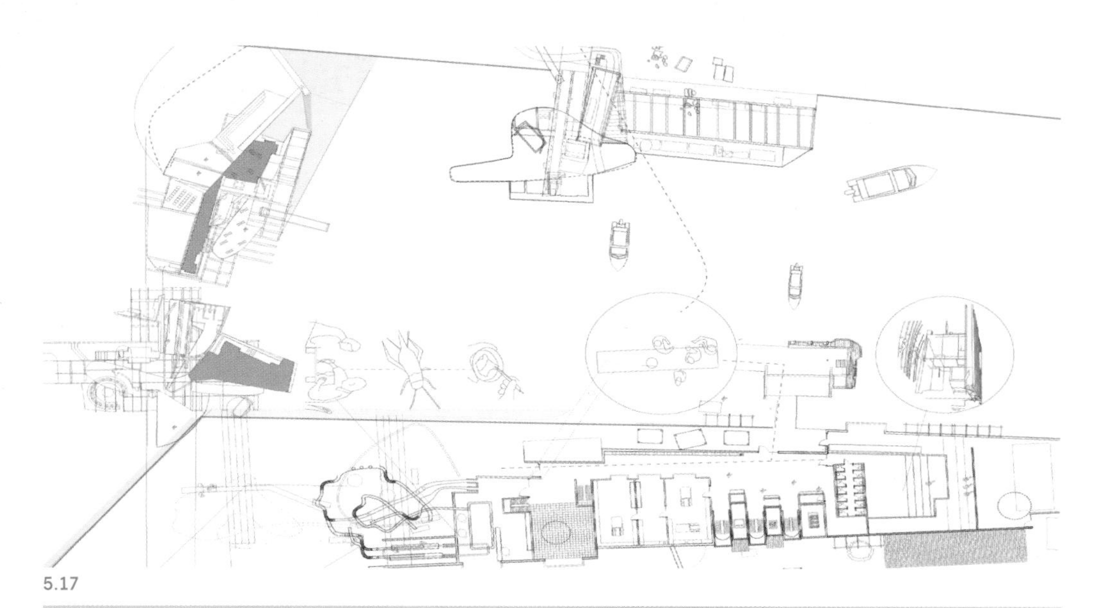
5.17

5.18

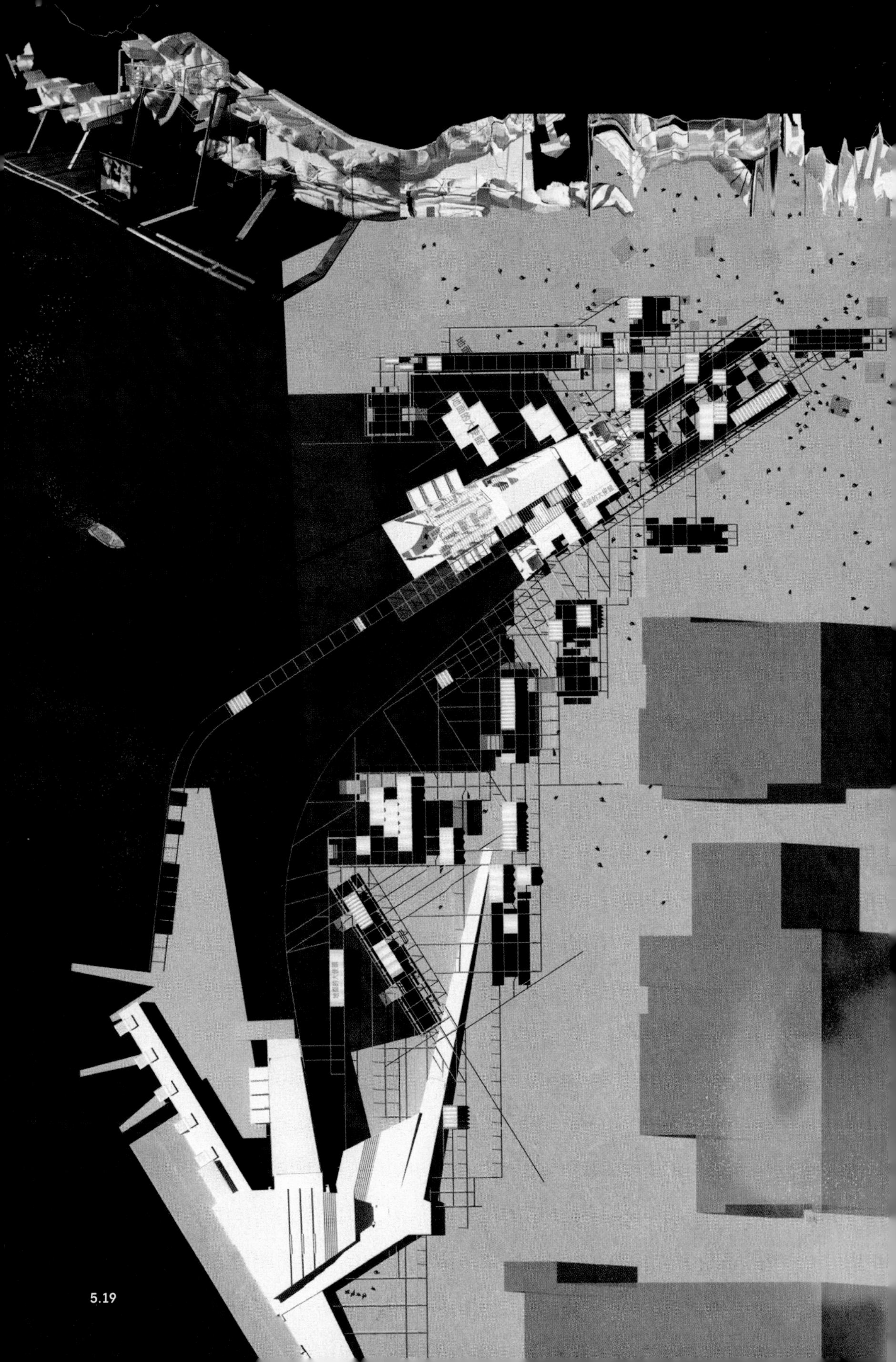

5.19

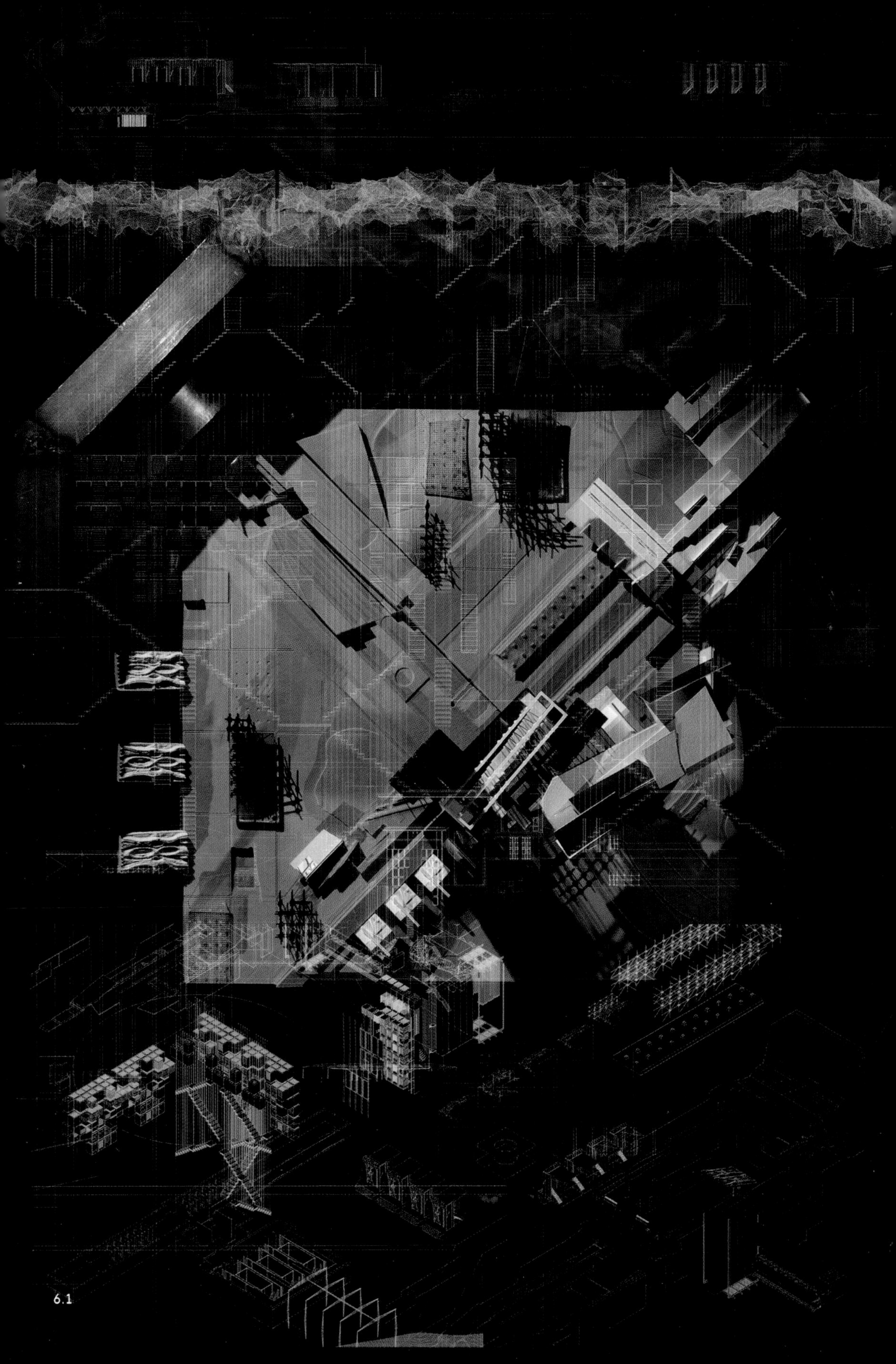

6.1

Tilt-Shift: Long Views Across the Edo

UG6

Farlie Reynolds, Paolo Zaide

Japanese *ukiyo-e* – meaning 'pictures of the floating world' – are woodblock prints that were intended to provide escapism from everyday 17th-century life in Japan during the Edo period. Stitching together stories of people, spaces in nature and the changing of the seasons, *ukiyo-e* depicted imagined societies where folklore, erotica and wild landscapes were in abundance. Today, Tokyo's dazzling neon backdrop is a dramatic shift from these dreamlike floating worlds. But between the subtle transience of the old capital and the digitally enhanced frenzy of Tokyo remains a culture inherently bound by tradition, craft and nature.

This dialogue between tradition and modernity is embodied in the tactility of the moss garden, the diffuse light of the *shoji* – traditional Japanese doors made with translucent paper – and the *engawa* – a narrow Japanese veranda that forms an ambiguous passageway between dwelling and garden. Caught between *shoji* screens and the outer storm shutters, the *engawa* exists as a blurred threshold – a space that is neither inside nor out – and is a space for conversation or for observation of the slow passing of the seasons. This space reflects Japan's traditional reverence for natural life and the environment. Originally absent from the Japanese language, 'nature' was considered so integrated with the everyday experience that there was no impetus to conceptualise it as its own entity. Technology was embraced as a means to adapt to the natural world and to passively extract resources, establishing a symbiosis between traditional Japanese craft and nature. Architecture, thus, became dependent upon its context rather than an artificial imposition within it.

Today, the paradox between Eastern and Western approaches in Japan typifies the tension between nature and culture: both are in constant motion, slowly tilting between extremes, forcing us to speculate on how our environment might recalibrate when one radically shifts. This year, UG6 confronted this changing environment. We negotiated small tilts and big shifts – shocks caused by abrupt changes in nature or culture – and questioned how everyday spaces and urban landscapes can adapt to accommodate environmental uncertainty. Our focus was Tokyo Metropolis, a model 'disaster-resistant city' that has undergone a number of changes to withstand potential environmental impacts over the years. Searching beyond the pragmatic, we interpreted the notion of 'shocks' and the 'environment' from a cultural perspective. This year's brief was an invitation to journey through Japan's traditional and contemporary narratives, to stitch into the rhythmic tempo of Tokyo and to bind age-old techniques and materials with new technological inventions.

Year 2
Renee (Soraya) Ammann, Tengku (Sharil) Bin Tengku Abdul Kadir, Cira Oller Tovar, Ewa Roztocka, Natalia Sykorova, Chak (Anthony) Tai, Milon Thomsen, Long (Ron) Tse, Suzhi Xu

Year 3
Chun (Jason) Chan, Hiu (Victor) Chow, Migena Hadziu, Zhongliang (Abraham) Huang, Yuen (Peter) Kei, Kit Lee-Smith, Owen Mellett

UG6 would like to thank our guest critics: Laura Allen, Barbara-Ann Campbell-Lange, Edward Denison, Christine Hawley, Ness Lafoy, Inigo Minns, Caspar Rodgers, Gregory Ross, Emory Smith, Kit Stiby Harris, Sabine Storp, Jessie Turnbull; and friends of the unit, Theo Clarke, Maxim Goldau, Kerry Lan, Shiyin Ling, Jerome Ng, Yip Wing Siu

Thank you to Robert Newcombe for our photography workshops, to our computing tutor Jack Holmes and our technical tutors Clyde Watson and Dimitris Argyros

For their warm hospitality we would like to thank Toshiki Hirano from the Kengo Kuma Lab, Kaz Yoneda and Momoyo Kaijima for introducing Tokyo from the Atelier Bow Wow Terrace. Finally, we would like to thank the Daiwa Foundation and the Great Britain Sasakawa Foundation for their generous support this year

6.1 **Migena Hadziu, Y3** 'Archipelago/Dichotomy'. This project proposes a DNA research and archive facility for the ex-military Daiba Park island in Tokyo Bay. The architecture bridges the gap between time and materiality by reacting to the conditions set out by the process of preservation and manipulation of the site, allowing the building to keep evolving in parallel to the research development.
6.2 **Natalia Sykorova, Y2** 'Museum of Forgotten Territories'. This project accesses the inaccessible through reconstruction of a non-existent village. A territory of the *Burakumin* – an outcast community considered to be at the bottom of Japanese society – the village has been left and consciously forgotten to suppress discrimination. The proposed building communicates collisions and disassociations within Japanese society through the process of leather-making.
6.3–6.5 **Kit Lee-Smith, Y3** 'Anthropogenic Tectonics'. The UNESCO Intangible Cultural Heritage programme promotes education and preservation, adopting traditional Japanese attitudes, rather than Western material archiving. The design for a 'seismic proving ground' within Tokyo Bay aims to celebrate new technologies, investigates seismic activity around liquefaction – whereby the strength of soil is affected through an earthquake or similar force – and searches for a future treatment for design on reclaimed land.
6.6 **Long (Ron) Tse, Y2** 'Juku with the Falling Eggs'. In response to the rigid yet inefficient Japanese education system, the project explores the new typologies of learning environment for students aged between 3 and 13. Inspired by Bruno Munari's 'Tactile Workshops', the scheme proposes a learning landscape and chicken farm that encourages children to learn through physical interaction, play and creativity.
6.7 **Hiu (Victor) Chow, Y3** 'Hesei Shrine Complex'. This project looks at the deconstruction and desecularisation of the traditional Japanese religion Shinto, with the aim of creating shrines with metaphysical boundaries, in contrast to traditional walls and gates, where enshrined objects have been closed-off and people have been forgotten. The project reminisces on the memories of the Tsukiji Fish Market and Heisei era, whilst looking forward to the revitalisation of Shinto and the future of the new emperor.
6.8–6.9 **Suzhi Xu, Y2** '*Kyo no Shiki* – Four Seasons of Kyoto'. By studying the daily rituals of geisha, the tradition of 'revealing and concealing' is reinterpreted in this project through the redesign of a kimono and in a performance. The performance became the foundation of an installation on Tokyo's streets, revealing and concealing fragments of Kyoto and the dying beauty of geisha culture.
6.10 **Owen Mellett, Y3** 'The Flooding Japanese Garden'. This landscape intervention sets a precedent for the further development of Tokyo, integrating flood control with the creation of new public garden spaces. By inhabiting and reconstituting the bottom floors of buildings close to important flood points, the project creates an ever-shifting garden space. Surrounded by a forest of support columns, among which the inhabited structures sit, the garden retreats, shifts and unfolds as the water level changes to ensure this public space is always inhabitable, regardless of the changing environmental conditions around it.
6.11–6.12 **Tengku (Sharil) Bin Tengku Abdul Kadir, Y2** '*Nha* – Home for the Vietnamese Immigrant'. A proposal for a co-housing scheme for the new Vietnamese immigrant and the Japanese university student, designed in response to a controversial immigration bill by the Japanese government. Learning and exchange are facilitated onsite through the use of adapted vernaculars and myths from both cultures.
6.13 **Chak (Anthony) Tai, Y2** 'Salaryman's *Genkan*'. Inspired by social problems relating to harsh working conditions in Japan, this project investigates extensions to the home that help people to de-stress after work. Using the *engawa* spaces commonly found in traditional Japanese homes, a series of scripted, organic landscapes in the form of 'plug-ins' create a new conversation around the conventional daily routine.
6.14 **Yuen (Peter) Kei, Y3** '*Mikoshi* Lion Festival'. Due to the redevelopment of Tsukiji Fish Market in Tokyo, the annual *matsuri* (festival) is disappearing. This project incorporates public and private spaces allocated to the festival's parade route and, also, workshop facilities for building celebratory structures. A *mikoshi* lion head is constructed above the workshop area as a symbolic display of Tokyo's dynamic cityscape.
6.15 **Renee (Soraya) Ammann, Y2** 'A Night-time Retreat'. Situated in Dogenzaka, Tokyo – where the night is always young, and the drinks never stop coming – this programme offers a place of rest for those wanting to escape it. Designed for the average party-goer and worker, it incorporates laundry, bathing and sleeping facilities packaged in the format of a deconstructed Katsura Imperial Villa.
6.16 **Milon Thomsen, Y2** 'Towards a 'Bonsai' Architecture: Multigenerational Living in Tokyo 2090'. With Tokyo's ageing population set to halve by the end of the century, this project seeks new strategies that might preserve the city's vitality through subtle subtractions and additions to existing building typologies. By connecting the disjointed urban structure and breaking with the unsustainable 'demolish and rebuild' philosophy, insertions of hanging gardens create new common ground for social interaction, learning and care between the young, working and elderly populations.
6.17 **Zhongliang (Abraham) Huang, Y3** 'Arrow to the Sea'. This project counters the ecological damage caused by the Tokyo 2020 Olympics in the form of a traditional Japanese martial arts centre, located in Tsukiji. In order to bring tranquillity back to the site, bamboo forests will be planted in and around the main architecture, where people can practice martial arts and Japanese archery, and enjoy the peaceful view of the bamboo forest and Tokyo Bay.
6.18 **Ewa Roztocka, Y2** 'Renewal of Shitamachi'. This project is set on the historical border between the Yamanote and Shitamachi areas in Tokyo, constructing a bridge on the border for contrasting social and urban patterns to meet. In it, lost personal memories and belongings of the forgotten lowland Shitamachi cultures are celebrated through craft. The design seeks to revive the Shitamachi area, in particular its housing, and promotes local Shitamachi craft.
6.19 **Cira Oller Tovar, Y2** 'The Streetscape of Asakusa'. In contrast with the civic squares seen in Europe, villages and districts in Japan have an axial organisation. This village structure, with no visual endpoints, would appear to signify the lack of importance placed on spatial limits. The project explores how different elements merge interior and exterior, and private with public spaces in contemporary Japan.
6.20 **Chun (Jason) Chan, Y3** 'Aqua-Vitality Retirement Centre'. This proposal uses architecture to retain the memory of the Tsukiji Fish Market. The building redefines the memory of existing shops, structures and functions. An intersection between Tokyo's old and new, prefabricated building elements were designed to combine with the existing structure, creating a sustainable Japanese garden and an atmosphere of delight for the older and younger generations.

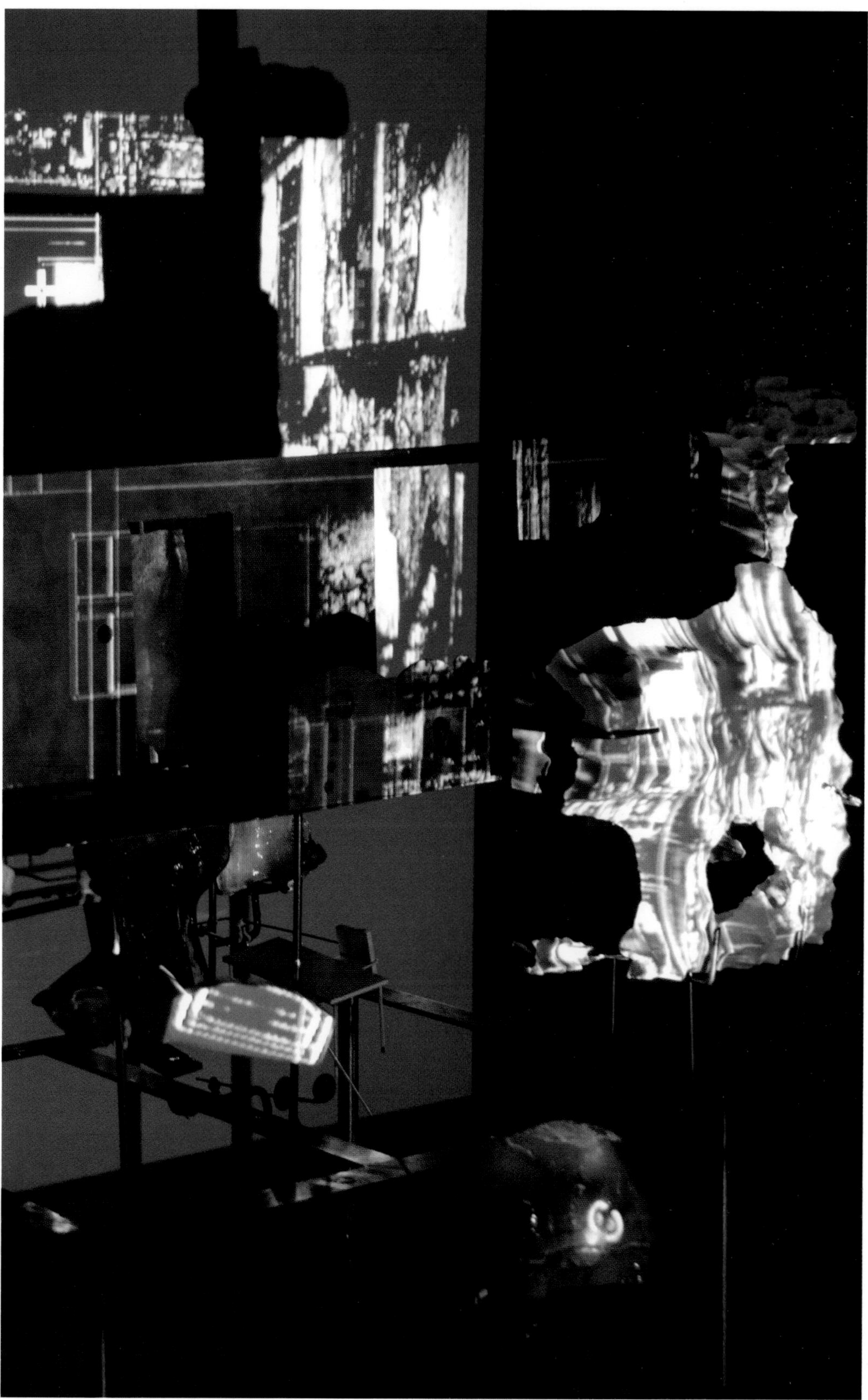

6.2

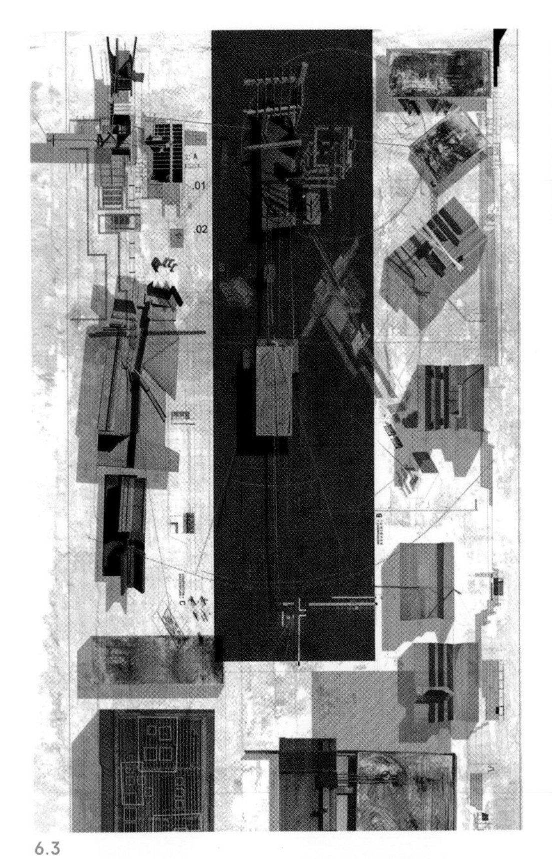

6.3

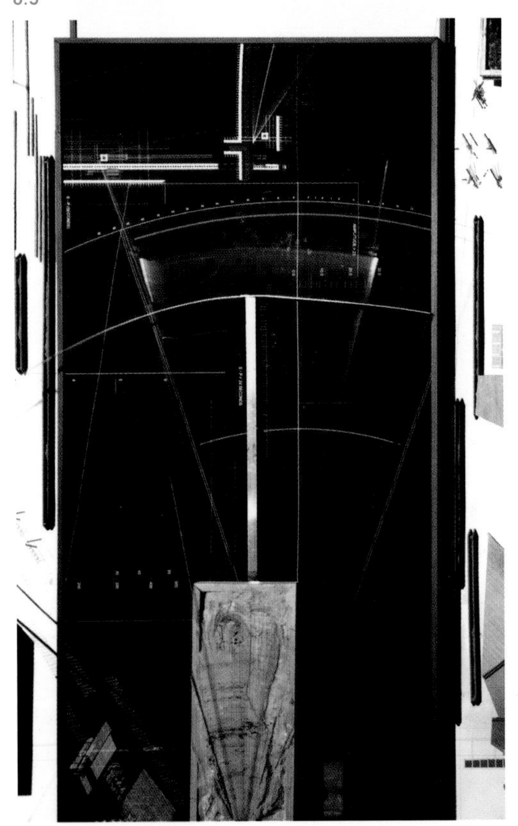

6.4

6.5

6.6

6.7

6.8

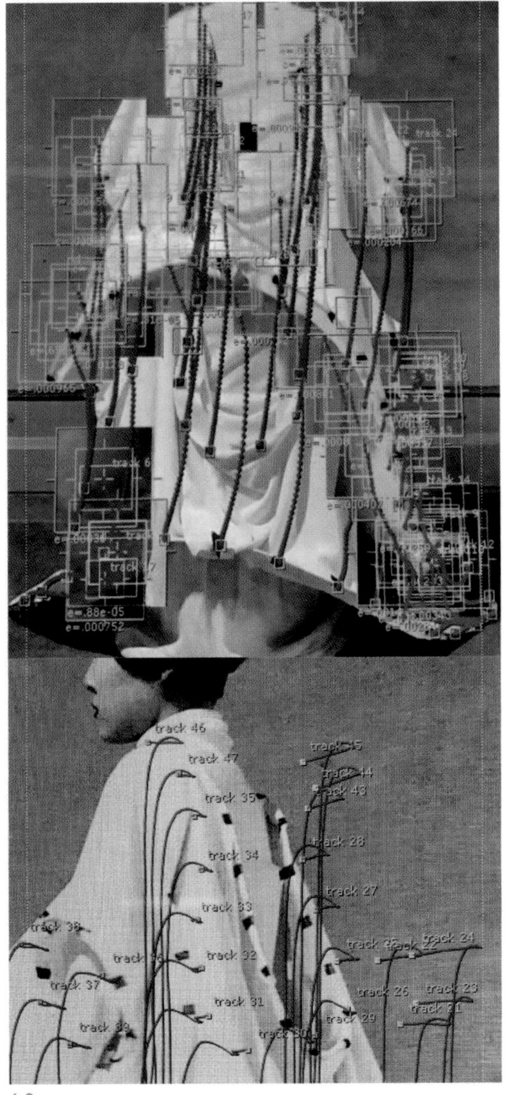
track 46
track 47
track 45
track 44
track 43
track 35
track 28
track 34
track 27
track 33
track 32
track 24
track 37
track 26
track 23
track 31
track 29

6.9

6.10

6.11

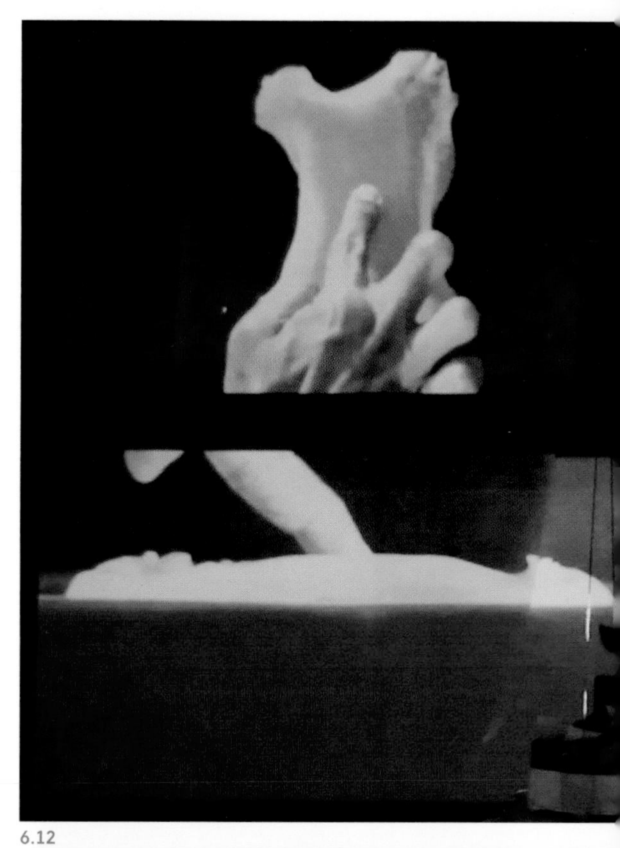

6.12

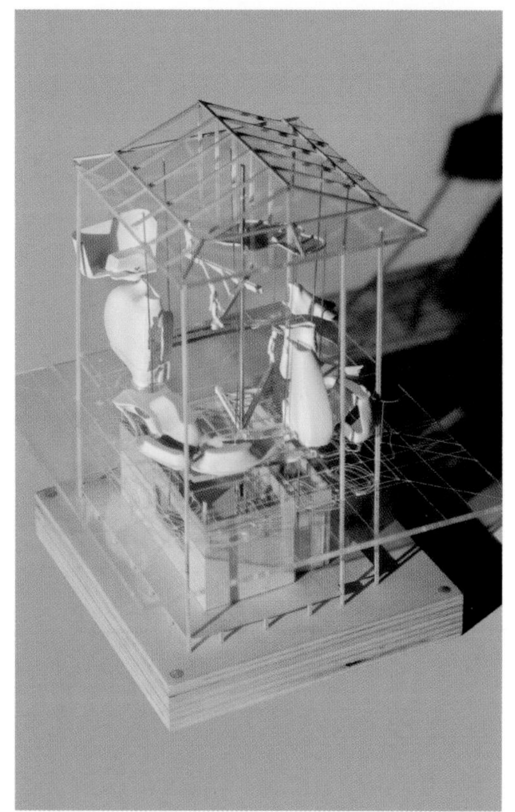

6.13

6.14

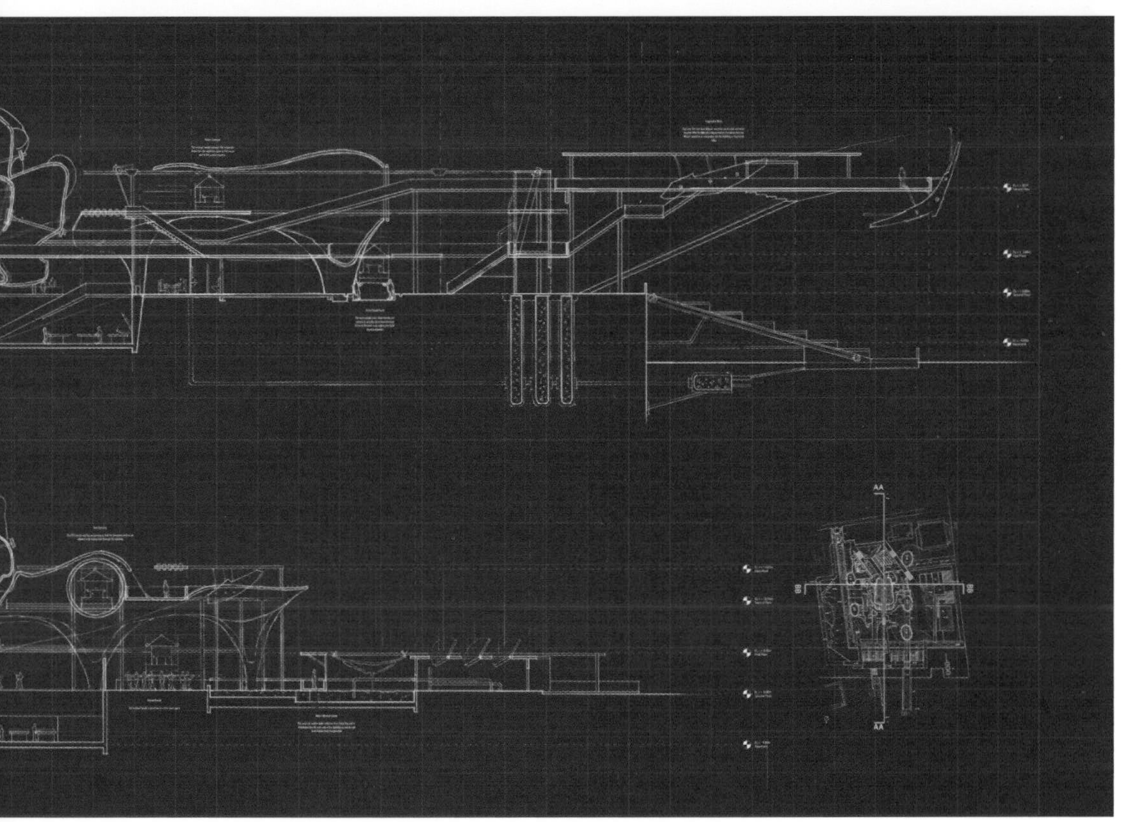

6.15

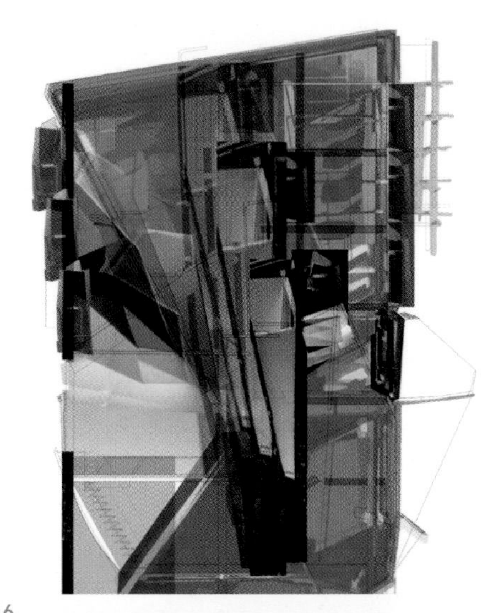

6.16

6.17

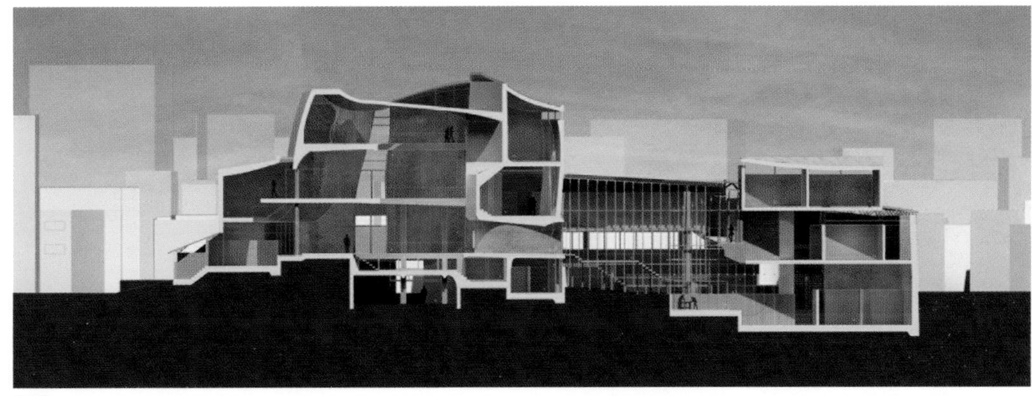
6.18

6.19

6.20

7.1

Surrender to the Seasons UG7

Pascal Bronner, Thomas Hillier

Our relationship with the weather has always been a fascinating one. Weather continually shapes civilisations, sculpts cities and inspires writers, artists and, especially, architects. It is arguably the single biggest influence on the evolution of architecture today.

Traditionally, we have attempted to design buildings and shelters to free us from the weather that surrounds us, but what if it rains inside? What if a snow blizzard dwells in our lounge? What if our kitchen is submerged in water or our bedroom is exposed to an ageing oak tree? Can the weather tell us the time? Can we choreograph decay to hide and reveal new worlds? Would this be wrong or just unusual? Or maybe even fantastical?

To explore these notions, the unit travelled to New York, a city of extremes that most certainly include its climate. New York's coastal proximity to the Atlantic Ocean creates excessive days of rain and long stretches of sun. The city experiences, on average, ten tornadoes per year. In 2012, Hurricane Sandy battered the city, during which the surf at New York harbour reached a record level; whilst in 2016, the city's largest snowstorm was recorded.

Before we set foot in New York, each of the students spent the first term exploring, researching and interpreting a specific weather condition that effects, or could effect, this great city, in an attempt to understand the city's history, masterplan, neighbourhoods and, importantly, its inhabitants and their connection to the changing conditions that surround them. Extrapolating their findings, students created a drawn, modelled or collaged weather narrative that culminated in a calibrated architectural or infrastructural innovation. These speculations were taken to New York and employed as a strategic compass (or weather vane) to help them discover their programme and site for the main building project.

We asked the students to respond to both the pleasures and discomforts caused by weather. Could their projects be designed to withstand and thrive in all weather conditions, or were they designed to crumble and deteriorate over time? Would they consider and engage with the subtlest of climatic shifts? Could their architecture explore the joy of the spring sun as it kisses one's skin or the trepidation of the cold breeze that hails the winter to come? How would these architectures 'feel' in the weather? Could they be calibrated to the New York climate so that they could shiver or sweat, spread themselves in the sun or curl up and hibernate during the winter months? As always, the work aimed to embody the unit's agenda of narrative, craft, speculation, experimentation, wonder and delight – with the only limit being the imagination.

Year 2
Inez Acquah-Aikins, Long Au, Hazel Balogun, Heather Black, Yeree Kim, Monika Kolarz, Sabrina Li, Ben Murphie, Carmen (Ligia) Poara, Hanna (John) Said, Matthew Semiao Carmo Simpson

Year 3
Theodosia (Ted) Bosy Maury, Sarah Jones, Rusna Kohli, Hau (Tini) Tang, Chuzhengnan (Bill) Xu

We would also like to thank our technical tutor, Martin Reynolds, and computing tutor, Sean Allen

Special thanks to our critics throughout the year: Sabina Andron, Peter Bishop, Alpa Depani, Stephen Gage, Kostas Grigoriadis, Soomeen Hahm, Will Jefferies, Maren Klasing, Holly Lewis, CJ Lim, Rahesh Ram, David Storring, Oliver Wilton and Stamatis Zografos

7.1 **Rusna Kohli, Y3** 'Sunsets and Scientists'. With New York State suing President Trump's Environmental Protection Agency for reversing the Clean Air Act, the building in this project filters the pollution of Manhattan, and stores the collected dust particles within its walls, to create a series of evolving spaces. Prominently situated in Times Square, the building acts as a barometer for the people of New York City. If the quality of the air remains the same, the building will be 'full' in 11.2 years, illustrating how little time there is left to address this problem.
7.2–7.4 **Theodosia (Ted) Bosy Maury, Y3** 'The Cast Courts of the Unlisted'. Situated on 42nd Street, close to Times Square and Broadway, 'The Cast Courts of the Unlisted' are designed as both a performative archive and a school for preservation techniques and building-relic maintenance. The project proposes a system of casting and performative maintenance to remember the many buildings that just miss 'Landmark' status, and questions 'How long should memories last?'
7.5 **Carmen (Ligia) Poara, Y2** 'The Fog House'. Fog can create an unearthly feeling; it can also confuse and obscure or create a sense of protection and safety. This project is situated in the Po Valley in Italy, which is known as one of the foggiest places on earth. The house manipulates fog to create a series of spaces, both tangible and intangible, where the architecture can be manoeuvred to alter the course of the incoming fog, exploring varying spatial relationships.
7.6 **Long Au, Y2** 'The Launderette of Sin'. Situated in Hell's Kitchen on the Upper West Side of Manhattan, this new laundrette strives to cleanse the sins of the city's hotel industry, both literally and metaphorically. The laundrette strives to purify the city through environmental means, serving as a symbol for green and sustainable industry by recycling and repairing old washing machines, drying laundry passively and using recycled rainwater.
7.7 **Long Au, Y2** 'The House of Houses'. Located on the coast of Staten Island, this proposal serves as a response to the aftermath of Hurricane Sandy in New York City. The building utilises fragments of the surrounding hurricane debris, knitting together broken remains to form a new assemblage: architecture that acts as both community storm shelter and as a symbol of resilience against future natural disasters.
7.8 **Monika Kolarz, Y2** 'The Lighting Strike Observatory'. The proposed observatory is sited on the Hudson River Palisades, opposite the Manhattan skyline. A series of interconnected pathways and viewpoints have been designed around the locations of famous lighting strikes across New York City, which carve up the architecture into a series of vertical planes. New views are constantly discovered as the inhabitants traverse this maze-like structure, in the hope of capturing the fleeting moment of a strike.
7.9 **Hazel Balogun, Y2** 'The Final Curtain Tree Nursery'. Located on the site of one of Manhattan's most catastrophic industrial fires, this project aims to counterbalance its history by using nature to bring life back to the neighbourhood. The nursery supports the production, exhibition and distribution of tree-grafted burial pods. Contained in biodegradable urns, the ashes from the departed aid in the growth of a living tree, transforming the ritual of death into an act of regeneration.
7.10 **Sabrina Li, Y2** 'The Water Tower Steam House'. Inspired by New York City's vast, invisible underground steam pipe system, the 'Steam House' posits a speculative approach to a new way of sustainable living. The 'steam keeper' inhabits one of the many rooftop water tanks of the city, where it is transformed into a new machine for living that harnesses the power of steam to fuel appliances and facilities.
7.11–7.12 **Inez Acquah-Aikins, Y2** 'The Rime Ice Refuge'. Rime ice forms when super-cooled water droplets found in fog freeze onto solid objects. 'The Rime Ice Refuge' explores the use of this weather phenomenon as a construction method. Temporary structures fabricated from timber and steel are placed on sites where rime ice commonly forms. During the right weather conditions these structures get coated in rime ice, creating a series of frozen enclosures. By their very nature, the structures and spaces are ever-changing, continuously evolving and reforming with the seasons.
7.13 **Yeree Kim, Y2** 'The New York Curling Club'. Nestled in Lower Manhattan, like a Japanese Zen garden, is a polished landscape of concrete and ice. Building on New York City's surprisingly long history with curling, this building aims to introduce the sport to a new generation. A courtyard of curling sheets is hugged by a continuous, inhabitable concrete ramp that slowly moves the public towards the cantilevered heart of the building, where the landscape of ice can be viewed.
7.14 **Hau (Tini) Tang, Y3** 'Manhattan's Exquisite Corpse'. This speculative masterplan maps the unique weather conditions that occur across Manhattan, creating a series of islands within islands, each with their own micro-climates. Site-specific weather strategies are employed across these islands, including inhabitable shading, ventilation devices and evaporative cooling systems.
7.15 **Sarah Jones, Y3** 'Exploring The Liquid City'. New York City is a city of constant historical, social and economic flux. Exploring historical journeys that have taken place across the city, this flux is mapped across time, creating a series of overlays in order to highlight its instability.
7.16 **Ben Murphie, Y2** 'Enter The Void'. Situated on the edge of Chinatown in Lower Manhattan, this new bathhouse is designed entirely around the concept of negative space, whereby the architecture seeps in between every crack of an existing courtyard surrounded by buildings. The medium of water, in its liquid and vaporous states, creates new tangible partitions and spaces that fill the negative voids and form a liberating communal hub of nudity within the privacy of clouds of mist.
7.17 **Heather Black, Y2** 'Occupiable Meteorology'. Using a combination of digital and analogue tools, this project experiments with various liquid viscosities to create a series of occupiable smoke clouds that, through scaled manipulation, take on a new life within New York City.
7.18–7.21 **Matthew Semiao Carmo Simpson, Y2** '16 – 35 – 70'. Set in Dumbo in Brooklyn – the riverside backdrop of many iconic moments immortalised on the silver screen – the primary mission of this new film institute is to promote the conservation, restoration and use of celluloid film. The building is a temple for a perennially 'at risk' cultural resource, which borrows from, and adapts, the principles, theories and qualities which have come to define the analogue medium and filmmaking process. In a bid to generate an architecture as rich and captivating as the culture it was formulated to serve, the building was conceived in screenplay form. In it, a series of interconnected scenes depict archetypal characters, spaces, sounds, moments and routines that animate the facility and immediate vicinity. A shot list was then devised, communicating the narrative essence of '16-35-70' through the juxtaposition of uninflected images.

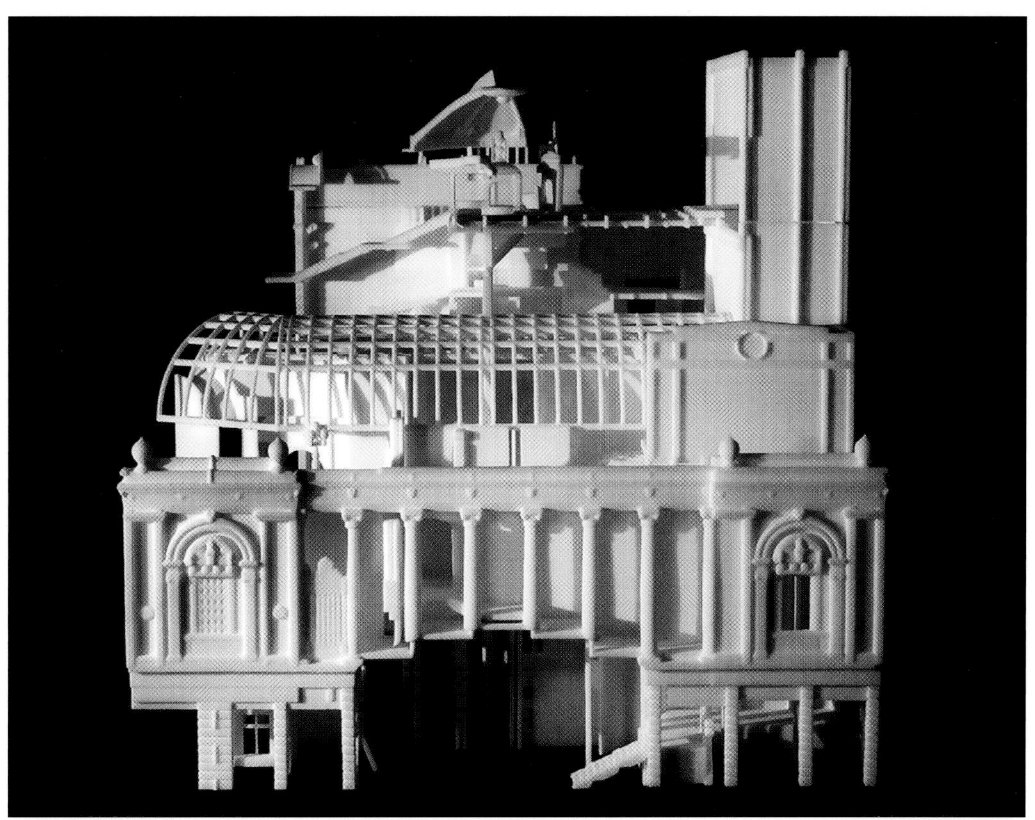

7.2

7.3

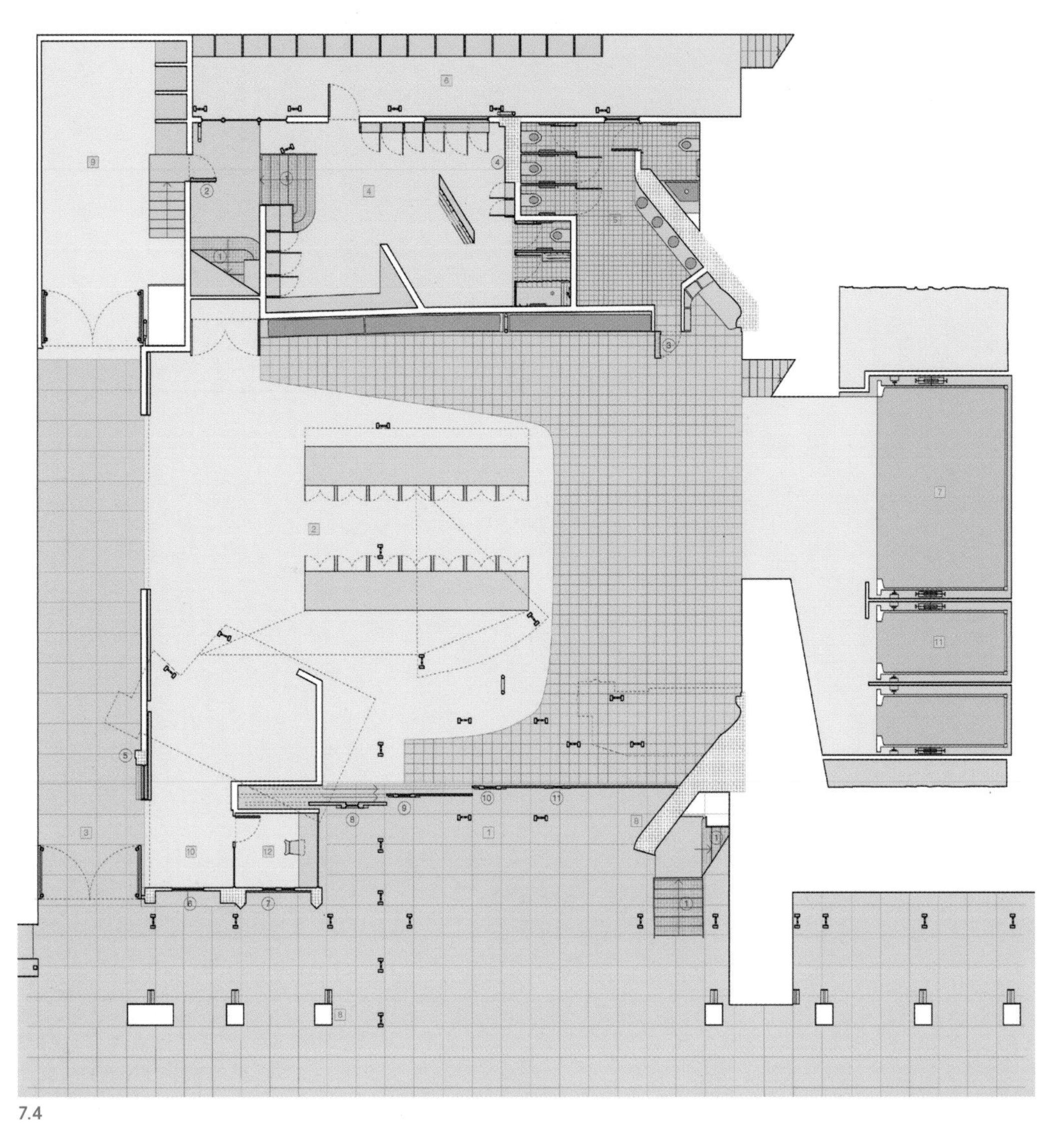

7.4

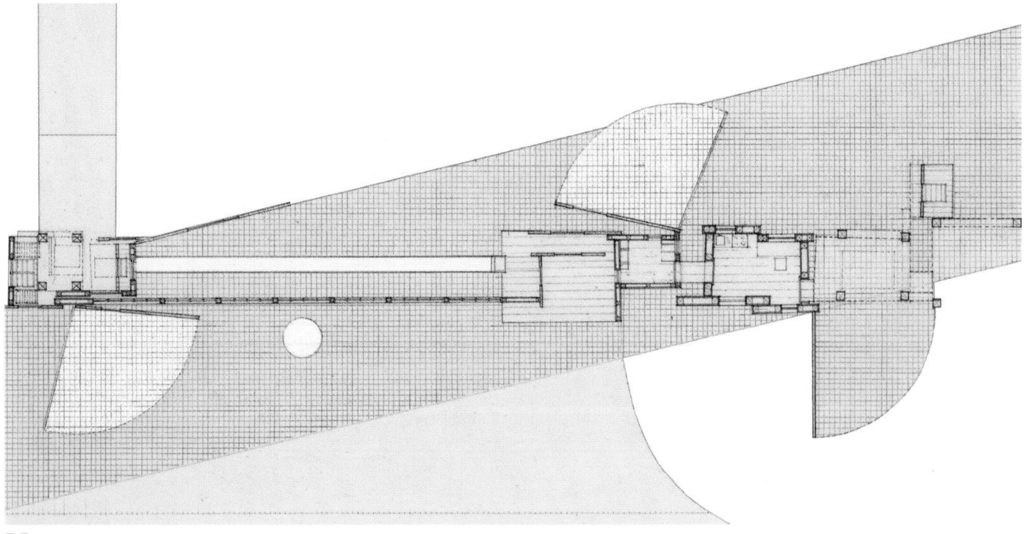

7.5

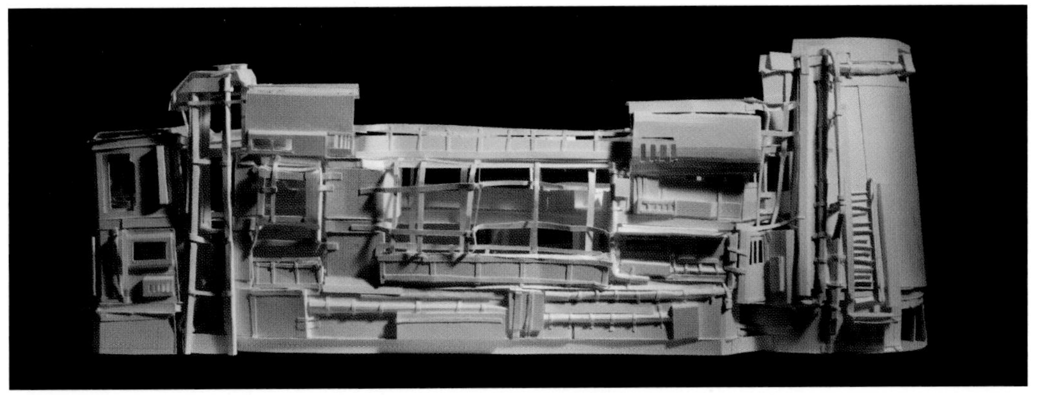

7.6

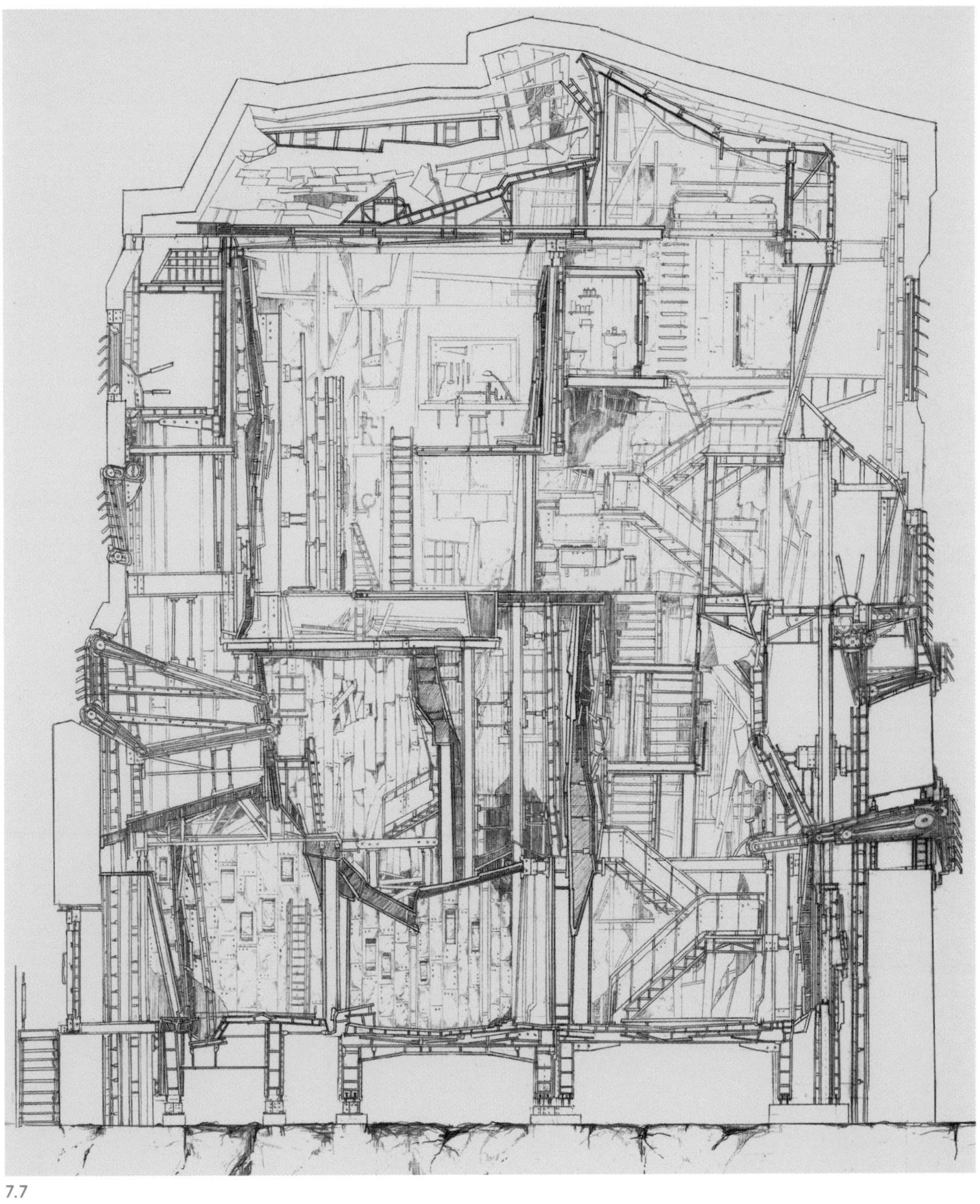

7.7

7.8

7.9

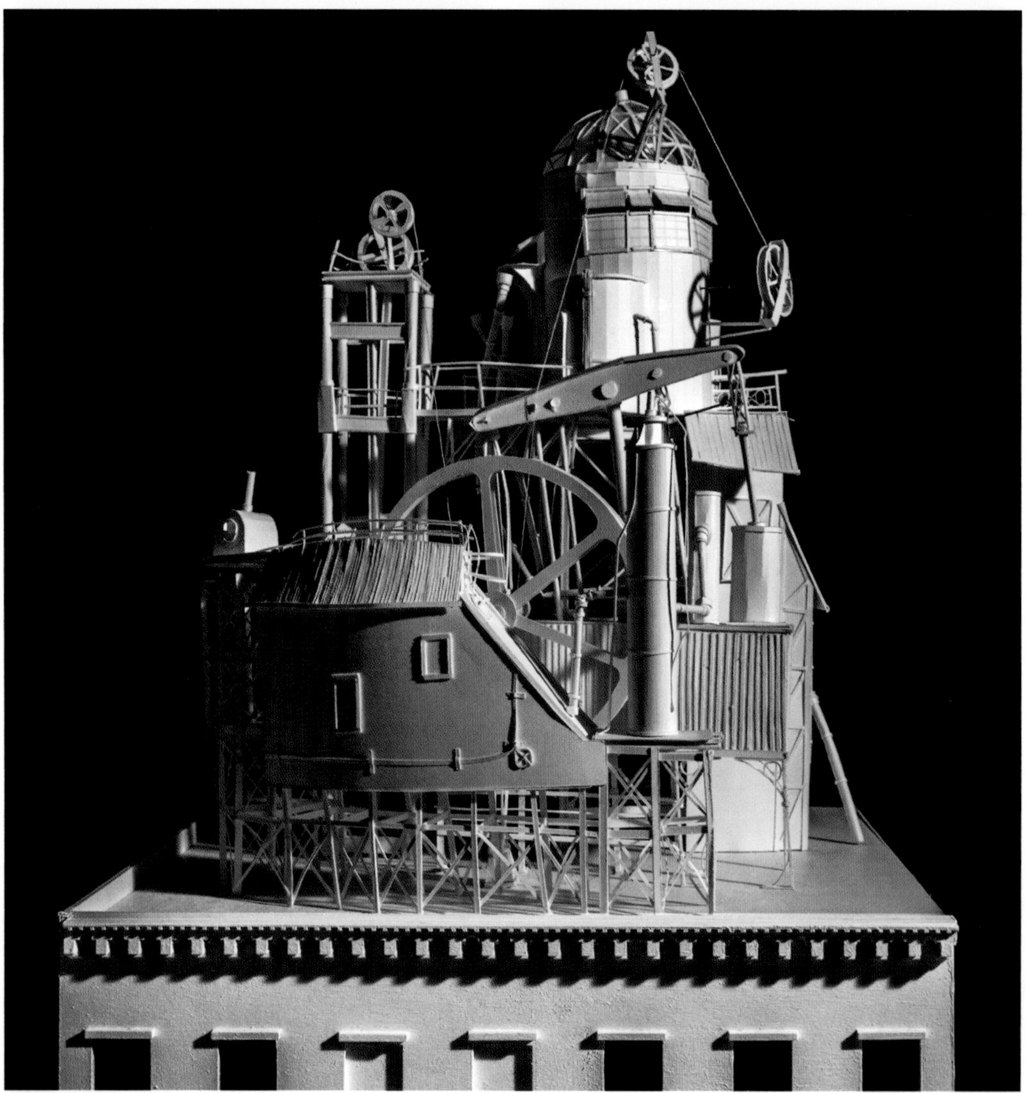

7.10

7.11

7.12

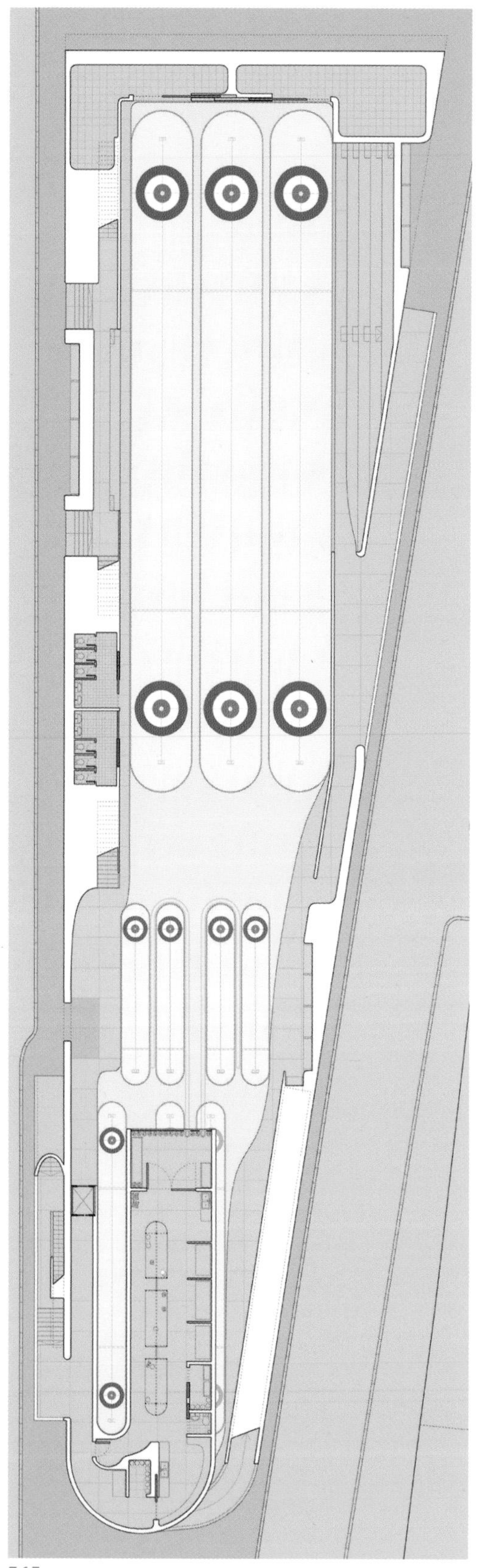

7.13

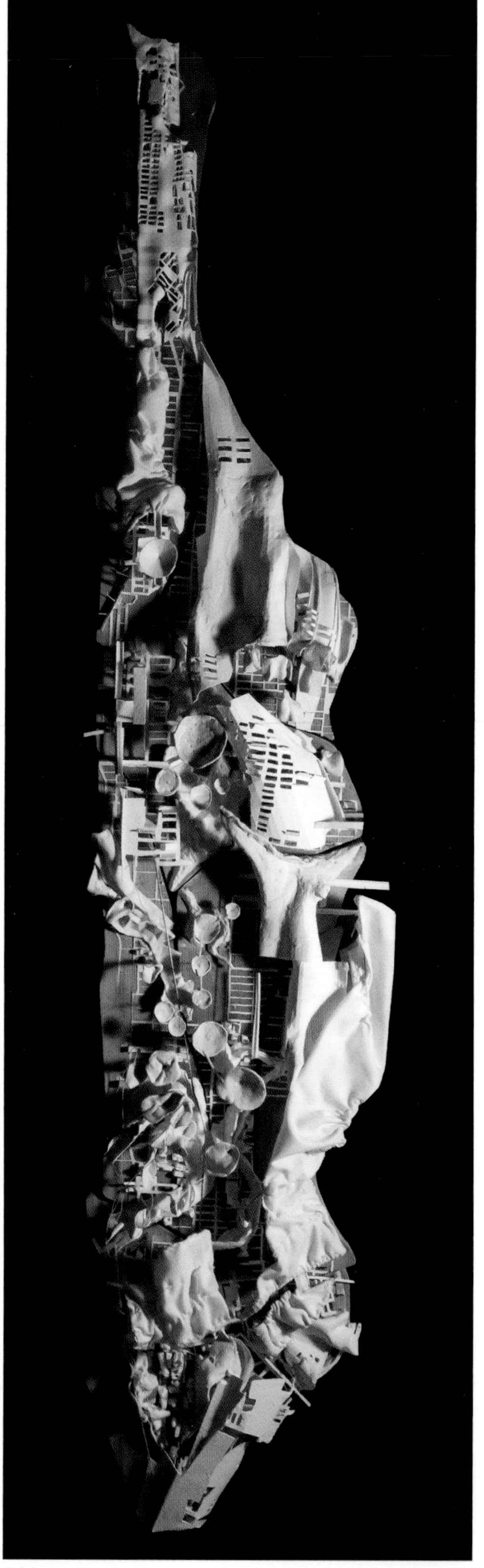

7.14

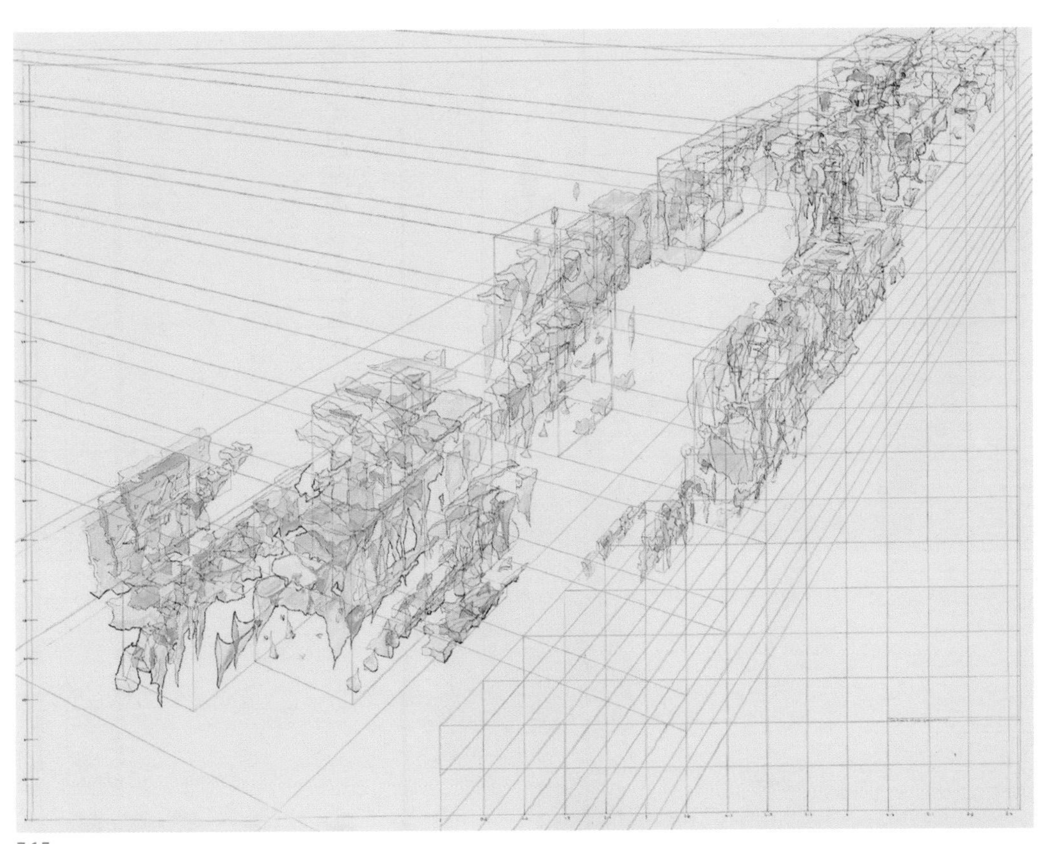

7.15

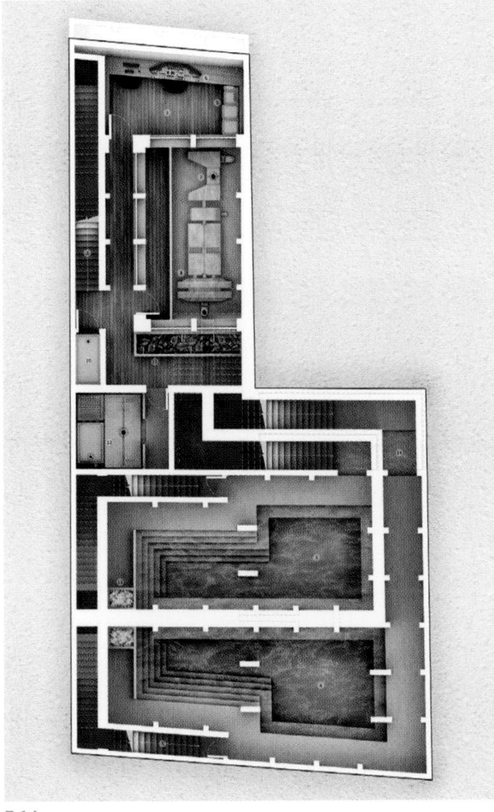

7.16

7.17

7.18

7.19

7.20

7.21

8.1

Unfinished Business

UG8

Thomas Pearce, Greg Storrar

The unfinished is a welcome antidote to the post-processed. It reveals the ruminations of invention and emanates a sense of possibility, of becoming rather than being. Flying in the face of predictability and determinism, it levitates, leaving space for imagination and letting us dream of alternative futures.

In 2019, we travelled to Sweden and Finland, where we explored notions of the unfinished. On our Nordic adventure, we looked beyond the nostalgic impression of the unfinished to instead revel in its opportunity for active reinvention. We learned how embracing openness and open-endedness is not just a critical part of a productive creative process, it is also our responsibility as designers and makers.

In our first project, we designed a spatial construction to house a found 'artifact of the unfinished'. We formulated speculative design strategies that questioned how we might deal with the unfinished, forensically studying the artifact to decode its texture and replace its phantom limbs, whilst celebrating the rupture, the edge condition between the inherited and the invented, inverting and perverting the rules of the artifact under study, seeing the old with new eyes, and tinkering with the recipe of the past to radically change the taste of the present. Having ventured between the modes of (un)finishing that constitute our creative process – media and models, drawn and made, digital and analogue, technical and psychological, and social and perceptual – we moved on to formulate building proposals for Helsinki.

Each project deployed our newfound understanding of the unfinished in a highly personal way: a theatre that stages the same play repeatedly within its frozen-formwork cast-concrete frame; a musician's residency generating alternative compositions in response to Finnish composer Jean Sibelius's abandoned symphony; a fire-free crematorium where the lives of those who pass through it are charred into its walls; a birthing sauna growing out of the armpits of Finnish mythological creatures; and the artifacts for a fictional architectural biography of the inventor of the Perlin noise algorithm. We found that seeking a design methodology for finishing the unfinished became a powerful tool for architectural invention.

Year 2
Maciej Adaszewski, Mohammad Aldoori, Alisa Baraboshkina, Albert Brown, Ana Dosheva, Yannick (Ocian) Hamel-Smith, Dilara Koz, Ziwei (Philip) Liu, Loukis Menelaou

Year 3
Miles Elliott, Charlotte Evans, Georgia Green, Bijou Harding, Hugo Loydell, Alessandro Rognoni, Imogen Ruthven-Taggart

Special thanks to our accomplices in design: technical tutor Steve Johnson and super-critic Simon Withers. Thanks also to all our critics and skills tutors, without whom we'd still be stumbling around in the great unknown: Charles Arsène-Henry, Theo Brader-Tan, Tom Budd, Barbara-Ann Campbell-Lange, Nat Chard, Kate Davies, Max Dewdney, Anna Drakes, Niamh Grace, James Green, Tom Parker, Rebecca Payne, Vseva Popov, Sophie Read, Farlie Reynolds, Bob Sheil, Jerry Tate, Emmanuel Vercruysse and Michelle Young. A final thanks to Steven Pippin, whose astonishing balancing pencil became the inspirational leitmotif to a year of experimentation and adventure

8.1 **Ana Dosheva, Y2** 'Mobile Tupa'. Challenging dominant notions of cultural preservation based on visual museum displays, this wearable travel companion simulates the physical experience of sleeping on a traditional northern-Finnish plank bed.
8.2–8.4 **Charlotte Evans, Y3** 'The Building as a Doula'. The 'Helsinki Home-Birthing Institute' aims to educate and redefine the sauna as a sacred space for birth, embracing Finland's reverse shift in development towards greater home birthing. Three protagonists – the midwife, the man and the woman – together simulate a symbiotic pseudo-sauna birthing experience within an architecture of membranes that sweat and breathe.
8.5–8.7 **Ziwei (Philip) Liu, Y2** 'Mark Agency'. Echoing Marcel Duchamp's Equation 'A Guest + A Host = A Ghost', this six-room hostel situated in central Helsinki sells tailor-made dreams for guests seeking immersive cosplay experiences. The building skeleton confuses the guests and disguises the 'host', Mark, who practices his subversive spying behaviour within the building's layered fabric.
8.8 **Loukis Menelaou, Y2** 'Building Sisu'. Inspired by the story of Tom Sukanen – a Finnish sailor who pulled a boat across the Canadian plains on an epic journey to Finland – this project exemplifies 'sisu', a Finnish word meaning hardiness and determination against all odds. The rehabilitation centre for social media addicts combats addiction by physically and psychologically separating the patient from their social media following and encouraging an investigation of the inner self.
8.9 **Georgia Green, Y3** 'Studies in Finnish White'. The Helsinki immigration centre aims to atmospherically acclimatise newcomers to the Nordic light and landscape through an organisation of spaces that reference the Finnish forest. Surface textures in the building highlight and modulate light, and are made using a design methodology structured around the representation of light in Finnish landscape painting.
8.10 **Albert Brown, Y2** 'City-Sami Sample Scape'. This project proposes an inner-city cultural centre for the Sami – an indigenous people originating from northern Finland – in Helsinki. Located on a street corner, the building's publicly-accessible roof topography samples the landscapes and settlements of the Sami. The vision of the building as a landscape is realised through the development of a lightweight structure.
8.11 **Yannick (Ocian) Hamel-Smith, Y2** 'Baby Fever: A City Oasis'. This project proposes a sacred realm for the Finnish child within a carved spatial landscape. Warped in scale, its inhabitants are perceived as giants. The project is a reminder that we are sensory beings with a primal need to surround ourselves with qualities that thrill our fingertips and possess our mind.
8.12 **Alisa Baraboshkina, Y2** 'The Rune Library'. Evoking runes – figural depictions of elements of the natural landscape translated into alphabet characters – 'The Rune Library' imports qualities of the rural Finnish landscape into the inner city, creating a place for quiet study and learning.
8.13 **Miles Elliott, Y3** 'Stories told by the Fire'. A proposal for a crematorium where the bodies are dissolved and the building is burnt. Stories of the deceased are digitally encoded and physically inscribed into the fabric of the building. These inscriptions filter precious sunlight onto the body as it is lifted into the ceremony space.
8.14 **Ana Dosheva, Y2** 'Finnish Tango: A Phantom Dance'. A proposal for a dance centre celebrating and preserving the tradition of Finnish Tango. Built upon the tradition of the frozen-lake *tanssilava* (dance hall), it provides an immersive experience of dance as ritual, using architecture defined by tools: the sand cast is eventually embedded in the building structure.
8.15–8.17 **Imogen Ruthven-Taggart, Y3** 'Forging Impressions in the Positive'. A bereavement centre appropriating jewellery-making techniques to develop a reusable metal formwork. Designed to empathise with the mourner, the building patinates with rainfall, and maps the passing of time.
8.18 **Hugo Loydell, Y3** 'Perlin's Descent into Digital Noise'. After growing tired of the machine-like computer graphics of the late 1970s, Ken Perlin developed 'Perlin noise'. This project explores the forgotten, obscure narrative that guided Perlin to his discovery and enacts its fictional architectural framing.
8.19–8.20 **Maciej Adaszewski, Y2** 'Helsinki Woodwork Academy'. At the intersection of the digital and analogue worlds of Finnish craftsmanship, the design of the academy is driven by the physical prototyping of a novel hybrid timber-lamination system. Through its experimental use of timber construction, the academy attempts to teach its students using its architecture.
8.21–8.23 **Alessandro Rognoni, Y3** 'Finns Just Eat Marinated Reindeer. Berlusconi Gets a Very Finnish Revenge'. Two building proposals for the Finnish fast-food chain, Kotipizza. In the first, the flagship store in Helsinki, the industrial process of smoking reindeer becomes a commercial spectacle. In the second proposal, located in Parma, Italy, a smokehouse imported from Finland retains a vernacular façade, challenging the Italians' curiosity and mistrust of foreign pizza.
8.24 **Dilara Koz, Y2** 'Following the Swan of Tuonela'. This project proposes a musician's residency and research facility that generates alternative compositions in response to Jean Sibelius' abandoned symphony *The Swan of Tuonela*. The building is a temporal space where layered patterns of light and shadow deconstruct musical dimensions.
8.25–8.27 **Bijou Harding, Y3** 'Dramatic Variations of Frozen Fabric Formwork'. A proposal for an independent theatre in central Helsinki that shows different renditions of the play *The Seven Brothers* based on the famous novel by Finnish author Aleksis Kivi. The building is fabricated by casting into the frozen fabric formwork which, as a result, drastically reduces the amount of waste material produced. Setting it apart from other fabric formworks, the concrete allows for moulds to be reused and generates different geometries.

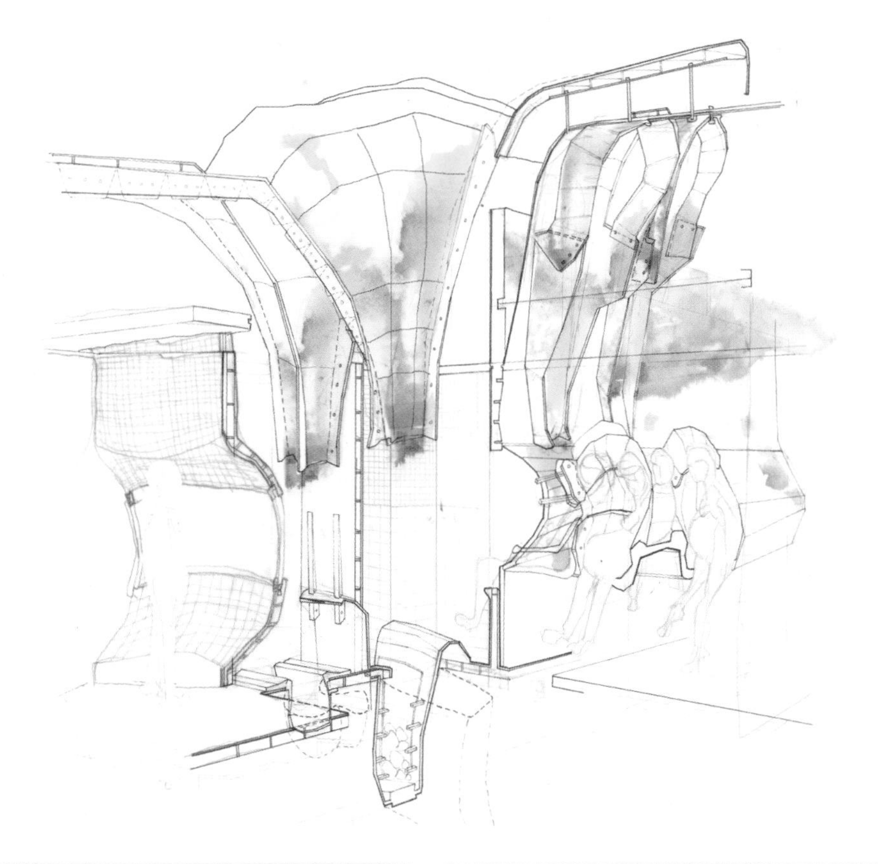

8.2

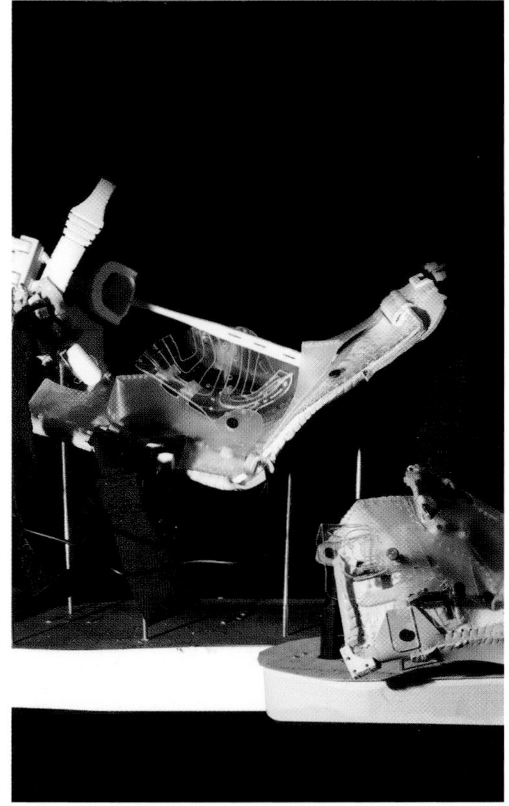

8.3

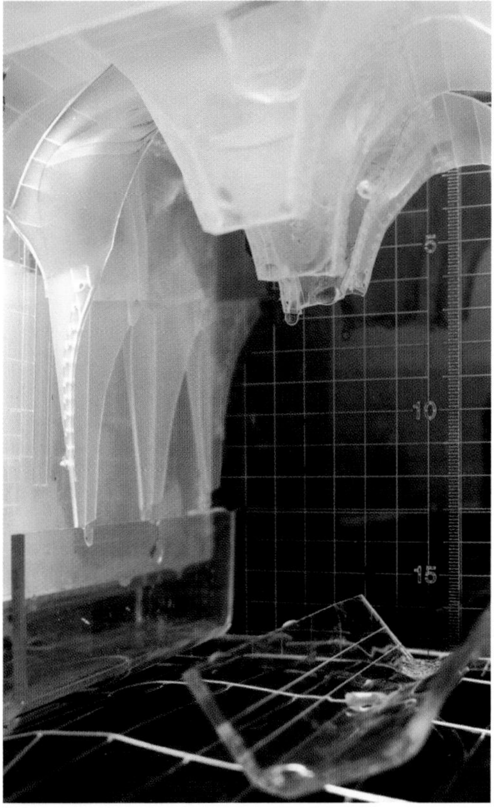

8.4

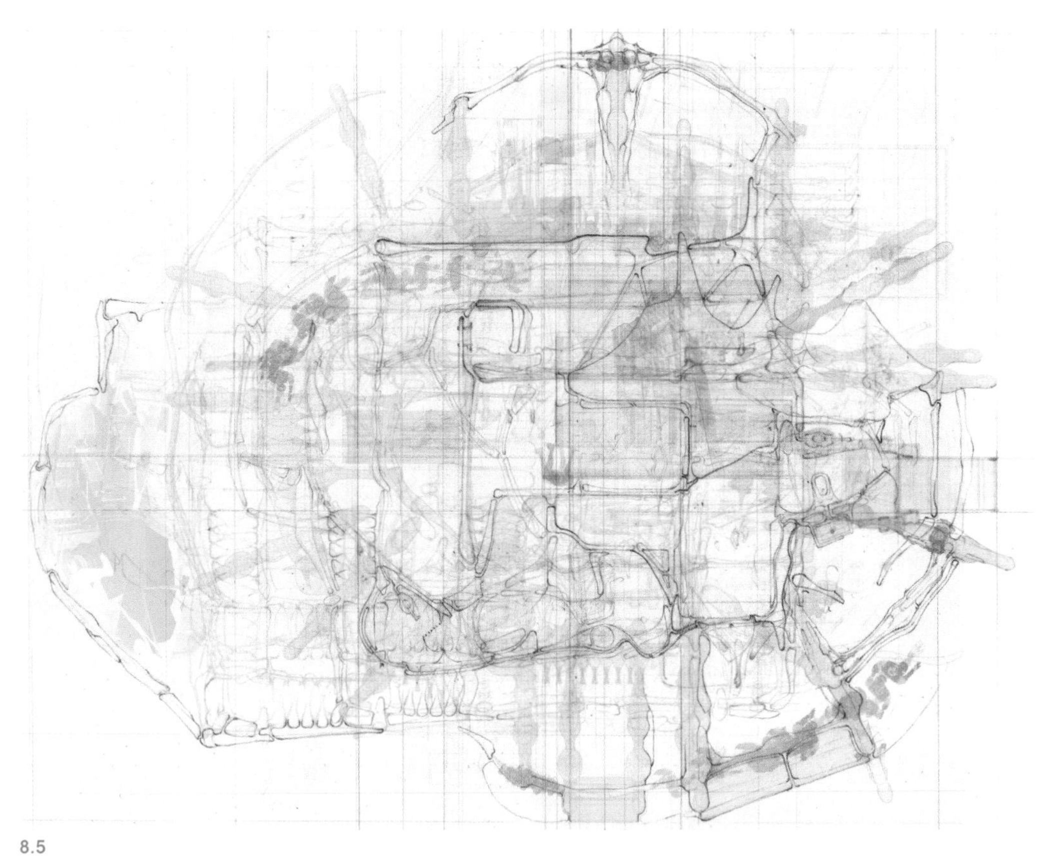

8.5

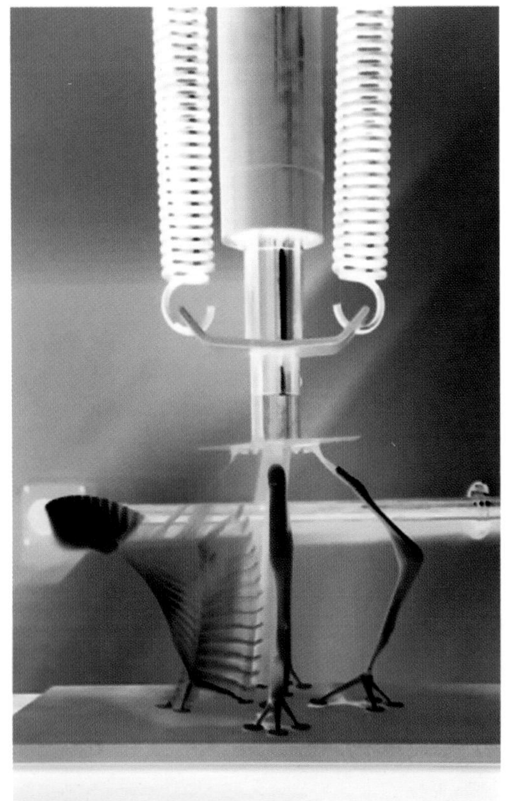

8.6

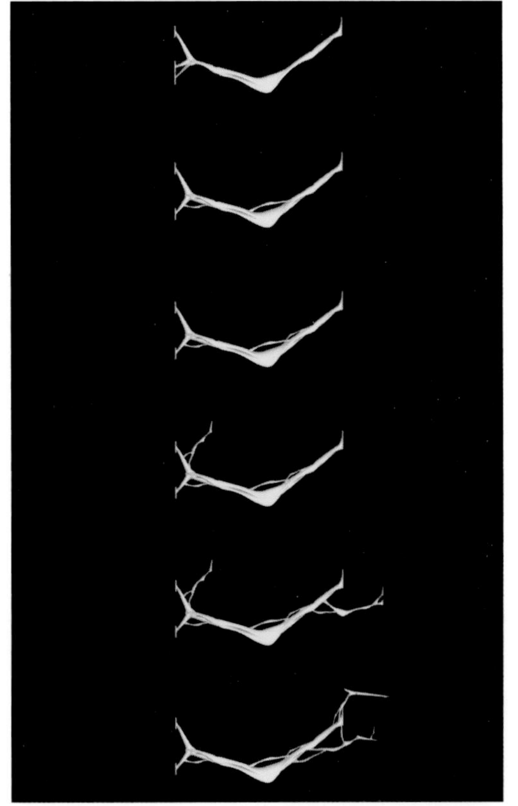

8.7

8.8

8.9

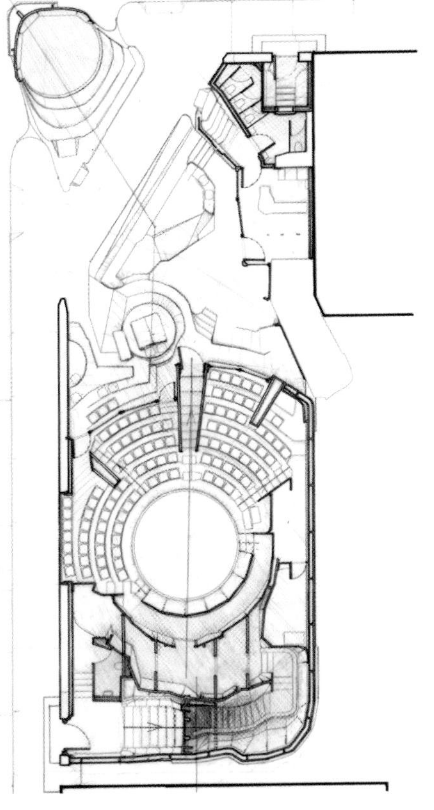

8.10

8.11

8.12

8.13

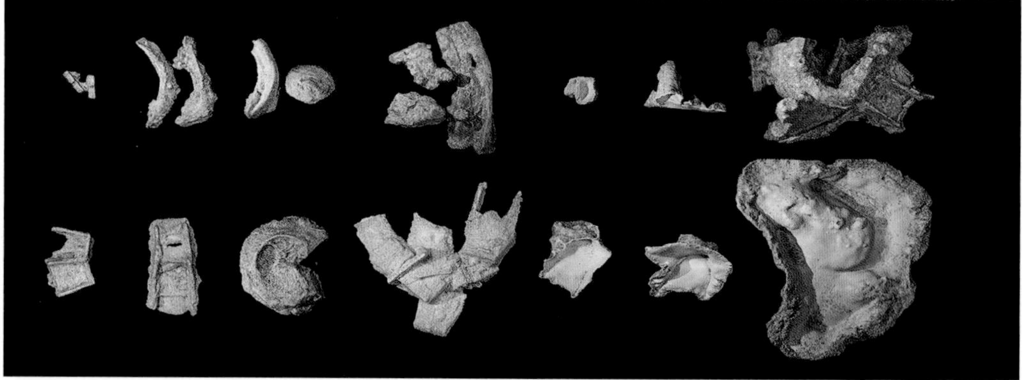
8.14

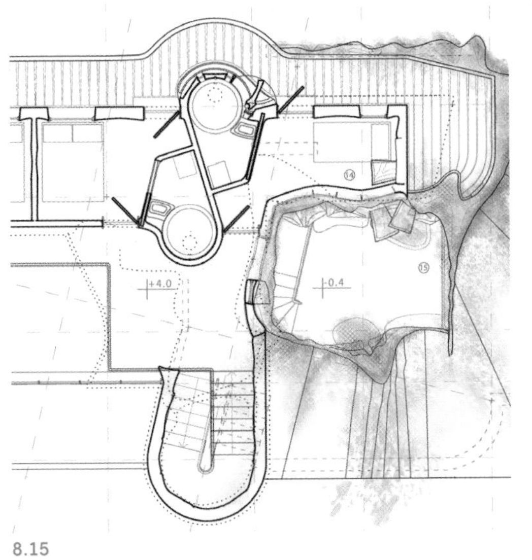

8.15

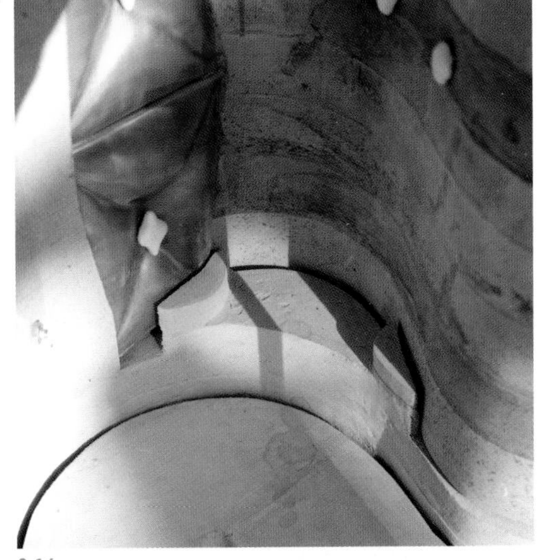
8.16

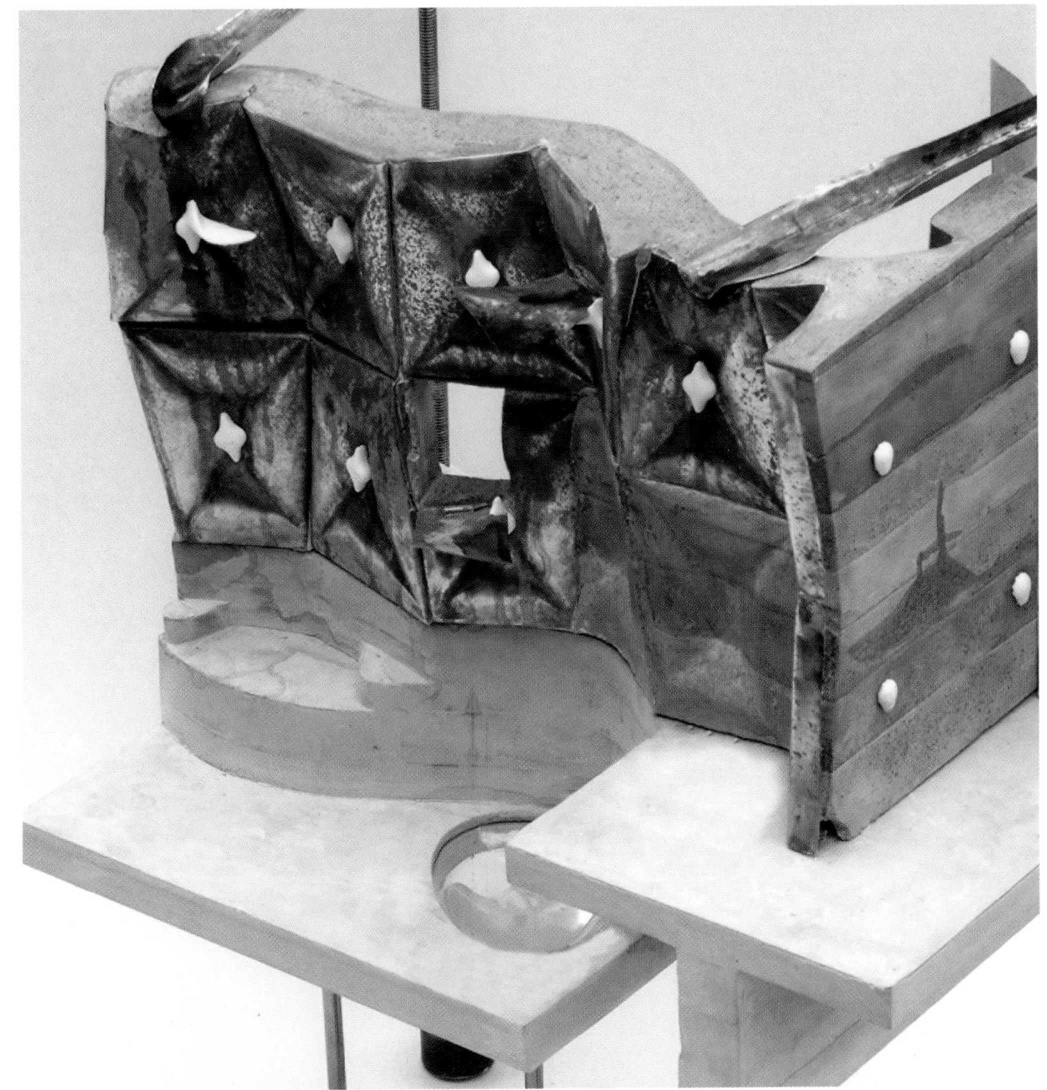
8.17

8.18

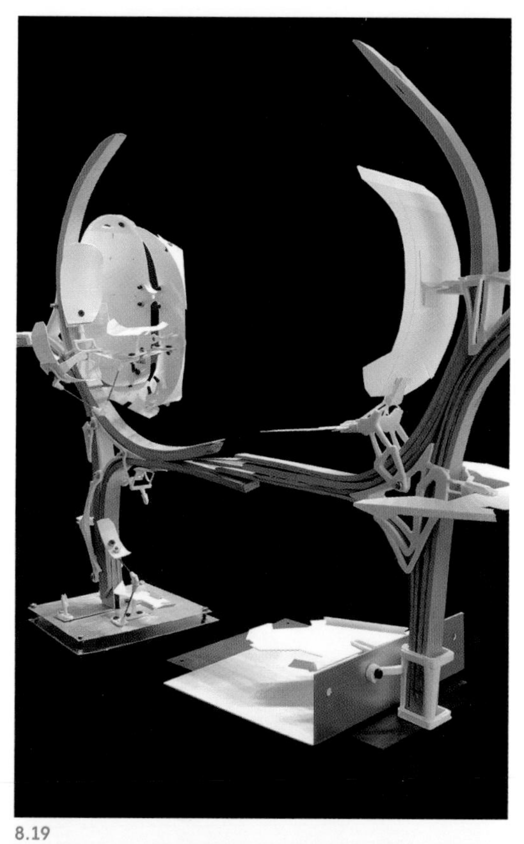

8.19

8.20

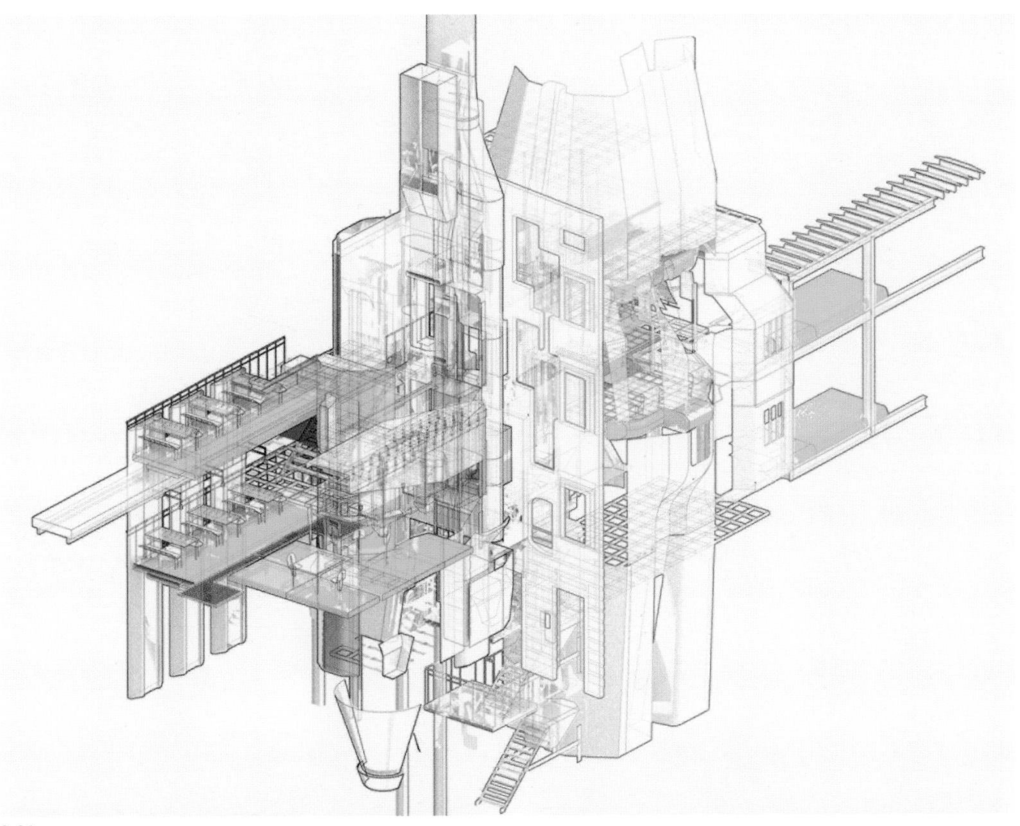

8.21

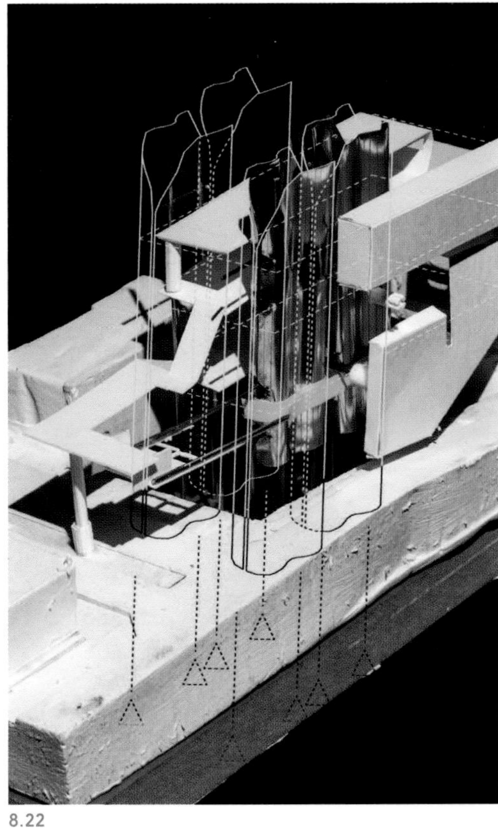

8.22

8.23

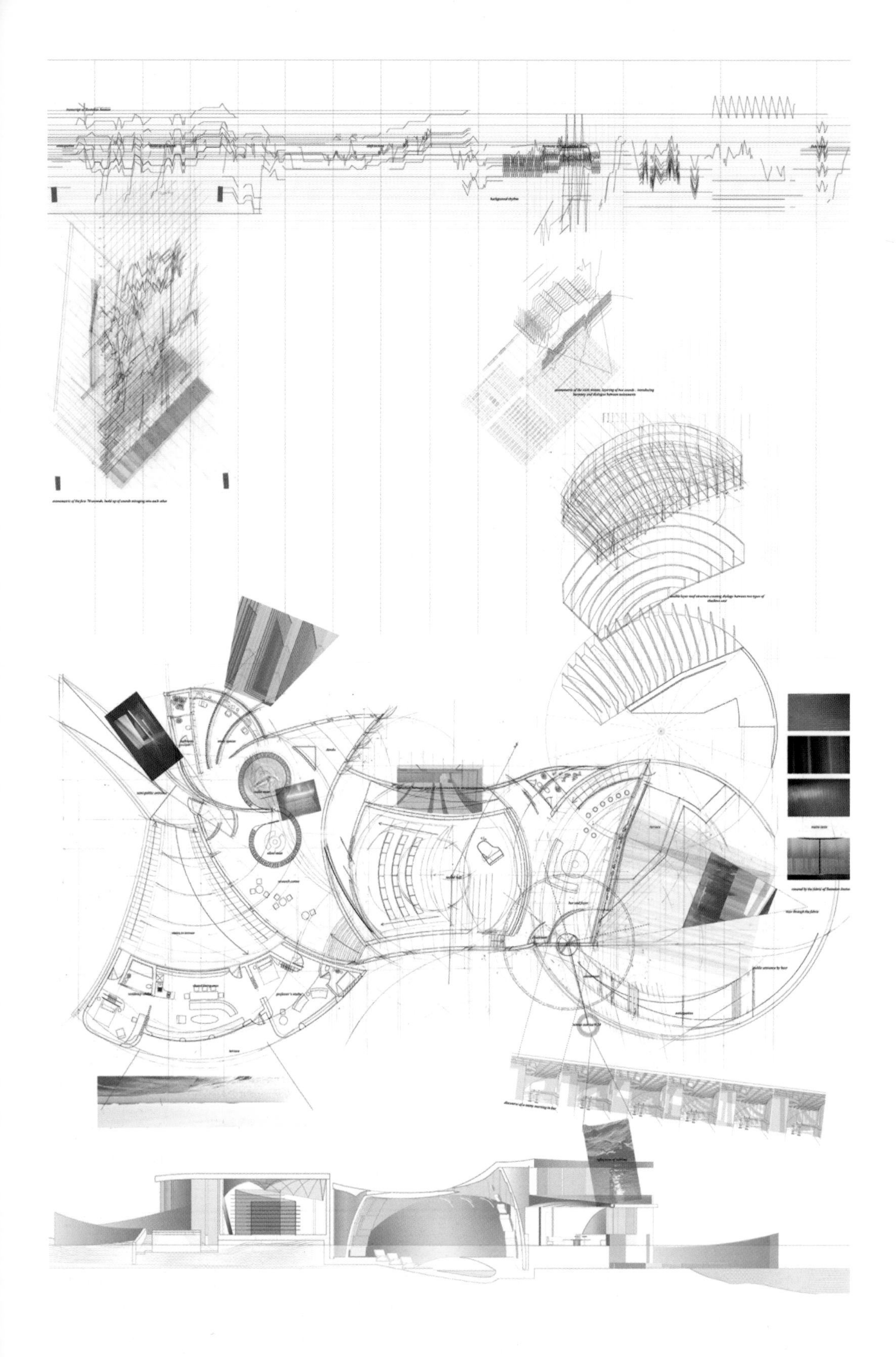

8.24

8.25

8.26

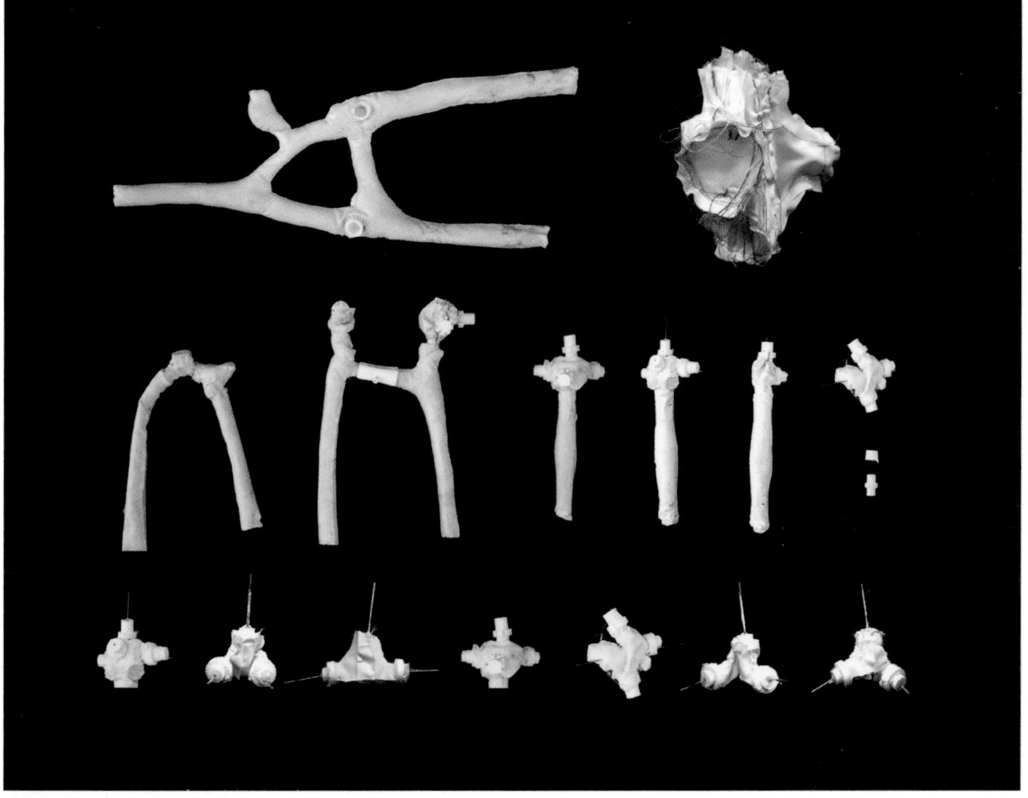

8.27

9.1

Superlatives

UG9

Jessica In, Chee-Kit Lai

This year, UG9 considered the possibilities of superlatives to explore and define architectural identities. Superlatives are about being true to yourself as a designer. By invoking a superlative state that explores the edges, exaggerations or extremes in conditions, language, behaviour and style, we aim to push and question the borders of the proper or 'normal'. Superlative architectures not only explore the extremes of the field but also solicit the best quality. We are critical of the use of superlatives in popular culture, where everything is reduced to the 'most important' and the 'best'. In UG9 this year, we re-examined this idea in the context of architecture.

Our field trip led us to Seoul, a city that embodies what the author Michael Breen observes in his book *The Koreans*: an ability to interpret foreign systems and develop them to the most extreme or successful, often outdoing their mentors. Our architectural propositions this year have ambitions of the same order, with projects considering superlatives across reality and illusion, collective and self-identity, and reconsiderations between viewer and occupant. In a city that has historically been seen as inward-looking, and that has raced through modernism and postmodernism within a couple of decades, our architectures offer a reframing of Seoul's identity on a global cultural stage. We aimed to address the qualities of the 'soft city' that Jieheerah Yun's *Globalising Seoul* identifies as priorities for invisible things: cultural, emotional and aesthetic measures that move beyond the hard, industrial city and emphasise speed and efficiency.

The mediation between matter and form, the relationship between design and occupation, the spatial implications of new technologies, and the subsequent restructuring of social relationships are all themes that continue to interest UG9.

Year 2
Weiting (Terry) Chen, Ernest Chin, Peter Cotton, Eudon Gray Desai, Dinu Hoinarescu, Ye Kim, Olivia Shiu

Year 3
Vitika Agarwal, Kai (Kelvin) Chan, Carlota Nunez-Barranco Vallejo, Wei (Eugene) Tan, Tom Ushakov, Sung (Ryan) Wong

Thanks to our consultants Marcus Cole, Matt Lucraft, Donald Shillingburg, Denis Vlieghe, and to Thomas Chu for our Summer Show mechanism design

Special thanks to our critics: Laura Allen, Iain Borden, Barbara-Ann Campbell-Lange, Nat Chard, Alessandro Conning-Rowland, Peter Cook, Christopher Daniel, Tamsin Green, Penelope Haralambidou, Simon Herron, Jonathan Hill, Freddie Hong, Steven Howson, Parker Heyl, Soohyeon Kang, Constance Lau, Evan Levelle, Claudia Orsetti, Bakul Pakti, Pedro Pitarch, Donald Shillingburg, Giles Smith, Mark Smout, Sarah Stevens, Sabine Storp, Mohammed Syafiq, Michael Tite, Michael Wagner

Special thanks to our show sponsors: Panopus Printing PRS Ltd

9.1, 9.15–9.17 **Ernest Chin, Y2** 'Itaewon Stacked Bathhouse'. A smorgasbord building proposal, showcasing a selection of media including hand sketches, conceptual models, unfolded drawings and a final model with animated projections. Sited on the boundaries of three distinct areas – Halal Hill, Homo Hill and Hooker Hill – the project proposes a double stacked bathhouse using layered drawings, an animated projection on a physical model and an exploded physical model. The lower tier consists of a series of salted soak baths, whilst the naturally warmer upper tier houses steam rooms. Strategic roof lights, voids, fenestration and double and triple height spaces offer glimpses of the site context to an otherwise deeply intimate building. The staircases connecting baths and steam rooms are on the outside of the building, allowing boundaries to be blurred between inside and out.
9.2, 9.18 **Wei (Eugene) Tan, Y3** 'South Korean Women's War Museum'. A museum proposal presented as an exploded large-scale model and a museum guide using unfolded orthogonal drawings. The museum's spaces sensitively combine the imperial with the domestic to evoke the memory of war as told by female survivors. Visitors are given a small unfolded museum guide to navigate the central space of the museum, including an exploded axonometric highlighting the different public and private zones of the museum. The proposed plan allows visitors to peel parts of the roof back to reveal internal plans underneath, with the inside of the roof showing perspective views of those areas. A section drawing shows visitors' experiences depending on the time of year.
9.3 **Tom Ushakov, Y3** 'Drawing a Parallel'. A proposal for an interactive painting device. In Korean culture, painted backdrops are used for formal events, such as a meeting between South Korean President Moon Jae-In and North Korean Supreme Leader Kim Jung Un. The device creates watercolour paintings of mountainscapes using recordings of up to two participants, and measures levels of intimacy between them.
9.4 **Tom Ushakov, Y3** 'Making a Scene'. A building proposal to be sited in front of the South Korean City Hall. The proposal allows for future summit peace talks between the South Korean president, the US president and the North Korean supreme leader. Optical illusion creates the appearance of fairness between the three when they meet.
9.5 **Carlota Nunez-Barranco Vallejo, Y3** 'Reinterpreting the Hanok House'. A 3D-printed model of a 360-degree multi-scale device, on a robotic arm used for animated projection.
9.6–9.7 **Carlota Nunez-Barranco Vallejo, Y3** 'Beehive Housing'. A proposed courtyard view and roof plan for a series of hyper-dense housing units that reinvent traditional beehive housing – homes made from circles of stones with domed roofs – allowing for triple occupancy per unit. The architecture plays with occupying the oblique, with certain conditions presenting a paradox of representation. This is a plan that looks like an isometric drawing.
9.8 **Olivia Shiu, Y2** 'Stereoscopic Photography Studio'. Sited in Itaewon in South Korea, this building proposal allows for five overlapping photography studios within a tight site. Inspired by cones of vision, the proposal is presented as isometric moment drawings.
9.9 **Sung (Ryan) Wong, Y3** 'Superlative Crit Machine'. A prototype for an interactive audio-visual monitoring device that tracks a panel of architectural critics through voice recognition. The device identifies generic superlatives in the critics' comments and, in turn, creates an uncomfortable consciousness.
9.10 **Kai (Kelvin) Chan, Y3** 'Virtual Dimensions'. An interactive installation of a spatial construct that exists only in social media space. The protagonist is able to have a dinner party, meeting or event with themselves by occupying the time lag that inherently comes with re-projecting a Facebook live feed.
9.11 **Weiting (Terry) Chen, Y2** 'Internet Spotter'. A dancer wears an interactive LED arm contraption that is responsive to an active internet signal. Through a carefully choreographed dance sequence, boundaries of internet black holes are revealed in the city, resulting in a light drawing.
9.12 **Weiting (Terry) Chen, Y2** 'Itaewon Cultural Centre'. An exploded axonometric projection of a building that acts like a giant staircase across a nine-metre drop site, thus, creating staggered platforms for cultural activities, market stalls and seating.
9.13 **Vitika Agarwal, Y3** 'Jongno-gu Sleep Centre'. A physical model inspired by *pungsu* (Korean geomancy) of a sleep centre sited next to the Changdeokgung Palace, that takes the shape of hills surrounding a valley. The outer buildings provide public activities, such as a tea house, baths and saunas, whilst the more intimate multi-tiered sleep pods are located in the central deep basements.
9.14 **Ernest Chin, Y2** 'Rain Show(er)' This installation recreates the sensation of Korean rain using only light and sound. Motion sensors detect the presence of people in the space and activate the upside down rain in recognition of Seoul being on the opposite side of the world to London.

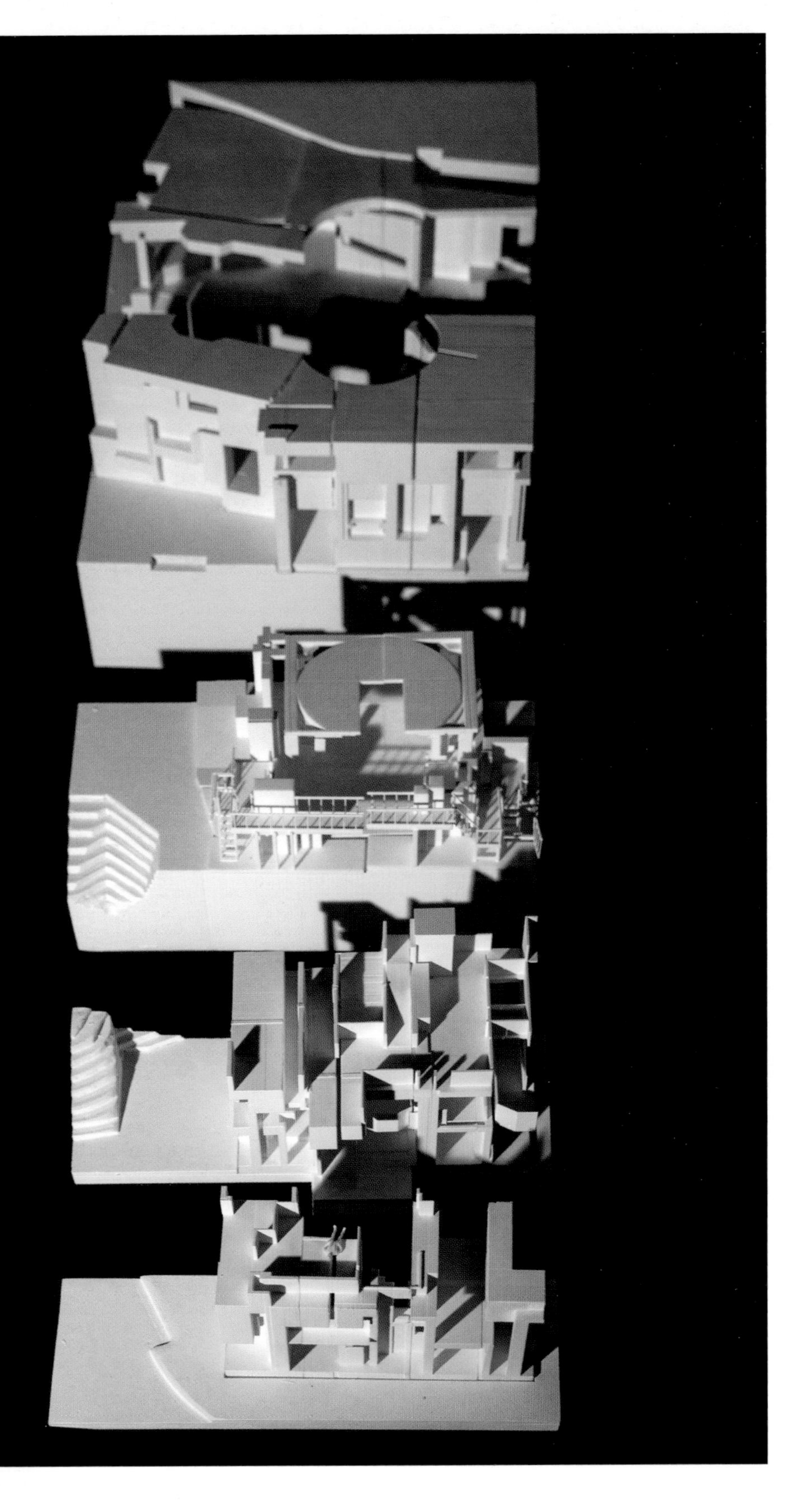

9.2

9.3

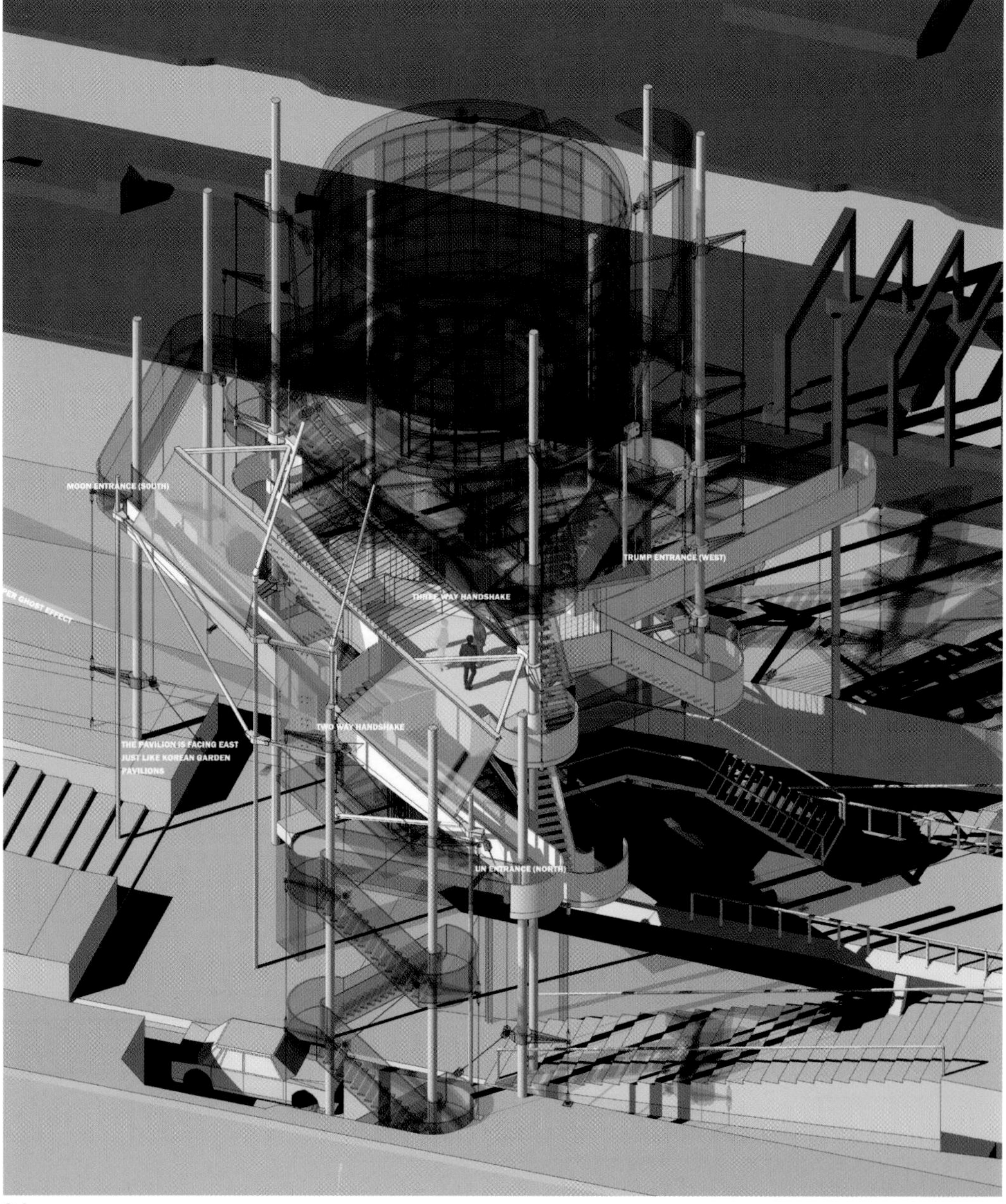
MOON ENTRANCE (SOUTH)
TRUMP ENTRANCE (WEST)
THREE WAY HANDSHAKE
TWO WAY HANDSHAKE
THE PAVILION IS FACING EAST
JUST LIKE KOREAN GARDEN
PAVILIONS
UN ENTRANCE (NORTH)

9.4

9.5

9.6

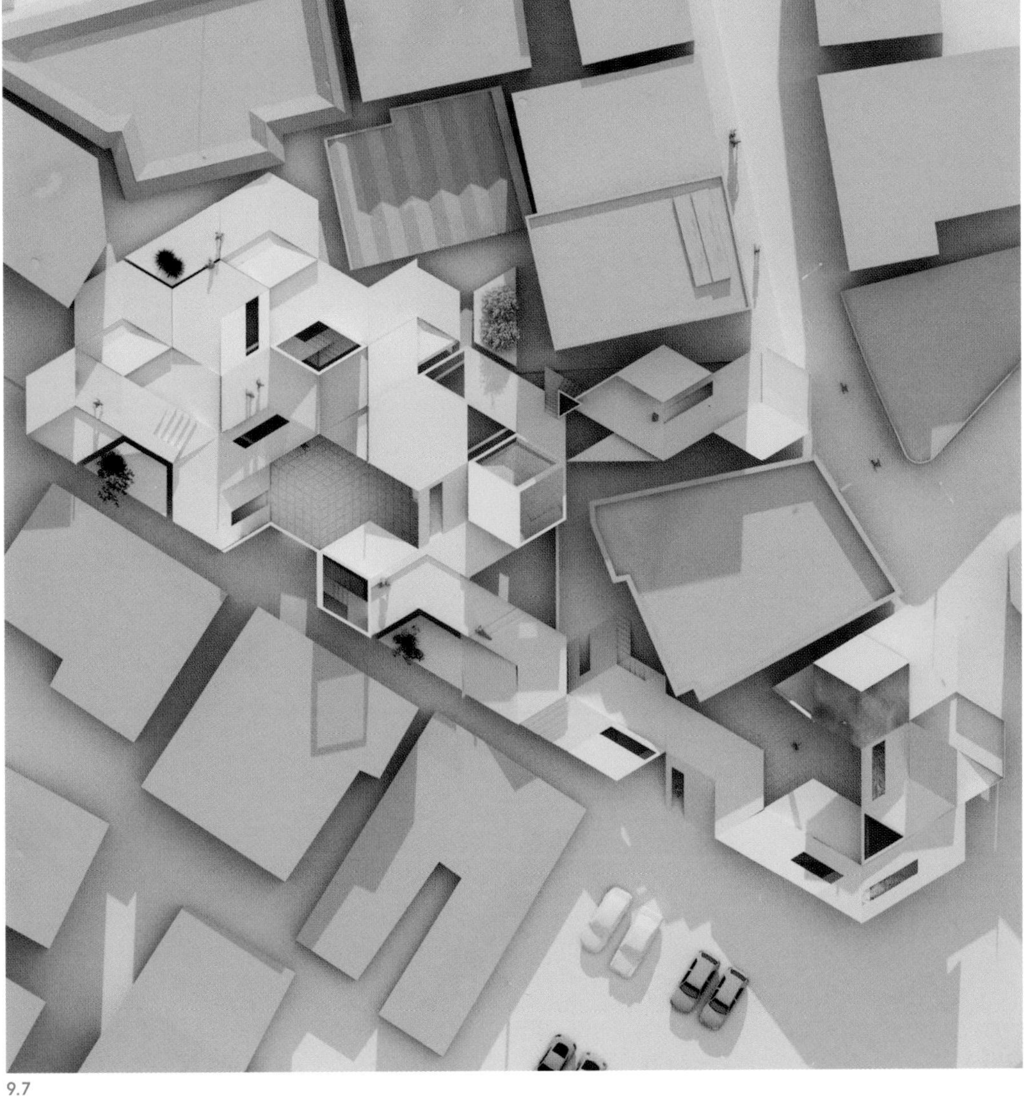

9.7

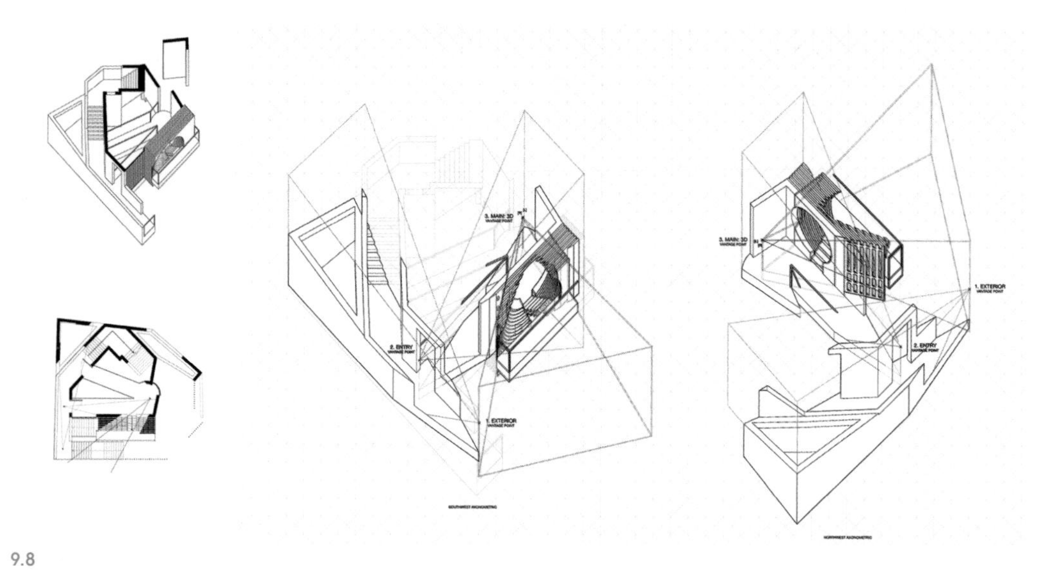

9.8

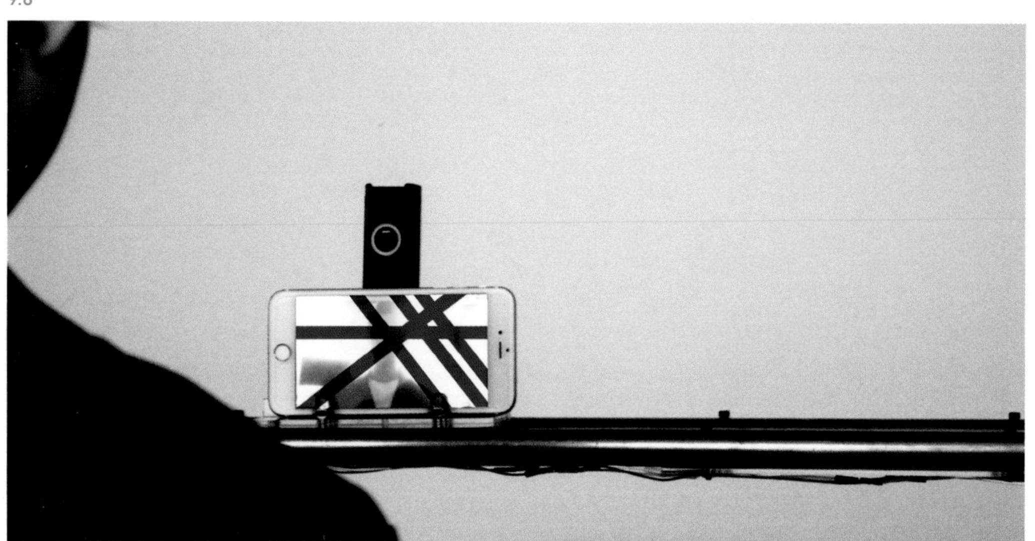

9.9

9.10

9.11

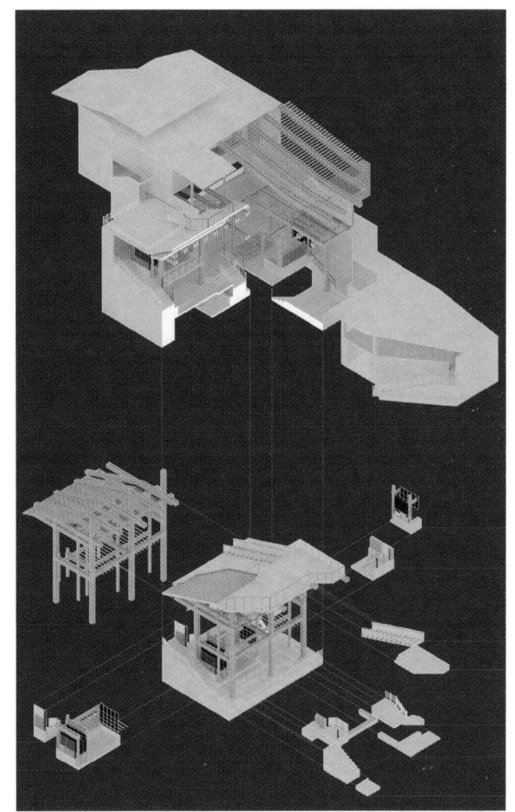

9.12

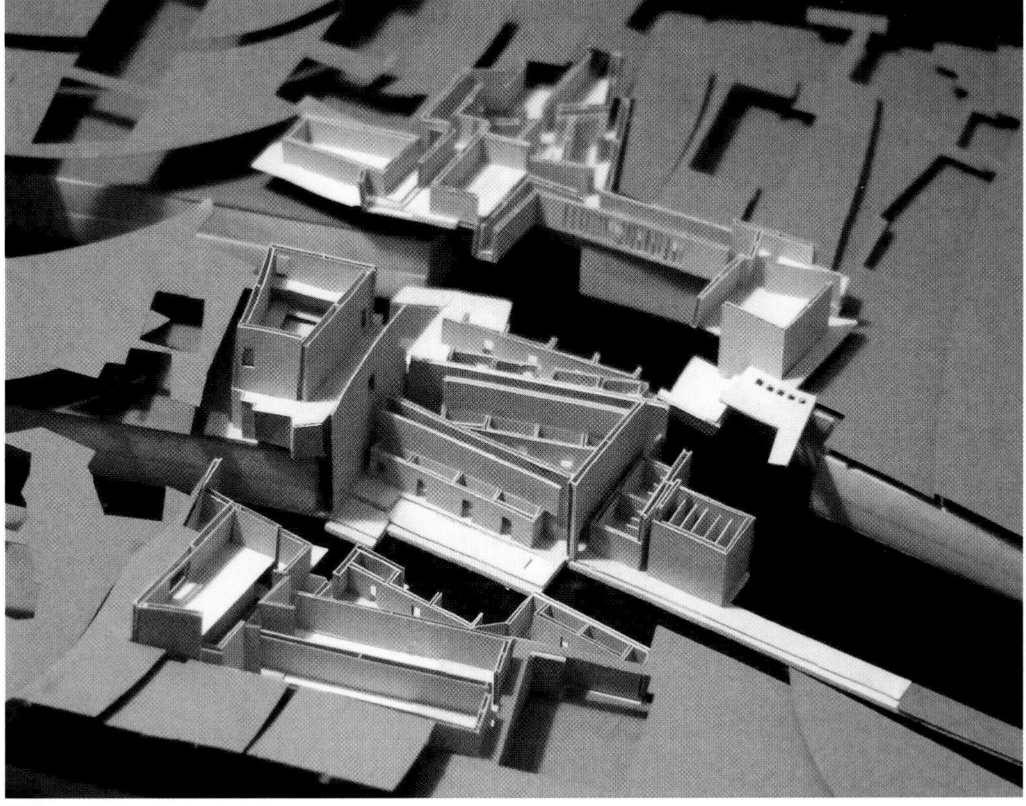

9.13

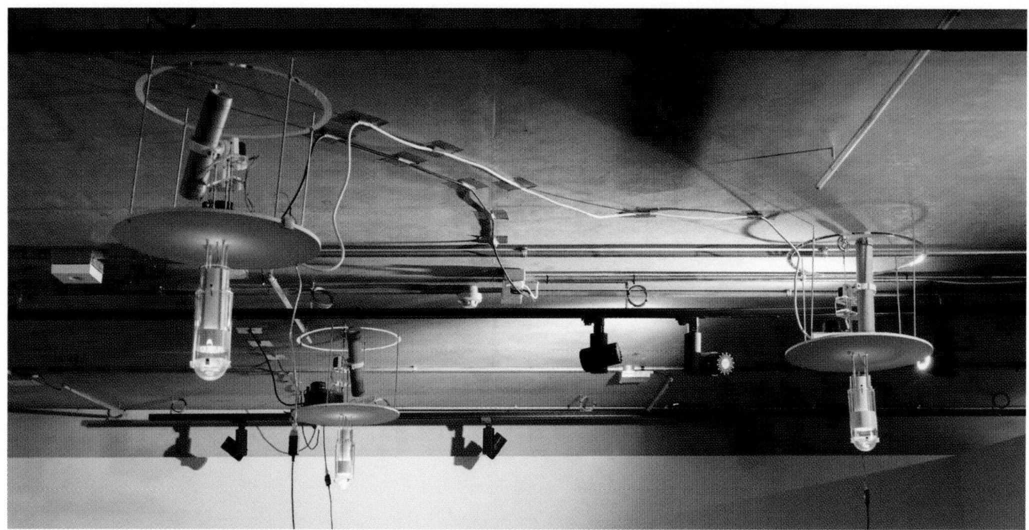

9.14

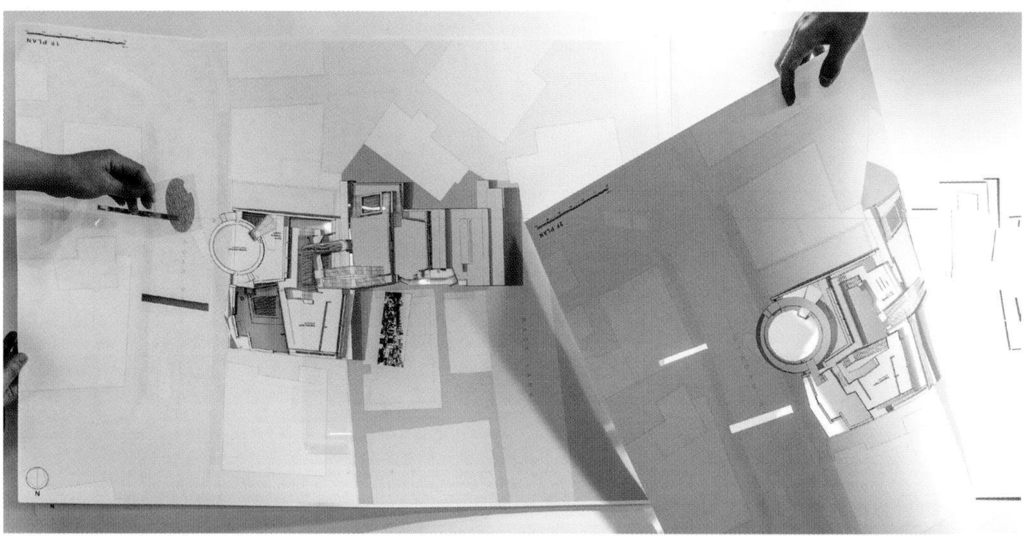

9.15

9.16

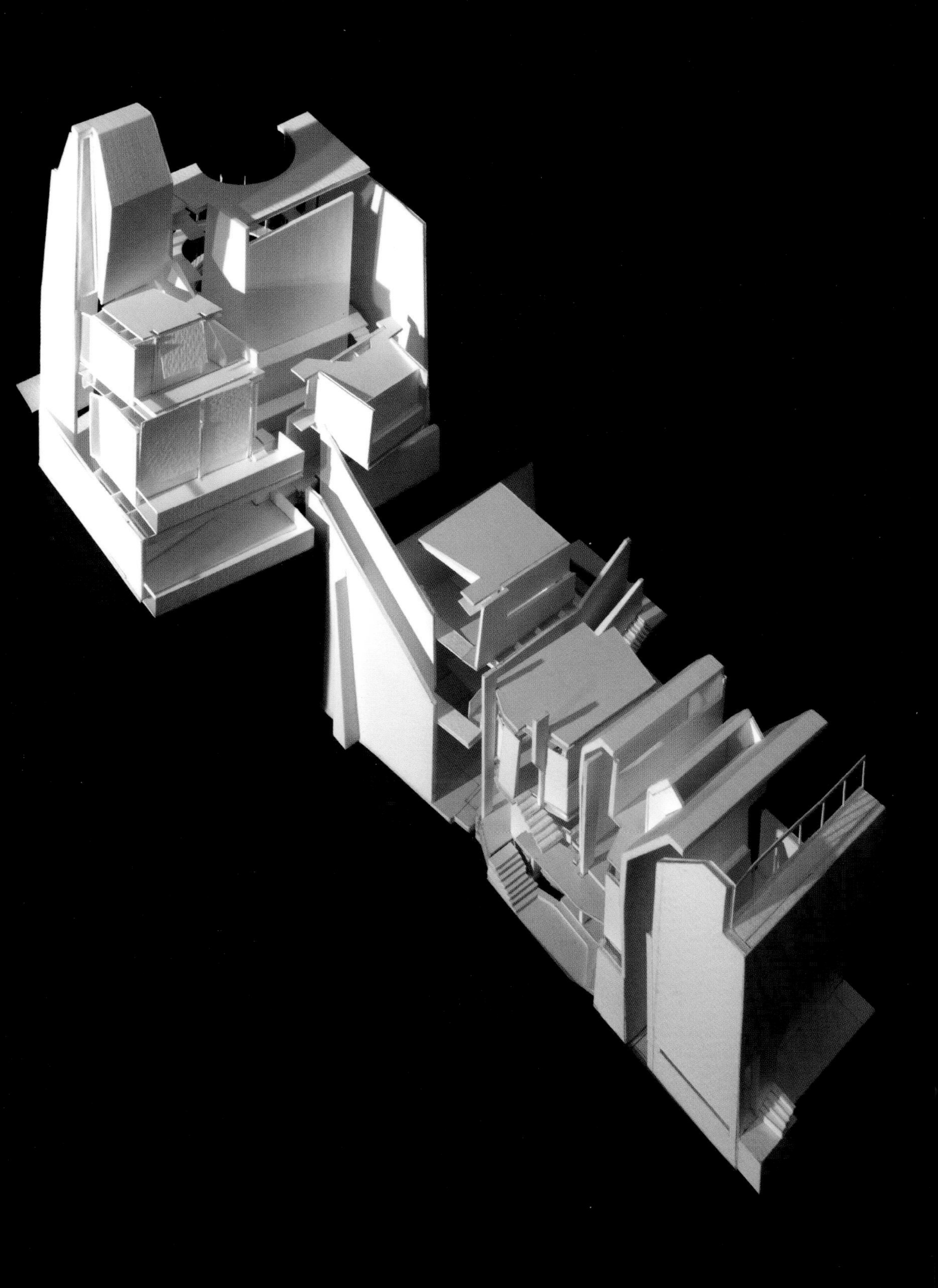

9.17

9.18

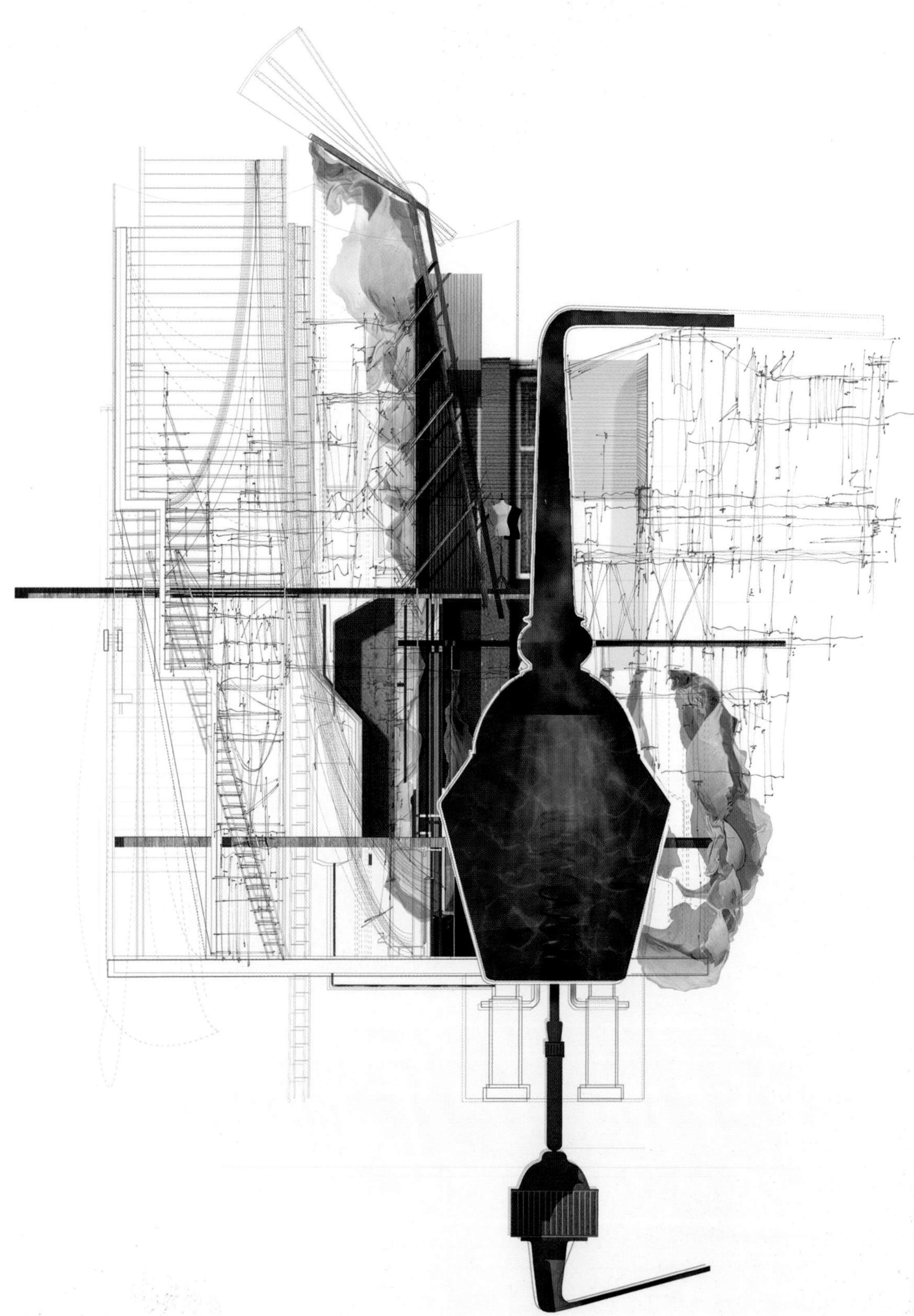

10.1

Reality and Other Stories UG10

Pedro Pitarch, Sarah Stevens

'What you're seeing and what you're reading is not what's happening.'
Donald Trump, 24 July 2018

This year, UG10 were interested in design as a way to challenge the stories we build around ourselves. These stories govern our world, defining our actions and their implications; from the stories we tell ourselves to those told to us, and the stories woven around us by the media that become more real than we are. Our built environment grows from these stories, offering them physical form so that they submerge us and influence our perception of reality. From the skyscrapers of Manhattan to King Ludwig's castles in Bavaria, all embody stories interpreted as truths. In challenging this, we draw forth architectures that inhabit alternate presents, making new realities visible through shifts in thought. Such architectural interventions offer a critique of contemporary society, whilst also proposing new routes forward. Research is rapidly superseded by individual architectural languages.

We explored the fractures in our constructed world to navigate crumbling landscapes of thought, divining individual trajectories to narrate stories from our own critical positions. Our stories lie shattered around us, as we attempt to navigate a world dominated by uncertainty and impermanence. Our desire for understanding is overwhelmed by a never-ending stream of information. Truth has become multiple; misinformation and 'fake news' contort our view and have become new threats to democracy. Brexit has threatened our belief in government, whilst the US enters a world inhabited by multiple truths, where history is being rewritten. All the while, unimagined storms ravage, heatwaves parch, mental health issues spiral and untold species silently disappear. We have reached an impasse, for which new stories are needed before our future is lost.

The Netherlands, a constructed breathing machine woven from stories, was home to many of UG10's explorations this year. We challenged assumed, emerging and infiltrated stories to propose new futures and realities in speculative proposals for new institutions sited within fabricated landscapes. We asked what architectures might inhabit such a world of uncertainty? What if we discard the false reassurances and illusions of control to seek out creativity in the contradiction and poetry of impermanence?

Year 2
Sumayyah Jannat, Evelyn Jesuraj, Su (Yen) Liew, Jiying (Emily) Luo, Sarfaraz Salim, Anastasiia Stoliarova, Sinziana Vladutu, Wenxi Zhang

Year 3
Alexander Balgarnie, Arseniy (Danya) Baryshnikov, Amanda Dolga, Noriyuki Ishii, Megan King, Thomas Roylance, Jake Williams

Special thanks to our technical tutors Peter Lenk, Jack Morton, and to Jason Coe, Matthew Turner, Charlotte Bovis and Sarish Yarish for their digital workshops

Our thanks to OMA and MVRDV, for generously opening their offices to us during our field trip, with particular thanks to Maria Aller, Ana Melgarejo and Stavros Gargaretas

Thank you to all our critics for their invaluable feedback: Laura Allen, Andrew Best, Iain Borden, Charlotte Bovis, Peter Cook, Simon Herron, Jessica In, Chee-Kit Lai, Ifigeneia Liangi, Bakul Pakti, Jonathan Paley, Matthew Rosier, Sara Shafiei, Giles Smith, Mark Smout, Sabine Storp, Uieong To, Martin Walsh

10.1, 10.12–10.16 **Megan King, Y3** 'The Lijnbaan Seam, Rotterdam'. Part of the 1950s reconstruction of Rotterdam, the Lijnbaan was the fashionable home of boutiques and jazz clubs. By the 1990s, however, it had descended into another form of notoriety: vandalism and crime. This project aims to revitalise the area, echoing its heritage in a sustainable couture fashion house for independent makers. Challenging fast fashion, it utilises organic fibres for the fabric of both the garments and the architecture. Embedded processes – such as the growing of organic fibres and natural dying and drying of fabric – feed the architectural language. The project is a social commentary on sustainable fashion and highlights the potential of organic fibres by offering an alternative sustainable reality that clothes both people and architecture. 10.1 shows the southern end of the site, highlighting the water tanks and drying racks used in the production of organic and recycled fabrics.
10.2–10.4, 10.6 **Amanda Dolga, Y3** 'Head in the Clouds, Rotterdam'. In this project, digitally induced weather inhabits a re-imagined data centre. There are over 7,500 data centres worldwide, with over 2,600 in the top global cities alone, and an estimated construction growth of 21% per year through 2018. The average data centre consumes over a hundred times the power of a large commercial office building, whilst a large data centre uses the electricity equivalent of a small US town. This project critically reflects on the physical ramifications of the digital world. Climatic gardens, warmed by the residual heat of the centre, serve as direct indicators of data consumption, as internal weather systems, mists, clouds and rain are induced when internal climate tipping points are reached.
10.5 **Su (Yen) Liew, Y2** 'Parliament Playground, London'. In the midst of the current political turmoil, this project takes a critical look at contemporary politics, challenging the separation of the populace from the governance of their country and the inner battles of the power hungry. The speculative proposal re-envisions the Houses of Parliament as a playground fuelled by commentary on its entrenchment in age-old traditions and rituals. A new 'House of Peoples' is proposed to remove the physical barriers and allow the populace to take an active, welcome role in the governing of their country.
10.7 **Jake Williams, Y3** 'Institute for Transient Populations, Rotterdam'. This project responds to dramatic changes in social patterning and the absence of an appropriate housing to compensate. The failure of the housing market to evolve with the rapidly changing patterns of living means that people not only cannot afford to live where they want, but often cannot live the way they want. A collective housing prototype views shared resources as an exciting prospect and a way of fostering a community.
10.8 **Alexander Balgarnie, Y3** 'Housing Prototype, Rotterdam'. This project proposes an institution that combines community facilities with temporary housing for displaced individuals and families, and understands architecture as a spatial and technical offering for the user/inhabitant. The approach is a structural response to questions of use, sustainability and ecological crisis. The strategies employed eliminate waste and throwaway culture.
10.9 **Arseniy (Danya) Baryshnikov, Y3** 'Unveiling the Unreal, Whitehall London'. Drawing on Jean Baudrillard's 'Hyperreality', this project challenges the existing symbolic landscape of Whitehall through the addition of architectures to re-frame it as 'pure form'. This subversion of the function of Whitehall's monumental architecture aims to challenge the saturation of overlaid narratives that are endlessly echoed by the media.
10.10–10.11 **Thomas Roylance, Y3** 'Van de Maas, Rotterdam'. A jenever distillery operates on a number of time-scales, from the finely tuned malting and distilling timetable to the centuries-old lineage of distillers on the Nieuwe Mass. This project challenges the notion of buildings as static. It promotes a vision of buildings as neverending continual processes, drawing them into a meaningful relationship with the locality.
10.17, 10.19 **Evelyn Jesuraj, Y2** 'Therapeutic Retreat from Cognitive Overload, Rainham Marshes, Thames Estuary'. Anxiety is seen as a new epidemic; in one study, one in five Londoners said that they had high anxiety. This project proposes a therapeutic retreat set within the salt marshes on London's outskirts, and offers a space for release from cognitive overload. Veiled by reeds encrusted with salt drawn up from the marshes, screens shield the occupants within. The project acts as a commentary on the impact of disconnection from the natural world, offering proposals for temporary respite within delicate pavilions of reed and salt that step across a fragile landscape within sight of the city. Experimental salt drawings explore the agency of salt within the work.
10.18 **Sarfaraz Salim, Y2** 'Conservational Research Facility, Southwark, London'. This project engages with the territory of memory within the fast changing infrastructure of Southwark. A re-imagined 19th-century warehouse acts as a repository for artefacts found during ever-present construction works. These artefacts become the focus of curiosity and research, as archaeologists populate hanging repositories of uncovered fragments.
10.20 **Noriyuki Ishii, Y3** 'Nature as Privatised Space, Parliament Square, London'. An invisible field of laws controls behaviour and construction in Parliament Square, making occupation or interventions a virtual impossibility. This speculative proposal subverts regulations, in the form of a transformational structure offering seating, shelter, water and nighttime lighting, under the guise of a maintenance platform that protects damaged grass and restores it with water and light.
10.21 **Amanda Dolga, Y3** 'Another Brick in the Wall, Whitehall, London'. This project explores the concept of 'hyper-surveillance' by establishing and mapping means of security, tracking and online data collection. It creates a testing ground for a space that exists between the physical and the digital. The plan reveals the unseen eyes of CCTV cameras that follow our every step within Whitehall. The act of seeing, the boundary between public and private, is being partially obliterated. The digital reality (the Internet), and data collection and tracking, reverse the act of seeing to the act of being seen, questioning one's privacy not only within the city but also within one's own room.

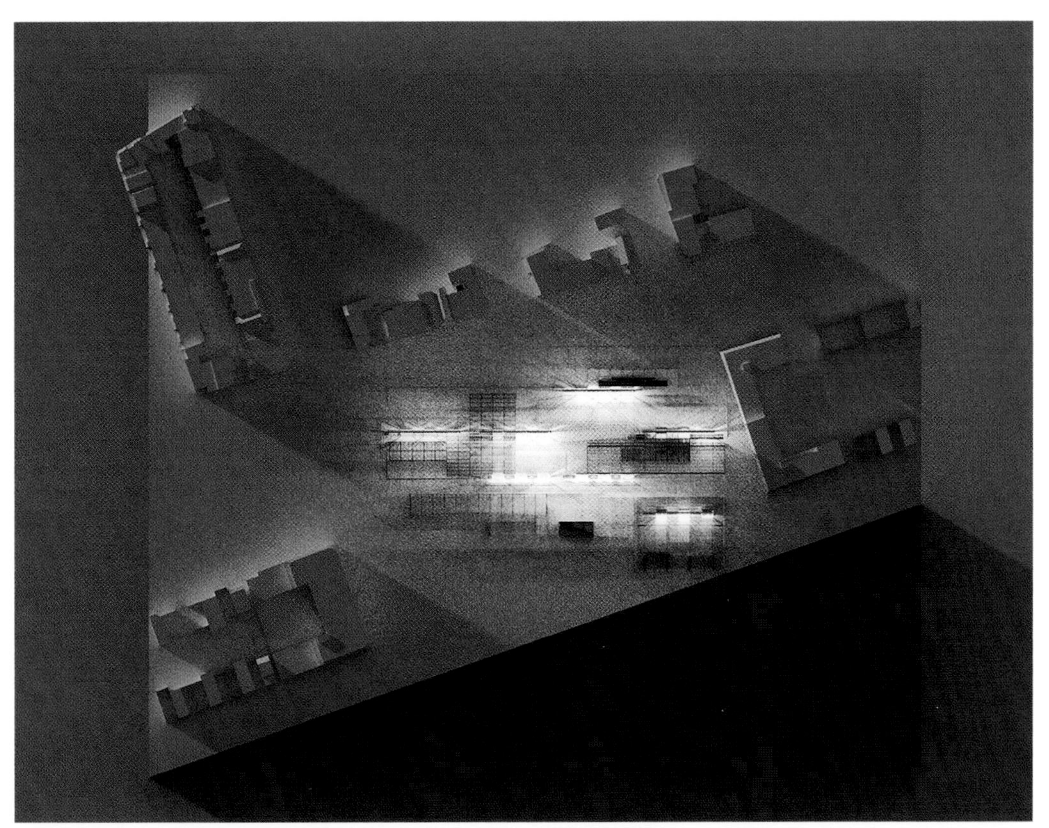

10.2

10.3

10.4

+28.0 m
+22.0 m
+18.0 m
+14.0 m
+10.0 m
+6.0 m
+0.0 m
-4.0 m
-8.0 m
-12.0 m
-16.0 m
-20.0 m

10.5

10.6

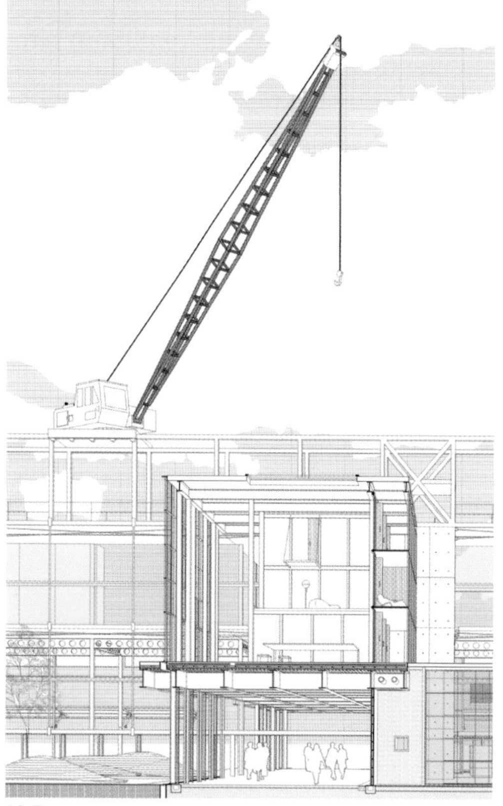
10.7

10.8

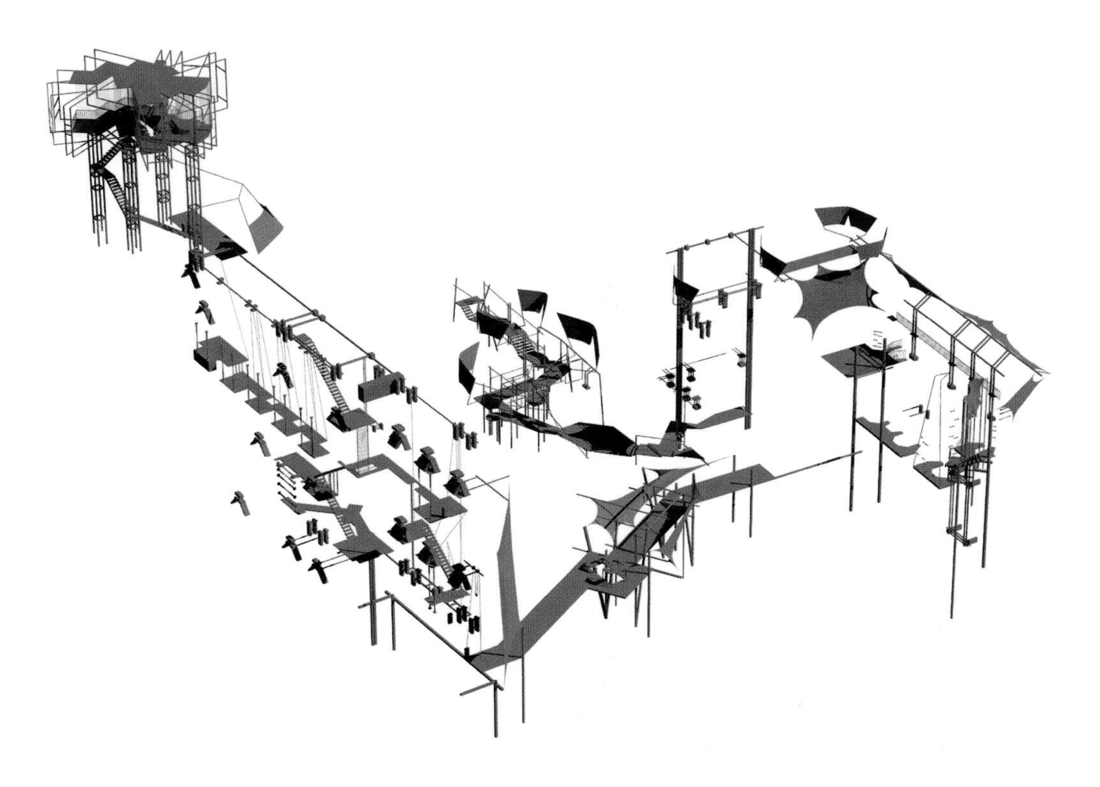

10.9

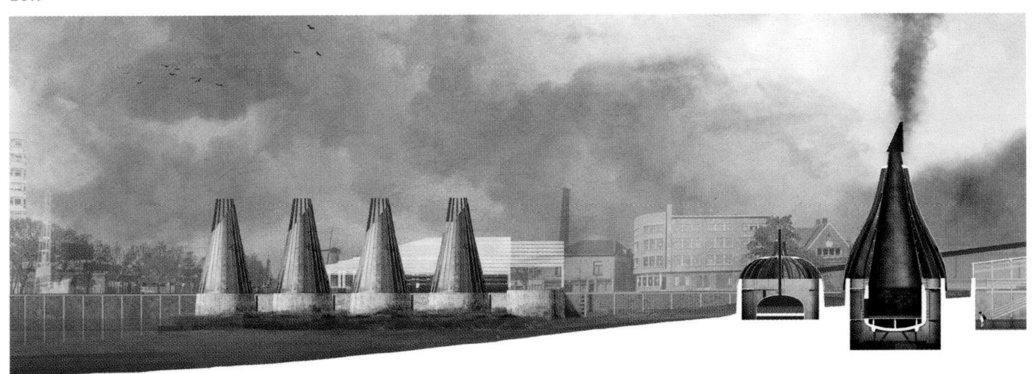

10.10

10.11

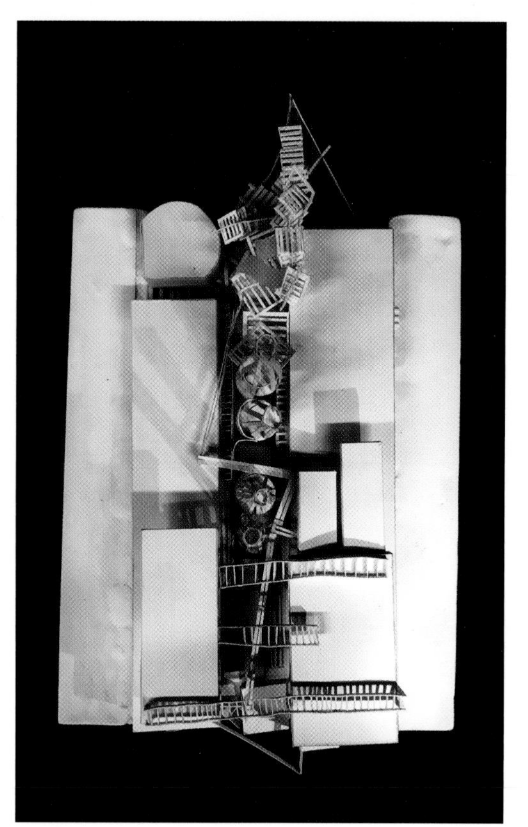
10.12

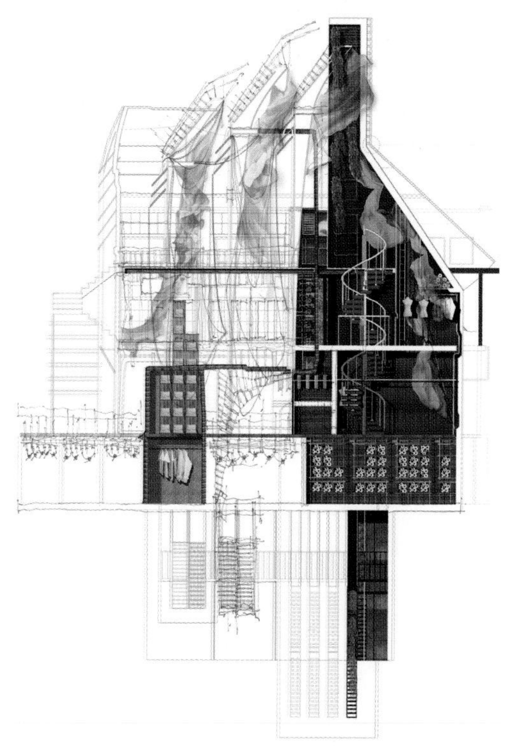
10.13

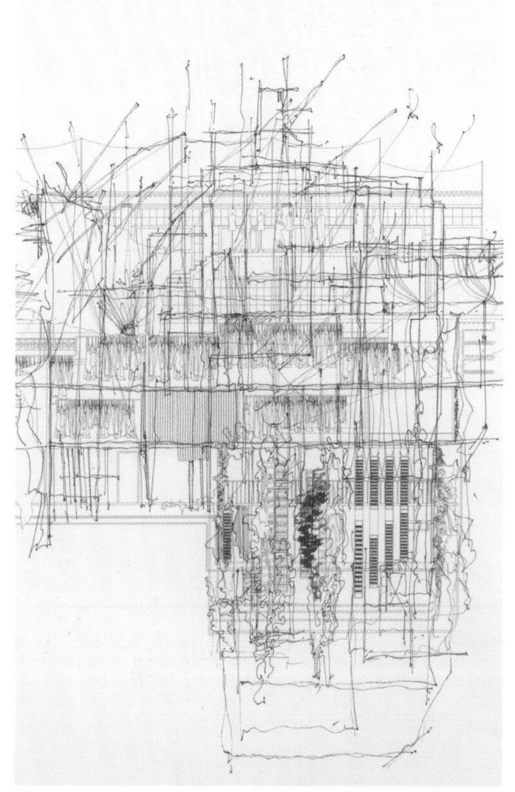
10.14

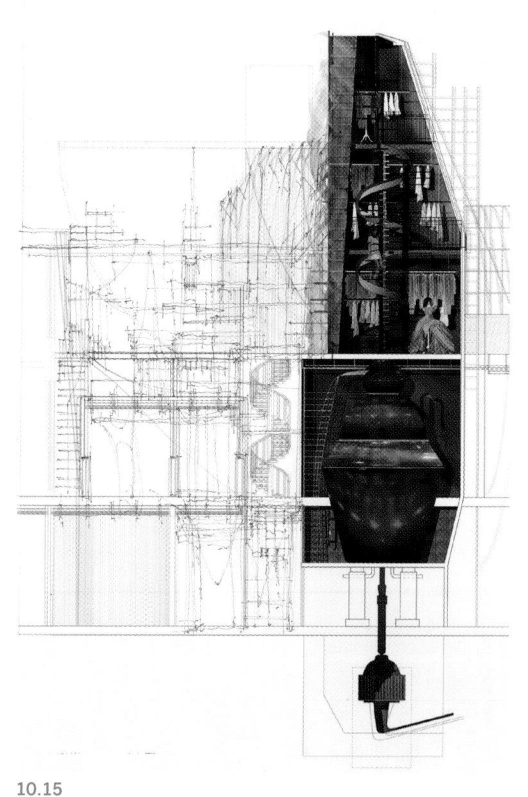
10.15

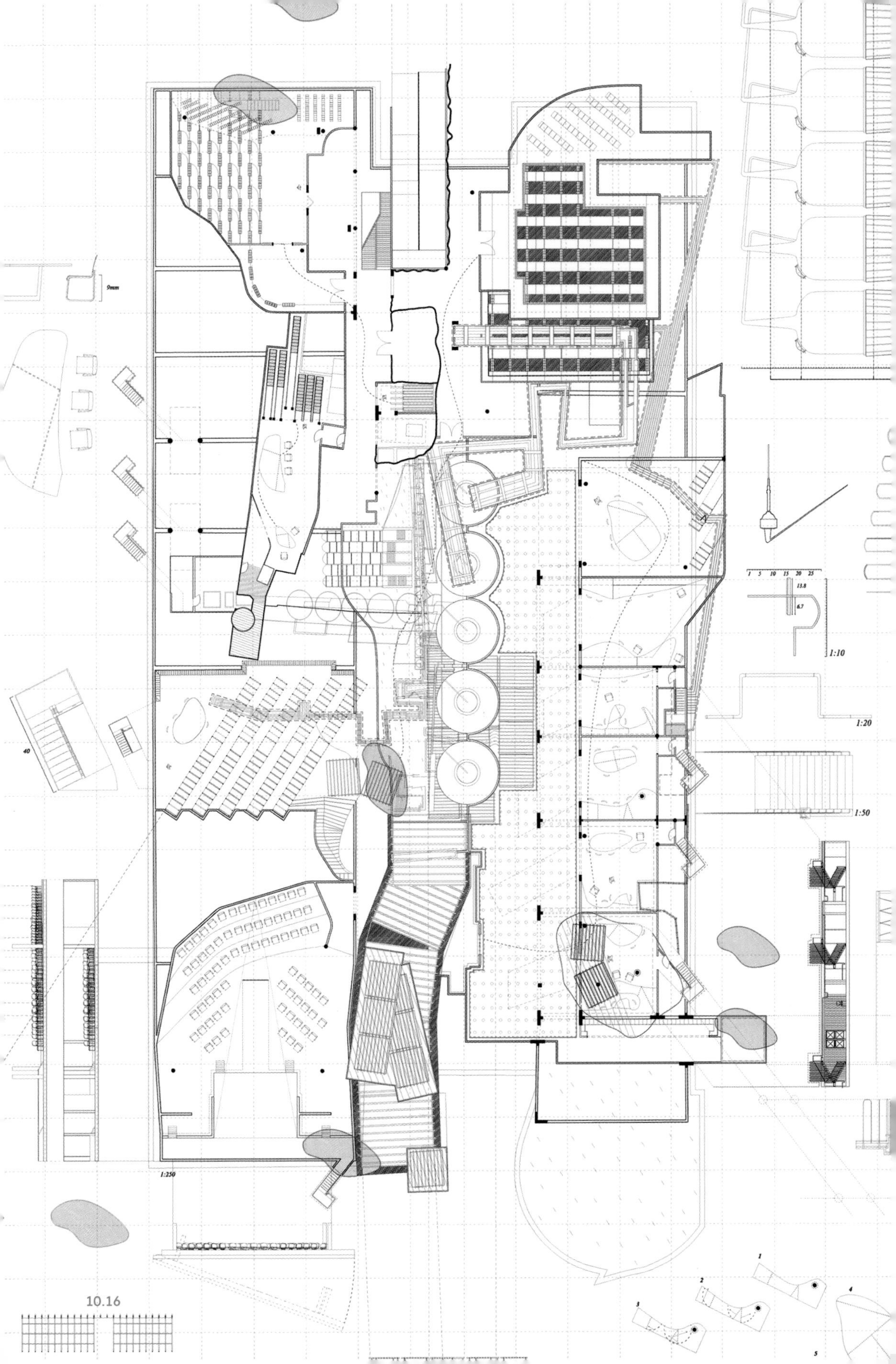

9mm
1 5 10 15 20 25
13.8
6.7
1:10
1:20
1:50
40
1:250
10.16
1
2
3
4
5

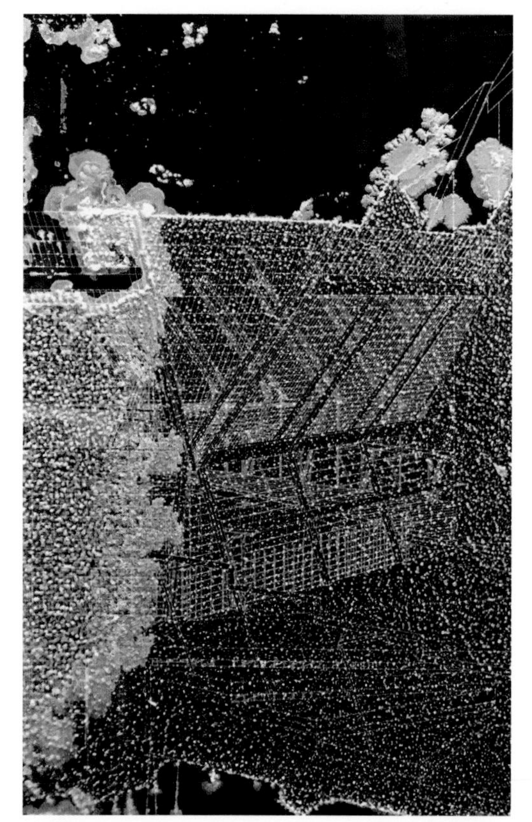
10.17

10.18

10.19

10.20

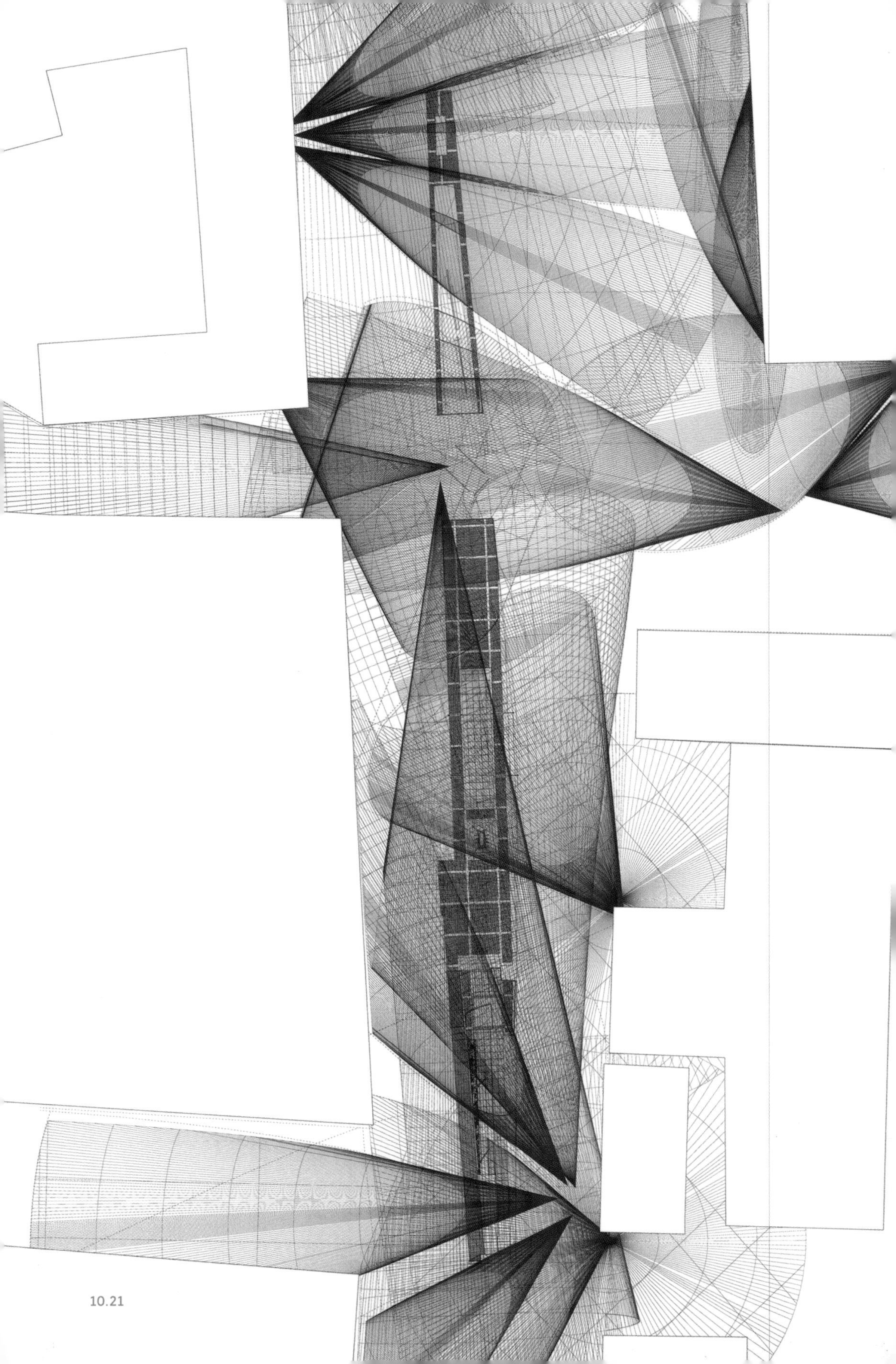

10.21

11.01

Entropic Encounters

UG11

Kostas Grigoriadis, Maren Klasing

UG11 operates with the idea of 'change' in mind. The aim of the unit is to embrace uncertainty in the digital age and address some of the increasing challenges of the Anthropocene. We argue that process-based, computational design thinking enables us to prepare for the complexity of an unpredictable future. The built environment needs to facilitate adaptation and abandon the unsustainable nature of static architecture and predefined, confined space. Contemporary times require a radically new repertoire and alternative design methodologies to cope with volatility and to deal with ambiguity. In UG11, we strive to create resilient and dynamic environments as a result of iterative processes, in response to major societal and environmental shifts. We aim for unique spatial experiences that achieve versatility through complexity, and discover distinct qualities through diverse unconfined and atmospheric spaces.

This year started off with physical, material experiments that explored notions of ambiguity, impermanence, emergence and entropy. We simulated natural processes of transformation where multiple forces resulted in surprising synergies and intriguing spatial ambiguities. Inspired and informed by these initial explorations, we identified computational design techniques that aimed to simulate such processes in the digital realm, generating various formations, versatile conditions and atmospheric qualities.

These experiments were then applied in the context of Moscow, where we visited mass-housing schemes with nondescript envelopes, abandoned buildings, obsolete facilities and monuments of past times, to observe and critique the impact and failures of repressive and purpose-built architecture. This dense urban fabric provided us with a fertile ground to formulate our briefs for architectural interventions that addressed environmental and societal issues like overpopulation and obsolescence, unregulated automation and alienation, unleashed consumerism and infrastructural collapse. We discussed how the inherent ambiguities of our process-based formations enabled our architectural concepts to adapt to the changing circumstances of a place, directly informed by the computational techniques we experimented with.

Alternative design methods served as thought vehicles with which to speculate on alternative architectures, investigating synergetic relationships between virtual, natural and artificial materiality with productive encounters of existing and envisioned environments. Architectural ecologies were developed that were relevant and resilient, comprised of diverse spatial qualities, characterised by ambience and immediacy, and ultimately redefined our perception of space and the way we relate to it.

Year 2
Hanna Abramowicz, Ahmed Al-Shamari, Poppy Becke, Angel Lim, Diana Marin, Zaneta Ojczyk, Jingxian (Jacquelyn) Pan, Chueh-Kai (Daniel) Wang, Kehui (Victoria) Wu, Sevgi Yaman

Year 3
Wan Feng, Celina Harto, Francis Magalhaes-Heath

Special thanks to our technical tutor Jeroen Janssen, and many thanks to our computing tutors and guest critics: Monika Bilska, Samuel Esses, Soomeen Hahm, Xuanzhi Huang, Martin Krcha, Igor Pantic

11.1–11.4 **Zaneta Ojczyk, Y2** 'Gallery Of Reclamation'. Moscow's landfills are reaching maximum capacity, due to the population only recycling 4% of their waste. This proposal aims to show the aesthetic side of recycling by demonstrating how disposed objects can have a second life. The gallery not only exhibits trash art, but is also an exhibit itself as it uses reclaimed plastic as a building material. The versatility of plastic is harnessed here to create varied internal spatial conditions that are manifested gradually as one walks through the gallery.
11.5–11.7 **Angel Lim, Y2** 'Transit Theatre'. The proposal for a drive-through theatre in the performance arts district of central Moscow provides an entertaining alternative to the frustration of being stuck in the city's seemingly neverending traffic jams. Three differently-sized stages are set along the road with pedestrian paths weaving above and below. Based on the varying lengths of each show, the road curvatures determine speed and time spent driving by these stages. The roof structure carefully curates light conditions and sightlines, whilst creating a sense of arrival. What was a congested 30-metre-wide motorway that was too difficult to cross is now a bridge over a continuous park, enabling a harmonious relationship between cars and pedestrians.
11.8 **Celina Harto, Y3** 'Grown Ornaments'. This project started with a series of material studies of salt and borax, observing the ornamental qualities and structural capacities that result from their growth over time. Following this, a series of urban interventions were designed across London that consist of bare frameworks to facilitate the growth of crystals that form pockets of space for people seeking refuge from the unpredictable London weather, whilst forming highly sculptural and ornamental aesthetic singularities in the urban fabric.
11.9–11.10 **Francis Magalhaes-Heath, Y3** 'Democratising the Edge'. This project salvages the vast amount of material produced by the demolition of the social housing developments in Moscow, and proposes their deposition on the city's river embankment. There, they are used to construct a landscape of living spaces that weave into public platforms and the corroded river bed to form a democratic landscape. Learning from the failures of other cities, the proposal aims to democratise the edge and reconcile public space so that it is accessible by all, with private housing that generates profit for the city. The diverse repertoire of spatial conditions and spectrum of building blocks established for the proposed reconstruction is informed by thorough research into deconstruction methods and weathering effects on materials in Russia's extreme climate.
11.11–11.14 **Jingxian (Jacquelyn) Pan, Y2** 'Youth Shelter'. This project proposes a shelter offering protection for teenagers that have been exposed to domestic violence. A range of spatial conditions are created with variably soft and hard materials to provide a unique sense of safety and relaxation for each occupant, whilst the organisation of the different interiors promotes the development of positive relationships amongst the teenagers.
11.15–11.19 **Kehui (Victoria) Wu, Y2** '*Krushchyovka* Disordered'. Responding to Moscow's demolition of the *Khrushchyovkas* – mass-housing built during the Soviet era – and arguing for the selective preservation of their architectural and cultural qualities, this project attempts to adaptively reuse two such buildings in Cheremushki by converting and extending them into a themed luxury hotel and *Khrushchyovka* museum. Observing the modular features of the existing buildings, the design disrupts and deforms the strict spatial grid whilst working with a programmatic transition gradient to bring the old and the new together in a coherent yet distinct proposal.
11.20–11.21 **Ahmed Al-Shamari, Y2** 'Parallel Pools'. In this project, a catalogue of variably porous walls are used to regulate atmosphere, light and ambience in a public bathhouse that acts as a vitrine for its concealed LGBTQ counterpart. The latter provides a network of spaces for bathing and relaxation for this persecuted and censored community in Moscow. Both parts remain contained in parallel realities, but they coexist in an architecture that enables their encounter through varying degrees of phenomenal and actual transparency, challenging that divide.
11.22, 11.25 **Hanna Abramowicz, Y2** 'Synthetic Garden'. This proposal is a response to the fact that we stigmatise technology by denying its natural aspects: mortality, fragility, complex interactivity, and its utter dependence on sometimes fitful flows of energy and material substance. An initial series of both physical and digital studies explore these abstract notions. The proposed landscape elicits a tender, reverential and nurturing attitude towards technology and artificiality.
11.23–11.24 **Chueh-Kai (Daniel) Wang, Y2** 'Communal Culinary Centre'. Inspired by the current Russian culinary revolution, this project creates a social hub for Moscovites, aiming to educate them through a shared dining experience. The building houses the ecology of cooking, from growing to recycling. At the intersection of three distinct volumes, spaces merge and transform towards an inner core of shared areas, where formal qualities shift and material properties adjust to the changing and overlapping spatial requirements.
11.26–11.27 **Wan Feng, Y3** 'Souvenir Tower'. This design proposal aims to promote traditional Russian crafts that have fallen under the radar despite their cultural significance and economic value, providing a livelihood for many. The building programme organises two main elements in a vertically spiralling arrangement that is part monument and part mall, incorporating functional workshop facilities for artisans with a visitor route that allows tourists to view and experience the various manufacturing processes and purchase their products. The tower is supported by an exoskeleton that inherits the ornamental quality of the souvenirs and identifies their structural potential.

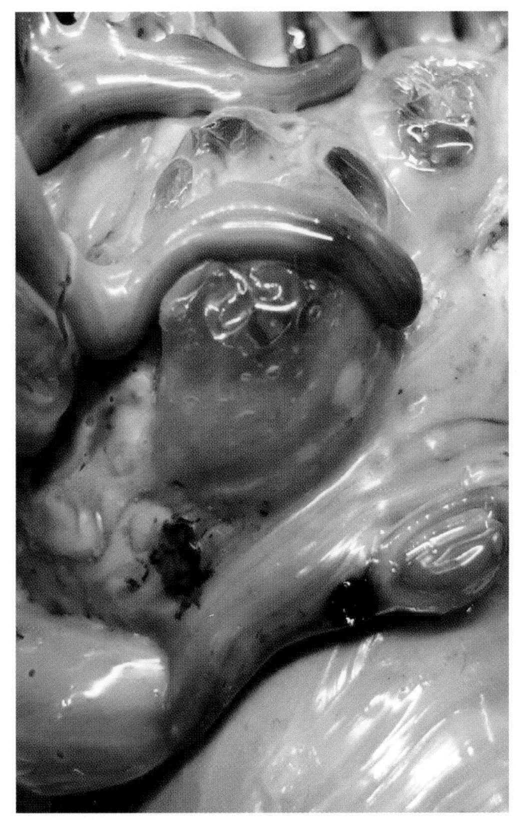
11.2

11.3

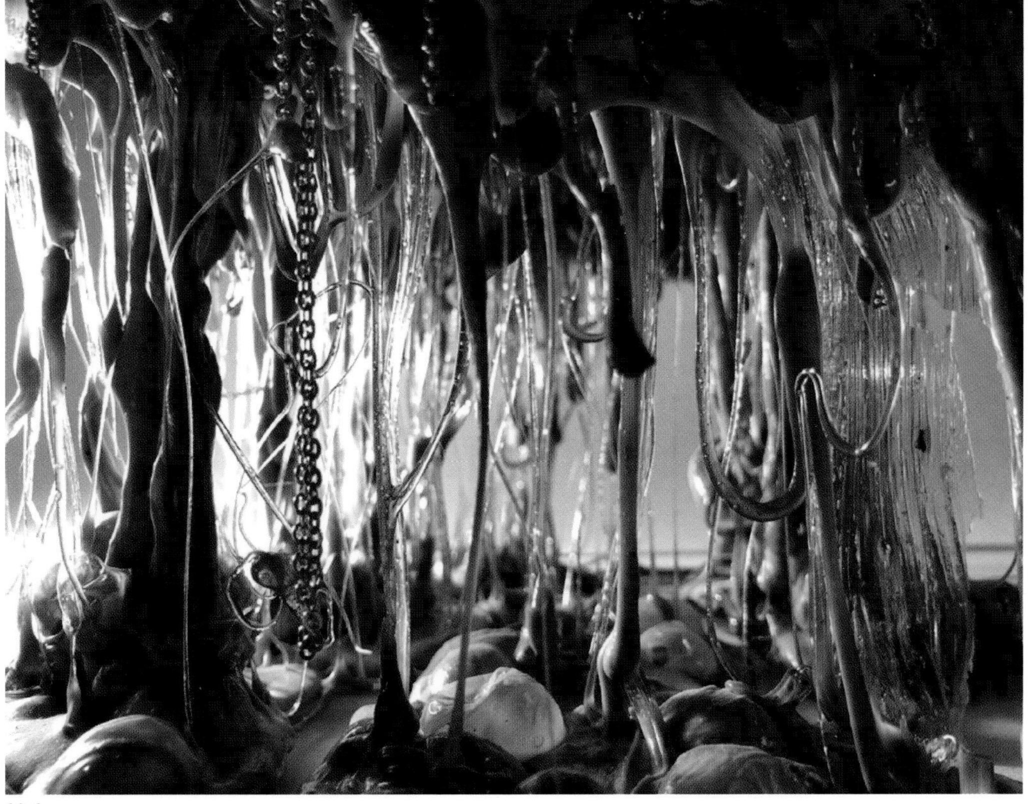
11.4

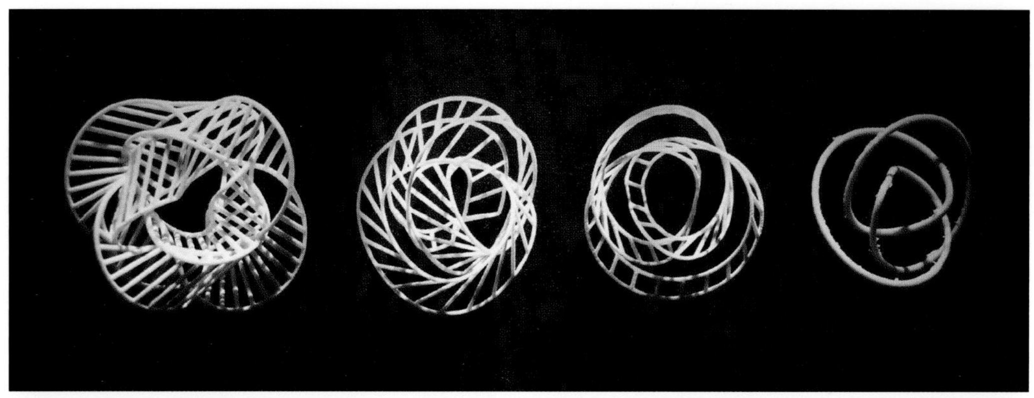

11.5

11.6

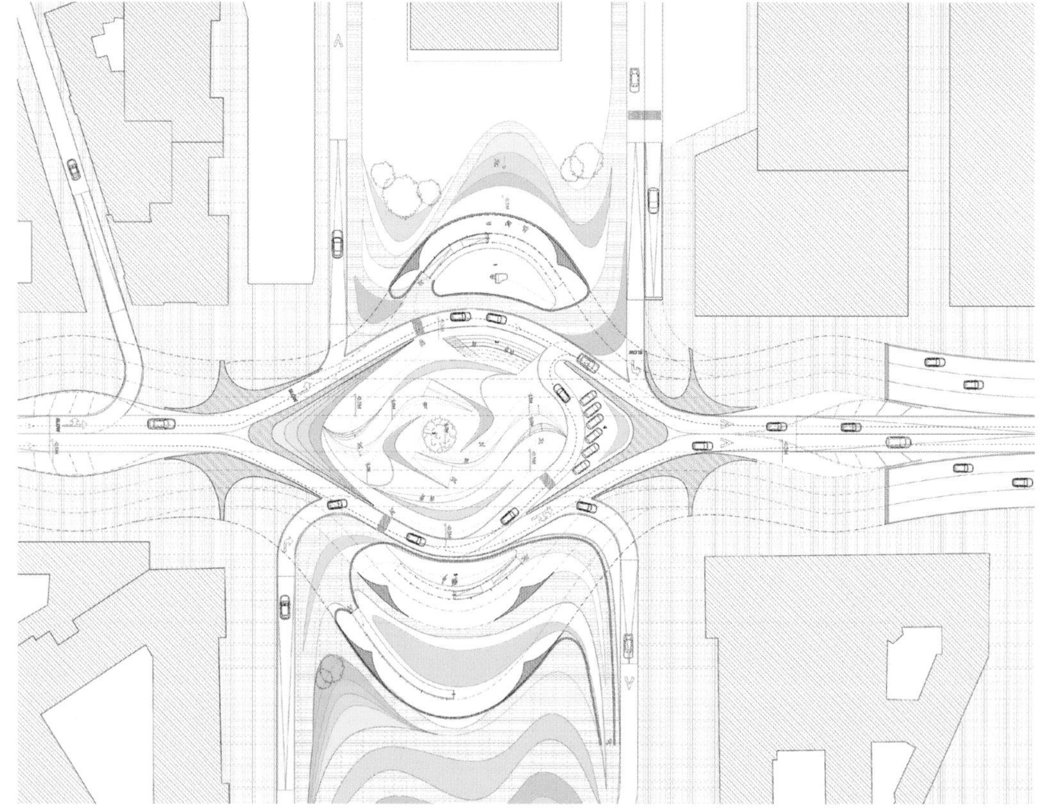

11.7

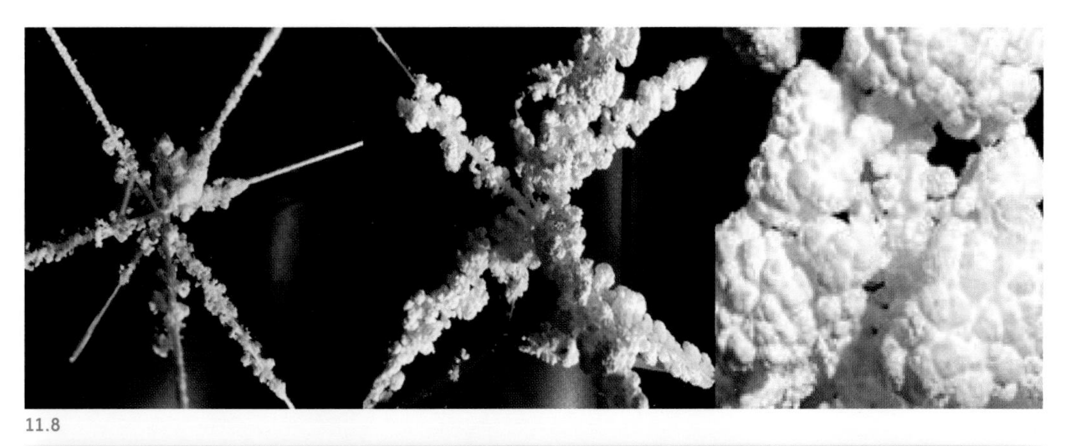

11.8

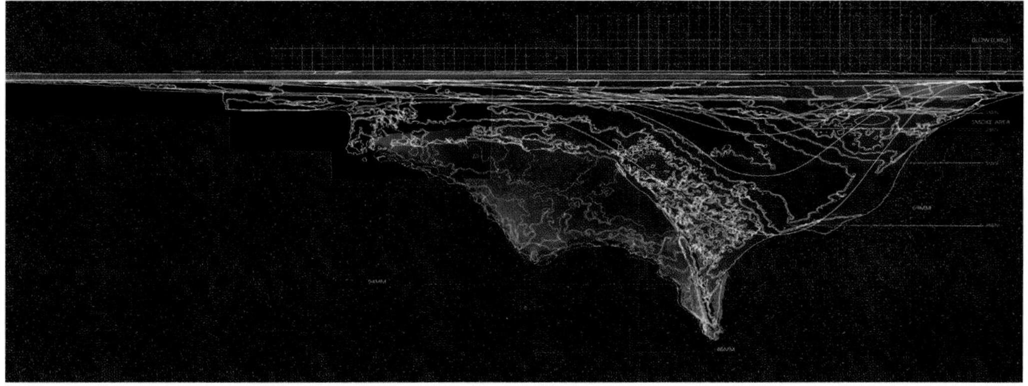

11.9

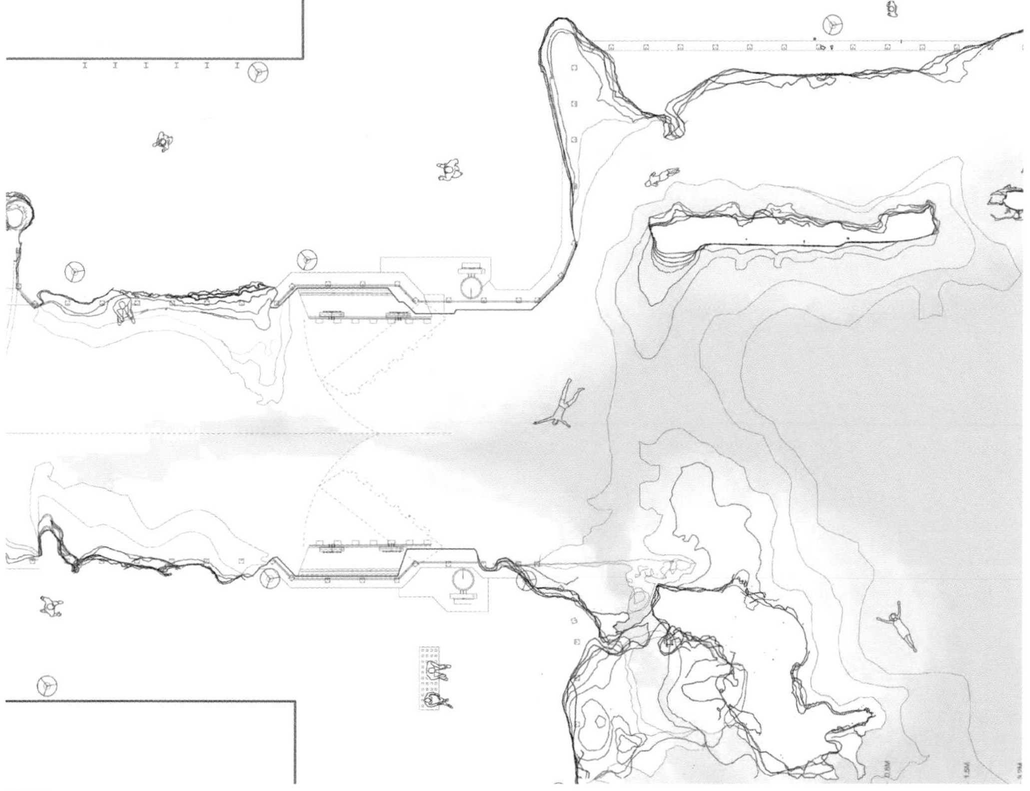

11.10

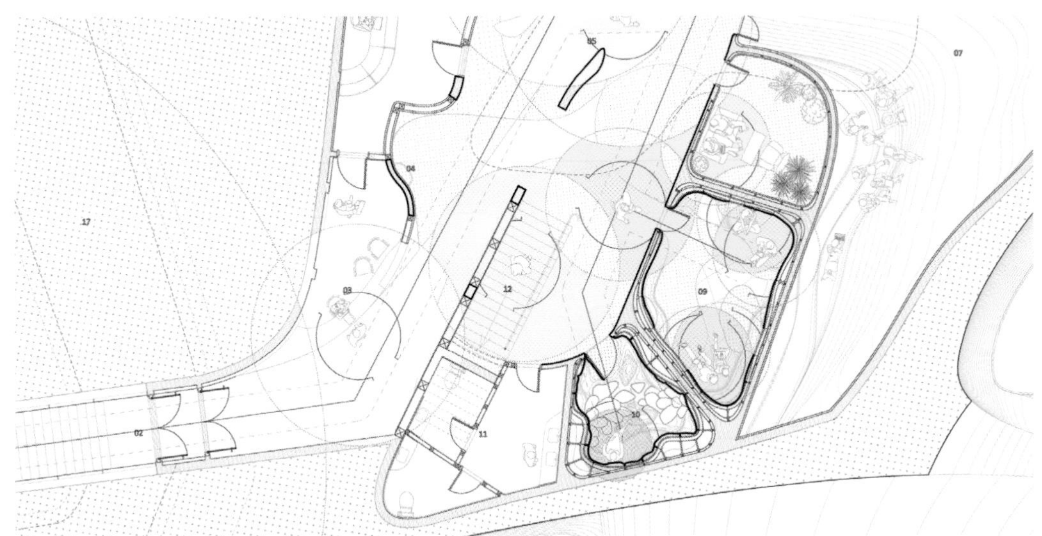

11.11

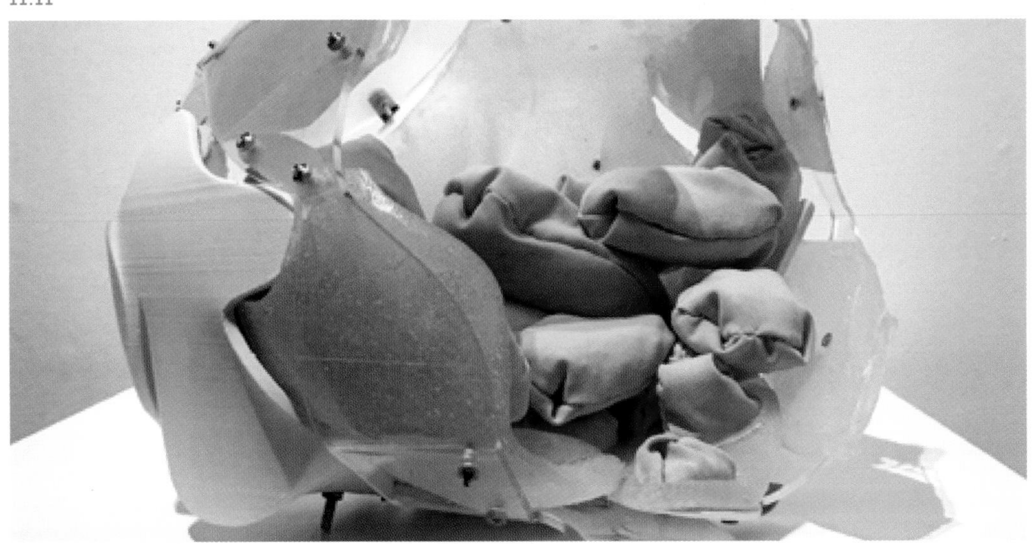
11.12

11.13

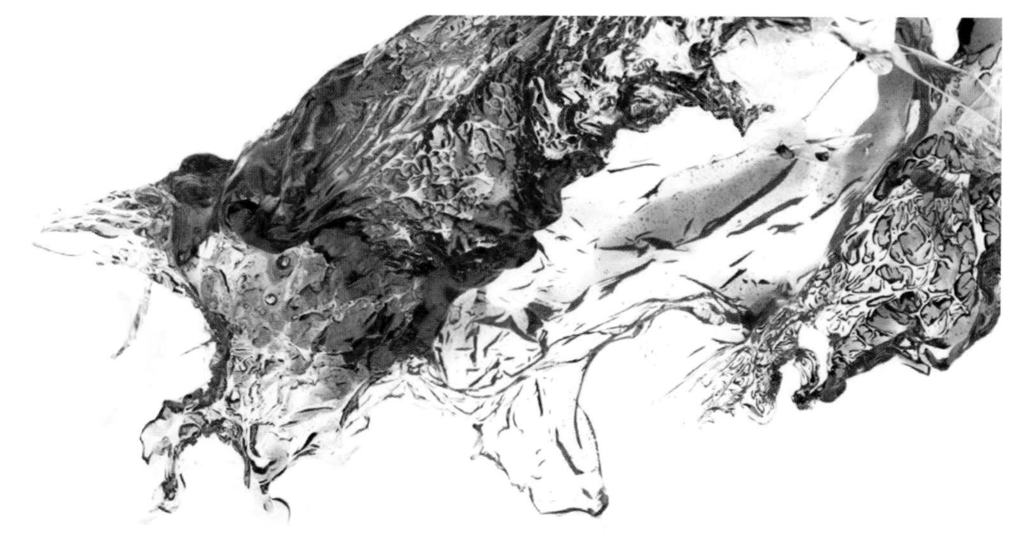

11.14

11.15

11.16

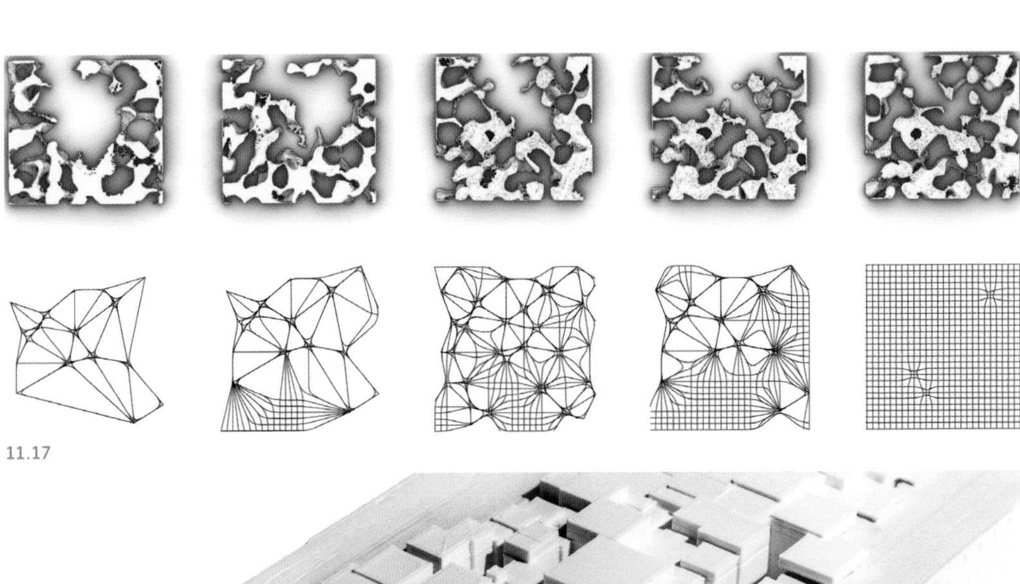

11.17

11.18

11.19

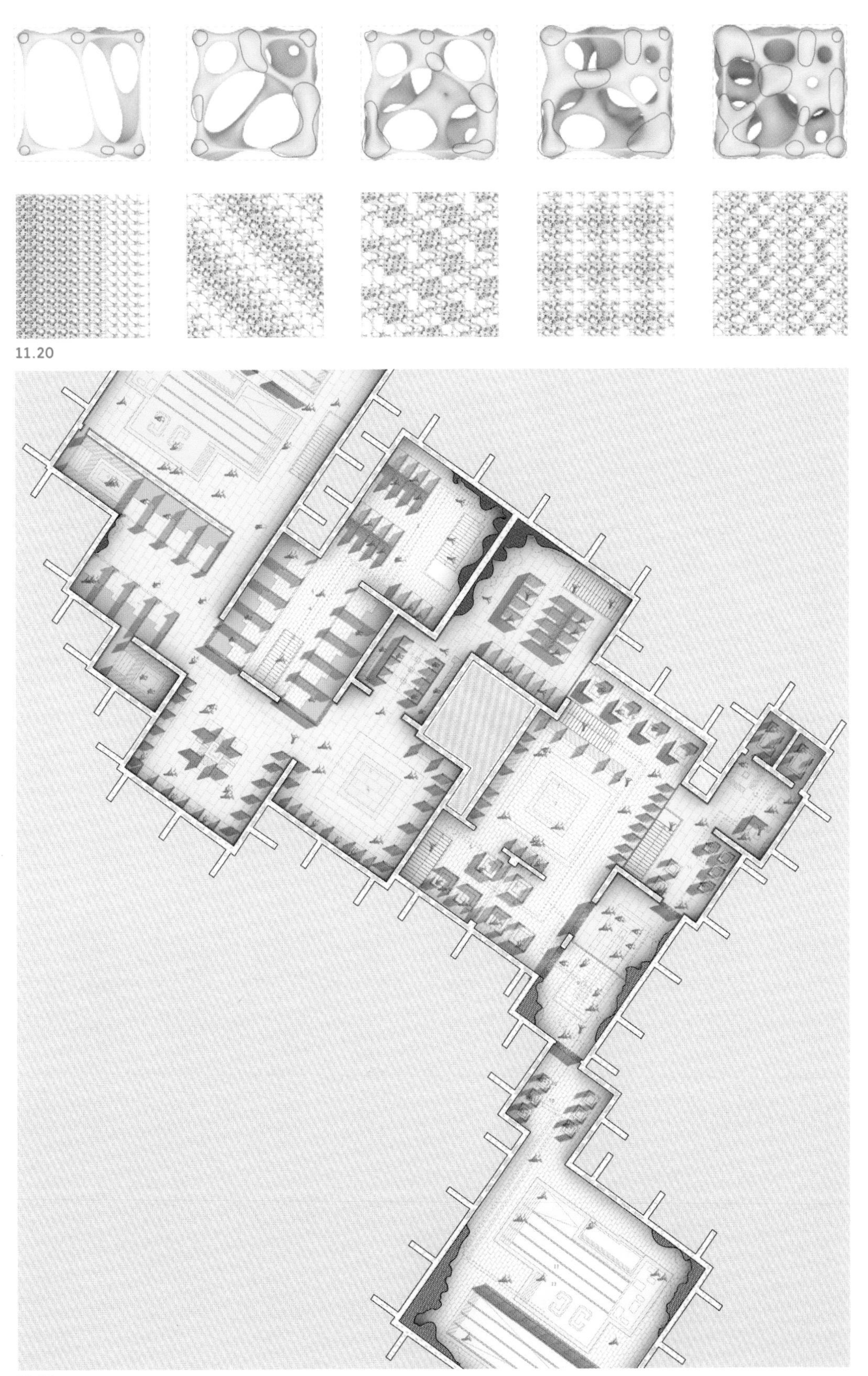

11.20

11.21

11.22

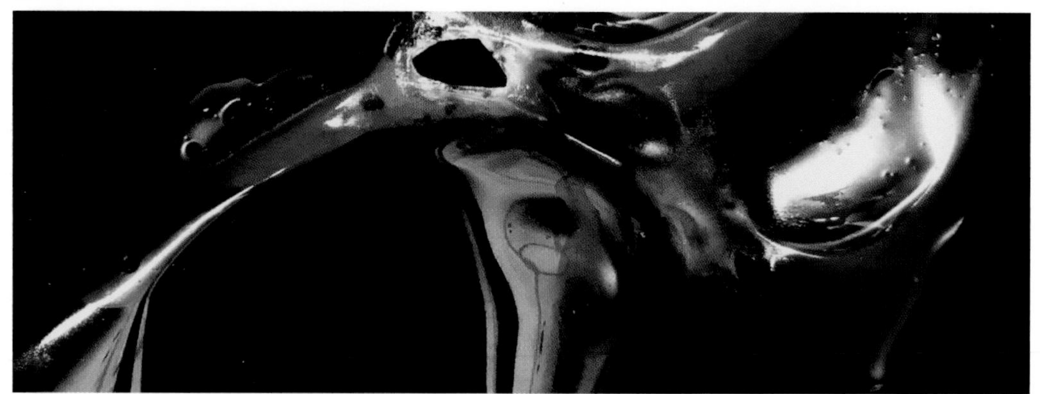
11.23

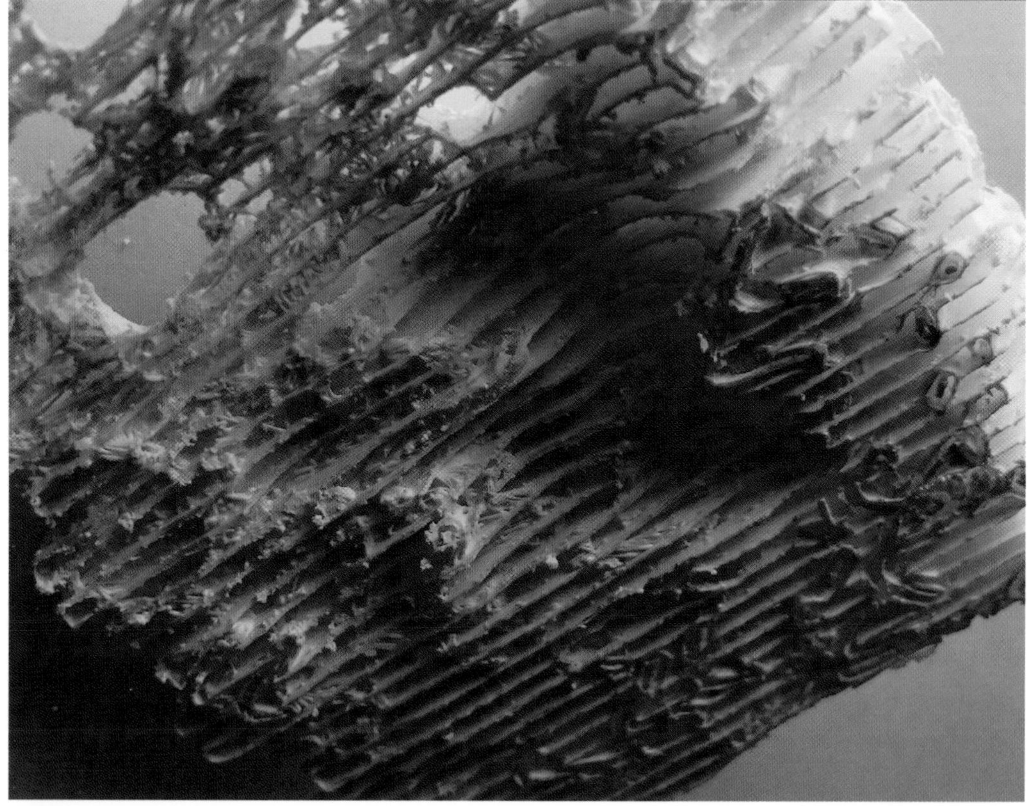
11.24

11.25

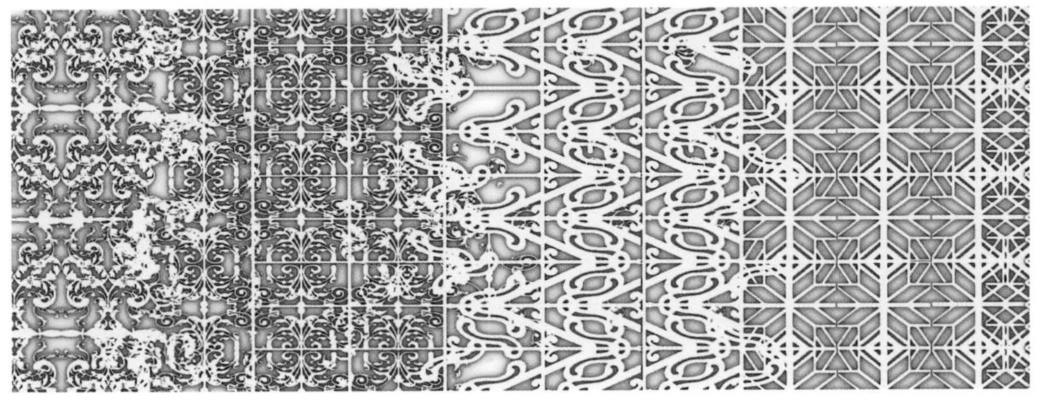

11.26

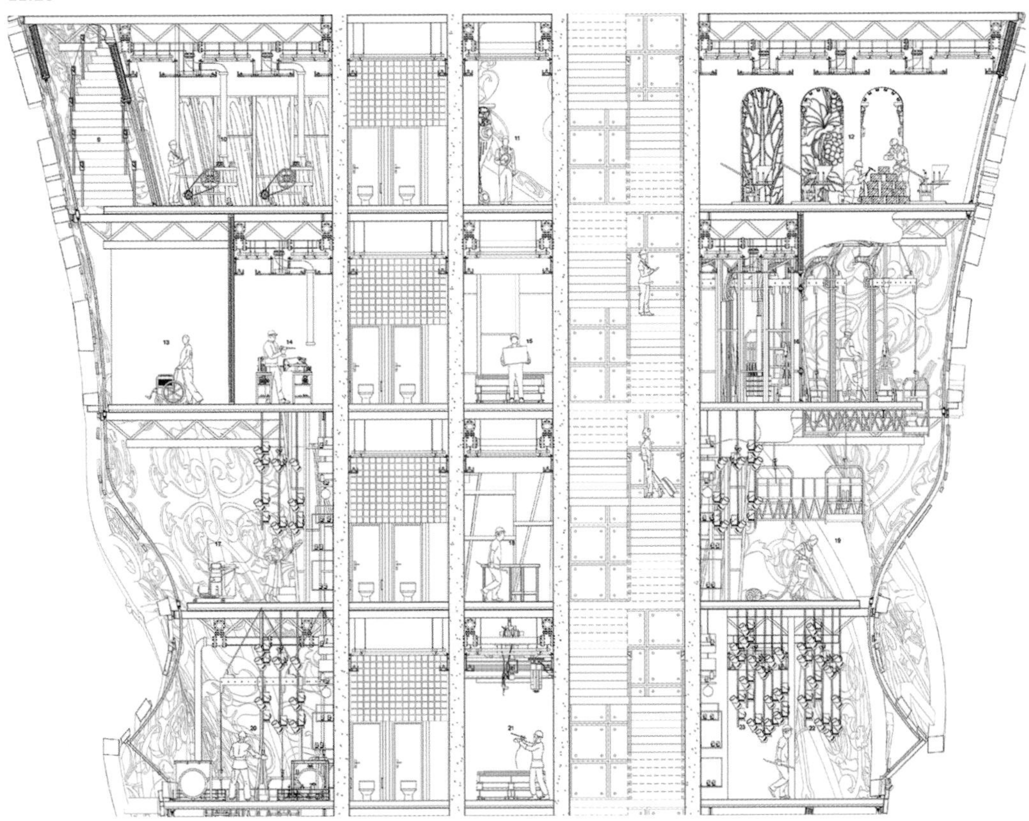

11.27

Anger Management

UG12

Johan Hybschmann, Matthew Springett

This year was the last chapter in UG12's trilogy of provocative explorations into American culture. In the first, we considered the notion of the 'embassy' and ideas of 'belonging' by looking at public buildings in New York and examining identity in the post-Obama era. In the second, we drew on the role of 'disrupters' in the development of the American city by exploring infrastructural buildings for alternative communities within Chicago. This year, two years into the Trump presidency, we explored the architecture of confrontation in response to injustice. We visited New Orleans, a city on the edge, in flux, and still rebuilding its communities after the destruction caused by Hurricane Katrina in 2005, whilst also navigating the societal turbulence of the Trump presidency.

Polarised societal anger appears to be a global phenomenon. Whilst such cultural enmity has always existed, recent technological revolutions have allowed it to be shared, presented and represented in more tangible, amplified ways, for anyone who chooses to listen. It truly feels like the world is an angrier place than when we started this American adventure. Politically, we are witnessing greater and faster sharing of unmediated opinion. Divisive political and cultural disputes and angry disagreements are characterising the Trump presidency. Similarly, we find our own country polarised and acrimoniously split.

There is, perhaps, no way of stopping the negative factors and influences of the pervasive media but, this year, we explored the possibility of mediating societal anger through architectural experimentation. We reflected on architecture as a response to anger and aimed to mediate, resolve and counter the negative trends of our times. We questioned whether a new architecture can locally recalibrate the status quo in a city or neighbourhood? We also asked whether an architecture can manage anger through the way we design, programme and make spaces? We considered these questions, tested the possibilities and found answers that would bring architectural delight.

The unit's final building projects are sited in New Orleans and respond to individual observations established by the students before and during the field trip. The result is a series of complex buildings for identified communities looking to change how they inhabit, work in and mediate the city of New Orleans.

Year 2
Dominic Benzecry, Samuel Dodgshon, Olivia Hoy, Marina Kathidjiotis, Maria Mendoza Guerrero, Ellen Nankivell, Jennifer Oguguo, Freya Parkinson, Amy Peacock, Evelyn Salt

Year 3
Yu (Pearl) Chow, Chit (Jessica) Liu, Lucy Millichamp, Harriet Orr, Malgorzata Rutkowska, Annabelle Tan Kai Lin, Maya Whitfield

Thank you to our technical tutor Rhys Cannon and computer tutor Pete Davies

Model photos by French+Tye

Thank you to our critics: Laura Allen, Kyle Buchanan, Barbara-Ann Campbell-Lange, Rhys Cannon, Pete Davies, Fiona MacDonald, Duncan McLeod, Ana Monrabal-Cook, Jonathan Pile, Peg Rawes, David Roberts, Bob Sheil, Mark Smout

12.1, 12.2, 12.21 **Annabelle Tan Kai Lin, Y3** 'Wetland Frontier'. Straddling a six-foot levee, this proposal facilitates the regeneration of the Lower Ninth Ward community and the adjacent wetlands – both currently ghosts of their former selves after prolonged neglect. Urban ecosystems, disaster-proof housing and sediment satellites make up the multi-scalar scheme, which speculates a new approach to nature in New Orleans.
12.3 **Samuel Dodgshon, Y2** 'Manchester–New Orleans Trade Consul'. This project aims to build on the historic trade between New Orleans and Manchester in a time when both are facing economic difficulties. The building is designed to showcase Manchester's cultural exports with internal views through the skeletal structure.
12.4 **Freya Parkinson, Y2** 'Hollywood South'. A proposal for a film studio and headquarters for Hollywood in New Orleans that aims to increase public engagement with the film industry in both the city and the state. The project also hopes to heal the wounds caused by tax benefits and cuts, and encourages Hollywood moguls to reinvest in the community.
12.5, 12.7 12.25 **Yu (Pearl) Chow, Y3** 'Building Resistance'. This project proposes a 15-year progressive business plan to kick start the local economy in the Lower Ninth Ward of New Orleans post-Katrina. Firstly, the scheme exists as a vocational construction training centre that equips the community with skills to rebuild the local area. There is a boarding house where the students can stay during the course, which evolves into a community hub and research centre for flood-proof vernacular construction.
12.6, 12.12 **Olivia Hoy, Y2** 'Bridging the Lower Ninth'. An investigation into ingrained conflicts within the social, political and environmental climate of the Lower Ninth Ward in New Orleans. The project seeks emancipations via the provision of a legal advocacy community centre branching over the levee at the site.
12.8 **Amy Peacock, Y2** 'A Community Centre for Mardi Gras Indians'. A proposal for a meeting place, workshop and teaching centre to support and cultivate the traditions of a community of costume-makers within one of the oldest African-American neighbourhoods in the US.
12.9 **Ellen Nankivell, Y2** 'A Workshop of New Orleans Historic Vernacular'. Taking inspiration from the historical construction techniques of old New Orleans, and looking to the future for a utilisation of these traditional methods, this project delivers an educational workshop and 'archive' of vernacular architecture for the community of Tremé.
12.10, 12.23 **Maya Whitfield, Y3** 'While Roe'. Women have the right to an abortion in most states in the US, yet violence at clinics by protesters represents one of the greatest deterrents. This project provides a new form of clinical architecture, with an entryway that aims to deter protesters. Simultaneously, it responds to the growing issue surrounding illegal sex trafficking within New Orleans by providing a space of sanctuary, with short respite care rooms and counselling facilities for those in need.
12.11, 12.22 **Chit (Jessica) Liu, Y3** 'The Ninth Ward Kindergarten'. A proposal for a kindergarten in the Lower Ninth Ward neighbourhood, based on the concept of 'building a school as a park', aims to create a new learning environment within a post-disaster environment.
12.13, 12.26 **Lucy Millichamp, Y3** 'Reclaiming Ritualism: The Sanctification of the French Quarter for Voodism in New Orleans'. As both a voodoo spiritual temple and a public performance space, this architecture aims to provide local worshipping communities with a sacred space in the historic heart of the city. If offers an authentic representation of a religion that has been commodified for the entertainment and leisure of tourists in New Orleans.
12.14 **Harriet Orr, Y3** 'Riverfront: Bridging the Boundary Between City and Water in New Orleans'. This project proposes the design of a single-pilot, dual purpose, community performance centre that will be able to transition into a temporary disaster-relief centre for up to 500 people. Focusing on the importance of the New Orleans riverside, the building will blur the boundary between the city and the water, becoming an extension of the land, diminishing fear and instead celebrating the natural phenomenon of the Mississippi River.
12.15, 12.20 **Malgorzata Rutkowska, Y3** 'Recalibration – New Orleans'. A proposal for an environmentally responsive art centre brought to the community by US Army Corps of Engineers in order to educate people about the Mississippi River and the effects of water on the manmade environment. Instead of focusing on problems and difficulties, the project explains the consequences of controlling the elements through positive actions. Merging activist art and canal engineering for positive human impact, it brings attention to the difficult topic of unpredictable environmental change.
12.16 **Jennifer Oguguo, Y2** 'Claiborne Place'. New Orleans – the birthplace of jazz – is slowly losing its sense of culture as people are pushed out of the city due to overwhelming rental prices. This is a proposal for an affordable temporary accommodation for young musicians, allowing them to stay near to the city, whilst giving the local community a new social environment that celebrates music, collaboration and the local vernacular.
12.17 **Maria Mendoza Guerrero, Y2** 'Nurturing Roots'. A study into the homeless people of New Orleans, this project proposes a building that acts as a bridge between the displaced and nature, and helps to reincorporate them back into society.
12.18 **Dominic Benzecry, Y2** 'A New Orleans'. This project is a response to the tension between the major oil companies and green energy startups based in New Orleans, and the response of said oil companies to global warming. The building provides co-working space for up-and-coming industries, under the pretence that it is being funded, and partially occupied, by Shell.
12.19 **Evelyn Salt, Y2** 'The Respite Centre'. This project provides a space for therapy and counselling of terminally ill patients in the French Quarter in New Orleans. The space allows patients to reflect and converse with other people in similar situations.
12.24 **Marina Kathidjiotis, Y2** 'A Year and a Day'. Directed at the few-remaining voodoo practitioners in New Orleans, this project encompasses a funeral home and crematorium based on the 'year and a day' commemoration that is followed by many voodoo families, during which the body of the deceased is stored in a mausoleum until it can be cremated. Situated in one of New Orleans' biggest cemeteries, the interior spaces and circulation of the building are defined by the timeline of rituals and events that take place there, creating two distinct journeys: one for those who attend the rituals and the other for the handling of the deceased.

12.2

12.3

12.4

12.5

12.6

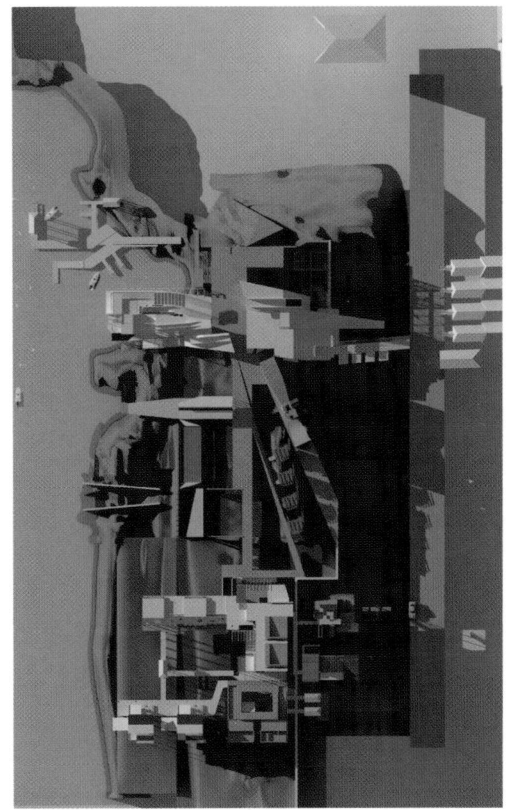

12.7

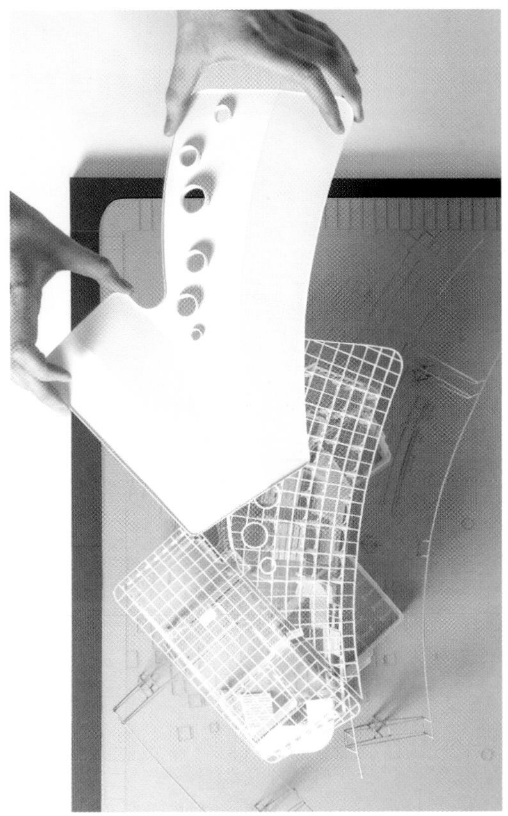

12.8

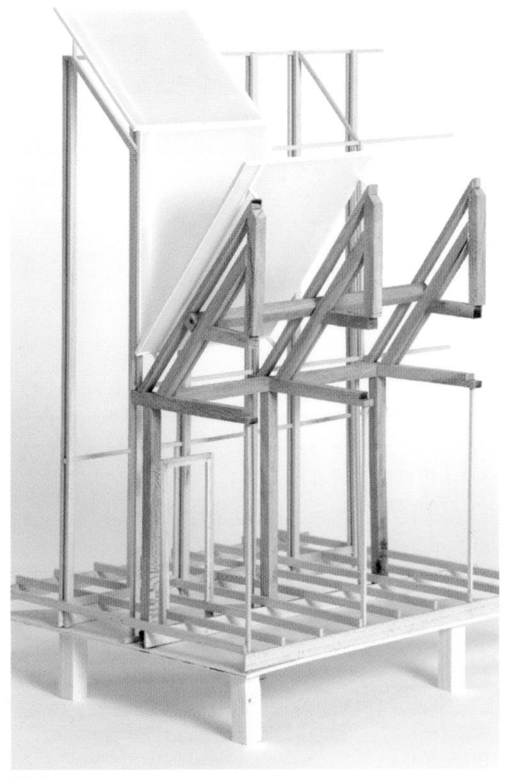

12.9

12.10

12.11

12.12

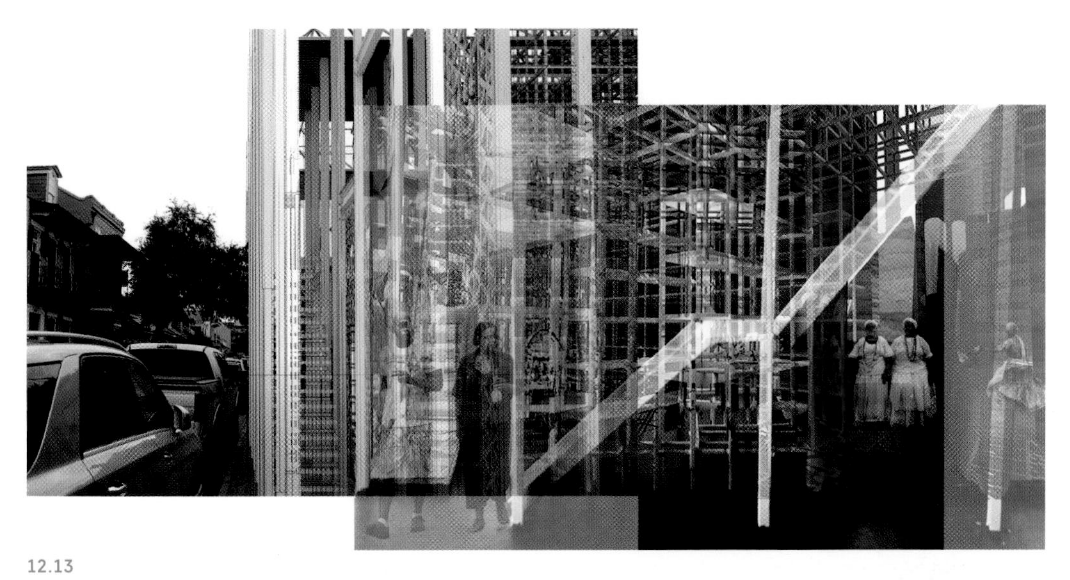

12.13

12.14

12.15

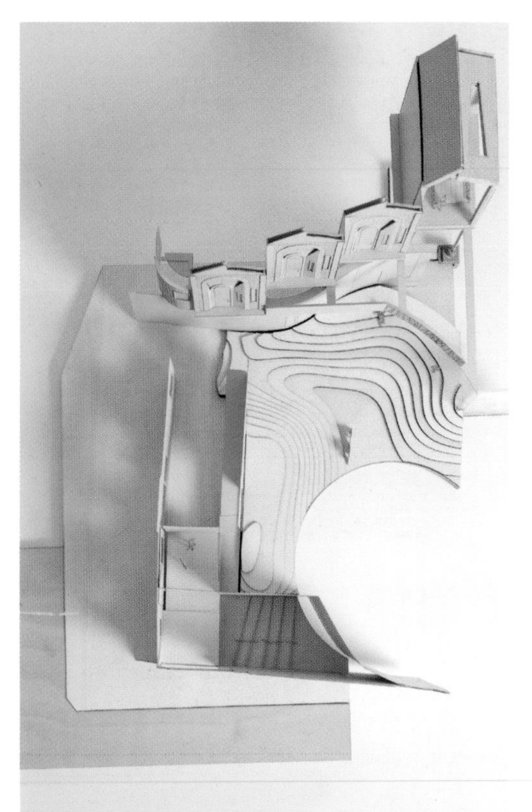

12.16

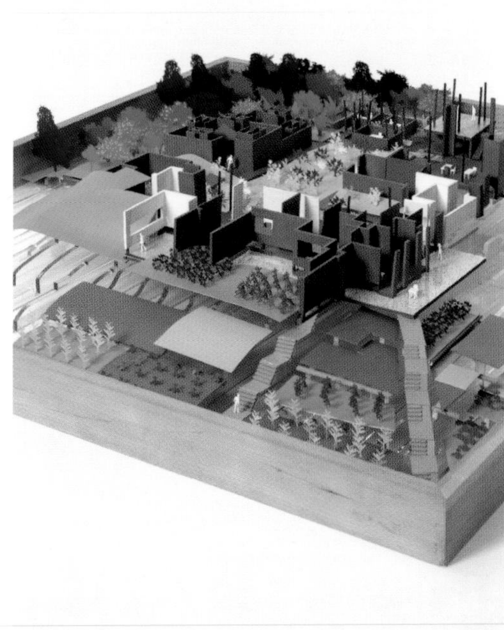

12.17

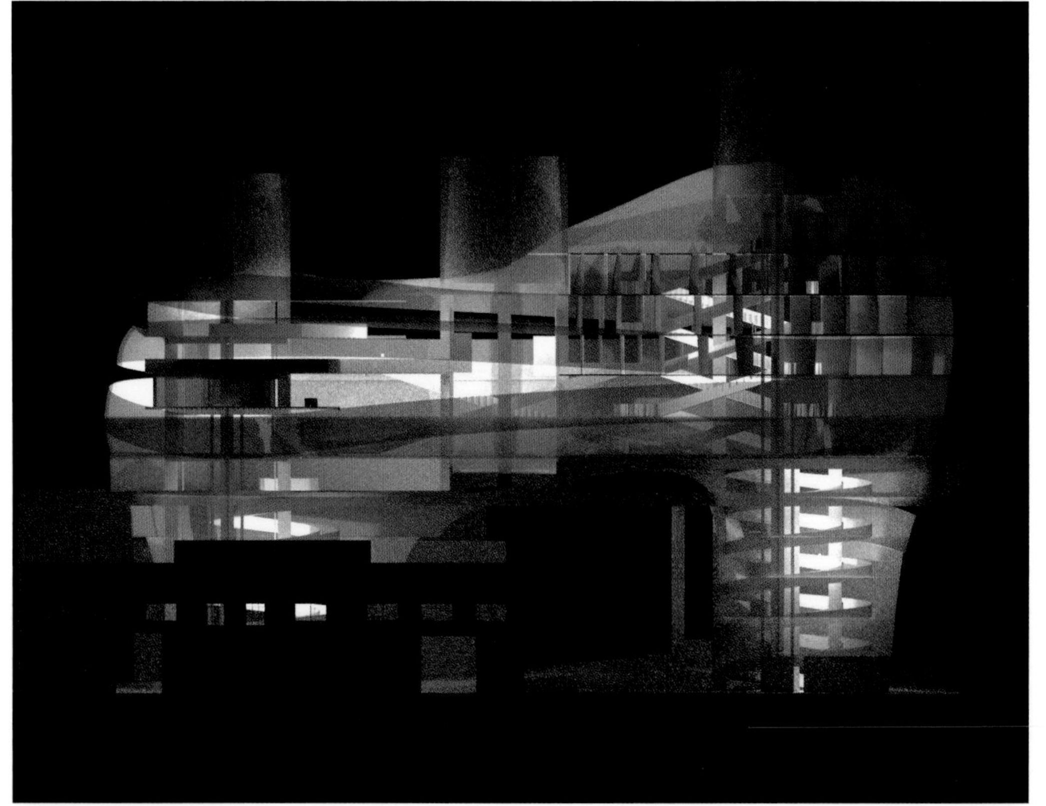

12.18

12.19

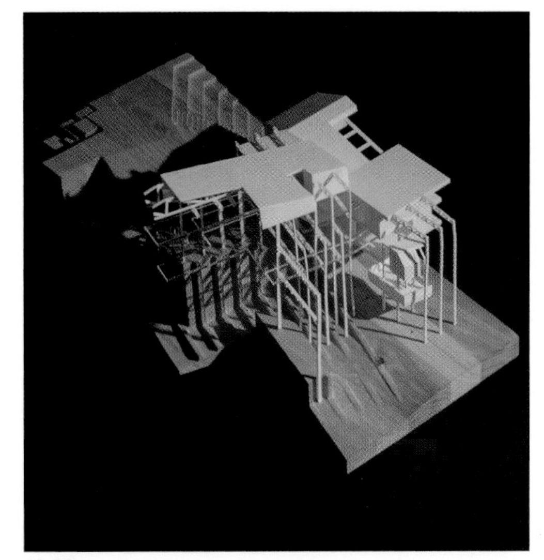
12.20

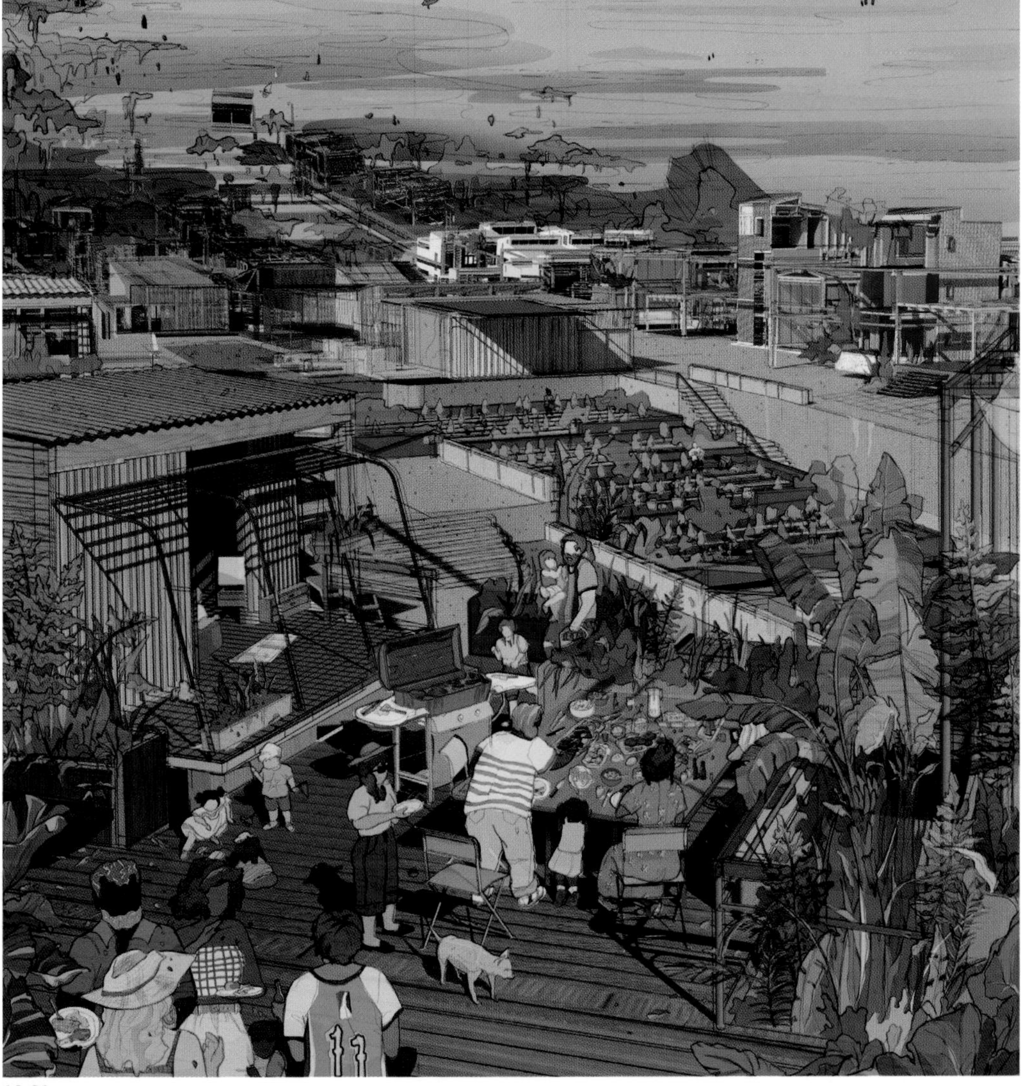
12.21

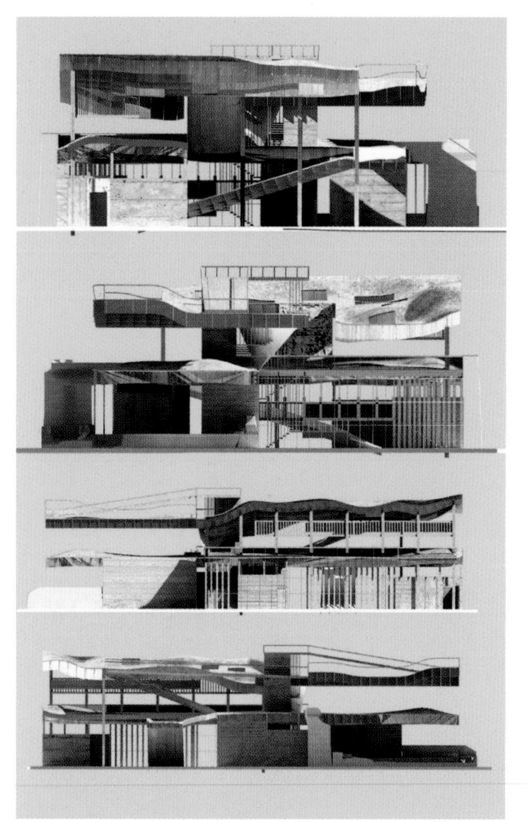

12.22

12.23

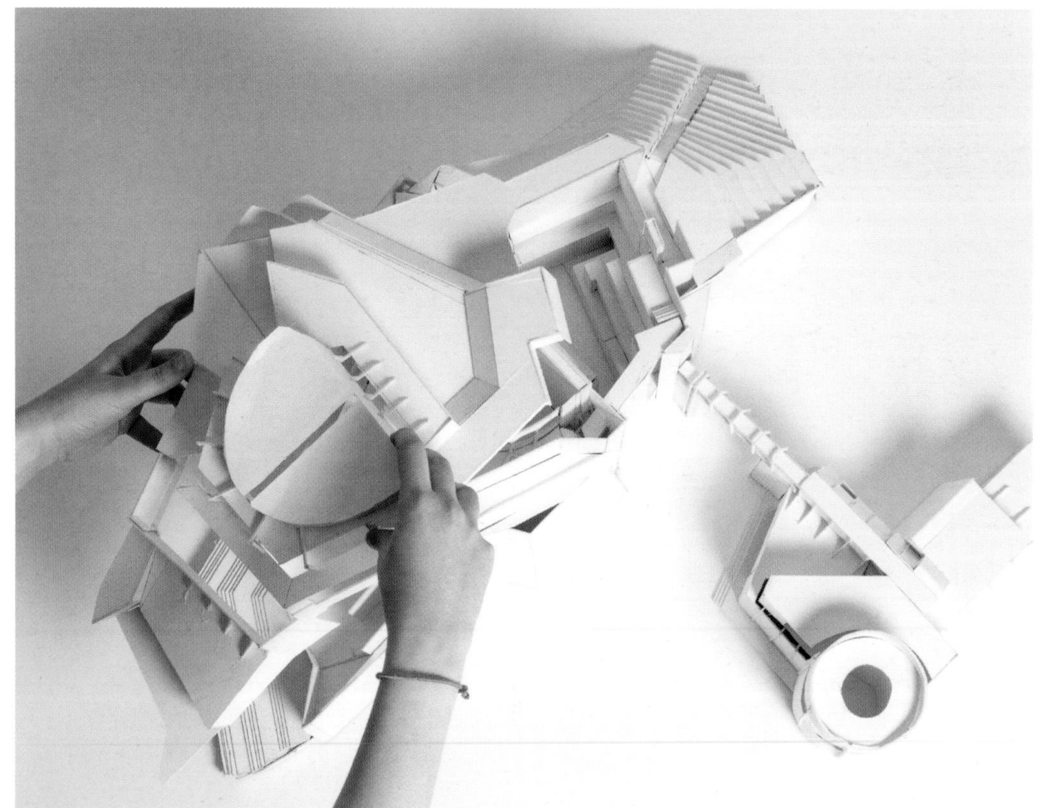

12.24

12.25

12.26

13.1

Registrations in the Feral Ground

UG13

Tamsin Hanke, Ralph Parker

Our inquiry into landscape this year leaves aside the picturesque and the garden for the wilderness, the feral, and the visceral engagement of ground, depth, space and body, found through adventure. We are the new explorers, registering the ground afresh. We are the transcribers of its strange histories, those who listen for its peculiar resonances, the keepers of its countless time and cartographers of its unholy dreams. We are intrigued by the human desire for conquest and the search for an improbable and previously impossible relationship between man and ground. Architectural opportunity lies in the spatial idea of this relationship – how we discover adventures and mark territory.

Charting a path towards an archaeology of future architectures that have an inexorable correlation with the terrain, we find new ground hidden in old landscapes. We create works as spatial registrations into the landscape; interventions borne of congruences, syncopations, phase shifts and alignments, dualities, ciphers and sequences across the vast stratification of place and people, where strange and meaningful architectures coalesce. What discoveries can we draw from an infinitely stratified landscape, to then be modulated and refigured into architectural action?

The unit favours the 'making' of ideas and space because physical production carries with it a degree of difficulty that allows the work itself to speak back, as it is fashioned through its subtle procession of successes and failures. We value work that – although often simple in its programmatic and verbal description – is delightfully complex in its architectural proposition and inventiveness. Achieving clarity is firmly respected within our experimental and explorative agenda. We nurture a challenging environment of experimentation in the as-yet-unknown, where students feel supported and equipped to take the chances required to achieve the exceptional.

This year, we have purposefully sought out difficult places set in challenging landscapes, to stimulate inventiveness in response to those landscapes, and to achieve propositional clarity not subservient to, but in balance with it. The projects engage with a swathe of sites uncovered on an ascension across Europe; from the glimmering sea level of Gaudí's Barcelona, via Ledoux's sublime salt works, the historical grain of ancient Lyon, the susurrating vine-clad shores of Lake Geneva and upwards, into the echoing footholds of heroic Alpinists at the high roof of the continent.

Year 2
Rory Cariss, Herui Chen, Andrew Cowie, Henri Khoo, Oscar Leung, Seng (Aaron) Lim, Diana Mykhaylychenko, Konrad Pawalczyk, Theo Syder

Year 3
Vasily Babichev, Vladyslav Bondarenko, Alys Hargreaves, Yu-Wen (Yvonne) Huang, Maria Jones Delgado, James McLaughlin, Arina Viazenkina

With thanks to visiting tutor Colin Herperger and technical tutor Sash Scott

Thank you to our critics: Nat Chard, Olivia Forty, Syafiq Jubri, Perry Kulper, Javier Ruiz

13.1, 13.19 **Alys Hargreaves, Y3** 'In Conversation With: A Glacier'. Set within the scar of a rapidly retreating glacier, the climate convention centre establishes an international space of collective discussion for the long-term catastrophe and short-term states of crises that are symptomatic of climate change. Consisting of a lecture theatre, an assembly hall, libraries and accommodation, the building addresses the need for soft and hard discussions linked to the pace and syntax of conversation. The architecture has a spatial temporality translated through the process of slip-casting.
13.2 **Yu-Wen (Yvonne) Huang, Y3** 'Swan Lake: An Immersive Theatre Hotel'. Inspired by Punchdrunk's immersive theatre productions, the public spaces of this boutique hotel transform into performance stages at designated times of the day. The architecture is the manifestation of performance as built pieces in space. An alternative approach to data-driven designs was explored by alternating between digital technology, 3D printing and traditional building methods, such as sand casting, and interpreted a contemporary adaptation of *Swan Lake*. The integration of structural and environmental building performance with theatrical productions, tests the intermediate boundaries between structure, form and function.
13.3 **Arina Viazenkina, Y3** 'The Institution of Dreams'. Taking inspiration from Carl Jung's dream theories, this project aims to materialise a dreamlike experience in a proposal for a public walkway in Tring Park in Hertfordshire. The design of the walkway is based on the novel *Monday Starts on Saturday* by Arkady and Boris Strugatsky.
13.4–13.5 **James McLaughlin, Y3** 'The Theatrics of Paper'. This project creates visual moments of performative disruption within a theatre, whereby the audience is presented to itself, blurring the boundary between performance and reality. The building mirrors and divides these brief moments of objectification and voyeurism by layering the typologies of theatre and set production. Paper elements of the architecture and the stage are cast within the various programmed spaces, further subverting the role of the audience into having an active involvement with the theatre's development, expansion and deterioration.
13.6–13.7 **Vasily Babichev, Y3** 'The Creature in the Arveyron River'. A proposal for an arts institution that fosters environmental responses to Mer de Glace, a melting glacier in the French Alps. As the glacier 'weeps', the building clings to the land with its tears.
13.8–13.9 **Maria Jones Delgado, Y3** 'The Harbinger of the Storm'. Born from the myth that dragons pre-empt and cause storms in the Alps, this botanical garden and seed bank research facility channels extreme weather into the building to preserve specimens threatened by the glacial retreat happening parallel to the site.
13.10 **Andrew Cowie, Y2** 'Post-Work Re-Education Centre'. A proposal for a community centre in Lausanne in Switzerland that fosters the re-education of pre-industrial Swiss crafts – specifically stone sculpture, sgraffito, tavillonage, wood-carving and decoupage. The centre aims to carve new histories into the land's abundant resources of timber and stone in a 'post-work' society.
13.11 **Seng (Aaron) Lim, Y2** 'Play Atlas'. This project is an inter-generational playhouse bringing together families and artists-in-residence to inspire horizontal learning, collaboration and experimentation. Grounded by the Reggio Emilia pedagogy – a student-centred preschool education philosophy – the playhouse is a haven for imagination that subverts daily domestic elements, routines and scales to encourage residents to use their innate curiosity in understanding the world they inhabit.
13.12 **Konrad Pawlaczyk, Y2** 'Trans-Musical Realm'. This project explores the spatial possibilities of architecture in facilitating shifts of human cognition through the sublime experience of music (vibration), and represents a transition between the typology of a chapel (silence) and a club (sound). The project looks at physical engagement with the experience of music.
13.13 **Theo Syder, Y2** 'Concrete Latex Plastic Latex'. A proposal for a micro-hotel with an interior that subtly reconfigures according to the different groups of inhabitants and the unique configurations of the seven types of Greek love experienced by them.
13.14 **Diana Mykhaylychenko, Y2** 'The Search of Inflection Point'. This project asks 'What is the best moment to perform the perfect shot?', 'How do you catch the inflection point between two different states and materialise opposite forces in the architecture?' and 'Can the sequential process of long-distance shooting be read as a transitional procession that helps you to understand the environment outside?'
13.15 **Vladyslav Bondarenko, Y2** 'Breath of the Landscape'. A proposal for an inflatable pavilion in Tring Park, constructed using a method of both metal and reflective fabric tailoring. The pavilion – constantly inhaling and moving with the air and wind – houses a meditation space creating a fluid yet tranquil experience using its materiality.
13.16 **Oscar Leung, Y2** 'BURD's Onsen'. A design proposal for a hot spring emporium for visitors and locals of the resort town, based on a mechanised bird. Abutting a saltworks-turned-museum, the building utilises its neighbour's original brine pipelines and stores its contents in iron basins to supply rust-infused saltwater to its various hot springs for a genuine 'iron onsen' experience.
13.17–13.18 **Henri Khoo, Y2** 'The Tringest Tring'. An invitation to explore the unseen territory of the composited spectacle: the reanimation of Tring Park.
13.20, 13.22 **Rory Cariss, Y2** 'An Archive of Alpine Misadventure'. The archive, situated in Le Trétien, Switzerland, is based on the history of man's failed attempts to conquer the Alps. The building houses a collection of objects and digital recordings, celebrating and preserving these stories of misadventure. A co-housing scheme forms a large part of the project, providing a home for the ex-mountaineers that run the archive.
13.21 **Herui Chen, Y2** 'Land/Soundscapes'. Experimentations on developing musical compositions into landscapes or converting spatial settings into music. The objective of this project is to find an alternative iterative tool to generate spatial designs.

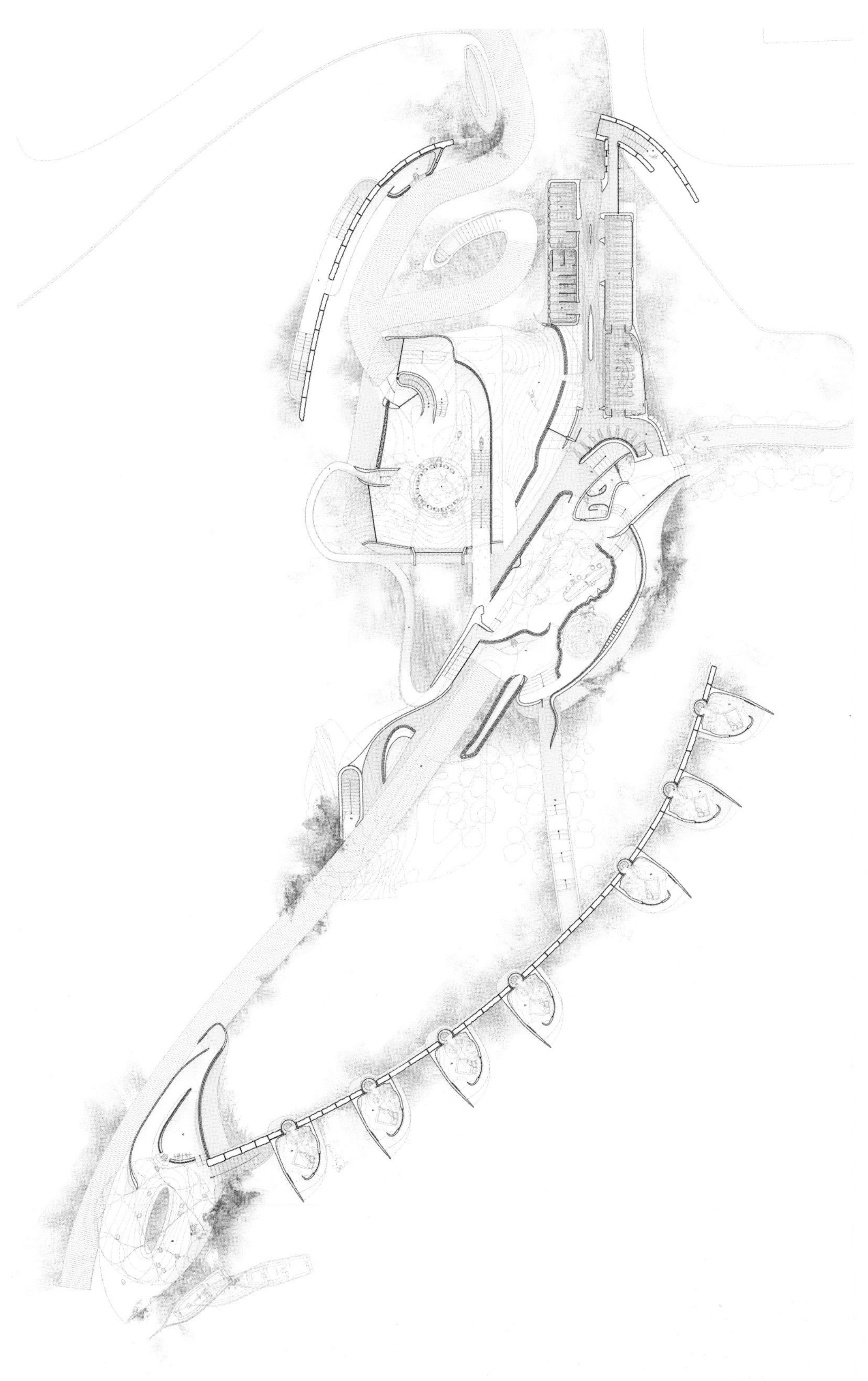

13.2

13.3

13.4

13.5

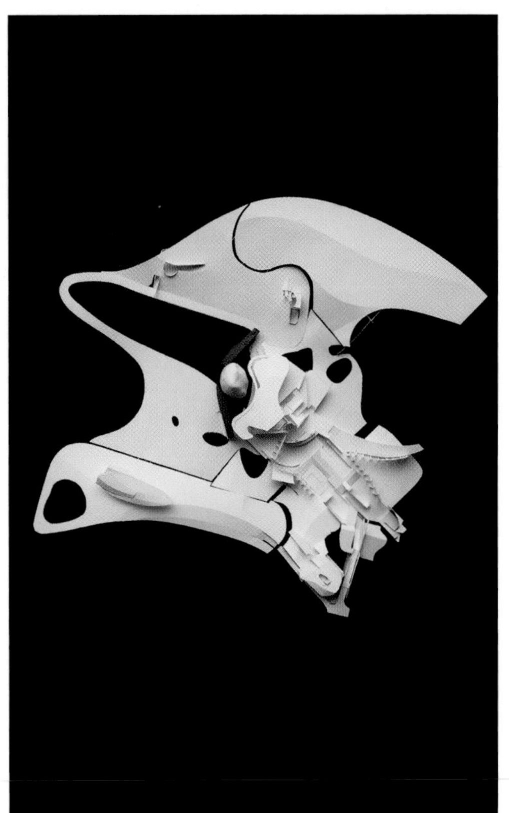

13.6

13.7

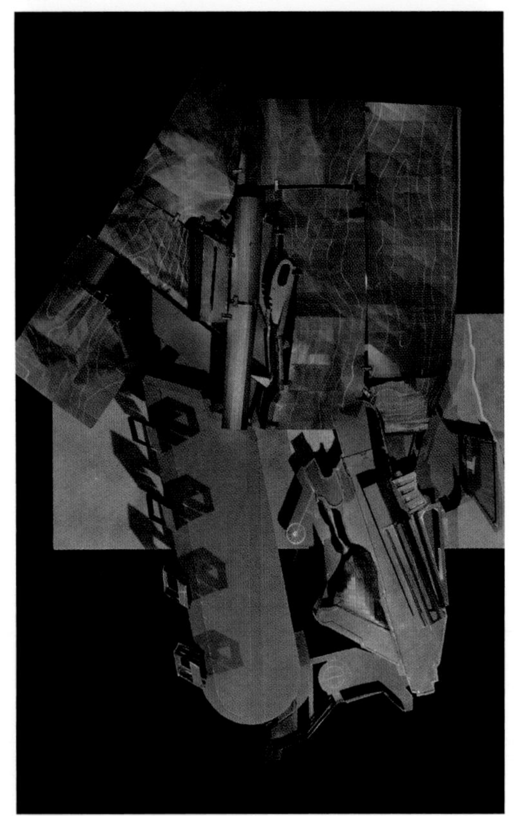

13.8

13.9

13.10

13.11

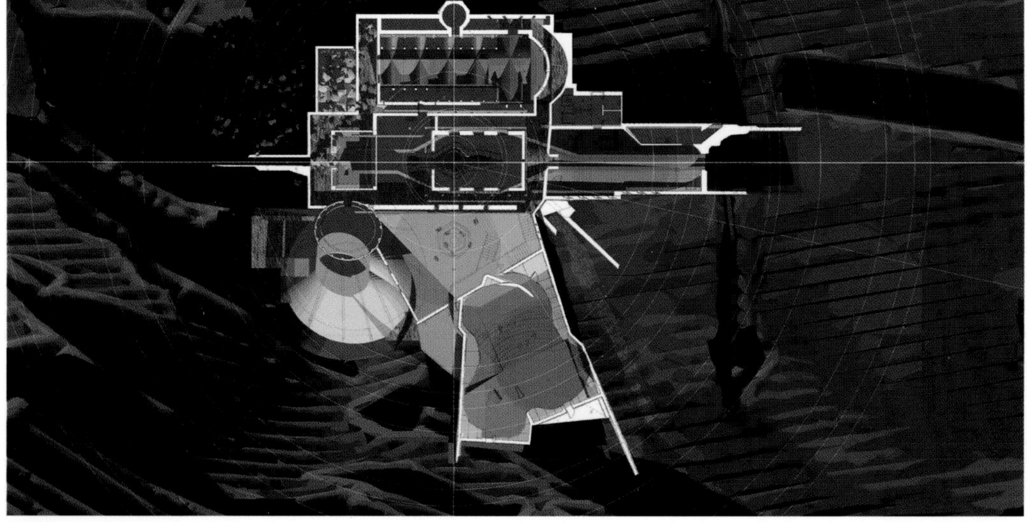

13.12

13.13

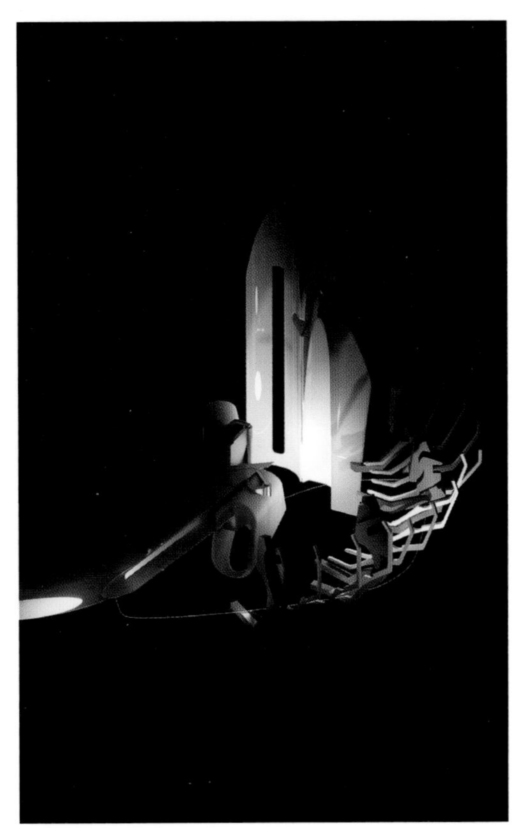
13.14

13.15

13.16

13.17

13.18

13.19

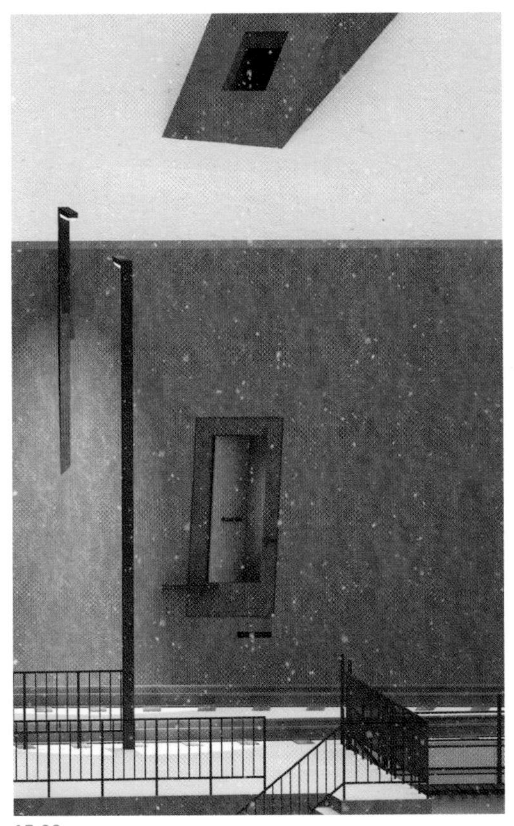

13.20

13.21

13.22

Undergraduate tutorial in the studio

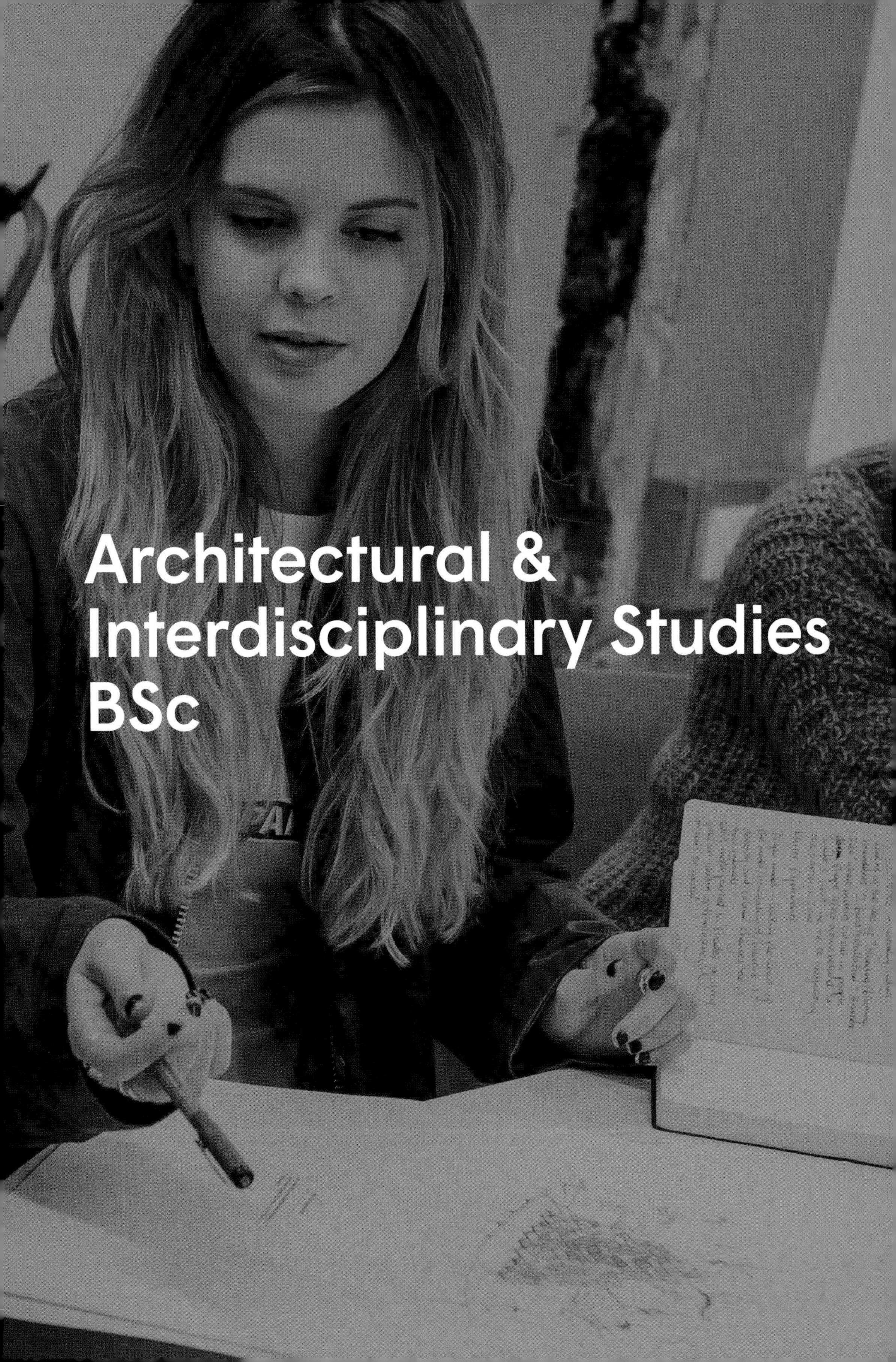
Architectural &
Interdisciplinary Studies
BSc

Architectural & Interdisciplinary Studies BSc

Programme Director: Elizabeth Dow

Architectural culture has never been exclusively produced by certified architects but now, more than ever, there are many other people working in related fields – film, media, curation, design and creative practice – who shape debates and ideas around architecture in significant ways. In bringing together architectural research with design and creative practice, Architectural & Interdisciplinary Studies students are participating in these significant and complex debates.

The greatest strength of the programme is its interdisciplinary nature. We encourage our students to navigate their studies in a focused manner, whilst choosing from a diverse range of modules from across UCL alongside their architectural studies. They develop a range of skills and build a unique knowledge-set tailored to their interests, empowering them to go on to apply themselves to careers such as journalism, art, design policy and activism, environmental and urban studies. The programme also serves to form a foundation for postgraduate study, with our current graduating cohort already having accepted places on Master's programmes.

This year, the programme has received two exchange students from Vienna and two of our own students have travelled to study in Vienna and Leiden. Our study abroad placements continue to allow students to take advantage of the wider curricula offered by our partner institutions and experience different and exciting cultural approaches to their studies that not only inform their work, but also inspire and provoke a broader pedagogic debate amongst the whole programme.

There are two specially tailored modules for Architectural & Interdisciplinary Studies students at The Bartlett, 'Design and Creative Practice' and 'Architectural Research'. Images from the resulting design projects and a summary of work produced on this year's 'Architectural Research III' essay-based module can be found on the following pages.

Architectural Research staff
Ruth Bernatek, Brent Carnell, Stylianos Giamarelos, Barbara Penner, Sophie Read, David Roberts, Huda Tayob

Design & Creative Practice staff
Kirsty Badenoch, Stef Gradinariu, Kevin Green, Tom Kendall, Chee-Kit Lai, Caroline Rebourdin, Freddy Tuppen, Gabriel Warshafsky, Michelle Young

Computing for Design & Creative Practice
Bill Hodgson

Special thanks to Vasilija Abramovic, Sabina Andron, Joseph Augustin, Sue Barr, Douglas Bevans, Nat Chard, Sabrina Chou, Luofei Dong, Taylor Enoch, Jack Hardy, Mads Hulsroy Peterson, Susanne Isa, Thomas Kador, Ifigeneia Liangi, Rob Lye, Eloise Maland, Caroline Mok, Afra van t'Land

Architectural Research III: Encounters

Module Coordinator: Brent Carnell

Students
Elizabeth Atherton, Lucy Brown, Anna Cabanlig, Jasmine Ceccarelli-Drewry, Esme Chong, Isabel Dorn, Roxanne Gonzales, Lillie Hall, Holly Hatfield, Sara Herrera Dixon, Julia Millang, Emilie Morrow, Vikrimjeet (Vikrim) Nagra, Syed (Tanzim) Naser, Ged Ribas Goody, Camilla Romano, Yasmine Zein El Abdeen, Mengxuan (Moe) Zhao

After a revision to the module, this year marks the first time students' final written work on Architectural Research III has been gathered in a collective publication. While students still undertake a substantial piece of individual, rigorous research in an architectural subject and disseminate this in a lengthy essay, the new group project presents shorter excerpts. In doing so, it begins to showcase and curate the interdisciplinary knowledge which Architectural and Interdisciplinary Studies students have accumulated across their degree. Our collection, *Encounters*, proposes a student-led framework for architectural research and studies, one that challenges the ways in which architecture today is constructed, engaged with, and discussed. Each text in this publication aims to engage with architecture from a distinct and original perspective, generating thought-provoking contributions to the discipline. Setting up a framework for future years, the works featured in this first publication question the production of space through cultural identities, interpersonal connections and social relations.

Curating Social Imaginaries
The works in this section of the student-edited collection bring together a mix of cultural practices such as language, performance, curation, film and literature in an attempt to uncover how these practices inform national identities and shape social imaginaries. Through analysing film, Mengxuan Zhao and Vikrim Nagra analyse the growing interdisciplinary connections between architecture and film studies, interrogating spatial qualities of the visual medium in representing political conflicts and our planet's future. In a similar vein, Elizabeth Atherton and Anna Cabanlig look at contemporary curatorial practices, as a way of translating architecture and spatially representing cultural identities. Roxanne Gonzales and Tanzim Naser in turn use drama and literature to examine the function of architecture in opening cultural debates, new realms of imagination and new dimensions of design.

Home Un/Making
Here, excerpts analyse processes of home-making and un-making conditioned by sociopolitical, economic or urban factors, whether unintentional or deliberate, temporary or permanent.

Emilie Morrow and Holly Hatfield look at how interpersonal connections can generate a sense of belonging and feeling of home, investigating sensory experiences, relationships, identity and ownership in both public spaces and the home itself. Camilla Romano and Julia Millang explore architecture's role in generating and reinforcing collective identities and societal structures, looking at housing estates in the United Kingdom and Sweden. And Lillie Hall and Esme Chong broaden the understanding of the diverse ways in which people have come to live and dwell around the world, investigating micro-housing and trends of flexible living.

In/Formal Infrastructures

In the final section of the book, students showcase different informal practices and the way they relate to formal structures or systems of control, as well as the management and government of urban space. The chapters cover a range of practices such as activism, community groups, community spaces and creative resistance, unpacking the ways irregularity and informality interact with and form spatial strategies. Lucy Brown and Jasmine Ceccarelli-Drewry investigate the formation of collective spatial identities through practices of urban appropriation such as squatting and skating. Ged Ribas Goody and Isabel Dorn explore the challenges and obstacles faced by more sensitive and often marginalised peoples in claiming, appropriating and inhabiting urban and social spaces. Yasmine Zein El Abdeen and Sara Herrera Dixon's texts revolve around the spatial transformations engendered by urban revolutions and political movements, establishing how these might allow the reclaiming of public spaces and reinforcement of resistance.

The papers in this first publication consider architecture and the built environment in creative and innovative ways, drawing inspiration from a diverse range of disciplines, contexts and histories. It is our aim that future cohorts will carry forward our agenda, adding to architectural debates with new forms of research, communication and practice, ultimately producing a catalogue of work that will grow in the years to come.

The collection is available to purchase at The Bartlett Summer Show and via The Bartlett website.

Design & Creative Practice 1, 2 & 3

Design & Creative Practice enables students to undertake a mode of working that particularly interests them and an independent practice-based project in which they can research and pursue a subject of their preference. Students are asked to think of architecture in interdisciplinary ways, explore alternative approaches to design and situate their work within a broader cultural context.

This year's Year 1 Design & Creative Practice students defined their investigations as a series of islands. Visual and textual techniques were used to trace the limits of physical sites and cultural phenomena: atmospheres, smells, subcultures, and intimate moments of contact between body and city. These early mapping exercises enabled the development of considered critical positions as the basis for spatial proposition. Writing and image-making workshops encouraged students to adopt the stance first of the archaeologist, then the tourist, and finally the diplomat, to move from investigation to articulation. The resulting proposals, developed through a continuous dialogue, interrogate the limits of the individual in social space.

Year 2 students worked collaboratively to build complex dioramas based on their observations of Gordon Square and Tavistock Square in London. Dioramas are commonly understood to be three-dimensional representations of specific scenes and their environments. They sit somewhere between the model and the painting, offering the viewer a carefully composed representation of the subject depicted, usually to be viewed from a particular given angle through a pane of glass. They are fabrications, interpretations, distortions and constructions. Each one of the students' dioramas invites the viewer to engage with a quality of the site in a very direct manner, whether through the handling of castings taken from the site, through specific positions necessary to recompose an anamorphic view, or through the reading of letters found in a secret cabinet.

In the third year, Design & Creative Practice is driven by an interest in interdisciplinary practice that looks outside of the institution and promotes public-facing, socially engaged projects. Combining group work and individual practice, we explore and experiment with strategies for creative practice that are sustainable within a wide cultural context, whilst collectively exploring a theme relating to architecture and the built environment. This year's brief centred around the theme of failure, both as a necessary condition of creative practice and a force for change in society. We asked how failures shape the cities we live in today: the failure of individual endeavours or communal ambitions; failed politics, failed masterplans, failed ideologies and failed designs. To accept and learn from failure is to move into new territory for exploration. It can motivate us to find new approaches and different perspectives, something we need today more than ever.

Year 1
Rasim Aroglu, Anna Chippendale, Yoon-A Chung, Gurmukh Dhanjal, Sandra Engardt, Camille Eymieu, Fran Green, Joseph Kingsley, Jeewoo Lee, Nelli Mazina, Erika Notarianni, Herb Ronson, Zhelin (Simon) Sun, Chetz (Chloe) Tan, Helen Visscher, Marcos Wolodarsky Newhall

Year 2
Rory Alexander, Moe Atsumeda, Sadika Begum, Sam Bloomfield, Yingqi (Jessie) Gao, Maya Garner, Mari Katsuno, Lily Ketzer, Alexia Koch, Inbar Langerman, Ashley Law, Tseng-Han (Christina) Lin Hou, Qiyin (Sienna) Liu, Ethan Low, Mimi Osei-Kuffuor, Uliana Shesterkina, Eloi Simon, Connie Stafford, Motong (Mog) Yang, Emma Yee

Year 3
Lizzie Atherton, Danhng (Dan) Bai, Philipp Behawy, Anna Cabanlig, Jasmine Ceccarelli-Drewry, Esme Chong, Isabel Dorn, Roxanne Gonzales, Hollie Hatfield, Sara Herrera Dixon, Sara Hill, Katarina Krajciova, Julia Millang, Emilie Morrow, Tanzim Naser, Max Pertl, Ged Ribas Goody, Camilla Romano, Jessica Thorpe, Yasmine Zein Elabedin, Mengxuan (Moe) Zhao

Year 4
Lucy Brown, Vikrimjeet (Vikrim) Nagra

DCP.1, DCP.14 Katarina Krajciova, Y3 'My Paradise: The Exploration into the Modern Sacred'. This film is an exploration into the nature of the new spirituality that took over the church garden of St Dunstan in the East. The beautiful architecture crafted for the purposes of worship is now overgrown with vegetation and turned into an picturesque backdrop for Instagram photographs. The spiritual nature of social media is addressed in the project, along with its relationship to the religious tradition of Christianity associated with the site.
DCP.2 Fran Green, Y1 'Drawing Twilight'. In a city dominated by artificial light, a system and a set of tools for enhancing and recording the evening's delicate shifts in colour and shadow seeks to restore and intensify our experience of the diurnal cycle .
DCP.3 Sandra Engardt, Y1 'A Sensory Playground'. In a critique of the modernist drive for efficient urban circulation, a collection of paving stones encourages the the walker to slow down, re-engage and reminsice, through the textures of the ground beneath their feet.
DCP.4 Anna Chippendale, Y1 'A Portable Subconscious Enabler'. Asserting the value of the bed as a fertile intellectual, creative and spiritual territory, a series of wearable textile prototypes seek to create similarly intimate environments in spaces beyond the domestic.
DCP.5 Helen Visscher, Y1 'Prayer Nut'. An artefact to support new pre-match rituals for West Ham United fans, bringing luck to the team in their new stadium.
DCP.6 Herb Ronson, Y1 'Medicine for Free-Thinking Individuals: façade study'. As ever more people reject modern scientific thought around immunisation, the architecture of the 'anti-vax' community expresses the ideals of a disparate global movement that must distance itself from the rest of the world for reasons of medical and ideological hygiene.
DCP.7 Helen Visscher, Y1 'Ken's Café'. A speculative reconstruction of West Ham United fan culture extrapolated from the physical and digital relics of the team's former home in Upton Park, centring on a legendary local café.
DCP.8 Ethan Low, Y2 'Flight of the Land Kite'. Hovering between flight and failure, a series of wind-driven devices explore contemporary restictions in airspace law, capturing the glory of attempted, ambiguous and impossible flights on film.
DCP.9–DCP.10 Yingqi (Jessie) Gao, Y2 'Landscape of the Past'. A reconstruction of the layered history of Regent's Park translates land ownership patterns, diverted architectural plans and natural interventions into a stratigraphic time capsule, buried onsite.
DCP.11 Moe Atsumeda, Y2 'The Secret Silk Factory'. Welcome to the hidden world within Regent's Park Lake, where the swans of the park secretly labour, plucking and weaving their own feathers into luxurious silks. A Japanese folk tale translates into a critique on power, money and contemporary convenience.
DCP.12 Yingqi (Jessie) Gao, Ethan Low, Emma Yee, Y2 'Distillation of Time'. An artificial limb clutches to the Friendship Tree in the centre of Gordon Square, fed by the falling leaves, extracting and distilling their essence and feeding it back to the roots from which they came. The natural and the artificial grow and wither in symbiosis.
DCP.13 Sam Bloomfield, Maya Garner, Jessica Thorpe, Motong (Mog) Yang, Y2 'Shifting Volumes'. An unfolding installation deconstructs the movements that underpin Tavistock Square, tracing interactions between the park and the people that create it. Its interlocking parts – a doorknob, a railing, the edge of a wall – are the memories, traces and containers of actions.
DCP.15 Roxanne Gonzales, Y3 'Sugar Sculptures: A sweet inquiry'. The project aims to examine the materiality of sugar and expose the environmental effects of sugarcane farming. By drawing together elements of the history of sugar, the work seeks to make sugar a spectacle again, but also to question where it comes from and how it can affect our planet.
DCP.16 Camilla Romano, Y3 'Breaking the Table'. Exploring the theme of etiquette, this project focuses on what it means for a woman to perform 'good etiquette'. The film, 'Breaking The Table', combines etiquette of posture, conversation and table manners into a rebellious act against longstanding notions of feminine etiquette.
DCP.17 Ged Ribas Goody, Y3 'Archives in Transmission: Object #001'. This is the first object to be given to and also taken from the Archives in Transmission (AIT) archive during our first workshop. The photograph is of the object in the hand of the person who took it. AIT is an immaterial archive of trans exchange, knowledge production and storytelling.
DCP.18 Jasmine Ceccarelli-Drewry, Y3 'Annotating the City'. Annotation can be used to keep track of our thinking as we read. It can also be used to tune into a text more efficiently, or as a feedback system to 'eavesdrop' on other people's ideas. This project develops an idea of 'spatial annotations', asking how we can capture the reactions, moods, emotions and decisions of people experiencing the city, and why these may be worth capturing. Supported by UCL's Urban Innovation and Policy Laboratory, on the 6 May 2019 the project brought together industry experts and researchers to explore what it means to 'Annotate the City.' In an interactive guided tour around Euston Station, participants were asked to engage in a spatial annotation process using photographs and note-taking to capture reactions to the urban landscape. The tour was followed by a panel discussion to reflect on how we can move towards a more holistic and inclusive policy and planning framework, develop models of community engagement and consultation, and encourage people to be alert to their position in the city.

DCP.1

DCP.2

DCP.3

DCP.4

DCP.5

DCP.6

DCP.7

DCP.8

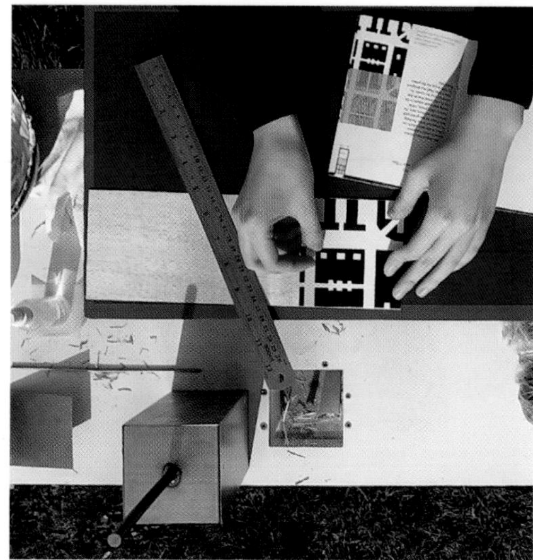
DCP.9

DCP.10

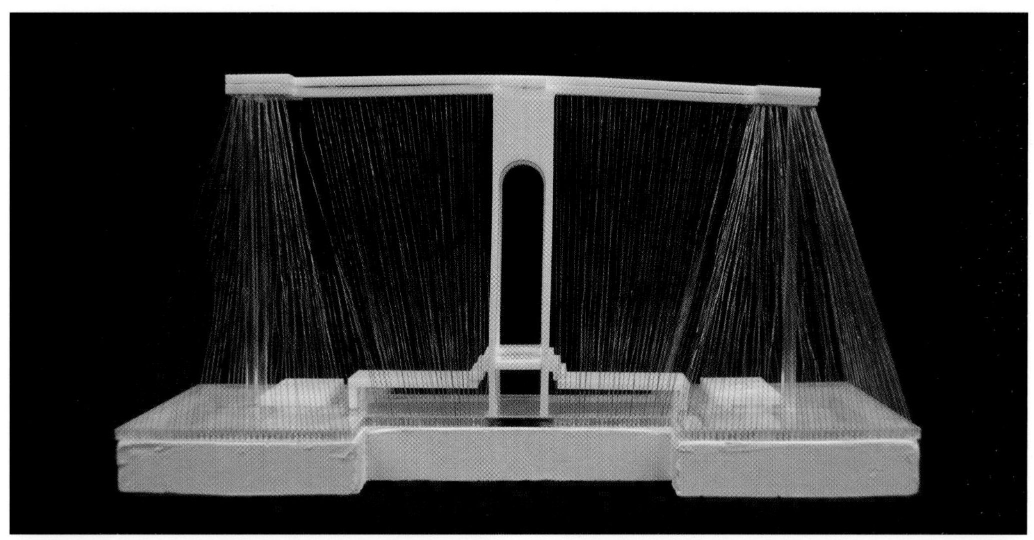

DCP.11

DCP.12

DCP.13

DCP.14

DCP.15

DCP.16

DCP.17

DCP.18

Inside the Engineering & Architectural Design pavilion 'WeValues', 2019

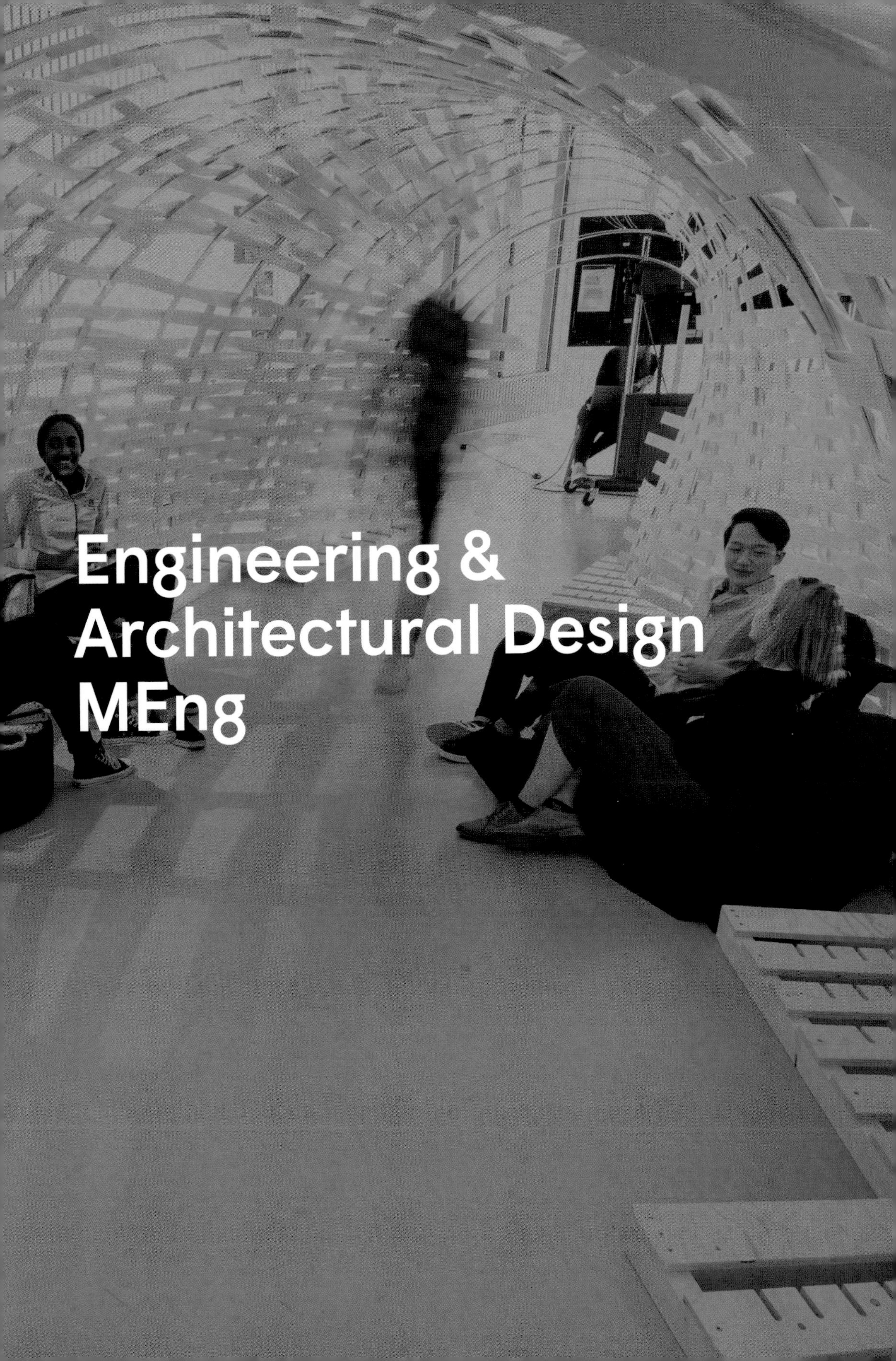

Engineering & Architectural Design MEng

Year 1

Tamanna Abul Kashem, Yuval Ben-Giat, Wenhui (Alex) Cao, Chongyu (Victor) Chen, Yuzhe (Eason) Chen, Yi (Alex) Chen, Ruiyi (Renae) Du, Andreea Dumitrescu, Victoria Ewert, James Grimmond, Panagiota Grivea, Sarah Hassan M Alsomly, Jessica Ho, Sichen Hu, Iman Jemitola, Young Choel Moses Jeon, Hans Kei Kaeppeler, Leo Kauntz Moderini, Tianhao Luo, Pedro Merino Ramon, Victor Noorani, Sarina Patel, Franca Pilchner, Jakub Plewik, Mateo Rossi Rolando, Kimberley Rubio Ugalde, Ralf Saade, Samuel Seymour-Blackburn, Nikie Siabishahrivar, Allegra Simpson, Johanna Stenhols, Harry Sumner, Emma Temm, Tahira Uddin, Igor Verkhoturov, Yile (Aloe) Wu, Zhuofan (Marco) Wu

Year 2

Cecilia Cappellini, Zhe Chen, Federico Chiavegati, Kasikit Dumnoenchanvanit, Luke Duncan, Michael Fordham, Simran Khurana, Michal Kierat, Maria Konstantinova, Clement Lefebure, Cheuk Liu, Yuhan Liu, Sheung Lo, Julie Motouzka, Olivia Narenthiran, Iuliana-Andra Padurariu, Fatema Panju, Praefah Praditbatuga, Jahnina Queddeng, Toekinah Sabeni-Lefeuvre, Xi Shen, Yan To, Tin Tse, Rabia Turemis, Lan Wang, Kaia Wells, Sheryl Wylie, Yibin Xu, Chenmuyuan Zhang, Hetian Zhang, Yunxian Zhu

Engineering & Architectural Design MEng

Programme Director & Architecture Lead: Luke Olsen

Designed in close collaboration with industry leaders, Engineering & Architectural Design MEng combines the major disciplines of the built environment, architecture and engineering, to prepare future industry leaders. With the first cohort now completing their second year, this pioneering programme is crossing the professional, pedagogical and cultural boundaries between architecture and engineering to expand further the biggest ecology of all – innovative design.

The degree is taught collaboratively by three UCL departments: The Bartlett School of Architecture, The Institute for Environmental Design and Engineering, and the Department of Civil, Environmental and Geomatic Engineering – across two sites in Bloomsbury and UCL at Here East. In Year 1, students complete core modules in building physics, the history and theory of engineering and architecture, and mathematical modelling, alongside design and material-led work within the studio. In Year 2, students undertake a substantial design practice module, along with advanced mathematical modelling and analysis, structural analysis, urban physics and environmentally responsible building systems.

This year, first-year students explored the theme of 'Tribal Gathering', working within the state-of-the-art fabrication facilities of Here East to explore how architecture and engineering can work at a practical, experimental and societal level to bring people together. Students designed, built and tested – sometimes to destruction – pavilions at 1:1 scale, with each project supporting a deeper understanding of the design process from concept to completion. Pavilions explored ideas including craft and the bespoke, digital fabrication and generative design, interactivity and puppetry and used materials ranging from birch ply to resonating steel tubes.

The collaborative and interdisciplinary work of first-year Engineering & Architectural Design students was celebrated in March as part of the Faculty's centenary events, when local practitioners and community members were invited to Here East for an exhibition, open crit and party to explore the pavilions. Three of the pavilions, 'WeaValues', 'The Expandables' and UCLoud', were also re-installed as part of Dulwich Picture Gallery's *Colour Palace*, part of the London Festival of Architecture.

Meanwhile, this year's second-year students worked individually and in collaboration to develop innovative buildings as a space of exchange. Ideas were explored and incubated within an interdisciplinary design studio, responding to the theme of 'Borders in Barcelona'. Students investigated the blurred edges and spaces within boundaries in El Poblenou, along Pere IV, developing and testing digitally crafted prototypical architectures, to straddle the seam of two or more contradictory spaces or conditions.

Structural Engineering Lead
Liora Malki-Epshtein

Environmental Engineering Lead
Dejan Mumovic

Bartlett School of Architecture staff
Bim Burton, Melis van de Burg, Matthew Butcher, Dan Carter, Satyajit Das, Dave Edwards, Laura Gaskell, Mark Hines, Clara Jaschke, Jonny Martin, Josep Miàs, Luke Olsen, Igor Pantic, Klaas de Rycke, Matt Ridsdale, Sam Riley, Andrew Scoones, Sara Shafiei, James Solly, Michael Stacey, Jerry Tate, Michael Wagner, Graeme Williamson

UCL Department of Civil, Environmental & Geomatic Engineering (CEGE) staff
Fabio Freddi, Laura Hannigan, Olivia Riddle, Marek Ziebart, Santosh Bhattarai, Matthew Coop, Yasemin Didem Aktas

UCL Institute for Environmental Design & Engineering (IEDE) staff
Sarah Bell, Esfand Burgman, Ivan Korolija, Sam Stamp, Farhang Tahmasebi, Jonathan Taylor, Isobel Why

EAD.1 **Kei Kaeppeler, Marta Hagermann, Victor Luo, Sarina Patel, Kimberley Rubio Ugalde, Y1** 'Momentum'. The project re-examines the 'Bennett Linkage', a beguiling deployable system first invented by UCL alumnus and mathematician Dr Geoffrey Bennett, a hundred years ago. The pavilion is made of a network of square aluminium beams with double-curve elastic membranes providing tension to almost prevent collapse at full expansion. Stronger titanium hinges are required to prevent softening of these precise nodal connections.
EAD.2 **Tamanna Abul Kashim, Io Griviea, Jessica Lo, Leo Kauntz Moderini, Ralf Saade, Tahira Uddin, Zhuofan Wu, Y1** 'The Expandables'. The project is designed as a relaxing comfortable place in a hectic environment using a flexible, lightweight and triangulated net structures with integrated responsive lighting systems. The pavilion works as a deployable anaechoic chamber to make an acoustically comfortable and visually atmospheric space for groups of people throughout the day and evening to relax in, even when it is noisy and dark outside.
EAD.3 **Sarah Hassan, Franka Pilchner, Jakub Plewik, Yile Wu, Y1** '2Blessed2BeStressed'. Incorporating weaving and pattern-cutting techniques into a geometry taken from the motif of Alice falling through a field of mushrooms, this pavilion uses flexible plywood and fabrics to form a large-scale structure. Arches filled with ornamental designs based on silhouettes from John Tinnel's drawings to create an enclosure that transcends the environmental conditions with psychedelic light, coloured shade and pattern.
EAD.4 **Wenhui Cao, Yi Chen, Victoria Ewert, Pedro Merino Ramon, Sam Seymour-Blackburn, Allegra Simpson, Harry Sumner, Y1** 'UCLoud'. This interactive pavilion is composed of three modular elements with strings in tension that are tuned to resonate audible polyphonic tones. Visitors are invited to either pluck the strings, walk on the waw-waw peddle producing varied vibratory sounds, or to rest in the sitting area that makes up the pavilion's centre. Each sound produces a recorded fall-off and adds this to a digital loop that resonates with changing colour lighting long after the original sound occurs, creating a collaborative sound- and lightscape.
EAD.5 **Yuval Ben-Giat, Yuzhe Chen, Andreea Dumitrescu, James Grimmond, Iman Jemitola, Nikie Siabishahrivar, Emma Temm, Y1** 'WeValues'. The project explores a building system of birch plywood arches and timber foundations designed to adapt to various configurations and landscapes. Alongside UCLoud and Expandables this pavilion was redeployed at London's Dulwich Picture Gallery. The pavilion is a cooperative exploration of space and the public are invited to manipulate the materials from outside the structure and within to adapt to various preferences for particular views or apertures.
EAD.6 **Toekinah Sabeni-Lefeuvre, Y2** 'Peeking Gallery, Barcelona'. The project investigates the visual relationships within spaces by introducing a series of 'cracks', through which visitors can catch unexpected glimpses of the city, or in some cases pass through them.
EAD.7–EAD.8 **Zhe (Gigi) Chen, Y2** 'Weaving Space, Barcelona'. A new entrance and café extension exploring textile weaving in architectural skin.
EAD.9 **Xi Shen, Y2** 'Yoga & Meditation Centre, Barcelona'. Half-submerged on the beach of Barcelona, the project explores serene spaces for yoga and meditation that are closely related to the coming and going of the tides in their arrangement and expression.
EAD.10 **Clement Lefebure, Y2** 'El Poblenou Co-Making Space, Barcelona.' The project aims to enable young startups to investigate the underlying collaborative and iterative processes of design, fabrication, and manufacturing, by providing facilities to drive their designs from initial concepts to physical prototypes.
EAD.11 **Sheryl Wiley, Y2** 'Public Library, El Poblenou Barcelona,'. The project explores fluid integration of skin and opening through software explorations. Each formal modulation is predicated on a relationship to the surrounding context.
EAD.12 **Fatema Panju, Y2** 'Fish Market, Barcelona sea front'. The site-specific intervention is carried on a set of concrete 'trays', each modulated to create countertops and display areas for the market. Water is channelled through the ground plane to manage cooling and hygiene within the spaces, while solar shading is controlled overhead through a canopy structure.
EAD.13 **Rabia Turemis, Y2** 'Illusive Yoga and Meditation Studio, Barcelona.' The project explores notions of creating infinite spaces through the application of tools of illusion and deception. The project proposes a journey of 'imagination becoming reality.'
EAD.14 **Ellie To, Y2** 'Carved Gallery Block, Barcelona'. The project explores a sculptural agenda, carving a sequence of small gallery spaces from a cubic form – generating void and solid space.
EAD.15 **Cecilia Cappellini, Y2** 'Craft Medina, Barcelona'. A highly crafted architectural response, the project explores a series of covered spaces in brickwork housing artisan production processes, set within an underused residential courtyard.
EAD.16–EAD.17 **Kaia Wells, Y2** 'Secret/Dark Garden'. This project explores notions of smell and texture through the design of a garden and centre for visually impaired people.
EAD.18 **Olivia (Phoeby) Narenthiran, Y2** 'Student Gallery Pavilions, Barcelona'. A landscape of brick is introduced within which a series of stand-alone gallery spaces are allowed to propagate. The external and internal elements of each gallery are collected under a variegated canopy of repeated timber elements.
EAD.19 **Praefah (Muse) Praditbatuga, Y2** 'The Canopy: A view to the sea'. A modern reinterpretation of El Poblenou's relationship with the seafront.

EAD.2

EAD.3

EAD.4

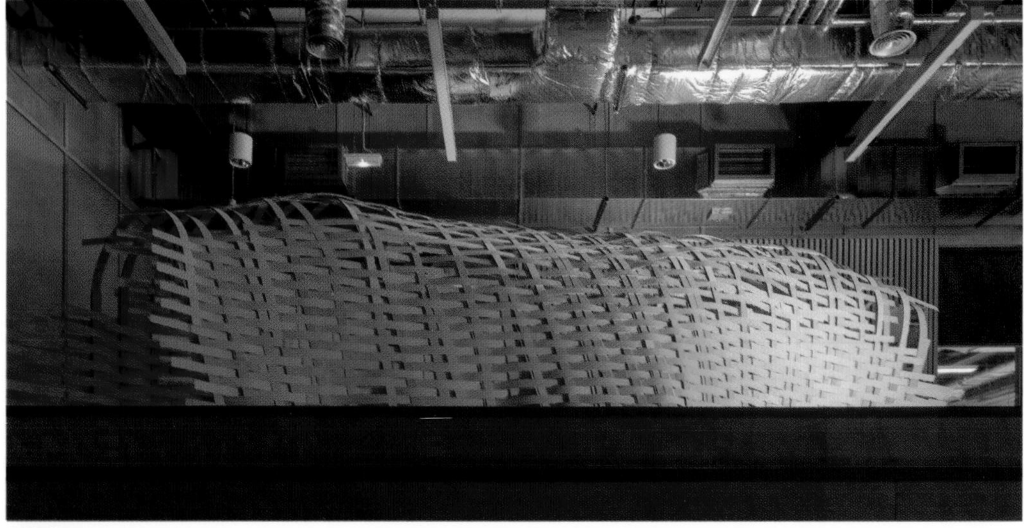

EAD.5

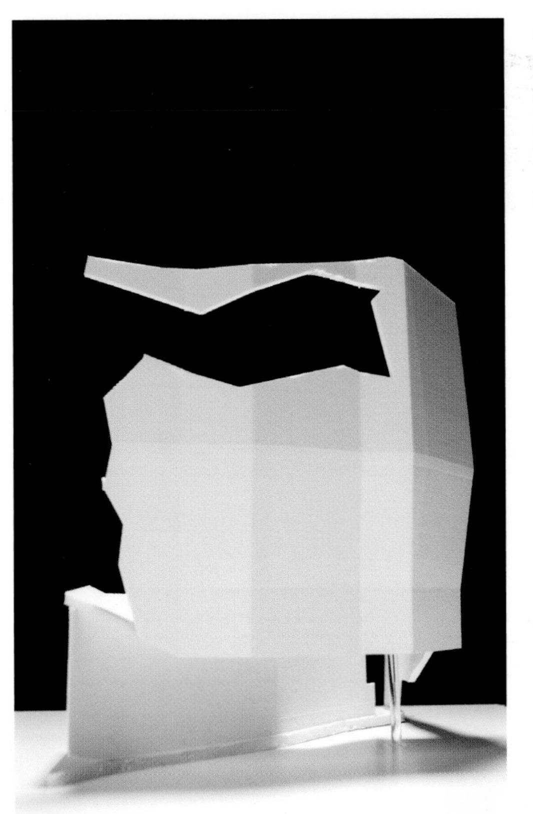

EAD.6

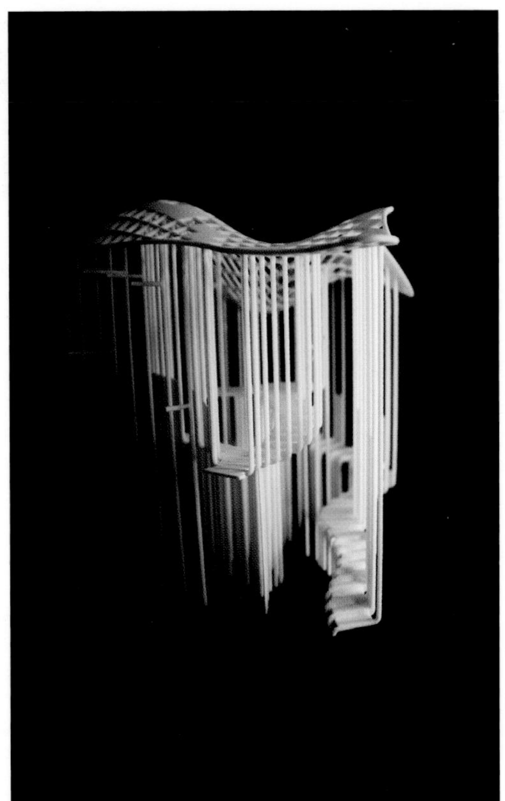

EAD.7

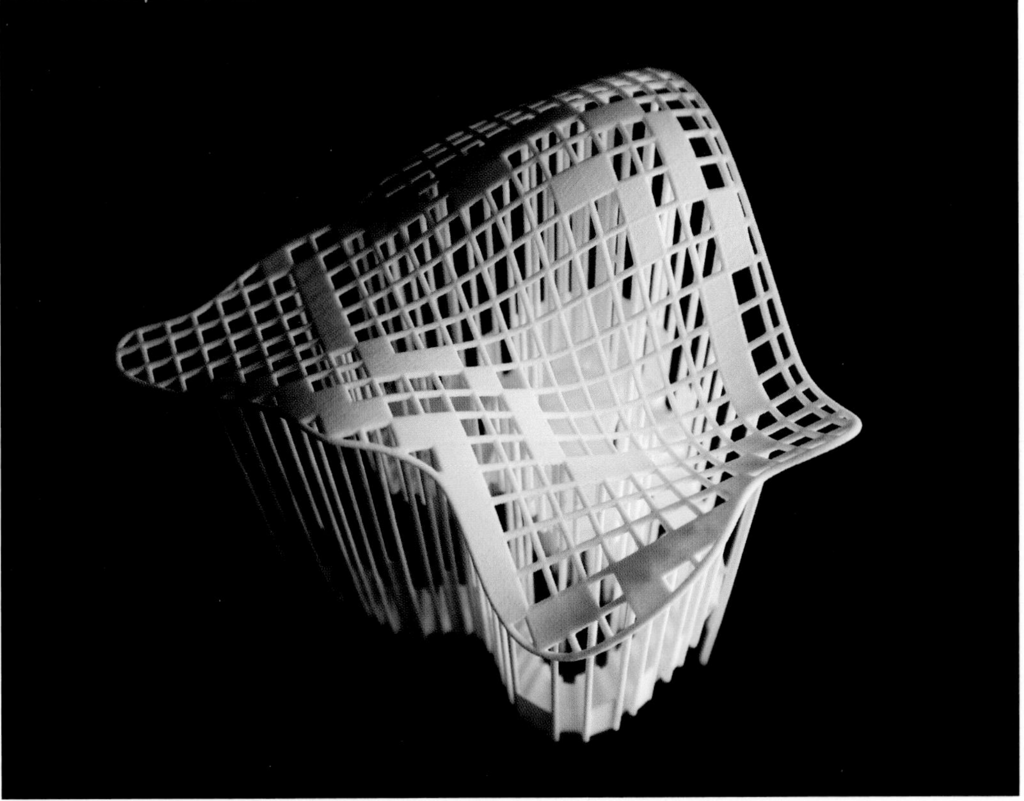

EAD.8

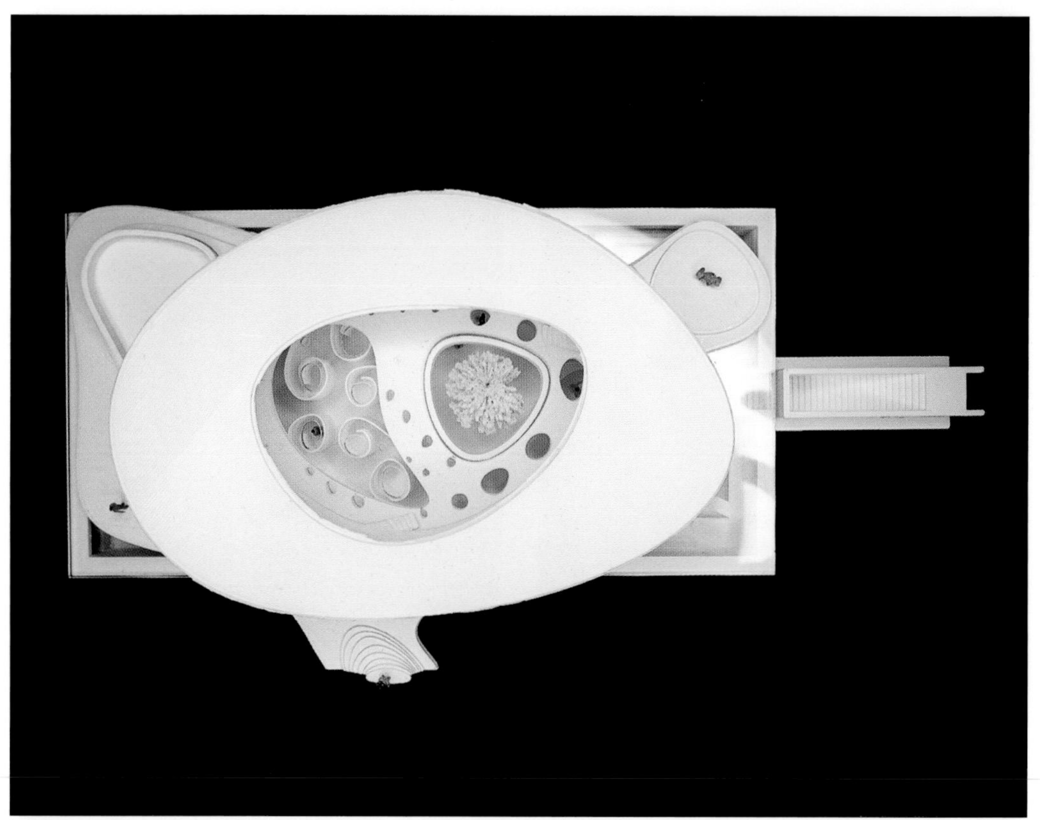

EAD.9

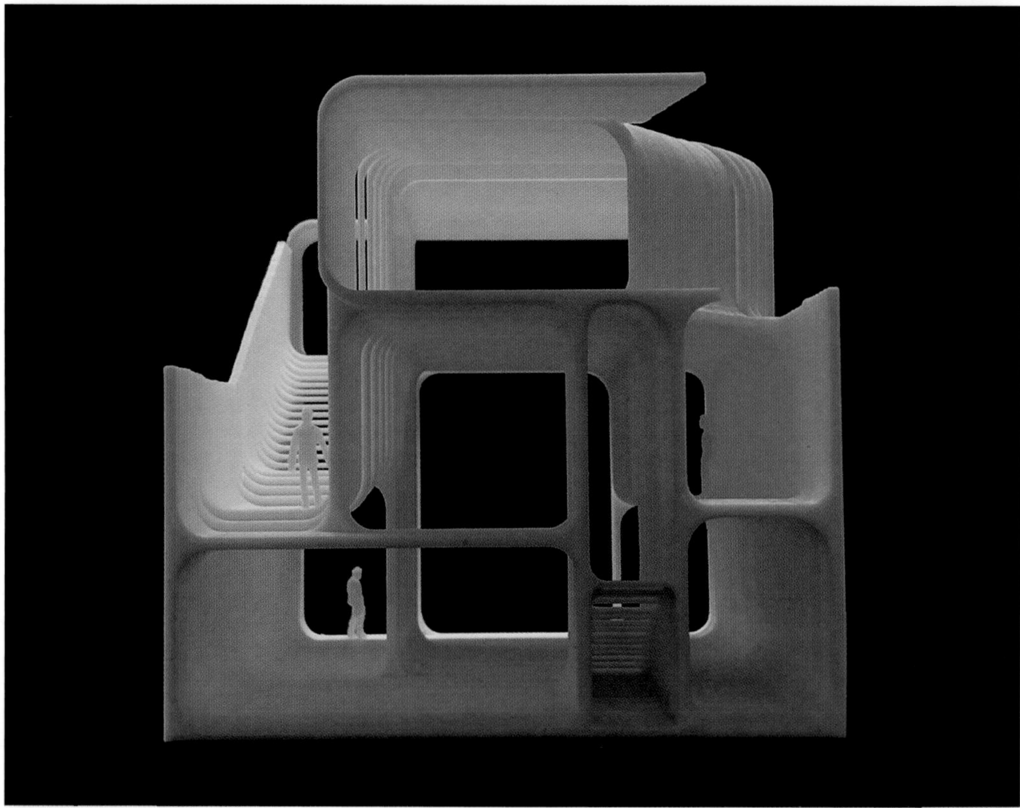

EAD.10

EAD.11

EAD.12

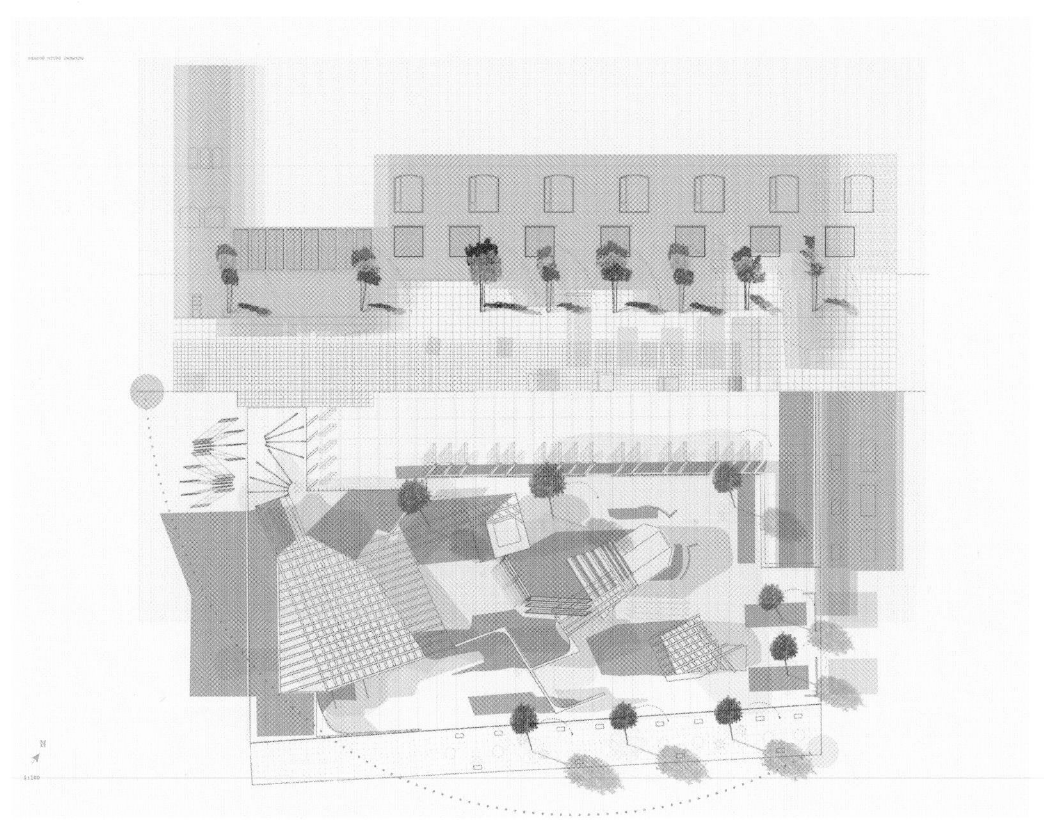
EAD.13

EAD.14

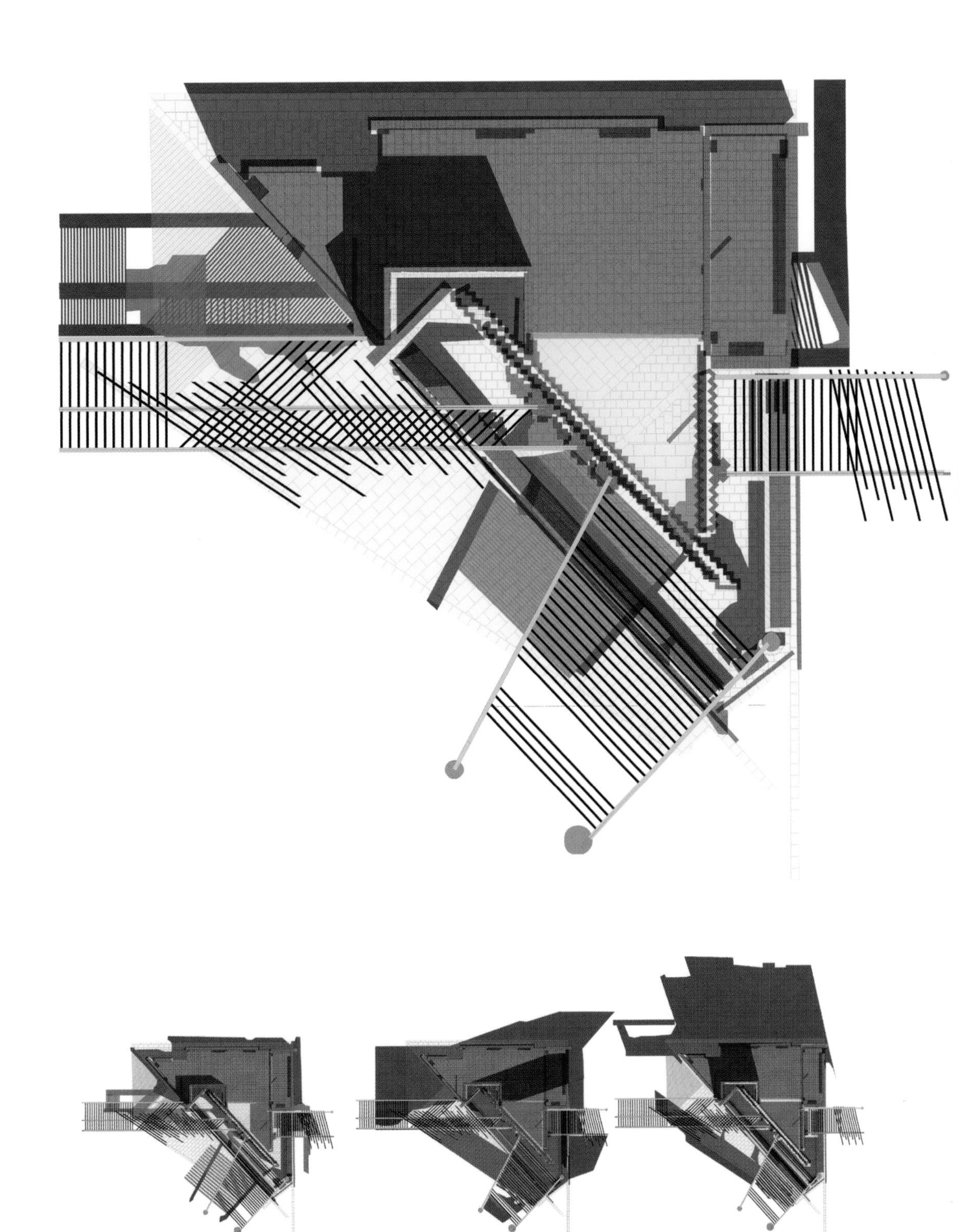

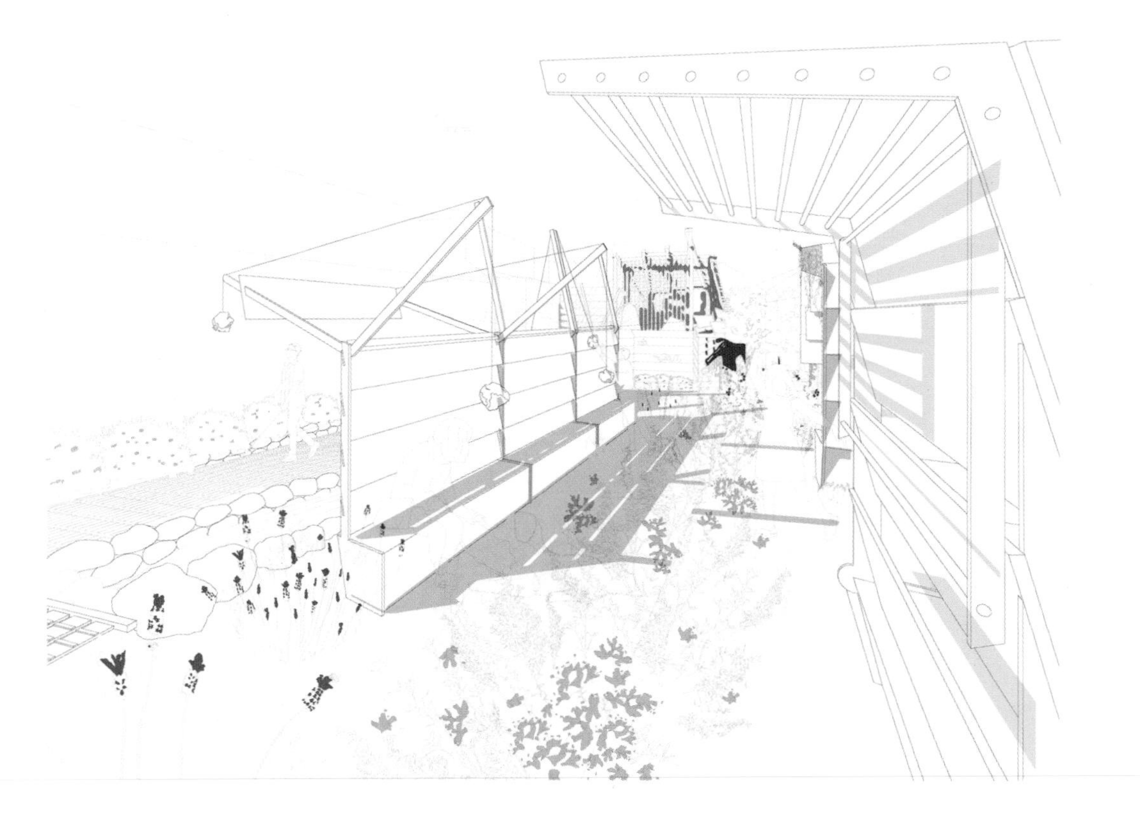

EAD.16

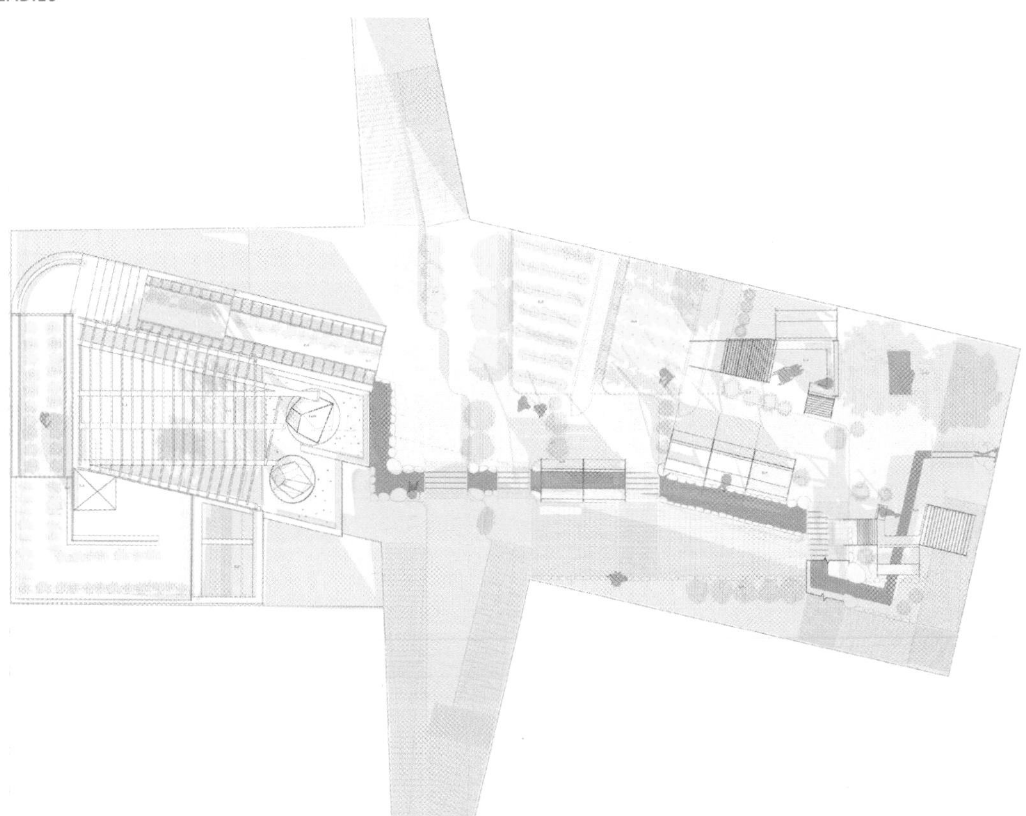

EAD.17

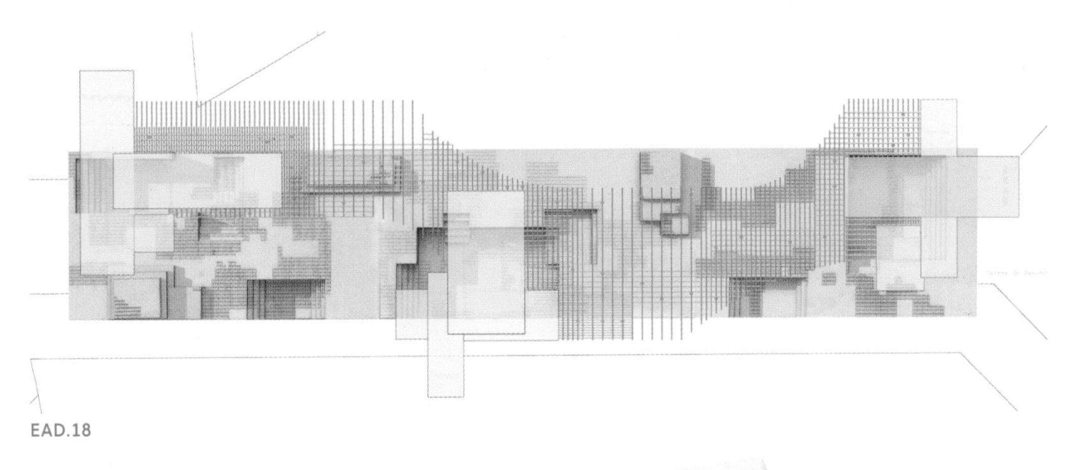

EAD.18

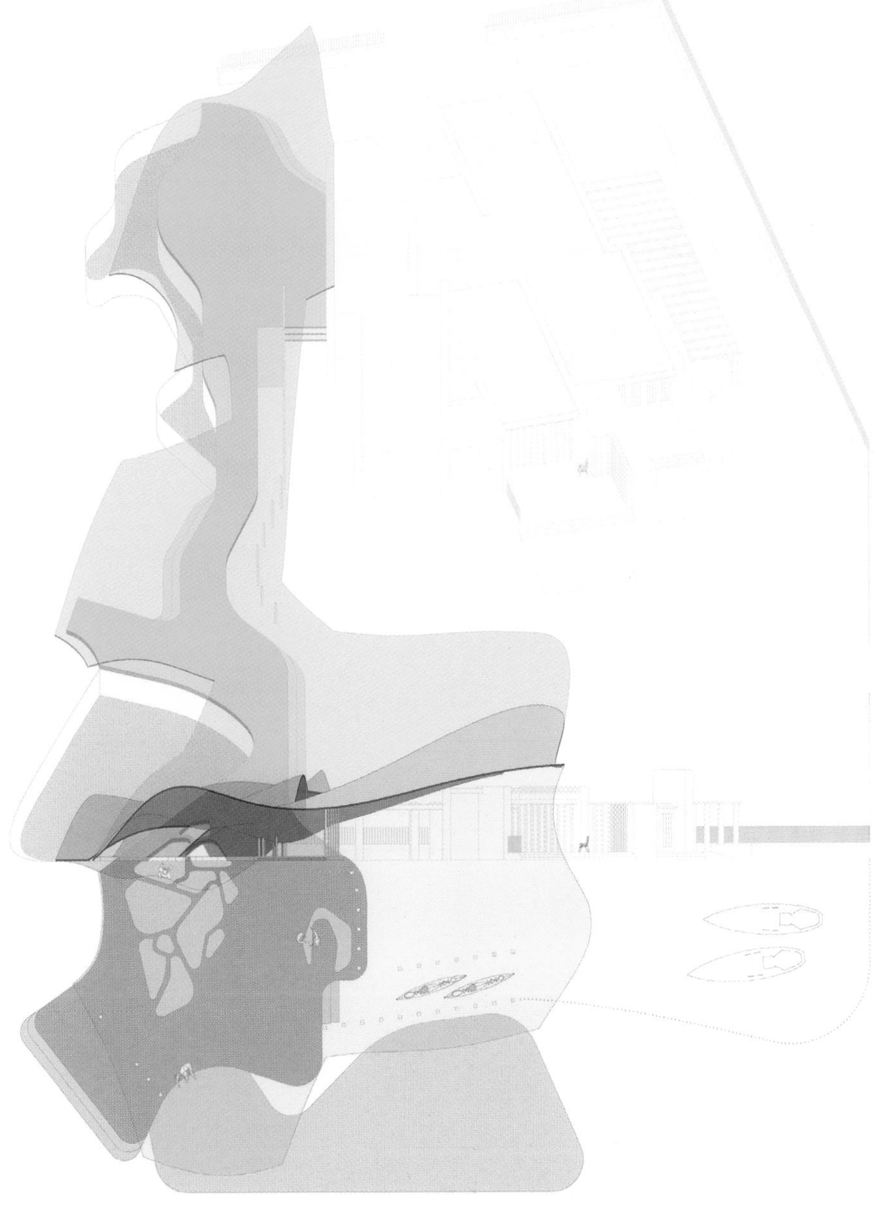

EAD.19

PG10 tutorial with CJ Lim and Simon Dickens

Architecture MArch (ARB/RIBA Part 2)

Architecture MArch (ARB/RIBA Part 2)

Programme Directors: Julia Backhaus, Marjan Colletti with Barbara-Ann Campbell-Lange

Practices of architecture are necessarily steeped in difficulty. There are no neat formulas, no easy wins, no clear answers, no simple solutions. There is no 'correct' medium in which to express an idea, no ideal material, no agreed version of history or vision of the future; no single way to design a city, a room or a detail. And we can never know enough, do enough, or care enough.

Yet still we attend. We watch, we listen, we converse, we ask, we wonder, we try. We irritate and iterate, doubt and disagree about ideas and methodologies that veer and err and swerve and rejoin in ragged pursuit of proposition and proposal. We evolve each other, learn to ask questions, to recognise assumptions and say when we don't know. We seek the overlooked and dare to imperfectly piece together the disjunct stuff of architecture for the diverse audiences we care about, some of whom may not be listening or able to hear.

Our units' practices are many and various, each expanding in a different way to develop projects that question how our discipline is rehearsed. Together, as tutors and students, we try to understand and speak about architecture: what it is, what it might do.

We are growing as polylingual makers and thinkers, entrepreneurs and policy-whisperers, ready to provoke architectures in socio-political force fields too complex to represent in any straightforward way. Our work opens up alternative models of collaboration, enabling intersections where none existed; it loosens tightly scripted dialogues to let in industries and institutions in less knowable, shifting territories and fragile ecosystems. Across these grounds of realities and ideals, of what is and what may be, knowledge is gained, challenged and adjusted.

Our projects span time from deep pasts to deep futures, engaging technologies and modes of production from disciplines outside our own. They work with faith and hope and charity to offer social change and resilience to established dogmas. They repair damaged landscapes, remaking terrains unknown and unimagined till now. Unloved and bypassed hinterlands of sprawling cities are re-presenced along transnational corridors. The hidden qualities of unassuming places are discerned and localness restitched into quiet spectacles. The experience and meaning of ordinariness, the matter and materials in our daily lives, is reframed and reformulated. Close readings of emerging vernaculars, where crafts meet technologies, unfold alternative educations.

We allow ourselves to slow down, to be sceptical towards industrialisation and look at technological progress as a means to restore quality to lives rather than an end in itself. We exhaust the possibilities of film, animation, virtual and augmented reality, and physical modelling techniques in order to push to its limits our exploration of architecture's relationship with time. A synthetic approach hybridising data and design encrypts and deciphers authorship in architecture. We draw distinctions and make decisions – premeditated, provisional and emergent, freed as much as possible from preconceptions, tested and revised in virtual and physical full-scale and no-scale installations.

We confront the crisis in reason and democracy.

All of us in education face the pressing need to work in another way: to connect our curricula and meet an uncertain future with socially and environmentally informed practices. And in the seams and at the thresholds of our joined work, we need to recognise the intimate link between ecological breakdown and global inequality.

In our discipline nothing made is easily won. We are not straightforwardly measurable, rateable, boxable or communicable, yet our practices strive to include and address, to build real relationships between peoples and places, and to create, through thought-filled arrangements of cherished materials, a sense of generosity with space and time. We do not turn from difficulty but engage with it, and though we fail, and fail again, we fail better in the belief that our thinking, our making, our collective care, carries the immense responsibility to improve the world we share.

10.1

The Virtues of Urban Resilience

PG10

Simon Dickens, CJ Lim

Faith, hope and charity are theological virtues, but they functioned as supremely civic virtues during the flowering of communes, guaranteeing good government. This is because love of the city one calls home has its roots in charity, and the actions of justice are animated by faith and by hope for divine guidance.[1]

It is certainly true that faith builds, as seen in the holy cities of Mecca or Varanasi, or in the hubris skyscrapers of Dubai that are propped up by belief in the oil economy. In the US in the 1920s and 30s, the Hoover Dam and Boulder City in Nevada came to symbolise hope for the millions of dispossessed Americans in the depths of the Great Depression. President Herbert Hoover feared public dependency on the federal government and realised the dam could unite public work and private enterprise, improve mass-employment and quality of life, support the economy and promote patriotism. In 19th-century Paris, urban planner Baron Haussmann (1809-1891) was both celebrated and despised for building much of what has since become synonymous with the city. By driving sweeping boulevards through the urban slums barricaded by the revolutionaries, he transformed Paris into a city of light and trees in an effort to improve living and working conditions.

Whether by bold gesture or subtle attrition, cities are constantly rewritten. Henri Lefebvre (1901-1991), the French sociologist and author of the seminal text *Critique of Everyday Life*, argued that every society produces its own spatial practice. At every critical juncture, the shape of the space that will help us contest climate change, social deprivation and deficiencies in food, water and energy has to be reimagined. In 1967, Le Corbusier lamented that, 'The world is sick. A readjustment has become necessary. Readjustment? No, that is too tame. It is the possibility of a great adventure that lies before mankind: the building of a whole new world.'[2] This comment might appear prescient, but it could have been written at any time in history. In the age of Trump and Brexit, Frugoni's virtues, faith, hope and charity, are key in redefining the built environment and the notion of citizenship: not only access to the rights guaranteed by the nation-state but more active and pluralistic forms of participation that promote community resilience.

For their project this year, Year 4 students chose a painting and employed a narrative that prioritised and redefined the spatial poetics of either faith, hope or love. The interpretations and identified issues provided a speculative programmatic framework for the year.

Year 5 students were required to identify a feature of their chosen site that qualified it as 'undesired', be it the weather, economy, geography, lack of inhabitation or indifference. The symbiosis between place and narrative informed their visionary urban design and architectural proposals.

Year 4
Lap Yan Chow, Xiaoliang Deng, Adrian Hong, Luke Hurley, Edmund Tan, Tyler Thurston, Ka (Karen) Tsang, Kit Wong

Year 5
Nicole Cork, Junchao Guo, Peter Hougaard, Jinrong Lai, Benjamin Simpson, Vilius Vizgaudis, Ananda Wiegandt

Thank you to Jon Kaminsky for his teaching of the Design Realisation module, David Roberts for the Manifesto Workshop and Matthew Wells for the Structures Workshop

Thank you to our consultants: Nathan Blades, Peter Brickell, Nathan Blades, Michela Martini, Chris Matthews, Sam Smith, Rachel Yehezkel

1. Chiara Frugoni, *A Day in a Medieval City*, (Chicago: University of Chicago Press, 2006), p21
2. Le Corbusier, *The Radiant City: Elements of a Doctrine of Urbanism to be Used as the Basis of our Machine-Age Civilisation*, (London: Faber & Faber, 1967), p92

10.1 **Ananda Wiegandt, Y5** 'The Valley of Harmony'. Grant Wood's *American Gothic* (1930) depicts the determination of the Midwestern rural population to work with the land during the Great Depression. The new landscape in 'The Valley of Harmony' promotes neighbourly love and provides earth-sheltered sustainable housing for the disenfranchised elderly and migrant populations, and facilitates an influx of seasonal cultural visitors. The extensive cultivation of pollen-emitting trees in the brown coal open-cast mines supports the creation of an environmental cooling spine through Europe, which aims to mitigate the effects of the changing climate, whilst the tree conveys notions of 'cohesion', 'resilience' and 'tomorrow'.

10.2 **Peter Hougaard, Y5** 'The Garden of Difference'. Yayoi Kusama's psychological illness and society's misfits are the creative inspirations behind her artworks. Similarly, in 'The Garden of Difference' weakness is strength, limitations are possibilities and difference is everyday's normal. Sexual and social misfits, disfranchised individuals and minority cultures work side-by-side with the citizens of Northallerton in Yorkshire to redevelop their high street and address increasing social monotony, prejudice and hostility. The architecture introduces social metaphors to unconventional construction techniques and materials, and questions conservative values: arcades made from living trees decorated with chandeliers of marijuana; hedges filled with worms fed to salmon in a park; cardboard box hotels; scaffolding platforms for selfie-taking tourists; and a carpark with former prostitutes eager to listen and discuss the state of the town.

10.3–10.4 **Jinrong (Jerome) Lai, Y5** 'The Appreciation'. This project draws similarities to Pieter Bruegel the Elder's *Netherlandish Proverbs* (1559) and is a propaganda to unmask human follies. Chinese President Xi Jinping believes that both morality and water quality in China are polluted. To bring faith and morality back into society and the environment, this project employs greed to cultivate awareness and encouragement in protecting against irresponsible outcomes, following the discovery of contaminated water resources due to unregulated industrialisation. Informed by *shan shui* paintings, the architecture creates not a perfect society but an acceptable equilibrium with nature.

10.5–10.6 **Ben Simpson, Y5** 'A Portrait of Self-Love and Self-Reliance'. In response to Theresa May's proposed 'Festival of Brexit', the project seeks not to revitalise national pride in clichéd short-lived event formats but, instead, invests in the regeneration of undesirable parts of the UK. A renewed ideology of 'Britishness' draws from the much-disparaged weather, agriculture and resources of pride identified in Lucas Cranach the Elder's *Cupid complaining to Venus* (c.1525): apples, timber, deer, honey, wool, myrtle and water. The new 'green corridor of self-love and self-reliance' protects areas of conservation that have seen recent industrial decline, as well as those that have lost industry due to Brexit. It provides a continuous passage for deer from Inverness to Cornwall, and is punctuated by community participation 'Self Stores', apple orchards offering employment, produce depots and intergenerational social spaces.

10.7 **Nicole Cork, Y5** 'The Renaissance of Burnley'. Derived from Alfred, Lord Tennyson's poem 'The Lady of Shalott' (1842), 'The Renaissance of Burnley' symbolises hope and depicts a pivotal moment of change empowered by nature. Under the new doctrine of the 'Post-Industrial Sisterhood', stems an appreciation of context and strategies to heal nature and rehabilitate the ground. By adopting the 2050 UK Climate Agenda and Fifth Carbon Budget, the post-industrial coal mining town is transformed into a clean-energy producing inhabitable landscape and nature reserve. It explores the opportunities of canal engineering with hybridised housing, addressing the issues of dereliction, unemployment, emigration of the working age, fuel poverty and contaminated waterways.

10.8 **Junchao Guo (Julian), Y5** 'V for Virtue: The Landscape of Tranquility'. The hope to relieve fraught political relations between China and Tibet is rooted in the principles of Buddhism and the harmony between human and nature. Within the 'Ring of Life' and the *qingke* barley landscape are five seasonal interventions made primarily from ice, appearing only in the coldest part of winter to teach the virtues of peace: 'Sky Road' (the path of forgiveness), 'Pavilion of Humility' (communal dining), 'Moonlight Podium' (a floating structure to contemplate afterlife), 'Bodhi Trees' (the library of enlightenment) and the 'Earthly Disciples' (short-term mud lodgings for Tibetan farmers). Through this sublime landscape, Tibet is offering China a form of salvation and spiritual repent from their relentless industrialisation.

10.9–10.10 **Vilius Vizgaudis, Y5** 'The Gift: Freedom, Equality and Diversity'. Analogous to the Hieronymus Bosch painting *The Conjurer* (c.1502), French President Emmanuel Macron hopes to convince American President Donald Trump to rejoin the Paris Climate Agreement. 'The Gift' rethinks the American city of Paris in Texas through the values of the Climate Agreement and the romantic French-Parisian lens symbolising freedom, equality and diversity. This new 21st-century Statue of Liberty promotes not only hope for urban climate resilience but, also, neighbourly love and humanity. The protagonist of 'The Gift' is a new, suspended River Seine that runs through the city and elevates the importance of water. The project provides shared housing, clean energy, local food, water and employment for an increasing number of American climate-change holidaymakers and refugees: people temporarily or permanently forced out of their homes due to extreme weather events.

10.2

10.3

10.4

SLAUGHTER
SCHOOL OF
SLAUGHTER
SCHOOL
OF
SLAUGHTER
MEATINGS
DAILY
SHABBY ROAD
10.5

10.6

10.8

10.9

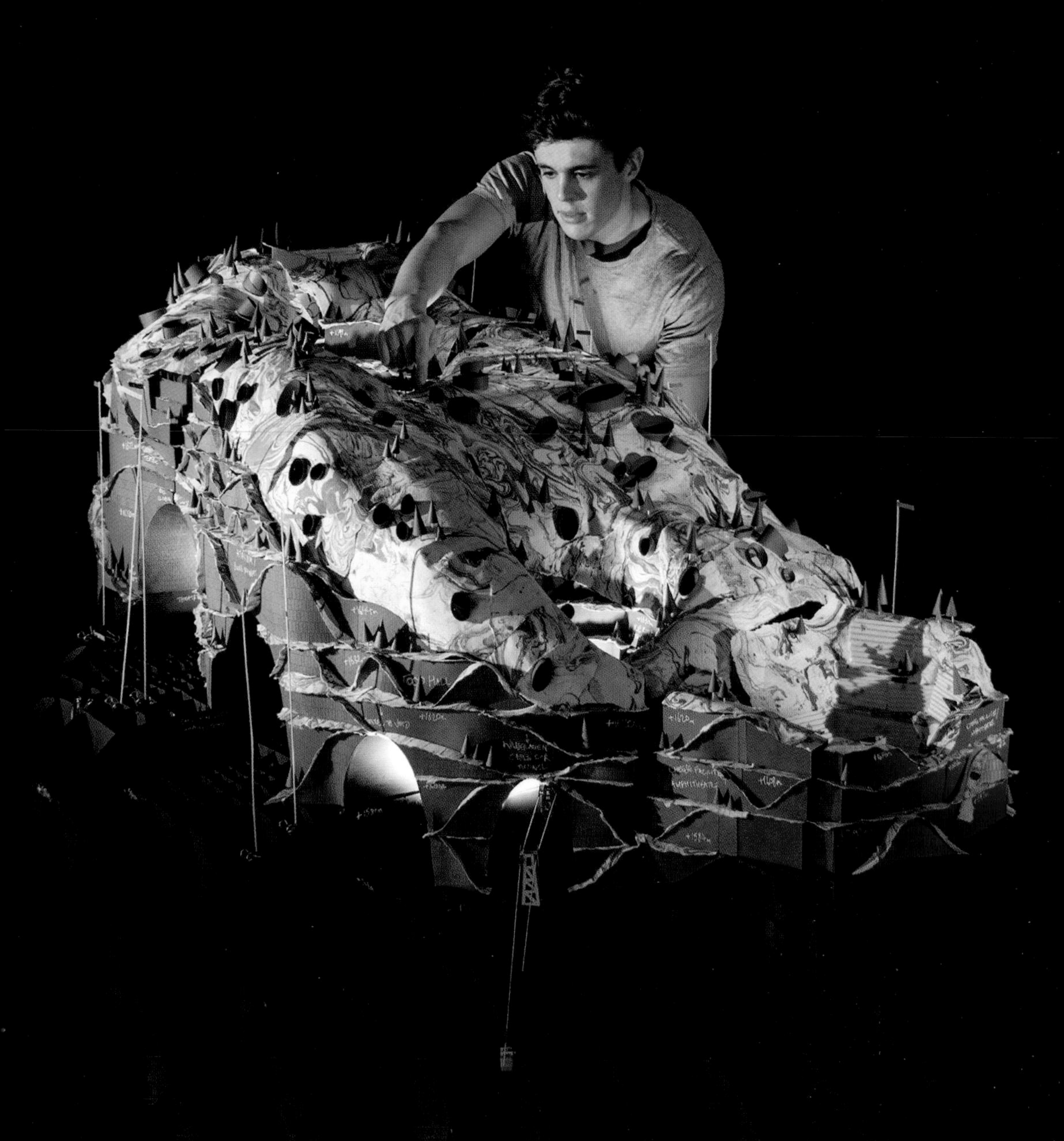

11.1

Terra Incognita

PG11

Laura Allen, Mark Smout

The Latin phrase *terra incognita*, meaning 'unknown land', was used by cartographers in the Age of Exploration (early 15th to early 17th century) to denote those territories of the globe that were unknown, unexplored or undocumented. Geographical *terra incognita* is now practically inconceivable, as the prospect of discovering uncharted land has all but disappeared. Myth and imagination are replaced by indisputable physical reality, as most of the Earth's surface has been digitally surveyed, if not charted, in minute detail. Yet, for reasons such as the shifting topographies of climate change, renegotiated political borders and evolving infrastructures, a map is outdated as soon as it is made. Flaws caused by digital glitches and the inaccuracies of new scanning technologies add yet another layer of redundancy and ambiguity. Our unremitting drive for 'progress' and search for knowledge has produced many Ages of Exploration, including missions to chart the ocean depths and voyages extending beyond our galaxy. '*Terra incognita*' is now more likely to be used metaphorically, to signify uncharted territories in other areas of exploration, such as fields of scientific research. This year, we asked: 'What is the current focus of global exploration?' and 'What is the role of architecture in future thinking?'

It is not down in any map; true places never are.[1]

Far from being 'lost in space', the unknown is, fundamentally, the territory of speculation and discovery. The unit focused on the moving target of the future at its most enigmatic, uncovering or proposing ideals and didactic models for living, evoking real or imagined scenarios and reviving forgotten innovations.

All who claim to foretell or forecast the future are inevitably liars, for the future is not written anywhere – it is still to be built.[2]

Following in the footsteps of the founders of the Alpine Club French architect Eugène Emmanuel Viollet-le-Duc (1814-1879) and English art critic John Ruskin (1819-1900), we endeavoured to develop a 'better knowledge of mountains through literature, science and art'[3] on a grand tour of the sublime Swiss Alps. The pristine wilderness is remarkably geotechnically manipulated and undergoes dramatic seasonal transformations, seen not only in the couture of the ski slopes but also in the ancient agricultural practice of 'transhumance': the moving of livestock from lowlands to upland grazing meadows. The awesome dominance of its sublime and elemental mountains – bucolic alpine panoramas with chocolate box views of bell-jangling cows grazing on wildflower meadows – belies a culture of modernity and scientific innovation. The majority of projects are sited amongst the visual abundance and landscape utility of this living laboratory.

Year 4
Siqi (Scott) Chen, Sacha Hickinbotham, Theo Jones, Karolina Kielb, Liam Merrigan, Rachel Swetnam, Maxime Willing

Year 5
George Bradford-Smith, Andrew Chard, Wei-Kai Chu, Oliver Colman, Stefan (Dan) Florescu, Paul Humphries, Douglas Miller, Naomi Rubbra, Nicholas Salthouse

Many thanks to Design Realisation tutor Rhys Cannon, and Stephen Foster for Structural consultancy

1. Melville, H., *Moby-Dick; or, The Whale* (London: Constable & Co., 1922)
2. Godet, M. and Roubelat, F.,'Creating the future: The use and misuse of scenarios', in *Long Range Planning*, Volume 29, Issue 2, April 1996, pp164-171
3. Alpine Club Rules, alpine-club.org.uk/ac2/about-the-ac/mission-2

11.1 **Oliver Colman, Y5** 'Alposanti'. In homage to the Alps as a source of Swiss national identity, 'Alposanti' takes compositional cues from the form of a mountain, to create a touristic, closed, world of the future. The project responds to declining tourism figures in Switzerland, partly due to diminishing snowfall due to climate change, and draws on the principles of hyperreality in duplicating and exaggerating culture to create an extensive architectural world of warped 'Swissness' within one mega-building.
11.2 **Andrew Chard, Y5** 'Reconfiguring the Rhône'. With retreating glaciers affecting river regimes throughout Switzerland, the creation of new water buffering dams is needed. Carved into the emerging granite landscape left behind by the fading glacier, these dams are sustained through the implementation of alpine farming communities, expanding from the growing water network deployed throughout the Rhône Valley over the next century.
11.3 **Karolina Kielb, Y4** 'Re(g)Rhône Glacier'. This project reinstates a Victorian research station on the Rhône Glacier in the Swiss Alps. The building is inspired by the Ice Stupa – a form of glacial grating that creates artificial glaciers – and uses meltwater from the glacier to artificially restore a fragment of the lost landscape.
11.4 **Wei-Kai Chu, Y5** 'Alpine City'. This project reflects on the environmental crisis, caused by rising temperatures, facing mountain ecology among alpine valleys. Initially, a thematic board game was created as a precursor for the scheme to speculate the potential and question the emergent botanic township.
11.5 **Naomi Rubbra, Y5** 'Who is London For?'. A masterplan is typically decided and drawn from the top-down. Here, instead, it becomes an activity by 'walking alongside' residents through the site. This site model is a manifestation of the findings; the bright ornaments and their associated timber swatch mimic design responses to issues of surveillance, safety, companionship and nature.
11.6 **Nicholas Salthouse, Y5** 'The Liquidity of Glacial Recession'. As Switzerland approaches 'peak water' taken from its glacial reserves, this project considers the relative social construct of 'water scarcity'. Since many struggling alpine towns depend on seasonal meltwater, a series of key infrastructural interventions form a resilient rind to protect the town, enabling further reconstruction of themselves by serving as 1:1 fabrication templates. This landscape of architectural jigs and civic prosthetics reconfigures the town, allowing rituals of harvest to come to the fore, thus catalysing their regeneration from within.
11.7 **Stefan (Dan) Florescu, Y5** 'Augmenting the Vernacular'. A new architectural ensemble in Albinen in Switzerland uses AR technology in order to make a step-by-step transition from the urban to the rural landscape, allowing newcomers to discover and understand vernacular architecture of alpine chalets. Initially encountered as a fully immersive AR experience, the virtual elements will gradually fade over time to reveal the physical reality.
11.8 **Douglas Miller, Y5** 'The Harderkulm Transect'. A restored hiking route runs from town square to mountain top in the city of Interlaken, Switzerland. Forming an alternative route to the recently installed funicular, a new transect is formed that crosses various mountainous biomes along which an array of buildings augment and protect the mountainside, whilst providing facilities for the local hikers.
11.9 **Paul Humphries, Y5** 'The End of Technology'. In this project, the city of Zurich in Switzerland is reimagined 50 years from now as Europe's first 'smart city' – but not as we imagine it to be today. This project explores our relationship with data as a series of architectural responses via a new, non-physical boundary – reinstating Zurich's 16th-century fortification as a data network.
11.10–11.11 **Siqi (Scott) Chen, Y4** 'Nomadic Farm'. Suffering from a dairy crisis, Switzerland is looking for a solution to save its traditional family farms. This project explores the relationship between nature, urbanity and industrialisation behind the Alpine dairy industry. Situated in Gruyères, the farm is made from timber, straw and hay, with an edible façade for cows.
11.12 **George Bradford-Smith, Y5** 'Manipulating Mont Blanc: Preparing for Martian Frontiers'. Located on the summit of Mont Blanc, this astronaut training facility passively simulates the Martian environment of the Alps, using an accessible extreme environment to recreate another.
11.13 **Sacha Hickenbotham, Y4** 'Immaterial Landscapes'. This installation explores the material and immaterial phenomenological qualities of scaled Swiss-landscape infrastructures. A series of suspended cast vessels produce a slow drip of water to replicate Swiss hydroelectric dam infrastructures. Subsequent models of light, sound and heat are activated through the impacting force of falling water.
11.14 **Theo Jones, Y4** 'Unfolding a home of diplomatic containment'. WikiLeaks founder Julian Assange lived inside the Ecuadorian embassy for six years. Leaked documents suggest that Ecuador considered transporting Assange out of the embassy in a diplomatic bag. In this project, the embassy is folded down inside the diplomat's jacket, secretly moving Assange and the territory of Ecuador that protected him.
11.15 **Maxime Willing, Y4** 'Woven Futures'. This project proposes a holistic environment designed to provide the people of Geneva with a building that changes in appearance with time and use. The architecture takes on the blue from the dyeing of textiles in the same manner that an artisan's hands change with work. Ornamentation developed from the Swiss vernacular process of 'sgraffito' is used as the vehicle for this layering of colour.
11.16 **Rachel Swetnam, Y4** 'Glasmuseum'. A process collage following a series of light studies testing the qualities of coloured light for a glassblowing museum and studio in Lucerne, Switzerland.
11.17 **Liam Merrigan, Y4** 'Neulandsgemeindeplatz'. For centuries, the Appenzeller community in northern Switzerland has resisted influence from beyond their territory, fostering a unique identity rooted in political debate, religion and their connection to the landscape. This project examines the past and future of this isolated culture, drawing on traditional costume and craft to convey architectural ideas. The scheme is a monument of statues, guesthouses, relics and festival spaces built around a new parliament square.

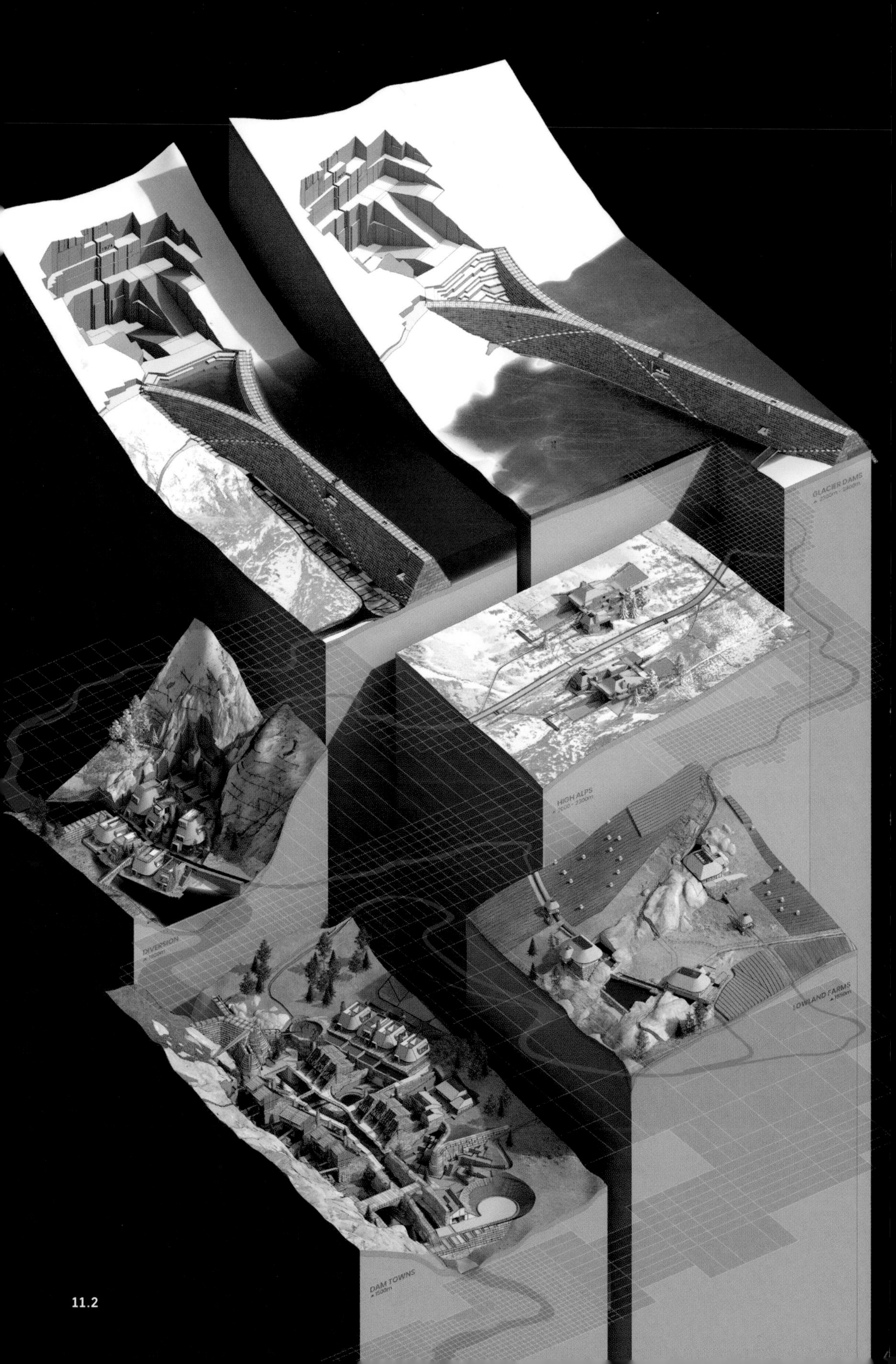

11.2

11.3

11.4

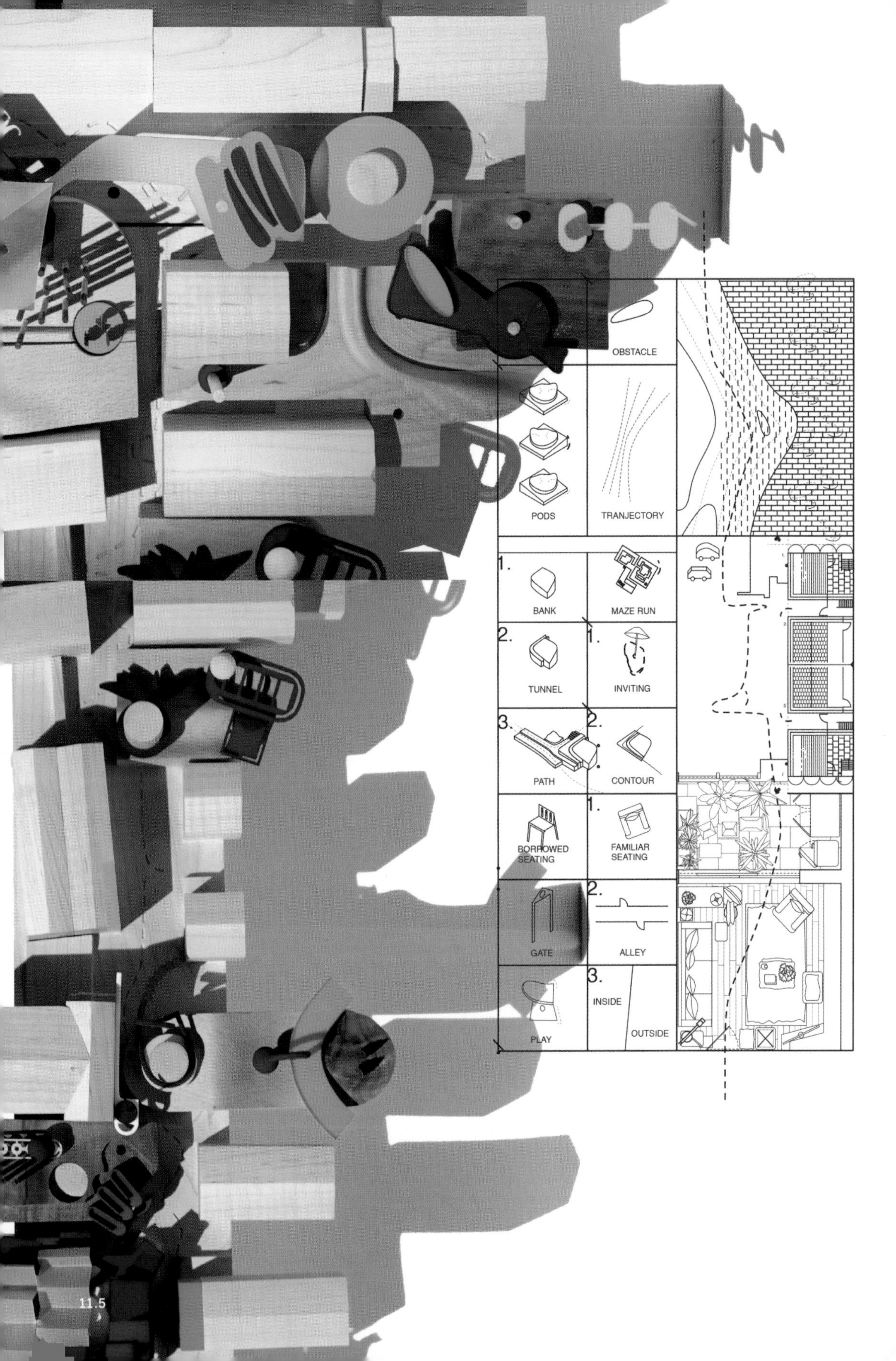

OBSTACLE
PODS
TRAJECTORY
1.
BANK
MAZE RUN
2.
TUNNEL
1.
INVITING
3.
PATH
2.
CONTOUR
BORROWED SEATING
1.
FAMILIAR SEATING
GATE
2.
ALLEY
PLAY
3.
INSIDE
OUTSIDE

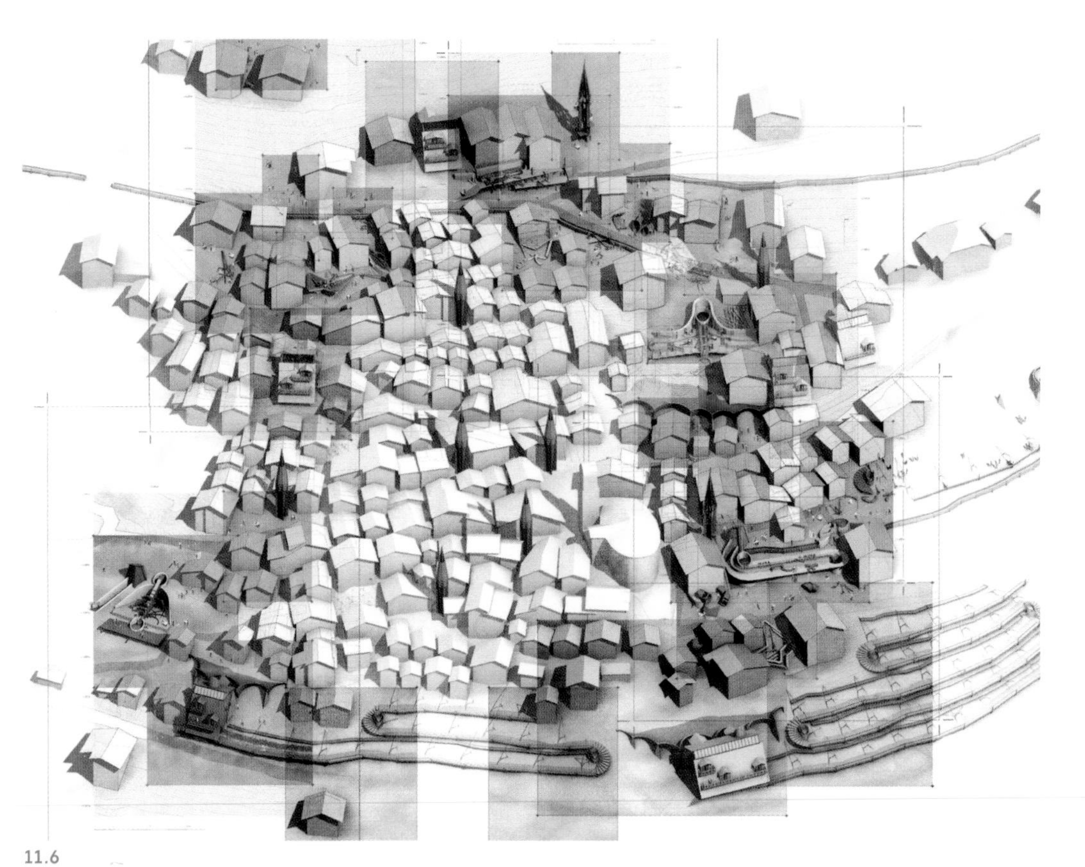

11.6

11.7

11.8

11.9

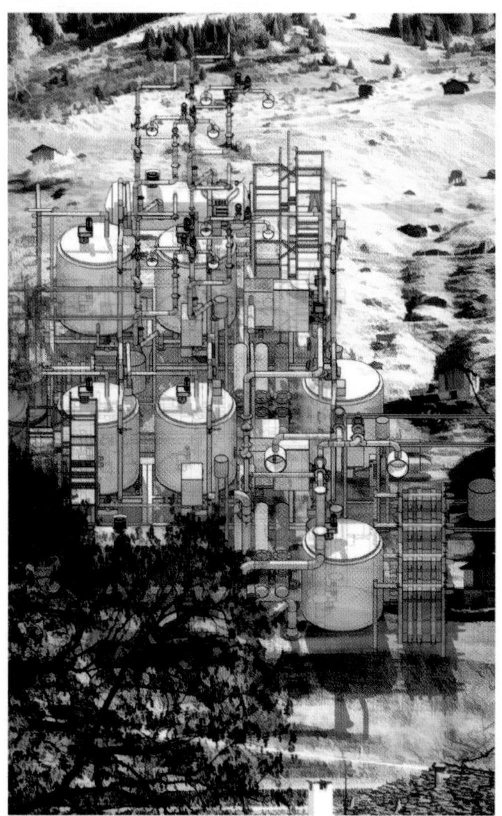

11.10

11.11

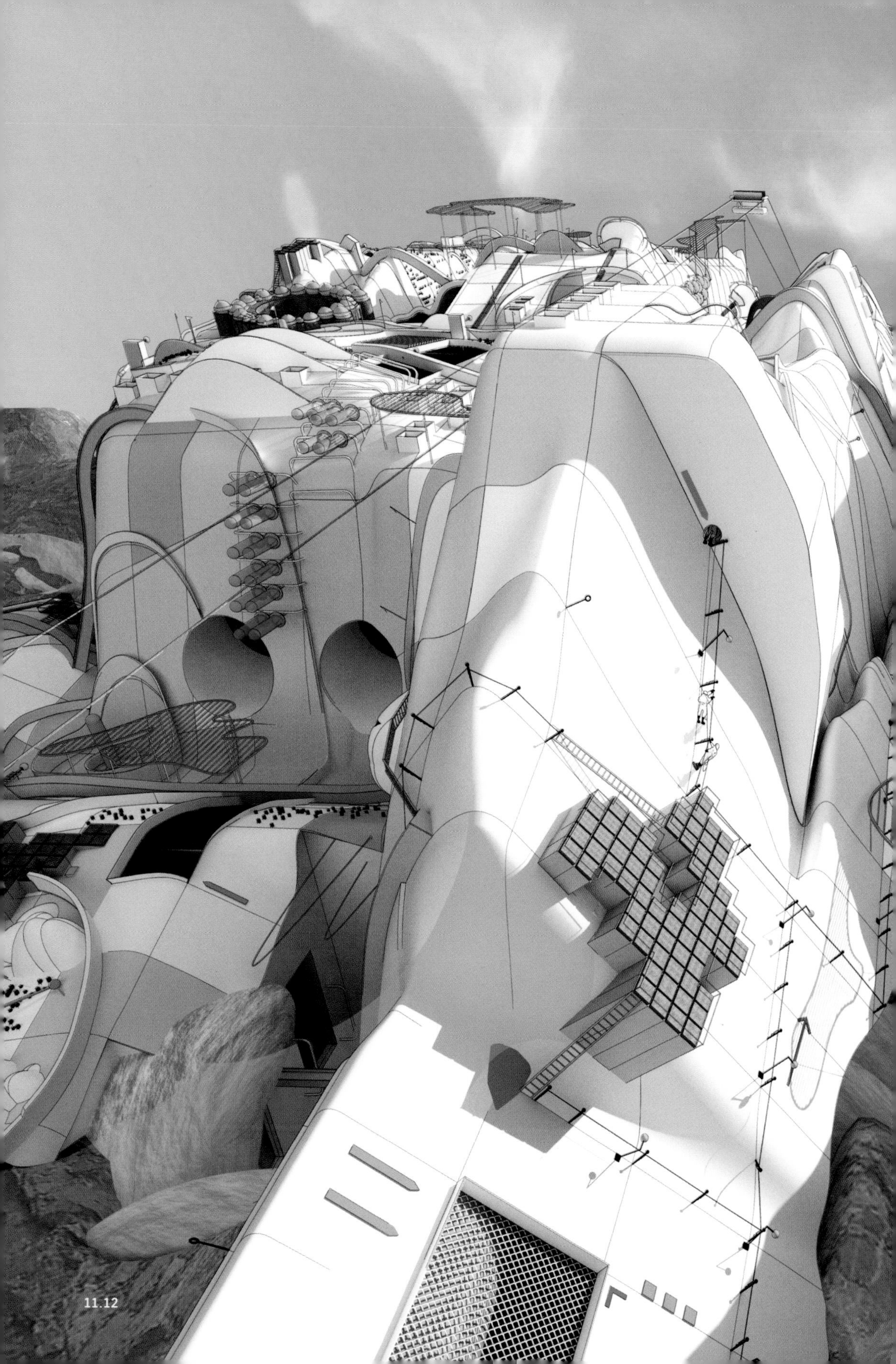

11.12

11.13

11.14

11.15

11.16

11.17

12.1

Designs on the Past, Present and Future

PG12

Elizabeth Dow, Jonathan Hill

The architect will 'always be dealing with historical problems – with the past and, a function of the past, with the future. So, the architect should be regarded as a kind of physical historian... the architect builds visible history',[1] wrote art historian Vincent Scully (1920-2017). The architect, therefore, is a 'physical novelist', as well as a 'physical historian'. Histories and novels both need to be convincing but in different ways. The historian acknowledges that the past is not the same as the present, whilst the novelist inserts the reader in a time and a place that feels very present, even if they are not. Although no history is completely objective, to have validity it must appear truthful to the past. A novel may be believable but not true. As a history is a reinterpretation of the past that is meaningful to the present, each design is a new history. Equally, a design is equivalent to a fiction, convincing users to suspend disbelief. We expect a history or a novel to be written in words, but they can also be delineated in drawing, cast in concrete or seeded in soil.

A building can be designed for the present in acknowledgement of contemporary contexts, needs and desires. A design can also be a selective, critical and creative response to the past. Equally, a prospect of the future can be implicit in a design, which is always imagined before it is built and may take years to complete. Some architects design for the present, some imagine for a mythical past, whilst others create for a future time and place. In many eras, the most fruitful innovations have occurred when ideas and forms have migrated from one time and place to another by a translation process that is stimulating and inventive. Thus, a design can be understood as specific to a time and a place, and also a compound of other times and other places. In conceiving a design as a history and a fiction, we encourage a simultaneous and creative envisaging of the past, present and future in a single architecture.

We began the year by studying unrealised architectures to understand how politics, economics and aesthetics undermined their construction. We wanted to understand the stories – some fact and others fiction – that surround their histories, and to speculate upon the question: 'How and why might this happen now?' Our project was to design a public building that imagined the past, present and future in a single architecture, representing and stimulating the values and practices of two interdependent organisations – national and international – and multiple populaces – local, regional, national and international – that collaborate and prosper for mutual benefit.

Year 4
Amelia Black, Jonathon Howard, Laura Keay, Przemyslaw Rylko, Isaac Simpson, Aryan Tehrani

Year 5
George Entwistle, Tasnim Eshraqi Najafabadi, Niki-Marie Jansson, Francesca Savvides, Yu (Nicole) Teh, Yat Chi (Eugene) Tse, Dominic Walker, Yushi Zhang

Thank you to our Design Realisation tutor James Hampton and structural consultant James Nevin

Thank you to our critics: Ana Araujo, Alessandro Ayuso, Matthew Blunderfield, Barbara-Ann Campbell-Lange, Sam Coulton, Mark Dorrian, Adrian Forty, Murray Fraser, Stylianos Giamarelos, Niamh Grace, Penelope Haralambidou, Bill Hodgson, Mary Vaughan Johnson, Brian Kelly, Perry Kulper, Chee-Kit Lai, Constance Lau, Ifigeneia Liangi, Lesley McFadyen, Barbara Penner, Rahesh Ram, Sophie Read, David Shanks, Sayan Skandarajah, Tania Sengupta, Dan Wilkinson, Alex Zambelli

1. Vincent Scully, *American Architecture and Urbanism*, (London: Thames and Hudson, 1969), pp221, 257

12.1 Tasnim Eshraqi Najafabadi, Y5 'Transforming Coryton Refinery to a Post-Petroleum Garden Town'. This project is a critique of oil culture and envisages post-petroleum imaginaries for a former refinery in south Essex. An experimental garden town in a refinery, the proposal oscillates between poetic and practical, suggesting gardening as an agency and a way of life to provide for society and rehabilitate the dilapidated ecology. Composed according to available resources, it comprises infrastructural interventions and architectural typologies which blend the land's past and future.
12.2 Niki-Marie Jansson, Y5 'The Ally Pally Annex: A masonry megastructure'. This project seeks to connect and dismantle established social and financial boundaries between London boroughs, in an attempt to address a group of urban, environmental, sociological and psychological problems. The design proposal manifests as a series of elevated and subterranean load-bearing masonry infrastructures that integrate themselves on a masterplan scale within London. They converege at a proposed megastructure undercroft at Alexandra Palace in north London. The infrastructure utilises the structural typology of the vault as a flexible building strategy.
12.3 Przemyslaw Rylko, Y4 'House of Leave and Remain'. This project reflects on the poor quality of discussion between so-called 'Brexiteers' and 'Remainers'. A sequence of acoustic, tactile and visual links attempts to connect people who might have different political opinions by establishing them as partners in conversation, instead of opponents to be defeated. The project is a response to the condition of Brexit, but is not 'for' or 'against' it; instead its primary aim is to foster principles of mutual understanding and respect.
12.4 Amelia Black, Y4 'The People's Republic of Foundlings'. A critique of the Garden City Plan, 'The People's Republic of Foundlings' is a micronation that uses the development of construction skills and community building to create a new egalitarian community typology. Each resident is fundamentally involved in both the material and immaterial construction of the community, utilising a systematic division of domestic and physical labour, as well as shared spaces, to alleviate pressures of a traditional 'female' caregiver role.
12.5–12.6 Jonathon Howard, Y4 'Sh*tHouse to Penthouse'. The project chronicles a selected sequence of domestic built interventions in unoccupied buildings in Hackney Wick that transfer from site to site and progressively accumulate into a complete building that recalls the memories of all the previous sites. The project narrates a renewal of current housing conditions through a variation of transformative processes that incorporate memories of the past and present, and that can be a suggestion for a potential future.
12.7–12.8 Laura A Keay, Y4 'Leyhalmode – The Fisheries Courthouse'. This project explores how a country might choose to rethink how it draws upon its own natural resources to build, govern and trade. It is set within a satirical Britain, in post-Brexit 2029, after a no-deal vote within parliament has led to to a halt in trade between the UK and EU. The architecture harks back to 'older' construction techniques, as the building industry is constrained by materials only produced and manufactured within the UK.
12.9 Isaac Simpson, Y4 'Terra Nullius: A vast land belonging to no-one'. The project's ambition is to challenge the national borders of West Africa with another border, in order to redefine the term 'border'; not as a line that splits cultures but as a line that connects. The West African institute of agroforestry will walk across the sub-Saharan lands planting rows of tree fields creating a reforestation border that re-fertilises the arid land for future agriculture. The locals decide the direction of these tree fields, in turn describing a new border mapped by the people, for the people.
12.10–12.12 Dominic Walker, Y5 'The Orkney Island Re-Forestry Commission'. This project seeks to understand the role of 'origins' and 'endings' in the production of architecture. The idea of 'endings' has become a growing theme in our comprehension of climate change, yet our minds are still captivated by the idea of salvation through technology. This project instead considers the idea that perhaps we have, as a species, reached a natural ending within the deep cycles of the world?
12.13 Francesca Savvides, Y5 'The Case for a New Architect'. The project is inspired by the recent movement to re-establish architecture departments in the public sector, and studies previous models of practice, such as the London County Council, to gauge what opportunities and capabilities would be afforded to architects in these new cross-boundary roles. The project proposes the 'Bishopsgate School of Building', a holistic school where architects, planners and construction workers would train together to develop a new age of 'civicness'.
12.14 Yat Chi (Eugene) Tse, Y5 'A Museum of Hong Kong, by Hong Kong, for Hong Kong'. The Museum of Hong Kong sets out an approach for Hong Kong's future in China. The result is a new reality of Hong Kong that contains China. The idea of reality in the architecture is expressed through symbolism. The project addresses the struggle of Hong Kong architects to retain a sense of their own cultural identity in modern international contexts by posing the questions: 'What is Hong Kong?', 'What should be remembered?' and 'What should be forgotten?'
12.15–12.16 Yushi Zhang, Y5 'The National Agricultural College 2028'. The project proposes a new model for the future of farming and rural dwelling under a 'no-deal' Brexit scenario. Taking the form of an agricultural college, the project proposes the possibility of a more democratic, cooperative-owned farm, with a new 'national agricultural conscription'. This is in order to regenerate a new attitude towards farming and making farming a life skill rather than a profession.
12.17–12.18 Yu (Nicole) Teh, Y5 'Institute for International Summit Negotiations'. As a reaction to the current de-globalisation movement, the project proposes an Institute for International Summit Negotiations, providing a space for press conference talks and private discussions. Sited in Singapore, a place seen as a neutral territory, it is a critique of the over-conditioned environment (both in terms of light and air) that itself seems to reveals a fear of darkness and disorder. The project focuses on the uses of darkness and natural ventilation, questioning how these 'fears' have brought about detrimental environmental consequences that should be addressed.
12.19–12.21 George Entwistle, Y5 'Wilding the City of London'. The project outlines a proposal for a town hall, set within a new forest planted in the heart of the City of London, replacing Guildhall as the seat of power. Covering ten acres of the Square Mile, the forest plays on historic precedent and folklore, and represents a place of liberty. The project is the antithesis of the current spatial conditions within the city and is divorced from its social, economic, and political hierarchies. Instead, it represents a more primal, natural order of governance.

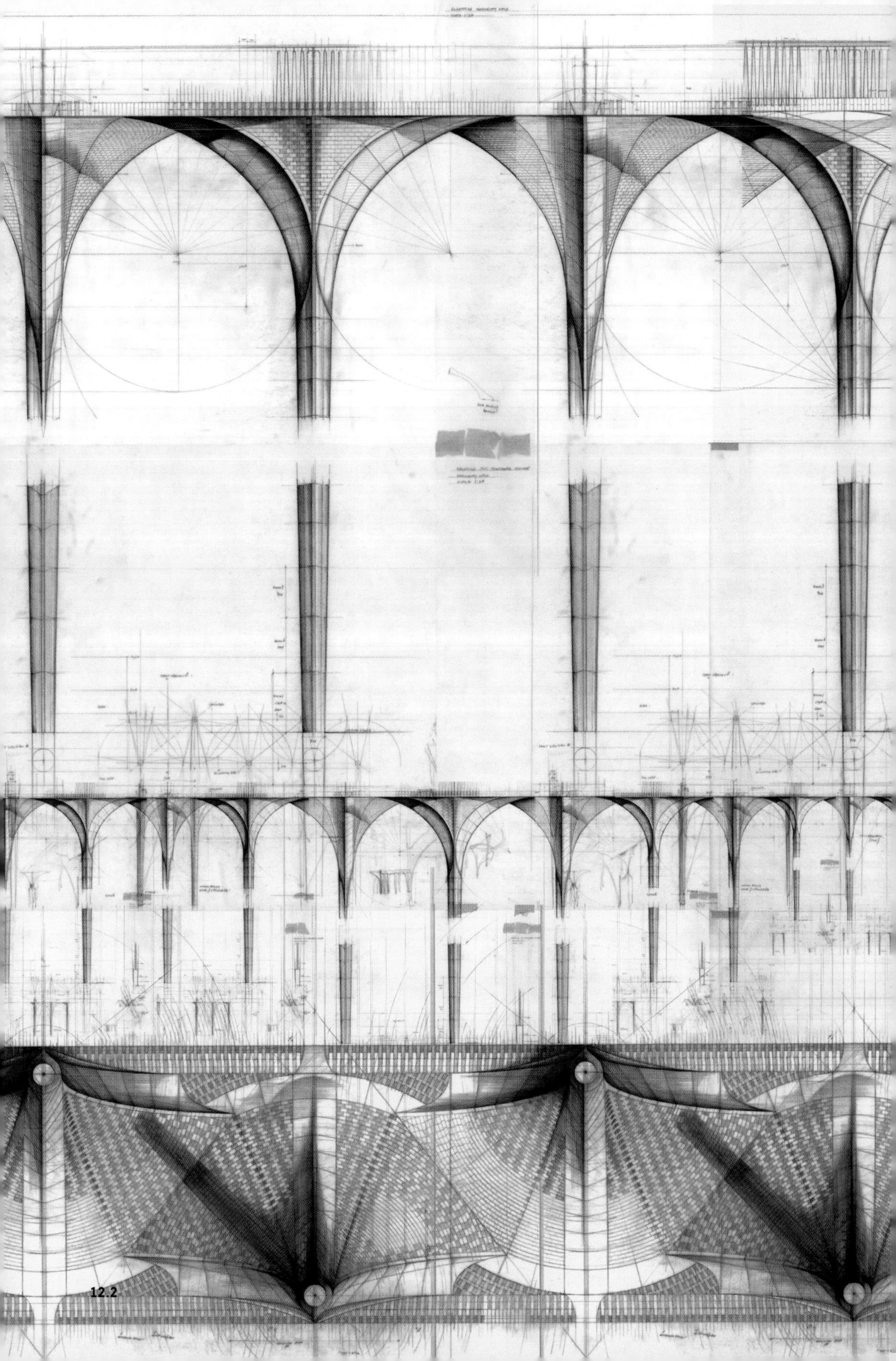

12.2

12.3

12.4

12.5

12.6

12.7

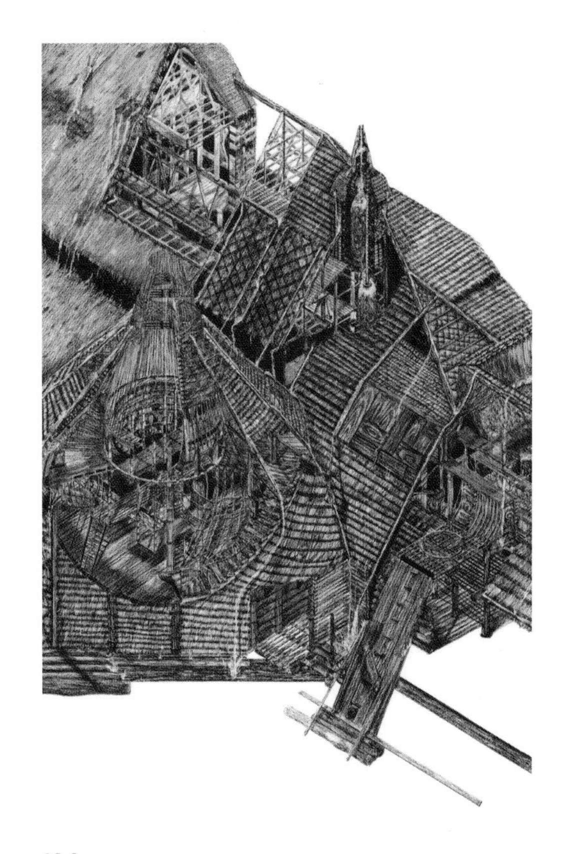

12.8

12.9

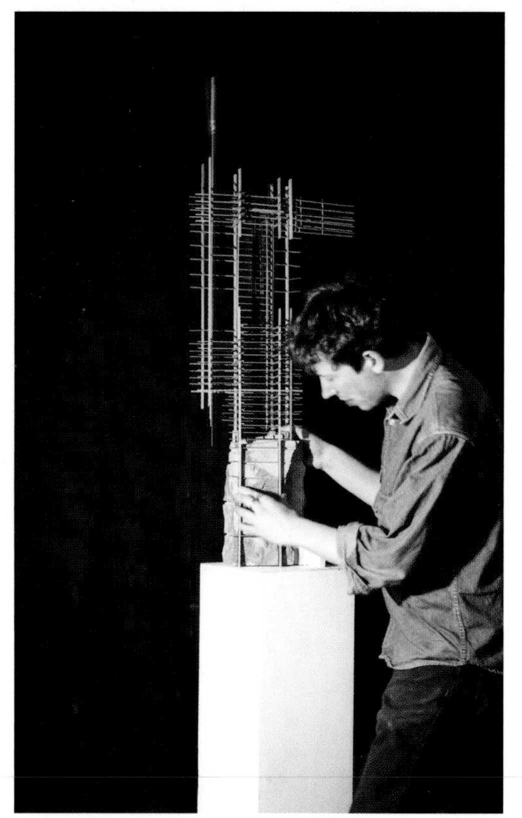

12.10

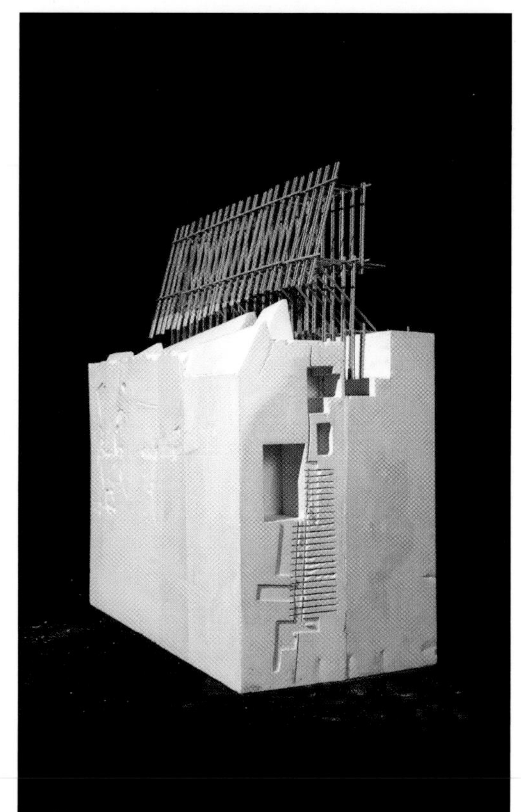

12.11

12.12

12.13

12.15

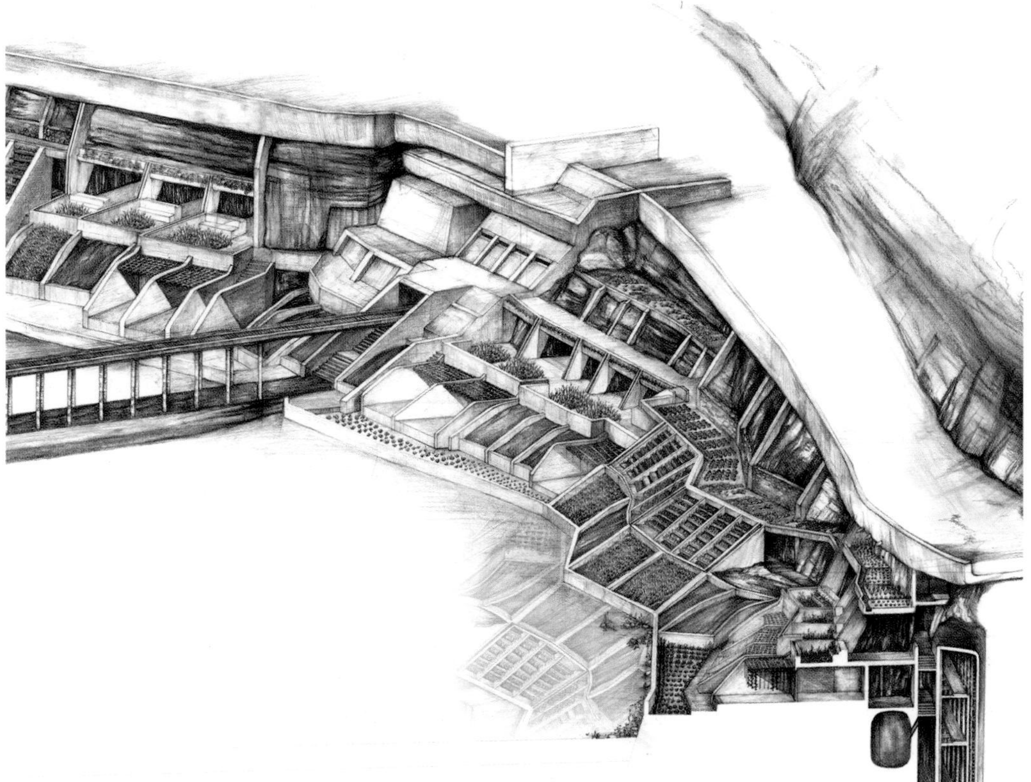

12.16

12.17

12.18

12.19

12.20

12.21

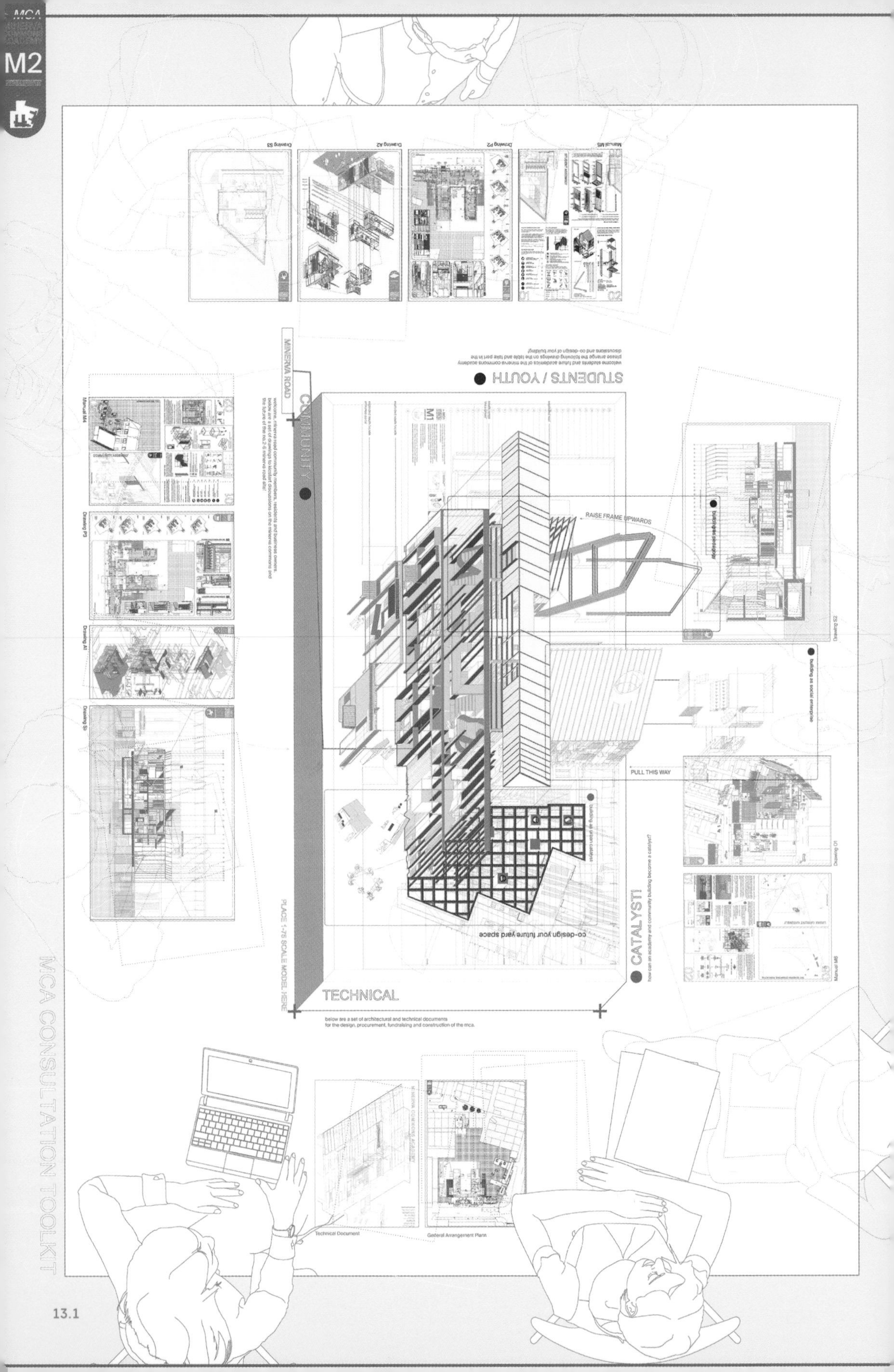
MCA
M2
RAISE FRAME UPWARDS
PULL THIS WAY
STUDENTS / YOUTH
COMMUNITY
MINERVA ROAD
CATALYST!
TECHNICAL
below are a set of architectural and technical documents
for the design, procurement, fundraising and construction of the mca.
co-design your future yard space
PLACE 1:75 SCALE MODEL HERE
Technical Document
General Arrangement Plann
MCA CONSULTATION TOOLKIT

Hidden Spectacles

PG13

Sabine Storp, Patrick Weber

In PG13, students propose creative new ways to inhabit the city by developing diverse spatial scenarios. This year, we looked at the embedded industrial urban fabrics of London and Seoul, and envisaged a new culture of sharing within urban communities, vital to the future of the sustainable city. We explored the inner working of a place and questioned what happens when 'back of house' becomes 'front of house' – is this the place where new models are tested and innovation happens? Some of the key terms we used as departure points were: 'sharing city', 'urban hacking', 're-acting', 'collective', 'community', 'trans-ient' and 'trans-loci'.

Presenting an alternative concept of living and working on the fringes of a city, students' projects were a testing ground for interdisciplinary cooperation and the methodologies used to make a city more liveable. Inventing new models for future inhabitation, we carefully observed fringe communities and challenged regulatory frameworks, setting ourselves a personal design research question and speculating on an imagined part of the city set within a real context.

Our Year 4 students worked on the Park Royal industrial estate in northwest London. They collaborated with the Old Oak and Park Royal Development Corporation on ideas for the future of the area, to be exhibited in London in autumn 2019.

Year 5 students challenged concepts of inhabitation for the city of Seoul in South Korea. We developed a close relationship with Seoul University and Hanyang University, and collaborated on a series of workshops in Seoul and London, which explored the idea of the 'sharing city' from two different cultural viewpoints. The ideas were expressed in collective drawings and models, which are to be presented at the Seoul Architecture Biennale in September 2019.

Year 4
Ka Chi Law, Shi Yin Ling, Mabel Parsons, Maïte Seimetz, Yip Wing Siu

Year 5
Daniel Avilan Medina, Nicola Chan, Thomas Cubitt, Naomi De Barr, Emily Martin, Giles Nartey, Robert Newcombe, Hoi Lai (Kerry) Ngan, Rebecca Outterside, Allegra Willder

Thanks to our partners: Hanyang University, Seoul; University of Seoul; Old Oak and Park Royal Development Corporation, London

Thanks to our critics and consultants: Jan Ackenhausen, Samson Adjei, Chris Bryant, Barbara-Ann Campbell-Lange, James Christian, Soyoung Kim, Fiona MacDonald, Guan-Yu Ren, Caspar Rodgers, Toby Ronalds, Henry Thorold, Ray Whittow-Williams, Paolo Zaide

13.1 Yip Wing Siu, Y4 'Minerva Community Academy'. With the arrival of Crossrail and HS2 in Park Royal, the traditional industrial fabric of food production and light manufacturing in the area is under threat; the socio-economic landscape is shifting, it is at an urban and theoretical juncture. Situated in one of London's most deprived neighbourhoods, the 'Minerva Community Academy' seeks to renegotiate the boundary between industry and living by introducing a vocational academy, transforming the site into a pedagogical and social catalyst.
13.2 Naomi De Barr, Y5 'Ceramic House in Pieces'. This project proposes a crafted installation for environmental diversity in homes in Seoul. The heated and ventilated floor of the traditional urban Hanok house encourages a sedentary living condition, harnessing thermal properties in the floor. This project examines craft on the scale of furniture and its influence on inhabitation.
13.3–13.4 Giles Nartey, Y5 'Finding Artefacts'. A new digital territory in Euljiro in South Korea is proposed for the relocation of the printing community, in reaction to proposed redevelopment. Critiquing the forced redevelopment of industrial areas and satirically playing with the limits of preservation, this project asks the question: 'How will we experience lost architectures and communities when they are gone?' It investigates whether the memory of what is lost can become architecture.
13.5 Allegra Willder, Y5 'The Cheonggye Baths'. Sited along the recently 'restored' Cheonggyecheon River in Seoul, this project looks to exhibit and utilise the phenomenal amount of artificial stream produced by the river through a series of interventions built along its course. Varying in scale, due to the fluctuating amounts of water available from site to site, the public buildings and spaces use water to describe and express the immediate surroundings.
13.6–13.8 Hoi Lai (Kerry) Ngan, Y5 'Bukchon Slow Town'. This project realises a piece of ageing landscape, romantically reimagined as a safe vessel for the elderly in a mythic, prelapsarian time. In response to the ageing crisis in South Korea, it unveils a sustainable ageing process for both the landscape and man. The exploration subtly critiques the unstoppable urbanisation in Seoul, which has resulted in a loss of diversity in ways of living.
13.9 Shi Yin Ling, Y4 'The Park Royal Partnership'. This co-living and working development is based on the concept of the 'circular economy'. From a social point of view, value is maintained through the act of sharing, learning and communication, prompted by the various spaces within the development. The building is raised on four cores, with an open internal courtyard and live-work spaces arranged around it. Reinventing the model of communal living, a flexible living typology is introduced, facilitating the growth and change of the building and occupants over time.
13.10 Mabel Parsons, Y4 'Minerva Multiplicities'. Situated above existing warehouses in Minerva Road in Park Royal, this project proposes affordable parasitic dwellings for a growing artists' community, consisting of co-living houses of various tenure, as a platform to grow connections. The proposal seeks to improve the image of the industrial estate, and values its existing character and communities by merging industrial and residential environments.
13.11 Ka Chi Law, Y4 'Safeguarding London'. Sited above the Grand Union Canal at Park Royal, the keyworker housing scheme is a response to London's land value and suggests an alternative of building on the free airspace above the canal. The building shelters a 'closed-loop' living system that not only harvests from the canal but also reactivates it through inhabitation. Its prefabricated design allows the scheme to expand along the London canal and provides homes close to work locations across the city.
13.12 Maïté Seimetz, Y4 'The Surplus City'. A prototype for temporary accommodation for women, combining experimental materiality, self-built construction and community participation to de-stigmatise homelessness and the treatment of surplus material. Set in the industrial zone of Park Royal, the scheme uses local industrial by-products as raw material for self-built components. Maker spaces become the catalysts for social reconnection and integration into the local community.
13.13 Robert Newcombe, Y5 'A Toolkit for an Architecture of Participation'. Collaborating with three real communities in the UK, South Korea and Chile, this project uses a set of experimental participatory tools to provide a common spatial language for architects and stakeholders.
By engaging in a meaningful, collective architectural dialogue that informs design decisions, the architecture embeds the collective briefing and is informed by users' living patterns, desired spatial qualities and relationships.
13.14 Nicola Chan, Y5 'The Slow Sewing Symposium'. This project explores the garment-making process as a new architectural typology for Seoul. The unique processes of pattern-making, cutting and toile-making are used as a methodology to manipulate and challenge space. The symposium becomes a living reminder of the craftspeople and craftsmanship of Changsin-dong in Seoul.
13.15 Rebecca Outterside, Y5 'A Circular Seoul'. This project introduces the idea of self-sufficient high-rise towers in Seoul. Tackling issues relating to food and construction waste, the project combines Korean food markets and kitchens with a new living typology. Spaces are designed for the inhabitants to grow and consume their own food, with any waste being regenerated into biomaterials for construction.
13.16–13.17 Emily Martin, Y5 'Community Catalyst'. This project negotiates the future of architectural practice by re-working the design process into an opportunity for community-driven development. By developing a new participatory method as a manual of engagement – through direct involvement and collective action within local communities – contemporary living opportunities are transformed and re-appropriated.
13.18 Daniel Avilan Medina, Y5 'Sewoon Archipelago'. An existing kilometre-long building in Seoul – currently the heart of the city's industrial complex – is reestablished as a pig farm for the city's inhabitants. Through a series of tectonic interventions, the farm becomes a new narrative for the people of South Korea, who have seen the city transform with the vanishing of its manufacturing heart. This new archipelago integrates Korean food culture and industrial growth into a rich environment for urban production.
13.19–13.21 Thomas Cubitt, Y5 '(Re) Placing the Urban Hanok'. This project questions the position of historic housing within the city. It proposes a higher-density evolution of Seoul's 1930s-urban Hanok houses and introduces a new construction method, re-configuring domestic spaces, whilst retaining a layout influenced by the courtyard typology. The project focuses on preserving the social characteristics of a neighbourhood, whilst allowing it to adapt and change.

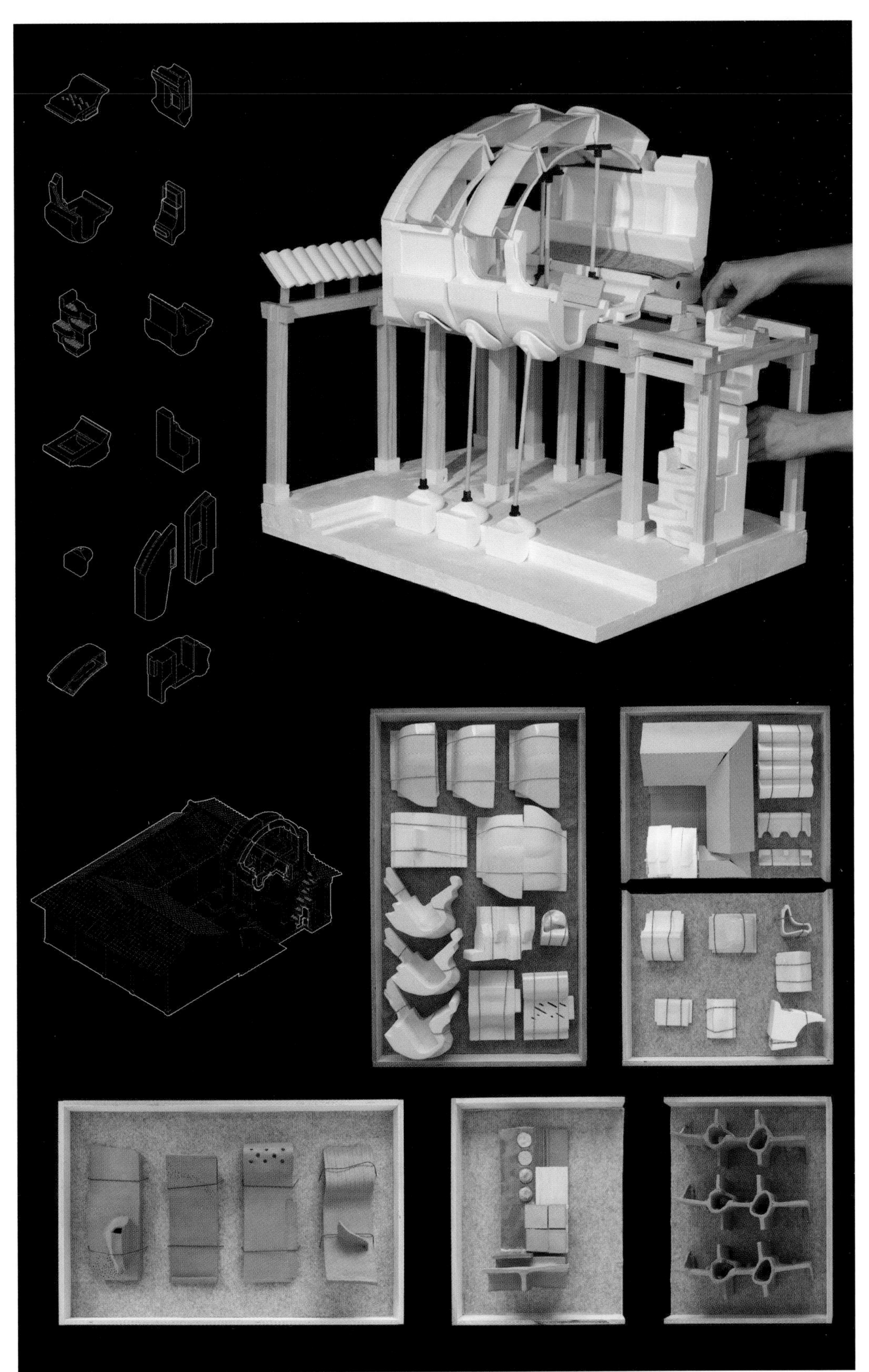

13.2

13.3

13.4

13.5

13.6

13.7

13.8

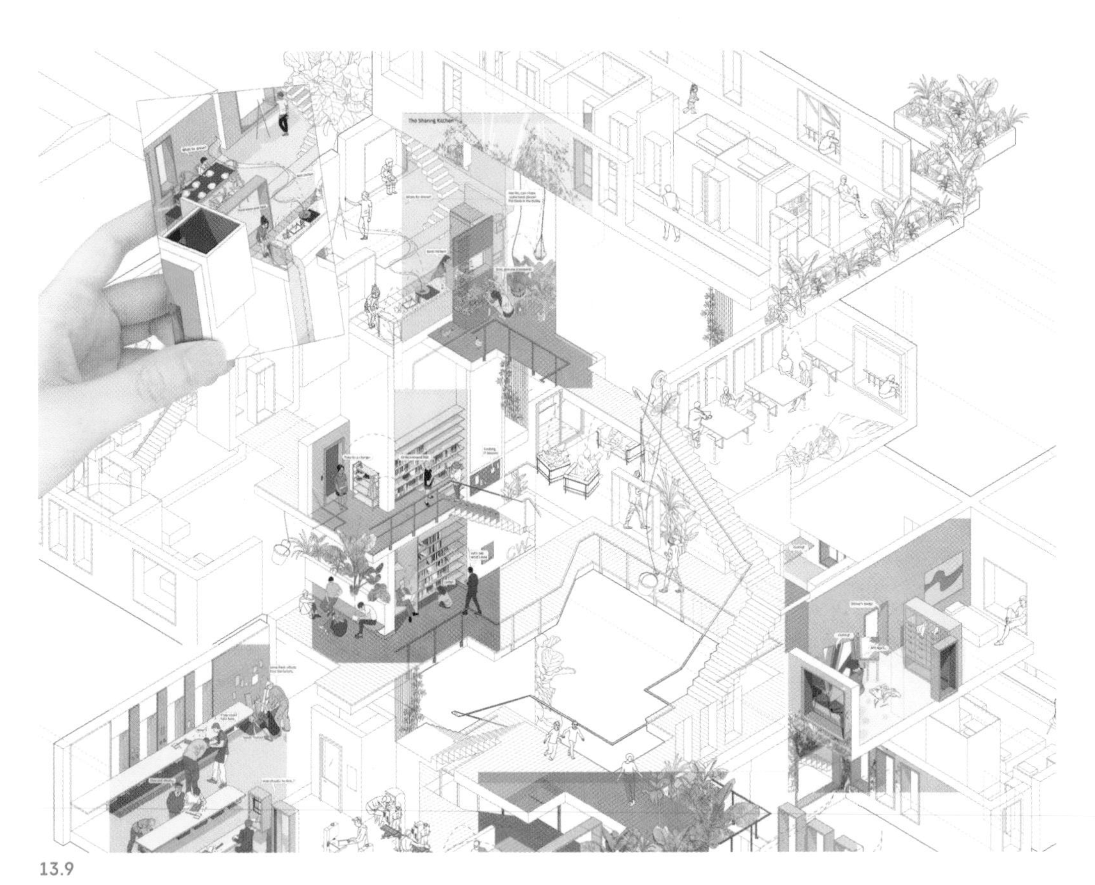

13.9

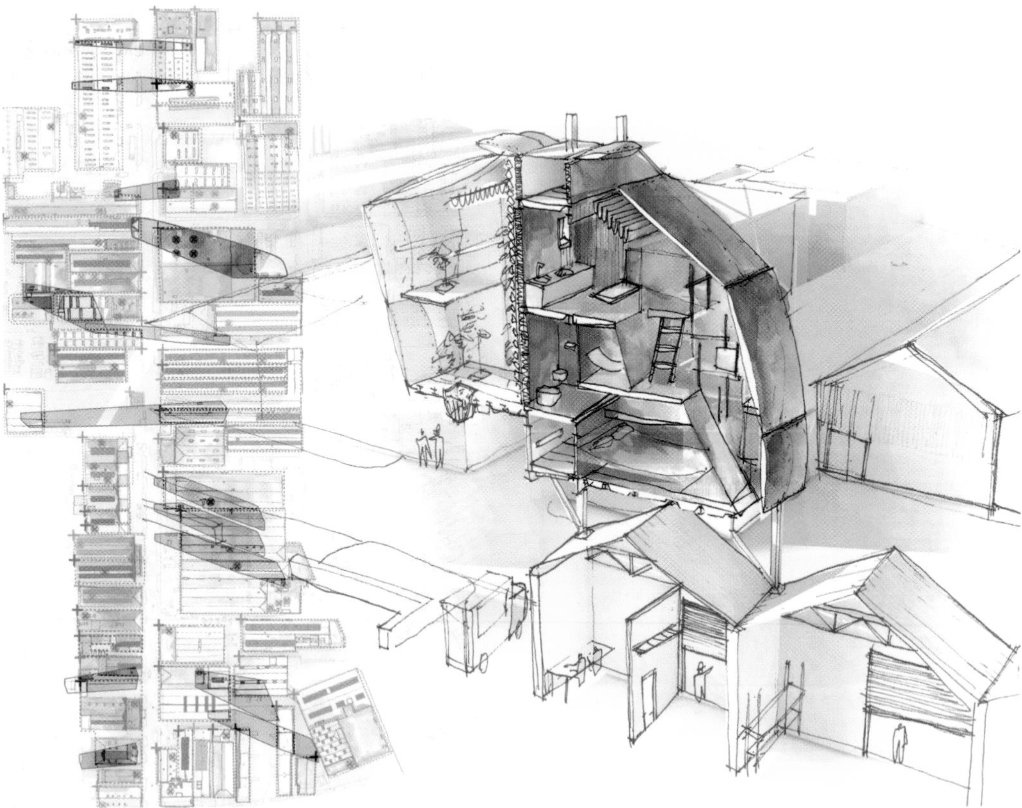

13.10

13.11

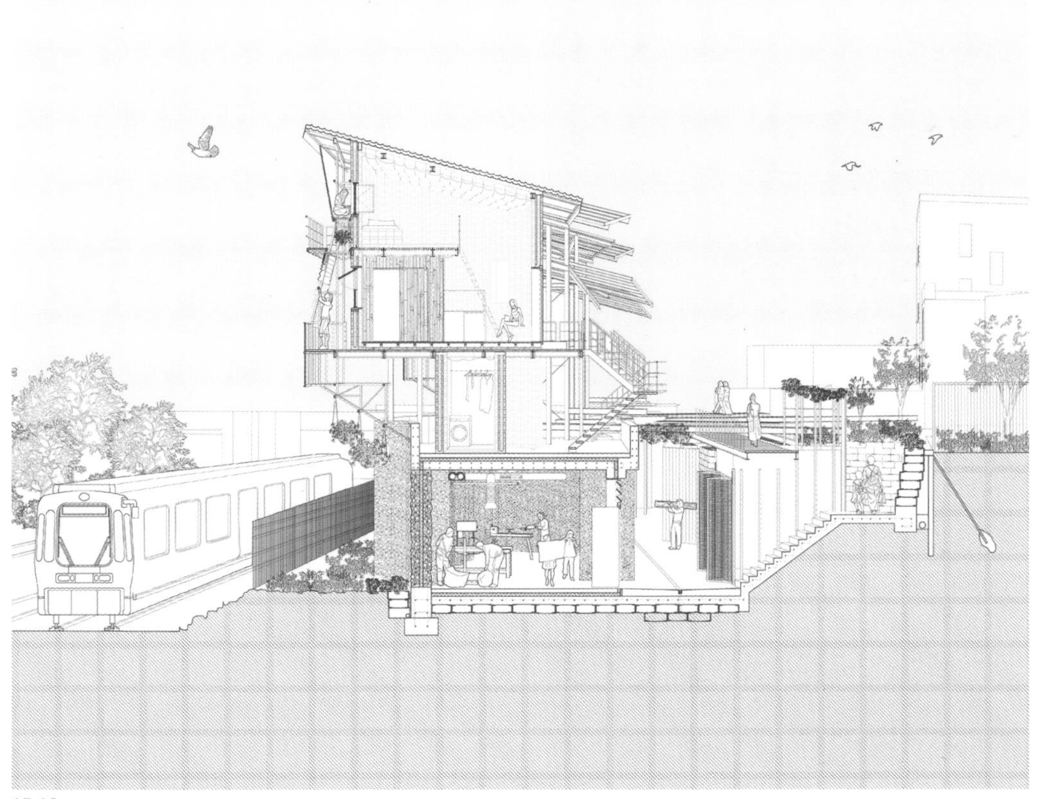

13.12

13.13

13.14

13.15

13.16

SOCIAL HOUSING
NOT
SOCIAL CLEANSING
THESE PEOPLE NEED HOMES

13.17

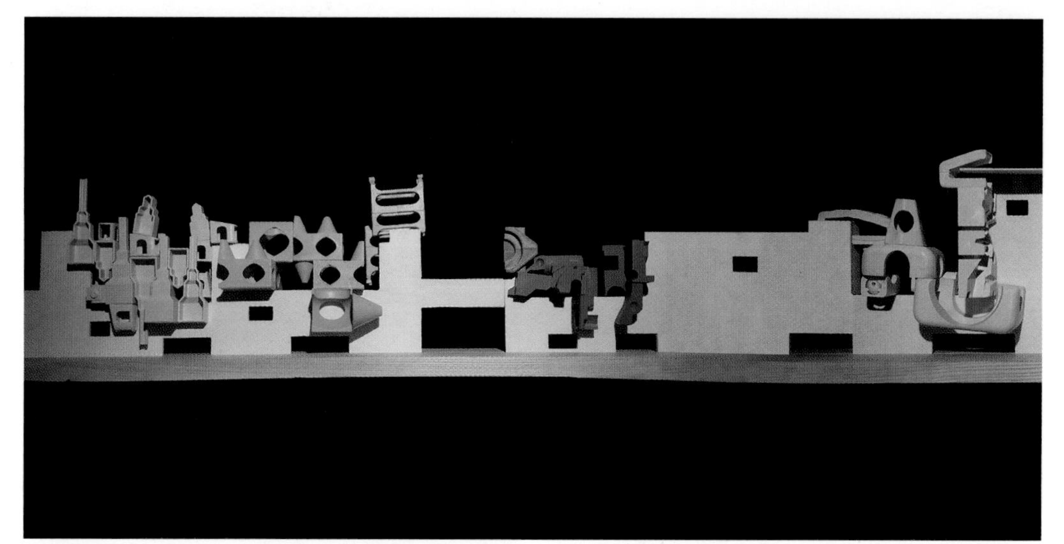

13.18

13.19

13.20

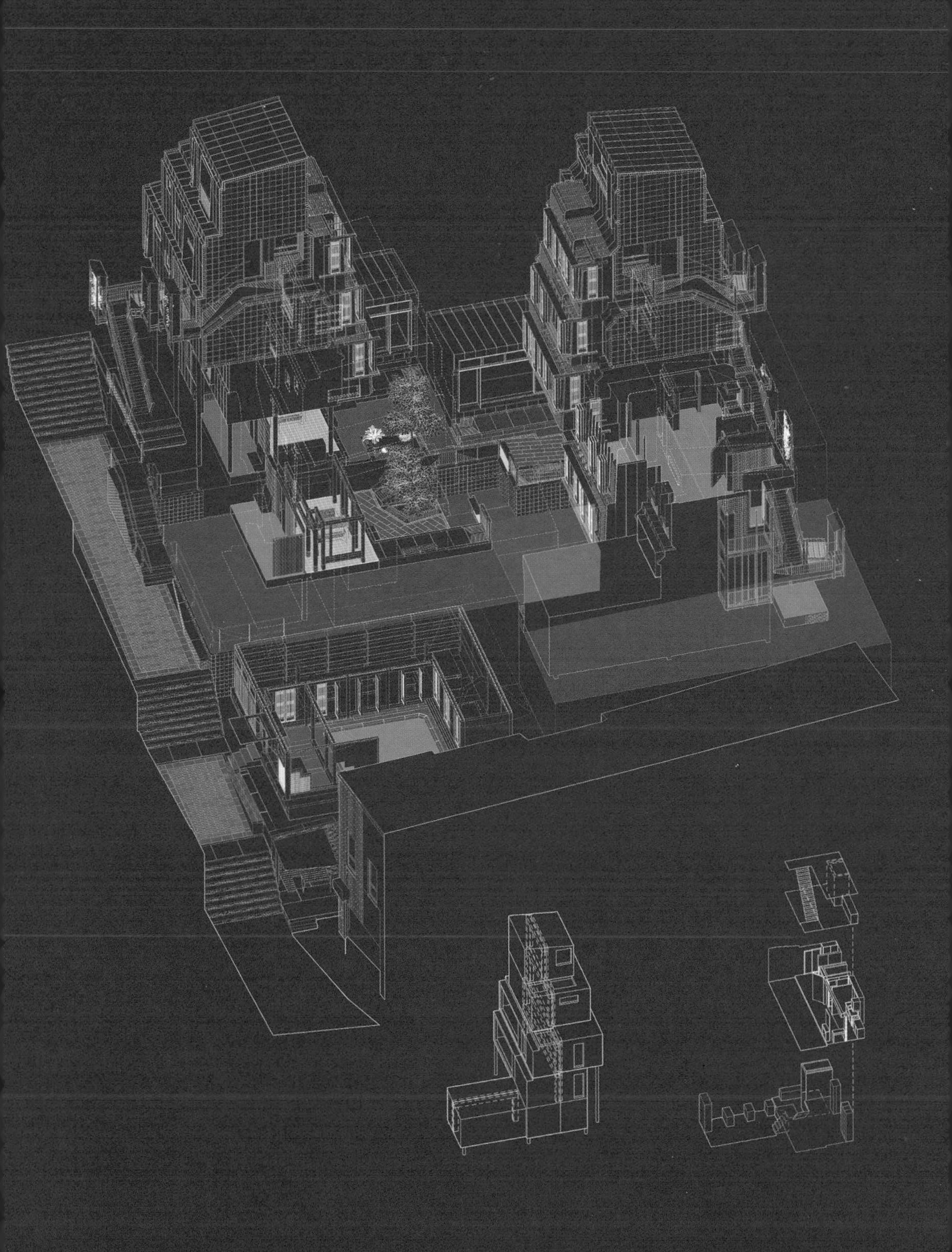

13.21

14.1

Modern Courage

PG14

Jakub Klaska, Dirk Krolikowski

At the centre of PG14's academic exploration is Buckminster Fuller's ideal of the 'the comprehensive designer': a master builder who follows Renaissance principles and a holistic approach.[1] Fuller (1895-1983), referred to this ideal of the designer as somebody who is capable of comprehending the 'integratable significance' of specialised findings, and is able to realise and coordinate the commonwealth potentials of these discoveries, whilst not disappearing into a career of expertise.[2] Like Fuller, we are opportunists in search of new ideas and their benefits via architectural synthesis and, as such, PG14 is a testbed for exploration and innovation, examining the role of the architect in an environment of continuous change.

We are in search of the new, leveraging technologies, workflows and modes of production seen in disciplines outside our own. We test ideas systematically by means of digital and physical drawings, models and prototypes. Our work evolves around technological speculation with a research-driven core, generating momentum through astute synthesis. We believe in the multi-objectivity of our design process, where the negotiation of different objectives becomes a source of architectural novelty and authorship. Our propositions are ultimately made through the design of buildings and the in-depth consideration of structural formation and tectonic constituents. This, coupled with a strong research ethos, generates new, unprecedented, viable and spectacular proposals.

This year, inspired by the audacity of the modernist mind, the unit's work aspired to reinstate the designer's engagement with all aspects of our profession. The observation and re-examination of developments in civilisation enabled us to project near-future scenarios and to position work as avant-garde, in the process of designing a comprehensive vision for the future. We explored how societal, technological, cultural, economic and political developments interlink, to shape strategies and determine a design approach. We investigated how human endeavour, desire and visionary thought interrelate to advance cultural and technological means, and drive civilisation. The underlying principle and observation of our investigations was that speculation can inspire and ultimately bring about significant change. The unit's work searches for modernist courage and aims to grow found nuclei into imaginative tales, with architectural visions fuelled by speculation.

Year 4
Iago natan Ferreira Souza, Michael Forward, Rupinder Gidar, Myfyr Jones-Evans, Ioannis Saravelos, Fan (Lisa) Wu, Qiming (Douglas) Yang

Year 5
Heidi Yat Ning Au-Yeung, Finbar Charleson, Matthew Gabe, Docho Georgiev, Charles Harris, Boyan Hristov, Sophie Tait, Nimrod Wong

Thanks to: RSHP, Zaha Hadid Architects, DKFS Architects, Heatherwick Studio, Amanda Levete Architects, Seth Stein Architects, Cundal Engineering, DaeWha Kang Design, Uni Stuttgart ITKE

Thanks to our critics and consultants: Andrew Abdulezer, Rasti Bartek, Barbara-Ann Campbell-Lange, Paulo Flores, Martin Gsandtner, DaeWha Kang, Jan Klaska, Melodie Leung, Filippo Nassetti, Ho-Yin Ng, Igor Pantic, Sam Saffarian, Ondrej Tichy, Charles Walker, Dan Wright, Bogdan Zaha

1. R. Buckminster Fuller, *Ideas and Integrities* (Baden: Lars Müller), 1963/2010, pp229-239
2. Ibid. p98

14.1, 14.13, 14.22 Finbar Charleson, Y5 'London Euston'. With comprehensive research into engineered timber as the primary design driver, this project draws upon historical references to situate what would be the first transit terminal structure constructed from wood. Experiments in wood lamination draw from a rich history, synthesising research into material science, sculpture, furniture design, naval architecture and aviation.
14.2, 14.9 Iago Natan Ferreira Souza, Y4 'The Campaign Pavilion'. This project uses airship technology to democratise the celebration of presidential campaigns in America. This new transportation method enables US presidential candidates to reach not just major cities in swing states but also the smaller towns in between. The design of the airship uses carbon fibre as a replacement to the existing, outdated, aluminium frame of modern airships.
14.3, 14.6, 14.7 Charles Harris, Y5 'Destination Docklands'. This project speculates a new 'multi-objective' approach to infrastructure for the 21st century, providing a core function with a locationally differentiated ancillary programme and contextual configuration.
14.4, 14.16 Matthew Gabe, Y5 'The London Philharmonic Hall'. A proposal for a new philharmonic hall on London's Southbank, which brings the grandeur of a night at the opera to modern music. A primary concert hall and external performance venue split the site, surrounded by public realm and covered by a timber canopy, which links the external and internal spaces.
14.5, 14.18 Heidi Yat Ning Au-Yeung, Y5 'Interstitial Play'. This project proposes a new typology of urban expansion as a critique of Hong Kong's current sea reclamation methods, easing the acute land shortage.
14.8 Sophie Tait, Y5 'Euroloop Leipzig'. This project proposes a 'European Hyperloop Network' – a new mode of transport that aims to enhance social, cultural and political solidarity amongst European countries. Carrying both goods and passengers, it travels up to 1200km per hour and enables the development of the European Single Market by creating better movement of goods, labour and services.
14.10 Ioannis Saravelos, Y4 'Googleplex Old Street'. This project speculates on an urban, privately-funded high-rise typology with intermediate pockets of public space. In this speculative context, the project funder is Google, being at the forefront of public space regeneration. The site is the Old Street Roundabout, tapping into the infrastructural opportunities and existing public space framework.
14.11–14.12 Michael Forward, Y4 'The Arctic Tap'. Situated in Tromsø in Norway, within the Arctic circle, 'The Arctic Tap' responds to the current cultural, climatic and economic position of the city. In partnership with Mack – the world's northernmost brewery – it is a modern take on the traditional railway pub, and serves as a gateway to the Arctic and a meeting point for locals, tourists, and educational and economic migrants.
14.14 Docho Georgiev, Y5 'Liberating Olympics'. The research aim of this project is to propose an architectural solution to the decreasing popularity of the Olympic Games, triggered by the negative financial and social impacts of purpose-built sports venues. Focusing on the design of the Olympic Stadium, it proposes a lightweight portable version, owned by the International Olympic Committee, to be hired by each host city.
14.15 Rupinder Gidar, Y4 'The British Leyland Transport Hub'. A proposal for a tower that sits on the proposed site for the HS2 terminal in Birmingham city centre. A subscription-based environment is imagined where individuals pay for access to the 'Future Type' vehicle instead of owning their own. The tower provides a system which uses packing algorithms and swarm behaviour to rapidly collect and dispense vehicles in the future-based context of 2040.
14.17 Boyan Hristov, Y5 'Warsaw High Speed'. This project speculates on an EU-funded regeneration of derelict pockets within Poland's central urban fabric using a bespoke mass-customised concrete construction. Cross-programming a new high-speed rail terminal with a food-market public plaza, it argues that typologies such as train stations are evolving to expand and include other programmatic uses, especially if situated within a dense urban area.
14.19 Qiming (Douglas) Yang, Y4 'Re-Occupying Gibraltar'. Gibraltar is the only British oversea territory that has a physical border with the EU. After Brexit, it is proposed that the UK government will tighten the strings for Commonwealth member states, and will seek new trading opportunities. Inspired by Boris Johnson's suggestion of a 'flagship' to strike deals around the world, this project proposes a 'Commonwealth Deal Making Headquarter' in Gibraltar, focusing on African trade deals.
14.20 Myfyr Jones-Evans, Y4 'e-Race Wales'. The 'Centre for e-Racing' aims to provide a post-Brexit beacon of research and development in e-technology in the heart of post-industrial Wales. Proposed to increase employment, provide apprenticeships and educational opportunities, improve the local economy, as well as the climate of innovation, the centre will also promote clean energy.
14.21 Nimrod Wong, Y5 'The International Trade Centre for the One Belt One Road Nations'. This new organisation is proposed as a reaction to recent incidents, protests and trade injunctions caused by the Basic Rate Interface (BRI). The new scheme serves as a democratic mediating arena that aims to foster multinational relationships, as well as regulate economic activity. The proposed 'International Trade Centre' (ITCOBORN) aims to capitalise on Chinese President Xi Jinping's trillion-dollar foreign policy offering improved integration of socio-economic interests to developing countries and emerging economies along the historic Silk Road route.
14.23 Fan (Lisa) Wu, Y4 'Chongwenmen Amateur Wine Gate' This project proposes rebuilding Beijing's city wall as fully enclosed highways for electric autonomous vehicles. The wall exterior is plugged with living modules, whilst the top is a belt of urban garden. The highway wall lifts off the ground in the locations of the old gates, allowing pedestrians to access the inner city from ground level. The nine gates are brought back as nodes, where different cultural or civic programmes are inserted, depending on their location and historical context. The gates are also transportation hubs, giving people access to the underground subway lines.

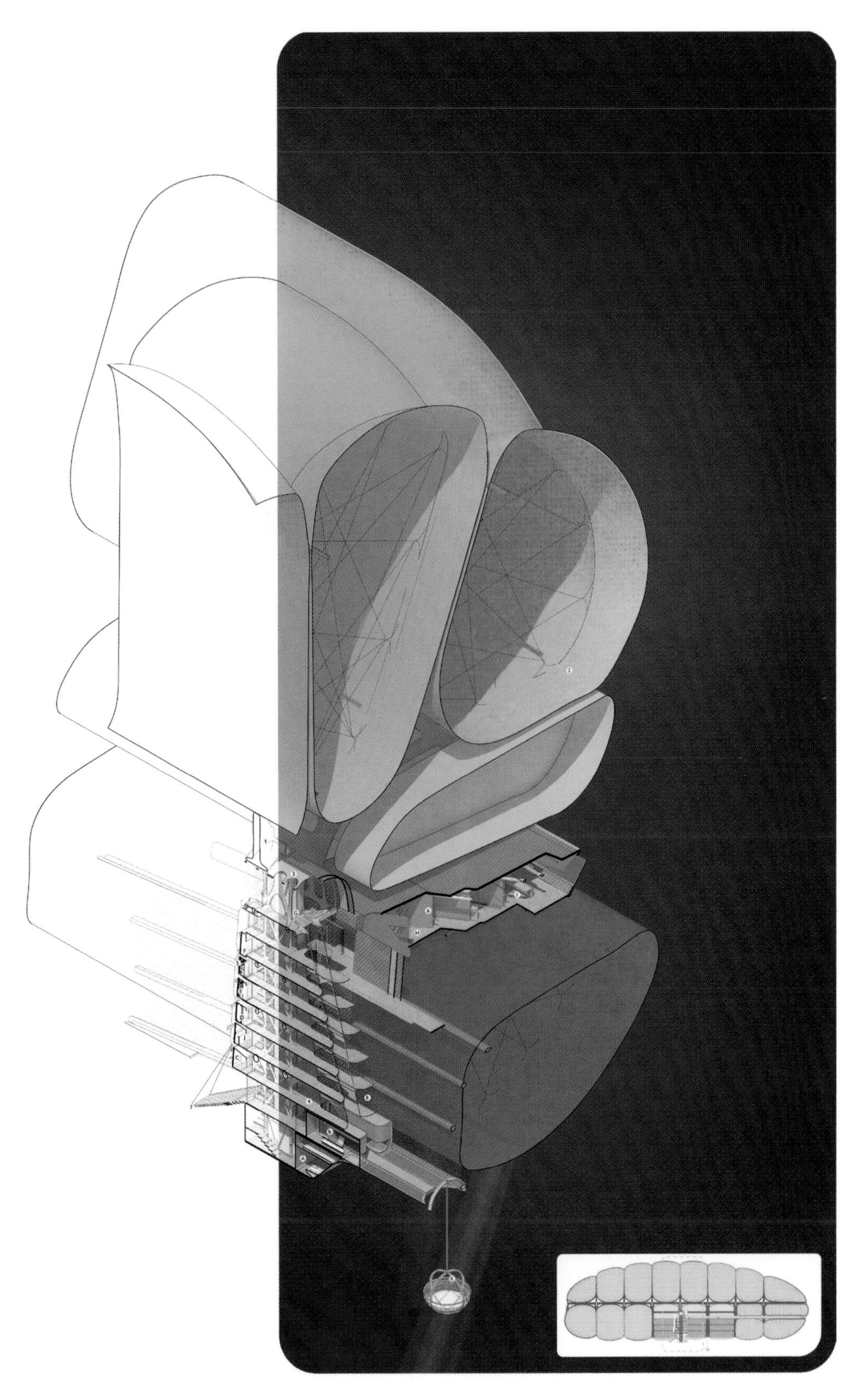

14.2

14.3

14.4

14.5

14.6

14.7

14.8

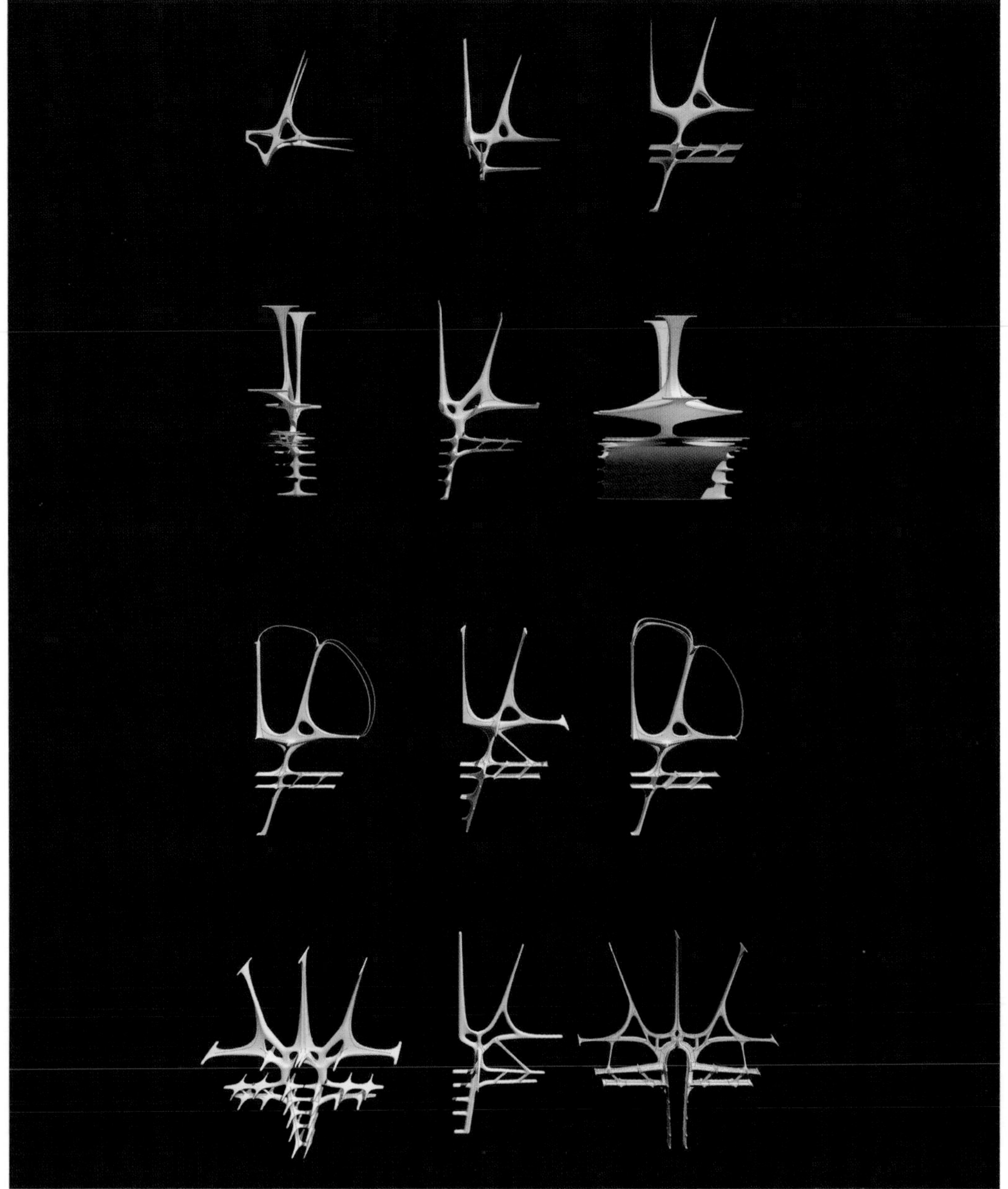

14.9

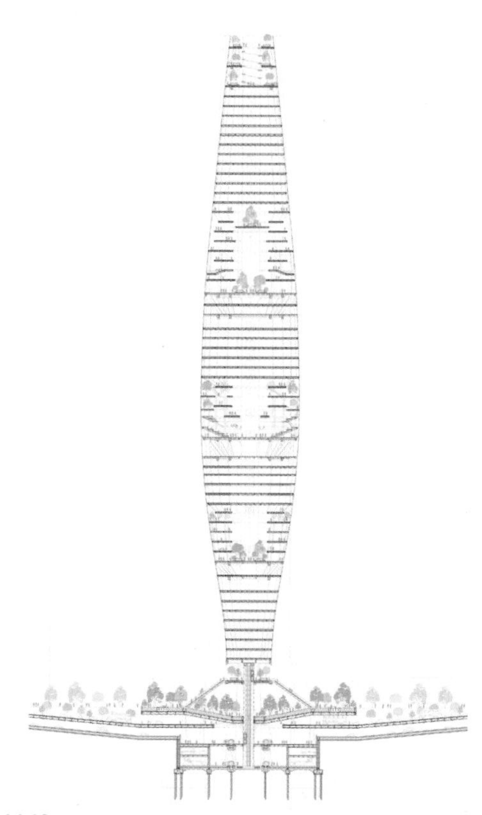

14.10

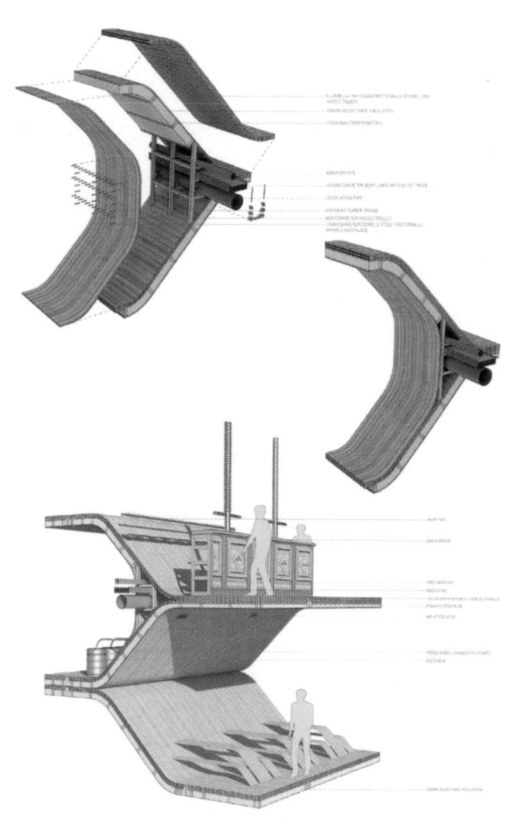

14.11

14.12

14.13

14.14

14.15

14.16

14.17

14.18

14.19

14.20

14.21

14.22

14.23

15.1

Lost Empires – New Tribes PG15

Max Dewdney, Susanne Isa

PG15 explores the transdisciplinary fields of art, architecture, museology and anthropology as a means to explore the psychology of places, narratives of history, mythologies, rituals and magic. We focus on collections, typologies and curation, and create episodic, surreal and transformational architecture, objects, spaces and landscapes.

'Lost Empires – New Tribes' was the theme for the year with the New Silk Road – a route that flows both ways from Yiwu in China to Barking in London – as our chosen site of investigation. In their research, students explored the following themes that underpinned investigations into 'deep time' and 'deep history':

1. Anthropo-Technology: A term coined by German philosopher and cultural theorist Peter Sloterdijk (b.1947), who describes how technological prosthetics and the merging of bodies and machines are radically altering our sense of self, shifting boundaries of nation(s), as well as our relationships with each other and bodies or 'clouds' of knowledge. It refers to the duality between technology and the body; home and exile; transit and stasis; shifts in imagination and how these alter how we draw, make and represent the scale of the body in space; and spaces of architecture between the object and body in motion.

2. Memory Institutions: As much as there is a need to conserve and preserve, there is also a need to rethink. How does the analogue have a digital afterlife? How can the digital and digital-born be preserved? The memory of place and journey are different for users and, in PG15, we are interested in discovering innovative ways to represent things geographically that can create new territories and landscapes.

3. Transcultural Exchange: The original Silk Road was as much an exchange of language as it was goods, and can be seen as the birth of globalism. Today, the physical infrastructure of ports, stations and airports, as well as transatlantic data routes, create greater connectivity and global synchronisation. Free-trade ports, and the towns surrounding them, generate markets, illicit trade and counterfeit goods. Art and biological exchange create spaces of multitude, transmutation, fluctuation and temporality. The pluralism of tongues creates cultural exchange.

The first project for PG15 was to design a 'New Silk Road Souvenir' and a 'Parallel Encyclopaedia' to enable each student to establish their own research topics. For Year 4 students, this developed into a small building project in Barking, East London, whilst Year 5 students established their own individual thesis project.

Year 4
Naysan Foroudi, Heman Galal, Stephany Govier, Oliver Hay, Wei Lau, Clement Laurence, Nhut Nguyen, Saria Saeed, Luke Sanders, Bogdan Stonciu, Jia Min Wong, Mengqiao Zhang

Year 5
Anastasia Leonovich, Phot Tongsuthi, Lu Wang

Special thanks to Marcel Rahm and Martin Sagar

Thanks to: Barbara-Ann Campbell-Lange, James A. Craig, Pedro Gil, Simon Herron, Alex Mark, Seán McAlister, Thomas Parker, Stephanie Reid, Marcus Seifermann, Mohammed Syafiq Hassan, Nicholas Szczepaniak, Jerry Tate, Jonathan Walker, Yeena Yoon

15.1, 15.14–15.17 **Anastasia Leonovich Y5**, 'The Living Organism of Karakum'. This project uses biological mechanisms of a camel as a backbone and imagines a structure in the desert that gathers water from an existing crater. The water is cleaned through the processes of aeration and filtration, and regulates its 'body temperature' by either cooling or heating the spaces.
15.2,15.6–15.7 **Clement Laurence Y4**, 'Pavilions for Conversation'. In light of the New Silk Road linking China to the UK, this project explores the notion of the tea ceremony as an act of conversation and cooperation between countries. Traces of movement are recorded on the table cloth, and are hidden from sight within the thermochromic shroud, revealed only when in contact with body heat. From these movements, pavilions are created to reflect the ritual. The architecture becomes elemental in nature, with the pavilions acting as sheltering stone caverns, which provide a place for conversation to flourish and disputes to be settled.
15.3, 15.12 **Stephany Govier Y4**, 'The Soil Institute'. Based upon research on myths and the duality of objects and materials, 'The Soil Institute' explores the passage of time and the process of healing, whilst indicating soil degradation and grieving over the global soil crisis. With the aim of achieving sustainable soils for future generations, the Institute is the first step towards a global intervention that uses phytoremediation and steam as healing methods.
15.4–15.5, 15.8, 15.22 **Oliver Hay Y4**, 'Scaling Disjuncture'. This project is an investigation into measurement and the disjuncture between different systems of measurement. The principles of the study were established through initial research into the 12,000km railway line that links Barking in London with Yiwu in China as part of the New Silk Road initiative. The subtleties and extremities explored within the initial investigations were then focused on Barking in East London in a design for a cricket pavilion that engages with themes of weight, measure and disjuncture.
15.9, 15.23 **Mengqiao Zhang Y4**, 'The New Silk Road Terminus, Barking International Station'. This project reveals the symbolic meaning of the New Silk Road. The arrival of the first New Silk Road freight train in Barking from Yiwu, allowed this project to imagine it as a passenger railway which links the east and west. Research into the signalling of rail systems across the landscape and neurological connections inside human bodies is embedded into the design to reimagine the typology of a train station. By translating the exchange status into lighting signals, the architecture celebrates the beauty of arrival and departure.
15.10–15.11 **Wei Lau Y4**, 'The Flaming Mountain'. Humans have always been fascinated with nature, thus, landscape is a constant source of inspiration in creating a work of art. 'The Flaming Mountain' in Barking represents transcultural exchange and is a slice of China's history transplanted into the UK. It is a diplomatic gift that addresses the new imperialism of China's 'Belt and Road Initiative' – a global development strategy – and is representative of the ties between the two countries post-Brexit.
15.13 **Bogdan Stonciu Y4**, 'Barking Institute of Hydrology'. Architecture usually responds to what is perceived as a threat by either retreating or defending. In response to rising sea levels, this project proposes a teaching and research facility that embraces its location and connection to the River Thames. Water is collected, filtered and allowed to enter the building. Sections of the roof direct rainwater either towards the inflatable pods located inside or, when these are filled, towards the central courtyard. The floating foundation sinks slightly after heavy rainfall, with the building appearing as an island.
15.18 **Luke Sanders Y4**, 'Transit House'. Focusing on the UK's automobile manufacturing industry, 'Transit House' used the Ford Dagenham Factory in Barking as an industrial landmark to explore car-metal stamping and mass production. The project offers an alternative solution to the London housing crisis, in the form of self-build mobile homes constructed from metal-stamped components prefabricated on the former factory site. The project makes use of under-utilised brownfield sites.
15.19, 15.21 **Nhut Nguyen Y4**, 'Making A Moon'. An attempt to bring the moon closer to us through multiple scales and methods, this project translates the unreachable subject into a more familiar system of reference that we can fathom: a birch ball viewed in the dark, a mirror with fingerprint smudges, a cafetière, a suction cup, a dance between two reluctant dancers or a plan to kidnap the moonlight.
15.20 **Jia Min Wong Y4**, 'Dagenham *Sankei Mandara*'. *Sankei Mandara* are representational maps showing a pilgrimage to the Buddhist sacred ground. A Buddhist retreat surrounded by man-made forest is reimagines the industrial site in Dagenham as a new Belt and Road Initiative city. Mogao Cave 61 in China, and the mural drawings within it, are studied to understand how to alter the perception of large and small, and near and far. This is then translated into the experience of approaching the Buddha statue in the centre of the *Sankei Mandara* landscape.
15.24, 15.25 **Lu Wang Y5**, 'Khorgos Trade Union Archive'. This project revolves around a protest held on 1 May 2020 in defence of the rights of workers in the city of Khorgos in China. The memory of the protest event is preserved in a clandestine visitor centre and archive adjacent to Trafalgar Square in London, exhibiting artefacts from the event. Its purpose is to inspire workers to develop ad hoc skills to promote their rights by establishing their own trade union.

15.2

15.3

15.4

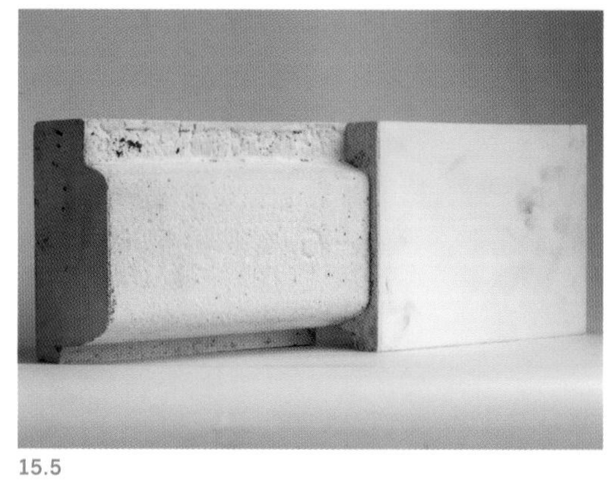

15.5

15.6

15.7

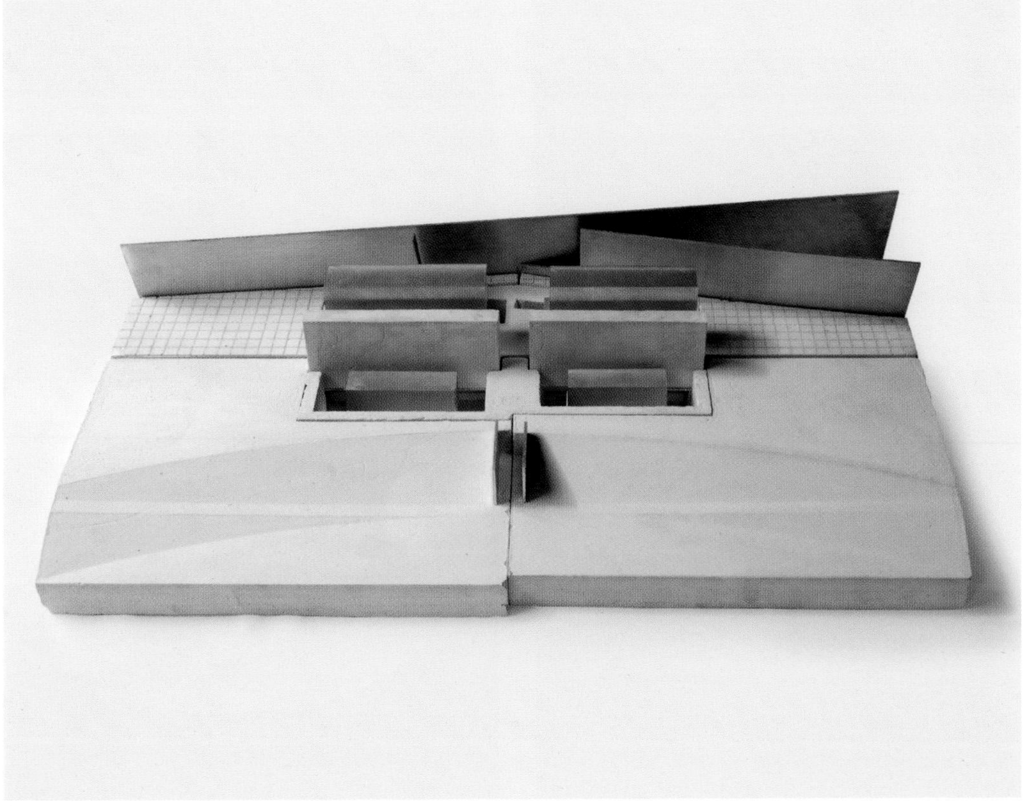
15.8

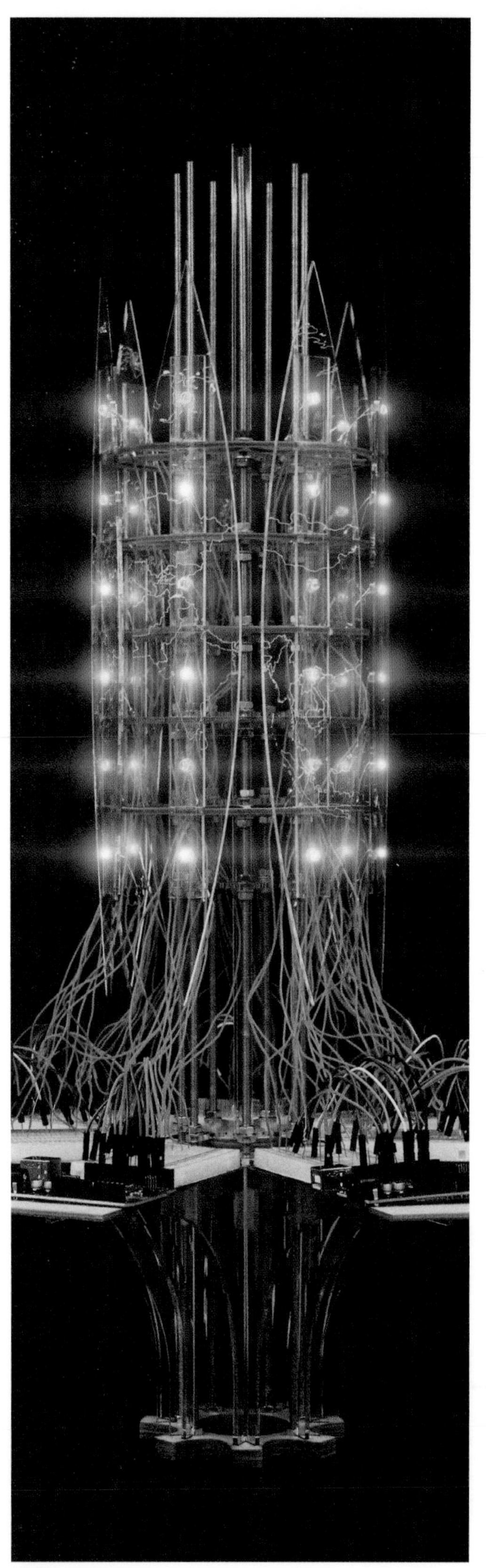

15.9

15.10

15.11

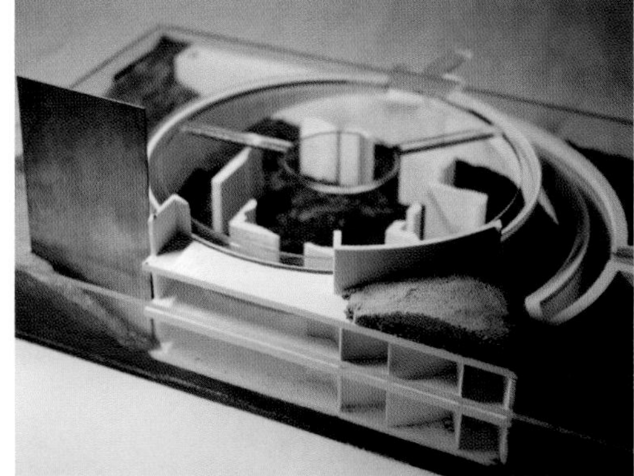

15.12

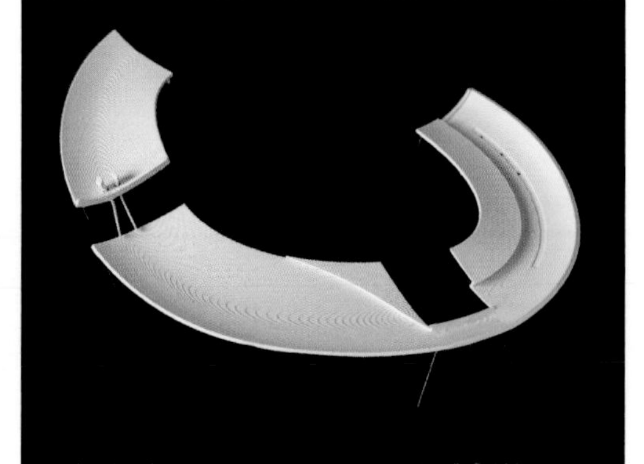

15.13

15.14

15.15

15.16

15.17

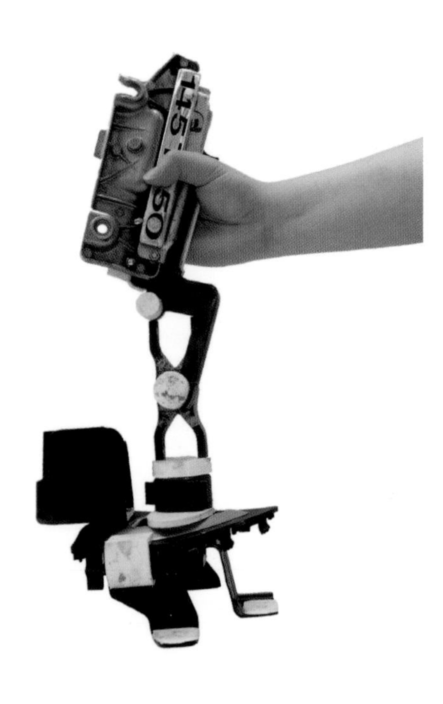

15.18

15.19

15.20

15.21

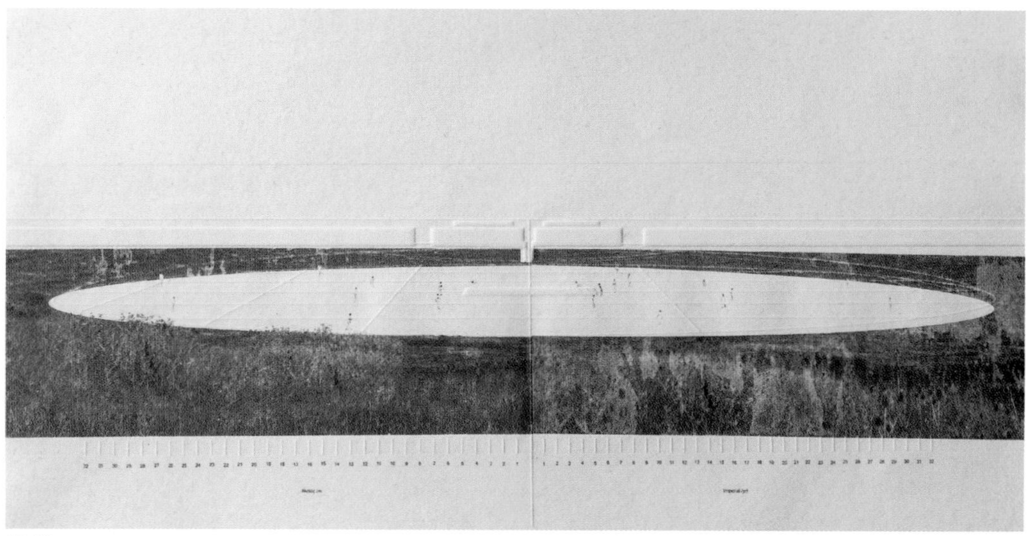

15.22

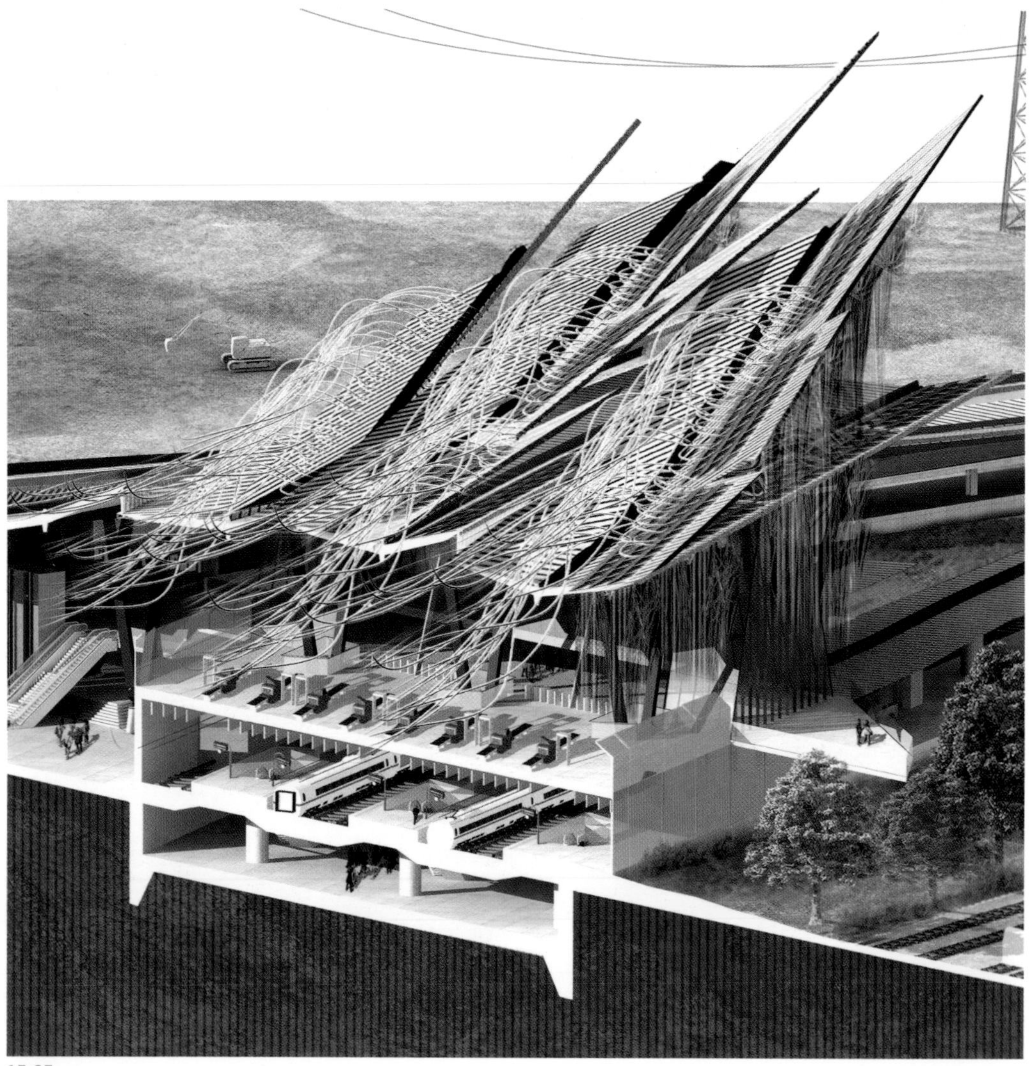

15.23

15.24

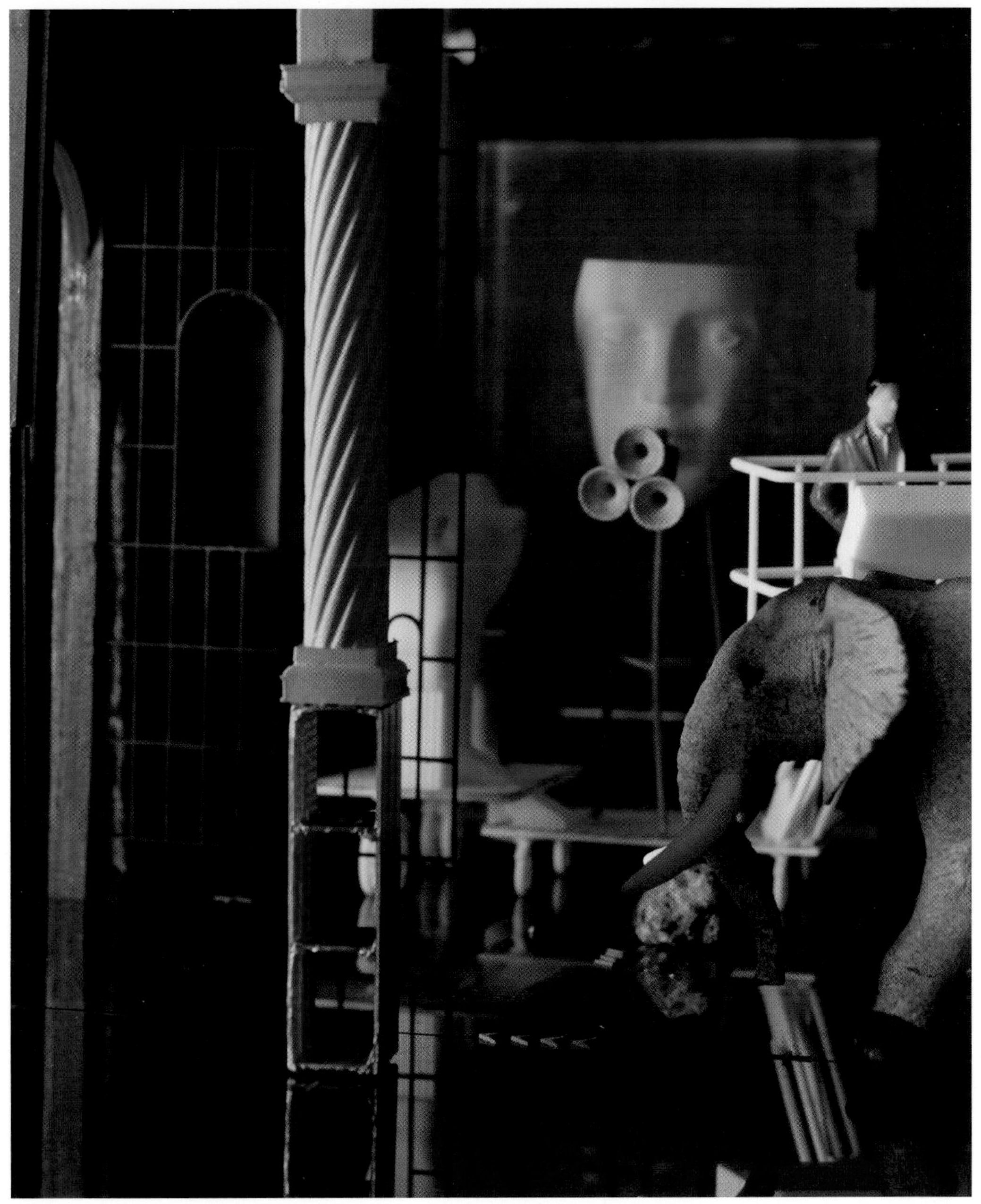

15.25

16.1

Quasi-Agents and Explorations on the Edge of the World

PG16

Matthew Butcher, Ana Monrabal-Cook

PG16 is interested in the exploration of architecture that emphasises our physical engagement with the environments we choose to inhabit. This year, we investigated the experience and meaning of matter, as well as the materials which frame and formulate our daily architectural experiences. Through research and experimentation, we revised our comprehension of materials and of matter more generally. We looked at the capacity of materials to act as 'quasi-agents'[1] and be a creative tool to reconsider the nature of the architectures we conceive.

Our site of enquiry was the region of Norrland in northern Sweden, largely defined by raw materials and natural resources, as well as vast areas of cultivated forest, iron ore mines and large developments for farming hydro energy; in the early 1900s, Norrland provided 25% of the world's timber. Although remote, the region's material resources link it to global networks of commerce and geopolitics through trade, defining both how it has been inhabited, and its identity, for hundreds of years.

As the global demand for iron ore has increased, over-mining threatens the stability of the ground in the northerly town of Kiruna, and the collapse of the mines there is now imminent. In response, the mining company plans to move the entire town two miles east, relocating 21 buildings, painstakingly, over 20 years. Vast infrastructural projects have also been instigated to connect the region with the rest of Europe, including railway networks for the transportation of resources. On our field trip, we collaborated with the architecture school based in Umea, and received invaluable input from local artists, activists and journalists. This exchange helped us draw on their knowledge of infrastructure, urban development and indigenous culture, as well as their global outlook.

In developing our investigations, PG16 questioned the impact, at various levels, of the use and abuse of natural resources as a catalyst for environmental strategies, structural deployments and new social models. Our students responded with projects that questioned the role of the architect in local policies, and the relationship between domesticity, forests and fire. Projects addressed the development of new vernaculars dealing with the loss of tradition and identity. We wondered at materials on a molecular level, exploring their response to the body and landscape. We engaged with a part of the world so defined by its infrastructure that is in danger of losing its identity to save itself. These are our explorations on the edge of the world.

Year 4
Jun Chan, Samuel Davies, Danny Dimbleby, Long Kwan, Ching Leung, Achilleas Papakyriakou, Przemyslaw Pastor, Wing (Michelle) Yiu

Year 5
Alessandro Conning-Rowland, Alex Kitching, Kin (Gigi) Kwong, Cameron Overy, Dimitar Stoynev

Many thanks to our technical tutor Will Jefferies for his dedication and insight. Thanks to all our critics for their invaluable feedback across the year: Andrew Belfield, Eva Branscome, Barbara-Ann Campbell-Lange, Christina Candito, Ian Chalk, Tom Coward, Tom Dobson, Nick Elias, Stylianos Giamarelos, Pedro Gill, Agnieszka Glowacka, Tamsin Hanke, Colin Herperger, Ifigeneia Liangi, Shaun Murray, Duncan McLeod, Robert Mull, Renee Searle, Matthew Springett, Ellie Ward, Owain Williams, Max Wisotsky

1. Phrase derived from: Jane Bennett, *Vibrant Matter: A Political Ecology of Things* (Durham, NC: Duke University Press, 2010), pviii

16.1, 16.23–16.24 Cameron Overy, Y5 'The Policy of Place'. This project questions the relationship between place and environmental policy-making, specifically laws that govern forest cultivation in Sweden. Whilst the vast majority of Sweden's natural resources are located in the northerly region of Norrland, the governmental bodies making decisions on these resources reside in the southern city of Stockholm. This has, historically, resulted in the idea that there exists a colonisation of the north by the south. This project is a proposal for a remote (or proximal) deliberation space for the Swedish parliament in order to reconfigure decision-making on the consumption of Norrland's natural resource of wood.

16.2 Kin Kwong, Y5 'Colourfield: Constructing Pigments on a Post-Industrial Landscape'. Raising awareness of the scarred landscapes created by the Anthropocene, this project proposes an architecture formed from chemical decay. Sited in the northern Swedish city of Kiruna, buildings purify waste from the adjacent mine, turning it into different-coloured pigments using a process of patination. Over time, the architecture slowly marks the ground with the pigments, transforming the deformed mining town with the colours created, and gradually replacing the vernacular Falu red as the main colour used to paint houses in Sweden.

16.3 Long Kwan, Y4 'White-Out Kiruna'. Celebrating the many visual and physical properties of snow in Kiruna, this proposal aims to reinforce the identity of the community at a time when it is being threatened by the relocation of the town due to over-mining. Positioned on a remote site to the east of the Kirunavaara Mine, the 'White-Out Centre' is a community and art centre, which facilitates a multitude of existing cultural activities that utilise snow and ice. The building seeks to bring these activities into one location, where certain climatic conditions needed to preserve and change the qualities of snow can be controlled and made manifest.

16.4–16.5 Jun Chan, Y4 'Inhabiting the Ecology: The Living Birchwood'. This project questions how we can challenge our perspectives on the ecological systems present in landscape through architecture, its materials and the environment it resides in? Situated in Sarek National Park – the most mountainous region in northern Sweden – the project functions as an outpost for the research and educational organisation, The International Bateson Institute, and focuses on the utilisation of birch wood, viewing the material as a body that is in constant negotiation with the environment.

16.6–16.8 Alex Kitching, Y5 'A Retreat for the Protagonists of the Swedish Forest Taskscape'. Focusing on the creation of a field condition in which the three protagonists of the Swedish forest 'taskscape' – logger, tourist and reindeer – are brought together, this project proposes a series of enclosures and viewing devices that generate subtle visual games and distortions in the forests of northern Sweden. Located in Dikanäs, the 'retreat' creates a choreographed orchestration of experience, highlighting the various ways that different individuals and groups inhabit and experience the landscape, simultaneously and in seclusion.

16.9–16.11 Samuel Davies, Y4 'Cookery and Apocalypse'. Responding to the prescribed burning of Swedish forests, this project proposes a series of houses as a meditative infrastructure that exists between the city of Umea and the forest that surrounds it. It explores the practical inhabitation of a place that is routinely burnt down and architecture that is emblematic of our conflicting attitudes and emotions towards domestic and landscape fires. It adapts fire control conventions and local policies to suit the conditions of forest fire and questions the way we manage building legislation.

16.12–16.14 Achilleas Papakyriakou, Y4 'Malmberget Centre for Relocation'. Due to extreme underground mining, a huge crater has split the Swedish town of Malmberget in two making it dangerous to live there. As a result, the community is undertaking a move to nearby towns in an evacuation effort set to last at least another decade. This project proposes three red pavilions that provide a warm and opulent sanctuary for the residents of the ailing Arctic town during the move.

16.15 Wing (Michelle) Yiu, Y4 'The Memory Kit'. The expansion of the mining activity in Kiruna has resulted in the city's church being demolished. This project examines how memory can alter and distort over time, changing the way we inhabit and remember buildings, using 'Memory Kits' that test against the reality and observe how physical and cultural memory is recorded and preserved.

16.16 Przemyslaw Pastor, Y4 'The Siedi Centre – An Observant Port Terminal'. Learning from specific perspectives on the environment from the Sami – the indigenous inhabitants of Sweden – this project animates a piece of the landscape and a building, utilising the changing states of certain materials, such as birch wood. Connecting the industrial and natural in the most northerly region of the country, the project proposes a port terminal and an observatory overlooking an 80-kilometre lake, located between the deepest mine in Europe and the tallest mountain in southern Sweden.

16.17, 16.19–16.20 Dimitar Stoynev, Y5 'Swedish Antiphony'. Set in the context of the proposed mass expansion of the mining industry in Norrland, this project explores the creation of a new northern Swedish vernacular, which seeks to preserve and expand upon traditional building typologies and practices. Through the use of 'architecture of collision', the new language seeks to disrupt the ongoing use of prefabricated and mass-produced structures as the default building typology in Sweden. To help develop this new architectural language, the project proposes techniques of building with rammed earth to create a tapestry of disjunction, material texture, memory and culture.

16.18 Ching (Albert) Leung, Y4 'Temporal Bathhouse, Kiruna, Sweden'. Exploring how architecture can frame and enhance the experience and understanding of multiple timescales – hourly, weekly, annually, etc. – this project aims to facilitate recovery from irregular working shifts and isolation from the outdoors that disrupts the Kiruna miners' circadian rhythms. It looks at how ephemeral events that occur repetitively, in different moments of time, gradually feel more permanent, whilst continuous events gradually fade away.

16.21–16.22 Alessandro Conning-Rowland, Y5 'New Nomads: Inhabiting the Moving City of Kiruna'. This project proposes an infrastructural framework for a moving city, designed to cater for the population of Kiruna, who have been forced to relocate due to the over-mining of Iron Ore. The proposal aims to address residents' fear of being forgotten through this forced move, as well as providing an alternative solution to the 'blanket housing typologies' of prefabricated construction and placeless masterplanning that is currently being imposed.

16.2

16.3

16.4

16.5

16.6

16.7

16.8

16.9

16.10

16.11

16.12

16.13

16.14

16.15

16.16

16.17

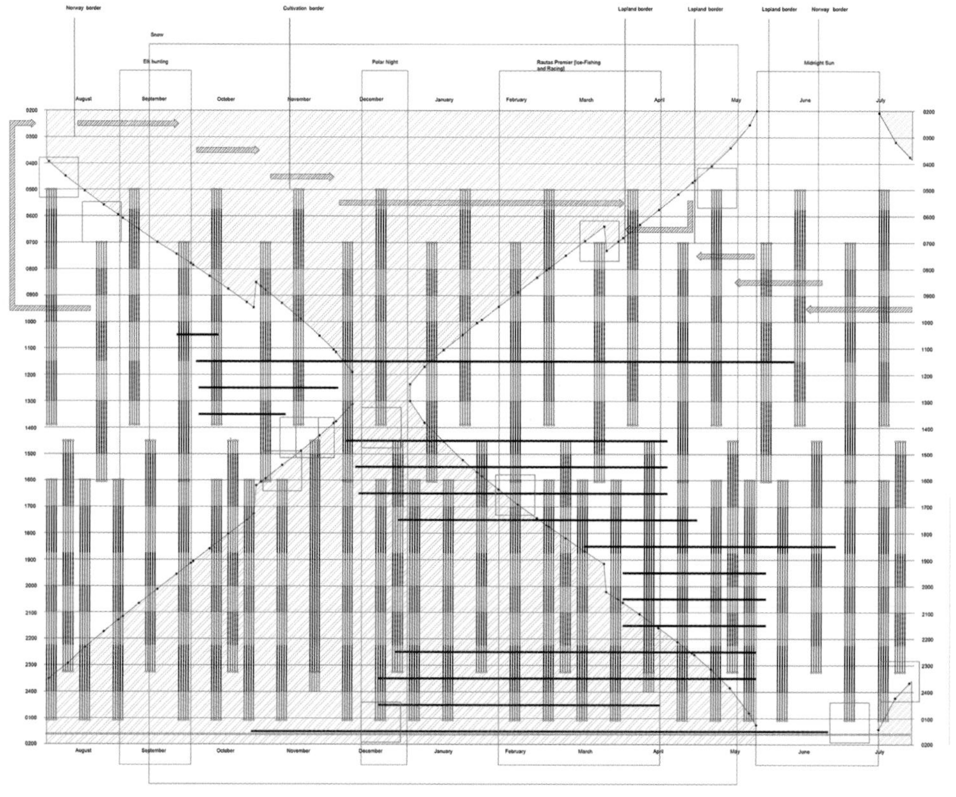

16.18

16.19

16.20

16.21

16.22

16.23

16.24

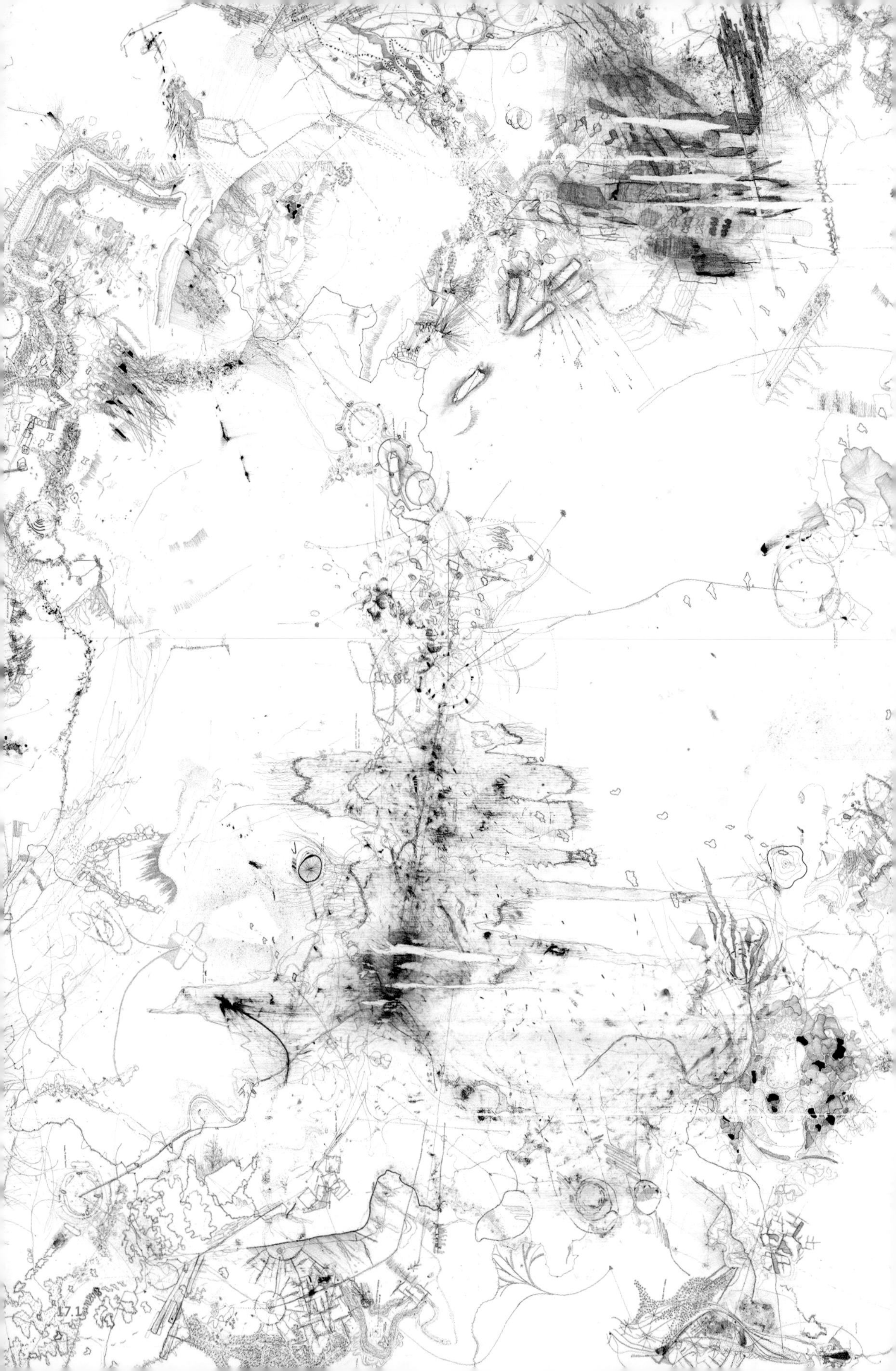
17.1

Deep Future, Deep Past

PG17

Yeoryia Manolopoulou, Níall McLaughlin

Our 'deep past' is inscribed on our consciousness and holds the key to our modes of perceiving, reasoning and acting within social settings. Even as we wonder about the challenges and possibilities of the far future, we are using cognitive tools which evolved over millions of years. PG17 is interested in the experience of design itself: that is, the design of the activity of design as an embodied action evolving in time and place. It is the very event of drawing and making, whilst being in the midst of it, that we interrogate, enrich and celebrate. Lines tell stories and cross each other as we strive to produce architecture with public meaning.

Mind and environment have evolved side-by-side for millennia. Architecture has not only emerged from this dynamic partnership but, to different extents, has influenced and determined the relationship between our consciousness and surroundings. If architecture is a mediator between a community and its buildings, how can it flourish in a new post-digital social condition? The human mind has not been devised as a discrete, logical computational apparatus, instead, it is an evolved biological network fully immersed in its physical and social environment. To understand our opportunities and needs as architects, we must fully explore this distinction.

This year, the unit investigated mind, community and land within time extremes. Our research and design processes were influenced by prehistory, anthropology, cognitive psychology, geology and emerging climate sciences. We considered animal and plant life, climatic uncertainty, the politics of land and artificial intelligence.

We visited the Orkney Islands – an archipelago of over 70 islands in the north of Scotland – which have been inhabited for at least 8,500 years and were, several thousand years ago, Britain's centre of innovation. We visited a vast hill covering more than six acres of land, which was thought to be made of glacial debris until, recently, it was discovered to have been made over 5,000 years ago by humans. Such enormous and timeless constructions on the Orkney Islands sit side-by-side with the newest facilities of wind and marine energy resources, stimulating a revived population of people who choose to live there. We worked intimately with this place, organising collective walks and drawing events.

Collaboration can break habits of mind, allowing other ways of seeing to influence our consciousness. Our drawing processes borrowed from modes of collaboration, performance, improvisation and chance in the aleatoric arts.

Year 4
Eleni Efstathia Eforakopoulou, Veljko Mladenovic, Iman Mohd Hadzhalie, Philip Springall, Harriet Walton

Year 5
Nathan Back-Chamness, Luke Bryant, Ossama Elkholy, Grace Fletcher, George Goldsmith, Hanrui Jiang, Rikard Kahn, Cheuk Ko, Alkisti Anastasia Mikelatou Tselenti, Andreas Müllertz

Thank you to Design Realisation tutors James Daykin and Maria Fulford

A special thanks to our critics: Barbara-Ann Campbell-Lange, Nat Chard, Hannah Corlett, Murray Fraser, Anne Marie Galmstrup, Pedro Gil, Agnieszka Glowacka, William Haggard, Tamsin Hanke, Chris Hildrey, Will Hunter, Susanne Isa, Sarah Izod, Matthew Leung, Anna Liu, Emma-Kate Matthews, Dean Pike, Sophia Psarra, Chenhan Wang, Tim Waterman, Victoria Watson, Izabela Wieczorek

17.1 PG17 Collaborative Drawing, Y4 and Y5 'Experiencing Landscapes'.
17.2 Nathan Back-Chamness, Y5 'Untitled'. Throughout this year-long project, the acts of doing and observing became a working method whereby architecture can be continually conceived and challenged, over thousands of years and within a single drawing.
17.3 Hanrui Jiang, Y5 'Fluidity between Land and Sea'. This project is based on the reading of Selkie – mythological 'seal folk' in Scotland – tales, which explore 'fluidity' within coastal regions. The site – the abandoned island of 'Eynhallow' – is investigated through its geographical features and the analogy that sealskin can be regarded as a transition between the land and the sea, and humans and seals. This study of 'fluidity' shapes the morphology of the island, reading the sea as a continuation of the land, with the water as only a thin membrane that separates the two.
17.4 Luke Bryant, Y5 'A Piece of Landscape'. This new intervention creates connections between isolated Neolithic monuments that were originally part of a processional path 5,000 years ago. 'A Piece of Landscape' seeks to interpret the historical sites, as well as engaging with the surrounding environment. Stones from Stromness – a nearby town at risk of flooding – are used to create a new structure; applying Neolithic principles to transport stones from previous communities across the landscape.
17.5 Alkisti Anastasia Tselenti Mikelatou Tselenti, Y5 'Orkney Tourism Association'. A series of archaeological studies of the scattered chambered cairns – Neolithic burial monuments – of the Orkney archipelago challenges the conventional understanding of 'archives'. This project argues that in order to envisage an archive for the islands, the only honest representation is the archipelago itself. The proposal aims to bridge the fragmented temporal and spatial gaps of Orkney, as well as to shed light on its marginalised past.
17.6 Veljko Mladenovic, Y4 'Temporal Strata'. Located directly on top of the Ness of Brodgar – a key Neolithic site currently under investigation – this project is a 'living archive', and explores architecture as a continual process without an end. 'Making in time' is a key theme where, through a dialogue of chance and intent, unpredictability is replicated to manifest an open-ended architecture.
17.7 Eleni Efstathia Eforakopoulou, Y4 'Living Geologies'. The romantic and picturesque sceneries that we see today are not static but, rather, are the result of a slow-motion car crash. This project interrogates this violent choreography and has sought to reimagine the landscape as in a perpetual state of change.
17.8–17.9 Ossama Elkholy, Y5 'Copinsay's Dark Uncanny'. Assuming landscape is a living process, this proposal plays out the impact of an imposed quarrying process, using a speculative quarrying tool that surveys Copinsay island's geological, meteorological, economic and ecological data to inform its movement and digging. It proposes that people manually carve the remaining stone, responding to what has already been excavated, simultaneously observing the unfamiliar ecologies that emerge.
17.10 Rikard Kahn, Y5 'Birsay Refuge'. This project seeks to provide a place for visitors to stay on the island of Birsay, accessible at only the lowest point of the tidal cycle. Interweaving itself with the archaeological remains of earlier Pictish and Viking settlements, the proposal provides a place for longing, contemplation and communal living whilst taking refuge on the historic site.
17.11 Harriet Walton, Y4 'Bog Queen'. Set in the landscape of Hoy, the sub-function provides a refuge for walkers on the island, made though the excavation of the peat bogs that cut through the landscape. The building hosts a seasonal music festival, whereby material removed from the subterranean peat chambers is assembled into structures above the cuts. The seasonal awakening of the structure is carried out by island residents and visitors during the summer to form a music chamber. In autumn the structure is disassembled and repacked into the main chamber and is preserved for another year in the peat.
17.12 Iman Mohd Hadzhalie, Y4 'Slowly Dyeing'. Natural purple dye in Orkney has become increasingly scarce due to the scarcity of the endangered purple flora from which it is made. In response, this proposed mill produces natural dye using a traditional process of fermenting lichen, as an alternative, sustainable solution to using purple flora. The building rejuvenates the abandoned ruin of the Earl's Palace, Birsay, connecting with the rich heritage of the Orkney archipelago whilst also creating a new future.
17.13 George Goldsmith, Y5 'Scapa Flow: An In-Situ Exhibition of Historical Knowledge'. This project explores ideas of exposing the unseen information stored within the islandscape of Orkney, and the amplification of nature and historical knowledge in the landscape. The project suggests a way of combining a museum and habitation with the need to generate renewable energy. The speculative proposal puts forward the idea that the exhibition of historical knowledge in-situ is superior to the removal of items from their context.
17.14 Grace Fletcher, Y5 'Stroma Salt Station'. This proposal seeks to regenerate the abandoned island of Stroma through the surrounding sea water and tidal energy of the Pentland Firth. The island has a dichotomous condition whereby the east is dry and fertile and the west is inhospitable and salty. A permeable membrane is constructed along the divide to enhance the existing differences, in turn setting up the island as a salt water battery for tidal energy. The battery accumulates in the centre of the island, in a power station built of salt and gypsum residue.
17.15 Philip Springall, Y4 'Leviathan'. The Stromness Maritime University reconnects the people of Stromness with the sea. Stranded whales, which are otherwise thrown into landfill, are transformed from raw material into building components, with each part of the whale utilised for its unique qualities. This whale tectonic combines bone, blubber, baleen, blood and oil into an inhabitable architecture.
17.16 Cheuk Ko, Y5 'Dynamic Body as a Measure and Projector for Architecture'. This project explores the conceptual relationship between the body and space, which is not necessarily recognisable on a daily basis unless intentionally examined. Actions, movements and processes are studied to design a farmhouse in Orkney, aiming to reintroduce pleasurable farming that reconnects the body and landscape.
17.17 Andreas Müllertz, Y5 'The Sea as a Room'. In this project, the Scapa Flow – a landlocked sea at the heart of the Orkney Islands – has been dammed and drained to reveal a vast landscape of shipwrecks, archaeological sites and scarred terrain. Timber infrastructure emerges from the practice of forestry under the previous water line, carrying boats and timber across the sea of trees.

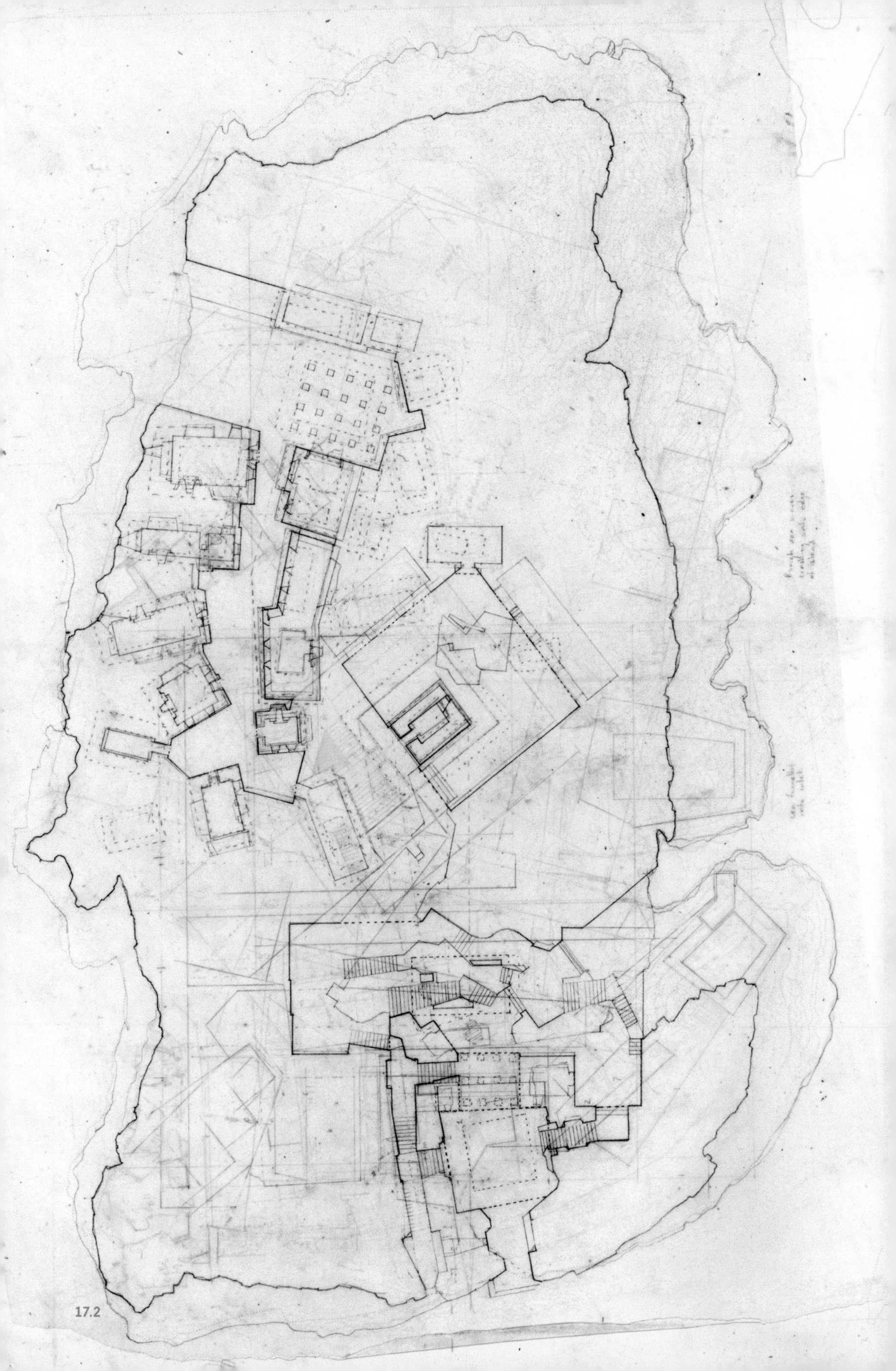

17.2

17.3

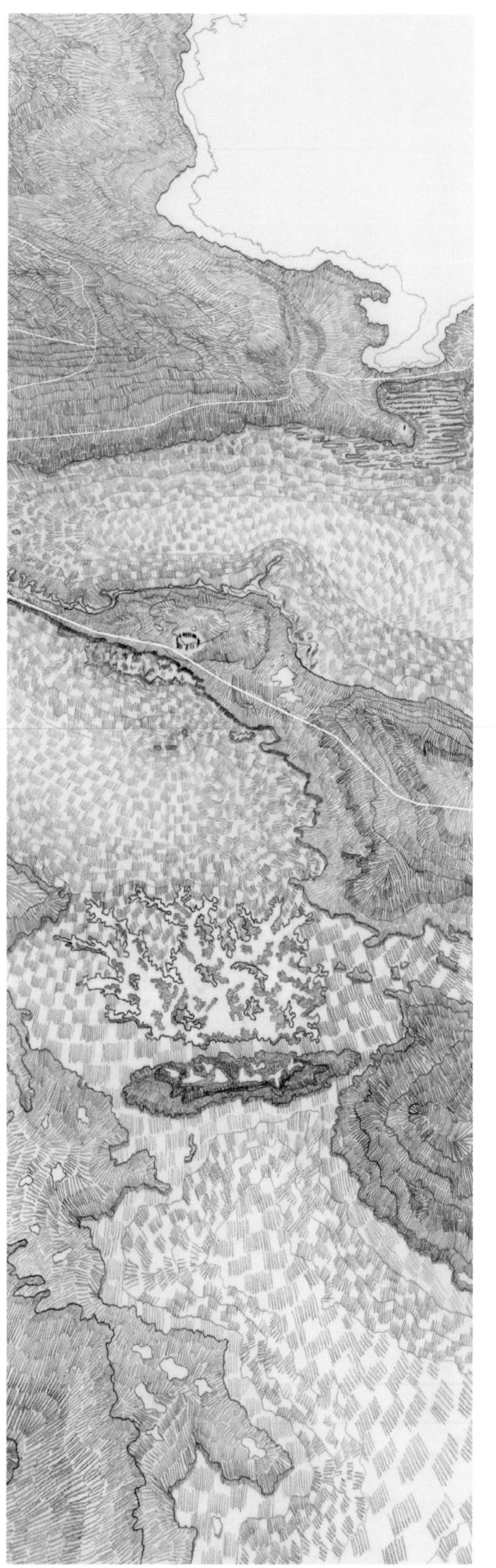
17.4

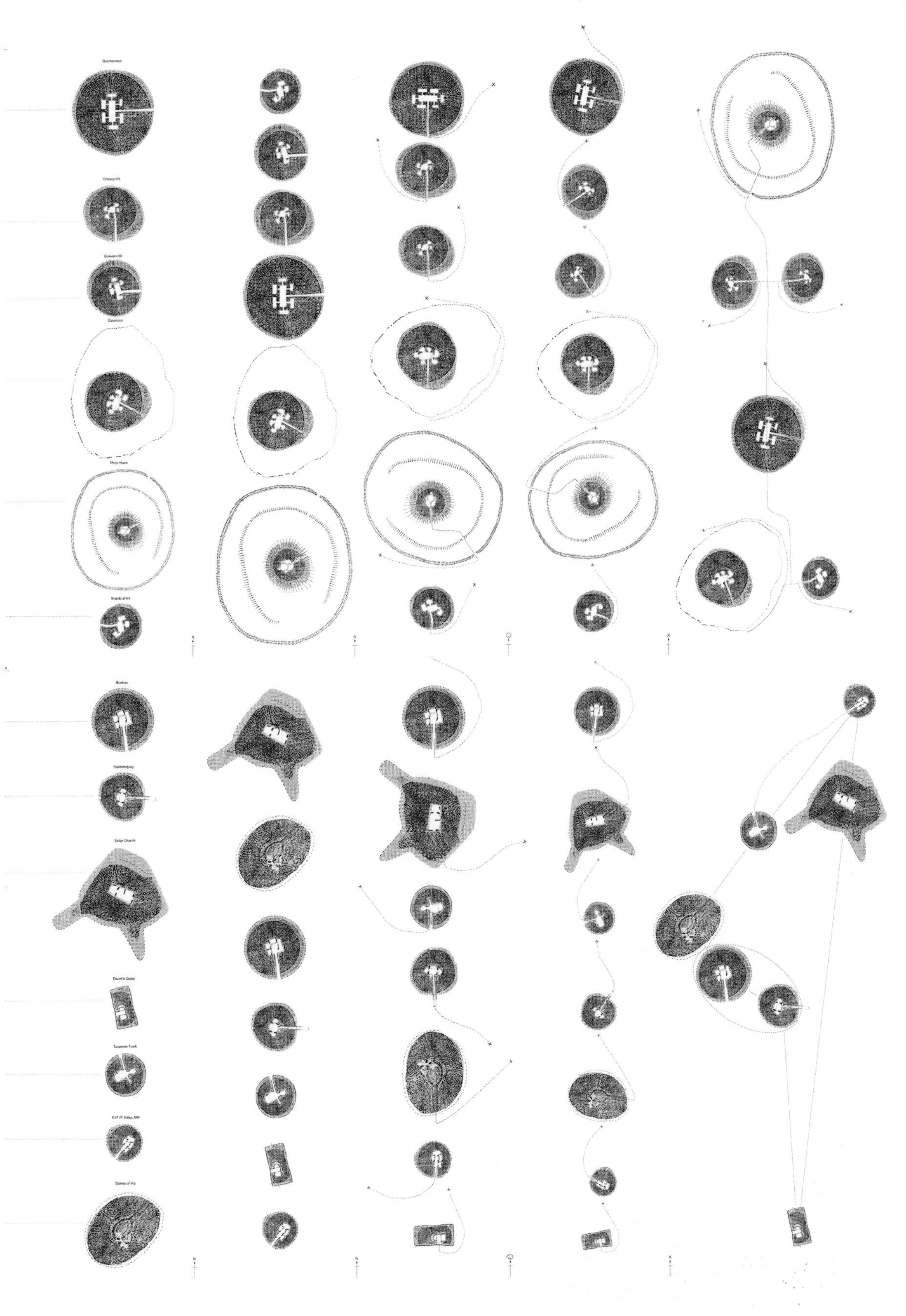

Quanterness
Vinquoy Hill
Cuween Hill
Quoyness
Maes Howe
Wideford Hill
Bookan
Huntersquoy
Eday Church
Dwarfie Stane
Taversoe Tuick
Calf of Eday, SW
Stones of Via

17.5

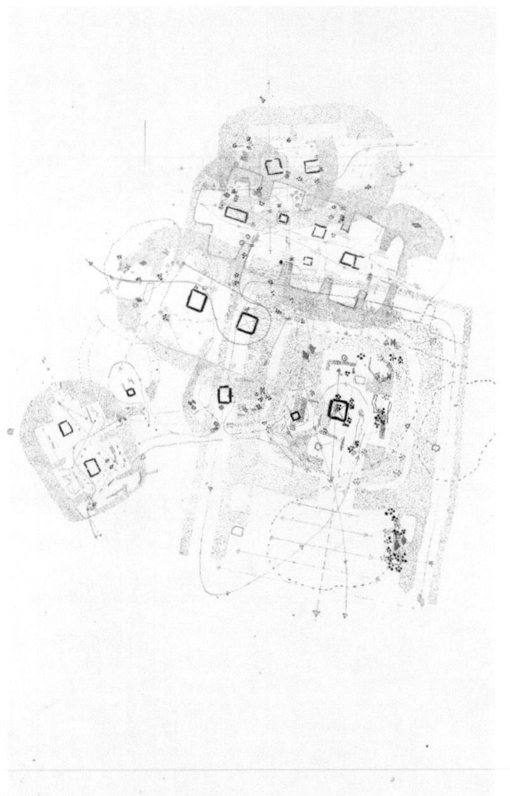

17.6

17.8

17.7

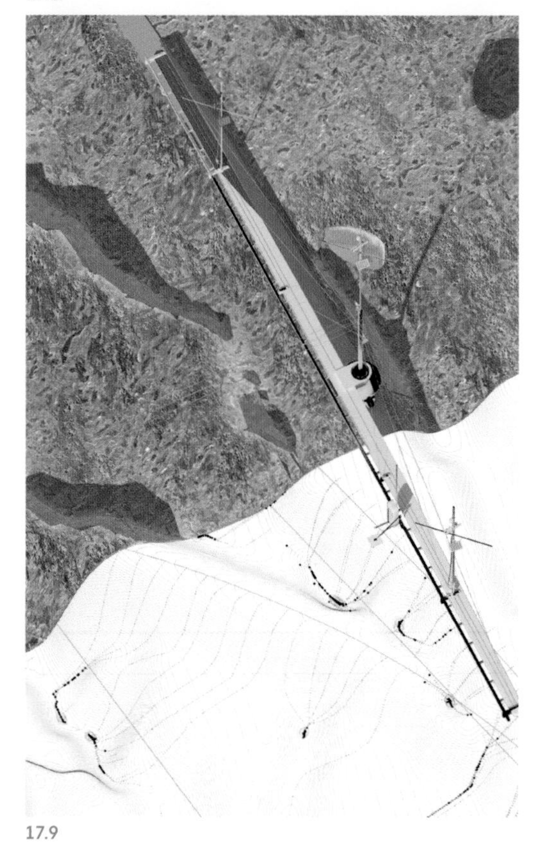

17.9

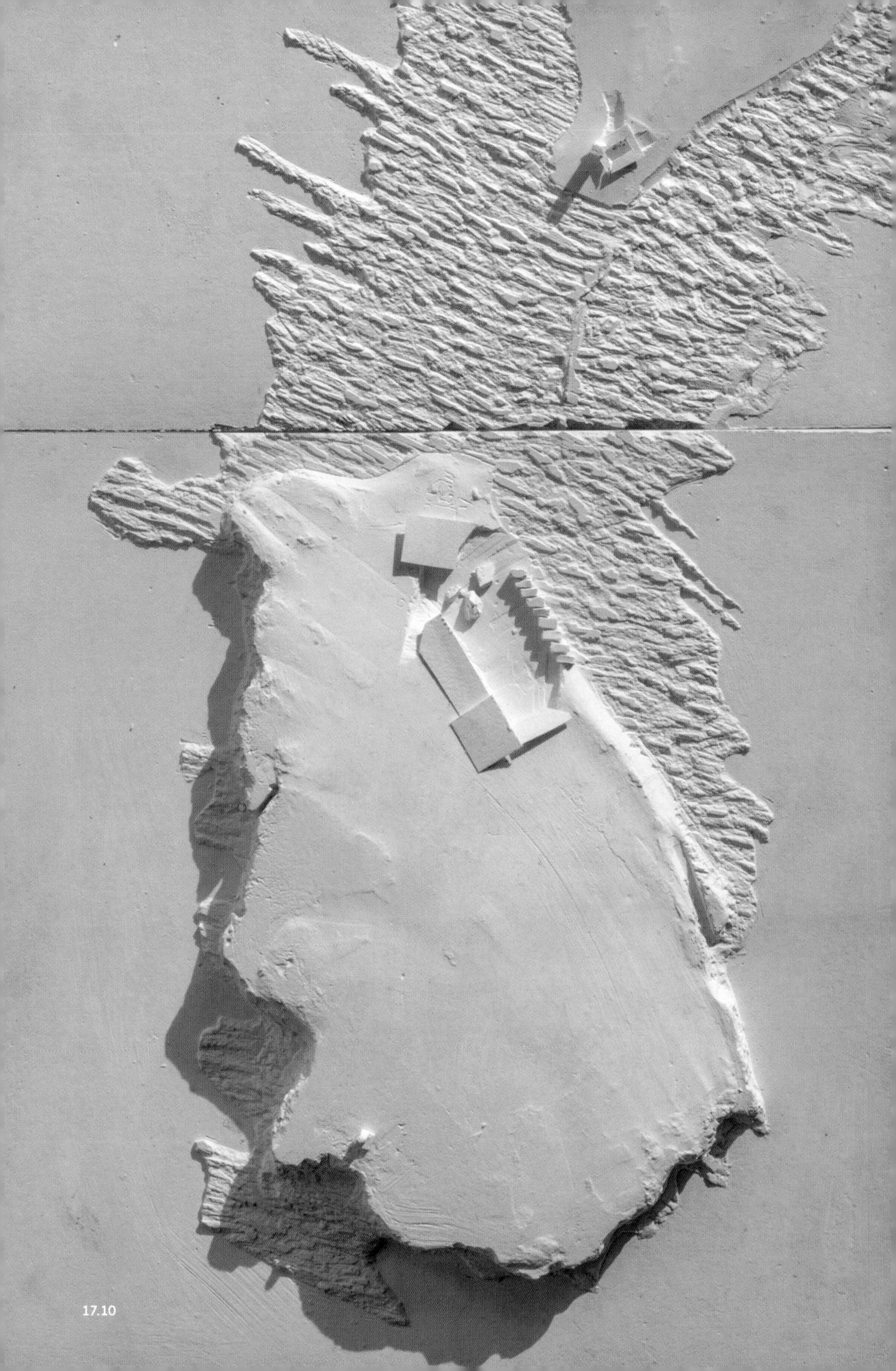

17.10

17.11

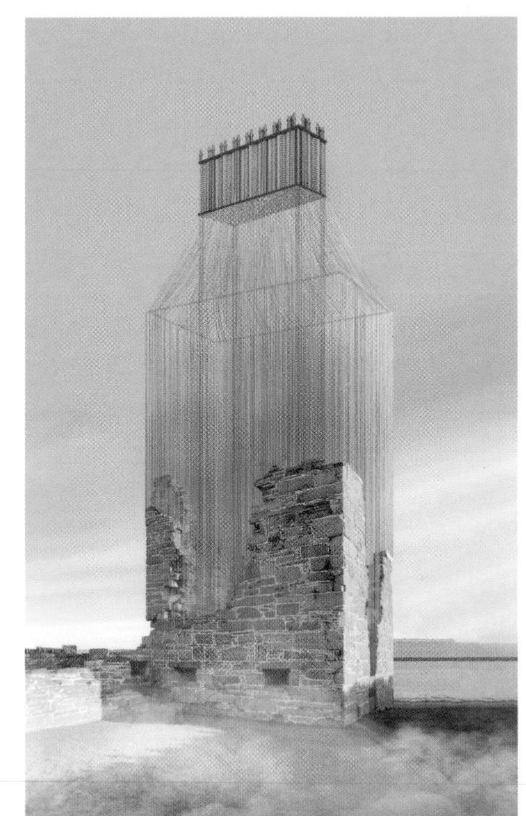

17.12

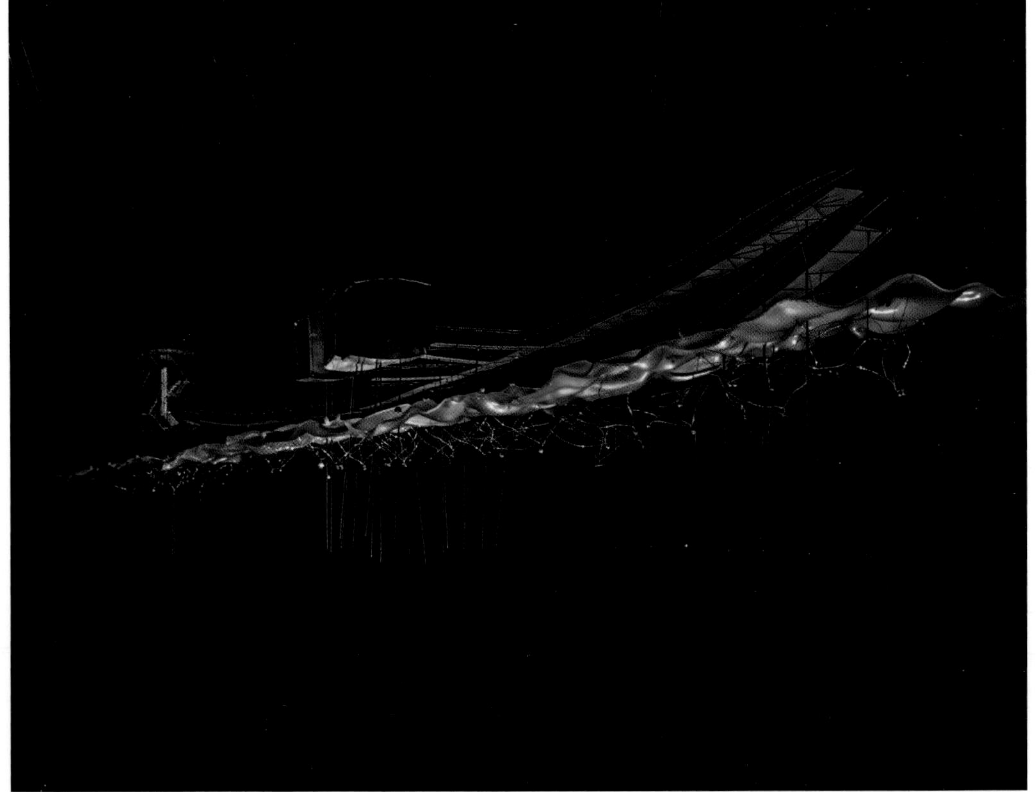

17.13

17.14

17.15

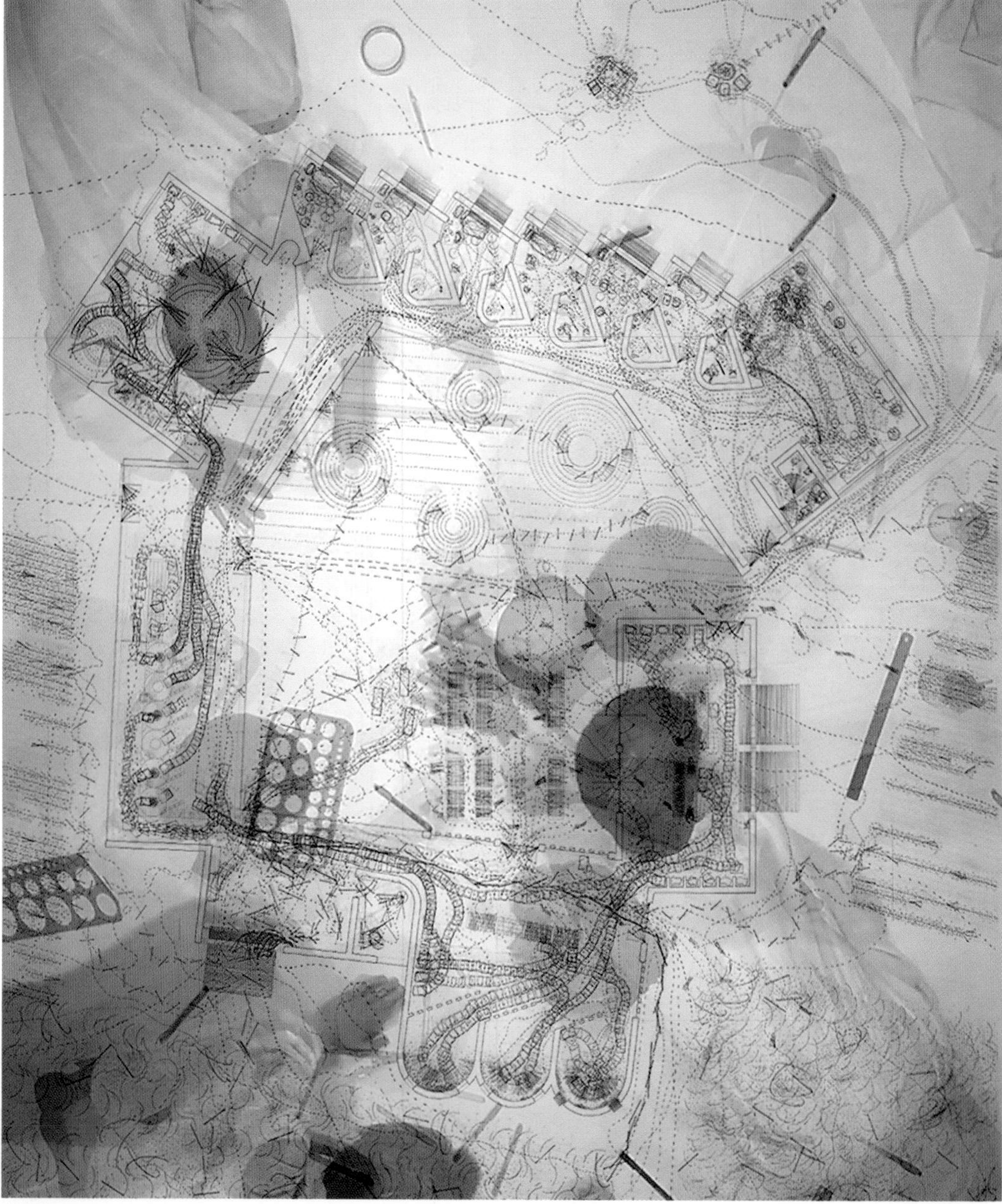

17.16

17.17

18.1

Earth Child / Education through Innovation

PG18

Isaïe Bloch, Ricardo de Ostos

A lot has been said about what makes culture local and specific, especially following recent debates on borders and identity. In PG18, we investigate the idea that the culture of a city is the meeting of tradition and innovation. We work with architecture as a place where knowledge is embedded in space, from the tectonic to the context of materials and uses. None of that is relevant, however, if we are not able to introduce concepts that challenge the status quo.

This year, the unit developed proposals for educational institutions in Ghana that focused less on the basics and more on innovation. Ghana is the fastest growing economy in Sub-Saharan Africa and, in 2017, the country's government announced a campaign 'Ghana Beyond Aid' to challenge its dependency on foreign aid, by focusing on innovation and technology to develop a long-term future plan instead of short-term measures. In response, this year, our students researched and proposed potential architectures. Focusing on both technical and intellectual skills, students were introduced to ways of thinking innovatively, in specific contexts with specific opportunities and challenges. In order to be innovative, students often had to go against current academic discourse, incorporating both local sensibilities and entrepreneurial know-how.

'The Accra Literacy Centre' by Jack Moreton responds to a local history of verbal learning by proposing a centre to facilitate the practice and education of reading and speaking. Located in the Jamestown district of Ghana's capital city Accra, the project mixes existing materials and practices with new forms of expression. Developed through model tests and in-depth material research, the building aims to create sheltered space for locals to read, write and debate.

For a rural area of Ghana, Christina Grytten designed a 'Bamboo Demonstration Farm' in collaboration with a real client, combining entrepreneurial principles with local sensibilities. The social, economic and sustainable demonstration farm aims to promote a more positive perception of bamboo.

By following a brief about education and innovation in Ghana, students explored the balance between passion and scepticism. Both qualities are crucial to any architect delving into the dangerous yet wonderful space of cultural development.

Year 4
Alex Desov, Christina Grytten, Maria Alessia Junco, Lucie Krulichova, Joanna Rzewuska, Alexis Udegbe, Andrei Zamfir

Year 5
Mahalah Attwell Thomas, Teodor Cuciureanu, Paalan Lakhani, Krasimir Mitrev, Jack Moreton, Farah Omar, Liang Qiao, Tul Srisompun, Rashi Vijan

Thank you to: Teoman Ayas, Barbara-Ann Campbell-Lange, Marjan Colletti, Oliver Domeisen, Pedro Gil, Robert Haworth, Nannette Jackowski, Stefan Necula, Elena Pascolo, Gilles Retsin, Nic Stamford, Risa Tadauchi, Anna Woodeson, Adrian Yiu, Yeena Yoon

18.1 Jack Moreton, Y5 'Written By Accra'. The 'Accra Literacy Centre' helps with reading, writing and speaking in the Jamestown area in Ghana's capital city. Ghana has a long history of verbal learning but the teaching of literacy is considered underdeveloped for a country that has the leading economic position in West Africa.
18.2–18.4 Christina Grytten, Y4 'Bamboo Demonstration Farm'. This project investigates the untapped potential of bamboo in Ghana. It aims to shift its current perception through a socio-economic and sustainable bamboo demonstration farm in Kumawu, where bamboo plays an alleviating role on forest resources. The building will educate current 'slash-and-burn' farmers to become agro-foresters at an established bamboo nursery. With integration, knowledge about the harvest and treatment of bamboo will better provide for the livelihoods of local farmers and the landscape they settle on.
18.5–18.7 Mahalah Attwell Thomas, Y5 'Aeolian Soundscapes'. This project researches the particular psycho-sensorial experience of the Brekete tribe in Ghana, and investigates how architectural interventions, through geometry and materiality, may manipulate and amplify traditional rituals and practices of the culture. The dance and drumming centre is intended to interact with the annual sand-laden wind in *Harmattan* – a season in West Africa – forming a space that links culture and place over time. Through the reconfiguration of a shifting landscape, the proposal manifests a collective cultural identity in the landscape that formed it.
18.8–18.9 Farah Omar, Y5 'Food and Landscape Narratives'. This project aims to address the idea of food as a social and cultural aspect by reflecting on the environment. It intends to understand the concept of the market as a place for education and awareness. The social purpose of the intervention is to celebrate the harvest of yam, West Africa's staple food, providing an educational exchange for women, a trading platform and a public entertainment arena.
18.10 Andrei Zamfir, Y4 'The [AR]Hub'. This project is a political hub for new policy making in regards to wildlife conservation. Data gathered on wildlife for scientific purposes can hold immense value for the communication of conservation efforts to a wider audience, hence the centre will act as a main data bank for the Ghanaian natural environment and its wildlife.
18.11 Paalan Lakhani, Y5, 'Education In Urban Parks'. In Accra, parks that could be valuable spaces for people are often neglected, including the derelict Efua Sutherland Children's Park located in the heart of the city. This project seeks to redevelop the park, integrating education into the design of the landscape for the benefit of children's development, providing an additional form of education to classroom learning, which is beneficial for low-income families in the developing country.
18.12 Rashi Vijan, Y5 '(D I S) P L A Y'. This project focuses on the power of 'play and display' as a means of education. It is a women-led initiative using datum shifts and canopy typologies to bring Ghanaian folklore back to life via ancient games (*Agoro*). It aims to protect the main cultural and crafts hub of Accra – the Centre for National Culture – and its 3,000 artisans. The waterfront of Accra will fight to keep its artisanal and cultural hub alive through the women-led 'Agoro Bazaar'.
18.13 Maria Alessia Junco, Y4 'The Drinking Lake: Prototype 1.0. 'The Drinking Lake' offers locals a congregation ground, where water acts as its key architectural element in the realm of spatial design, education, interaction and growth.
18.14 Teodor Cuciureanu, Y5 'Nkrumah Art Foundation'. Working with existing artistic manifestations in Ghana, this project proposes a foundation in order to celebrate art from the region. Exploring urban typologies, the design of the semi-detached galleries connects the city to the coast.
18.15–18.17 Tul Srisompun, Y5 'Outposts at the Worlds' Conjunction'. This project investigates a built environment within a conflicted landscape betweeen a forest preservation and a palm oil plantation. Situated along the border of Kakum National Park, the design aims to reconfigure a territorial relationship between forest and farmland, using a gradient strategy that enables indigenous forest restoration as a driver of environmental education.
18.18 Lucie Krulichova, Y4 'e-Jewellery'. This project works with local artisans to create treasure from trash. The goal is to empower low-wage, informal-sector workers, giving the community the opportunity to showcase their skills internationally by creating modern and beautiful jewellery and metal crafts. The project proposes a jewellery innovation hub and market space to promote formalised entrepreneurship through education and training.
18.19–18.20 Krasimir Mitrev, Y5 'Ethnocomputing'. Taking inspiration from African patterns and the mathematics behind them, this project proposes a territorial masterplan for an ethnocomputing centre in Accra, providing mathematics education to its residents. By understanding principles of spatial and social organisation, a new topological growth is speculated that uses a pattern-based rule system and incorporates cultural preservation and computational understanding.
18.21–18.22 Liang Qiao, Y5 'Un/foreseen'. With the advance of information technology, contemporary knowledge is exchanged through intangible data, and is a new way of storytelling. This project proposes a research institution in Ghana that creates a hub for resource-trading education and speculation via augmented reality. The project takes multi-layered reality as a driving force for the construction of experiential and educational landscapes, nested in academic research spaces. Without AR, the congregational spaces enable public engagement.
18.23 Teodor Cuciureanu, Y5 'Nkrumah Art Foundation'. A plan study organising open spaces, sculpture areas and entrances to gallery areas.
18.24–18.25 Jack Moreton, Y5 'Written By Accra'. In this project, modern facilities run through rammed earth structures constructed in collaboration with local specialists. Spaces for reading, writing and speaking have a tactile materiality referencing Ghanaian traditions of building using earth. The building is sited in a vibrant environment, so that it is integrated culturally and politically into the context without the reductive practice of drawing directly from the physical surroundings.
18.26 Joanna Rzewuska, Y4 'The Living School'. Inspired by the Barefoot College in India, this secondary education training centre equips local women with skills for creating a wide range of healthcare and sanitation products (e.g. mosquito nets and sanitary pads). Upon graduation, the students are able to stay onsite and construct their own workshop within the school. Due to the ever-changing community, the building comes alive and morphs its form, whilst the workshops are constructed and taken apart by the alumni.

18.2

18.3

18.4

18.5

18.6

18.7

18.8

18.9

18.10

18.11

18.12

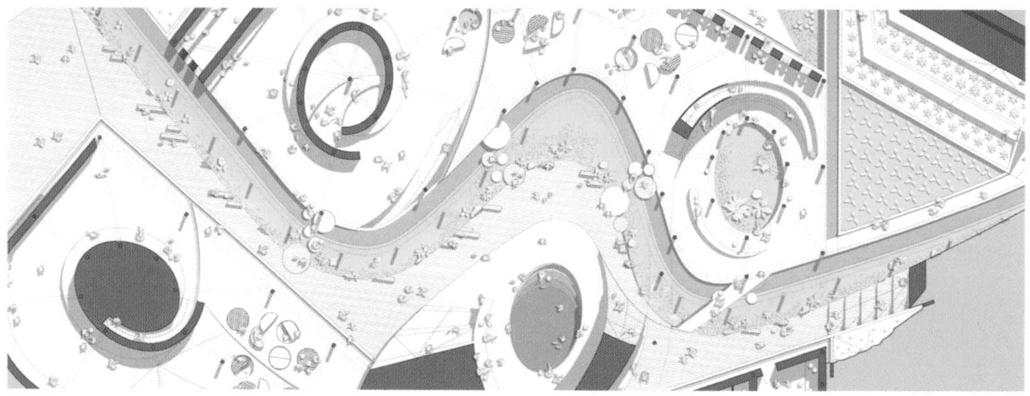
18.13

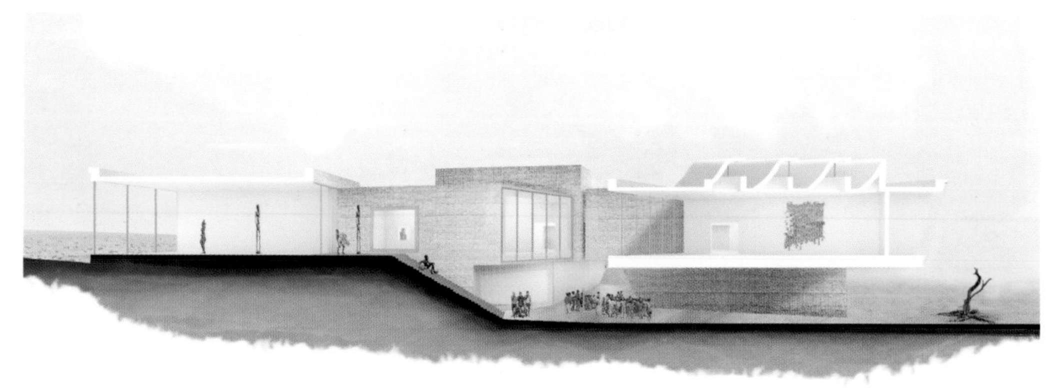
18.14

18.15

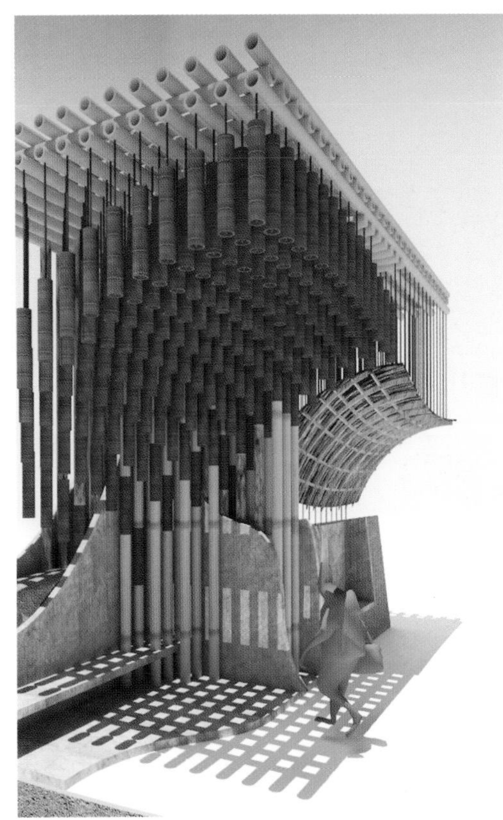

18.16

18.17

18.18

18.19

18.20

18.21

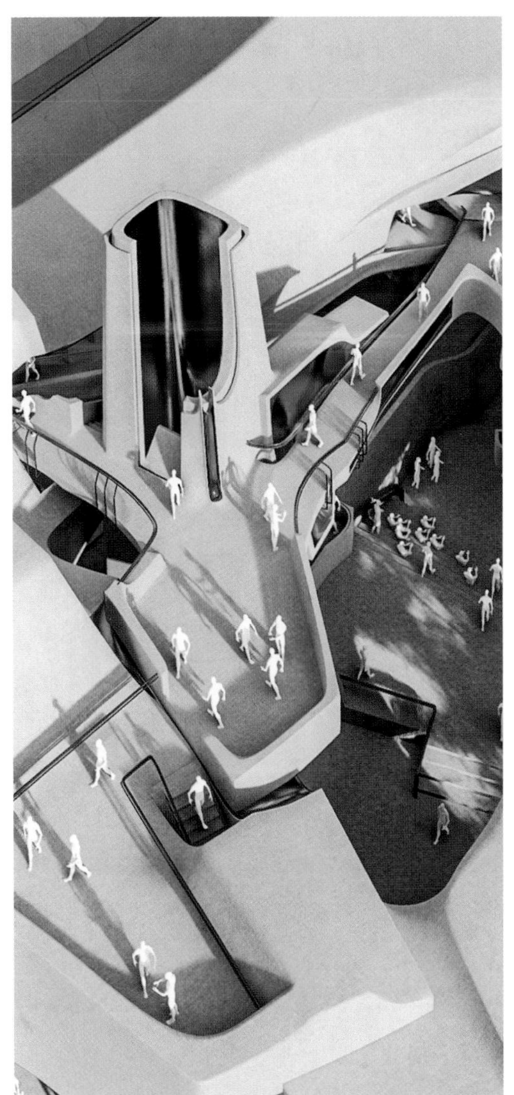

18.22

18.23

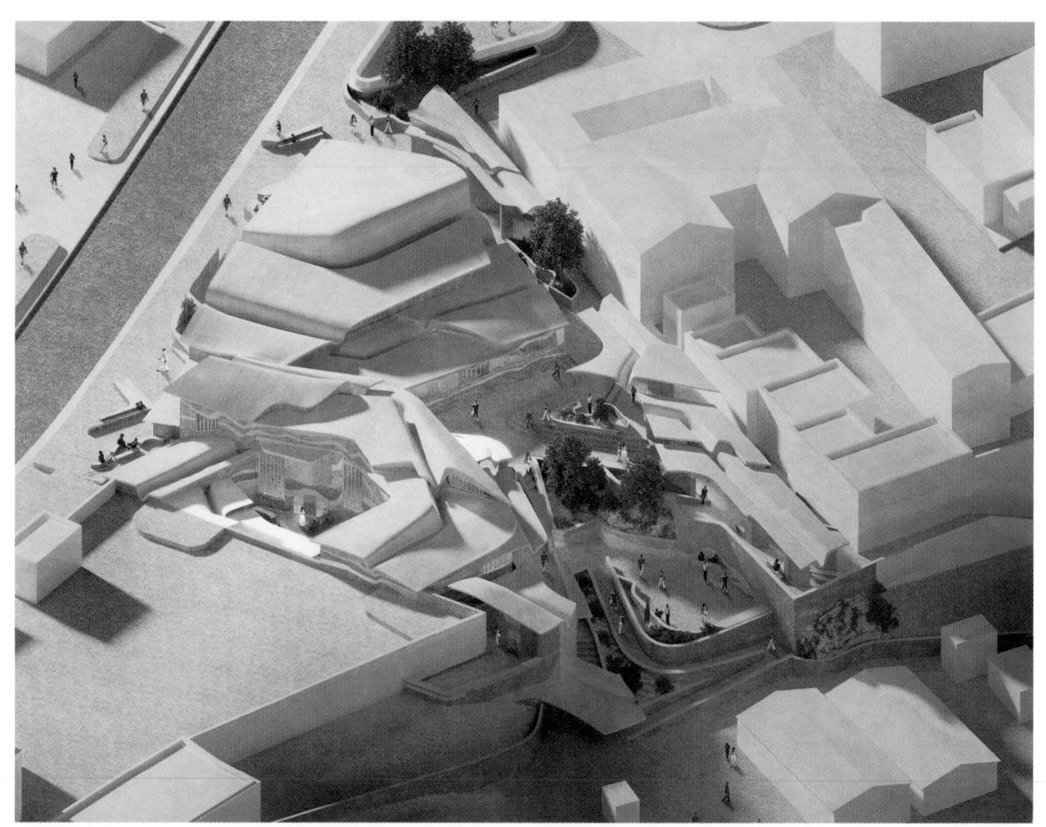

18.24

18.25

18.26

20.1

Post-Digital Practices: Past-Future Hybrids

PG20

Marjan Colletti, Javier Ruiz Rodriguez

At the dawn of the fourth Industrial Revolution, categorised by a wide range of technologies that are hybridising physical, digital and biological domains, the post-digital paradigm looks at learning and capitalising from the digital: initiating novel, synthetic, transdisciplinary processes that shift and disrupt disciplinary knowledge, financial models and political structures.

The term 'post-digital' does not refer to life after, without, or against the digital. On the contrary, it refers to life in which digital technologies have been assimilated into most aspects, from air travel to banking, from medical procedures to shopping. PG20 refuses to revert to an outdated *modus operandi* of pre-digital juxtaposition. We are in a world of interchange, where cross-fertilisation and constant negotiation present the possibility of a future in which our lives are more intertwined and cooperative, and less confrontational. If digital is a caterpillar, still voracious and rapidly growing, post-digital is a chrysalis, representing the potential for astonishing metamorphosis.

Post-digital hybridity challenges old and obsolete binary and juxtaposed conditions, such as past/future, nature/architecture, man/machine, material/data, biological/artificial, object/space, analysis/artificial intelligence, craft/machine learning, fact/fiction, hand/robot, entertainment/science, vernacular/sci-fi, collage/ecology, fragment/symbiont. It suggests far more complex, ambiguous and agile crossbreeds.

In Los Angeles and San Francisco we met architects, artists, space engineers, production designers, entertainment creators and teachers who make remarkable contributions to contemporary society. The resulting projects fuse architecture with ideas around artificial intelligence, machine learning, adaptive systems, biotechnology, fashion, multinational business, space colonisation, and more.

Year 4
Madalina-Oana Blaje, Magdalena Filipek, Tzu-Jung (Dexter) Huang, Hanadi Izzuddin, Ziyu (Ivy) Jiang, James Kennedy, Jonathan Rahimi (SCI-Arc exchange) Theodoros Tamvakis

Year 5
William Ashworth, Yan Ho (Brian) Cheung, Daniel Krajnik, Levent Özruh, Tobias Petyt, Shogo Suzuki, Hong Lien Tran, Hsin-Fang Tsai

Thanks to Michela Mangiarotti, Justin Nicholls, and Alexandra Toivonen

Thank you for generously hosting us in Los Angeles: Refik Anadol, Benjamin Ennemoser, Julia Koerner, Roberta Leighton, Clarence Major, Marcelo Spina, Madhu Thangavelu

We are grateful to the Directors Guild of America, Disney Imagineering, Goldstein Residence, UCLA, USC, SCI-Arc

20.1 Daniel Krajnik, Y5 'Tech-Hub Capriccio'. A machine learning-based design, which merges reality with architectural fantasy, this project looks beyond a single database and integrates design with alternative, publicly available sources. This embedded data allows for mining the past – here, understood as the reconstruction of past architecture provided by data extracted through photogrammetry. Based on the rocks and underlying soil, a generative script hybridises what was there with what could have been there.
20.2 Tobias Petyt, Y5 'Amazon 3.0: San Francisco'. The architecture of Amazon 3.0 proposes a centralised system of operations for the tech giant, fully integrated into an urban environment. The scheme reinvents the inventory into a high-resolution 3D-plane voxelisation system, where machines operate exclusively, collecting and distributing items bought by customers online. The architecture wrestles with the dimensional paradigms of the machine and people, forcing them to adapt their movements.
20.3 Yan Ho (Brian) Cheung, Y5 'Stony Ridge Observatory'. Culturally situated within Los Angeles' environment of constant reinvention and experimentation, the idea of an observatory as interface to the cosmos emerges from the process of computational morphological studies. The design language of the building and its interior spaces aims to inspire awe in users as they look up to the stars.
20.4–20.6 Shogo Suzuki, Y5 'Cyborgian Homes'. What if the spatial conditions of our homes could respond to our emotional states? As we enhance ourselves with artificial intelligence (AI) wearables and in effect become cyborgs, architecture too will become cyborgian. Extrapolating swarm 3D printing with a hypothetical reversible additive fabrication material, the project speculates how hi-res psychometric data available from wearables may manipulate a hi-res physical environment.
20.7-20.8 Hong Lien Tran, Y5 'MMM-Martian Magnetic Module'. The research studies the influence of magnetism on architectural design. Through form-finding and morphogenetic process, the project explores the interaction of ferromagnetic materials – with metal threads interwoven into fabrics – in accordance with the particularity of powerful magnetic crystal fields on Mars' surface. These form potential landing sites for future human adventures.
20.9 Hsin-Fang Tsai, Y5 'Mars Colonisation'. In response to the extreme climate on Mars, a semi-underground, sand dune-like shelter is designed as a daylight-responsive inhabitable machine. Printed using locally-sourced materials, the shelter provides radiation protection and thermal stability for future human inhabitation, using inflatable membranes, mechanical systems and lava tubes.
20.10 Levent Özruh, Y5 'First of the Trojans'. In response to the growing interest in asteroids, the project proposes a colonisation process for a peculiar group of asteroids known as the Trojans, which are in a stable position in deep space. A hybrid approach of both procedural design steps and explicit modelling techniques is developed to deal with the unique morphology of each asteroid, in order to house ring-shaped rotating space stations.
20.11 Ziyu (Ivy) Jiang, Y4 'Therapeutic Landscape of Contemporary Tibetan Buddhism'. Located in Los Angeles, the project proposes an Anthropocene landscape for contemporary Tibetan Buddhism. Embedded in the terrain is a retreat for the growing Buddhist population of Los Angeles. The institution is organised by imprinting a digital reading of the Tibetan Mandala as a geological condition. This artificial and pixelated landscape becomes a device for spiritual enlightenment.
20.12, 20.17 Hanadi Izzuddin, Y4 'Deep-Space Structures Laboratory (DSSL-1)'. A training facility that trains astronauts using its compartmentalised configuration and indoor neutral buoyancy pool. A classified 'space coral' research laboratory that forms an integral infrastructural system is embedded within the building. The building operates systematically like an engine, drawing and filtering resources from the extreme and varying desert climate to test spacecraft technology on a micro-scale through its cooling capillary skin.
20.13 James Kennedy, Y4 'Kuuyam Centre'. The Tongva are the indigenous inhabitants of Southern California. They regard themselves as guests (*Kuuyam*), of the land on which the city of Los Angeles was built, and seek restoration of the landscape and the people through the healing properties of food and culture. The project addresses homelessness in the city, proposing a programme where people can work and live in a restorative, native landscape.
20.14 Tzu-Jung (Dexter) Huang, Y4 'Sutro Performance'. An alternative bathhouse explores performative and vernacular ornament by implementing atmospheric devices, which regulate the environment through the exchange of fluids. The building showcases this mesmerising behaviour in nature and suggests a prototype for a sustainable paradigm in San Francisco.
20.15 Magdalena Filipek, Y4 'Bioluminescent Lab'. Based in Los Angeles, this NASA biochemical laboratory explores concepts of food production, oxygen and supplements for astronauts living on Mars during their eight-month mission. These products are obtained from algae located in the building's roof tiles, which also supply samples for laboratory experiments. Photosynthesis within algae tiles produces electricity and illuminates the building at night.
20.16 Theodoros Tamvakis Y4, 'The Icarus Silo Complex'. This project is set in a speculative future, in which a secret religious group repurposes a Cold War missile silo into a cultist cathedral. The complex explores negotiation and hybridity between the crude functionality of the silo and the spiritual significance of a cathedral.
20.18 Madalina-Oana Blaje, Y4 '3D-Printed Fashion Store'. A fashion store for unique, luxury 3D-printed dresses informs a filigree multidimensional façade. Its sculptural morphology protects the store from excess heat gain during summer, and allows for optimum light in winter.
20.19 William Ashworth, Y5 'The Pneumatic Terminal'. This project proposes a radical shift in the design of the train station typology, bringing together pneumatic technologies and embedded computation to enable programmatic flexibility. The Hyperloop train system provides large quantities of extracted pressurised air to feed the mechanisms of the terminal through a conduit structure.

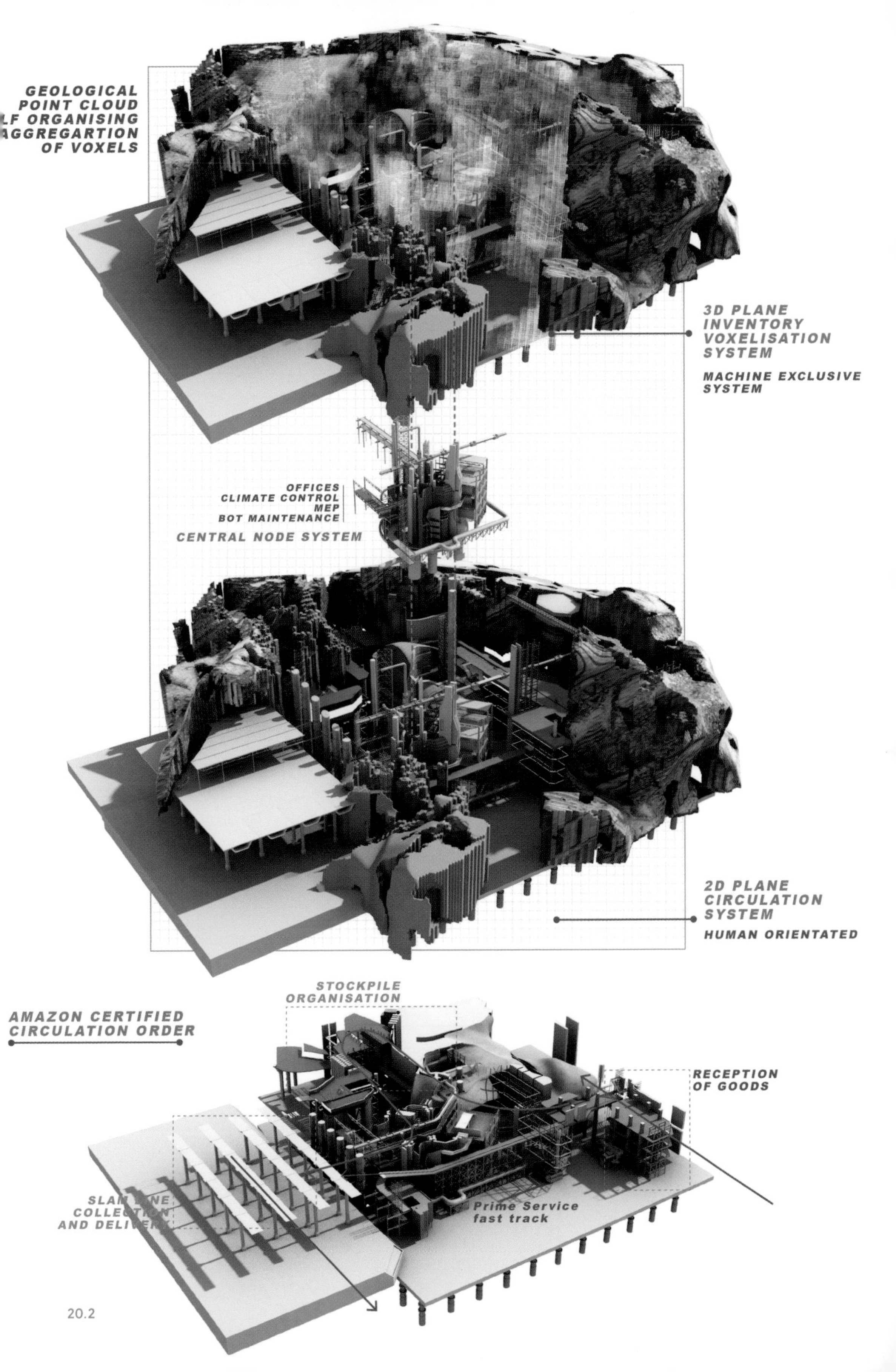

GEOLOGICAL
POINT CLOUD
LF ORGANISING
AGGREGARTION
OF VOXELS
3D PLANE
INVENTORY
VOXELISATION
SYSTEM
MACHINE EXCLUSIVE
SYSTEM
OFFICES
CLIMATE CONTROL
MEP
BOT MAINTENANCE
CENTRAL NODE SYSTEM
2D PLANE
CIRCULATION
SYSTEM
HUMAN ORIENTATED
STOCKPILE
ORGANISATION
AMAZON CERTIFIED
CIRCULATION ORDER
RECEPTION
OF GOODS
Prime Service
fast track
20.2

20.3

20.4

20.5

20.6

20.7

20.8

20.9

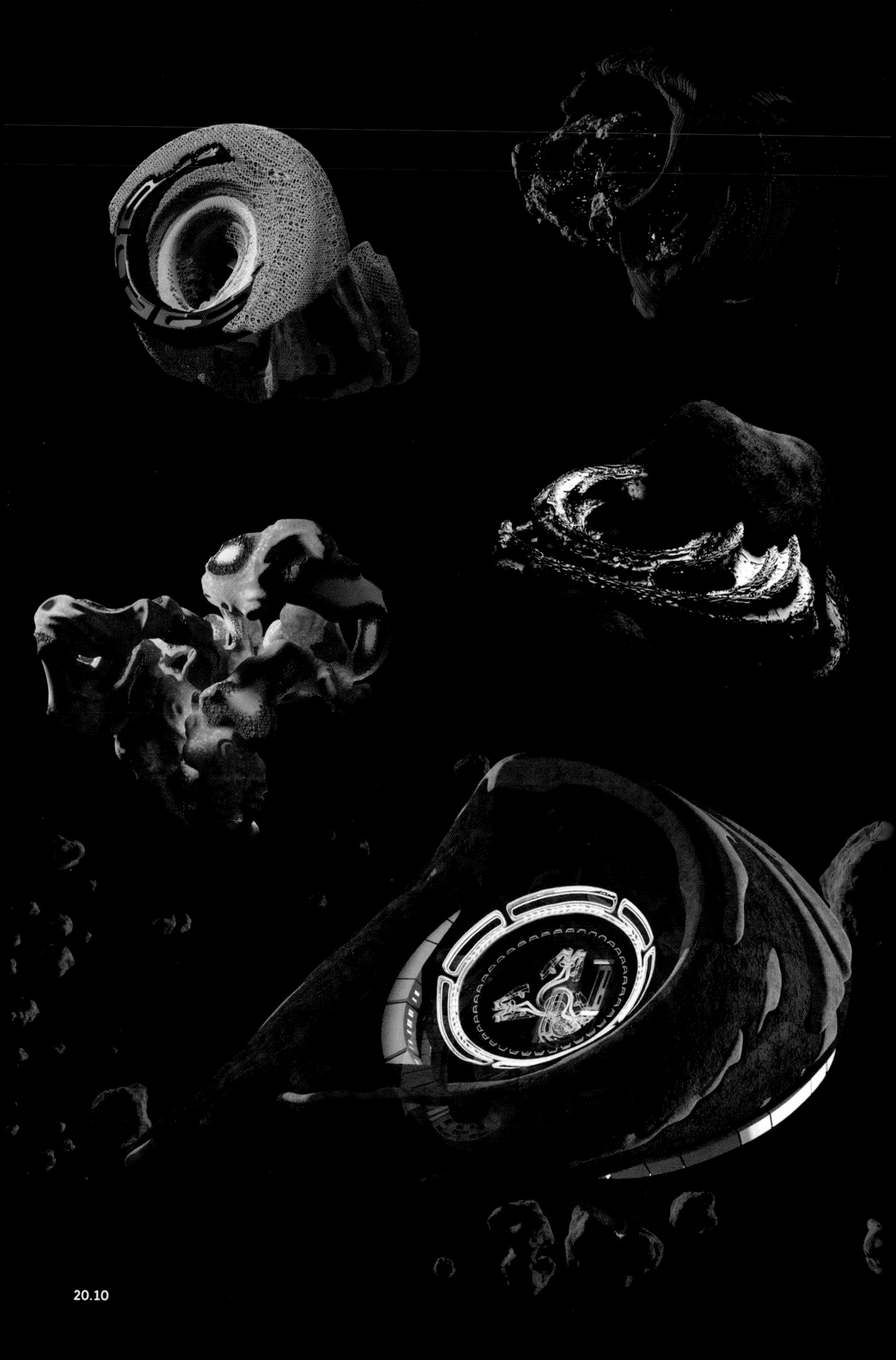

20.11

20.12

20.13

20.14

20.15

20.16

20.17

20.18

20.19

21.1

Exchange and Trade

PG21

Abigail Ashton, Tom Holberton, Andrew Porter

What Athens was in miniature, America will be in magnitude.[1]

We are living through a modern crisis in reason and democracy. The ancient urban life of Athens was a golden age where law, philosophy and art flourished and, subsequently, was mythologised and used as a foundation for 20th-century nation states. In 2019, we find that collective confidence in trade, democracy and truth is fraying. A new digital and global era that promises many freedoms seems to be undermining our instincts. This year, we explored Athens, a city that is both physically and economically at the edge of the EU. Emerging from its recent crisis, this 'arrival city' now acts as an entry point for both goods and people entering Europe. The Port of Piraeus, which has enriched the city, both culturally and physically, for thousands of years has been sold for redevelopment to the Chinese shipping company COSCO. It is to be expanded as part of the New Silk Road project, becoming one of the main entry points for containerised goods into Europe; it is already Europe's biggest passenger port.

Architects find themselves addressing the processes of exchange and trade in many ways. The complexities of making buildings involves exchanges and negotiations with many agencies. On a prosaic level, the machinations of the planning system are a constant source of negotiation. Building regulations and advanced construction technology often require trade-offs and, of course, the ever-present exchange between client and cost often dominates. In *Translations from Drawing to Building and Other Essays*, Robin Evans considered how things may get 'bent, broken and lost' in the process.[2] A contemporary reworking of this theme could be to consider how the digital (the drawing) might translate to the physical (the building). Whilst there are obvious benefits to this process, there are also opportunities for creativity and surprise through intervention and disruption of the processes that are parallel to the 'mistakes' referred to by Evans.

This year, we explored what a 'trade' might be: where physical movement of goods can create enormous economic opportunity, tariffs or duties, or where people may physically trade great risks to secure basic rights or safety. We looked at the exchange of the physical for the digital and of rights for obligations. We used exploratory drawings, models and building proposals to develop radical ideas on trade, reciprocity and exchange, physical and digital movements through time, balancing behaviours and duties. We investigated the role of architecture in creating or removing these moments in the city to connect physical demands with spatial freedoms and digital behaviours.

Year 4
Rahaf Abdoun-Machaal, Kelly Au, Julian Besems, Alexandra Campbell, Maya Chandler, Nicholas Chrysostomou, Qiyu (Jennifer) Ge, James Potter, Bethan Ring, Chengbin Shou, Ziyuan (Oliver) Zhu

Year 5
Ahmed Al Gamal, Lester Chung, Ching (Jin) Kuo, Alan Ma, Mishbah Mahmood, Yu Chen Pan, Oliver Parkinson, Duangkaew (Pink) Protpagorn, Cristobal Riffo Giampaoli, Emilio Sullivan, Minh Tran, Ernest Wang, Pricilla Wong

Thank you to our practice tutor Tom Holberton and structural engineer Brian Eckersley

Thanks to our critics: Paddi Benson, Roberto Bottazzi, Barbara-Ann Cambell-Lange, Emma Carter, Stephen Gage, Naomi Gibson, Mina Gospavic, Diony Kypraiou, Farlie Reynolds, Sayan Skandarajah, Camilla Wright

1. Thomas Paine (1792) *Rights of Man*, reprinted in B. Kuklick (ed.) *Political Writings*, (Cambridge: Cambridge University Press, 1989), p170
2. Robin Evans, *Translations from Drawing to Building and Other Essays*, (Cambridge: MIT Press, 1997), p154

21.1–21.2 Oliver Parkinson, Y5 'Learning from Raphael's School of Athens'. Situated upon Pnyx Hill in Athens, this proposition uses photogrammetry as a 2D/3D translation process to derive a new public planning forum alongside its ancient counterpart. This results in a changing civic landscape, which facilitates current planning policies and addresses the lack of organised public debate space for Athenians.
21.3 Yu Chen Pan, Y5 'Learning Through Play'. Severe educational inequality in Greece has led to a 'shadow education' system taking root. This proposal for a revolutionary Greek school uses architecture as a testing bed to improve the current situation, and challenges conventional ways of teaching by imposing the idea of 'learning through play'.
21.4 Lester Chung, Y5 'Piraeus Archipelago'. Based on cruise schedule data, this redevelopment masterplan for the cruise port of Piraeus in Greece reimagines it as a time-based waterfront urban park. It promotes Piraeus as a new tourist destination created for cruisers, tourists and residents alike.
21.5 Duangkaew (Pink) Protpagorn, Y5 'The Casino Garden'. This project proposes a casino with both semi-enclosed and outdoor casino areas. The building contrasts the existing casino typology, making it a tourist attraction for its individuality. The rooftop public park provides green space for locals, creating an exchange between the building, the city and its people.
21.6 Nicholas Chrysostomou, Y4 'Passports for Gold'. This homeless shelter in Athens is built using money from Golden Visa Greece, which gives a passport to foreign nationals who invest in Greek property. Buyers select elements from a catalogue and any cost fluctuations are mitigated by adding bespoke additions to base pieces.
21.7 Julian Besems, Y4 'Books as Bytes'. This project pursues the development of a software programme that generates a building based on user information, such as a university library where the relationship between books and how they are organised determines the configuration of the shelves, walkways and external envelope.
21.8 Alexandra Campbell, Y4 'Scaling Skalisma'. A cross-programming of a bathhouse and community theatre. The spaces in this project explore *skalisma* (stone-carving) processes and finishes at different scales. Both proposals reference Ancient Greek architecture and use natural stone for construction, building performance and architectural expression.
21.9 James Potter, Y4 'A City of Routes'. This project examines Athens as a series of labyrinthine networks, adopting a scheme where drawings become irrelevant, coding replaces lines and time becomes a collection. The building acts as an archive, exhibiting and collecting memories of the residents' representations of the city, within a series of archival routes.
21.10–21.11 Alan Ma, Y5 'The Ruin in the Sky'. This project explores the idea of transforming digital images into a series of 21st-century monumental ruins, aimed at celebrating Athenian heritage. It investigates perverse image analysis methods and their ability to create new, digitally-based, image-generated architectural spectacles.
21.12 Mishbah Mahmood, Y5 'The Athens of Euripides'. This project uses the playwright Euripides as inspiration, translating literary devices into behavioural, spatial and architectural gestures. Three of the devices – 'myth', 'chorus' and 'stichomythia' – provide the basis for an algorithmic toolkit, which allows for the development of a new architectural vernacular in Athens.
21.13 Maya Chandler, Y4 'Kinderkípos'. A new kindergarten for children and their parents in Athens, this project reimagines the Garden of Epicurus – a symbol of the philosophy promoted by the Greek philosopher Epicurus who lived in Athens in 307/306BCE. Those visiting the site proceed through separate programmatic spaces based on various philosophical subjects: for example, theology, epistemology, ethics and politics.
21.14–21.15 Pricilla Wong, Y5 'The Manual to (Un) Archaeology'. This project seeks to re-assess the ways in which we engage with sites and object-deemed archaeology. Through a series of playful material investigations and subversion of archaeological practices, the project proposes an alternative heritage practice where the archaeology and architecture coalesce, mediated by a hierarchy of material language.
21.16 Ahmed Al Gamal, Y5 'A Personal Athenian Restaurant'. This project proposes a restaurant and residential quarters for a local chef, based on movement mapping of meal-preparation. It prompts individualistic action as a way to revitalise the city, in response to social issues and a stagnant built environment.
21.17 Cristóbal Riffo Giampaoli, Y5 'Inhabiting the Shoreline'. This project proposes a new city hall that addresses social instability through the idea of an 'open city', encouraging encounters with strangers through ambiguous edges, incomplete forms and unresolved narratives. It takes the form of a shoreline, where a former marble quarry meets the area of Exarcheia in Athens.
21.18 Ching (Jin) Kuo, Y5 'Re-Discover Athens'. A series of six landmarks that set a new datum to the context of Athens. Individually themed interventions aim to offer a new method of exploring to help locals identify culture and pass down the legacy of the city.
21.19 Rahaf Abdoun-Machaal, Y4 'A Bureau for Customs Fraud'. Situated on a rocky islet just off the coast of Piraeus in Greece, the 'Bureau for Customs Fraud' is conceived as a series of dispersed programmatic spaces, shrouded by a fragmented shell structure. The design imitates and exaggerates the existing terrain, yet presents an uncanny artificial intervention.
21.20 Chengbin Shou, Y4 'New Rovertou Galli Park'. This project is a renovation of a park near the Acropolis which allows visitors to determine the appearance. Exploring the new meaning of sightseeing and human relations in the digital age, it encourages visitors to leave their information and existence in the park.
21.21 Minh Tran, Y5 '(St)oc(k)ulus'. The 'Oculus' is a stock exchange based on the translation of quantitative phenomena in Athens. The parameters are derived from digital 'footprints', the sun and stock movement. The building negotiates pure algorithmic design and the realisation of space at a human scale.
21.22–21.24 Ernest Wang, Y5 'The Athenian Shadow Monument'. Visitors work collaboratively to produce and manipulate the shadows that comprise this public, participatory monument. It uses the relationship between Greek gods and man to explore the roles of designer and participant, and interrogates the role of the model in architectural practice.
21.25 Kelly Au, Y4 'A House Built in 24 Hours'. As an extension of peculiar building regulations from the 1800s, this project proposes a house that acts as a sundial. Shadows and light over 24 hours choreograph the design, to show the user how the house should be built.
21.26 Ziyuan (Oliver) Zhu, Y4 'Athenian Referendum Centre'. Questioning transparency in government building, this project aims to design a debate and referendum centre in Athens that promotes the concepts of 'I don't know' and 'Change of mind'.
21.27 Emilio Sullivan, Y5 '(En)Powering the Polykatoikia'. In recognition of the growing waste management issue in Athens, this project looks to process food waste at a hyper-local level. Three power plants are proposed to process waste and provide amenity and resources to an under-served community in Athens.

21.2

21.3

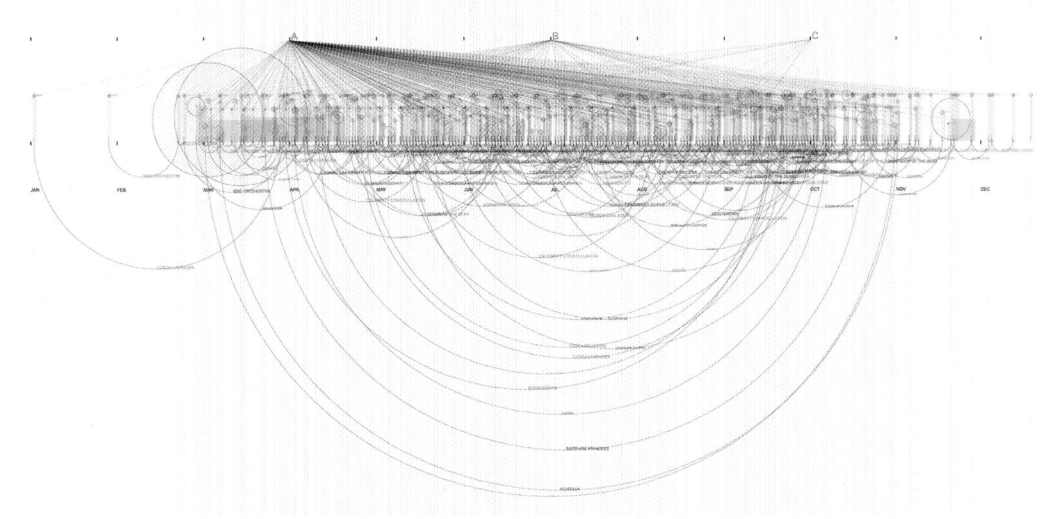
A
B
C
JAN
FEB
MAR
BBC ORCHESTRA
APR
MAY
JUN
JUL
AUG
SEP
OCT
NOV
DEC
SAPPHIRE PRINCESS

21.4

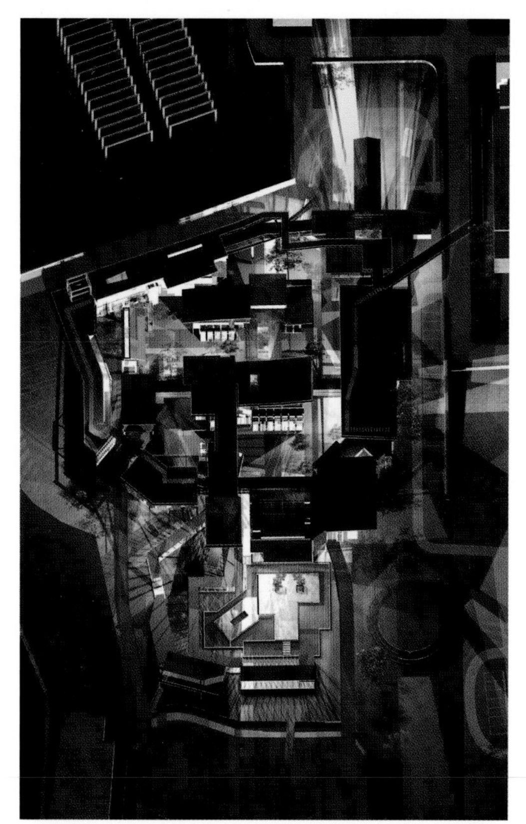
21.5

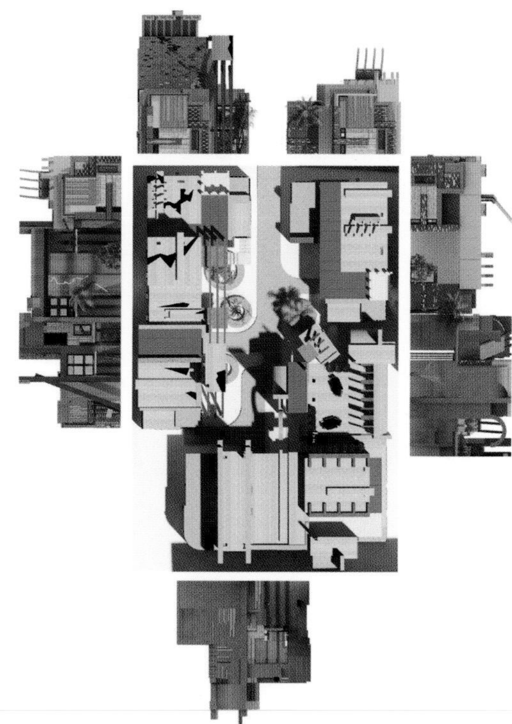
21.6

21.7

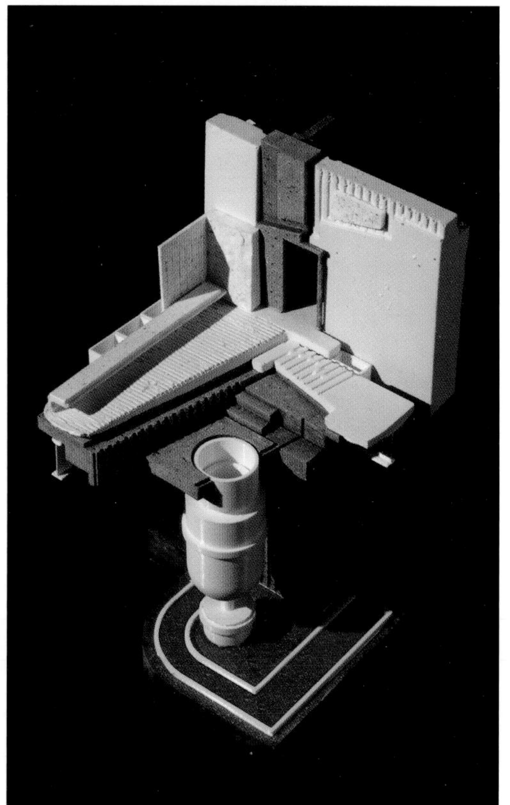
21.8

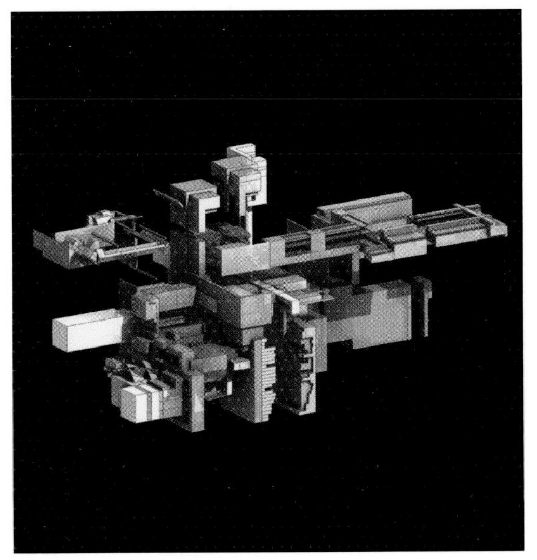

21.9

21.10

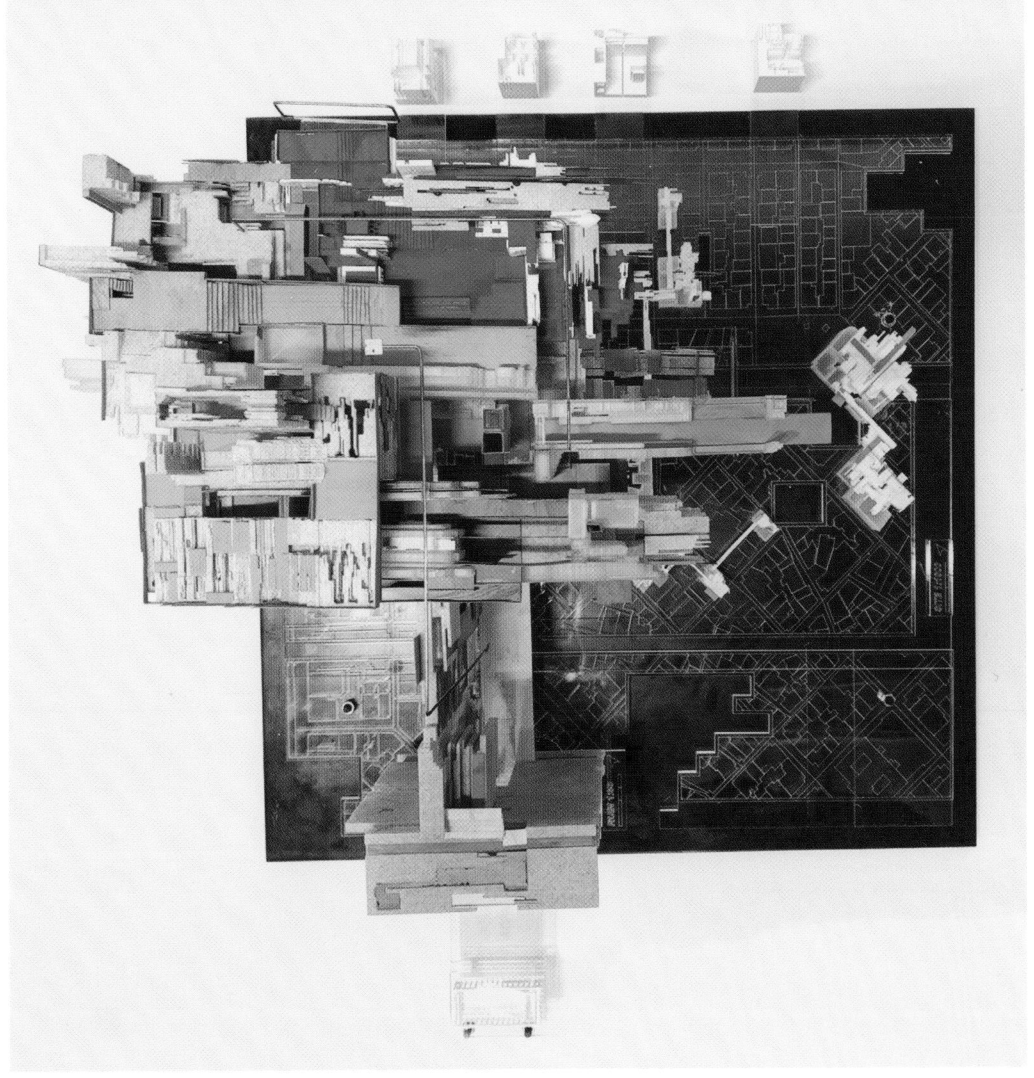

21.11

21.12

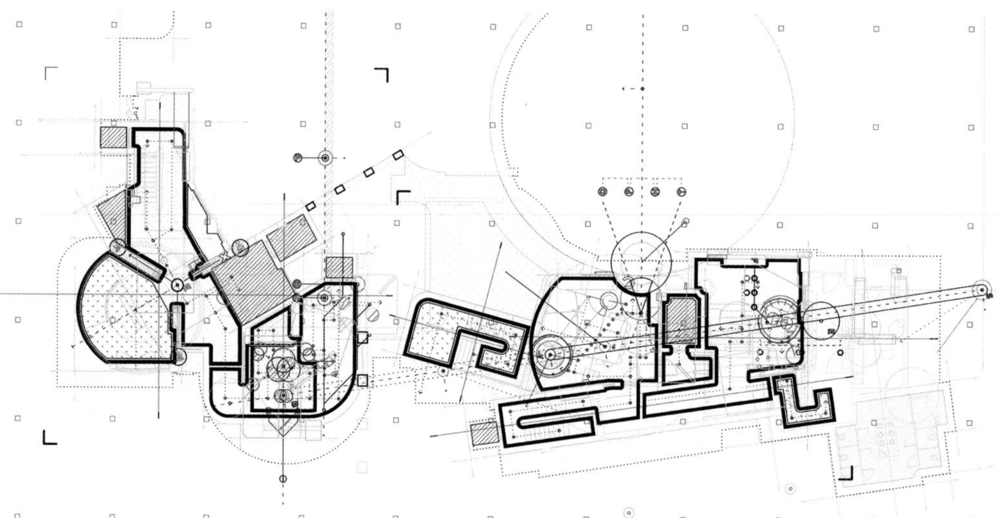

21.13

21.14

21.15

21.16

21.17

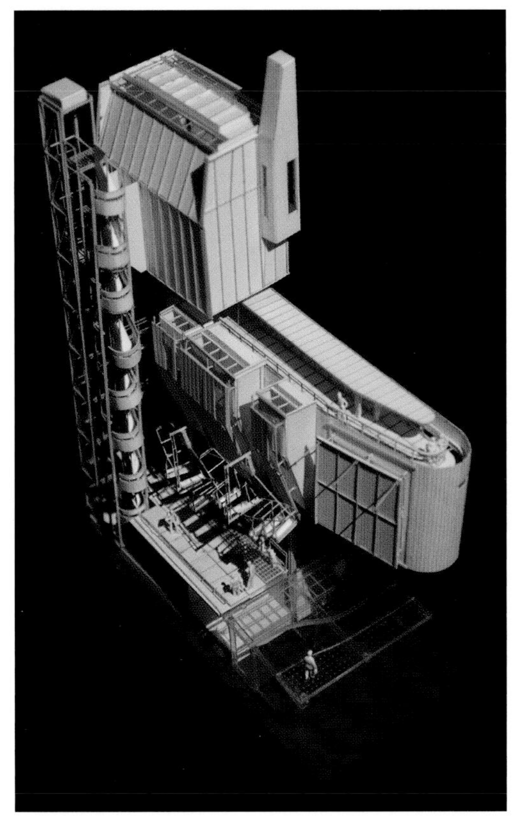

21.18

21.19

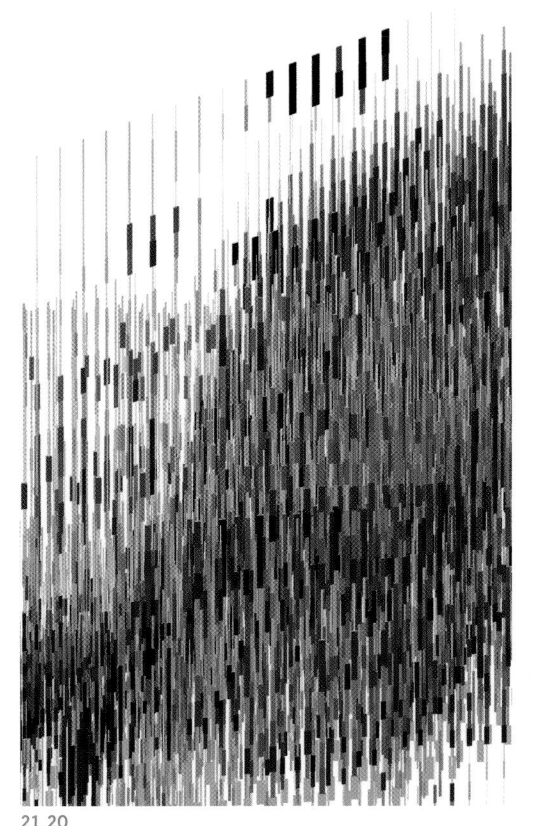

21.20

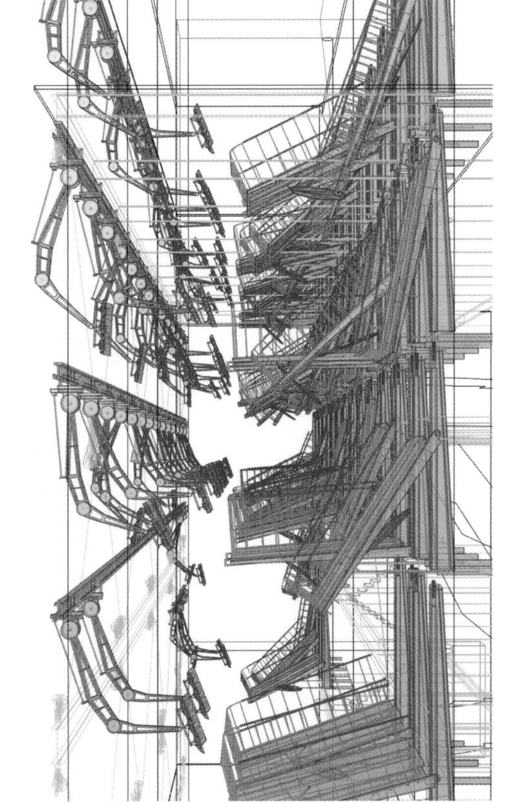

21.21

21.22

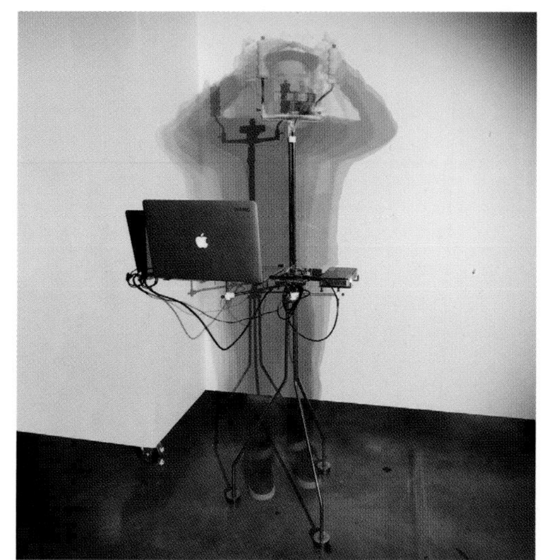

21.23

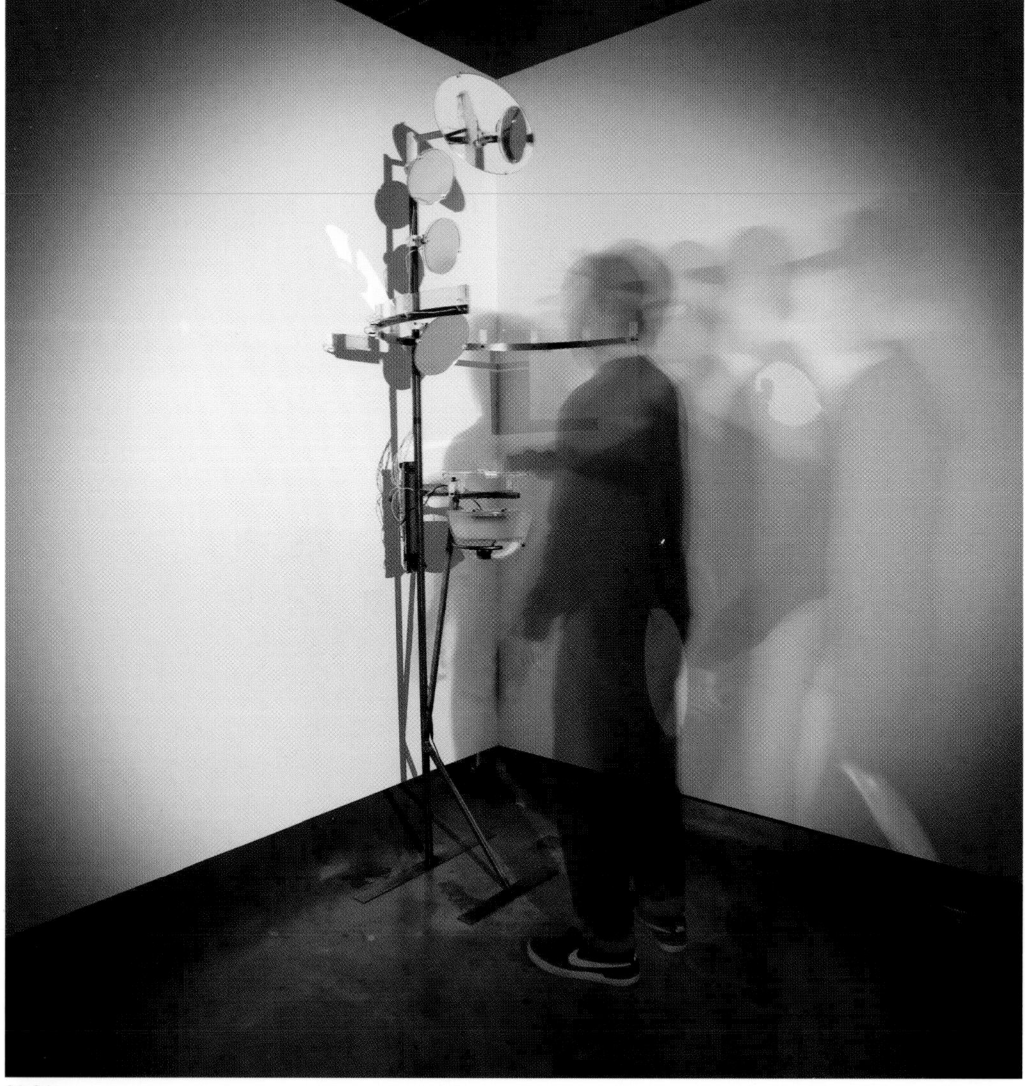

21.24

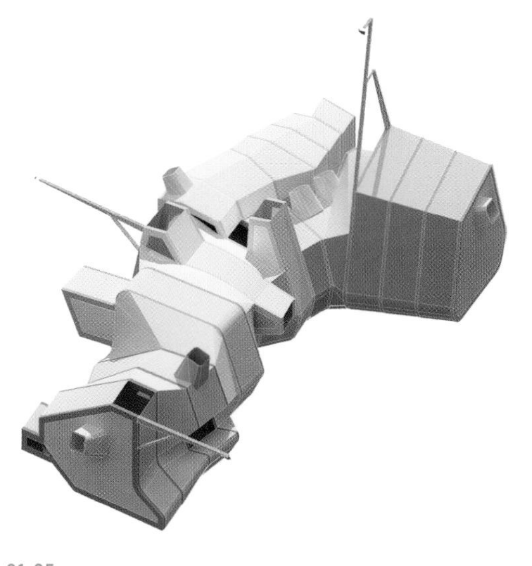

21.25

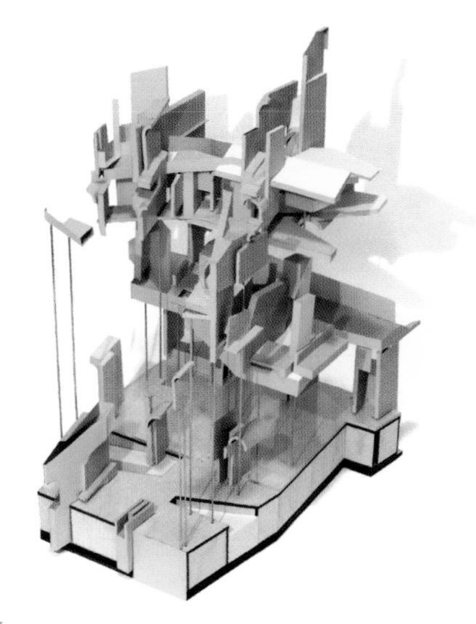

21.26

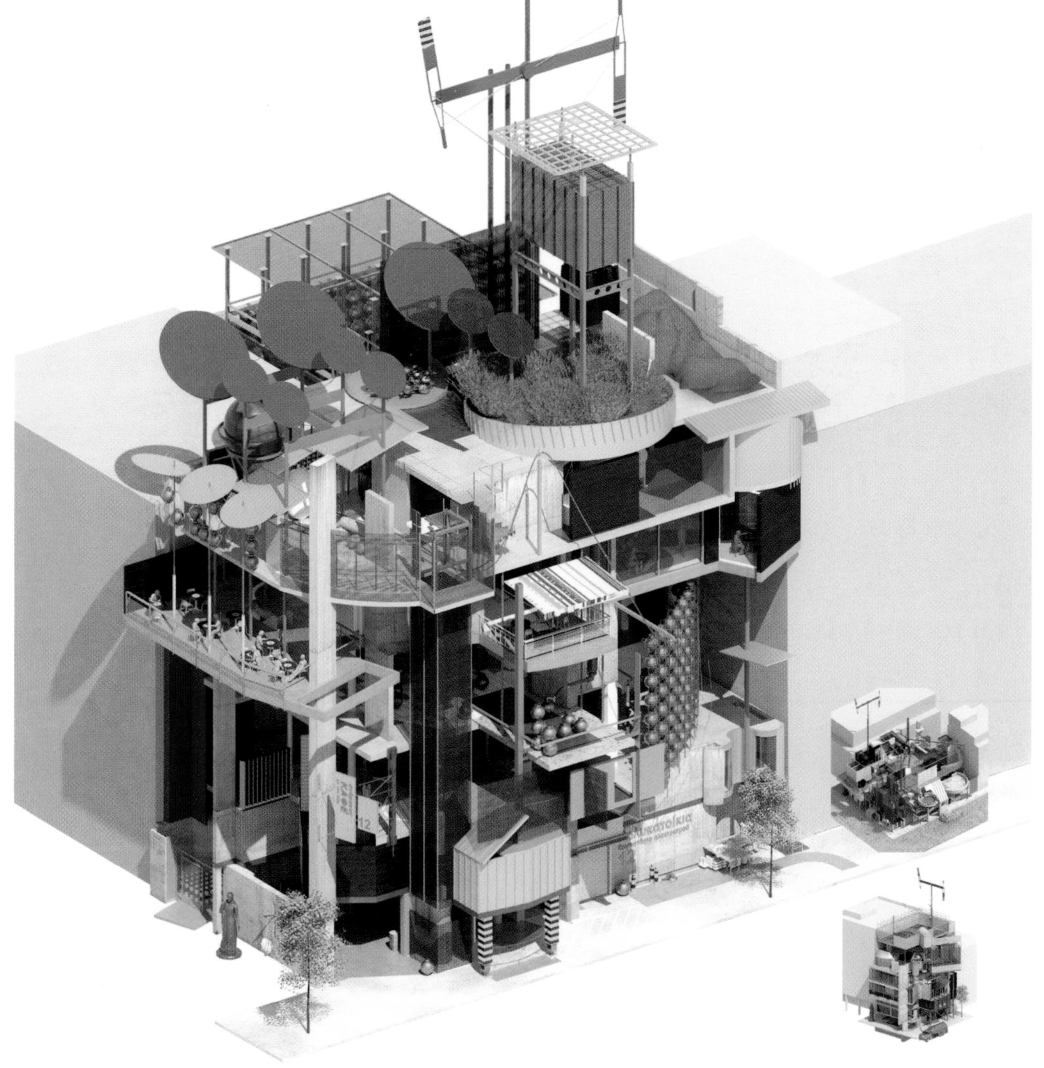

21.27

22.1

The Mediterranean Perspective

PG22

Izaskun Chinchilla Moreno, Daniel Ovalle Costal

Europe has historically been organised through a network of 'south-to-north' and 'periphery-to-centre' trade connections. These trade relationships were some of the core development questions Europe confronted early on and are embedded in its DNA.

Growing up in a southern, or peripheral, European country means being conditioned to see northern and central Europe as synonyms for professional development, the welfare state, financial success, stability, cosmopolitanism and cutting-edge trends. Besides the infrastructural construction of the south-to-north connection, there has been an aspirational consolidation of that same link, with citizens of southern European countries aspiring to access the opportunities that northern countries provide.

This year, the unit's research has been focused on Mediterranean culture, which has traditionally valued quality of life over progress. It seems that central and northern Europe have accepted that industrialisation and technological development are the best partners for welfare. Societies on the Mediterranean shore, meanwhile, seem to be more sceptical of industrialisation and technology, an attitude which has gained in consciousness and has become part of the region's cultural and social identity. Students addressed this cultural particularity from a series of perspectives: firstly, that of the family – looking at both the nuclear and extended family, and cultural approaches to ageing and retirement; food – looking at preferences for eating 'clean' or 'real' food, processes of growing and ideas on communal cooking and dining; skills – whether workers are hyper-specialised or multi-skilled; and tourism – how it affects quality of life, discussing ideas on discovery, and over-tourism and its impact on local communities.

This year, students looked at notions of 'slowness' and 'disengagement', in particular the Slow Food movement, which began in 1986 as a protest against the opening of a McDonald's restaurant in Rome, and advocates a cultural shift towards slowing down the pace of life. 'Slowness' celebrates the Mediterranean legacy, but its success and development require a global network. Many of the issues affecting Europe and the Mediterranean, such as migration, cannot be confronted in isolation. Using three shores as their focus – the UK, European Mediterranean and Asian Mediterranean – students implemented programmes that not only had individual relevance but also dealt with common problems: empowerment of citizens in different areas – balancing equity, education, research, languages, job opportunities, entrepreneurial support, vocational schools, food production and consumption; insertion programmes – social housing and the integration of migrants and refugees; and reconstructing quality of life – through slow communities, organic farming, and the preservation and revitalisation of traditional craft.

Year 4
Byungjun Cho, Siu Yuk (Daniel) Chu, Faye Greenwood, Janis Ho, Funto King, Yang Ting (Lorraine) Li, Yuqi Liew, Yinghao Wang, Lewis Williams, Kate Woodcock-Fowles

Year 5
Florence Bassa, Jun Wing (Michelle) Ho, Alastair Frederick Johnson, Jonah Luswata, Rui Ma, Yehan Zheng

Thanks to our fabulous critics: Barbara-Ann Campbell-Lange, Freya Cobbin, Gabi Code, Sarina da Costa Gómez, Elanor Dodman, Laurie Flint, Cristina Garza, Kaowen Ho, Ann Kelly, Ifigeneia Liangi, Ana Monrabal-Cook, Arantza Otaeza Cortázar, Adam Peacock, Tania Sengupta, Barry Wark, Timmy Whitehouse, Izabela Wieczorek

Thank you to Gonzalo Coello de Portugal, Marta Granda Nistal, Nacho López Picasso, Roberto Marín Sampalo and Ajay Shah

22.1–22.3 **Alastair Frederick Johnson, Y5** 'Augmenting Kayaköy'. After the fall of the Ottoman empire, the population exchange forced Greek residents out of the Turkish town of Kayaköy, previously a unique model of religious tolerance. This project proposes the redevelopment of the town in line with the Historic Urban Landscape approach: to truly protect delicate sites, inhabitation is essential. A phased programme of reconstruction, preservation of local crafts and active tourism is proposed. The programme is supported by a mixed reality platform to enhance Kayaköy's history.
22.4–22.5 **Florence Bassa, Y5** 'Co-Komi'. 'Co-Komi' is the community cooperative of the farming village of Komi, on the Greek island of Tinos. The project demonstrates how the community can use local skills and EU funding with the goal of becoming a 'Competitive Village', tackling population decline and low incomes. The village engages with global discourses, such as plastic waste and the future of work. The architecture contributes to Komi's new identity and breaks stereotypes about rural areas.
22.6, 22.8 **Faye Greenwood, Y4** 'The Boxed Sandwich Revolution'. This project aims to slow down the UK's relationship with food, taking influence from Mediterranean food culture. With remote and co-working trends becoming more popular, this project aims to integrate flexible working spaces and communal cooking and dining programmes in London's commuter belt. A modular system is proposed, with cooking at the core, within a landscape of allotments. The building's construction, materials and organisation aim to use spare resources.
22.7, 22.9 **Jun Wing (Michelle) Ho, Y5** 'City as a House'. In the context of landmark-focused over-tourism in Mediterranean cities, this project proposes a family-friendly alternative. A series of domestic spaces is scattered around the city at sites with strong connections to local heritage and population. By shifting the focus from landmarks to experiences, heritage is redefined around everyday life. Proposed architectural preservation does not freeze buildings in time but boosts their use. New layers of intervention act as mechanisms for learning about heritage as a historic process.
22.10 **Rui Ma, Y5** 'Hospitable Nomads' Living Posts'. This project aims to update the living conditions of the Yörük nomads of Turkey whilst preserving their unique lifestyle. The proposal consists of posts that provide infrastracture for a revisited nomadic tent built in several layers. The scheme allows active tourism to be part of the nomads' life and income.
22.11 **Yan Ting (Lorraine) Li, Y4** 'A Resilient Strategy Against Over-tourism and Seasonality'. The economies of many Mediterranean countries rely on tourism. The seasonality of the sector affects their economy by putting stress on public services and housing. This project explores the possibility of introducing residential units into an existing 1970s hotel in Ibiza, via small-scale demolition, retrofitting, and by creating new spaces. A series of timber trusses provides structural support for cantilevered floor slabs, acting as a buffer between residential and temporary hotel units.
22.12–22.13 **Kate Woodcock-Fowles, Y4** 'A New Town Square for Worksop'. Low-income families often lack the choice to eat healthy foods. In post-industrial, working-class communities like Worksop, the resulting obesity epidemic is placing a huge strain on the NHS. Inspired by the Mediterranean diet, the new town square proposes to tackle this issue with a permanent programme of restaurants, kitchens and learning areas to promote healthy eating. The design takes inspiration from the rich industrial heritage of Worksop, with a focus on one of the town's major exports: the Windsor chair.
22.14 **Janis Ho, Y4** 'Transport for Santorini'. Due to overtourism, Santorini's authorities have limited the number of visitors to the island by half. This project proposes to enhance local agriculture as a second source of income. A system of bus stops celebrating the island's agriculture introduces its products to tourists. The bus terminal doubles up as a market in which visitors can learn about and buy local produce. Built on reinforced local volcanic rock, the terminal aims to bring together locals and tourists in a new sustainable economy.
22.15 **Yehan Zhen, Y5** 'The Built Pension'. The 'young-old' are an emergent demographic of 50-70 year-old retired people with specific needs. The research questions the nature of pensions as a monetary entities and proposes a 'socio-spatial' pension as a flexible alternative. The Mediterranean 'in-between' condition inspires a split-level typology that integrates existing industrial communities with a retirement layer and an alternative 'street', linking disparate spaces. The built pension spans the domestic and corporate, resulting in an architecture of needs rather than economics.
22.16 **Lewis Williams, Y4** 'Museum of Mediterranean Memories'. British tourists, with the uncertainty of Brexit looming above them, can escape to a playful fairground full of tongue-in-cheek Mediterranean experiences. This project is strategically located in Dover, England. Making their way through border control, tourists embark on their own itinerary through a series of fairground-style rooms, harking back to the days of the Grand Tour, in a space designed to encourage irregular discovery.
22.17 **Yuqi Liew, Y4** 'The Giving Island'. This project aims to foster close ties between locals and refugees by participating in each other's traditions and cultural practices. Architectural events around the island celebrate local traditions, trades, and landscapes. The main focus is an artisanal cheese-making facility where both communities can come together in sustainable craft. The building materials are made from the goat's milk and hair in a bid to use local renewable resources.
22.18 **Funto King, Y4** 'Growing Gorreto: Repopulating Italy's oldest town'. This project addresses the depopulation and ageing of rural areas across Europe. Through a masterplan of flexible housing and workspaces in touch with nature, the town is set to become a family-friendly, rural place where millennials can settle.
22.19 **Byungjun Cho, Y4** 'Extended Boundaries for the Integration of Locals and Refugees in Lesvos'. Across Europe's Mediterranean shore, refugees are housed in camps that often lack basic infrastructure, and some of the communities where they first arrive are amongst the most underfunded. This project focuses on the Greek island of Lesvos and proposes to divert resources into building new infrastructure that helps integrate refugees in the local community, provides dignified housing and also fills gaps in local infrastructure.
22.20, 22.22 **Yinghao Wang, Y4** 'Working in the Garden'. Located in Athens, this project is a start-up incubator for Greek millennials to regain confidence in their future careers in the country, whilst emphasising a slow-paced, high-quality working lifestyle. Working spaces are outdoor or in-between spaces, creating a unique biodiversity-rich working environment that makes a positive contribution to the city's microclimate.
22.21, 22.23 **Jonah Luswata, Y5** 'Socilising Childcare: A Strategy for Slow Living in Konuksever, Antalya'. A lack of childcare is preventing Turkish women from accessing the labour market. Through a series of urban interventions in the city of Antalya, this project aims to provide a form of childcare that engages the community to empower mothers. Turkish vernacular is reinterpreted in a scheme modelled on the pedagogic ideals of learning through play and discovery.

22.2

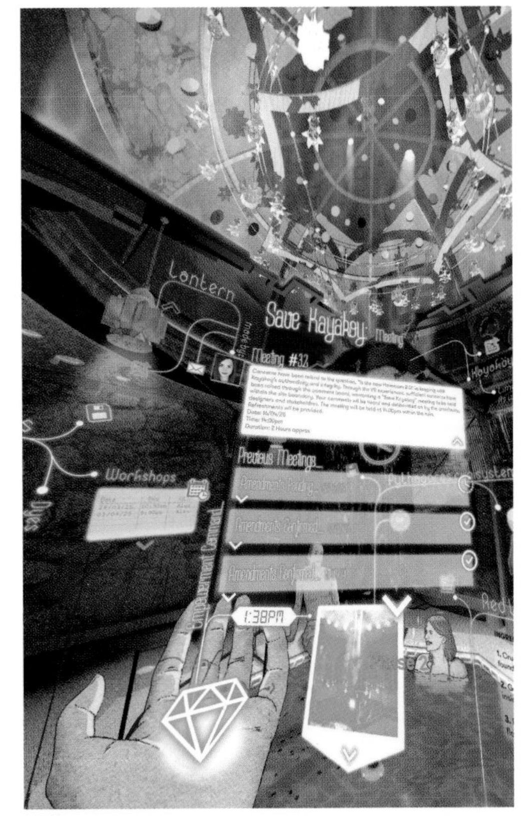

22.3

22.4

22.5

22.6

22.7

22.8

22.9

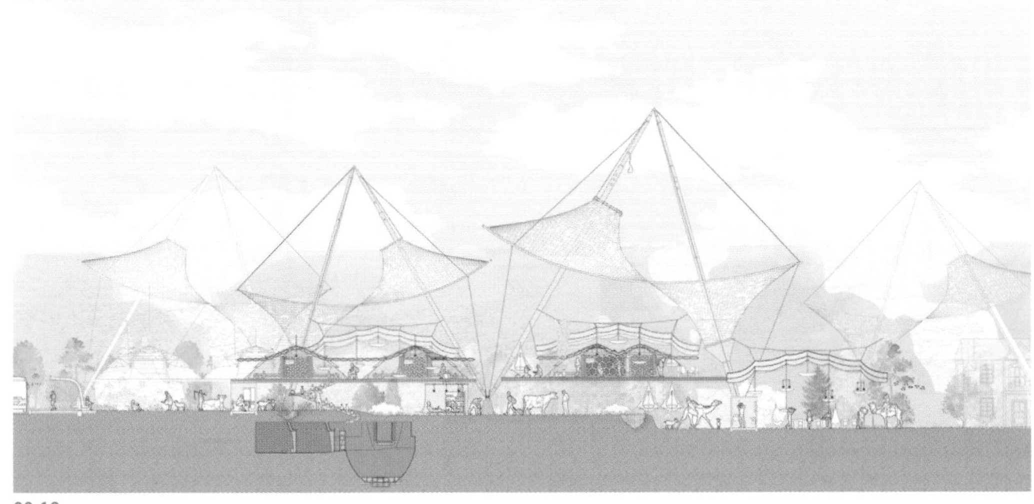

22.10

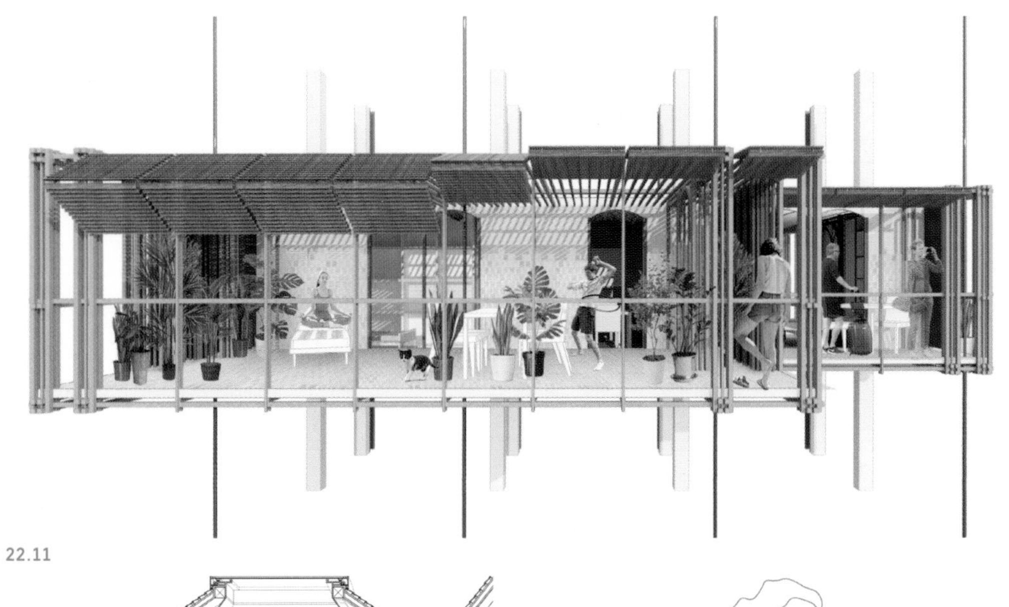

22.11

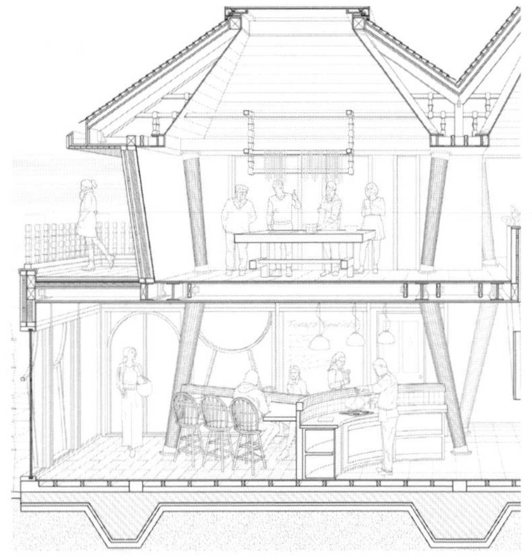

22.12

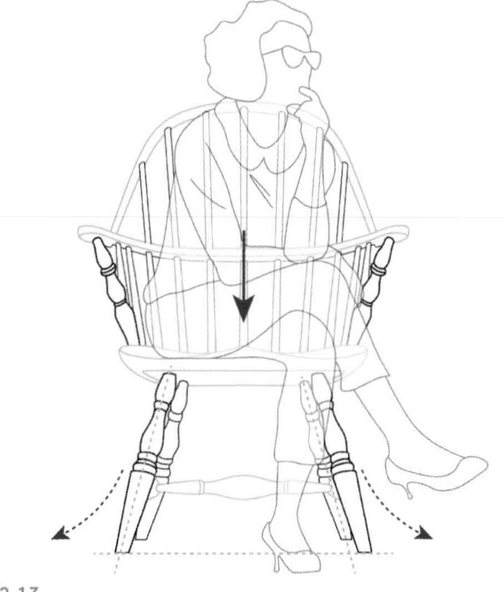

22.13

22.14

22.15

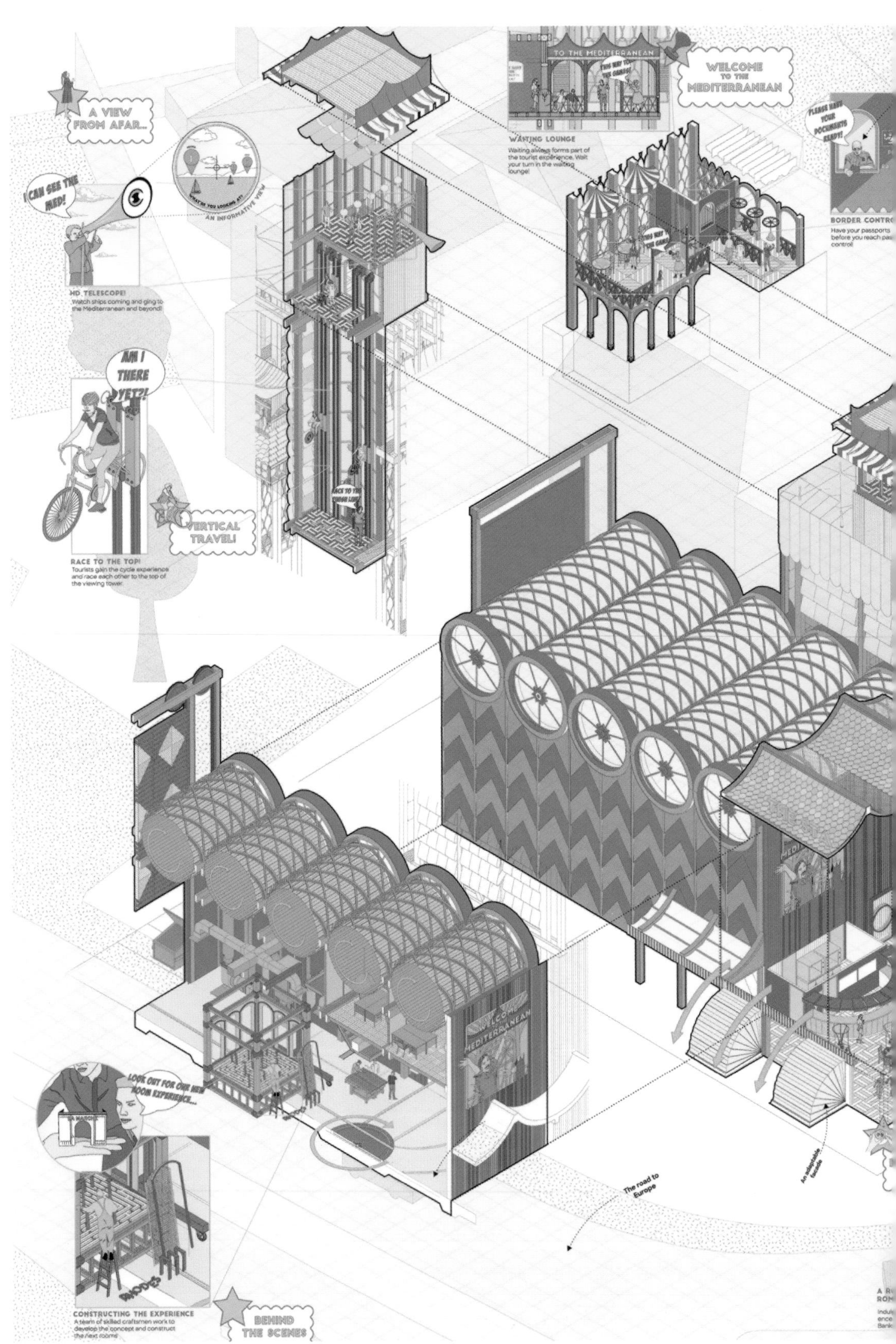
A VIEW FROM AFAR...
I CAN SEE THE MED!
AN INFORMATIVE VIEW
HD TELESCOPE!
Watch ships coming and ging to the Mediterranean and beyond!
AM I THERE YET?!
VERTICAL TRAVEL!
RACE TO THE TOP!
Tourists gain the cycle experience and race each other to the top of the viewing tower.
TO THE MEDITERRANEAN
WAITING LOUNGE
Waiting always forms part of the tourist experience. Wait your turn in the waiting lounge!
WELCOME TO THE MEDITERRANEAN
PLEASE HAVE YOUR DOCUMENTS READY!
BORDER CONTRO
Have your passports before you reach pa control!
LOOK OUT FOR OUR NEW ROOM EXPERIENCE...
WELCOME MEDITERRANEAN
The road to Europe
An adaptable facade
CONSTRUCTING THE EXPERIENCE
A team of skilled craftsmen work to develop the concept and construct the next rooms
BEHIND THE SCENES

22.16

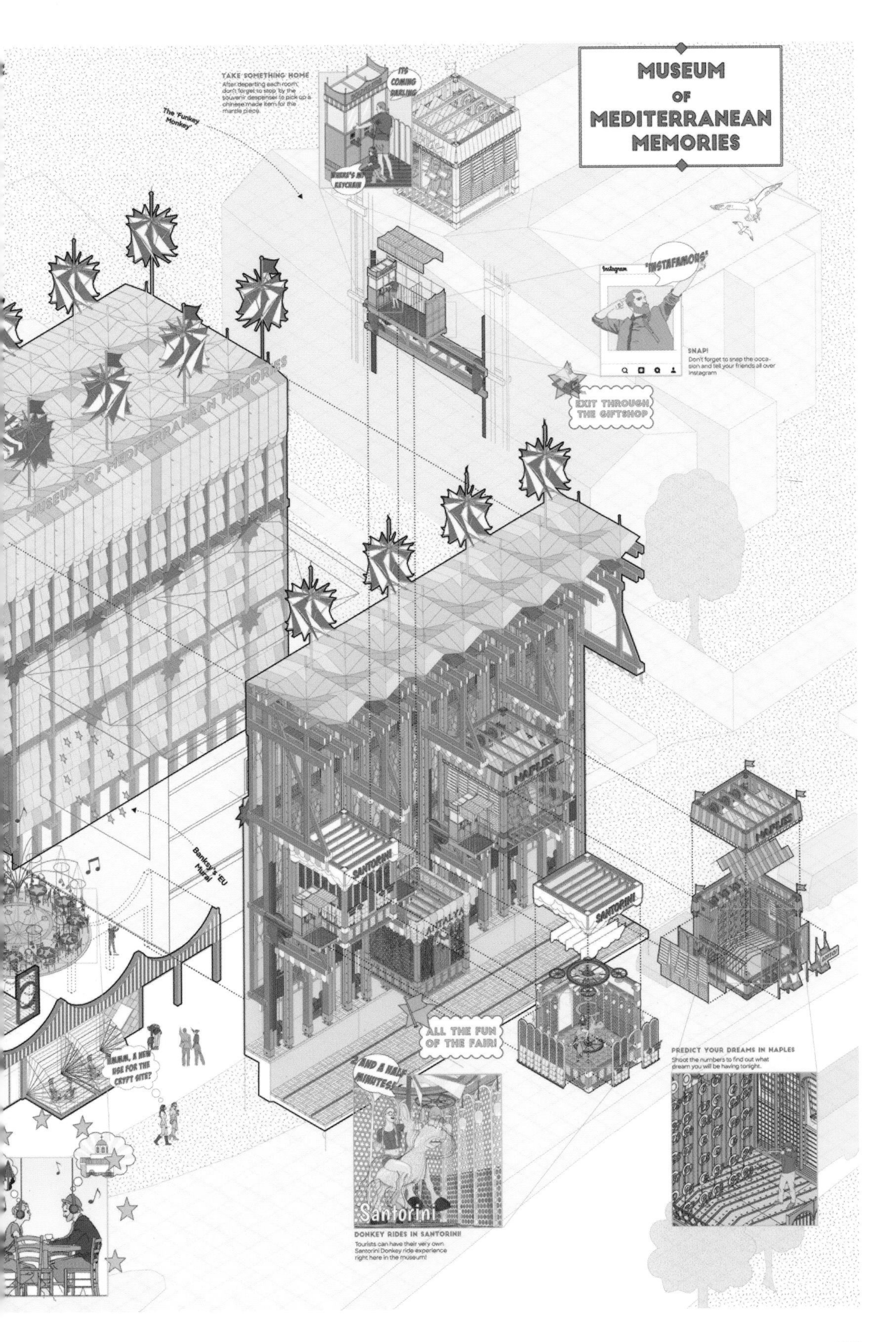
MUSEUM OF MEDITERRANEAN MEMORIES
TAKE SOMETHING HOME
After departing each room, don't forget to stop by the souvenir despenser to pick up a chinese made item for the mantle piece.
The 'Funkey Monkey'
ITS COMING DARLING
WHERE'S MY KEYCHAIN
Instagram
"INSTAFAMOUS"
SNAP!
Don't forget to snap the occasion and tell your friends all over Instagram
EXIT THROUGH THE GIFTSHOP
MUSEUM OF MEDITERRANEAN MEMORIES
NAPLES
SANTORINI
ANTALYA
Banksy's 'EU Mural'
ALL THE FUN OF THE FAIR!
MMM, A NEW USE FOR THE CRYPT SITE?
PREDICT YOUR DREAMS IN NAPLES
Shoot the numbers to find out what dream you will be having tonight.
Santorini
DONKEY RIDES IN SANTORINI!
Tourists can have their very own Santorini Donkey ride experience right here in the museum!

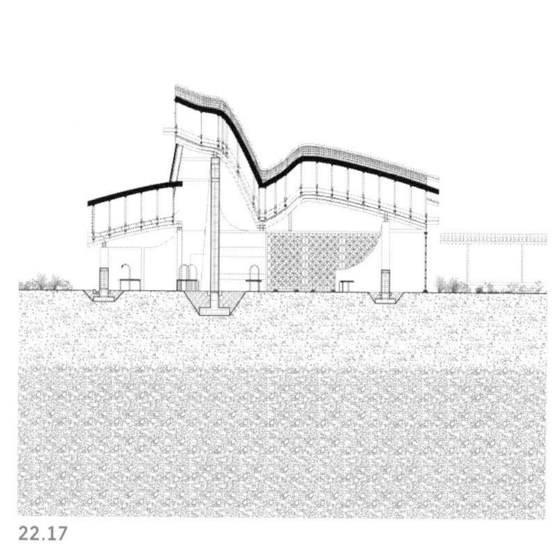

22.17

22.18

22.19

22.20

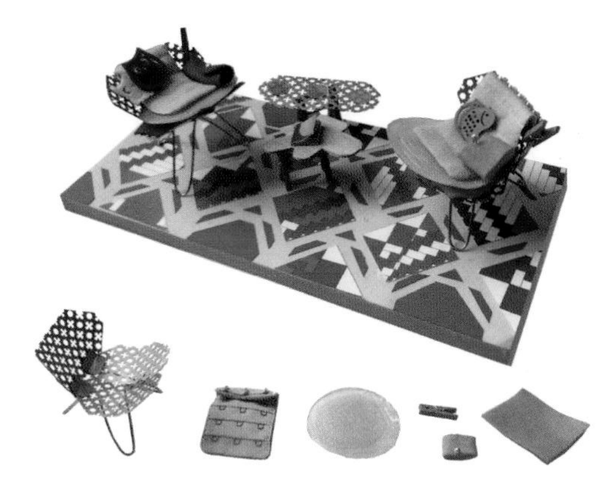
22.21

22.22

22.23

24.1

Redrawing the Rural

PG24

Penelope Haralambidou, Michael Tite

In PG24, we employ film, animation, virtual reality (VR), augmented reality (AR) and physical modelling techniques to explore architecture's relationship with time. We nurture free thinkers and storytellers who find inspiration in both film and architecture, studying their intertwined histories and seeking the myriad possibilities arising from their merger.

This year, we turned our attention to the fast-changing nature of architectural drawing. Time charges and enlivens space in drawing. It can reveal the process of assembly, predict responses to weather, calculate future patterns of occupation, connect with the past, imagine the future, unfold a narrative, build atmosphere, engage with sound and light, and relink architectural composition with the senses. Filmic drawings lead to empathetic design. At the same time, ubiquitous computer-aided design (CAD), building information modelling (BIM) and artificial intelligence (AI) have the potential to eradicate the need for drawing entirely. If a building can draw itself, what is the role of the architect? Has the digital mechanised the hand? Can we draw 1:1 and inhabit the drawing whilst it is being drawn? Can we close the loop between drawing, manufacture and inhabitation by allowing instantaneous feedback between the three? Can digitally disseminated drawings democratise architecture, expand the impact and reach of architectural ideas, and bring communities together?

According to Rem Koolhaas, 50% of the global population now lives in cities and, as a result, we tend to ignore 98% of land: the countryside. Economically and socially overlooked, the rural is the realm of the most rapid and radical change, and the testbed for the future of the world. A colossal 'back-of-house' that feeds, maintains and entertains ever-growing cities, the countryside has historically been the site of utopic visions, centres for study and contemplation, labs for testing new building paradigms, spiritual retreats, sanctuaries for healing and art collections. It can be dreamed up as paradise and idyll, but also demonised as the location of existential horror.

Inspired by our visit to Niall Hobhouse's remarkable Drawing Matter archive at Shatwell Farm in Somerset and our road trip through Europe, we cast off our urban predilections and ventured into the rural. Beyond farmed land, we looked for sites in the wilderness – forests, mountains, oceans and even the atmosphere – and used digital drawing and cutting-edge technologies to narrate new architectural prototypes that change the way we conceive and inhabit space.

Year 4
Krina Christopoulou, Lucca Ferrarese, Alex Haines, Hanna Idziak, Maria Konstantopoulou, Maria Afrodite Moustroufi, George Proud, James White

Year 5
Alexander Ball, Flavian Berar, Uday Berry, Lee Kelemen, Pascal Loschetter, Jerome (Xin) Ng, Sylwia Poltorak, Marie Walker-Smith

Special thanks to Keiichi Matsuda. Thank you also to our Design Realisation tutor Matt Lucraft; our consultants Kevin Pollard, Ali Shaw and Ben Sheterline; workshop/ seminar leaders Finbar Fallon and Jack Holme; and Niall Hobhouse and Susie Dowding at Drawing Matter, Somerset

Thank you to our critics: Laura Allen, Ollie Alsop, Barbara-Ann Campbell-Lange, Rhys Cannon, Nat Chard, Nigel Coates, John Cruwys, Elizabeth Dow, Ava Fatah gen. Schieck, Maria Fedorchenko, Maria Fulford, Pedro Gil, Kate Goodwin, Stefania Gradinariu, Kevin Green, Sean Griffiths, Colin Herperger, Niall Hobhouse, Jack Holmes, Jessica In, Chee-Kit Lai, Matt Lucraft, Abel Maciel, Thomas Millar, Matei Mitrache, Caireen O'Hagan Houx, Sophia Psarra, Nick Shackleton, Jasper Stevens, Stefania Tsigkouni, Nimrod Vardi, Kevin Walker, Tim Waterman, Simon Withers

24.1 **Flavian Berar, Y5** 'Engines of Creation'. In response to existential threats posed by climate change, artificial intelligence and nanotechnology, 'Engines of Creation' explores potential new directions that architecture might take, reacting to and against these potent forces. Located in the heart of Europe, within the neutral, yet hostile, territories of the Swiss Alps, the project begins as an alternative Future of Humanity Institute. Conceived as a mythical research laboratory, where 'Citizens of Nowhere' gather to shape our Post-Anthropocentric interplanetary future, the building slowly evolves over a long time period in response. A radical landscape of the sublime, this is a visionary regenerative architecture born out of the merger of art, nature and technology.
24.2 **Lee Chew Kelemen, Y5** 'Proxima Estacion: Via (De)Colonial'. Over the last four decades, the Argentinean railway network has slowly fallen into ruin, leaving many rural communities disconnected and struggling for survival. The crumbling town of Mechita – once home to the largest railway workshop in South America – finds itself hollowed out: its citizens, having long since migrated away to urban areas, have left behind the carcasses of thousands of disused trains. A new 'De-Colonial Line' emerges from these ashes; a line that will awaken the spirit of the trains once more. Wearing 'architectural masks' given to them by the remaining community, the train carriages house new mutating programmes such as micro-banks, *Pulperia*, football pitches, protest walls and carnival floats. The trains act nomadically, not knowing when they will leave or return, bringing with them a dynamic exchange of civil disobedience as well as cultural, economic and social events according to the needs of the rural population.
24.3–24.5 **Pascal Loschetter, Y5** 'The Unnatural History Museum'. Emerging from a coastal landfill site on the Thames Estuary and telling the story of a landscape of waste, 'The Unnatural History Museum' is a new kind of building that is part-museum, part-monument, part-land art. The museum exhibits markers of our time which contribute to the geology of the future. The architecture itself acts as a monument to the current age of excess by displaying petrified 'memories' of landfill objects within the building's skin. The process carried out to create the building – whereby material is excavated and transformed into plasma rock – remediates the entire landscape, recreating a habitat of salt marshes for the local fauna and flora. Gradually constructed as a remnant of the transformed landscape, the building draws value from the materials found on the site, whilst mitigating against the environmental damage associated with the archaic processing of landfill.
24.6 **Marie Walker-Smith, Y5** 'The Last Forest: Rothiemurchus 2098'. The year is 2098. The Rothiemurchus Project in the Scottish Cairngorms stands as the 'Last Forest', the final remnant of a doomed UN experiment to protect global biodiversity. A central 'ark' building, designed initially to protect plant life in perpetuity, has been left to ruin. Yet, against the odds and for better or worse, the intelligent robotic infrastructure, designed to maintain the forest, appears to have adapted and grown. As an inquisitive biologist infiltrates the Last Forest, we accompany him to discover how corruption and disorder might be forces for survival. The mysterious world we find there asks us to consider who its architecture is for, how custodianship might shape space and how the idea of 'nature' itself might evolve in time.

24.7–24.9 **Alexander Ball, Y5** 'Dreaming in the Shadows'. Streaming services such as Netflix and Disney+ are not only transforming the way that films are produced and distributed, but are also threatening the film theatre as an urban artefact. Inspired by the horror genre, 1950s visions of domesticity and *The Twilight Zone*, a strange installation is imagined on the sacred ground of the recently demolished Marble Arch Odeon. Blurring the boundaries between the architectural home and architectural cinema, the film charts the slow disintegration of the central protagonist. Where is his identity centred? In the home or the cinema? Or an uncomfortable strange place belonging to neither?
24.10–24.12 **Sylwia Poltorak, Y5** 'The Independent State of Melanfolly'. What is architecture? How long can it last? Can it help us endure time itself? The answer is definitively, yes it can! The Independent State of Melanfolly is a secretive cultish island state, lying somewhere in the South Pacific. The rebellious insiders, who refer to themselves as 'lobsters' have developed a mysterious bio-scientific system to extend their existence through the cryogenic growth of artificial organs. Trees twitch with gossip, walls flow with mysterious red liquid and all is watched over by the mysterious 'banner girl'. Give in to this wild, noxious, moonlit party-architecture; you cannot escape it.
24.13–24.16 **Uday Berry, Y5** 'The Tower of a Forgotten India'. Exploring the politics, cultural forces and power struggles underlying architectural heritage and conservation in India, this project proposes an extraordinary tower that acts as a living museum, protecting the nation's threatened and under-valued buildings. Threats come from every direction: religious fundamentalism, rampant modernisation, the culture of collectability and political corruption. In a rapidly developing and ever-changing nation, heritage is seen here as a living part of the city, rather than a site for displaying museum pieces. The tower breathes life back into these forgotten building fragments, reintegrating them into the city's urban fabric. Firing us into the heart of the sprawling chaos of Delhi, 'The Tower of a Forgotten India' is a modern parable spanning decades that seems to suggest that taking control of a city's past is, in the end, a fool's paradise.
24.17 **Jerome Ng Xin Hao, Y5** 'Metabolist Regeneration of a Dementia Nation'. Singapore's Golden Mile Complex is celebrated in many countries as an important icon of 1970's Metabolist urbanism, yet, in its home city, it faces imminent demolition. More than 80 similar sites have already been destroyed, as part of a progressive nation-building programme. More will follow. This project speculates on an alternative vision for this huge residential block, that not only saves the building, but allows it to absorb physical artefacts from Singapore's threatened urban infrastructure. It acts as a prototype for an alternative pattern for future development, allowing residents to forge new memories, whilst giving space for the past to breathe. The animated film documents the lives of a series of Golden Mile residents, urging us all to resist the power structures that see our urban memories so readily erased.

VIA DECOLONIAL
La marea del cambio
Despide a lo estático
Las olas reconocen
La huella
Siguiéndola al origen
MECHITA

24.2

24.3

24.4

24.5

24.6

24.7

24.8

24.9

24.10

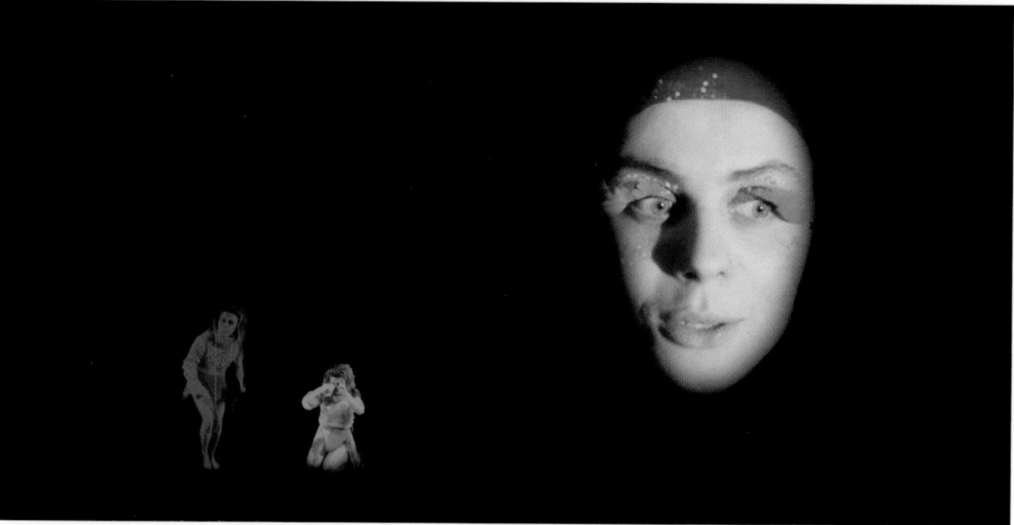
24.11

24.12

24.13

24.14

24.15

24.16

24.17

25.1

Practice and Simulation PG25

Nat Chard, Emma-Kate Matthews

PG25 focuses on developing experimental research methods and processes. We value the production of tacit knowledge and encourage practices that tease this out in research. We are also interested in the role of media in the development of ideas, and the way in which this might provide a critical resistance or resonance in discussion. This particularity leads to a diverse range of means of representation in the unit, often developments of existing processes or fresh inventions. We see the reciprocity between design, material and processes of representation as parallel to the ways that ideas can be embodied in architecture. Many of the students in the unit, therefore, make use of the wide range of manufacturing techniques available at The Bartlett.

This year, we have concentrated on developing ideas of practice along with the means to simulate them. Our projects and fascinations were diverse, with projects ranging from explorations into the world of geological action to observing how speed mediates our experience of architecture; also understanding what is to be learned from the spaces implicated in still-life painting; experiencing sensual architecture; improvising architecture, and more. Each student developed the means to test their ideas through content-related modes of simulation. In most examples, this involved the construction of the apparatus through which ideas are tested and that nurtured the character of the subsequent architecture. On our field trip to Sweden and Denmark, we visited projects in Stockholm, Gothenburg, Klippan, Malmö and Copenhagen, by architects such as Lewerentz and Asplund.

This year, Professor Perry Kulper from the University of Michigan was the Sir Banister Fletcher Visiting Professor, and made a wonderful contribution to our reviews, seminars and tutorials.

Year 4
Callum Campbell, Pete Markos, Tse Hin Matthew Poon, Blake Walter

Year 5
Yuezai Chen, Vlad Daraban, Patrick Dobson-Perez, Egmontas Geras, Ren Zhi Goh, Isaac Leung, Gaoqi Lou, Carys Payne, Toby Preston, Roshan Sehra, Ben Spong

Critics: William Victor Camilleri, Barbara-Ann Campbell-Lange, Peter Cook, Yeoryia Manolopoulou, Shaun Murray, Thomas Parker, Alex Pillen, Mark Ruthven, Bob Sheil, James Solly, Jerry Tate, Emmanuel Vercruysse, Simon Withers

Thank you to Geoff Morrow, Jerry Tate and the B-made workshop team

25.1–25.3 **Patrick Dobson-Perez, Y5** 'Digging Matter(s)'. This project, based in Portland, investigates architectural possibilities on a geological timescale. Habitable machines manipulate the landscape and become buried, only to be rediscovered in deep time.
25.4–25.7 **Egmontas Geras, Y5** 'Haunts'. This project interrogates a personal photograph of a manor house which sits in ruin amongst the trees. The forest is usurping: the roof is off, the manor shuts its two visible eyes. The rest can fit between the overexposed sky and the unknown darkness of the shade.
25.8–25.9 **Roshan Sehra, Y5** 'Accelerating Hotel'. Speed, velocity and acceleration are parameters associated with motion. This project utilises a spatial score as a method for spatio-temporal investigation in the context of a hotel situated in the gaps between Charing Cross station and the Southbank in London.
25.10–25.12 **Ren Zhi Goh, Y5** 'In Nature's Shadow'. This extraordinary office block is situated in the spaces between the Blackfriars Bridge in London. Somewhere between architecture and infrastructure, these individually-scaled spaces provide habitats for birds, humans and horses.
25.13–25.14 **Ben Spong, Y5** 'House at 685 Degrees'. This design/research-based project explores how still-life painting can function in an architectural context. Several fundamental questions are asked: 'How can objects have the capacity to 'discuss' content from other worlds?' 'What spatial relationships are defined when site and architectural objects are assembled within a still-life composition?' and 'Does the concept of 'blackness' have the ability to describe indescribable spatio-temporal depths?'
25.15 **Callum Campbell Y4** 'Thurston's Match Hall'. This project proposes a space for practicing and learning snooker, in the heart of London's Soho. The project has been investigated using pinhole photography and the making of large cameras.
25.16 **Pete Markos, Y4** 'Collaging Markets: An architecture of production'. This market, on the edges of Edgware Road, acts as a gathering device for spatio-cultural phenomena. The project provides a reliable infrastructure whilst the products on sale are visually curated in a way that generates its own architectural character.
25.17 **Vlad Daraban, Y5** 'Fantastic Realities (and Where to Find Them)'. Hackney Wick is the site of a project which investigates how normal spaces can become shaped by personal fascinations, in a world where residential architecture is becoming increasingly generic.
25.18–25.19 **Toby Preston Y5** 'Improvising Architecture'. This project is a proposal for a primary school in Frostrow Fell, Yorkshire Dales National Park. Several drawing instruments were developed as a means to interrogate the site and the practice of improvising architecture in an educational context.
25.20 **Yuezai Chen, Y5** 'Time Clinic'. Based on the white cliffs of England's south coast, this project is a proposal for a medical clinic which celebrates and makes visible the passing of time on a range of timescales. This research was conducted through a series of paintings, material studies and time-based site studies.
25.21 **Blake Walter, Y4** 'Inverted Museum'. A building which exhibits scale models of projects which never existed or no longer exist. The concept of 'the frame' is investigated as a spatial construct for housing these exhibits on multiple scales.
25.22–25.23 **Gaoqi Lou, Y5** *'Le corps a l'envers l'architecture en verlan'*. This project proposes a club in the heart of Paris for those who are fond of dressing in extravagant and whimsical ways. The research was conducted through a series of 1:1 garments which dress the performance of an elaborate architecture, on a large-scale site model.
25.24 **Matthew Poon, Y4** 'Spatial Monosodium Glutamate'. This project investigates the uncanniness between the reality that we experience on a day-to-day basis, and the unreal encounters that we are free to explore within the world of videogames and virtual reality technologies. The resultant architecture is 'alive' with character, behaviour and reaction.
25.25 **Carys Payne, Y5** 'Complementary Therapies'. This research project uses a series of drawing devices which encourage the architect to 'feel' space as opposed to seeing it. Situated by the water in Berlin, the project offers a series of spaces which are designed to emit an 'energy' which can often only be felt and not seen.
25.26 **Isaac Leung, Y5** 'Tuning the Acousmatic Veil'. This radio station in the Regent's Canal broadcasts found sound, performed music and sound art. A grand piano acts as an analogy for the site, which can be performed, improvised and articulated as an acoustic representation of designed architectural space.

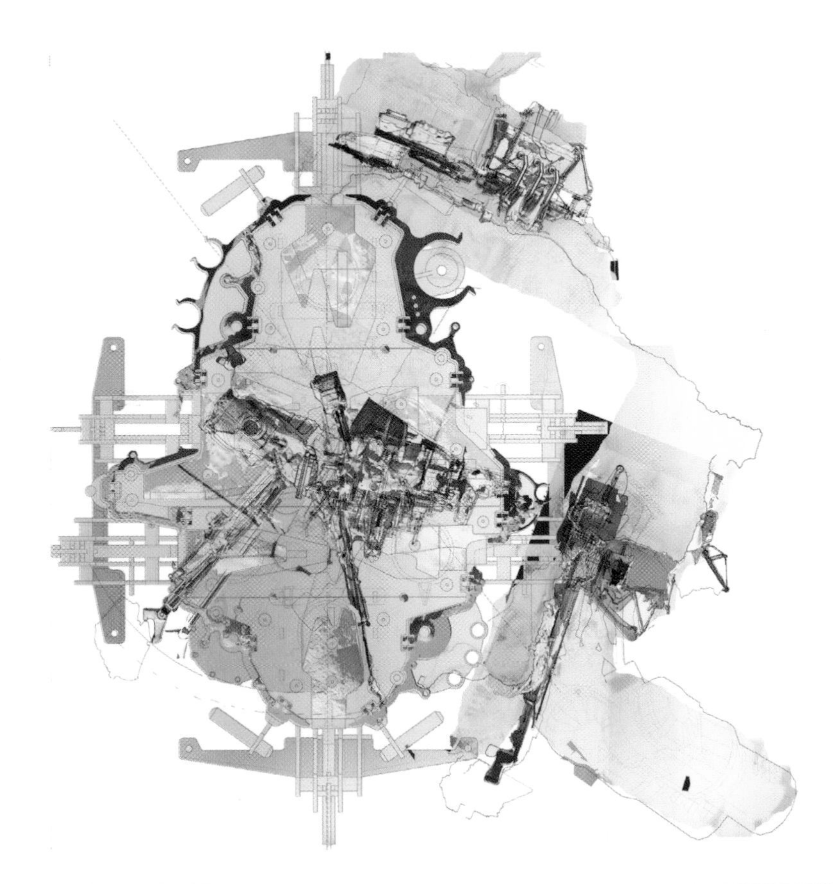

25.2

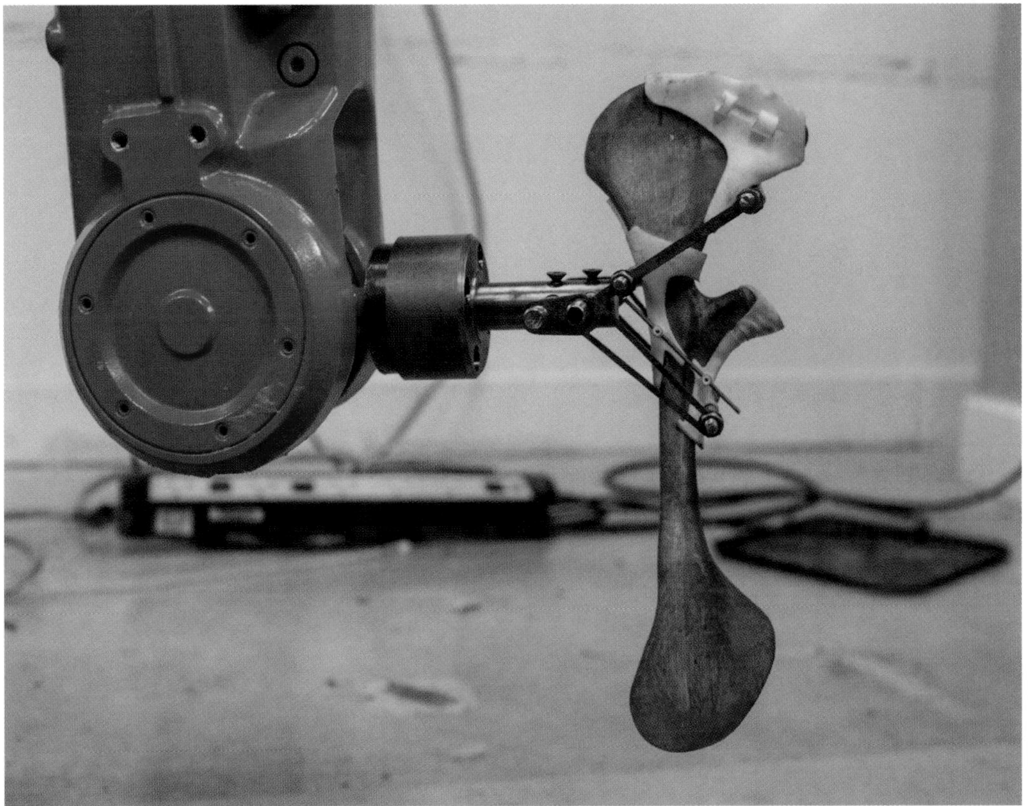

25.3

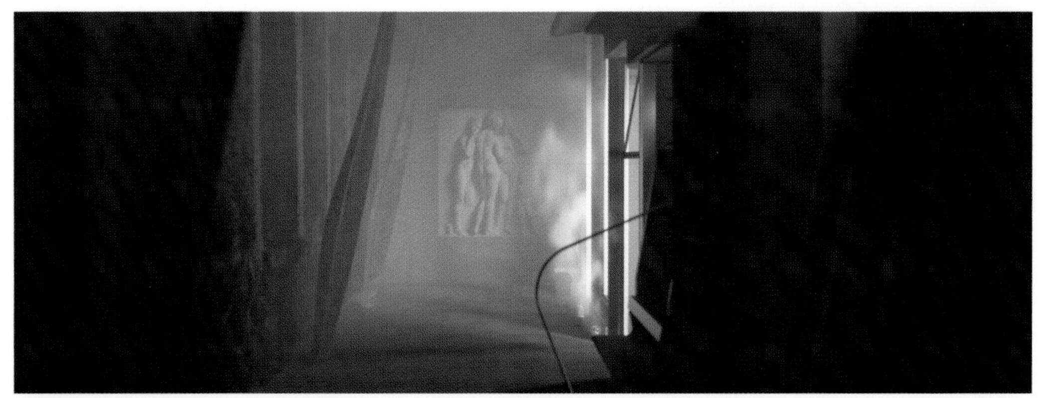

25.4

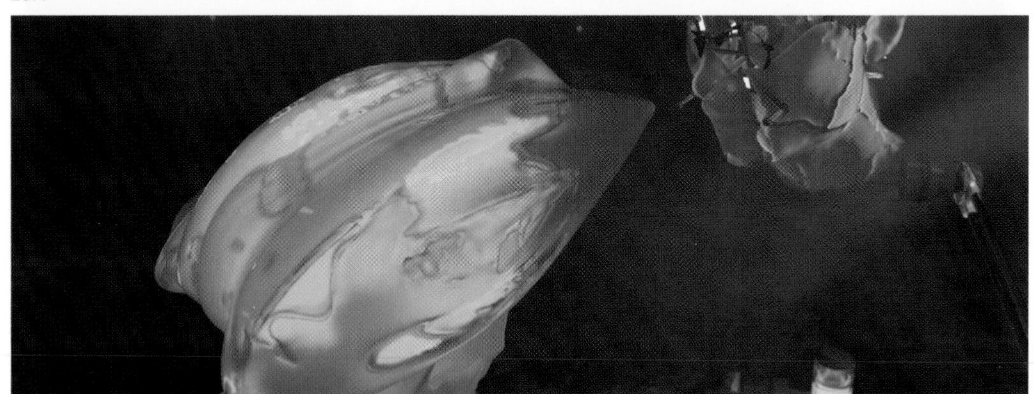

25.5

25.6

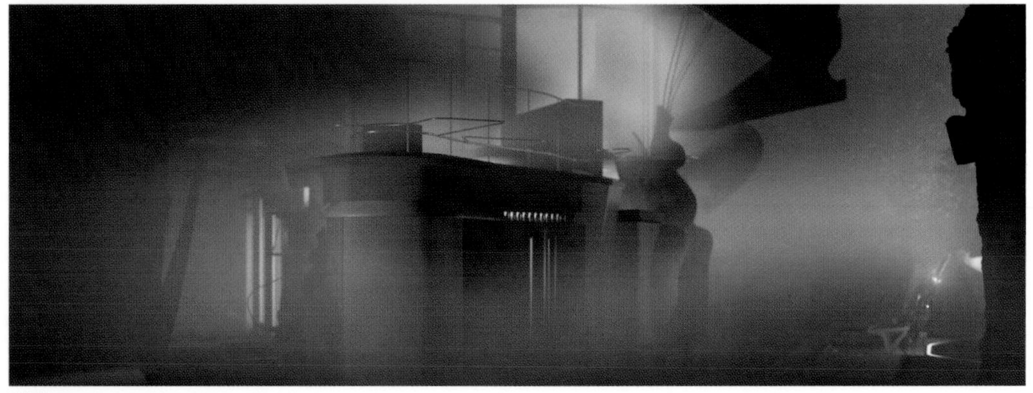

25.7

25.8

25.9

25.10

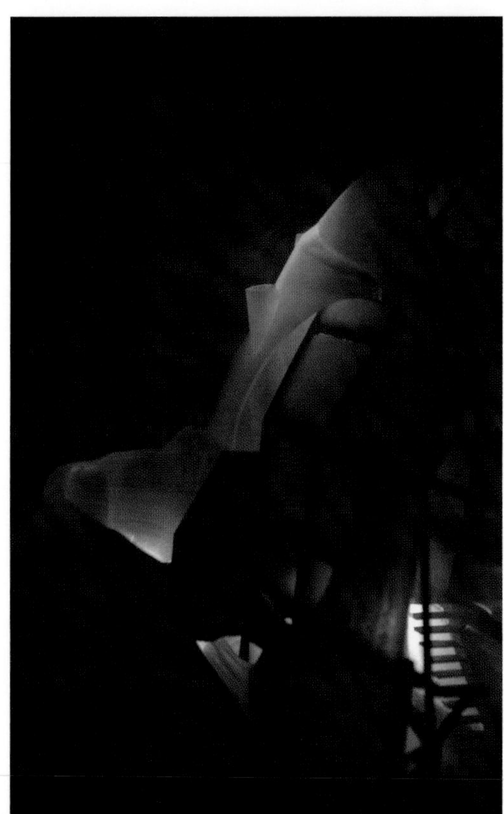

25.11

25.12

25.13

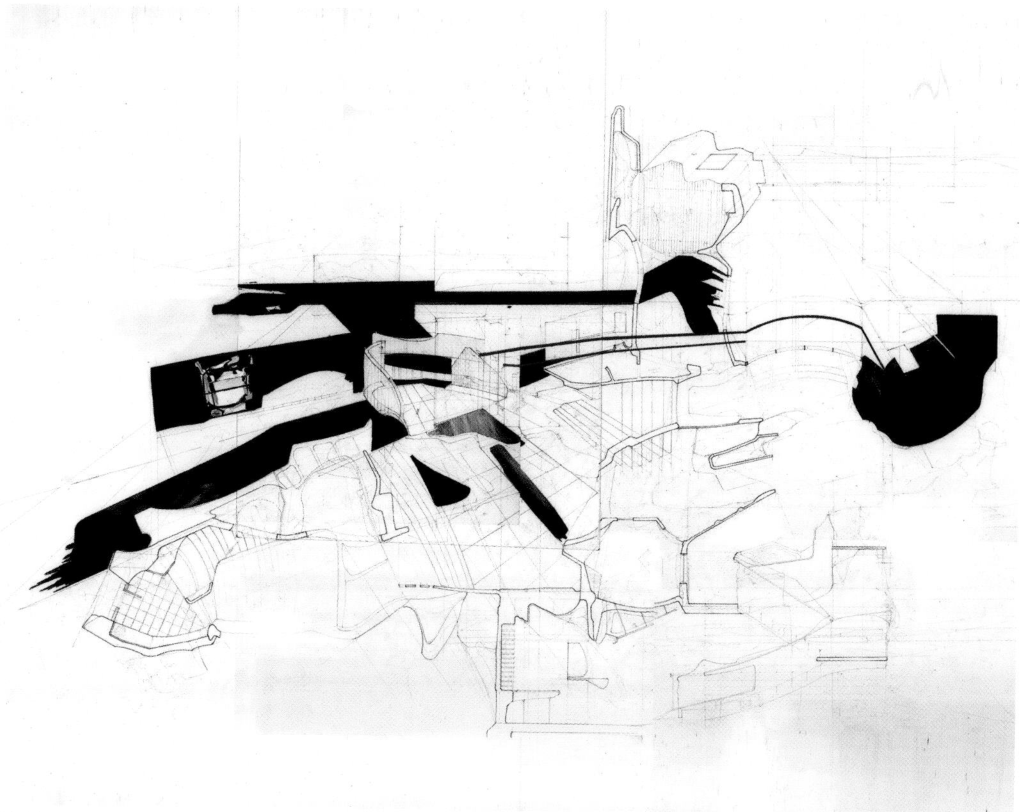

25.14

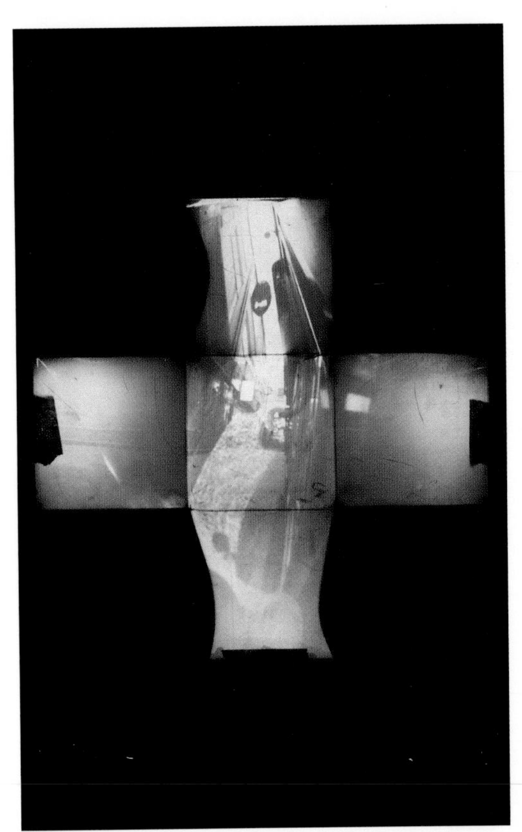
25.15

25.16

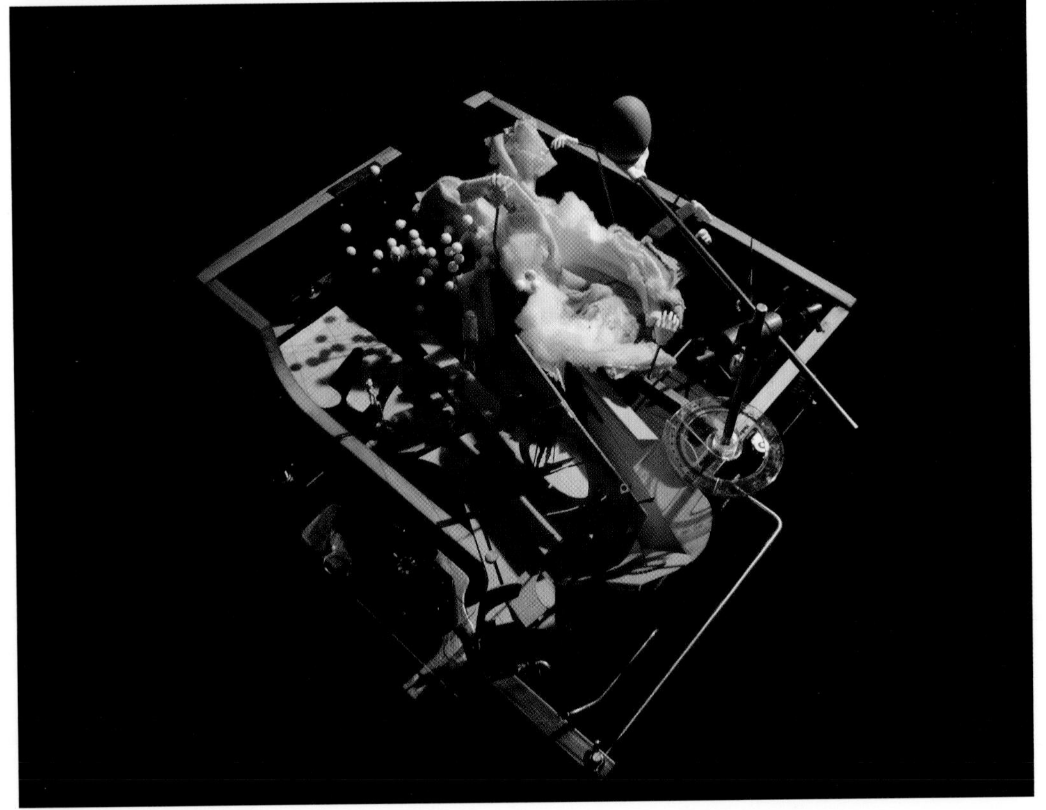
25.17

25.18

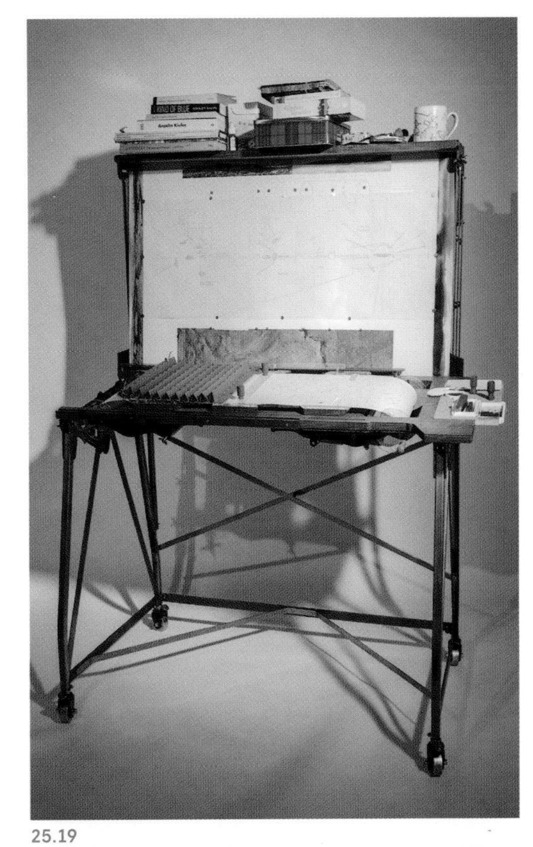

25.19

25.20

25.21

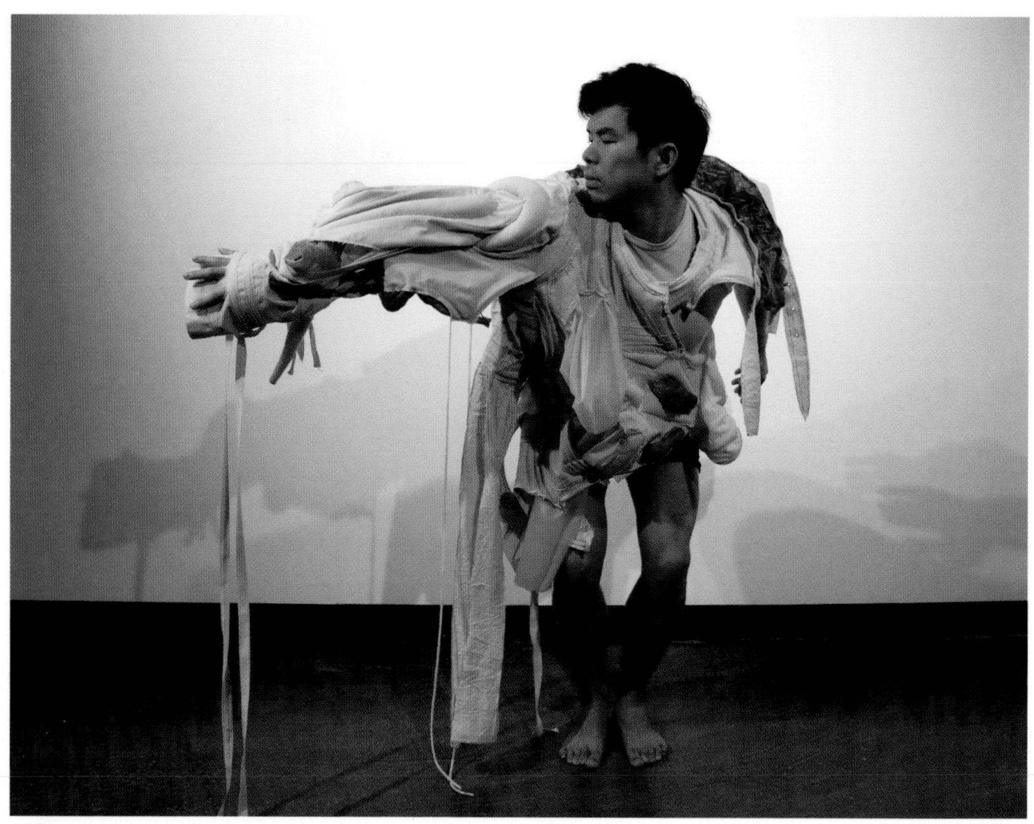

25.22

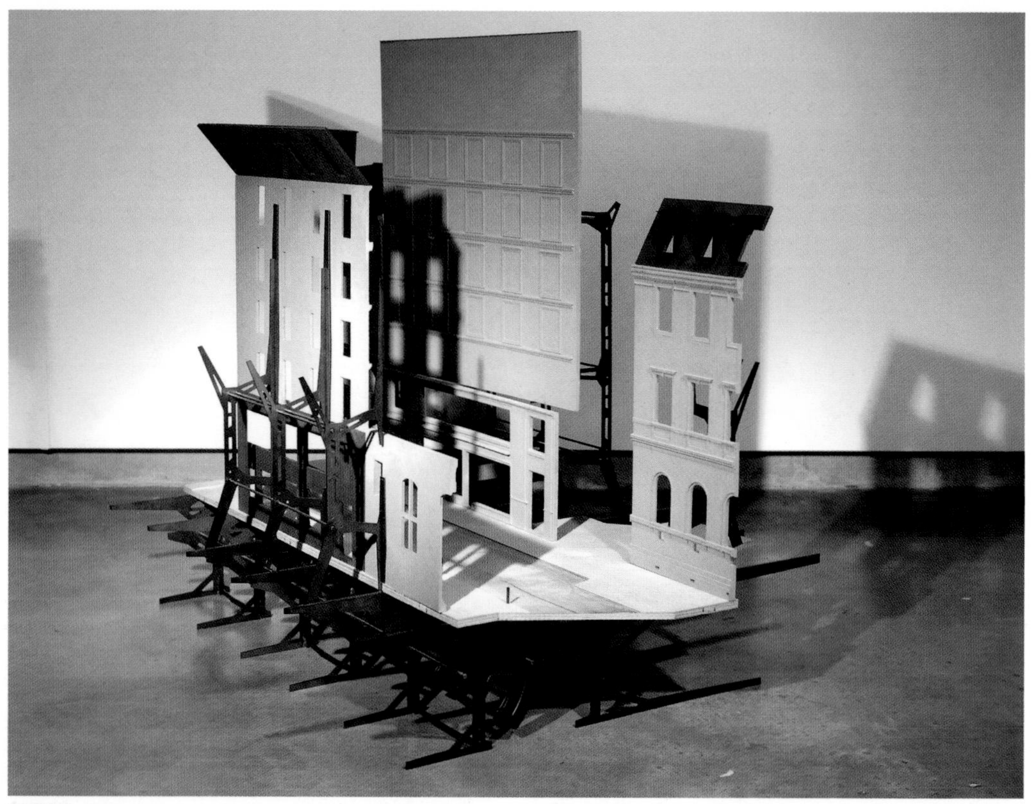

25.23

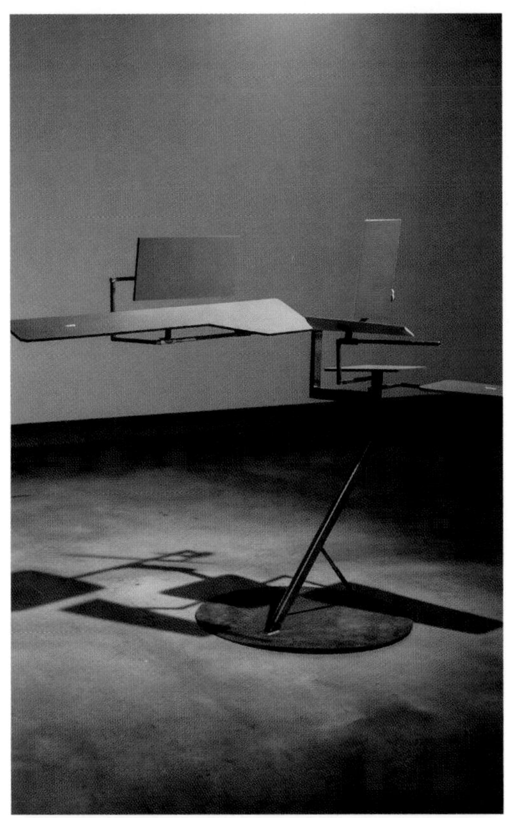

25.24

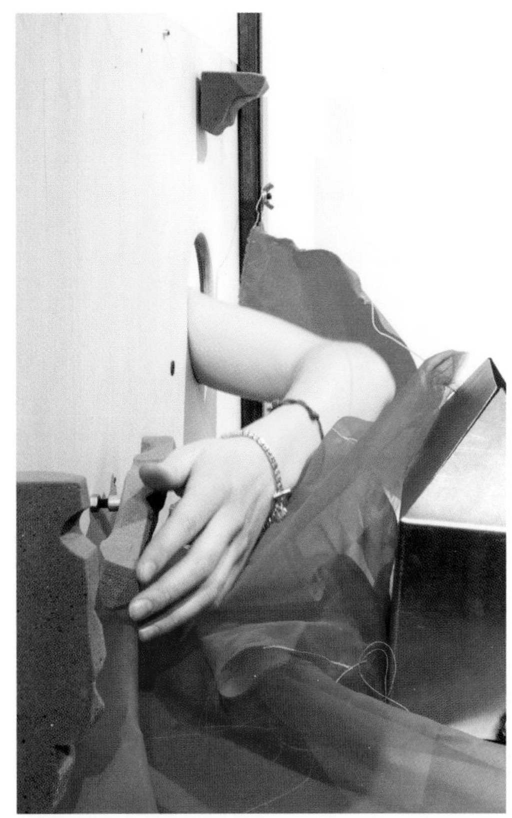

25.25

25.26

PAPER
JAM
YOUR
GET YOUR TICKETS NOW

Description, Invention, Reality

PG26

David Di Duca, Tetsuro Nagata

Art and design have historically challenged and explored our society. Our unit continues this by observing and forming critical positions on what we see around us. We are interested in how architecture is able to evoke emotion and prompt conversation. We consider our role as active observers and participants, and are interested in testing out theories by making films and 1:1 installations. There is a common misconception that architects design experiences, but in PG26 we would rather suggest that architects design places and objects to be experienced. This position leads to a design process with a focus on how people perceive, interact with and remember space, and the connection between body, imagination and memory.

The world around us is changing fast and, with it, the ubiquitous and continuous exposure to technology is making audiences to digital arts less responsive, as new possibilities arrive faster than they can be explored. Personal data, connected technologies, and interactive and predictive products are all current topics of debate. Cynicism towards technological progress is not new but we are experiencing a rapid rise in anxiety about automation and surveillance, which is leading to a growth in neo-luddite, off-grid lifestyles. Architecture is integral to this, as cities and buildings can increasingly be seen as systems to utilise technology to control the currents of weather, nature, power, heat, water and data. In PG26 this year, we looked at how we can embrace, ignore and disrupt these 'controlled' systems and, as a result, the architectures that the unit designed were both reactive to, and interactive with, the uncontrollable.

We began the year by creating small-scale installations in a brewery in Walthamstow that explored how buildings can react to the actions of people and the environment around them. Embracing the performative aspects that this brought, we moved towards larger-scale architectural proposals in London and beyond. We actively encouraged our students to work with varied approaches: to utilise the workshop to fabricate haptic devices, develop code and electronics to test interactivity, and create physical and virtual spaces to evoke emotional responses and challenge ideas. We produced films incorporating four-dimensional drawings and viewer-driven non-linear narratives. Above all, our work was iterative and reflective, and we learned to criticise and question our own processes.

Year 4
Alexander Borrell, Darren Buttar, Andrei-Ciprian Cojocaru, Ross Gribben, Sze (Viola) Poon, Ryan Tung

Year 5
Pitchaya Chayavoraprapa, Jolene Hor, Klaudia Kepinska, Kin (Glynnis) Lui, David Majoe, David Park, Baifan Tao, Artur Zakrzewski

Thank you to: Barbara-Ann Campbell-Lange, Stephen Gage, Alexis Germanos, Stefana Gradinariu, Mike Hutchison, Simon Kennedy, Ted Krueger, Henry Pelly, Henrik Pihlveus, Grace Quah, Daniel Sonabend

Sponsor: BAT Studio

26.1, 26.5 Pitchaya Chayavoraprapa, Y5 'Mundane to Mad'. The process of imagining spaces and places for others' needs is based on assumptions about shared experiences and our ability to empathise with others. Assumption is a device rather than a fact; we all experience the world uniquely depending on our past experiences and physiology. This project explores how the imagination is as potent in our experiences as the physical things around us. The work culminates in a non-linear interactive film, which viewers engage with by moving in space, relative to the screen and a tracking camera.
26.2–26.4 David Park, Y5 'Insta[nt] Virality'. Instagram is directly influencing our engagement with the public realm. If a place sees a spike of interest on Instagram, it leads to a corresponding popularity in real-world visitors. These visitors post images of the places and the cycle becomes self-fulfilling. This gives Instagram's algorithms increasing influence on our urban behaviour, especially relating to tourism. This project explores what this means and imagines a figurative architecture designed for this emerging scenario in which the social media representation of a place is as important as the physical.
26.6 Darren Buttar, Y4 'Digital Theatre'. Site-specific theatre and arts have become increasingly popular and technology has resulted in the prevalence of installation work. However the majority of this work either relies on found spaces or adapting work into traditional theatres and galleries. This project imagines a new typology of theatre and arts building to facilitate new types of performance.
26.7 Andrei-Ciprian Cojocaru, Y4 'Date Hub'. Responding to the brief for a public house, a place for socialising beyond one's domestic environment, this project evolved from an interest in how people form new personal relationships. The proposed building, an architectural representation of a dating algorithm, is a reaction to relationships mediated through smartphones.
26.8 Sze (Viola) Poon, Y4 'Made in Camden'. The site currently occupied by a large supermarket in Camden is due to be transformed into a residential development, creating a new community for thousands of people. This project proposes a garden and craft centre which would form an ambitious community asset and social hub for this new development.
26.9 Alexander Borrell, Y4 'Cloud Courts'. This project proposes a parliament building for the age of digital communication and data-based capitalism. The design strategy employs the metaphor of 'echo chambers' surrounding a debating hall through which disputes in the digital world are resolved. These disputes might range from the petty to the extremely important; either way, the outcomes are cast in iron and placed into a public garden for all to see.
26.10 Ryan Tung, Y4 'Amphibious Living for Later Life'. This building is designed for a specific community group; people who live on canal boats in London. As people grow older and their mobility decreases, living on a barge becomes increasingly difficult. This project imagines a retirement home for a boating community in Camden, enabling people to live on their boats for as long as possible. Ideas related to the slow way of life, travelling by canal are used as a design metaphor throughout the building.
26.11 Ross Gribben, Y4 'Post-Primark'. This project facilitates slow conversations between strangers, and explores the changing social activities surrounding retail. It proposes a future building on Oxford Street based around ethical clothing production, recycling and mass-customisation.
26.12–26.13 Klaudia Kepinska, Y5 'Digital Memories'. This project imagines a landscape museum and archive based on the life of a Finnish architect who is largely forgotten. The project explores the boundaries between documentation, facsimile and imagination. It directly acknowledges the role of the designer's own imagination as a source of inaccuracy but also creativity in the process of representing a history that cannot be recreated. The project is portrayed using experimental film and drawing techniques.
26.14–26.15 Jolene Hor, Y5 'Unprivate Mansion'. Our society is heavily influenced by aspirational lifestyles portrayed through various forms of media. This project began with an examination of architectures created for reality television. This led to a test installation which explored the ideas, and a parallel thesis focused on domesticity and privacy. The project culminates in a film which extrapolates observable behaviours in our current society, portraying a unique and potentially disturbing building in a near-future Camden.
26.16 Artur Zakrzewski, Y5 ' Ministry of Wellbeing'. GDP and continuous growth as a measure of development are a capitalist constructs which are no longer compatible with the challenges of climate change and social inequality we face. Progressive societies are starting to value measures of happiness and wellbeing. This project imagines a new 'Ministry of Wellbeing' for London. The proposed building, in the most prominent of locations, the Serpentine lake, features a skin which is animated so that people may perceive the building as expressing emotions.
26.17 Kin (Glynnis) Lui, Y5 'West Pier Life Garden'. The project's key themes are transition, in-between states and rituals associated with loss, mourning and reinvention. The project developed through an experimental installation which combined animation and tactile objects to depict the serendipity of transitional states. The major project is sited in the remains of Brighton Pier, a building famous for being lost multiple times and existing in states of transition for long periods. It draws on ideas from winter festivals, seasonal cycles and rebirth.
26.18 Baifan Tao, Y5 'Metropolitan Yu'. This project imagines a near future in which the urban realm can be augmented and themed depending on a persons mood or interests. The project was researched and developed through a series of augmented reality apps, and culminated in a composited film shot on location in Chongqing, depticting a journey inspired by a famous Chinese myth.
26.19–26.22 David Majoe, Y5 'Haptic Virtuality'. This experimental project comprised practical research and a thesis-led investigation into how perceptive traits can be explored and exploited in virtual reality. The project aspires to create new forms of architecture that may transcend the possibilities of the conventional palette. In the near future, the plausibility of things we encounter and the mixed sensory inputs we receive from both the physical and virtual components of our environment, will become part of the architect's armoury of design tools.

26.2

26.3

26.4

26.5

26.6

26.7

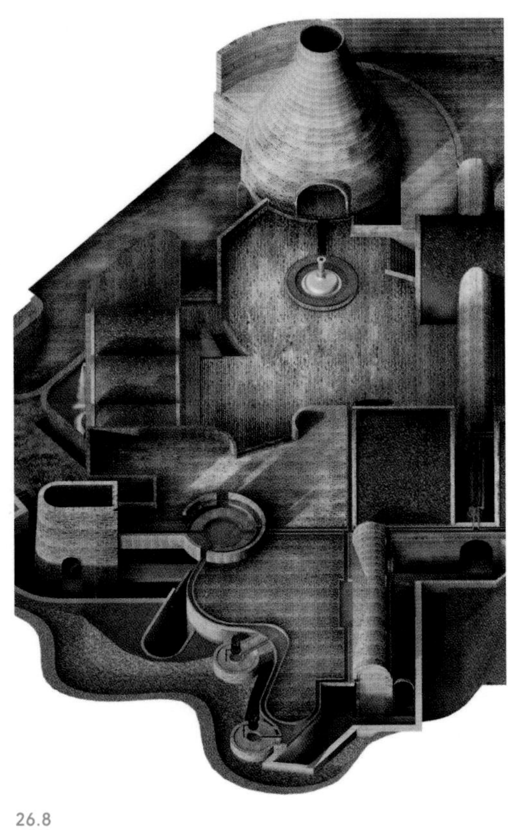

26.8

26.9

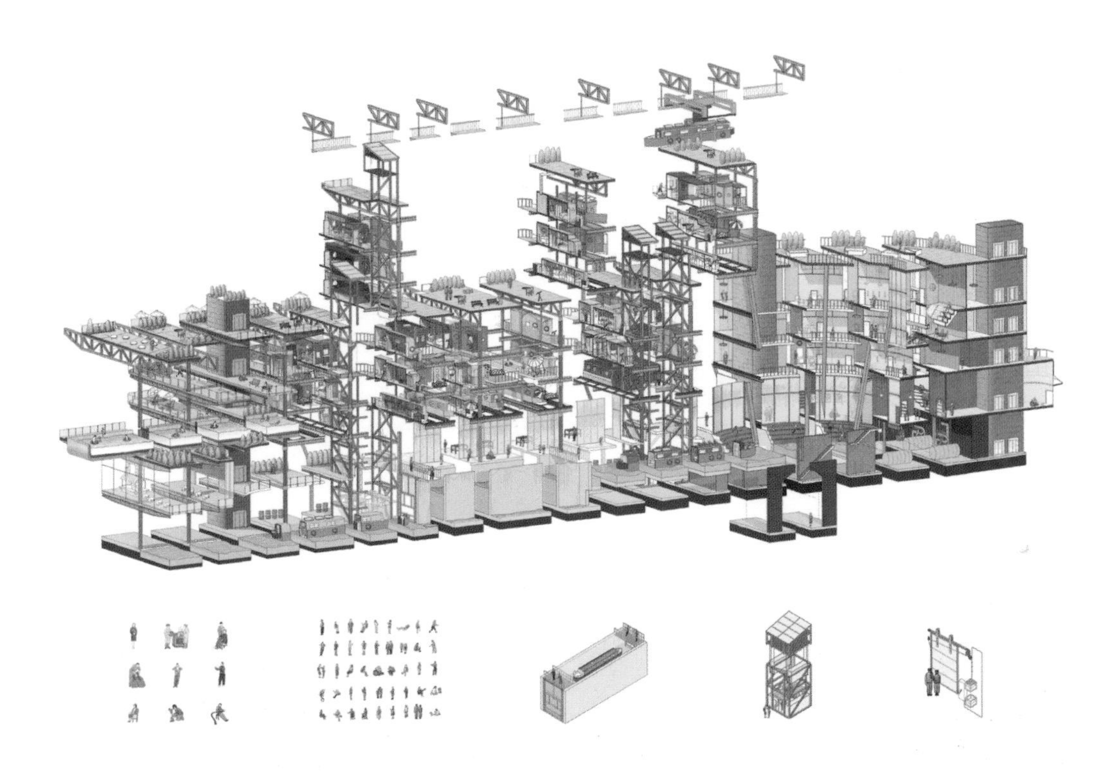

26.10

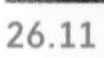

26.11

26.12

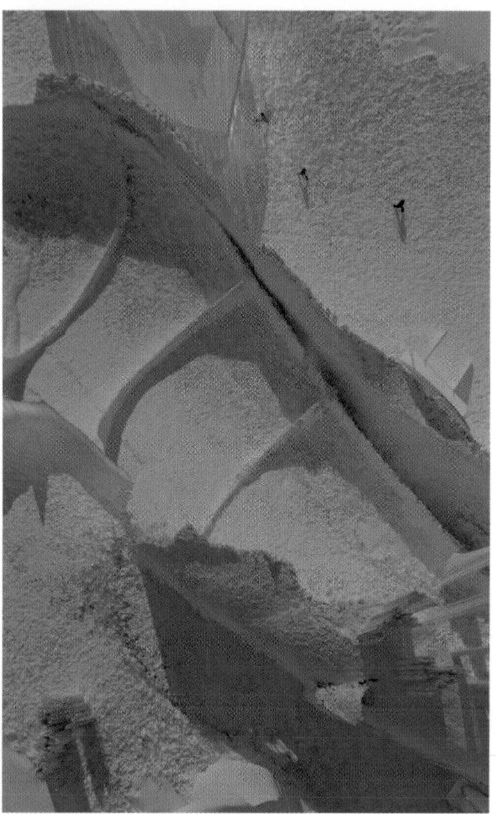

26.13

26.14

CAMDEN

26.15

26.16

26.17

26.18

26.19

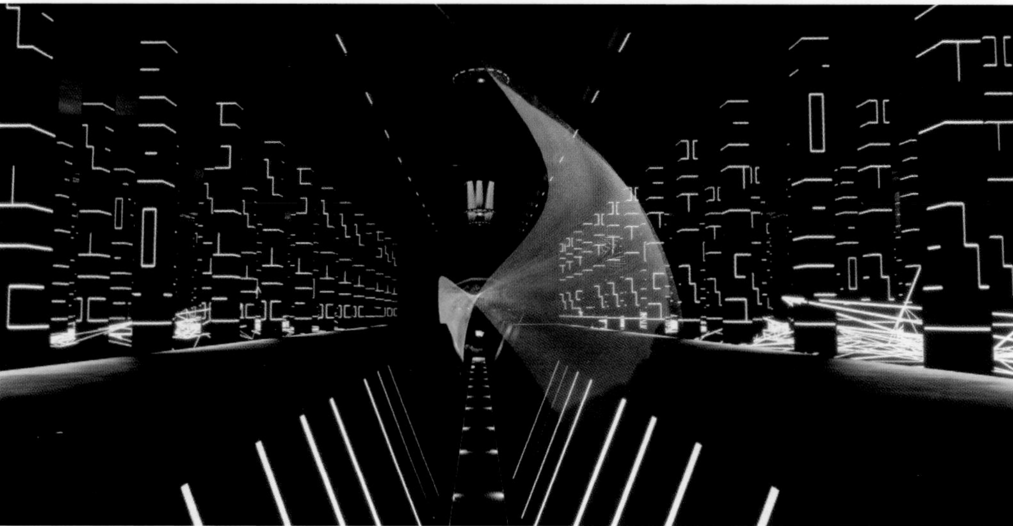

26.20

26.21

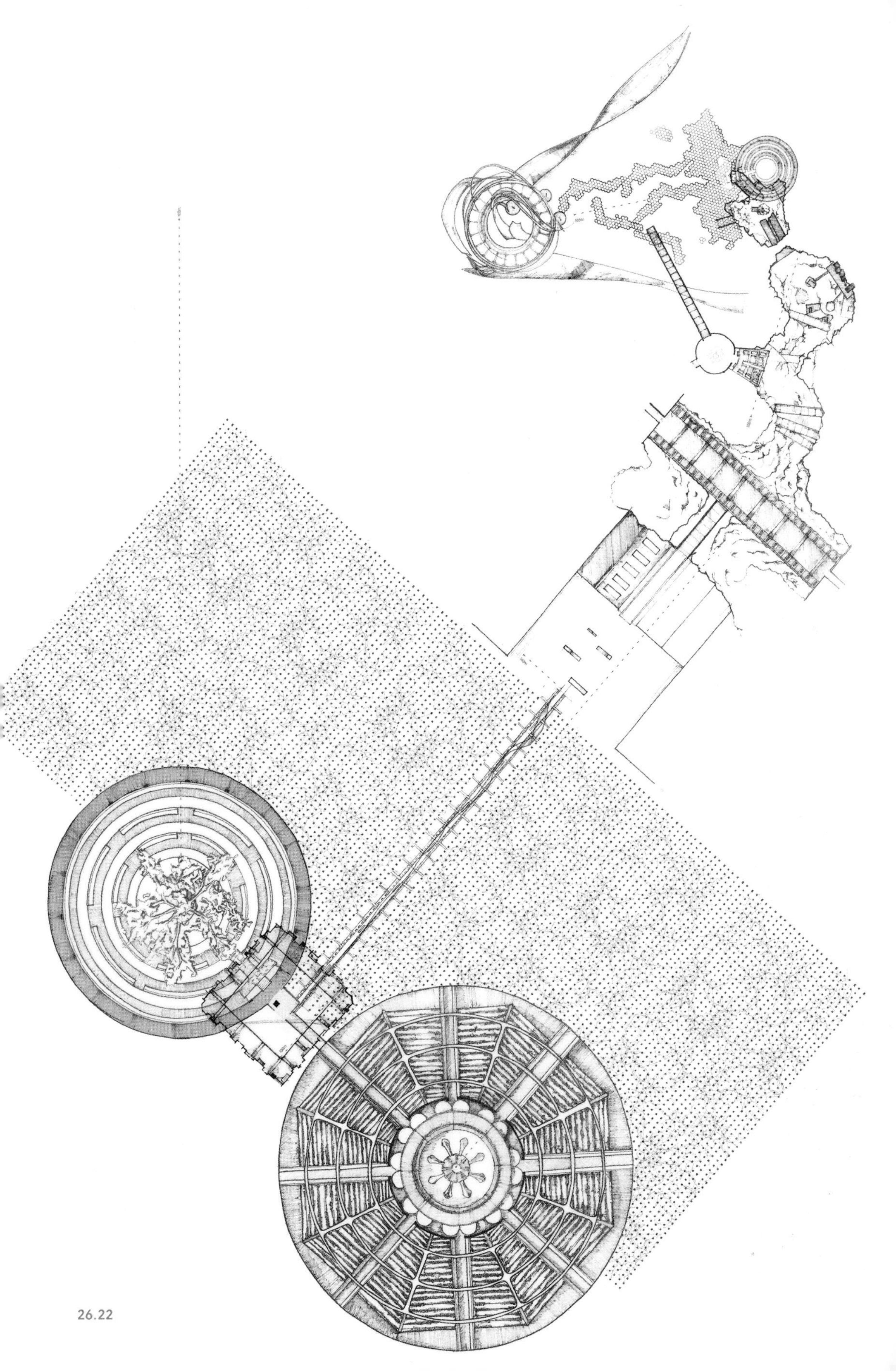

Design Realisation

Year 4

Module Coordinators: Pedro Gil, Dirk Krolikowski, Stefan Lengen

The Design Realisation module provides an opportunity for all Year 4 Architecture MArch students to consider how buildings are designed, constructed and delivered. It provides a framework to facilitate experimentation through the design of buildings, and encourages the interrogation and disruption of technical ideas and principles.

Students propose their ideas at a variety of scales and represent them using drawings, diagrams, animations, physical models and 3D digital models. They are encouraged to take risks in their design thinking and strategy.

The module bridges the worlds of academia and practice, engaging with many renowned design practices and consultancies. A dedicated practice-based architect, structural engineer and environmental engineer support each design unit, working individually with students to develop their work throughout the module.

This year, we have seen a magnificent bounty of projects that test, explore and innovate across a wide spectrum of principles and mediums. Students have produced an array of breathtaking work that pushes the boundaries of technical and professional practice disciplines. Projects include inventive structural systems, environmental strategies, buildings for challenging sites, community engagement proposals, infrastructural projects and entrepreneurial proposals, to name but a few.

Thanks to all the structural consultants who have worked with individual students to realise their projects; to Atelier Ten, Max Fordham, and WSP, environmental consultants to all design units; and to our practice tutors for their remarkable commitment and dedication.

Image: James White, PG24, 'Augmented Rehabilitation', Somerset, UK

Lecturers
Andrew Abdulezer (Seth Stein), Damian Eley (Expedition Engineering), Pedro Gil (The Bartlett / Studio Gil), Jan Guell (Nikken Barcelona), Adam Holloway (AHA), Dirk Krolikowski (The Bartlett / DKFS), Tim Lucas (Price & Myers), Ho-Yin Ng (Amanda Levete Architects), Victor Orive (Zaha Hadid Architects), James Parker (Expedition Engineering), Joanna Pencakowski (RSHP), Hareth Pochee (Max Fordham), Andrew Segwick (Arup), Dan Wright (RSHP)

Practice Tutors
PG10 Jon Kaminsky (Hawkins\Brown)
PG11 Rhys Cannon (Gruff Limited)
PG12 James Hampton (Periscope)
PG13 Rae Whittow-Williams (EWE Projects)
PG14 Jakub Klaska (The Bartlett, UCL)
PG15 Marcel Rahm (Milk Studio), Martin Sagar (Undercover Architecture Ltd)
PG16 Will Jefferies (Rogers Stirk Harbour + Partners)
PG17 James Daykin (Daykin Marshall Studio), Maria Fulford (Fulford Majer)
PG18 Robert Haworth (LTS Architects), Anna Woodeson (LTS Architects)
PG20 Justin Nicholls (Fathom Architects)
PG21 Tom Holberton (The Bartlett, UCL)
PG22 Marta Granda Nistal (Binom Architects) Gonzalo Coello de Portugal (Binom Architects)
PG24 Matt Lucraft (Galmstrup Ltd)
PG25 Jerry Tate (Tate Harmer)
PG26 Alexis Germanos (3X Architects)

Advanced Architectural Studies

Year 4

Module Coordinator: Tania Sengupta

Teaching Assistant
Miranda Critchley

The Advanced Architectural Studies module, taken in the first year of the Architecture MArch programme, focuses on architectural histories and theories. Here we reflect on architecture within a broader, critical, intellectual and contextual field – simultaneously producing and being produced by it. We look at architecture's interfaces with other disciplinary and knowledge fields – from the scientific and technological to the social sciences and the humanities. We straddle empirics and theory, design and history, the iconic and the everyday.

Depending on individual interest, the module helps the students engage with architectural history and theory as a critical approach to augment design, as a parallel domain to test out design approaches or as a discrete or autonomous domain of architectural engagement. It focuses on three key types of academic development: first, a reflective, critical and analytical approach; second, research instinct and investigative methods; and third, skills of synthesis, writing and articulation. The module also acts as foundational ground for the thesis that the students produce in the final year of the Master's degree.

The module consists of a lecture series called 'Critical Frames', which examines six themes: the museum and the city; the home and the social; architecture, discourse, public sphere; building systems, social and material relations; radical frames; and architectural imaginations and 'other vantages'. These lectures are followed by the core of the module, which is a set of six tutor-led seminars. The seminars straddle, geographically, the architectural histories of various global contexts, and, thematically, issues such as buildings, urbanism, typology, ecology, politics, technology, production, public participation, urban regeneration, phenomenology, historiography and representation. At the end, based on their learning from the lectures and seminars, the students formulate a critical enquiry around a topic of their choice and produce a 4,500-word essay.

2018-19 Seminars

- *Flexible Bodies, Flexible Selves*, Tijana Stevanović
- *Architecture On & Off Screen*, Christophe Gerard
- *U-topographics: Utopic Journeys into Postmodern Culture*, Robin Wilson
- *Architecture and The People: unpicking the politics of how places are made (and what that means for practice)*, Daisy Froud
- *Criticism and the History of the Architectural Magazine, Anne Hultzsch*
- *Senses and the City*, Jacob Paskins
- *The Ecological Calculus*, on Goodbun
- *Buildings as 'types' or 'kinds of things': Architecture, Spatial and Cultural Practice*, Tania Sengupta
- *Architecture, Art and the City*, Eva Branscome
- *Architectural Splendour: The History and Theory of Ornament 1750 to Present*, Oliver Domeisen
- *Architecture and the Image of Decay*, Paul Dobraszczyk
- *The Dialogic Imagination: Landscape/Landship and Practices of Worlding*, Tim Waterman

Free (us) from the city: The potential of territorial secession as a sustainable freedom enabler

Maïté Seimetz
Tutor: Tijana Stevanović

Abstract:
In 1977, an anarchist squatter commune drew a line around their Notting Hill building block and declared it the 'Free Independent Republic of Frestonia'. Amidst London's surge of gentrification, densification and rapid urbanisation, this micro-nation successfully fought eviction with a peaceful parade of passport-stamping and diplomacy, resulting in some of its members living in their 'homeland' to this day.

Frestonia's secessionist urban revolution alludes to the sociopolitical role of territorial boundary in the coexistence of the expanding city (urbanisation) and the limited city (intra-urban squatting), thus requiring a critical interrogation of the geopolitical consequences of territorial separation. The idea of architectural form as 'limit' and 'boundary' within an urban fabric has previously been explored in concepts such as 'Stop City' (2007) and 'absolute' architecture (2011) by Pier Vittorio Aureli and Martino Tattara. Both theories suggest 'form', in the sense of physical architectural intervention, as a political enabler and a liberating counter-movement to expansive urbanisation. However, by taking a purely formal approach to demarcation, the social complexity behind territorial segregation and the degrees of socio-economic permeability involved to sustain it are easily overlooked. When applied to an existing urban context, it would be naïve to ignore the inherent risk of hostile confrontation, nationalism and territorial warfare that secession holds. The exact behaviour of a community within an architecture can neither be predicted, nor forced without resorting to bio-political means and consequently encroaching on human liberty. In a scenario where the city fabric is programmed to eventually absorb any distinct urban pocket, the idea of coexistence is described by theorists, such as Felicity D. Scott in *Outlaw Territories* (2016), as a heterotopic ideal. In the quest for freedom, one can physically stop the process of urbanisation, but the social implications of separation and re-absorption under neoliberal capitalist directive remain the weak link of secessionist thought.

The success of such practice thus strongly depends on the transformation of the agonistic struggle of separate parts – Frestonia versus London – into an emancipated state of co-existence. The 'Republic of Frestonia' is one of few urban niches that have achieved freedom within their bounds in the form of anti-hierarchical detachment from biopolitics and urbanisation. Physical boundaries may have set the base condition for the rise of this independent nation, but what ultimately overcame the geopolitical tension was the Frestonians' strong sense of diplomacy and readiness to cooperate with the surrounding city.

Image: The Embassy café, Mortimer Road, one of the few physical reminders of Frestonia. Photo by the author

The Silent Hearth: Conviviality and Thermal Care

Sam Davies
Tutor: Tim Waterman

Abstract:

'Strangers are not a modern invention – but strangers who remain strangers for a long time to come (...) are.' [1]

The interrelations between the strangers who occupy our modern cities require warming. This demands a reconsideration of the systemic tools we have developed and their role in the relationships we form. While it may be the failing of global, institutional tools that has estranged the modern city dweller, the tools we use as architects have a direct influence on our local, social landscapes. Heating is one such tool in need of re-evaluation.

In this essay I use Ivan Illich's theory of the 'tool' to establish heating as an architectural tool for conviviality. Secondly, I identify the tipping point at which mechanised heating systems prioritised their own efficient function over the autonomy of their user. I hope to show that dominant notions of thermal comfort are defined by this industrial watershed and therefore limit opportunities for care in the work of the architect.

In order to investigate the interplay between comfort, care and conviviality, we will warm ourselves by a series of historical hearths. These case studies act as 'postholes' to trace not only the general trajectory of technical advancements but also the role of warmth in arousing convivial scenes and stories. From Vitruvius' open hearth and the first fireplaces, to the chilly ideals of Modernism and the invention of that most tyrannous of tools, the thermostat, we find that, through its industrialisation, thermal comfort has become a prescriptive ideal.

The essay concludes by sketching a path towards an architecture of thermal care. Relational feminist theory describes the relinquishing of control inherent in the emotional act of caring. The role of the architect, then, is not to provide comfort, but to provide the tools with which to comfort. In their use of the tool, the occupants are caring for one another. I encourage a more tender approach to our entrenched views of thermal comfort that might help kindle delight in company. In our 21st-century cities of strangers, this would be a small yet significant success.

1. Zygmunt Bauman, *City of Fears, City of Hopes.* (London: Goldsmith's College, 2003.)

Image: Exploration of the open hearth in Swedish smoke-house typologies. Drawing by the author

Is Museumification Detrimental to the Artist? How the Victoria & Albert Museum Made Frida Kahlo Up

Amelia Black
Tutor: Eva Branscome

Abstract:
This essay develops the art historian Tim Barringer's assertion that, 'the meaning of an object is inflected, even reinvented, by the context in which it is displayed'.[1] The critique is an exploration of museumification and the curatorial responsibilities of blockbuster exhibitions, with reference to the Victoria and Albert Museum's recent show *Frida Kahlo, Making Her Self Up* (16 June-18 November 2018).

The research suggests that within this exhibition the female painter was featured not for her art but as a fetishised icon through the display of her very personal medical prosthetics and make up, her everyday clothing, as well as her depiction through photography by her father and husband, and thereby the male gaze. The author argues that while these personal objects associated with this female artist have been put on display, allowing them to transcend into objects of art, they were never intended as such. The actual importance of Frida Kahlo as an artist is thereby undermined as her personal items are integrated into her identity beyond her creative intention. Two very similar recent blockbuster exhibitions that featured male pop and fashion icons are shown as a comparison, where the objects on display, such as the clothing in the Alexander McQueen exhibition, or the stage wardrobe of David Bowie had been shown as intentional artistic outputs.

The V&A has always been a forerunner in utilising the gift shop for generating revenue, and the importance of 'delivering a profit' is evident in the 'Making Her Self Up' gift shop. Accounting for one third of the exhibition's footprint, this excessive commodification of Frida Kahlo sits in direct opposition to her communist ideology. And again, like the exhibition, the curation of items on sale refuses to prioritise her artworks, where the only references to her oeuvre fetishise them.

The argument is made for an urgent reassessment of how female artists are put on display, represented in their entirety. This cannot mean displaying intimate items such as lipstick and pain medication as intentional artefacts that help to 'make up' the artist as part of her oeuvre, but accurately representing her work, politics and heritage.

1. Barringer, T., Flynn, T. (eds), *Colonialism and the Object: Empire, Material Culture and the Museum* (London: Routledge, 1998), p12

Image: *The Absence of Kahlo's Oeuvre.*
Photograph by the author

Thesis

Year 5

Edward Denison, Robin Wilson, Oliver Wilton

The thesis enables Year 5 Architecture MArch students to research, develop and define the basis for their work, addressing architecture and relevant related disciplines such as environmental design, humanities, engineering, cultural theory, manufacturing, anthropology, computation, the visual arts, physical or social sciences, and urbanism.

Students undertake the work in depth, supported by specialist tutors who are individually allocated to them based on their stated areas of interest, in consultation with their design unit tutors. The result is a study of 9,000 words or equivalent, that documents relevant research activities and outcomes, and typically includes one or more propositional elements that may include the development of an argument or hypothesis, the development of a design strategy or the development and testing of a series of design components in relation to a specific line of inquiry or interest.

The thesis is an inventive, critical and directed research activity that augments the work students undertake in the design studio. The symbiotic relationship between thesis and design varies from being evident and explicit, to being situated more broadly in a wider sphere of intellectual interest.

We anticipate that a number of theses from this year's academic cohort will be developed into external publications.

Thesis Tutors
Hector Altamirano, Alessandro Ayuso, Matthew Barnett-Howland, Carolina Bartram, Paul Bavister, Sarah Bell, Ruth Bernatek, Jan Birksted, Camillo Boano, Roberto Bottazzi, Eva Branscome, Rhys Cannon, Brent Carnell, Simon Carter, Nat Chard, Mollie Claypool, Gillian Darley, Meredith Davey, Edward Denison, Paul Dobraszczyk, Murray Fraser, Stephen Gage, Stelios Giamarelos, Polly Gould, Gary Grant, Jane Hall, Sean Hanna, Elain Harwood, Anne Hultzche, Jan Kattein, Zoe Laughlin, Guan Lee, Stephen Lorimer, Luke Lowings, Tim Lucas, Abel Maciel, Richard Martin, Claire McAndrew, Euan Mills, Harry Parr, Hareth Pochee, Alan Powers, Sophia Psarra, Rokia Raslan, Guang Yu Ren, David Rudlin, Tania Sengupta, Alistair Shaw, Bob Sheil, Neil Spiller, Emmanuel Verycrusse, Tim Waterman, Robin Wilson, Oliver Wilton, Simon Withers, Stamatis Zografos

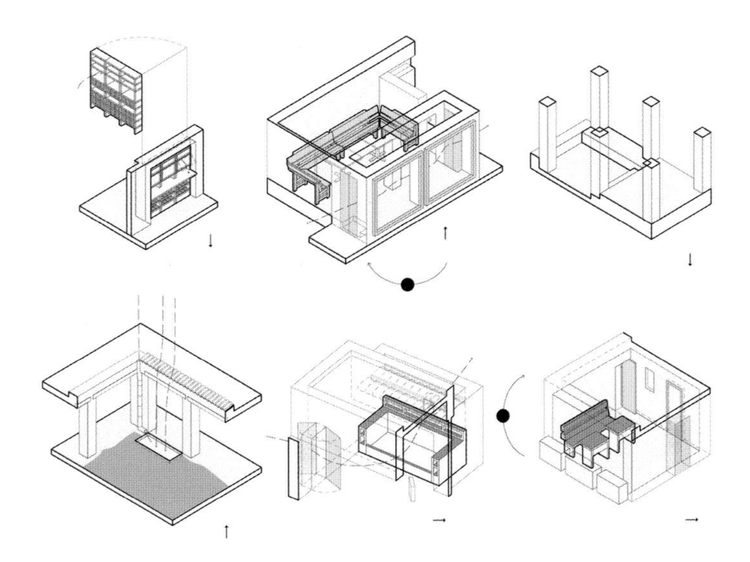

Furnishing Comfort in Can Lis: from A to Z
Naomi De Barr
Thesis Tutor: Guan Lee

The thesis addresses environmental diversity, earthen materials and Jørn Utzon's house in Mallorca, Can Lis.

Can Lis was built in 1973 and occupied by Utzon and his family. Earth-based materials of sandstone, glazed and unglazed ceramic in the house respond differently to the local climate, creating a diverse environment. 'Furnishing Comfort in Can Lis' is an exercise in noticing and documenting the spatial diversity within this domestic space. It analyses the techniques Utzon used in his design of the house which challenge the controlled, uniform and mild environments often connected with the idea of comfort.

This account of a journey through Can Lis was constructed over three months after my first and only visit on 13th January 2019. The 24 hours 'lived' at the house was warped by my expectations of it and this thesis builds upon my original subjective recordings (photography, notes, sketches) in an effort to contextualise my experience within the wider discourse of environmental diversity and discover why I found the house comfortable, when objectively it was uncomfortably cold.

As I was in the house for a short time, the environmental diversity recorded is predominantly spatial, not temporal. The essay is structured around the immovable furniture of the house, labelled with letters A to Z. The micro-architecture of Utzon's built-in furniture orchestrates the human experience of Can Lis and offers points from which to observe the surrounding environment. The essay intends to provide a spatially chronological account of the spaces surrounding the furniture and record the transitions between them. A map of the house is used in conjunction with this essay to assist in orientating the reader on a personal journey through Can Lis.

Within this account, two recorded moments instigated my own material tests, examining the properties of ceramic. These suggest how ceramic materials might be used to create a similar environmental diversity to that found at Can Lis.

The thesis observes how Utzon provided environmental diversity in Can Lis, in contrast with comfort 'norms', and it forms part of a wider criticism of homogenous comfort. Environmental diversity within domestic space has become a rarer phenomenon in the context of an increasingly homogenous perception of comfort. Whilst optimum environmental conditions vary greatly according to building location and use, this environmental variation is not experienced in spaces now easily (and affordably, for many in wealthy countries) controlled by mechanical systems used to create uniform environments.

Image: Worktop and storage, fixed wooden bench, floor bench, flowerbed, bed, and breakfast table within Can Lis. Drawing by the author

Towards Effective Architectural Practice: Lessons from the Elthorne Housing Estate
Naomi Rubbra
Thesis Tutor: Edward Denison

What shapes architectural practice and how could it be more effective? This thesis critically reflects on what people need to live a good life and argues that, by better understanding these needs, we might achieve an effective architectural practice, achieving lasting benefits for health, wealth, community and society. At the heart of this enquiry is the question of how the architect's 'image' of current or future users informs their practice and to what extent the formation of this image relies on assumed 'conjectures' [1] or situated engagement.

Patrick Abercombie's *County of London Plan* (1943) endorsed by the government's *Housing Manual* (1944), provided a 'new broom', pioneering a user-centred approach to architecture for Britain's postwar society.[2] Mass housing, a national health service, free education, and urban renewal programmes saw architects, planners, social scientists, and policymakers collectively 'engaged in the large-scale reorganisation of everyday life'.[3] Notwithstanding wide variations in quality, professional interpretation and public reception, when this programme worked well, the lasting benefits have been profound.

Focusing specifically on housing, this study revisits this aspirational programme to explore what, if anything, might be learned when seeking an effective architectural practice fit for the twenty-first century. Based on a specific kind of situated practice with residents on the Elthorne Housing Estate where I live, this work re-examines the 1961 Parker Morris Report that was influential in shaping the architects' 'standardised' image of the occupiers as 'young, nuclear families', raising questions about those who did not fit the mould.[4] It also draws on the work of social scientist Jane Darke, who explored the dichotomy between architects and users, and users and their estates; and who I was able to interview for this piece. Darke's work is instructive not only for its content, but also for its timing in offering a snapshot of Britain as it embraced a neoliberal economic programme that, after half a century, has profoundly altered Britain's housing landscape. The Right to Buy scheme, under-funding of public housing, and historically low levels of construction in public and private sectors have led to a 'housing crisis' that, combined with the selling of public land and property, has altered the urban environment in ways that challenge the architects' foundational presumption that they were advantageous to 'the citizens' and 'the public improvement' [5] of our cities.

1. Darke, J. 'The Primary Generator and the Design Process', Design Studies, Volume 1, Issue 1, July 1979, p36
2. Hardiman, C. 'Our Story - A History of Caxton House and the St. John's Way Site', caxtonhouse.org
3. Cupers, K. (ed.), *Use matters: an alternative history of architecture.* (New York: Routledge, 2013), p7
4. Darke, J. *Architects and user requirements in public-sector housing* (Planning and Design, 1984), 389
5. Royal Institute of British Architects, *Transactions of the RIBA*, vol 1/1. (London: John Weale, 1836), viii

Image: The Collective Memory Workshop

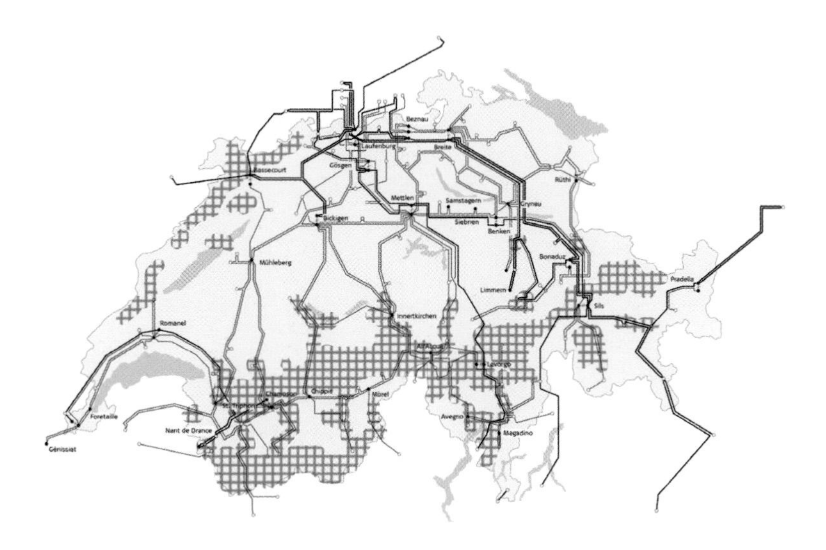

Hydrological Hinterlands
Nicholas Salthouse
Thesis Tutor: Oliver Wilton

We are officially in a glacial recession, as Switzerland approaches 'peak water' abstracted from its glacial reserves. Based on present climate change trajectories, global warming is distorting seasonal access to glacial meltwater and whilst the net annual mass balance is negative, surplus meltwater presents an opportunity for hydroelectric energy generation. However, this abundant glacial 'fuel' has a half-life that needs to be capitalised upon to offset future hydrological stress in the region. 'Put directly, what else can infrastructure do? ... it is incumbent upon us to open up new channels for cooperation and to engender a shared desire for a common project of world-making rather than one of world-draining, if infrastructure is to truly take command.'[1]

The study is set out at two scales: first, a proposed intensification of large-scale hydrological buffering through the increased use of hydroelectric batteries (dammed reservoirs) and second, a proposed smaller-scale mesh network of hydroelectric capacitors (micro-dams and infrastructural architectures) to supplement the combined systems' capacitance. The proposal of a national hydro-grid of penstocks would complement and augment the electrical grid and extend its supply and demand dynamic, introducing a level of relative local autonomy. Diagrammatic hypotheses speculate an evolution of the Swiss energy system, proposing forms of generation and storage as alternatives to those set out in the European Energy Roadmap 2050.

The core pumped storage technologies that are needed to decarbonise the energy sector have existed since 1890, but this research reveals that a networked approach is imperative. A hydro-grid could store vast quantities of latent energy and, assuming renewables become prevalent, will be capable of banking these alternative forms of energy production alongside primary hydroelectric generation. The existing electrical grid therefore becomes ancillary, solely distributing power. This offers a tiered scalable solution with the potential to disrupt future energy markets. Water may subsequently come to dominate geopolitics on a global scale as oil does today.

Energy production has long been the largest contributor to carbon emissions. Alternative production processes and buffered hydroelectric storage systems could be the key to reversing climate change. Whilst Europe contributes a comparatively small proportion of global carbon emissions, technologies such as these – developed in the Alpine massifs – could be applicable in other regions of the world, also improving resilience in less wealthy regions.

1. Angélil, M., & Siress, C., *Infrastructure Takes Command: Coming out of the Background.* (Berlin: Ruby Press, 2017), p20

Image: Europe's Alpine Battery – a proposed national hydro-grid offering hydrological buffer capacitance to augment the Swiss transmission grid on a continental scale. Drawing by the author

The Myth and the Tectonic
Dominic Walker
Thesis Tutor: Jan Birksted

'The Myth and the Tectonic' investigates ways in which we engage with history when we produce and analyse architecture. Two conditions are presented. Firstly, the translation of elements of history into abstract principles or 'laws' that guide architectural practice. This condition is then presented with its antithesis, as the translation of history into that which is experienced phenomenologically. The first condition is treated as 'myth' – an abstraction – while the latter is considered as 'tectonic' – something real and tangible.

The notion of 'myth' is developed through Gottfried Semper's intepretation of the origins of architecture in *The Four Elements of Architecture* (1851). Semper took a real artefact, a primitive 'Caribbean hut', and abstracted it into a series of universal, typological laws. The tectonic became a myth. These tectonic myths were instrumental in the development of tectonic themes within modernism, such as the 'curtain wall'. In this sense, the true potential of Semper's theory was reduced to a typological manifesto when, in fact, it was a theory that suggested materials and techniques could mutate over time, rather than remain universal.

I visited two late modernist buildings, La Tourette by Le Corbusier and St. Peter's Church by Sigurd Lewerentz, in order to develop personal, tectonic and phemenological interpretations. I demonstrate how both buildings intermix materials and techniques in order to convey complex symbolic messages, as opposed to fixed, universal, architectural laws. The concrete walls of La Tourette are cast to be read like stone; the journey into St. Peter's is not dissimilar to entering into a cave. Myths are seen to take on a more complex tectonic reality. Most importantly, they are made real by the observable qualities of their tectonics, such as the visceral reminders of the challenges of casting brickwork in St. Peter's.

The comparison of phenomenological readings of the case studies against a critique of abstraction allows one to assess the ways we can work dynamically with history in architecture. The thesis argues that a myth or an element of history in architecture is not simply made tangible by constructing it from something real. Instead, it is made real by bringing it into the context of the present day, by using contemporary tectonic references. In this respect, the thesis challenges universality in architecture, proposing instead that the myths of the past can be a fruitful way to enrich experiences of the present.

Image: The interior of St. Peter's Church. Photograph by the author

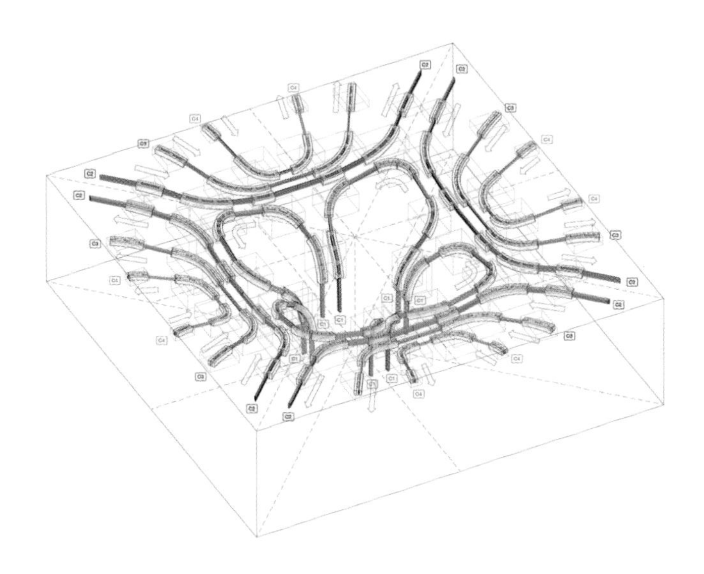

Free-Form
Matthew Gabe
Thesis tutor: Tim Lucas

Advances in digital design and simulation techniques have opened the door to the creation of more complex geometries during the architectural design process. However, these forms come with specific challenges during construction. Inspired by the experimental work of Frei Otto and his emulations of natural principles, this thesis proposes a methodology to transform complex geometrical surfaces into materially efficient frames. The work creates possibilities for structural forms where the integration of performative objectives informs the discretisation of the surface, focusing on the relationship between shape and structural strength.

Two integrated workflows are established: the digital design in which the geometric arrangement of the structure is developed, and the physical testing which explores the material and construction constraints. This culminates in the production of a prototype timber structure.

The first section focuses on the development of a digital workflow by which key stress paths can be identified in a master surface. An iterative methodology is proposed for focusing these stress vectors to concentrate the tensile and compressive forces into discreet, linear structural members, which follow the general form of the master surface. The primary outputs from this process are a set of curves in the 3D design space, representing the tensile and compressive forces.

The second section explores the design and construction of a timber frame structure, composed of laminated dowels, which follows the curve network developed previously. Through a series of small-scale prototypes, a system is developed which uses steam-bending, lamination and parametrically designed, 3D-printed formwork pieces to precisely manipulate the form of each member. In this way, the anisotropic properties of wood can be aligned to the direction of the stress vectors at each point in the master surface.

The thesis reaches its conclusion in the construction of a scaled prototype, constructed of curved, laminated timber dowel members and steel wire, each holding compressive and tensile forces respectively. The use of 3D printing and parametric design are key elements in the design and fabrication workflow and expand the possibilities for implementation of this work on a larger scale. The final structure demonstrates the feasibility of the design methodology in creating a structural frame and proposes a materially efficient alternative to a conventional grid-based approach.

Image: Construction diagram of the final prototype showing the assembly and indicating the 3D-printed formwork used to shape each component

Installing The Bartlett Summer Show 2018

Installing The Bartlett Summer Show, 2018

Our Programmes

The Bartlett School of Architecture currently teaches undergraduate and graduate students across 25 programmes of study and one professional course, with a new integrated Master's, Architecture MSci, opening for applications this autumn.

Across the school's portfolio of teaching, research and professional programmes, our rigorous, creative and innovative approach to architecture remains integral.

You will find below a list of our current programmes, their duration when taken full time (typical for MPhil/PhDs) and the programme directors. Much more information, including details of forthcoming open days, is available on our website.

Undergraduate

Architecture BSc (ARB/RIBA Part 1)
Three-year programme,
directed by Luke Pearson & Sara Shafiei

Architecture MSci
New, five-year programme,
directed by Sara Shafiei

Architectural & Interdisciplinary Studies BSc
Three or four-year programme,
directed by Elizabeth Dow

Engineering & Architectural Design MEng
Four-year programme, directed by Luke Olsen

Postgraduate

Architecture MArch (ARB/RIBA Part 2)
Two-year programme,
directed by Julia Backhaus & Marjan Colletti

Architectural Computation MSc/MRes
12-month B-Pro programmes,
directed by Manuel Jiménez Garcia

Architectural Design MArch
12-month B-Pro programme,
directed by Gilles Retsin

Architectural History MA
One-year programme,
directed by Professor Peg Rawes

Architecture & Digital Theory MRes
One-year B-Pro programme,
directed by Professor Mario Carpo
& Professor Frédéric Migayrou

Architecture & Historic Urban Environments MA
One-year programme,
directed by Dr Edward Denison

Bio-Integrated Design MSc/MArch
Two-year B-Pro programmes,
directed by Professor Marcos Cruz
& Dr Brenda Parker (MSc only)

Design for Manufacture MArch
15-month programme,
directed by Dr Chris Leung

Design for Performance & Interaction MArch
15-month programme,
directed by Ruairi Glynn

Landscape Architecture MA/MLA
One (MA) and two-year (MLA) programmes,
directed by Professor Laura Allen &
Professor Mark Smout

Situated Practice MA
15-month programme,
directed by James O'Leary

Space Syntax: Architecture & Cities MSc/MRes
One-year programmes,
directed by Dr Kayvan Karimi

Urban Design MArch
12-month B-Pro programme,
directed by Roberto Bottazzi

Advanced Architectural Research PG Cert
Six-month programme,
directed by Professor Stephen Gage

Architectural Design MPhil/PhD
Three to four-year programme,
directed by Professor Jonathan Hill

Architectural History & Theory MPhil/PhD
Three to four-year programme,
directed by Dr Ben Campkin

Architectural Space & Computation MPhil/PhD
Three to four-year programme,
directed by Dr Sean Hanna

Architecture & Digital Theory MPhil/PhD
Three to four-year programme,
directed by Professor Mario Carpo
& Professor Frédéric Migayrou

Professional

Professional Practice & Management in Architecture PGDip (ARB/RIBA Part 3)
7, 12, 18 or 24-month course,
directed by Professor Susan Ware

Short Courses

The Bartlett School of Architecture welcomes hundreds of students from around the world to participate in summer short courses. We also run pop-up workshops locally and internationally, working closely with architectural institutions and practices.

The Bartlett Summer School

Our Summer School is ideal for students looking to bridge the gap between school and university, and bolster their understanding of architecture school. Taught through a series of tutorials and workshops over either one, two or three weeks, the Summer School culminates in an open sharing session. **Applications for 2020 will open in November 2019. A limited number of scholarships are available each year.**

The Bartlett Summer Studio

Our Summer Studio is an academic and architectural adventure, enabling students to build their design skills and conceptual and critical thinking within a playful atmosphere of experimentation and fabrication. It is ideal for students already studying architecture or a related discipline, and is taught over three consecutive weeks. **Applications for 2020 will open in November 2019.**

Pre-Master's Certificate in Architecture

Designed for applicants interested in applying to a Master's Programme in Architecture at The Bartlett, the Pre-MArch prepares students for further study, developing a range of key skills alongside their English language skills.

Beginning in January each year, the programme provides 15 hours' teaching contact time on average per week by the Centre for Languages & International Education and additional tuition at The Bartlett, to develop research skills and critical thinking, understanding of the issues related to architecture and a small design portfolio. **Applications for 2020 are currently open.**

Find out more

Visit our website to find out more and to see this year's pop-up workshops.

Contact

Bartlett.shortcourses@ucl.ac.uk

At work in the B-made workshop

Open Crits

The Open Crits are a chance for distinguished external critics to critique the work of our Architecture BSc Year 3 and Architecture MArch Year 5 students. Each year, the Open Crits generate fascinating exploratory dialogues, showcasing The Bartlett's diversity at its best.

Critics

- **Stephen Barrett, Rogers Stirk Harbour + Partners**
- **Diann Bauer, Laboria Cuboniks**
- **Nera Calvillo, Architectural Association**
- **Barbara-Ann Campbell-Lange, The Bartlett**
- **Esther Choi**
- **Nigel Coates**
- **Peter Cook, CRAB Studio**
- **Sarah Featherstone, Featherstone Young Architects**
- **Stephen Gage, The Bartlett**
- **Sarah Handelman, Drawing Matter**
- **Simon Herron, University of Greenwich**
- **Lucy Jones, UCA Canterbury**
- **Ross Lovegrove**
- **Joe Morris, Morris+Company**
- **Vicky Richardson**
- **Eszter Steierhoffer, Design Museum**
- **Jane Wong, Architectural Association**

Participating Students

Jahba Anan, Yat Ning (Heidi) Au-Yeung, Daeyong Bae, Alexander Balgarnie, Arseniy Baryshnikov, Flavian Berar, Uday Berry, Theodosia Bosy Maury, Finbar Charleson, Imogen Dhesi, Patrick Dobson-Perez, George Entwistle, Charlotte Evans, Docho Georgiev, Egmontas Geras, Bijou Harding, Eleanor Harding, Yu-Wen (Yvonne) Huang, Paul Humphries, Kit Lee-Smith, Gaoqi Lou, Emily Mak, Owen Mellett, Jack Moreton, Carlota Nunez-Barranco Vallejo, Cameron Overy, Levent Ozruh, Carys Payne, Toby Preston, Joshua Richardson, Alessandro Rognoni, Naomi Rubbra, Malgorzata Rutkowska, Justine Shirley, George Stewart, Hsin-Fang Tsai, Arina Viazenkina, Dominic Walker, Benjamin Webster

Presenting at the Open Crits, 2019

Public Lectures

The Bartlett International Lecture Series

Attracting guests from across the capital, our International Lecture Series has featured over 500 distinguished speakers since its inception in 1996. Lectures in this series are open to the public and free to attend. Many of the lectures are recorded and made available to watch online.

Speakers this year included:

— **Kai-Uwe Bergmann, BIG – Bjarke Ingels Group**
— **Jane Burry, Swinburne University of Technology**
— **Izaskun Chinchilla, Izaskun Chinchilla Architects**
— **Fenella Collingridge, Salter + Collingridge**
— **Adrian Forty, The Bartlett**
— **Hsinming Fung, Hodgetts + Fung**
— **Jeanne Gang, Studio Gang**
— **Manuelle Gautrand, Manuelle Gautrand Architecture**
— **Stephen Graham, Newcastle University**
— **Francine Houben, Mecanoo**
— **Eva Jiřičná, Eva Jiřičná Architects**
— **Momoyo Kaijima, Atelier Bow-Wow**
— **Hanif Kara, AKT II**
— **Perry Kulper, University of Michigan**
— **Jing Liu, SO-IL**
— **Mariana Mazzucato, UCL Institute for Innovation and Public Purpose**
— **Niall McLaughlin, The Bartlett School of Architecture**
— **Kyle Miller, Syracuse University, New York**
— **Tobias Nolte, Certain Measures**
— **Alina Payne, Harvard University, Boston**
— **Wang Shu and Lu Wenyu, China Academy of Art**
— **Michael Webb, Archigram**
— **Jenny Wu, Oyler Wu Collaborative**

The Bartlett International Lecture Series is generously supported by Fletcher Priest Architects.

Constructing Realities

An informal event series at UCL at Here East, Constructing Realities welcomes a diverse range of speakers on themes of performance, interaction, design and manufacturing.

This year's speakers were:

— **Ramon Amaro, Goldsmiths University of London**
— **Stephanie Chaltiel, architect**
— **Carole Collet, Central Saint Martins, UAL**
— **Sonya Dyer, artist**
— **Sasha Engelmann, Royal Holloway University of London**
— **Barbara Imhof, LIQUIFER Systems Group**
— **Mitchell Joachim, Terreform ONE [Open Network Ecology]**
— **Martin Knight, Knight Architects**
— **Zoe Laughlin, Institute of Making, UCL**
— **Ho-Yin Ng, AL_A**
— **Brenda Parker, The Bartlett**
— **Pier Schneider, 1024 Architecture**
— **Malkit Shoshan, FAST: Foundation for Achieving Seamless Territory**
— **Helene Steiner, Open Cell**
— **Jol Thomson, artist**
— **Chris Williamson, Weston Williamson + Partners**
— **François Wunschel, 1024 Architecture**

Constructing Realities is generously supported by Populous.

Prospectives

The Bartlett's B-Pro history and theory lecture series offers a platform for presentation, discussion and theoretical reflection on the links between digital thought, architecture and urban design.

This year's speakers were:

- **Roberto Bottazzi, The Bartlett**
- **Raoul Bunschoten, Technische Universität, Berlin**
- **Silvio Carta, University of Hertfordshire**
- **Emmanuelle Chiappone-Piriou**
- **Mollie Claypool, The Bartlett**
- **Keller Easterling, Yale University**
- **Delfina Fantini van Ditmar, Royal College of Art**
- **John Frazer, architect**
- **Adam Greenfield, writer**
- **Ludger Hoverstadt, Swiss Federal Institute of Technology, Zurich**
- **Giorgio Lando**
- **Dan McQuillan, Goldsmiths, University of London**
- **Frédéric Migayrou, The Bartlett**
- **Euan Mills, Future Cities Catapult**
- **Luciana Parisi, Goldsmiths, University of London**
- **Casey Rehm, Studio Kinch**
- **David Rozas**
- **Jose Sanchez, Plethora Project**
- **Philip Steadman, UCL Energy Institute**
- **Jordi Vivaldi Piera, Institute of Advanced Architecture of Catalonia**
- **Michael Young, Young & Ayata**

Situating Architecture

Situating Architecture is an architectural history lecture series, affiliated with our renowned Architectural History MA and designed for both current students and members of the public alike.

Recent speakers have included:

- **Roberto Bottazzi, The Bartlett**
- **Rosi Braidotti, Utrecht University**
- **Eva Branscome, The Bartlett**
- **Tim Brittain-Catlin, Kent School of Architecture**
- **Paul Dobraszczyk, The Bartlett**
- **Laurent Stald**

Michael Webb delivering his International Lecture Series lecture

Events & Exhibitions

The Bartlett plays host to a range of events throughout the year, ranging from PhD conferences to workshops and hackathons. This year we hosted *EUGIC*, an international conference focused on greening cities, and *Innoskate*, a day-long celebration of skateboarding with specially designed obstacles, workshops and skate-related talks.

In addition, a vibrant programme of exhibitions runs throughout the year at 22 Gordon Street. These include displays of student, staff and alumni projects, as well as work by invited guests. As well as our major Summer and B-Pro exhibitions, in winter 2018 we staged our first *Fifteen* show, celebrating fifteen months of innovative work by graduating Design for Manufacture, Design for Performance & Interaction and Situated Practice Master's students.

Our 'Kiosk' is a permanent micro-exhibition space in the front window of the school, exclusively displaying student and staff projects, at street level.

Kiosk exhibitions this year have included:

- *Bartlett Ceramics* curated by teaching fellow Dan Wilkinson
- *The Diplomatic Bags* by student Theo Jones
- *EMO* by students Jung-Tu, Ping-Chieh Hsieh and Wimonwan Wichaikhamjorn
- *Future Hoxton* by teaching fellow Bill Hodgson and Jan Kattein Architects
- *Focus E15 Victory Village* by student Emily Martin

Family Day at The Bartlett Summer Show, 2018

Alumni

The Bartlett's diverse and vibrant alumni play a vital role in the life of the school, as staff, visiting lecturers, mentors, sponsors, donors and participants.

Every year we organise several alumni events, including the R&V Dinner, founded by and for alumni as the 'Rogues and Vagabonds' over 60 years ago. The event offers great food, an interesting venue, thought-provoking speakers and a chance to catch up with friends. This year's dinner took place at 22 Gordon Street, with guest speakers including Professor Sir Peter Cook and prizewinning alumna Sonia Magdziarz. The dinner is chaired by Paul Monaghan, Director at Allford Hall Monaghan Morris.

Other events for alumni include a lively Spring Social which this year was held on the rooftop at Derwent London's White Collar Factory. We also invite alumni to join us for drinks and guided tours of the The Bartlett Summer Show at an exclusive Alumni Late.

All Bartlett School of Architecture alumni are invited to join UCL's Alumni Online Community to keep in touch with the school and receive benefits including special discounts, UCL's Portico magazine and more.

Registered alumni have access to:

- Thousands of e-journals available through UCL Library
- A global network of old and new friends in the worldwide alumni community
- Free mentoring and the opportunity to become a mentor yourself
- Jobs boards for the exclusive alumni community

aoc.ucl.ac.uk/alumni

Alumna Sonia Magdziarz presenting at the R&V Dinner

Staff, Visitors & Consultants

A
Thomas Abbs
Ana Abram
Vasilija Abramovic
Phoebe Adler
Visiting Prof Robert Aish
Prof Laura Allen
Dimitris Argyros
Azadeh Asgharzadeh Zaferani
Abigail Ashton
Edwina Attlee
B
Julia Backhaus
Kirsty Badenoch
Edward Baggs
Tim Barwell
Stefan Bassing
Paul Bavister
Richard Beckett
Ruth Bernatek
Shajay Bhooshan
Vishu Bhooshan
Jan Birksted
Prof Peter Bishop
Isaïe Bloch
William Bondin
Prof Iain Borden
Daniel Bosia
Roberto Bottazzi
Visiting Prof Andy Bow
Matthew Bowles
Dr Eva Branscome
Pascal Bronner
Alastair Browning
Giulio Brugnaro
Tom Budd
Bim Burton
Matthew Butcher
C
Joel Cady
Thomas Callan
Blanche Cameron
William Victor Camilleri
Barbara-Ann Campbell-Lange
Dr Ben Campkin
Alice Carman
Dr Brent Carnell
Prof Mario Carpo
Martyn Carter
Dan Carter
Ricardo Carvalho De Ostos
Tomasso Casucci
Dr Megha Chand Inglis
Frosso Charalambous
Prof Nat Chard
Po-Nien Chen
Laura Cherry
Prof Izaskun Chinchilla Moreno
Sandra Ciampone
Ed Clark
Mollie Claypool
Jason Coe
Prof Marjan Colletti
Emeritus Prof Sir Peter Cook
Marc-Olivier Coppens
Hannah Corlett
Miranda Critchley
Prof Marcos Cruz
Lisa Cumming
D
Gareth Damian Martin
Satyajit Das
James Daykin
Klaas de Rycke
Luca Dellatorre
Dr Edward Denison
Pradeep Devadass
Max Dewdney
Dr Ashley Dhanani
Ilaria di Carlo
David Di Duca
Simon Dickens
Visiting Prof Elizabeth Diller
Paul Dobraszczyk
Oliver Domeisen
Elizabeth Dow
Tom Dyckhoff
E
Sari Easton
Gary Edwards
David Edwards
Ruth Evison
Vanessa Eyles
F
Pani Fanai-Danesh
Ava Fatah gen. Schieck
Donat Fatet
Timothy Fielder
Lucy Flanders
Alex Flood
Zachary Fluker
Emeritus Prof Adrian Forty
Emeritus Prof Colin Fournier
Prof Murray Fraser
Daisy Froud
Maria Fulford
G
Emeritus Prof Stephen Gage
Leo Garbutt
Laura Gaskell
Audrey Gbato
Christopher Gerard
Egmontas Geras
Alexis Germanos
Octavian Gheorghiu
Dr Stelios Giamarelos
Pedro Gil
Emer Girling
Dr Ruairi Glynn
Alicia Gonzalez-Lafita Perez
Dr Jon Goodbun
Dr Polly Gould
Niamh Grace
Stefana Gradinariu
Marta Granda Nistal
Kevin Green
Emmy Green
James Green
Sienna Griffin-Shaw
Dr Sam Griffiths
Dr Kostas Grigoriadis
Peter Guillery
Seth Guy
H
Soomeen Hahm
James Hampton
Tamsin Hanke
Dr Sean Hanna
Dr Penelope Haralambidou
Visiting Prof Itsuko Hasegawa
Emeritus Prof Christine Hawley
Robert Haworth
Ben Hayes
Jose Hernandez Hernandez
Colin Herperger
Simon Herron
Parker Heyl
Prof Jonathan Hill
Prof Bill Hillier
Thomas Hillier
Mark Hines
Bill Hodgson
Tom Holberton
Adam Holloway
Tyson Hosmer
Oliver Houchell
William Huang
Dr Anne Hultzsch
Vincent Huyghe
Johan Hybschmann
I
Jessica In
Anderson Inge
Susanne Isa
Cannon Ivers
J
Jeroen Janssen
Clara Jaschke
Will Jefferies
Manuel Jimenez Garcia
Steve Johnson
Helen Jones
Nina Jotanovic
K
Jon Kaminsky
Dr Kayvan Karimi
Dr Jan Kattein
Anja Kempa

Jonathan Kendall
Tom Kendall
Maren Klasing
Jakub Klaska
Fergus Knox
Maria Knutsson-Hall
Daniel Kohler
Kimon Krenz
Dirk Krolikowski
Dragana Krsic
Sir Banister Fletcher Visiting Prof Perry Kulper
Diony Kypraiou

L

Chee-Kit Lai
Elie Lakin
Stephen Law
Ruby Law
Jeremy Lecomte
Roberto Ledda
Dr Guan Lee
Stefan Lengen
Dr Chris Leung
Sarah Lever
Visiting Prof Amanda Levette
Ifigeneia Liangi
Prof CJ Lim
Enriqueta Llabres-Valls
Alvaro Lopez
Tim Lucas
Genevieve Lum
Sian Lunt
Samantha Lynch

M

Abel Maciel
Nazila Maghzian
Alexandru Malaescu
Shneel Malik
Prof Yeoryia Manolopoulou
Jonny Martin
Emma-Kate Matthews
Claire McAndrew
Hugh McEwen
Prof Niall McLaughlin
Dr Clare Melhuish
Visiting Prof Jeremy Melvin
Prof Josep Miás
Bartlett Prof Frédéric Migayrou
Sarah Milne
Ana Monrabal-Cook

N

Tetsuro Nagata
Elliott Nash
Filippo Nassetti
Rasa Navasaityte
Jack Newton
Chi Nguyen
Justin Nicholls

O

James O'Leary
Andy O'Reilly
Luke Olsen
Visiting Prof Raf Orlowski
Alan Outten

P

Yael Padan
Igor Pantic
Marie-Eleni Papandreou
Annarita Papeschi
Thomas Parker
Dr Brenda Parker
Ralph Parker
Jacob Paskins
Claudia Pasquero
Jane Patterson
Thomas Pearce
Dr Luke Pearson
Prof Alan Penn
Prof Barbara Penner
Drew Pessoa
Mads Peterson
Frosso Pimenides
Tomaz Pipan
Pedro Pitarch Alonso
Maj Plemenitas
Danae Polyviou
Andrew Porter
Alan Powers
Samuel Price
Arthur Prior
Prof Sophia Psarra

R

Dr Caroline Rabourdin
Marcel Rahm
Carolina Ramirez Figueroa
Robert Randall
Prof Peg Rawes
Dr Sophie Read
David Reeves
Dr Aileen Reid
Guang Yu Ren
Prof Jane Rendell
Gilles Retsin
Charlotte Reynolds
Eduardo Rico Carranza
Sam Riley
Rosie Riordan
Dr David Roberts
Gavin Robotham
Martina Rosati
Javier Ruiz Rodriguez
Alice Russell

S

Martin Sagar
Dr Kerstin Sailer
Prof Andrew Saint
Dr Shahed Saleem
Anete Salmane
Carina Schneider
Peter Scully
Dr Tania Sengupta
Sara Shafiei
David Shanks
Alistair Shaw
Prof Bob Sheil
Don Shillingburg
Naz Siddique
Amy Smith
Colin Smith
Paul Smoothy
Prof Mark Smout
Jasmin Sohi
Vicente Soler Senent
James Solly
Harmit Soora
Matthew Springett
Prof Michael Stacey
Simon Stanier
Brian Stater
Emmanouil Stavrakakis
Tijana Stevanovic
Sarah Stevens
Rachel Stevenson
Catrina Stewart
Emily Stone
Sabine Storp
Greg Storrar
David Storring
Kay Stratton
Michiko Sumi
Tom Svilans

T

Jerry Tate
Huda Tayob
Philip Temple
Colin Thom
Michael Tite
Martha Tsigkari
Freddy Tuppen

V

Melis Van Den Berg
Kim Van Poeteren
Afra Van't Land
Dr Tasos Varoudis
Prof Laura Vaughan
Hamish Veitch
Emmanuel Vercruysse
Viktoria Viktorija
Jordi Vivaldi Piera
Dr Nina Vollenbroker

W

Michael Wagner
Andrew Walker
Adam Walls
Prof Susan Ware
Barry Wark
Gabriel Warshafsky
Tim Waterman
Clyde Watson
Visiting Prof Bill Watts
Patrick Weber
Paul Weston
Alice Whewell
Amy White
Andy Whiting
Rae Whittow-Williams
Daniel Widrig
Freya Wigzell
Dan Wilkinson
Henrietta Williams
Graeme Williamson
Dr Robin Wilson
Oliver Wilton
Simon Withers
Katy Wood
Anna Woodeson

Y

Sandra Youkhana
Michelle Young

Z

Paolo Zaide
Emmanouil Zaroukas
Fiona Zisch
Dominik Zisch
Stamatis Zografos

Exploring The Bartlett Summer Show 2018

Supporters

We are grateful to our generous supporters:

Summer Show Main Title Supporter 2019
Allford Hall Monaghan Morris

Summer Show Sponsors
Foster + Partners
Brewer Smith Brewer Gulf

Summer Show Opener's Prize
Wilkinson Eyre

Summer Show Alumni Late
Adrem

Bartlett International Lecture Series
Fletcher Priest Architects

Constructing Realities Lecture Series
Populous

Prizes
Max Fordham
Council for Aluminium in Building

Architecture BSc Scholarship
Norman Foster Foundation

Architecture MArch Bursaries
Hawkins\Brown
Kohn Pedersen Fox Architects
Rogers Stirk Harbour + Partners
WES Lunn Design Education Trust

ALLFORD HALL MONAGHAN MORRIS

Foster + Partners

WilkinsonEyre

fletcher priest architects
london + köln + riga

POPULOUS

Foster + Partners
fosterandpartners.com

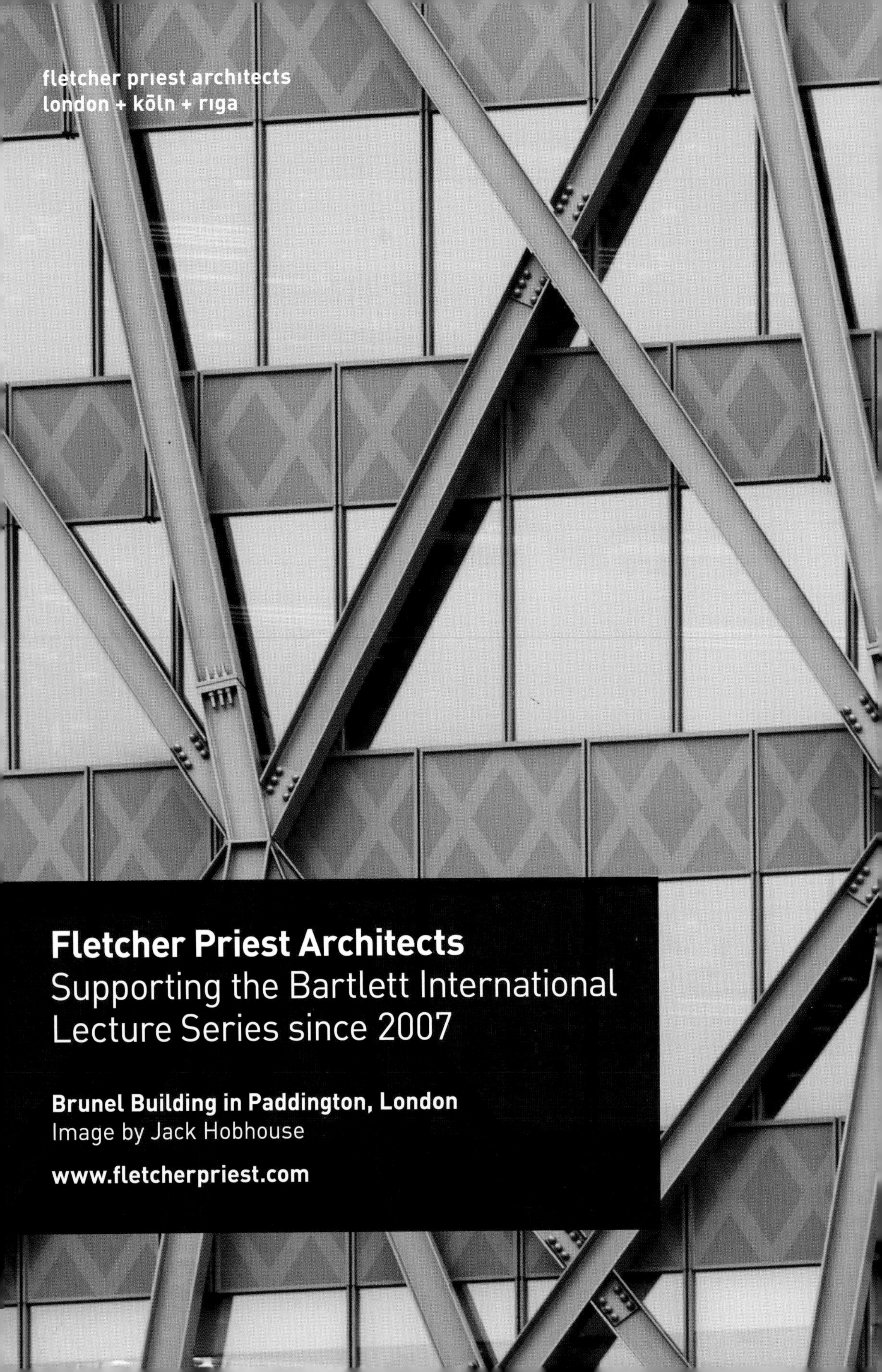
fletcher priest architects
london + kōln + riga
Fletcher Priest Architects
Supporting the Bartlett International Lecture Series since 2007
Brunel Building in Paddington, London
Image by Jack Hobhouse
www.fletcherpriest.com

We design the places where people love to be together

Sharing innovative ideas and exciting stories from unique multidisciplinary perspectives, Populous is delighted to sponsor The Bartlett's Constructing Realities Lecture Series.

POPULOUS

adrem

London's original architecture,
construction and design
recruitment agency.

adremgroup.com
+44 207 562 8282

MORE THAN ARCHITECTURE

An award winning, international practice with offices in Ho Chi Minh, Dubai and London, Brewer Smith Brewer Group provides a multi-disciplinary proposition founded upon three pillars; architecture, engineering and interior design.

+ architecture
+ interior design
+ engineering

t +971 4 294 2042
f +971 4 294 2101
e info@bsbgulf.com
w www.bsbgltd.com

ucl.ac.uk/architecture
Find us on

Publisher
The Bartlett School of Architecture, UCL

Editor
Laura Cherry

Copy-Editor
Phoebe Adler

Graphic Design
Patrick Morrissey, Unlimited
weareunlimited.co.uk

Executive Editors
Penelope Haralambidou, Frédéric Migayrou, Bob Sheil

Bartlett life photography included taken by Ana Escobar, Kirsten Holst and Richard Stonehouse.

Copyright 2019 The Bartlett School of Architecture, UCL. Works copyright the students named, unless otherwise stated.

No part of this publication may be reproduced or transmitted in any form or by any means, electronic or mechanical, including photocopy, recording or any information storage and retrieval system, without permission in writing from the publisher.

We endeavour to ensure all information contained in this publication is accurate at the time of printing.

ISBN 978-1-9996285-5-0

The Bartlett School of Architecture, UCL
22 Gordon Street
London WC1H 0QB

+44 (0)20 3108 9646
architecture@ucl.ac.uk

This is a carbon-balanced publication printed by Impress Print Services Ltd (Reg. 2220) in support of the World Land Trust.

The Bartlett School of Architecture